Palestine Membership in the United Nations

Palestine Membership in the United Nations: Legal and Practical Implications

Edited by

Mutaz Qafisheh

CAMBRIDGE SCHOLARS

PUBLISHING

Palestine Membership in the United Nations:
Legal and Practical Implications,
Edited by Mutaz Qafisheh

This book first published 2013

Cambridge Scholars Publishing

12 Back Chapman Street, Newcastle upon Tyne, NE6 2XX, UK

British Library Cataloguing in Publication Data
A catalogue record for this book is available from the British Library

ISBN (10): 1-4438-4656-2, ISBN (13): 978-1-4438-4656-1

This book is dedicated to

My wife, Rana
My daughter, Bana

CONTENTS

Part II. Specific Implications of Palestine's UN Membership

Part III. The State of Palestine: Past and Future

CONTRIBUTORS

Mutaz M. Qafisheh is a Professor of International Law and Legal Clinic Director, Hebron University, Palestine. He holds a PhD in International Law, Graduate Institute of International and Development Studies, Geneva. He is a practising international lawyer, advising a number of international organizations, including the UN and the PLO. He has formerly worked as Human Rights Officer, UN Office of the High Commissioner for Human Rights in Geneva, Beirut and Ramallah; Regional Director, Penal Reform International, Middle East and North Africa, Amman; Director, Security Sector Reform, Birzeit University; Director, Legal Education, Palestinian Law Schools, Jerusalem; Legal Advisor, Palestinian Parliament; Co-Founder, Human Rights Program, Al-Quds-Bard Honors College, Jerusalem and New York. His twenty-five studies include: *The International Law Foundations of Palestinian Nationality* (Leiden and Boston: Brill, 2008); 'Article 1D: Definition of the Term 'Refugee,'' in A. Zimmermann, ed., *The 1951 Convention Relating to the Status of Refugees and its 1967 Protocol: A Commentary* (Oxford: University Press, 2011); 'The Dilemma of Legislative Reform in Line with International Standards on Gender Equality in the Islamic World: The Case of Palestine', *International Journal for Legislative Drafting and Law Reform* (London 2013); 'The Ability of the Palestinian Legal System to Secure Adequate Standards of Living: Reform or Failed State Duty,' *Asian Journal of International Law* (Cambridge 2013).

Richard Falk is Professor Emeritus of International Law at Princeton University and the United Nations Special Rapporteur on the situation of human rights in the Palestinian territories occupied since 1967. He is the author or co-author of 20 books and the editor or co-editor of another 20 books, and a speaker and activist on world affairs. He obtained a BA in Economics from the Wharton School, University of Pennsylvania, a Bachelor of Laws from Yale University, and a Doctor of Laws from Harvard University.

Saeb Erikat is the Head of the Palestine Negotiations Office, Palestine Liberation Organization. He holds a PhD in peace studies, University of Bradford, UK; a BA and an MA in Political Science, San Francisco State

University, USA; and he is a member of the PLO Executive Committee. He has been a Professor of Political Science at Al-Najah National University; a co-editor of *Al-Quds* newspaper; deputy head of the Palestinian delegation to the Madrid peace conference; Minister of Local Government; Chief Negotiator since 1995; member of the Palestinian Parliament.

Guy S. Goodwin Gill is a Senior Research Fellow, All Souls College, and a Professor of International Refugee Law, University of Oxford. He is also a barrister and a member of Blackstone Chambers, London. He has worked extensively with the UN, including twelve years with UNHCR, has advised the Inter-Parliamentary Union and the Center on elections and international law, has been a member of the Council of the Overseas Development Institute since 2007, a Patron of Asylum Aid since 2008, and from 1997 to 2010 he was President of Refugee and Migrant Justice. He is the Founding Editor of the *International Journal of Refugee Law*. His publications include, 'The Right to Seek Asylum: Interception at Sea and the Principle of *Non-refoulement*,' 23 *International Journal of Refugee Law* 443-57 (2011); 'The Challenge of the Child Soldier,' in Hew Strachan & Sibylle Scheipers, *The Changing Character of War* (Oxford 2011); 'The West Bank and Gaza: Free and Fair Elections, Human Rights and the Transition to Democracy,' in S. Bowen, ed., *Human Rights, Self-Determination and Political Change in the Occupied Palestinian Territories* (Dordrecht: Kluwer, 1997); *Brownlie's Documents on Human Rights*, with I. Brownlie (Oxford 2010); *The Refugee in International Law*, with J. McAdam (Oxford 2007); and *Free and Fair Elections* (Geneva: Inter-Parliamentary Union, 2006).

Winston P. Nagan is Director of the Institute for Human Rights, Peace and Development, University of Florida, USA, Sam T. Dell Research Scholar, Professor of Law, University of Florida; Affiliate Professor of Anthropology; Affiliate Professor of Latin American Studies; Affiliate Professor of African Studies; Chair, Program Committee, World Academy of Art and Science. He holds a BA, University of South Africa; BA and MA, University of Oxford; LLM, MCL, Duke University; JSD, Yale University. He has widely published in international law and human rights. He is an expert and eyewitness on the apartheid system in South Africa.

Aitza M. Haddad is a PhD candidate at Howard University, Washington, DC. She holds a BA in Political Science from the University of Puerto Rico, Mayagüez, a JD from the Inter American University of Puerto Rico,

Law School, Hato Rey, Puerto Rico, and an LLM in Comparative Law from the University of Florida. She is a Fellow of the University of Florida Institute for Human Rights, Peace, and Development and a Junior Fellow of the World Academy of Art and Science.

Basheer Al-Zoughbi is a Researcher and Project Manager for Middle East HURIDOCS, Geneva. He holds an LLM in European Union Law, Reading, UK, an MA in Human Rights Law, Malta, and an MA in International Relations, Milan, Italy. He worked with Facilitate Global, UK, the Applied Research Institute, Jerusalem, and taught at Birzeit University. His research interests focus on public international law: human rights, humanitarian law, criminal law, State responsibility and diplomatic law.

Floriana Fabbri holds an LLM in International Humanitarian Law and Human Rights from the Geneva Academy of International Humanitarian Law, an MA in International Relations/International Law from the Università degli Studi di Firenze, Italy, and a BA in International Studies from the same university. She has worked for the UN Committee on Economic, Social and Cultural Rights in Geneva.

Jacopo Terrosi holds an LLM in International Humanitarian Law and Human Rights from the Geneva Academy of International Humanitarian Law and a BA in International Studies from the Università degli Studi di Firenze, Italy. He has worked for the UN Committee on Economic, Social and Cultural Rights in Geneva.

Valentina Azarov is a lecturer on the Human Rights and International Law Program at the Al-Quds Bard College, Al-Quds University, Palestine. She formerly worked as a legal researcher with Al-Haq, a Palestinian human rights group, on corporate accountability cases and on the Palestinian statehood initiative file, and with HaMoked, Center for the Defence of the Individual, on Palestinian residency rights in East Jerusalem. She obtained LLB in European Legal Studies (Honours) from the University of Westminster in London, and LLM in International and European Law, University of Geneva. She is currently completing her PhD in Public International Law at the Irish Centre for Human Rights, National University of Ireland, Galway.

Magdalena A. Pulido holds an MA from the Geneva Academy of International Humanitarian Law and Human Rights and a BA in Law from the Universidad Nacional Autónoma de México, Mexico. She worked at the UN Development Programme in Mexico and at the International Criminal Tribunal for Rwanda.

John Quigley is President's Club Professor of Law, Ohio State University, USA. He is the author of many studies, including: *The Statehood of Palestine: International Law in the Middle East Conflict* (Cambridge 2010); *The Six-Day War and Israeli Self-Defense* (Cambridge 2012); *Flight into the Maelstrom: Soviet Immigration to Israel and Middle East Peace* (Ithaca 1997); *The Case for Palestine* (Duke 2005), *The Genocide Convention: An International Law Analysis* (Ashgate 2006); *Soviet Legal Innovation and the Law of the Western World* (Cambridge 2007); *Consular Law and Practice* (Oxford 2008); and *The Ruses for War: American Interventionism Since World War II* (Prometheus Books 2007).

Valentin Jeutner is a PhD candidate at the Faculty of Law of the University of Cambridge. He holds an LLM from Georgetown University, USA, and a BA in Law, Pembroke College, University of Oxford. His research interests pertain to international water law and the philosophy of international law.

Nael Sayed-Ahmad is a Lecturer at the Faculty of Finance and Management, Hebron University, Palestine. He holds a BSc in Accounting and Finance, Hebron University, an MSc in Accounting and Finance from the University of Westminster, UK. He is currently completing his PhD in accounting in International Islamic University, Malaysia. His research interests range from corporate social responsibility of Islamic Banks, risk appraisal, management and current financial markets trends, to the impact of international polices on the Palestinian economy.

Lauren Banko is a PhD candidate at the Department of History, School of Oriental and African Studies, London University, UK. Her research focuses on the history of citizenship discourses of the populist leadership during the Mandate, and is entitled 'The Invention of Palestinian Citizenship: Discourses and Practices, 1918-1936.'

David F. Chavkin is a Professor of Law, College of Law, American University, Washington, DC. He received a BA in Science from Michigan State University and a JD from the University of California at Berkeley, USA. He has served as a presidential appointee under Jimmy Carter and in numerous other government positions. He is a frequent consultant to foreign governments and universities and an author of many studies on human rights and clinical legal education.

Uri Davis is an Erstwhile Associate Professor, Israel Studies Track, Institute of Area Studies, Al-Quds University, Jerusalem, Palestine. He is a member of the Middle East Regional Committee of the *International Journal of Citizenship Studies*; Honorary Research Fellow, Institute of Arab and Islamic Studies, University of Exeter, UK, Institute for Middle Eastern and Islamic Studies, University of Durham, UK; and a member of the Palestine National Council. He is the author of *Citizenship and the State: a Comparative Study of Citizenship Legislation in Israel, Jordan, Palestine, Syria and Lebanon* (London: Garnet & Ithaca Press, 1997).

Said Zeedani is a Professor of Philosophy and Vice-President for Academic Affairs, Al-Quds University, Jerusalem, Palestine. He holds a PhD and an MA in Philosophy from the University of Wisconsin, USA, and a BA in Philosophy and English Language from the University of Haifa, Israel. He is a former Director General of the Palestinian Commission for Citizens' Rights; Dean of Students, Al-Quds University, Palestine; Dean, Faculty of Arts, Birzeit University, Palestine; Program Director, Al-Haq Human Rights Group; and Chairman, Department of Philosophy and Cultural Studies, Birzeit University. He has published and edited numerous studies on democracy, human rights, politics, ethics, aesthetics and the Israel/Palestine conflict.

FOREWORD

RICHARD FALK

On 29 November 2012, the UN General Assembly voted (138-9) to upgrade the status of Palestine from being a 'permanent observer entity' to that of 'non-member statehood.' The date had symbolic significance as it is the UN official 'Day of Solidarity with the Palestinian People,' observed in many places around the world, underscoring the plight of millions of Palestinians living under occupation, often as refugees, and many others scattered in an involuntary Palestinian diaspora throughout the world, a set of dismal conditions endured by some of the Palestinian people since the *nakba* of 1948 and for the rest (other than the 1.5 million living as a discriminated against minority within Israel) since the Six Day War of 1967.

The initial reaction among Palestinians was to declare victory, and to celebrate this symbolic recognition as a political step closer to the goal of self-determination, expressed by way of the establishment of a sovereign Palestinian State within secured and acknowledged borders associated with the 1967 'green line,' and including having its capital in Jerusalem, either in joint administration with Israel or in that part of the city known as East Jerusalem occupied by Israel since 1967.

It should be realized that this move by the Palestine Liberation Organization and the Palestinian Authority in the General Assembly was a sequel to the stalled effort in 2011 to achieve full-fledged UN membership. This initiative, eloquently presented to the world community by Mahmoud Abbas in his speech of a year ago to the General Assembly, was blocked, as had been anticipated by the United States, which threatened to cast a veto if necessary to ensure that the membership (which implied statehood) bid did not go forward. The preferred mode of the United States was to bottle up the issue indefinitely in the tangled procedures of the UN bureaucracy, which it succeeded in doing, raising serious questions about the ability of a single powerful State to control the operations of the Organization on matters such as membership, which should not depend on the presence of a geopolitical consensus among the permanent members of the Security Council. Such a threatened use of the veto power, while technically consistent with the UN constitutional framework, is highly irresponsible, and should signal other countries to circumscribe the use of the veto along with other reforms that would make the UN Security Council more responsive to the needs and values of the organized world community in the early 21st century.

Few on either side of the controversy over Palestinian statehood paused to evaluate its real effects on the long struggle to realize Palestinian rights. On the Palestinian side, many assumed that any measure that was so intensely opposed by Israel and its junior partner, the United States, must be of benefit to the Palestinians. Hamas reinforced this understanding by abandoning its original opposition to the statehood bid to one of political support, part of a renewed politics of reconciliation as between Fatah and Hamas. Although a Hamas spokesperson clarified this show of support by saying that it should not be understood as waiving its objections to the establishment of a Jewish State in historic Palestine, it was nevertheless a momentous step toward achieving a compromise on Palestinian goals that corresponded to the global consensus on a two-State solution as articulated originally in Security Council Resolution 242 adopted unanimously in 1967 and numerous subsequent reaffirmations, including by Israeli and American political leaders. For his part, President Abbas made very clear the realistic scope of Palestinian ambitions when he said in his speech to the General Assembly, '. . . we do not seek to delegitimize an existing State—that is Israel: but rather assert the State that must be realized—that is, Palestine.'

More questionably, in contrast with the language of the statehood resolution (A/67/L.28, 29 November 2012), Abbas in a recent interview seemed to imply a waiver of Palestinian rights of return when he said that he made no claim of a right to return to his birthplace in Safed, a town in pre-1967 Israel, although he would look forward in the future to the opportunity for a visit. The UN resolution, in contrast to such an imprudent weakening of refugee rights, refers to the resolution of the refugee problem 'in conformity with resolution 194(III),' which unequivocally confirms the Palestinian right of return. Such a right is declaratory of international law on the matter. It is important that the text of the statehood resolution did not foster the impression that the establishment of Palestine as a State was *only* about 'land for peace,' with abandonment of non-territorial demands.

Israel and the United States argue without any qualifications that Palestinian statehood can only be achieved by direct negotiations between the parties. Any effort to reach such an outcome by a shortcut or symbolically is, in the words of Susan Rice, US Ambassador to the UN, 'unfortunate and counterproductive,' as well as creating 'further obstacles in the path of peace.' President Obama and the Secretary of State, Hilary Clinton, all utter this mantra of opposition whenever the Palestinians seek to enhance their status as a political actor. This is a diplomatic posture that seems cruel and unreasonable for at least two principal reasons: (1) there is scant prospect for negotiations, which have been suspended since they collapsed in September 2010 when the Israeli Prime Minister, Benjamin Netanyahu, refused to extend the moratorium on settlement expansion, and since then steadfastly refused to suspend settlement building even while negotiations are in progress while at the same time cynically calling for negotiations 'without preconditions;' (2) the reality of an occupation that has lasted since 1967, and shows no credible signs of ending in the foreseeable future, makes it humane and reasonable to take some compensatory steps that might at least offer the protection of the daily rights of the Palestinian people as well as uphold their collective dignity while subject to an occupation that looks more and more like annexation. International humanitarian law, including the Fourth Geneva Convention and the Geneva Protocols of 1977, are deficient to the extent that they do not make special provisions on behalf of a civilian population entrapped in an ordeal of 'prolonged occupation.'

The Israeli response to the statehood bid is as disproportionate as is their use of force contra Palestinians in the name of security. Israel has announced a series of accelerated and controversial settlement moves that annoyed even Washington, and antagonized Israel's supporters in Western Europe. So far announced, justified as a reaction to the General Assembly vote, was the approval of 3,000 housing units in the long deferred E-1 settlement that has the effect of isolating Palestinian neighbourhoods in East Jerusalem from the West Bank. Additionally, Israel has also declared that it was moving toward final approval for an additional 1,500 units in the Ramo Shlomo settlement located in north Jerusalem. It is my view that Israel used the statehood vote as a pretext for retaliation so as to proceed with the accelerated expansion of the settlement phenomenon, which was part of its game plan in any event. On another level this form of response is a further expression of Israeli rejection of UN (and international law) authority as it directly flaunts the clear language of the resolution, which calls for the 'complete cessation of all Israeli settlement activities in the Occupied Palestinian Territories, including East Jerusalem.'

The deeper issues as to the value of this statehood resolution remain uncertain and contested. It does not dramatically alter the role of Palestine within the UN, which since 1998 has extended special privileges not available to other actors with an observer status, including the right to participate in the general debate at the start of all General Assembly annual sessions as well as the right to cosponsor resolutions. The further rights that membership in the UN would confer include the right to vote and to initiate resolutions and other activities. Depending on how statehood is used in the UN System it could give the Palestinians options to join other actors that determine access by statehood criteria rather than on the basis of UN membership. This includes the International Criminal Court, and such specialized agencies as the International Labour Organization, the World Health Organization, the International Monetary Fund and the World Bank. It also gives Palestine the opportunity to adhere to human rights treaties, and build a stronger normative foundation for their claims to become a truly sovereign State that is a constructive member of international society.

Beyond this, prolonged occupation of a political entity that constitutes a State in the eyes of the United Nations would seem to open Israel to contentions that it is in violation of a series of fundamental rules of international law to the contrary, including Charter Article 2(4), reaffirmed in the Statehood resolution, and Security Council Resolution 242, to the effect that it is inadmissible to acquire territory by force. Especially in light of such extensive and sustained unlawful settlement activity, as well as the separation barrier and ethnic cleansing in Jerusalem, it would seem appropriate for the General Assembly to follow up with a resolution requesting an Advisory Opinion from the International Court of Justice as to the legality of continued Israeli occupation of the West Bank, East Jerusalem, and Gaza in light of Palestinian statehood.

It is against such a background that this collection of contributions to a scholarly appreciation of Palestinian statehood issues is to be welcomed with gratitude by all of us concerned with the protection of Palestinian rights and the strengthening of international law and the United Nations. Complex issues of representation, as well as the confusing situation of Palestinian nationality given the multiple residential circumstances in which Palestinians are forced to live, are explored with unsurpassed clarity and depth. This is an invaluable contribution to the scholarly literature on the Palestinian struggle for self-determination, and offers students of the subject throughout the world an ideal point of departure for understanding the core issues as they exist at this time.

The volume goes beyond the direct implications of Palestinian statehood within the UN to consider the prospects for a resolution of the underlying conflict with Israel. The statehood resolution reaffirms the two-State consensus and the Quartet's endorsement of 'the roadmap,' which to many seems increasingly a desert mirage without any prospect of being realized. What self-determination might mean in light of this background, where the two-State solution seems to be nearing the end of its sunset phase and the one-State secular democracy alternative is generally put to one side in deference to the strong Zionist commitments of the overwhelming majority of Israelis, is explored in creative ways by several authors in this volume.

In concluding, I congratulate Professor Mutaz Qafisheh for gathering such an outstanding group of scholarly interpreters of the Palestinian reality and so expertly editing this collection in a manner that creates a sense of coherence and comprehensiveness. I can only hope that this volume will receive the readership and critical appreciation that it so richly deserves.

20 December 2012
Santa Barbara, California

INTRODUCTION

MUTAZ M. QAFISHEH

The Palestine Liberation Organization declared in early 2011 that if the peace negotiations with Israel fail, it would apply as an alternative for full statehood membership in the United Nations. On 23 September 2011, Palestinian President Mahmoud Abbas submitted an official letter to the UN Secretary-General Ban Ki-moon requesting membership as a State. Although the process of application for full membership has yielded no result owing to the Security Council's inability to take a decision, the PLO was determined to pursue the matter further. On 31 October 2011, Palestine was admitted as a full member to the United Nations Educational, Scientific and Cultural Organization (UNESCO). It also filed an application to the UN General Assembly to acquire the status of an observer State, which was approved by the Assembly's Resolution 67/19 on 29 November 2012 by a majority of 138 States in favour, 9 against, 41 abstentions and 5 absent States.

There has been a great deal of speculation about the legal and political implications of Palestine's membership of the UN as a State. While positions have been taken by various States, depending on their general political stance with regard to the Palestinian-Israeli conflict, no in-depth analysis has been undertaken to date on the concrete implications of the Palestine UN membership. The media have dealt with the issue extensively, and civil society institutions have held seminars and organized symposia at which opinions, mainly political or personal ones, have been expressed. At the academic level, however, few or no scientific studies exist, although short notes, comments and expert 'talks' have been publicized, chiefly by the media and online blogs, and in many cases have led to misunderstandings at the academic and public levels.

This book aims to bridge the scientific gap that exists in this regard. As international law cannot operate and be understood outside the context of the global political atmosphere, the book focuses on the international legal dimension as well as the practical/political perspectives of Palestine's membership in the world's organization.

The book is largely the outcome of a series of papers presented at an international conference on Palestine membership in the UN organized by the Legal Clinic of Hebron University (Hebron, Palestine), 18-19 April 2012. Papers were discussed by specialists in the fields of law, political science, history and economics from various universities in Palestine and abroad (Hebron, Al-Quds, Al-Azhar, Al-Najah, Istiqlal, Birzeit, Oxford, Ohio, Geneva, Georgetown, Florida, London, and American University Washington DC) and by a number of Palestinian officials and independent experts. The papers offered substantive analysis relating to such a move.

The conference, which was attended by hundreds of people from different countries, including ministers, ambassadors, UN officials, judges, lawyers, professors, and independent experts, urged the PLO to continue its efforts to seek full UN membership by applying to the Security Council or directly to the General Assembly to acquire either full membership based on the Assembly's specific power to determine the status of mandated territories, or the status of a non-member State. The PLO should do so regardless of progress achieved in the negotiation process, since membership of the UN stems from the Palestinian people's right to self-determination, sovereignty and statehood (Erakat, Chapter One).

In order to effectively represent the Palestinian people worldwide, the PLO's role in leading the Palestinians should be strengthened by including representatives of the younger generation in its ranks, elections to the Palestinian National Council should be held in Palestine and abroad, and all Palestinians, wherever they may be, should be given the chance to register, participate in the elections and be represented (Goodwin-Gill, Chapter Two). The experts attending the Conference asked the PLO to grant identity papers, such as passports, identity cards or certificates of citizenship, to all Palestinians, wherever they may be, in order to confirm their Palestinian citizenship through the enactment of a law on Palestinian nationality, and to grant the right of citizenship to every person belonging to historical Palestine, whether born to a Palestinian father or a Palestinian mother (Qafisheh, Chapter Three). In parallel to their efforts to acquire UN membership, the Palestinians are urged to activate popular resistance by peaceful means as a strategic goal in order to achieve actual independence. This could be done, for example, by invoking international law rules, devising an improved media strategy, encouraging movements of solidarity with the Palestinian people, formulating a precise Palestinian strategy relating to American foreign policy and showing that the Palestine statehood is an American interest as it is for the Palestinian as well as Israeli benefit (Nagan and Haddad, Chapter Four).

Notwithstanding the rejection of the Palestinian request for an investigation of Israeli crimes by the Prosecutor of the International Criminal Court on 3 April 2012, Palestine needs to try to accede to the Rome Statute of the International Criminal Court as expeditiously as possible after Palestine's admission to the General Assembly. It can alternatively request the Court to accept Palestine as a member by applying through the Assembly of States Parties to the Rome Statute (Azarov, Chapter Eight). Palestine needs to ratify forthwith the International Covenant on Civil and Political Rights, the International Covenant on Economic, Social and Cultural Rights, and other core human rights treaties; as Palestine meets the conditions for accession to these treaties since becoming a member of UNESCO. The State of Palestine should thus modify its domestic legislation and institutional practices to ensure compliance with the provisions of the aforementioned treaties at the local level. Palestine should not hesitate to ratify other available treaties, such as those dealing with protection of the cultural heritage, diplomatic and consular relations, the law of the sea, humanitarian law, refugees, apartheid, and the environment (Qafisheh, Chapter Six).

The book deals in some detail with selected issues arising from the membership of Palestine in the United Nations. It discusses the question of humanitarian law and in particular the applicability of Geneva Convention IV after admission to the UN (Fabbri and Terrosi, Chapter Seven). The situation of Palestinian prisoners, whose status affects hundreds of thousands of families, is explored in connection with the possibility of Palestine becoming a party to Geneva Convention III in order to take advantage of the mechanisms for the protection of prisoners of war envisaged in the Convention (Pulido, Chapter Nine). The status of Jerusalem (Quigley, Chapter Ten) after UN membership or observer status as well as the distribution of water resources between the States of Palestine and Israel (Jeutner, Chapter Eleven) are studied in depth.

Palestine may apply for the membership of other international organizations and UN agencies, such as the World Trade Organization (Sayed-Ahmad, Chapter Twelve), the International Labour Organization, the World Bank, the International Monetary Fund, the World Health Organization, and the Food and Agriculture Organization, since membership of these organizations would serve as an indicator of the existence of the State and might be regarded as a step towards full UN membership (Al-Zoughbi, Chapter Four). To this end, Palestine should reform its diplomatic staff by developing unified rules for its embassies and consulates, and should improve the performance of the Ministry of Foreign Affairs by supplying it with trained staff able to provide protection for Palestinians abroad effectively and to represent Palestine professionally.

Some chapters adopt historical and comparative approaches in discussing the implications of Palestine's UN membership. In Chapter Thirteen, Banko addresses the creation of Palestinian nationality and citizenship under the British Mandate and its influence on nationality in the future State of Palestine. Nagan and Haddad in Chapter Fourteen compare the experience of other States that engaged in peaceful resistance, particularly the liberation of Namibia from apartheid South Africa, with the independence of Palestine. Chavkin (Chapter Fifteen) discusses the desired legal system of Palestine and ways in which it may offer a model for institution-building based on justice. In Chapter Sixteen, Davis outlines the principles that should underlie the Palestinian constitution in a single bi-national State for Arabs and Jews. Lastly, beyond UN membership, Zeedani in Chapter Seventeen proposes a creative alternative to the two-State solution: a bi-national single land that shares two peoples with two citizenships.

However, these are only some of the key implications of Palestine's membership in the United Nations. The book does not claim to be inclusive or comprehensive or to address all potential dimensions of such membership. Questions relating to the future of negotiations, Israeli settlements within the occupied territory of the State of Palestine, borders, entry into the country, security, economic relations with Israel and other States, diplomatic relations, to name just a few other issues, ought to be considered by scholars.

A note should be added on the aforementioned UN General Assembly Resolution of 29 November 2012, which was adopted after most chapters of this book had been written. This resolution might constitute a historical breakthrough for the Israel-Palestine conflict. But it might also be similar to the hundreds of previous UN resolutions on the conflict if the move is not followed by a series of measures that should be undertaken in the near future by the Palestinians themselves.

At the global level, the Palestinians should as expeditiously as possible approach the International Criminal Court, utilize judicial and diplomatic channels available under international humanitarian law, human rights law, refugee law, diplomatic and consular law, the law of the sea, and join further UN specialized agencies. Equally important, at the local level, the State of Palestine should enact legislation and take measures relating to citizenship and passports, elections, constitution, currency, legal reform, and institution-building. Such global and domestic measures are briefly highlighted here, while some other issues are more thoroughly explored in various chapters of the book.

The Prosecutor of the International Criminal Court (ICC) would not hesitate as of now to accept Palestine's application to accede to the 1998 Rome Statute that established the Court. The former ICC Prosecutor justified his decision of 3 April 2012 to defer the Palestinian application to the ICC chiefly on the ground that Palestine was not a State then. Now the Prosecutor would be compelled to investigate and might issue arrest warrants, through Interpol, to the police of 121 States members of the Rome Statute who would be under an obligation to deliver accused war criminals to The Hague. This is the main reason why Israeli politicians fear Palestine's UN bid. Once ICC jurisdiction is triggered in the case of Palestine, the Israeli military will think twice before using indiscriminate force against Palestinian civilians, including children, as was the case during the November 2012 offensive on the Gaza Strip. Hence, ICC jurisdiction – either through ratification of the Statute or acceptance by the Court of Palestine's declaration under Article 12(3) of the ICC Statute – might serve as a preventive measure that would contribute to a reduction in the violence and harm caused to civilians.

Yet, more significantly, Israeli politicians, military officers and settler leaders might be accused by the ICC of committing war crimes owing to settlement activity in the West Bank, which is prohibited under Article 49(6) of Geneva Convention IV and considered as a 'grave breach' under Article 147 of the said Convention and a 'war crime' under Article 8(2)(b)(viii) of the ICC Statute. The Palestinians, while resisting the occupation, would likewise be under an obligation to avoid targeting Israeli civilians. This in turn might prompt the Palestinians to invent more peaceful resistance techniques. Besides, Palestinian security personnel might be accused of committing crimes against humanity if they commit acts of torture or other serious human rights abuses against their fellow Palestinians.

Two international humanitarian law instruments should be ratified by Palestine immediately: Geneva Conventions III and IV. The enforcement of Convention III indicates that Palestinian prisoners in Israeli jails – currently treated as ordinary criminals by Israel – would be accorded the status of prisoners of war (POWs) in the eyes of the international community. Such POWs, by virtue of Article 118 of the said Convention, should be released upon cessation of hostilities. In the likely event of Israel's non-compliance, Palestine could resort to remedies available under the Convention, including calling upon the High Contracting Parties, under Article 132, to turn to the ICC, under Article 8(2)(a)(vi) of the

Rome Statute, which considers arbitrary detention or the failure to adhere to fair trial standards as a war crime.

Similarly, Palestine could ratify Geneva Convention IV by sending a request to the Swiss Confederation in Bern (under Articles 152 and 155 of the said Convention), asserting the importance of ensuring proper protection for the civilian population in the occupied State of Palestine. Although the Convention has, in theory, been legally applicable in the past and current state of affairs, ratification of the said Convention would enable victims to file complaints before Palestinian courts that would be able to exercise universal jurisdiction, based on Article 146 of the Convention, to issue arrest warrants and to prosecute war criminals, regardless of the their nationality and the place of commission of the crime. Such warrants might be addressed via Interpol to the courts and police of other High Contracting Parties to arrest, extradite and prosecute perpetrators in the local courts of nearly all States.

Palestine could now accede to all human rights treaties. The State was able to become a Party to certain treaties, such as the two human rights covenants as indicated above, after its admission to the UNESCO on 31 October 2012, as per Article 48 of the International Covenant on Civil and Political Rights and Article 26(1) of the International Covenant on Economic, Social and Cultural Rights. Now, all human rights treaties are open to the State for ratification, including the other seven core conventions (i.e. conventions on torture, women, children, disability, disappearance, migrant workers). Article 46 of the Convention on the Rights of the Child, for instance, provides that it 'shall be open for signature by all *States*' (emphasis added). Palestine could thereafter become a party to the UN treaty monitoring bodies, appoint Palestinian experts to such bodies, submit State reports and file complaints against other States, where applicable. The ratification of these legal instruments would also impose certain obligations on Palestine to ensure respect for the provisions of the treaties, including by harmonizing its legislation with the treaty's provisions and undertaking the necessary reforms of its institutions and their legal practice. Individual victims might be able to file complaints against Palestinian authorities as well.

With almost half of Palestinians being refugees, international refugee law would be no less relevant than the other branches of law mentioned above. While the right of return for Palestinian refugees to Israel continues to be applicable notwithstanding Palestine's recognition by the UN (Qafisheh, Annex to Chapter Three), three key points should be stressed: (1) the State of Palestine is obliged to readmit or allow the return of those persons who left or were forced to leave the West Bank or Gaza at any point from 1948 until today (about 1,200,000 persons); (2) Palestine could accord its citizenship to any refugee originating from the territory of Israel and protect him or her abroad—it should be noted that the admission of such refugees to Palestine would not undermine their right of return to their original places of residence in Israel; (3) Israel, which currently controls the borders of the State of Palestine as an Occupying Power, might deny the return of refugees to the West Bank. At this point, Palestine could become a party to the 1951 Convention relating to the Status of Refugees and automatically resort to the International Court of Justice under Article 38 of the Convention to complain about any of Israel's violations thereof.

International diplomatic and consular law, set out respectively by the Vienna conventions of 1961 and 1963, could provide the State of Palestine, after accession, with the right to send and receive diplomatic and consular missions as it wishes. A problem would arise if Israel prevents certain States from sending diplomatic or consular personnel into Palestine. In such cases, the States concerned, as well as Palestine, would have the right to complain against Israel before the International Court of Justice under the optional protocols to these conventions concerning the compulsory settlement of disputes. The State could, as a matter of right for Palestine and as an obligation in the case of the receiving States, afford diplomatic protection to its citizens abroad and serve them through its consular staff.

The law of the sea is applicable to the coastal area overlooking the Mediterranean in the Gaza Strip as well as to the West Bank, which is landlocked territory. By ratifying the 1982 United Nations Convention on the Law of the Sea, the State of Palestine could claim sovereignty over its territorial waters (12 nautical miles or 22,224 km) and jurisdiction over its contiguous zone (24 nautical miles) and exclusive economic zone (200 nautical miles or just over 370 km at the Gaza coast). If the Israeli navy prevents the Palestinians from using these areas – for any purpose such as transport, fishing, constructing ports or exploring for gas – Palestine may resort to the optional settlement measures recognized in Article 287(1) of the Convention: the International Tribunal for the Law of the Sea in Hamburg, the International Court of Justice, or arbitration. Although Israel is not presently a party to the Convention, Palestine could still use diplomatic means to approach the Convention's 163 State Parties.

Joining international organizations had become possible even before the aforementioned UN General Assembly vote by virtue of the admission of Palestine as a full Member State to UNESCO in October 2011. Palestine was already a member of other intergovernmental organizations such as the League of Arab States and the UN Economic and Social Commission for Western Asia. The latest vote would make it easier for Palestine to join further UN specialized agencies, including the World Health Organization (WTO), the International Labour Organization (ILO), the World Bank and the World Trade Organization (WTO). Article 3 of the WHO Constitution, for instance, stipulates that 'Membership in the Organization shall be open to all States.' Palestine could resort to the Dispute Settlement Body of the WTO to complain against Israel if this State continues to impose restrictions on Palestinian imports, exports, taxes, customs and price control. The WTO is expected to take certain measures against Israel should it continue imposing restrictions on the Palestinian economy and Palestinian freedom to trade.

Enacting a Palestinian citizenship law would have different effects today from those it would have entailed before the General Assembly vote. Palestine may define its population as it deems fit. It could, based on citizenship law, issue Palestinian passports that would *ipso facto* be recognized by other States—or at least by the States that voted in favour of Palestine's statehood. Palestine could then claim diplomatic protection for its citizens abroad, as mentioned above. Citizenship is a precondition for filing cases concerning violations against citizens under international criminal law, humanitarian law, refugee law and human rights law, including extradition, and for the context of elections to the Palestinian parliament.

It is high time for Palestine to initiate elections to its State institutions in view of the lack of popular legitimacy of the 'governments' that are in place in both Ramallah and Gaza. In Ramallah, the term of President Mahmoud Abbas, who was elected in 2004, lapsed in 2008, and the term of the Hamas government in Gaza, which won a parliamentary majority in the 2006 elections, ended in 2010. Elections should be comprehensive and include all Palestinians, who should be defined based on the citizenship law just mentioned, in Palestine and abroad. The elections should include the Palestinian National Council which would represent both the State and the PLO. The Council might well be broken down into two chambers, one representing the State in the West Bank and Gaza and the other representing the Palestinians in the diaspora, with agreed functions for each chamber and general functions for both chambers. The elections should be preceded by a process of reconciliation between the existing governments in order to form a unity government between the West Bank and Gaza. Without elections, effective unity between the West Bank and Gaza cannot be achieved—and this is a precondition for avoiding the situation of a failed State scenario.

The constitution is a fundamental instrument for constructing and sustaining the political system of Palestine and laying the basis for its ability to act as a State. The current 2003 Amended Palestinian Basic Law was drafted for an authority that was expected to function for a transitional period. It is not sufficient to regulate the political system of a State. A committee which was set up to draft the Palestinian constitution has produced a number of bills. These might be considered as a starting point for finalizing a constitutional draft that reflects the establishment of a democratic State of Palestine, which should ultimately be submitted for a referendum to the Palestinian people. The new constitution should avoid the pitfalls that weakened the Basic Law. In particular, it should clearly define the relationships among the three powers, and unequivocally embrace international human rights standards, particularly with regard to the death penalty, women rights, torture, and the declaration of a 'state of emergency'—all of which are issues that are vaguely formulated in the current Basic Law. In this regard, the 'parliamentary system' is the preferred mechanism to be adopted by the constitution. Such a system would permit the parliament to choose a prime minister and a cabinet that might be changed from time to time depending on the coalitions and balances created on the basis of the electoral system and parliamentary groupings. The electoral system should be based, as it is now, on proportional representation.

One of the features of any State is a national currency. According to the Paris Protocol that was signed between the PLO and Israel in 1994 as part of the Oslo Accords (Palestinian-Israeli Interim Agreements), Palestine could have adopted a national currency at an earlier stage. If it had been adopted in the absence of a formally recognized State, the recognition of this currency might have been questionable. This concern has now been diminished, as very few would be able to question the validity of the 'Palestinian pound' after its issuance by a formally sovereign central bank.

Legislative reform is an indispensable tool for the execution of most international and local measures highlighted here. Such reforms would involve ensuring that domestic law is in line with Palestine's international human rights obligations and providing for implementation of the ICC Statute, the Geneva conventions and other legal instruments. Palestine's prospective admission to international organizations would require the amendment of a number of laws. For example, a reform of business and investment law is necessary to adhere to WTO's standards, an improvement in labour law is required for ILO membership, and the adoption of a modern cultural heritage law is important for membership of

UNESCO, which Palestine has already acquired. Reform is also necessary to harmonize the law applicable in the West Bank and Gaza, whose laws differ considerably due to the legal systems that were inherited from the Ottoman, British, Egyptian and Israeli regimes over the past 100 years.

Enacting legislation, ratifying treaties, approaching international tribunals and entering global organizations are all steps that require technical preparation and institutional reform. They similarly require actions to recruit and build the capacity of individuals who can undertake analytical studies, provide reports to international forums, plead before international courts, represent the country in embassies abroad, be hired by global organizations as staff members and experts, offer consular and diplomatic services to citizens oversees and elaborate strategic plans for legislative reform. All these steps demand the allocation of adequate financial resources.

This book consists of three parts. Part I presents the framework of Palestine's UN membership, its legal and political foundations, its implications for PLO representation, Palestinian refugees and population status, and its impact on relevant parties. Part II focuses on selected issues that arise in relation to the Palestine UN membership, including human rights, humanitarian law, international criminal law, prisoners, Jerusalem, water and the accession to the WTO. Part III connects the history with future solutions for Palestinian-Israeli conflict.

I would like to expresses my deepest gratitude to Patricia Deane for her excellent editing and proofreading work and for correcting the language of significant parts of the volume. I do not know how the book would have been completed without her support. Thanks are also due to Rana Tamim, Carol Koulikourdi, Richard Falk, Saeb Erakat, Said Zeedani, David Chavkin, Guy Goodwin-Gill, Winston Nagan, John Quigley, Uri Davis, Basheer Al-Zoughbi, Magdalena Pulido, Valentin Jeutner, Nael Sayed-Ahmad, Lauren Banko, Aitza Haddad, Valentina Azarov, Jacopo Terrosi, Floriana Fabbri, Hendam Rjoub, Rashad Twam, and Yasin Sayed.

April 2013
Hebron, Palestine

PART I

SIGNIFICANCE OF THE MEMBERSHIP
OF PALESTINE IN THE UNITED NATIONS

The five chapters in this part present a framework indicating the general consequences of the membership of Palestine, as a State, in the United Nations.

Chapter One deals with the fundamental foundations on which the Palestinian people can form an independent State. It shows that self-determination for the Palestinians, namely the right to establish and live in a sovereign State of their own on the 1967 borders, has long been universally recognized by the international community. For two decades the PLO, as the legitimate representative of the Palestinian people, has undertaken to achieve this national aspiration peacefully through negotiations with Israel. However, Israel's refusal to halt its illegal settlement activity is endangering the very viability of the two-State solution. This 'compels us, the Palestinians, to take the path Israel took more than 60 years ago by seeking international recognition of the State of Palestine,' as Palestine meets all the legal criteria for statehood.

Chapter Two explores the international legal challenges to the Palestinian UN bid. In particular, the distinguished author reminds us of the implications of Palestine's membership in the UN for PLO representation of the Palestinian people, with specific reference to Palestinian refugees. After demonstrating that the right of the Palestinian people to self-determination has been clearly recognized in international law, the author notes that current moves to secure recognition of statehood do not appear to reflect fully the role of the Palestinian people as a principal party in the resolution of the Middle East situation. The interests of the Palestinian people are at risk of prejudice and fragmentation, unless steps are taken to ensure and maintain their representation through the PLO until such time as there is in place a State competent and fully able to assume these responsibilities towards its people at large. The exercise of the right to self-determination is closely linked to 'representation' and the right of the people to make known their views. An inherent aspect of self-determination is representative and democratic government. There is an essential link between the State and the people it claims to represent. The best evidence of that link is through elections which are based on the enfranchisement of the people at large.

Chapter Three conducts a survey regarding persons eligible to become citizens of the State of Palestine, focusing on the future of the 1948 Palestinian refugees, if the State is established in the territory of the West Bank and Gaza Strip occupied in 1967. It examines the different legal and political scenarios pertaining to Palestinians living in various parts of the world, whatever their status in the countries where they find themselves at present. At a time when the PLO is approaching the UN for statehood, it is useful to address the status of the inhabitants who would form the citizens of that State. In one sense, this chapter identifies those who would be represented by the PLO and might vote in its institutions in order to avoid the risks of 'fragmentation' described in Chapter Two. The chapter divides the individuals who would potentially be entitled to Palestinian citizenship into fifteen groups and analyses each group's status under international law. Citizenship may be conferred on the basis of the legal right recognized by international law or on the basis of the individual's choice. Palestine is under an obligation to grant its passport to any eligible person who opts for its citizenship, regardless of whether the person concerned could enter Palestine or not. This chapter answers the question: 'Who is Palestinian?' or 'Who is entitled to be a citizen of Palestine?'

Chapter Four discusses selected policy considerations and legal conditions relating to the membership of Palestine in the UN. It explains that the idea of a 'Greater Israel' remains a centrepiece of the agenda of various Israeli administrations, which seek to justify the idea on the ground that the ancient boundaries of the 'land of Israel' are based in antiquity, and argues that this trumps Palestinian territorial rights. While the parties are negotiating on this matter, the Israeli authorities have continued to support settlement expansion. The Israeli right wing has tremendous assets in Europe and the United States and has sought to mobilize those assets to block a decision in favour of Palestinian statehood. While the Palestinians have managed to develop sympathy, goodwill and remarkable ties in Asia, Africa, Latin America, and (albeit to a letter extent) Europe; they still need to develop a strategic policy *vis-à-vis* the United States.

Chapter Five tackles the issue of the *de jure* State of Palestine that is expected to remain under Israeli belligerent occupation even after its admission to the United Nations. The chapter examines the admission of new States to the UN from the standpoint of international law and global politics. It further touches upon the privileges of UN membership from the standpoints of diplomatic law, human rights, humanitarian law, international criminal law and affiliation to UN specialised agencies. The major question posed in this chapter is that: to what extent and under what conditions the non-admission of the *de jure* State of Palestine as a full UN member can affect Palestine's status under international law?

CHAPTER ONE

PALESTINE LIBERATION ORGANIZATION LEGAL BRIEF IN SUPPORT OF RECOGNITION OF THE STATE OF PALESTINE

SAEB ERAKAT

Introduction

The right of the Palestinian people to self-determination in a sovereign State of their own on the 1967 borders has been universally recognized by the international community. For two decades, the PLO, the legitimate representative of the Palestinian people, has undertaken to achieve these national aspirations peacefully through negotiation with Israel. However, Israel's refusal to halt illegal settlement activity is endangering the very viability of the two-State solution. This compels us to take the path Israel took more than 60 years ago by seeking international recognition of the State of Palestine.

Palestine meets the legal criteria for statehood. The fact that it has yet to establish effective control over all of its territory is a result of the continuation of Israel's military occupation of the West Bank, including East Jerusalem, and the Gaza Strip, in violation of international law and the right of the Palestinian people to self-determination. This fact should not impede international recognition of Palestine. Rather, it provides the very reason why the international community must uphold international law and facilitate Palestinians' exercise of self-determination by recognizing Palestine and admitting it as a State into the United Nations and other international organizations.

The State of Palestine remains committed to negotiating a peaceful resolution to the conflict between it and the State of Israel. Palestine will also continue to cooperate with Israel in security and civil matters; as it has done throughout the almost two decades of negotiations with Israel. Now on, as a State, Palestine will do so on the basis of sovereign equality.

Palestinians Right to Self-determination and Sovereignty

Self-determination under the League of Nations

As early as 1922, the Palestinian people's right to self-determination and sovereignty was confirmed by the League of Nations with respect to the entire land area encompassing present-day Israel and the 1967 occupied Palestinian territory ('OPT'). According to the League of Nations, historic Palestine, along with certain other communities comprising the Turkish Empire, was deemed developed enough to warrant provisional recognition as an independent nation. However, it was temporarily placed under the administration of a Mandatory Power (Great Britain) as a 'sacred trust' 'until such time as [it was] able to stand alone.'[1] In this regard, it was clear that the Mandatory Power had only temporary administrative power and a main responsibility to assist the people of Palestine to achieve full self-government and independence at the earliest possible date.

The Palestinian people's right to self-determination in an independent State of their own was also recognized by the League of Nation's successor, the United Nations, when in 1947 its Subcommittee 2 to the *Ad Hoc* Committee on the Palestinian Question reported, *inter alia*, that 'the people of Palestine are ripe for self-government and that it has been agreed on all hands that they should be made independent at the earliest possible date. It also follows, from what has been said above, that the General Assembly is not competent to recommend, still less to enforce, any solution other than recognition of the independence of Palestine.'[2]

Despite the *Ad Hoc* Committee's report, the General Assembly undertook on 29 November 1947, in its Resolution 181 (II) ('the Partition Resolution'), to partition the territory of Mandatory Palestine into two States. Although the Partition Resolution did not reflect the wishes of the majority of the population of Palestine, it does constitute an affirmation of the Palestinian people's right to sovereignty and self-determination. Each State was required to establish a democratic government and guarantee to 'all persons equal and non-discriminatory rights in civil, political,

---

[1] Article 22 of the Covenant of the League of Nations states that 'the ultimate objective of the 'sacred trust' was the 'self-determination and independence of the peoples concerned.' International Court of Justice (ICJ), *Legal Consequences for States of the Continued Presence of South Africa in Namibia (South West Africa) Notwithstanding Security Council Resolution 276, Advisory Opinion,* para. 53 (hereinafter 'ICJ Wall Opinion').

[2] UN Doc. A/AC.14/32, and Add.1, 18 (1947).

economic and religious matters and the enjoyment of human rights and fundamental freedoms.' [3]

The State of Israel was established only months after the General Assembly adopted the Partition Resolution. However, the State for Palestinians did not gain independence as the 1948 war broke out and, as a result, significant portions of the territory allotted to the Palestinian State were forcibly seized by Israel, reducing the territory of that State by more than half. In 1967, the remainder of historic Palestine – the territory comprising the West Bank, including East Jerusalem, and the Gaza Strip – came under Israeli belligerent occupation.

The UN and Palestinian Self-determination and Sovereignty

Consistent with the United Nations Charter and the Universal Declaration of Human Rights, and in recognition of the historic injustice endured by the Palestinian people, the United Nations has repeatedly called for the exercise of the Palestinian people's inalienable right to self-determination and sovereignty. In 2004, the International Court of Justice (ICJ), the principal judicial organ of the United Nations, ruled that 'the existence of a 'Palestinian people' is no longer an issue' and affirmed its right to self-determination.[4]

The ICJ ruling on the Palestinian right to self-determination found support in years of General Assembly resolutions on the matter. In 1970, the General Assembly declared that the Palestinian people entitled to self-determination in accordance with the UN Charter,[5] and in 1974 it reaffirmed 'the inalienable rights of the Palestinian people in Palestine,' including their right to 'independence without external interference' and 'national independence and sovereignty.'[6] The General Assembly condemned the government responsible for denying the people of Palestine the right to self-determination, considering the denial of that right a gross violation of the United Nations Charter.[7]

The most recent General Assembly resolution supporting the Palestinian people's right to self-determination is Resolution 65/202 which reaffirmed 'the right of the Palestinian people to self-determination, including the

[3] UN Doc. Res/181(II)[A-B] 10(d) (1947).
[4] ICJ Wall Opinion, *op. cit.*, para. 162.
[5] UN Doc. Res/2672 (XXV) C (1970). See also General Assembly Resolution 2535 B (1969) which previously affirmed 'the inalienable rights of the people of Palestine.'
[6] UN Doc. Res/3236 (XXIX) (1974).
[7] UN Doc. Res/2649 (XXV) (1970).

right to their independent State of Palestine,' and further urged 'all States and the specialized agencies and organizations of the United Nations system to continue to support and assist the Palestinian people in the early realization of their right to self-determination.'[8]   The resolution was adopted by an overwhelming majority of 177 States.

Israel Accepted the Palestinian's Self-determination

As a condition precedent to Israel's admission to the United Nations, Israel committed itself to comply with the terms and conditions of General Assembly Resolution 181 which called for the establishment of a Palestinian State.[9] Israel has also recognized, in Prime Minster Rabin's letter to PLO Chairman Arafat on 9 September 1993, the political rights of the Palestinian people and that the sole legitimate representative of those rights is the PLO. The Israeli letter stipulated that '. . . the Government of Israel has decided to recognize the PLO as the representative of the Palestinian people . . . .' This unilateral declaration by Israel is an international legal obligation that is binding on Israel.[10]

Israel recognized the right of the Palestinian people to self-determination in the 1993 Declaration of Principles on Interim Self-Government Arrangements (DOP) and the 1995 Interim Agreement on the West Bank and Gaza Strip ('Interim Agreement'). The DOP preamble describes the PLO as 'representing the Palestinian people' and provides that Israel recognizes the 'legitimate and political rights' of the Palestinian people. Similarly, the Interim Agreement describes the PLO as the 'representative of the Palestinian people,' and its preamble provides that the parties 'reaffirm . . . the mutual legitimate and political rights' of the other and 'reaffirm . . . the mutual recognition' expressed in letters between the Government of Israel and the PLO. It also refers to the 'legitimate rights of the Palestinian people.' These references and stipulations indicate clearly that Israel has recognized the right of the Palestinian people to self-determination.

---

[8] UN Doc. RES/65/202 (2010).
[9] General Assembly Resolution 273 (III) of 11 May 1949, admitting Israel to membership in the UN.
[10] See *Norway v. Denmark*, Permanent Court of International Justice (PCIJ), Series A/B, No. 53, 71 (1933). In that case, the PCIJ considered as binding a declaration made by a representative of the Government.

The Self-determination Recognized in the 1967 Territory

That the basis for the territorial unit of the State of Palestine is the 1967 border is in line with Security Council Resolution 242 which asserted the international law principle that any attempt by Israel to acquire Palestinian territory by force is inadmissible and demanded that Israel should withdraw from the territories it had occupied since 1967.[11] The Security Council has specifically recognized that the occupied Palestinian territory will form the basis for the Palestinian State.[12]

The Security Council pronouncements are to be seen in the context of clear resolutions of the General Assembly declaring that the 'inalienable rights' of the Palestinian people are 'an indispensable element in the establishment of a just and lasting peace in the Middle East.'[13] A just and lasting peace is understood today by the international community as necessitating the exercise of independence and sovereignty by the Palestinian people over 'their territory occupied since 1967.'[14] General Assembly Resolution 58/292 in particular affirmed both 'the need to enable the Palestinian people to exercise sovereignty and to achieve independence in their State, Palestine,' and that 'the status of the Palestinian territory occupied since 1967, including East Jerusalem, remains one of military occupation, and affirms, in accordance with the rules and principles of international law and relevant resolutions of the United Nations, including Security Council resolutions, that the Palestinian people have the right to self-determination and sovereignty over their territory.'[15]

The ICJ also recognized and affirmed that the Palestinian people are entitled to exercise their right to self-determination in the Palestinian territory occupied by Israel since 1967. In its Wall Opinion, the Court stated that Israel's action inside the OPT that prejudices Palestinian rights to a homeland there 'severely impedes the exercise by the Palestinian people of its right to self-determination, and is therefore a breach of Israel's obligation to respect that right.'[16]

---

[11] UN Security Council Resolution 242 (1967).
[12] See, for example, UN Security Council 1860 (2009) ('Stressing that the Gaza Strip constitutes an integral part of the territory in 1967 and will be part of the Palestinian State . . . .')
[13] UN Doc. Res/2672 (1970).
[14] UN Doc. Res/43/177 (1988).
[15] UN Doc. RES/58/292 (2004).
[16] ICJ Wall Opinion, *op. cit.*, para. 122.

These UN resolutions, confirmed by the ICJ, coupled with clear provisions in the agreements between the PLO and Israel incorporating the same and calling for preservation of the OPT as a 'single territorial unit,' support the conclusion that the self-determination unit for the Palestinian people is the Palestinian territory occupied by Israel since 1967.

Palestinian Self-determination as an *Erga Omnes* Right

According to the ICJ, international law has developed such that the principle of self-determination is a right *erga omnes* applicable to all non-self-governing territories.[17] The World Court further determined that the *erga omnes* obligations being violated by Israel are 'the obligation to respect the right of the Palestinian people to self-determination, and certain of its obligations under international humanitarian law.'[18]

The Court also called on all States 'to see to it that any impediment' arising from Israel's construction of the Wall in the OPT, to the exercise of the Palestinian people of its right to self-determination, be brought to an end. In light of the fact that the Wall constituted an attempt by Israel to *de facto* annex land constituting part of the territory internationally recognized for the exercise of Palestinian self-determination, the Court's opinion can be understood as protecting the territorial integrity of the Palestinian State.

Illegal Israeli Settlements

According to Article 49(6) of the Geneva Convention relative to the Protection of Civilian Persons in Time of War, of 12 August 1949 ('Fourth Geneva Convention'), the deportation or transfer by the occupying power of parts of its own civilian population into the territory it occupies is prohibited. Moreover, settlement activities are considered a war crime under Protocol 1 Additional to the Geneva Conventions and under the Rome Statute of the International Criminal Court. Israel's settlement policy and practices in the OPT, including East Jerusalem, have been determined by the UN Security Council to have 'no legal validity,' constituting 'a flagrant violation' of the Fourth Geneva Convention and 'a serious obstruction to achieving a comprehensive, just and lasting peace in

---

[17] *Ibid.*, paras. 87-88.
[18] *Ibid.*, para. 155.

the Middle East.'[19] Likewise, Israel's measures aimed at changing the *de facto* and *de jure* status of Jerusalem are also illegal.[20]

The Quartet's Performance-Based Roadmap to a Permanent Two-State Solution (2002) ('Quartet Roadmap'), which has been endorsed in Security Council Resolution 1515 (2003), provides that a settlement to the Israeli-Palestinian conflict will include 'an end to the occupation that began in 1967' based on 'the principle of land for peace.' In the first phase of the Quartet Roadmap, which was accepted by both the PLO and Israel, Israel is required to freeze all settlement activity.

Despite Security Council determinations declaring settlement construction illegal, and the clear prohibitions contained in the Fourth Geneva Convention and the terms of the Quartet Roadmap, Israel has refused to freeze settlement activity throughout the OPT and, particularly, in and around occupied East Jerusalem. Between 2002 and 2011, tens of thousands of housing units were tendered for settlement construction. During 2008 alone, the year of Annapolis negotiations, Israel actually tendered more housing units for settlements than it had in the year before Annapolis. Most of those units were for settlements in and around occupied East Jerusalem.

The State of Israel, the occupying power, has continued to provide incentives for Israeli citizens to move into the OPT. Those incentives include subsidized housing, tax exemptions, preferential prices and access to services, higher salaries and free education, among others. As a result, the Israeli settler population in the OPT, including East Jerusalem, has increased from under 420,000 in 2002, when the Quartet Roadmap was presented, to over 500,000 today.

Third States have the Legal Authority to Recognize the State of Palestine on the Basis of the 1967 Border

Recognition of the State of Palestine on the basis of the 1967 borders is an act consistent with international law, United Nations resolutions and the international consensus on the two-State solution for a peaceful settlement of the longstanding Israeli-Palestinian conflict. It is a legally and politically sound step in line with legal obligations and political responsibilities *vis-à-vis* the question of Palestine.

---

[19] UN Security Council Resolution 446 (1979) adopted by 12 votes to none, with 3 abstentions; UNSC/Res/452 (1979).

[20] UN Security Council resolutions 252 (1968) adopted by 13 votes to none, with 2 abstentions; 267 (1969); and 465 (1980) adopted unanimously.

Each State, as sovereign, has authority to recognize other States through the exchange of diplomatic letters or through the conduct of diplomatic relations. The recognition of a new State is the free act by which one or more States acknowledge the existence on a definite territory of a human society politically organized, independent of any other existing State, and capable of observing the obligations of international law, and by which they manifest their intention to consider it a member of the international community.[21]

As a quintessential political act, a State may only be deemed to be acting against international law in recognizing a State if such recognition would be sanctioning the illegal use of or acquisition of territory by force, or violations of peremptory norms of international law such as racial discrimination. Thus, recognitions by third States of the racist minority regime's declaration of statehood in Southern Rhodesia (known as Zimbabwe today) were seen as illegitimate. Similarly, States created through the unlawful use of inter-State force are not recognized States even if they fulfil the factual predicate for statehood.

According to the Arbitration Commission of the International Conference on Yugoslavia which represents the dominant understanding of acts of recognition:

> 'While recognition is not a prerequisite for the foundation of a State and is purely declaratory in its impact, it is nonetheless a discretionary act that other States may perform when they choose and in a manner of their own choosing, subject only to compliance with the imperatives of general international law, and particularly those prohibiting the use of force in dealings with the other States or guaranteeing the rights of ethnic, religious or linguistic minorities.'[22]

In the case of recognition of the State of Palestine, States will be upholding international law, i.e., recognition will validate Security Council resolutions declaring the inadmissibility of the acquisition of territory by force and calling for a withdrawal of Israel from the OPT, including East Jerusalem. Likewise, States will be complying with their international legal obligation to bring to an end to the impediments to the exercise of the

---

[21] H. Kelsen, 'Recognition in International Law: Theoretical Observations,' 35 *American Journal of International Law* 605 (1941); H. Lauterpact, *Recognition in International Law* (Cambridge: Cambridge University Press, 1947).

[22] Badinter Commission, Opinion No. 10, Paris, 4 July 1992, para. 4. Reproduced in 4 *European Journal of International Law* 90 (1993). See also C. Warbick, 'States and Recognition in International Law,' in M. Evans (ed.), *International Law* (Oxford: Oxford University Press, 2006), p. 250.

right to self-determination by the Palestinian people and thus upholding their *erga omnes* obligations.

Palestine Fulfils all the Legal Criteria for Statehood

Palestine Qualifies as a State under the Montevideo Convention

The Montevideo Convention on the Rights and Duties of States is understood as expressing the most accepted formulation of criteria for statehood. According to that instrument, the following conditions must be met for statehood: (1) a permanent population; (2) a defined territory; (3) government; and (4) capacity to enter into relations with other States.[23] The criteria are aimed at discerning whether or not a given territorial unit has the requisite 'effectiveness' to function as an independent self-governing entity.[24] Despite these criteria, cases abound in which States have been recognized by the international community without meeting these requirements fully, or the effectiveness principle in particular.

From State practice, it is clear that the Montevideo Convention criteria are not the decisive or the only relevant considerations in ascertaining whether a territorial unit is a State. Additional considerations on whether to recognize a State and how to apply the Montevideo Convention criteria include whether to do so would comport with principles of legality and legitimacy.[25] One of the most important principles counselling in favour of recognition of a new State is advancing the exercise of the right to self-determination. If an entity is an internationally recognized territorial unit of a people exercising their right to external self-determination, the necessary degree of effectiveness needed for statehood is lower.[26]

The State of Palestine clearly qualifies as a State under the Convention's criteria:

---

[23] *Montevideo Convention on the Rights and Duties of States,* 26 December 1933, 165 LNTS 19, Article 1.

[24] J. Crawford, *The Creation of the State in International Law* (Oxford: Clarendon Press, 2006), p. 46.

[25] M. Shaw, *International Law* (Cambridge: Cambridge University Press, 2003), p. 178.

[26] Crawford, *op. cit.*, p. 387, said that 'it is difficult to accept that the normal requirement of effective government has been entirely displaced. Rather, the criterion in this type of case would appear to be one of qualified effectiveness . . . . In such a case the principle of self-determination legitimizes what might otherwise be premature recognition by other States.'

- The Palestinian people have been internationally recognized as a people entitled to external self-determination in a State of their own;
- The Palestinian territory occupied since 1967, including East Jerusalem, is a defined territory, as made clear by the ICJ,[27] within which a permanent Palestinian population has the legitimate right to exercise its right to self-determination. The size of this territory, 6,258 square km, and the Palestinian population therein, over four million, is significantly higher than some UN member States such as Nauru (area 21 square km; population 11,000), Tuvalu (area 26 square km; population 10,000) and San Marino (area 61 square km; population 32,000);[28]
- International law does not require that all of a State's boundaries be clearly agreed before the State is recognized. Parts of the boundaries of Israel, India and China, for example, remain unsettled, but that has not impeded recognition of those States;
- The State of Palestine has capacity to enter into international relations as it has been recognized by over 120 nations and has active diplomatic relations with these countries and maintains diplomatic missions;
- Palestine is a member of international organizations, including the Non-Aligned Movement,[29] the G-77,[30] the League of Arab States,[31] the Council of Arab Economic Unity, the Arab Monetary Fund, the Arab Bank for Economic Development in Africa, the Arab Fund for Social and Economic Development, the Greater Arab Free Trade Area, the Organization of Islamic Cooperation,[32] the Islamic Development Bank, and the Economic and Social Commission for Western Asia;[33]

---

[27] ICJ Wall Opinion, *op. cit.*, para. 136.

[28] According to the US representative to the Security Council during consideration of Israel's application for admission as a State: 'Both reason and history demonstrated that the concept of territory did not necessarily include precise delimitation of the boundaries of that territory.' Report of the Security Council to the General Assembly, UN Doc. A/945/Add. 1 (1949), p. 87.

[29] See http://www.nam.gov.za/background/members.htm (visited 21 June 2010).

[30] See http://www.g77.org/doc/members.html (visited 21 June 2010).

[31] See http://www.arableagueonline.org/las/arabic/details_ar.jsp?art_id=3349& level_id=61 (visited 21 June 2010).

[32] See http://www.oic-oci.org/member_States.asp (visited 21 June 2010).

[33] Palestine was admitted to membership of ESCWA pursuant to ECOSOC Resolution 2089(LXIII); Annual report of the Economic Commission for Western

- Palestine exercises considerable control over domestic and foreign policy, despite the constraints imposed on it by the ongoing belligerent Israeli occupation. Israel recognizes the Palestinian National Authority (PNA) as having territorial jurisdiction over at least part of the West Bank and Gaza Strip[34] and Palestine has well-developed government institutions and a strong police force with jurisdiction over significant parts of Palestinian territory,[35] effectively upholding public order and security.

Palestine's competence in governance, the readiness of its national institutions for self-government and indeed its readiness for independence have been recognized and affirmed by the World Bank, the International Monetary Fund and the United Nations in recent reports.[36] In fact, the Special Coordinator for the Middle East Peace Process found after reviewing institution-building in six different areas including governance, rule of law and human rights, labour, education and culture, health, social services, and infrastructure and water, that 'Palestinian governmental functions are now sufficient for a functioning government of State.'[37]

It is primarily the continuation of Israel's occupation that hinders further development of the institutions of State in Palestine. Precisely because the case of Palestine involves the denial of a clearly recognized right of self-determination and gross violations of internationally recognized human rights and humanitarian law, the State of Palestine presents the strongest argument in favour of statehood where not all the criteria for statehood may be fully fulfilled.[38] Israel should not be

---

Asia, Resolution 2089 (LXIII), UN ESCOR, 63rd Sess., Supp. No. 1, UN Doc. E/6020 (1977), p. 1.

[34] Article IV of the DOP.

[35] *Ibid.*

[36] The Office of the United Nations Special Coordinator for the Middle East Peace Process, *Palestinian State-Building: A Decisive Period* 1 (13 April 2011) (hereinafter 'Special Coordinator's Report'); *Building the Palestinian State: Sustaining Growth, Institutions, and Service Delivery* 5, 30, The World Bank (13 April 2011); E. Bonner, *Bid for State of Palestine Gets IMF support, New York Times*, 6 April 2011; Remarks by European Union High Representative C. Ashton after the donor coordination group for the Palestinian Territories, 13 April 2011 ('Today Palestinian institutions compare favourably with those in established states').

[37] Special Coordinator's Report, *op. cit.*

[38] 'Legitimacy as endorsed by the international community plays an important role in the acknowledgment of Statehood and sometimes overrides an ineffectiveness of

permitted to prevent the emergence of a Palestinian State and benefit from its internationally wrongful conduct.[39]

Palestine Fulfils the Obligations for UN Membership

Article 4(1) of the United Nations Charter States that 'Membership in the United Nations is open to all other peace-loving States which accept the obligations contained in the present Charter and, in the judgment of the Organization, are able and willing to carry out these obligations.' The State of Palestine expressed its commitment to the United Nations Charter in the Palestinian Declaration of Independence of 15 November 1988. The Declaration clearly states that the State of Palestine is committed 'to the purposes and principles of the United Nations, to the Universal Declaration of Human Rights and to the policy and principles of non-alignment.' It also rejected 'the threat or use of force, violence and intimidation against its territorial integrity and political independence or those of any other State,' and the use of 'terrorism in all forms, including State terrorism.' The State of Palestine also accepted all obligations contained in the four 1949 Geneva Conventions and the 1907 Hague Regulations on Land Warfare.

The State and Parameters for the Conflict Resolution

Recognition of the State of Palestine supports the two-State solution and the parameters accepted by the international community as the basis for peaceful resolution of the Israeli-Palestinian conflict. These parameters include the delineation of the boundaries of the State of Palestine based on the 1967 lines, with possible agreed minor modifications equal in size and value. This understanding has been expressed recently by the United States President Barack Obama:

'The United States believes that negotiations should result in two States, with permanent Palestinian borders with Israel, Jordan, and Egypt, and permanent Israeli borders with Palestine. The borders of Israel and Palestine should be based on the 1967 lines with mutually agreed swaps, so that secure and recognized borders are established for both States. The

---

control.' J. Quigley, *The Statehood of Palestine: International Law in the Middle East Conflict* (Cambridge: Cambridge University Press, 2010), pp. 238-239.
[39] International Law Commission, *Second Report on State Responsibility,* UN Doc. *Add. 2*, A/CN 4/498/Add.2 (1999), para. 314.

Palestinian people must have the right to govern themselves, and reach their potential, in a sovereign and contiguous State.'[40]

The Quartet's Roadmap, endorsed by the Security Council,[41] also supports parameters that would be based on the withdrawal of Israeli forces from occupied Palestinian land and an end to the occupation that began in 1967.[42] With respect to the European Union, it has confirmed that the borders of Israel and Palestine will be based on the 1967 lines with mutually agreed swaps.[43] The Arab Peace Initiative of 2002, endorsed by all 22 Arab States, 57 Muslim countries of the Organization of Islamic States, and the Security Council, includes a call for complete Israeli withdrawal from all territories occupied since 1967, implementation of Security Council resolutions 242, and 'the establishment of the sovereign, independent Palestinian State on the Palestinian territories occupied since June 4, 1967 in the West Bank and Gaza Strip, with East Jerusalem as its capital.'

The Oslo Accords and Security Council Resolution 242

The PLO signed the Oslo Accords and entered into the peace process on the understanding that a sovereign Palestinian State—including the West Bank with East Jerusalem, and the Gaza Strip—would gain independence after the conclusion of the five-year transition period. Article I of the DOP stated: 'The aim of the Israeli-Palestinian negotiations . . . is, among other things, to establish a Palestinian Interim Self-Government Authority, the elected Council (the 'Council'), for the Palestinian people in the West Bank and the Gaza Strip, for a transitional period not exceeding five years, leading to a permanent settlement based on Security Council Resolutions 242 and 338.' However, almost 20 years have passed since the signing of the DOP and Israel continues to expand Israeli settlement-colonies upon land which was meant to form the basis for the Palestinian State. In fact, Palestinians in the OPT face land confiscations, home evictions, and demolition orders at a greater rate today than they did before the peace process began. The Palestinian national economy is severely damaged by Israeli occupation policies, and the settler population has more than tripled in the West Bank.

---

[40] *The Guardian,* 19 May 2011.
[41] Security Council Resolution 1515 (2003).
[42] *A Performance Based Roadmap to a Permanent Two-State Solution to the Israeli-Palestinian Conflict,* p. 7, available at
http://www.un.org/media/main/roadmap122002.pdf.
[43] EU Council Conclusions on the Middle East Peace Process of 8 December 2009.

PLO Sought Statehood before Agreements with Israel

The State of Palestine declared its independence in 1988 prior to the conclusion of any agreements between the PLO and Israel. Following that declaration, over 100 countries moved to recognize the State of Palestine, and the State sought to accede to various multilateral treaties and to gain admission to international bodies. Efforts to obtain additional bilateral recognitions and admission to the United Nations is a continuing Palestinian diplomatic initiative; it is not a new one. This diplomatic activity is consistent with agreements signed between Israel and Palestine, as those agreements envisioned an end to the Israeli occupation of Palestinian land consistent with UN Security Council resolutions 242 and 338.

Recognition of the State of Palestine is also compatible with the commitment contained in Article XXX(7) of the Interim Agreement which provides that neither party will 'initiate or take any step that will change the status of the West Bank and the Gaza Strip pending the outcome of the permanent status negotiations.' Since 1967, the legal status of the West Bank and Gaza Strip has been recognized, including by Israel's Supreme Court,[44] as that of an occupied territory. The conclusion of the interim agreements between the PLO and Israel did not change this status and neither will bilateral or multilateral recognition of the State of Palestine or admission of the State to the United Nations. The territory of the State of Palestine will remain under Israeli occupation until the Israeli government withdraws its occupation forces.

Israel has no legal claim to any part of the OPT. Irrespective of the conclusion of the agreements between Israel and the PLO, Israel's status is that of an occupier. An occupier cannot by definition occupy a territory of its own, meaning that Israel did not and could not have acquired any title over the OPT. Rather, the title over the territory lies with the people of that territory, i.e., the Palestinian people whose internationally recognized legal right to exercise self-determination in the OPT has long been established.

Any claim that efforts to gain further recognition of the State of Palestine constitutes a violation by the PLO of signed agreements with Israel has no bearing on the legality of a decision by third States to recognize the State of Palestine. While it is clear that modern international law treats breaches of *peremptory* or fundamental norms of international law as legal impediments to statehood, this does extend to *all* of

---

[44] See, for example, Israeli Court of Justice, *Beit Sourik Village Council v. Government of Israel et al.* (2004): 'Since 1967, Israel has been holding the areas of Judea and Samaria [the occupied West Bank] . . . in belligerent occupation.'

international law or bilateral treaties.[45] The Oslo Accords created only a temporary regime of administration of the OPT and did not in any way constitute a permanent settlement of the Israeli-Palestinian conflict such that it would deprive Palestinians of their right to establish their State on territory internationally recognized as theirs.

Breach of Agreements Destroys the Two-State Solution

Israel has violated all of the agreements that it has signed with the PLO, including the DOP and the Interim Agreement. Most significantly, all past Israeli governments have systematically transformed the physical and demographic landscape of the OPT to entrench Israeli control over Palestinian land that Israel seeks to annex, while at the same time displacing Palestinians from those same areas. Israel has done so by building its wall of separation and settlements and by instituting its closure regime, international law and its commitments under agreements notwithstanding. In 2010, Israeli Military Order 1560 legalized Israel's *de facto* control and jurisdiction over the West Bank, including those areas that were supposed to be under Palestinian control under the Interim Agreement, referring to the West Bank once again as 'Judea and Samaria.'

Although Israel undertook to remove obstacles to movement separating Palestinian communities in the West Bank and Gaza Strip from one another under both the *Agreement on Movement and Access* (AMA) of 2005 and the Interim Agreement, Israeli authorities have, over the years, significantly restricted the movement of people and goods between Palestinian communities in the OPT, and between the OPT and the rest of the world. Today, there are over 550 obstacles to movement in the OPT. Gaza remains cut off from the rest of the world and East Jerusalem has been severed from the rest of the West Bank. Unless something is done now, Israel will forever destroy the prospects of achieving a lasting peace on the basis of the two-State solution.

Conclusion

While the Palestinians have been, and remain, unwavering in their commitment to reach a negotiated peace agreement based on two States, Israel has persisted in its prolonged occupation and settlement enterprise in the OPT. This is eroding the viability—indeed, the very possibility—of a two-State solution.

---

[45] See Crawford, *op. cit.*, at 102.

In an attempt to advance the cause of freedom, self-determination, independence and human rights and to prevent the demise of the two-State solution, the Palestinians are calling on the international community to make good on its promises and to uphold its responsibilities towards international law and the Palestinian people. This is the rational underpinning for the Palestinian call for international recognition of the State of Palestine and for its admission to the United Nations as an equal member among the community of nations. Gaining recognition and admission for the State of Palestine is not intended as a diplomatic stunt in response to Israel's intransigence. Rather, it is an existential matter for both the Palestinian and Israelis.

CHAPTER TWO

PALESTINE, UN MEMBERSHIP AND POPULAR REPRESENTATION: INTERNATIONAL LEGAL CHALLENGES AND STRATEGIC OPTIONS[1]

GUY S. GOODWIN-GILL

Introduction

The bid by Palestine for full UN membership in September 2011 generated controversy, discussion, reflection, and doubt, all now helped along by UNESCO's decision to admit Palestine as a State of full capacity. The questions arising here are not just sterile, academic ones about the incidents and criteria of statehood, relevant though some of them are to the general question. Rather, this is an intensely political moment, one of deep-seated frustration on the part not only of Palestinians, but also, once again, of a large part of the world community which sees justice for the people of Palestine endlessly obstructed.

In this highly contested context, Palestinian statehood can seem indeterminate and uncertain, when considered against traditional, Montevideo Convention criteria[2] – a fluctuating and hitherto uncounted population,

---

[1] This chapter is the revised text of two papers presented at the International Conference on 'Membership of Palestine in the United Nations: Legal and Political Implications,' Hebron University Legal Clinic, Hebron University, Palestine, 18-19 April 2012. The chapter draws on related work by the author, including a talk given at the Seminar, 'Discussing the Palestinian bid for Statehood,' organized by *Lawyers for Palestinian Human Rights*, Garden Court Chambers, 57-60 Lincolns Inn Fields, 28 November 2011; and an Opinion and Background Paper drafted and circulated informally in August 2011.

[2] See Article 1, 1933 Montevideo Convention on the Rights and Duties of States, referring to the following criteria for Statehood: (1) a permanent population, (2) a

borders at the mercy of realignment by superior force, daily restrictions on the capacity to govern itself. And yet the conception of the Palestinian State and the goal of full representation in the United Nations continue to exert their pull, for they have their uses. In particular, they would seem to offer Palestinians the chance to put their complaints, their disputes, their rights and their claims on a higher plane, and to access more directly a variety of international mechanisms to assist their cause, bringing about or closer that goal of a national home for the people of Palestine which has been the stated aim of the international community for over sixty years.

Within its traditional legal contours, territory, population, government, capacity and recognition, the State is seen as the paradigm actor on the international plane, able to assert its rights as a sovereign equal within the international community; to resist encroachment or violation of its rights by others; to help to bring an end to foreign territorial claims; to access, as of right, the available means of peaceful settlement of disputes; to seek and to receive the assistance of other States or international organisations without being subject to the diktat of another, whether in economic development, social, or cultural matters; and to fulfil its role in domestic and external affairs without interference.

It is the State which is competent to negotiate its boundaries, to determine who shall be its citizens, to regulate investment, to organise itself internally. It is the State which is competent to agree alliances, to conclude trade agreements, to participate fully in the United Nations and its associated agencies and organisations, to draw the benefits of membership, to ratify international covenants. And just as the State is competent to ratify treaties and to contribute to the development of international law, so too it is the State which has responsibilities, and which must fulfil its obligations in international law, both in its dealings with other States and in its relations with its citizens and inhabitants.

For all of these reasons, rights and responsibilities, statehood also has attractions for the people of Palestine which are not strictly legal, but which draw strongly on the State as the prospect and embodiment of a national home, a place in which national identity can be located, a place to return to. Statehood and full membership of the United Nations will thus signal a major achievement, including representation internationally and, in principle, a status of sovereign equality with others. Of course, political realities will likely continue to qualify aspirations. There is all the more reason, therefore, to ensure that the State of Palestine, domestically, is able

---

defined territory, (3) government, and (4) capacity to enter into relations with other States. See generally and further, J. Crawford, *The Creation of States in International Law* (Oxford: Oxford University Press, 2006), Chapters 1-5.

to fulfil its international obligations and that, above all, the government of the State derives its authority from the will of the people and remains accountable to the people.

This chapter, therefore, focuses not so much on statehood or the membership of international organizations as such, but rather on the question behind the question, the question that we can and should ask of *every* State, actual and potential. And that question is about *who* represents the State in its relations with other States, and by what right or claim, and about whether this is a matter of international legal concern.

Self-determination and Representative Government

Although it opens with the resounding words, 'We the Peoples of the United Nations . . .,'[3] the UN Charter remains the constitutional basis for an international organization of *States*, and it is States which are its members and directly represented, rather than the people or peoples who stand behind them.

At the 1945 San Francisco Conference, some delegates did in fact speak of self-determination as necessarily reflecting the free and genuine expression of the will of the people, although any talk then of a 'right' to representative or democratic government would have been premature. But the idea that the right to govern is intrinsically linked to representation persists. Article 21(3) of the Universal Declaration of Human Rights, adopted three years later, declares in all simplicity that: 'The will of the people shall be the basis of the authority of government . . . .' Some thirty years ago, the noted international lawyer Antonio Cassese remarked that the exercise of self-determination implies the freedom of the people to choose their model of internal and external governance, and that in turn requires opportunity and, among others, effective protection of related freedoms of association and speech.[4]

But *who* are the people, *how* are they to be empowered, and *how* are their rights to be made real and effective? The United Nations affirmed the right of the people of Palestine to self-determination in the 1970s, and thereafter began to treat Palestine as more or less equivalent to a Member State. In 1988, for example, following the Palestinian Declaration of

---

[3] Preamble, Charter of the United Nations.
[4] A. Cassese, 'Political Self-Determination – Old Concepts and New Developments,' in A. Cassese, ed., *UN Law/Fundamental Rights* (Dordrecht: Martinus Nijhoff, 1979), p. 137; A. Cassese, 'The Self-Determination of Peoples,' in Louis Henkin, ed., *The International Bill of Rights – The International Covenant on Civil and Political Rights* (New York: Columbia University Press, 1981), p. 92.

Independence, the General Assembly voted to use the word 'Palestine'[5] rather than 'PLO,' (Palestine Liberation Organization) and later it gave Palestine the right to participate in a wide variety of UN agenda items, not just those related to itself.[6] The Palestinian claim to self-determination, of course, is indisputable today, endorsed not only by the United Nations (the General Assembly, the Security Council, the International Court of Justice), but also by Member States, including Israel.

Moreover, the people of Palestine have been clearly identified by the General Assembly as '*the principal party*' to the processes of peace and self-determination,[7] just as the PLO has also been recognized as the sole representative of the people. These issues come together in a telling way, for those displaced since 1948 and their descendants constitute more than half of all the people of Palestine. In repeatedly stressing that 'the Palestinian people is the principal party to the question of Palestine . . .,' the General Assembly has never drawn any distinctions on the basis of place of residence. It is thus the people of Palestine, as a whole, who possess the inalienable rights to self-determination, national independence and sovereignty, and the right to return to their homes and property from which they have been displaced and uprooted.[8]

In the practice of the UN, therefore, neither the Palestinian people nor the right to self-determination is territorially limited to the space currently referred to as the 'Occupied Palestinian Territory.' It may be challenging to identify 'the people' in this context, at least pending a viable and effective system of registration for the purposes of voting or referendum, but the intent of successive General Assembly resolutions has been clearly to include both Palestinians in the occupied territories and those who remain displaced in other countries. The identification of the people is clearly a matter for the people, irrespective of their place of residence, but it is also a matter of international legal concern when considered within the political context of the bid for UN membership.

Historically, these have been among the critical constituent elements in the movement for liberation. Given the obstacles faced by the people – not the least being exile and a divided land – it is hardly surprising that the modalities for achieving democratic, representative and accountable

---

[5] UN General Assembly Resolution 43/177, 15 December 1988.
[6] UN General Assembly Resolution 52/250, 7 July 1998, 'Participation of Palestine in the Work of the United Nations.'
[7] UN General Assembly Resolution 3210 (XXIX), 14 October 1974; UN General Assembly Resolution 3236 (XXIX), 22 November 1974, para. 4; UN General Assembly Resolution 3375 (XXX), 10 November 1975.
[8] UN General Assembly Resolution 3237 (XXIX), 22 November 1974.

government in a future State and in the interests of *all* Palestinians have either been sidelined by momentarily greater concerns, or left pending for later, in some imagined period to come of calm transition and reflection.

Nor is this exceptional. In practice, States commonly emerge and are accepted during ongoing conflict, or during the chaotic aftermath of State-building. At such times, often only the distant promise of elections can be offered to a people whose struggle for national liberation seems best achieved for now by the international recognition of their State. What is different in the Palestinian case, however, is the emphasis given both to return and to self-determination.

Self-determination and Democratic Representative Government

The exercise of the right to self-determination being so closely linked to the issue of representation opens up a raft of issues touching on the political rights of individuals, of the people.[9] Professor James Crawford, giving his inaugural lecture at the University of Cambridge in March 1993, referred to Article 1 of the 1966 Civil and Political Rights Covenant and suggested that 'self-determination is a continuing matter, not a once-for-all constitution of the State. Thus, in addition to its familiar role in the decolonization process, Article 1 can be read as affirming the self-direction of each society, and thus as affirming *the principle of democracy at the collective level.*'[10]

He went on to add, however, that under international law '[t]here was no requirement that the government of a State, to be a government, should have been democratically elected or even that it should have the general support of its people.'[11]

Twenty years later, it is again worth asking whether a State seeking membership of the United Nations, and the government which claims to represent the people of that State, should be democratic and representative. Or is it still the case that all that is required to qualify for membership is

---

[9] Although different perceptions remain, it is increasingly accepted that popular participation is necessarily linked to rights – the right to be recognized as a person at law and hence to be registered and enabled to vote, the right of universal suffrage, the right to associate for political purposes, to establish political parties, to freedom of expression, to the secret ballot, and to a transparent and verifiable ballot count, among others.

[10] Revised and published as 'Democracy and International Law' 64 *British Yearbook of International Law* 113 (1993), p. 116 (emphasis added).

[11] *Ibid.*, p. 117.

that, in accordance with Article 4 of the Charter, it should simply be 'peace-loving,' should accept the obligations of the Charter and, in the judgement of the organisation, be able and willing to carry out its obligations? The question, twenty years later, may remain the same, but the legal context has undoubtedly changed.

The 'democracy debate' was given another kick-start by UN Secretary-General Boutros Boutros-Ghali in the 1990s;[12] it may have tailed off institutionally since then, but it is certainly back in the frame now, with the financial crisis and the resurgence of popular movements against authoritarian and non-accountable governments. Indeed, since Secretary-General Boutros-Ghali put democracy centre-field in his proposals for peace, development and international organization, the General Assembly, the Commission on Human Rights, the Human Rights Council, and the Human Rights Committee have each played a role in keeping the democratic imperative in focus.[13] At the regional level, too, the radical idea that intervention is acceptable in support of democratically elected governments has gained traction in Africa and Latin America, while the UN itself has continued to provide electoral assistance to new and restored democracies.

For its part, the Human Rights Committee has confirmed the link between elections and representative democracy, noting that it is implicit in Article 25 of the 1966 International Covenant on Civil and Political Rights that representatives who exercise governmental power are accountable through the electoral process for their exercise of that power.[14] A clear link to the *system* of international legal obligation

---

[12] See, in particular, *An Agenda for Peace* (1992), *An Agenda for Development* (1994), and *An Agenda for Democratization* (1996). See also T. Franck, 'The Emerging Right to Democratic Governance,' 86 *American Journal of International Law* 46 (1992); G. Fox and B. Roth, eds., *Democratic Governance and International Law* (Cambridge: Cambridge University Press, 2000); S. Marks, 'What has become of the emerging right to democratic governance?' 22 *European Journal of International Law* 507 (2011).

[13] As the UN Secretary-General noted presciently in 2003 '. . . just as the price of exclusion is often violence, the benefit of political inclusion is a much better prospect of stability.' 'Strengthening the role of the United Nations in enhancing the effectiveness of the principle of periodic and genuine elections and the promotion of democratization, Report of the Secretary-General.' UN Doc. 58/212, 4 August 2003, para. 4.

[14] Human Rights Committee, General Comment No. 25, 'The right to participate in public affairs, voting rights and the right of equal access to public service,' 12 July 1996, collected in 'Compilation of General Comments and General Recommendations

nevertheless remains unclear and in a society configured by principles of sovereignty and non-intervention, who represents the State continues to hover on the edges, if not entirely beyond the reach of international law.

'Statehood' remains the necessary qualification for membership of most international organizations, and in the UN context, the *political* process of acceptance and admission as a State is by decision of the General Assembly on the recommendation of the Security Council.[15] An additional twist in the overall picture, however, is provided by the law and practice of *recognition* of States and governments. At one ideal level, this might just be a matter of declaring the facts – a State exists – but historically other States have often also included a *discretionary element* in their practice. Beyond the appreciation or assessment of the facts, recognition has been employed to express their willingness or not to enter into normal diplomatic relations with the new State on the block, or with a new government which has established effective authority over all or part of the territory of an already existing State.

That discretionary element, that open door, has certainly allowed the intrusion of other 'non-legal' criteria into the practice; sometimes, they have reflected blatant political self-interest, but at other and more recent times, that discretion has also been used to accommodate issues of wider, *international* concern – human rights, good governance, democratic legitimacy, the rule of law.

There is thus an uneasy connection, moderated and muddied by politics, between statehood, eligibility for UN membership, self-determination, and emerging notions of democratic entitlement, particularly at the point of international representation. The collective right of peoples must necessarily be exercised through the choices made by individuals, however, and this in turn raises the question of facilitation and the challenge of making rights real and effective. In addition, things move on, and international law is no different. Over the last fifteen to twenty years, both States and international organizations have started to review assumptions about sovereignty, and to ask whether the right to represent a State internationally should perhaps be contingent on a clear link to a valid expression of the will of the people. International law has moved on and the Charter can or should be interpreted consistently with that international law. Alternatively, if this is wrong and international law is still in an evolutionary stage, then there are good strategic reasons for an emerging

adopted by Human Rights Treaty Bodies;' UN Doc. HRI/GEN/1/Rev.9, 27 May 2008.
[15] Article 4(2), Charter of the United Nations.

State seeking UN membership to align or develop its policy, practice and institutions with international law as it is evolving.

Although it is formally correct to say, as a matter of law, that 'democracy' is not a requirement for membership of the UN, let alone a pre-requisite condition for the recognition of statehood, the characteristics commonly associated with a democratic State are acquiring increasing weight. There is thus growing institutional expectation that States should so organise themselves internally as to demonstrate accountability and commitment to the rule of law,[16] including the principle that the authority of government be found in the expressed will of the people, and that the State should ensure and protect human rights for all. In addition, the specific principle of gender equality, especially in political life, is needed. In 1995, the Beijing Declaration and Platform for Action recognised that 'the goal of equal participation of women and men in decision-making will provide a balance that more actually reflects the composition of society and is needed to strengthen democracy and promote its proper functioning.'[17]

An inherent aspect of the principle of self-determination today is *representative* and democratic government, and there is an essential link between the State (for example, as a member of the United Nations), and the people it claims to represent. The best evidence of that link – representative government – is through elections based on the enfranchisement of the people at large.[18] This is not to say that free and fair elections are the hallmark of democracy, only that they are necessary conditions – but very necessary conditions.

---

[16] For details and explanation of the UN's engagement with rule of law issues, see http://www.unrol.org.

[17] Beijing Declaration and Platform for Action, Fourth World Conference on Women, UN Doc. A/CONF.177/20, 15 September 1995, Chapter IV, 'Strategic Objectives and Actions), para. 183. But see also UN General Assembly Resolution S-23/3, 'Further actions and initiatives to implement the Beijing Declaration and Platform for Action,' 16 November 2000, paras. 22-3; UN General Assembly Resolution 61/145, 'Follow-up to the Fourth World Conference on Women and full implementation of the Beijing Declaration and Platform for Action and the outcome of the twenty-third special session of the General Assembly,' 19 December 2006, para. 7(c).

[18] See generally G. Goodwin-Gill, *Free and Fair Elections* (Geneva: Inter-Parliamentary Union, 2006).

Palestine and the Challenge of Popular Representation

The PLO is accepted by the UN and by the international community of States,[19] including Israel, as the *sole representative* of the Palestinian people.[20] In this representative capacity, both inside and outside the UN, the PLO's mandate encompasses the totality of issues arising from the continuing displacement of Palestinians and the struggle for self-determination, including, among others, the questions of return and compensation highlighted in UN General Assembly resolution 194 (III), and the question of national boundaries, which is implicit in Security Council resolution 242. These, necessarily, are matters for the Palestinian people as a whole. Given its internationally recognized status, could the PLO be replaced, substituted within the UN, by the State of Palestine as the legitimate representative of the Palestinian people? Anything can happen institutionally, of course, although it is telling that in presenting the 23 September 2011 application for UN membership, Mahmoud Abbas signed off as 'President of the State of Palestine' *and* as 'Chairman of the Executive Committee of the Palestine Liberation Organization.'[21]

Among others, 'representation' raises a number of 'constitutional' problems (in that they engage the Palestinian National Charter and the organization and entities which make up the PLO); secondly, it brings in the question of the 'capacity' of the State of Palestine effectively to take on the role and responsibilities of the PLO in the UN; and thirdly, it invites a close focus on the will of the people.

It is somewhat presumptuous to speak to issues of internal governance and about choices which only the people of Palestine can make. What follows, therefore, is intended to highlight those matters which have an international legal dimension and which can be considered as matters in which other States and relevant international institutions have a lawful interest.

Following the Oslo Accords of 1993, the PLO, with the subsequent endorsement of the Palestinian National Council, established the Palestinian Authority as a short-term, *administrative entity* charged with the limited governance of those areas of the West Bank and Gaza which were placed under Palestinian responsibility. Its mandate, originally five

---

[19] See, for example, League of Arab States, Seventh Arab League Summit, Rabat, Morocco, 'Resolution on Palestine,' 28 October 1974, para. 2, affirming the PLO as 'the sole legitimate representative of the Palestinian people.'

[20] UN General Assembly Resolution 3236 (XXIX), 22 November 1974.

[21] Letter dated 23 September 2011 from Mahmoud Abbas to Ban Ki-moon, UN Secretary-General.

years, was extended in 1999. The Palestinian Authority thus has limited legislative and executive competence, limited territorial jurisdiction, and limited personal jurisdiction over Palestinians not present in the areas for which it has been accorded responsibility.

Within the constitutional structure of the PLO and the governance of the Occupied Palestinian Territory, therefore, the Palestinian Authority is a *subsidiary* body, competent only to exercise those powers conferred on it by the Palestinian National Council. By definition, and applying basic public law principles, it does not have the capacity to assume greater powers, to 'dissolve' its parent body, or otherwise to establish itself independently of the Palestinian National Council and the PLO. Moreover, it is the PLO and the Palestinian National Council which derive their legitimacy from the fact that they represent all sectors of the displaced Palestinian people, no matter where they presently live or have refuge.[22]

The move to enhance the Palestinian presence in the United Nations through full State membership carries the *risk* of fragmentation and disenfranchisement (the emphasis here is on *risk*, not certainty), where the State represents (some or all of) the people within the UN and the PLO represents (some or all of) the people outside the UN. Such a division of representation would run counter to the *status quo* and to the original intent of the international community of States in recognizing the PLO. The challenge is to maintain unity in these unique circumstances, and the question is whether that would be achieved by having the PLO as the representative of the State in the UN. It might well do, if the appropriate form of words and the right institutional guarantees could be found. The bottom line, however, remains the will of the people.

Popular Representation and International Law

The bid for full UN membership, for international recognition and acceptance of statehood in the fullest sense, reveals the tension between the formal criteria — what constituent facts make up the State — and the principle of self-determination considered as the actual freedom of the people to choose their model of internal and external governance.

The possibility of reconfiguring the self-determination unit by substitution, and without the consent of the people behind the competent

---

[22] The elections proposed under the Oslo Accords took place in January 1996 and were repeated in 2006 for the Palestinian Legislative Council. However, they were limited to the Palestinians of the West Bank and Gaza and did not include the Palestinians in the diaspora.

institutions, raises the 'external' question of its consistency, not only with the long-standing acceptance of the PLO as the sole, legitimate representative of the Palestinian people, but also with what can be argued to be the essential democratic underpinnings for a settlement.

Law and politics evolve. The question here is about change and development and about how that process can and must be legitimated. As repeatedly mentioned already, the long engagement of the UN and its member States in the Palestinian question means that it is a matter of international legal concern and not, as it were, a purely domestic, local or regional affair. The representation of the people of Palestine is also just such an international legal question. Their silence, or a failure to consult them, cannot be taken as acquiescence in other closely related matters, such as: Who is a citizen? Who is competent to ratify treaties? Who speaks to refugee return and compensation? The starting point when looking for answers is and must remain the principle of self-determination.

The General Assembly's 1947 plans for a future independent Arab State were premised, among others, on elections to a constituent assembly to be 'conducted on democratic lines,' and on voting to be open to those, including women, aged eighteen or over. The Constituent Assembly, in turn, was to draft a democratic constitution, establishing 'a legislative body elected by universal suffrage and by secret ballot on the basis of proportional representation, and an executive body responsible to the legislature . . . .'[23]

In many ways, this is still a strikingly modern agenda, so what then are the options and constraints? The basic working principle must be that only the people of Palestine should now determine who will represent them in the UN. Any change in who represents the people or a part of the people, therefore, requires an expression of the popular will and international recognition equivalent to that given in the past by the General Assembly and the Arab League. In the absence of that expression of popular will and international recognition, we will likely be faced with yet another crisis of legitimacy, going to the roots of the self-determination issue.

What might this mean in practice? In recent years, numerous international, regional and non-governmental organizations have striven to flesh out what it means, as a matter of international law, to require of States that they follow the path of free and fair elections. Although different perceptions remain, it is increasingly accepted that popular participation is necessarily linked to rights – the right to be recognized as a

---

[23] UN General Assembly Resolution 181(II), 'Future government of Palestine,' 29 November 1947.

person at law and hence to be registered and enabled to vote, the right of universal suffrage, the right to associate for political purposes, to establish political parties, to freedom of expression, to the secret ballot, and to a transparent and verifiable ballot count, among others.

The move to enhance the Palestinian presence in the United Nations through 'statehood' risks fragmentation. It cannot be ignored that the majority of Palestinians are refugees living outside of Palestine, and that they have an equal claim to be represented, particularly given the recognition of their rights in General Assembly resolution 194 (III), among others. It is not clear that they will be enfranchised through the admission of the State of Palestine to full membership in the UN, in which case the PLO must continue to speak for their rights in the UN until they are implemented.

Democracy, in the words of the 1997 Universal Declaration on Democracy adopted by the Council of the Inter-Parliamentary Union, presupposes a 'genuine partnership between men and women,' 'free political competition,' and 'open, free and non-discriminatory participation by the people, exercised in accordance with the rule of law, in both letter and spirit.'[24] In Beetham's words, 'representative' means 'reflecting the most important characteristics of the electorate, in the matter of geographical distribution, political opinion, and social composition,' while political equality means that 'everyone counts for one.'[25]

'Accountability' is a further relevant consideration. In the sense used here, political accountability requires a representative electoral system, which guarantees universal suffrage, the secret ballot, equality of the vote, and periodicity of elections. This in turn requires legislation and the institutions necessary to make a law effective, including an independent electoral commission.

The rule of law, moreover, is not just a matter of judges, independent of the executive and able conscientiously to review governmental conduct and to provide remedies for the citizen or resident whose rights are breached. Important as these things are, the rule of law is also about the separation of powers between the executive, the legislature and the judiciary; about there being laws in place which are known and agreed, and about the constitutional approach to government. One central element in the rule of law is the protection of human rights, especially those that

---

[24] Inter-Parliamentary Union, *Universal Declaration on Democracy*, adopted without a vote by the Inter-Parliamentary Council at its 161st Session, Cairo, 16 September 1997.
[25] D. Beetham, *Democracy and Human Rights* (Oxford: Blackwell Publishers, 1999).

are linked to the goal of political accountability; that is, the political rights: to associate, to organise, to form and join political parties, to express one's views, to register as an elector, to vote, to stand for public office, to participate. For a democratic State, a State fit for the twenty-first century, must clearly engage its people effectively, including and ensuring the representation of all groups and sectors of society. This is a programme, then, not something that can be achieved overnight. Popular participation, accountability, the rule of law, gender equality – are these yet conditions of statehood or UN membership as a matter of international law? Clearly not, but they are all matters upon which international law has something to say and the State seeking the fullest recognition and acceptance by the international community, the State anxious to show its willingness to fulfil its international obligations, will be best placed in the twenty-first century if it can demonstrate in real, practical, legal, institutional and effective terms, its commitment to these democratic imperatives.

The right of the Palestinian people to self-determination has been clearly recognized as a matter of international law.[26] The peaceful and effective exercise of this right in accordance with the UN Charter has further been recognized as requiring the representation of the Palestinian people at large in the work of the United Nations. Is there any reason why, in the case of Palestine, any of this should wait? The challenge for the people of Palestine and for those who speak for them today is probably unique in the perspective of 'State-building' and democratic development. It is to move consciously and openly from a first level of internationally accepted representation, into an evolved version of the traditional State model, without losing the legitimacy that comes from the voice of the people – to a model, therefore, in which all Palestinians continue to be represented, and are seen to be represented, in and through the UN.

Obviously, the situation in the West Bank and Gaza and among the diaspora has produced conditions different from those which have configured statehood in the past, but this is the source of both challenges and opportunities. Can mechanisms not be devised and put in place which would ensure the most free and ample participation of the people of Palestine in determining their future system of governance and, in the immediate and short term, the nature and composition of their representation at the international level?

---

[26] International Court of Justice, *Legal Consequences of the Construction of a Wall in the Occupied Palestinian Territory*, Advisory Opinion, 9 July 2004, para. 118.

Why should the people not be registered, for example? Voting by refugees and the displaced is nothing new; both the Office of the United Nations High Commissioner for Refugees (UNHCR) and the Inter-Parliamentary Union (IPU), as well as host States, have contributed in the past to the processes of registration, balloting, and the count. I have argued above that, in the particular case of the people of Palestine, the question of representation is to be considered a matter of international legal concern; but the reverse of the coin is that the international community of States and the United Nations also have responsibilities here, and an opportunity to apply their considerable experience in building and strengthening capacity. Moreover, that interest of the international community of States is accompanied by responsibilities to assist in building national capacity in pursuit of good governance and democratization.[27] This is not just a matter of allowing voices to be heard, therefore, but of translating voices into representation and political action.

Already, there is coming into place an extraordinary popular initiative for registration, which may finally allow Palestinians at large not only to be counted, but also to make known their views.[28] It needs to be endorsed by presently existing governmental institutions, guaranteed by appropriate international mechanisms, and given the widest and fullest international support, if it is to play its essential role in allowing the voice of the people to be heard.

International law may not yet make democratic representative government a condition of statehood, or even a condition of membership of the United Nations (regional organizations are another matter). But the character of government and representation *is* increasingly a matter of international concern and inquiry, while the people also increasingly embed their claims and their right to accountable government not only in local principles and precepts, but also in the rules and standards endorsed internationally.

Traditionally, a State for the purposes of international law presupposed territory, population, government and the capacity to enter into international relations. Today's world expects more, particularly where representation in the UN is concerned, and the State should be representative of the people for whom it speaks and directly accountable to them. One way to establish representative democracy is by elections, though elections should also meet certain international standards and be seen to advance the goals of popular representation, democratic

---

[27] See, among others, UN General Assembly resolutions 64/12, 9 November 2009; and 64/155, 18 December 2009.

[28] See http://www.palestiniansregister.org.

government, and the protection of human rights. States which are imposed, top-down, or which are created without an exercise of the popular will are, by definition, not representative. And as recent events remind us, the lack of representative and accountable government is a sure-fire recipe for disaster.

CHAPTER THREE

CITIZENS OF THE STATE OF PALESTINE AND THE FUTURE OF PALESTINIAN REFUGEES: LEGAL AND POLITICAL SCENARIOS*

MUTAZ M. QAFISHEH

Introduction

By virtue of 'nationality' or 'citizenship,' an individual becomes a 'citizen' of a State as opposed to a 'foreigner.' (In this chapter, the terms 'nationality' and 'citizenship' are used as synonymous.) The test of citizenship that determines the status of the people of any State is an integral part of international law. The formation of the 'people' who, together with 'territory' and 'government,' constitute the pillars of any State, stems from citizenship. Citizenship is the legal bond whereby individuals belonging to the people of a given State are connected.

Citizenship is the 'right of rights.' Based on citizenship, citizens, unlike foreigners, can vote in elections and referenda, be elected, obtain public employment, have the unconditional right to practise professions

* This chapter is based on five previous works conducted by the writer: (1) 'Article 1D of the 1951 Convention,' in A. Zimmermann, ed., *The 1951 Convention Relating to the Status of Refugees and its 1967 Protocol: A Commentary* (Oxford: Oxford University Press, 2011); (2) *Citizenship in the State of Palestine* (Ramallah: Palestinian Negotiations Office, 2011); (3) 'Genesis of Nationality and Migration in Palestine and Israel 1917-1925,' 11 *Journal of the History of International Law* 1 (The Hague: Martinus Nijhoff, 2009); (4) *The International Law Foundations of Palestinian Nationality: A Legal Examination of Palestinian Nationality under Britain's Rule* (Leiden/Boston: Brill , 2008); (5) *Nationality and Domicile in Palestine* (Birzeit: Institute of International Studies, 2000). The writer expresses his gratitude to the following for providing insightful comments on an early draft of this chapter: John Quigley of Ohio, Suzan Akram of Boston, Abbas Shiblak of Oxford, and Lance Bartholomeusz of UNRWA-Jerusalem.

and engage in business, own immovable property, form political parties, hold passports, travel abroad, be protected by State diplomatic missions, be immune from deportation, have an absolute right of residence and be allowed to return to the country of their citizenship.

As citizenship is inherently related to sovereignty, any attempt to understand the current status of Palestinian citizenship should start from the moment at which 'Palestine' became a separate entity that granted citizenship, namely after the separation of its territory from the Ottoman Empire. From 9 December 1917 until the present day, due to the *de facto* sovereignties exercised over Palestine, various statuses have shaped Palestine's inhabitants. Certain statuses emerged due to the policy pursued and the legislative acts undertaken unilaterally by individual States, chiefly Israel and Jordan.

The citizenship law of the State of Palestine, if it is to be based on international law, should grant citizenship to persons who have the right to acquire it. As citizenship is an individual right, it should be conferred on the following two grounds: (1) the right as recognized by international law; (2) the individual's choice. The State of Palestine is therefore under an obligation to confer its citizenship on any eligible person who opts for its citizenship, regardless of whether the person concerned is able to enter Palestine. For example, a refugee in Lebanon could acquire Palestinian citizenship and might be unable to set a foot in the State of Palestine because of the likely Israeli control of the State's border. As a Palestinian citizen, however, this person could obtain a number of benefits from citizenship if Palestine is considered a State. He/she could be protected abroad, travel by means of Palestinian passports, be employed as a Palestinian citizen by international institutions through national competitive examinations, serve in international courts, vote and be elected to the Palestinian parliament and other representative bodies, etc.

The goal of this chapter is to define the factual and legal status of Palestinians all over the world in order to clarify the basis of their citizenship with a view to elaborating policy actions to be translated into Palestinian citizenship law.

To this end, the chapter has the following objectives:

(1) To answer the question 'who is Palestinian citizen,' using a rights-based approach;
(2) To clarify the status of Palestinians worldwide for citizenship-granting purposes;
(3) To define the basis applicable to all types of Palestinians for granting the right of citizenship;

(4) To elaborate policy actions that can be taken by the State, or by the Palestine Liberation Organization, to realize Palestinians' right of citizenship in the event that full recognition/membership of Palestine is the United Nations is delayed.

A citizenship law of the new State of Palestine should be drafted on the basis of the foregoing considerations. The law should include various bases for nationality acquisition: nationality by birth (*jus soli*), by blood (*jus sanguinis*), by naturalization, and by marriage. The Palestinian citizenship law should reflect modern developments in both international human rights law and comparative citizenship laws, including equality between spouses regarding the granting of citizenship by marriage, transmission of citizenship to one's children when one of the parents is a citizen, fixing of a reasonable time for naturalization, and granting of citizenship by the State based on application in special cases. Other technical issues should be addressed by the said law, including citizenship revocation, abandonment by choice, and dual citizenship. A set of by-laws and procedures should accompany the bill.

In order to provide a clear legal basis for the concept of 'Palestinians,' this chapter will seek to categorize each population group relating to Palestine as the group stands today and to present the position of international law on each category. As there are many such categories, they may overlap and be re-categorized narrowly or widely. However, the precise features of each group can be accurately characterized only by using a legal approach as defined in international law.

Broadly speaking, people who relate to Palestine may be divided, in terms of citizenship features shared by each group's members, into three categories: (1) the inhabitants of the occupied Palestinian territory or the West Bank and the Gaza Strip; (2) Palestinian refugees who voluntarily left or were forced to leave their homes in the area of Mandate Palestine in which Israel was established; and (3) the inhabitants of the State of Israel. Each typological component comprises sub-categories.

The inhabitants of the occupied territory belong to three groups:

- West Bankers and Gazans;
- East Jerusalemites;
- The 1967 refugees.

Palestinian refugees constitute many different groups, depending on the status accorded to them in their places of residence. Thus, they may be considered as ordinary refugees, stateless, immigrants, permanent residents, or citizens. The feature they all share is their right of return to Israel according to international law. In this chapter, Palestinian refugees will be broken down into five groups:

- Palestinian refugees residing in the West Bank and the Gaza Strip;
- Palestinian refugees who acquired the citizenship of another State;
- Stateless Palestinian refugees within UNRWA (United Nations Relief and Works Agency for Palestine Refugees) areas of operation;
- Stateless Palestinian refugees outside UNRWA areas of operation;
- Palestinians stripped of their citizenship after 1925.

Despite holding Israeli citizenship, the status of the inhabitants of Israel requires clarification to include or exclude certain groups from the scope of Palestinian citizenship based on justified legal reasoning. This category includes five groups:

- Israeli Arabs in their original places of residence;
- Israeli Arabs internally displaced within Israel;
- Israeli Jews who were native Palestinians before 1917-1918;
- Israeli Jews naturalized by acquiring Palestinian nationality;
- Newcomer Israelis.

Before starting to address such categories on an individual basis, it is first necessary to address and understand the foundations of the right to Palestinian citizenship under international law. These foundations relate to the status of each group or sub-group to be studied. For the sake of clarity in surveying the various groups of 'Palestinians,' the foundations of Palestinian citizenship may be found in the annex to this chapter.

The Inhabitants of the Occupied Palestinian Territory

Palestinians of the West Bank

The West Bankers, who numbered about 2.58 million in mid-2011 according to the Palestinian Central Bureau of Statistics, include inhabitants who resided in the eastern part of Palestine which became known as the West Bank after the annexation of that area by Jordan in 1950. Three groups of West Bank inhabitants are discussed under separate headings below in order to clarify the rights relating to their particular status: (1) inhabitants of East Jerusalem; (2) inhabitants of the West Bank (and the Gaza Strip) who arrived from parts of Palestine that became Israel in 1948 and afterwards (occupied territory refugees); and (3) those who were residents of the West Bank (and the Gaza Strip) and were displaced during the 1967 war and its aftermath. Under British rule, the West Bank was an integral part of Palestine and did not form a political or administrative entity. Its inhabitants were Palestinian citizens. During the 1948 war, the Jordanian army entered parts of Palestine. The West Bank emerged as an entity after Jordan's conclusion of an armistice agreement with Israel in 1949. This agreement created what has become known as the 'green line,' i.e. armistice lines drawn up on the maps attached to the aforesaid agreement. As it is located on the western side of the Jordan River, this area of Palestine was *de facto* called the 'West Bank' as opposed to the 'East Bank' of the same river, namely the Hashemite Kingdom. Jordan continued ruling the area until 4 June 1967; the West Bank was occupied by Israel the following day. Under Jordanian rule, the West Bank incorporated East Jerusalem.

Gradually, Jordan granted its citizenship to the inhabitants of the West Bank, as well as to all Palestinian refugees who ended up on the West or East Banks of the Jordan River and who were prevented by Israel from returning to their homes within its territory. On 13 January 1949, by Law No. 56, Jordan amended its 1928 nationality law. This amendment provided that 'all persons habitually residing in Trans-Jordan or in the western area that is currently being administrated by the Hashemite Kingdom of Jordan who hold Palestinian citizenship shall acquire Jordanian citizenship, and enjoy all citizen's rights and responsibilities on the same footing as Jordanians' (Article 2). On 7 February 1949, Jordan enacted a law on passports. Article 2 of this law gave any 'Arab person holding Palestinian nationality' the right to obtain a Jordanian passport. Jordan confirmed the granting of its citizenship to all West Bankers by the Nationality Law of 2 February 1954. Article 3 of this law stated that 'the following persons shall be considered Jordanian citizens: . . . (2) Those who acquired Jordanian citizenship in accordance with Law No. 56 of 1949; and (3) All non-Jewish persons who were holding Palestinian citizenship prior to 15 May 1948 and who reside at the date of the enactment of this law in the Hashemite Kingdom of Jordan [which included the West Bank after the annexation].' Palestinians of the West Bank, via this process, were considered to be Jordanian citizens. They could as such participate in legislative elections, be elected to parliament, hold public office, become ministers, bear passports, and be provided with diplomatic protection by Jordanian embassies abroad.

The 1954 Jordanian Nationality Law adopted the common citizenship rules recognized in comparative law. It relied on *jus sanguinis* as the main principle, so that children born to a Jordanian father (not mother) would become Jordanians regardless of their place of birth (Article 9). Naturalization was made possible under Article 12 for any foreigner who resided in the country for four years and was literate in Arabic. Foreign women who married Jordanian men could acquire Jordanian citizenship upon application according to Article 8. Articles 18 and 19 provided for revocation of Jordanian citizenship by the government in cases of 'disloyalty,' such as serving in an enemy military force or committing a security-related offence. Dual citizenship was not permitted under Jordanian law. Thus, Article 17 required the approval of the Council of Ministers for the acquisition of a second citizenship and Article 4 stipulated that any citizen of an Arab State might acquire Jordanian citizenship after abandoning his former citizenship. However, the renunciation of previous citizenship was not a precondition for naturalization, as there was no provision to that effect in the law. In practice, applicants for Jordanian citizenship might be requested to submit proof of renunciation of their former citizenship as part of the naturalization procedures (Article 4). In such cases, the person might find himself compelled to renounce his previous citizenship. But, as the practice of States proves, the withdrawal of former citizenship does not depend on Jordanian law but rather on the domestic law of the State of former citizenship. Hence, the provision of evidence of expatriation does not necessarily result in the loss of one's existing citizenship. As a result, Jordanians may effectively retain former citizenships or acquire new nationalities without losing Jordanian citizenship. A major amendment to the 1954 law took place on 7 March 1963 in the form of the Amended Nationality Law. One of this law's provisions recognized non-Jewish holders of Palestinian citizenship who had been residing in Jordan from 20 December 1949 to 16 February 1954 as Jordanian citizens. The purpose of this amendment was apparently to halt the granting of Jordanian citizenship to more Palestinians who move to settle in Jordan. A second provision within the amended law applied the *jus soli* principle in exceptional cases: it granted citizenship to those born in Jordan to a Jordanian mother and to a stateless father, or to a father with unknown citizenship, or to an unknown father or unknown parents.

This situation continued until June 1967. From the beginning of the occupation until 1994, Israel closed the borders with Jordan and controlled the whole of the West Bank. No one could leave, or land in, the West Bank without Israeli permission. The inhabitants were considered by Israel at this time as permanent residents of the West Bank, not as residents of Israel because the area had not been annexed by the Israeli State. The status of West Bankers has then become similar to that of citizens, in terms of citizens' rights, albeit under occupation, according to the applicable law in the area. Israel issued orange-coloured identity cards to the West Bankers as an indication of residency. As a result, a sort of *de facto* 'West Bank nationality' was invented. Inhabitants could travel abroad using Jordanian passports. For a number of years prior to 1994, Israel obliged those travelling abroad to remain outside for at least nine months. Thousands of West Bankers who travelled abroad, however, were not allowed by Israel to return. Israel adopted the system of absentees, i.e. those who left the West Bank and failed to return within three years would lose the right to return. This policy created a category of West Bankers called 'identity card losers,' who virtually became refugees as will be shown below. Yet Israel allowed a limited number of non-West-Bank residents to return to the West Bank from abroad and obtain permanent residence in the occupied territory under the formula of family reunification.

Jordan continued at the time to treat the inhabitants of the West Bank as Jordanian citizens, despite their being under Israeli occupation. West Bankers could travel abroad, i.e. outside Jordan, using Jordanian passports (they travelled from the West Bank to Jordan using Israeli-issued identity cards and permits for each journey). Jordan also continued to protect the West Bankers abroad. West Bankers were allowed to reside in the territory to the east of the Jordan River, to own immovable property, to practise professions, and to hold public office—just like East Bankers/Jordanians.

The same status continued intact until 31 July 1988. On that date, the King of Jordan decided to end the Kingdom's already nominal sovereignty over the West Bank. This meant that all Jordanian citizens who were residing in the West Bank would *ipso facto* lose their Jordanian citizenship. To that effect, the Jordanian cabinet issued instructions to strip West Bankers of Jordanian citizenship. The Jordanian courts upheld the King's decision and considered West Bankers as 'Palestinians,' i.e. foreigners, while they were in the East Bank. Jordanian passports were withdrawn from West Bankers. As they did not have any other travel document, Jordan granted the West Bankers temporary Jordanian passports. These passports allowed the inhabitants to travel outside Jordan but not to reside in the Kingdom or to exercise citizens' rights therein. Hence, the temporary Jordanian passports, which had been issued for a two-year period, were treated as 'travel documents' rather than as passports by Jordan and other States. It should be noted that Jordan's sovereignty in the West Bank was questionable in international law since the vast majority of States had not recognized the Jordanian annexation. The Palestine Liberation Organization, as the legal representative of the Palestinian people, has always considered the West Bank to be part of Palestine.

Palestinians of the Gaza Strip

This group, which included some 1.59 million persons in mid-2011 according to the Palestinian Central Bureau of Statistics, incorporates the inhabitants of the part of Palestine that became known as the 'Gaza Strip' in 1948 when the Mediterranean enclave fell under the administration of Egypt. Two groups of 'Gazans' are addressed below: the 'refugees of Gaza' who moved to the Strip during the 1947-1949 war, and those who were displaced from the Gaza Strip (as in the case of the West Bank) and moved to other States after the Israeli occupation in 1967 and afterwards.

Although the Gaza Strip constitutes with the West Bank the Palestinian territory occupied in 1967, it has always had a separate political and social character from the West Bank after 1948. This character produced certain legal effects. The Gaza Strip, like the rest of Palestine, was occupied by Britain from 9 December 1917and remained under the Mandate until 14 May 1948. During its war with Israel, Egypt occupied the territory that has become known as the Gaza Strip. The Strip emerged within its current borders with Egypt and Israel after the signing of the armistice agreement between Egypt and Israel in 1949. Egypt retained its military administration of the Gaza Strip, without annexing it until 1967—unlike what Jordan had done in the West Bank as explained above. In June of that year, Israel occupied the Gaza Strip and continued controlling it until 1994 after the signing of the Oslo agreement with the Palestine Liberation Organization.

Citizenship in the Gaza Strip under Egyptian administration (1948-1967) had a particular, *de facto*, character. As Egypt had not annexed the Gaza Strip, the Strip's inhabitants retained a form of Palestinian citizenship, comparable to the citizenship that existed under British rule in Palestine as described above. The Palestinian Citizenship Order of 1925 continued to be applicable and the 'Gaza government' set up by Egypt treated the inhabitants as Palestinian citizens. Although Egypt granted Egyptian travel documents to the Gaza Strip's inhabitants, the inhabitants needed a visa to enter Egypt. At the time, persons could retain and recover Palestinian citizenship. Acquisition of Palestinian citizenship by naturalization was possible too. For example, a non-Palestinian woman who married a Palestinian man residing in Gaza could acquire permanent residency in the Strip and would be registered as a Palestinian citizen naturalized by marriage, as demonstrated by naturalization decisions published in the *Palestine Gazette*, the official journal of the Egypt-run government of Gaza. Citizenship was also accorded to persons who had been residing abroad and returned to the Gaza Strip. Such persons were obliged to renounce other nationalities that they might have acquired as a condition for obtaining Palestinian citizenship. Like naturalization decisions, decisions relating to such revocations of citizenship were also published in the *Palestine Gazette*. It should be noted that this 'Gaza citizenship' constituted an anomalous Palestinian citizenship. Its nature depended on the way in which States regarded such citizenship. Many States viewed the inhabitants of the Gaza Strip as refugees because they held Egyptian travel documents that Egypt granted to both refugees and non-refugees in the Strip. However, citizenship status produced fully-fledged local effects in the Gaza Strip. Its holders enjoyed citizens' rights, including participation in parliamentary elections, the holding of public office, and permanent residence.

Gazans were viewed as foreigners in Egypt, as just mentioned. However, they were treated on the same footing as Egyptians in regard to a number of social rights, such as admission to public schools and access to public health institutions. While abroad, Palestinians from the Gaza Strip were protected by Egyptian diplomatic and consular missions— similar to the protection enjoyed by Palestinians under British rule. Hence, in the Gaza Strip there was a special citizenship that can be described as 'Gaza citizenship.' This anomalous status is merely one of the many anomalous circumstances stemming from the absence of the State of Palestine. Such anomalies have shaped Palestinian citizenship from 1917 until, we may safely generalize, the present day; the citizenship of the Gaza Strip's inhabitants was no exception.

This situation continued until 5 June 1967 when Israel occupied the Gaza Strip. Israel then closed the borders with Egypt and did not allow the Gaza Strip inhabitants to leave the Strip by sea. No one could leave, or land in, the Strip without Israeli permission. The Gaza Strip inhabitants were considered by Israel at that time as permanent residents of the Strip. Their status had become similar to that of citizens, albeit under occupation, as was the case in the West Bank. Israel granted the Gaza Strip inhabitants orange-coloured identity cards as proof of residency. It allowed Gaza inhabitants who applied for permits to the Israeli military commander of the Strip to leave their areas of residence and to return. Thousands of them, however, were not allowed to return. Others were forcibly deported. Israel adopted the system of absentees, i.e. those who left the Gaza Strip and failed to return within three years would lose the right to return. This policy created a category of Gaza Strip inhabitants called 'identity card losers.' Yet Israel allowed a limited number of Palestinian refugees and non-Palestinians from abroad to obtain permanent residence under a family reunification procedure, as it had done in the West Bank.

The situation changed somewhat from 1994 when the Palestinian Authority was established in most areas of the Gaza Strip after the signing of the Oslo Accords. In 2005, Israel withdrew its forces from the Gaza Strip but it maintained control over the Strip's borders, airspace and territorial waters. Israel, Egypt and the Palestinian Authority signed an agreement in November 2005 placing the crossing point between the Gaza Strip and Egypt under joint Egyptian-Palestinian administration, with a European Union presence and remote monitoring by Israeli personnel. After Hamas assumed control over the Gaza Strip in June 2007, Israel imposed a blockade on the Strip and closed the crossing between Egypt and the Gaza Strip. However, the border crossing is opened from time to time. The inhabitants, notwithstanding the recent difficulties, have been able to travel abroad using Palestinian passports as in the case of the West Bank. After the Egyptian revolution of January 2011, Hamas *de facto* government could control the Rafah crossing from the Gaza side, while Egypt continued control its side of the border. Egypt and Hamas administrate the passage with limited or no Israeli interference. Since then, the movement of persons from and into Gaza has been substantially eased. For example, Palestinians from the West Bank, unlike in the past, could enter Gaza from Egypt using Palestinian passports.

A word must be added concerning the relationship, or the movement of Palestinians, between the Gaza Strip and the West Bank. After the establishment of the Palestinian Authority in 1994, Israel isolated the West Bank from the Gaza Strip. West Bank residents could not travel to the Gaza Strip, and *vice versa*, except with the permission of Israel. Gaza Strip inhabitants could reside in the West Bank only for as long as Israel determined. Israel reserved the power to deport inhabitants of the Gaza Strip from the West Bank. It likewise reserved the right to grant permanent residence to some of the Gaza Strip inhabitants in the West Bank, chiefly on grounds of family reunification or public employment. In August 2011, for example, Israel allowed 1,956 persons from the Gaza Strip, who had already been residing in the West Bank for years, the right to change their address to the West Bank and thereby acquire permanent residency in the West Bank. In practice, such persons became West Bankers and were unable to travel to the Gaza Strip without an Israeli permit. Israel also deported some West Bankers to the Gaza Strip and prevented their return to the West Bank. The status of the inhabitants of the Gaza Strip thus resembled that of *de facto* foreigners in the West Bank, and *vice versa*.

Citizenship under the Palestinian Authority

After the establishment of the Palestinian Authority in 1994 in certain parts of the West Bank and the Gaza Strip ('Occupied Palestinian Territory' or 'OPT') upon the signing of the 'Declaration of Principles' between Israel and the Palestine Liberation Organization on 13 September 1993 ('Oslo I') and after the signing of the 'Israeli-Palestinian Interim Agreement' on 28 September 1995 ('Oslo II'), the situation changed to some extent. Both of these instruments, commonly known as the 'Oslo Accords,' gave the Palestinian Authority the right to issue identity cards for OPT inhabitants and to print Palestinian passports after notifying Israel (Oslo II, Article 28, paragraph 7). Yet Israel continued controlling the OPT's border. The inhabitants could travel using Palestinian passports but required the permission of Israeli authorities located at the border crossing points with Jordan (West Bank) and Egypt (Gaza Strip). Palestinian passports are now recognized by most States of the world. States grant entry visas to Palestinian passport holders and deal with them according to the regulations governing other aliens enforced in these States on the same footing as foreigners from independent States.

A number of changes relating to Palestinian citizenship occurred after the signing of the Oslo Accords. A joint Israeli-Palestinian police force was stationed at the border crossing points. West Bankers travelling abroad via Jordan were required to pass through Israeli and Palestinian security checks; the same applied to Gaza Strip inhabitants travelling abroad through Egypt. For a number of years after the establishment of the Palestinian Authority, Gaza Strip inhabitants (and to a lesser extent West Bankers) were able to travel abroad through Gaza International Airport, which the Israeli army destroyed after the outbreak of the second *intifada* (uprising) in 2000. Also after the *intifada*, Israel prevented holders of Palestinian passports from travelling through its airports—they had in fact rarely travelled through those airports. Israel had the final say on whether passage was permitted at all locations from which Palestinians travelled. Thousands of inhabitants were banned from travelling abroad for 'security reasons.' Further, at the beginning of the second *intifada*, Israel ended the presence of the nominal Palestinian police force at border crossing points and retained exclusive control over the movement of persons. However, the Palestinian Authority maintained separate police control points near the border in the cities of Jericho (West Bank) and Rafah (Gaza Strip). Travellers were required to undergo Palestinian Authority police checks and passport registration before proceeding to the Israeli side of the border. Passengers were required to do the same on their way back from Jordan or Egypt. The Palestinian Authority could prevent certain West Bankers from travelling to Jordan by means of this procedure. Hamas, as a *de facto* authority, was able to operate a similar procedure after taking over the Gaza Strip.

Furthermore, the Oslo Accords affected Palestinian citizenship in a number of – albeit limited – positive ways. Thousands of persons were enabled to acquire permanent residency in the West Bank or the Gaza Strip and to obtain Palestinian identity cards and passports. The persons concerned, commonly known amongst the local population as 'the returnees,' belong to five categories: (1) officers recruited by the Palestine Liberation Organization from abroad (i.e. from among non-permanent residents of the West Bank or the Gaza Strip), mostly Palestinian refugees with Jordanian passports or Egyptian travel documents; (2) employees recruited to work for the Palestinian Authority who are mostly officials of the Palestine Liberation Organization; (3) 'investors, for the purpose of encouraging investment,' who are mostly Palestinian refugees from the business community; (4) 'spouses and children of Palestinian residents;' (5) 'other persons, for humanitarian reasons, in order to promote and upgrade family reunification.' The first category was recognized by Oslo I (Annex II, Article 3, paragraph c) and the other four categories were covered by Article 28 of Oslo II. The Palestinian Authority was enabled to grant such permanent residency in agreement with Israel on a case-by-case basis, effectively after the approval of Israel. Israel could block any decision on the granting of permanent residency, and it did so when it stopped approving family reunification requests after the outbreak of the *intifada* in 2000. In addition, the Accords defined the citizens of the occupied territory for the purpose of participation in general presidential and legislative elections in the West Bank and the Gaza Strip. Any permanent resident of the West Bank or the Gaza Strip over eighteen years of age was considered to be a Palestinian citizen for that purpose, based on Oslo II, Annex II, Article II. According to paragraph 1(g) of the latter article, certain persons who were not registered in the population register, i.e. who did not hold Palestinian identity cards, could acquire such identity cards and become permanent residents of the West Bank or the Gaza Strip.

Oslo II institutionalized population registration in the West Bank and the Gaza Strip (Article 28, Annex III). In particular, the agreement recognized identity cards issued by Israel for the population under occupation and replaced such cards with Palestinian cards as a sign of permanent residency. The Palestinian Authority assumed responsibility for population affairs relating to citizenship, including births, deaths, marriages, addresses, and the like. The Authority received from Israel 'the population registry for the residents of the West Bank and the Gaza Strip in addition to files and records concerning them [including] . . . records of births and deaths and the indexes from 1918 till 1981.' The Authority was mandated to register children under sixteen years of age who were born abroad 'if either of their parents is a resident of the Gaza Strip and West Bank' (Article 28, paragraph 12). The latter provision constitutes acceptance in practice of the *jus sanguinis* principle whereby any child born to a West Banker or Gazan father or mother is entitled to permanent residency, since such residency is effectively equivalent to citizenship. By allowing both parents to transmit their status to their children, this provision took gender equality into consideration.

Oslo II gave the Palestinian Authority, after Israeli clearance, the power to issue visitors' permits for persons from States that had no diplomatic relations with Israel (Article 28, paragraph 13). Requests for such permits were to be filed by any relative or acquaintance of the visitor residing in the West Bank or the Gaza Strip. Such visitors were permitted to remain in the occupied territory for a period of up to three months with the possibility of extension for an additional four months. The Palestinian Authority could also issue visitors' permits to foreigners for the purpose of study or work in the OPT for an extendable period of one year. Thousands of persons who entered the OPT under these provisions overstayed, especially spouses who had married local inhabitants and started families. While the status of many of these persons was regularized through family reunification procedures whereby they acquired identity cards and Palestinian passports, the cases of many others are still pending. Furthermore, a smaller number of persons from States that have diplomatic relations with Israel, who visited the OPT by obtaining visitors' permits from the Palestinian Authority (based on Oslo II, Article 28, paragraph 14) or by obtaining Israeli visas (under the 1952 Entry into Israel Law), also overstayed and are deemed to be illegal residents. These persons, mostly spouses of local inhabitants, may face deportation by the Israeli authorities if they are discovered.

This overview shows that the Oslo Accords have not significantly changed the *status quo* relating to Palestinian citizenship that was in place before the establishment of the Palestinian Authority. They broadly maintain that status with minor modifications that have affected the lives

of some individuals. Since the Accords, Palestinian citizenship in the OPT has become akin to permanent residence. Such *de facto* citizenship can be proved and claimed by means of two key documents: locally by means of Palestinian identity cards, and abroad by means of Palestinian passports. The current situation shows that Palestinian citizenship may be effectively acquired by a person born to a Palestinian citizen, who may be the father, mother or both parents, residing in the West Bank or the Gaza Strip, regardless of the place of birth—within the territory or abroad. Citizenship may also be acquired by marriage based not on local law but on the formula of family reunification which may be granted or withheld by Israel. There is no clear rule relating to naturalization, but one may view the cases enumerated above involving the granting of permanent residence in the West Bank or the Gaza Strip as cases akin to naturalization in practice. No rules are in place regarding citizenship revocation, but one may consider the deportation of inhabitants or the denial of return to those who travel abroad as a means of denationalization or citizenship revocation. Neither Israel nor the Palestinian Authority opposes the acquisition of one or more nationalities by permanent residents of the West Bank or the Gaza Strip, many of whom hold other nationalities in addition to their Palestinian passports and reside either in the OPT or abroad. Hence, it may be concluded that dual or multiple citizenship is *de facto* permissible for West Bankers and Gazans. Such dual nationals (e.g. French-West Banker, American-Gazan) are treated as Palestinians by the Palestinian Authority within the OPT, not as foreigners—for instance for participation in elections, ownership of immovable property, practising of professions, and holding public office. Likewise, Israel considers OPT inhabitants who hold foreign passports to be local Palestinians; such persons cannot use their foreign passports in Israel.

In an attempt to pave the way for further regularization of the inhabitants' status, the Palestinian Authority drafted a citizenship law. The bill was prepared in 1995 by the Ministry of the Interior. It took most of its provisions from the 1925 Palestinian Citizenship Order, as amended, that was implemented in Palestine under the Mandate and the 1954 Jordanian Nationality Law, as amended, that was enforced in the West Bank under Jordanian rule. In its twenty-five articles, the draft defined who is a Palestinian, fixed the modes of citizenship acquisition, naturalization, revocation and repatriation, covered issues such as the citizenship of spouses and children, and contained other provisions that normally exist in the citizenship laws of independent States. Despite the existence of the Palestinian Legislative Council since 1996 and its adoption of many laws, the citizenship bill has not been the subject of further deliberation. The reasons for this are the absence of an independent State that can confer its citizenship and obtain international recognition thereof, and the lack of a strategy for dealing with the question of citizenship in the event of a delay in the establishment of the State at the end of the transitional period in May 1999.

Diplomatic protection is the main manifestation of citizenship abroad. The Palestinian Authority was prevented under Oslo II from exercising certain types of diplomatic relations (Article IX, paragraph 5). Yet this restriction did not apply to the Palestine Liberation Organization. Nor, it can be argued, did it apply to the Palestinian Authority after the Oslo transitional period lapsed. Thus, nothing in international law would prevent the aforementioned Organization or Authority from exercising diplomatic protection on behalf of Palestinians abroad. Diplomatic protection may be extended to any Palestinian as defined in this chapter. It may be exercised through bilateral agreements between the Palestinians and other States with which the Palestine Liberation Organization has any type of diplomatic representation. Diplomatic protection takes various forms and can be exercised at different formal, informal or personal levels. It includes assistance to Palestinians abroad in regard to civil status matters, such as registration of marriage, divorce, birth or death, defence of persons facing criminal charges, certification of educational diplomas obtained abroad, mediation on behalf of Palestinians with international organizations in these countries (supporting the rights of persons to obtain refugee status by intervening with the Office of the United Nations High Commissioner for Refugees or defending the labour rights of Palestinian workers employed by international companies), assistance to Palestinian investors abroad by providing technical advice and facilities, and the issuing of Palestinian passports. Such protection needs to be institutionalized. It may be exercised by existing Palestinian embassies, consulates, missions or representative offices. These diplomatic institutions should be strengthened by hiring trained staff to exercise protection as a technical function.

The OPT Arab inhabitants (unlike Jewish settlers who hold Israeli citizenship) currently hold green-coloured Palestinian identity cards, which indicate their right of residence. Under Palestinian Authority rule, OPT inhabitants enjoy most citizens' rights. They can vote in legislative elections, be elected to parliament, obtain public employment, become ministers or judges, form political parties, establish associations, and peacefully assemble. The Palestinian Authority can, at least in theory, exercise diplomatic protection on behalf of West Bankers under bilateral agreements with host countries through its representative missions abroad.

Yet certain citizens' rights are still restricted due to the ongoing Israeli occupation. These restrictions include travel bans that affect some individuals travelling abroad, since Israel has retained the final say regarding departures from the West Bank, restrictions on travel within the OPT through a system of checkpoints, prohibitions on residency or the building of homes in certain areas, and denial of inhabitants' right to bring their foreign spouses into the OPT, save in exceptional cases (family reunification has been frozen since October 2000).

Consequently, the status of the 4.17 million West Bank and Gaza Strip inhabitants is close, albeit not identical, to the status of citizens belonging to sovereign States. There is, so to speak, *de facto* 'West Bank citizenship' and 'Gaza citizenship.' This citizenship is, in certain respects, akin to ordinary citizenship. It can be regarded as full citizenship for certain purposes at the local level in the West Bank or the Gaza Strip; such purposes include permanent residency, election, holding of public office, and travelling abroad. OPT inhabitants may also be considered by other States and by international organizations as citizens of the OPT for various legal purposes, for instance in cases involving private international law issues, refugee status termination (including *non-refoulement* to Israel or the Palestinian Authority), migration, and employment in international or regional organizations. However, certain legal effects do not ensue from such West Bank or Gaza citizenship, such as the possibility of extradition of OPT 'nationals' to other States or their repatriation to the OPT by the Palestinian Authority if necessary, the freedom of citizens to import or export goods without Israel's permission, and their freedom to travel abroad without Israeli bans.

In the future citizenship law of the State of Palestine, the inhabitants of the West Bank and the Gaza Strip should be collectively granted Palestinian citizenship with automatic effect by the operation of law, or *ipso facto*. The State of Palestine is under an international legal obligation to grant its citizenship *en masse* to these inhabitants. This obligation stems from the law of State succession. The State of Palestine would become a successor State to Mandate Palestine, as Palestinian citizenship has never been settled since the dissolution of Palestine in May 1948. In addition, the said State would become a successor to all the States that have exercised *de facto* control in the West Bank or the Gaza Strip (Jordan, Egypt, Israel, and the Palestinian Authority) and have taken action with respect to the inhabitants' citizenship. For example, if Jordan in the West Bank or Egypt in the Gaza Strip (before 1967) or Israel in the West Bank and Gaza Strip (after 1967) granted *de facto* Palestinian citizenship, or permanent residency, to certain persons in these areas, the State of

Palestine should confirm this status and grant Palestinian citizenship to such persons. The obligation of the State of Palestine can be deduced from the above-mentioned customary rule as codified in Article 1 of the International Law Commission's Draft Articles on Nationality of Natural Persons in relation to the Succession of States. It obliges each successor State to grant its citizenship to every individual who had the citizenship of the predecessor State and who has his or her habitual residence in the successor State.

The obligation of the State of Palestine to grant its citizenship should hold 'irrespective of the mode of acquisition of that [predecessor] nationality.' Thus, Jordan might have granted its citizenship to some foreigners in the West Bank during its rule before 1967. Some East Jordanians might have moved to the West Bank at that time, since residence within Jordan, east and west, was possible as part of the local law under which all citizens were free to live in any part of the State. The two groups of persons might have become permanent residents of the West Bank after the Israeli occupation. Israel, too, might have granted family reunification to a certain number of non-Palestinian men or women during its rule in the West Bank and the Gaza Strip. Some of these persons are currently permanent residents in the West Bank or the Gaza Strip, holding Palestinian identity cards and passports just like the rest of the local population. Similarly, the Palestinian Authority has granted permanent residency in the West Bank and the Gaza Strip to the foreigners mentioned above. Simply put, the test for conferring Palestinian citizenship on the inhabitants of the West Bank or the Gaza Strip in the citizenship law of the State of Palestine would be the possession of Palestinian identity cards or passports.

The new Palestinian citizenship would emerge, by and large, as a legalization of the pre-existing *de facto* Palestinian citizenship in the OPT. The new citizenship would be likely to have significant effects, most of them relating to international law. These would include: admission of Palestinian citizens as international staff members to United Nations bodies and other international organizations; nomination of Palestinian citizens to membership of international courts and United Nations convention-related mechanisms such as human rights treaty bodies; treatment of Palestinians on the basis of the principle of reciprocity with respect to the rights of non-citizens in certain States (e.g. the right to work, to own property, to practise professions); *de jure* diplomatic protection; invocation of International Criminal Court jurisdiction to prosecute those who assault Palestinian citizens once Palestine ratifies the 1998 Rome Statute of the Court; treatment of Palestinians as citizens for the purpose of the right of return and *non-refoulement*; and treatment of Palestinians as citizens while resolving cases relating to conflicts of law concerning personal status and inter-State business disputes.

Palestinians of East Jerusalem

This group (totalling about 288,900 persons at the end of 2009 according to the Israeli Central Bureau of Statistics) forms part of the West Bank population. It is, however, considered separately here due to the particular status that Israel unilaterally created for the group after annexing East Jerusalem in 1967. The members of the group do not hold Palestinian passports and are considered by Israel as permanent residents of Israel. A considerable number of East Jerusalemite Arabs have acquired Israeli citizenship pursuant to the 1952 Israeli Nationality Law upon satisfying the Law's naturalization requirements, i.e. residency, Hebrew-language literacy, and application.

A special status for inhabitants of Jerusalem (both west and east) was envisaged in 1938 by Britain and then in 1947 by the United Nations Partition Plan, when the idea of the internationalization of Jerusalem was deliberated at the international level. 'The City of Jerusalem,' as the Plan called Jerusalem and a wide area of surrounding towns, was intended to have a special international status. The citizenship of the inhabitants was formulated accordingly. The Plan conferred Jerusalem's citizenship with automatic effect on all residents of the city, irrespective of their citizenship, race or religion. It stated that 'all the residents shall become . . . citizens of the City of Jerusalem unless they opt for citizenship of the State of which they have been citizens.' By the end of 1944, the settled population of east and west Jerusalem numbered 240,880. Of these, 140,530 were Arabs and 100,200 Jews, and there were 150 others (Survey I: 152). The Arab and Jewish residents were given the right to opt for the citizenship of the Arab State or the Jewish State respectively. In such cases, the person in question would lose his or her Jerusalem status and become a citizen of either the Arab State or the Jewish State. The United Nations Trusteeship Council was expected to make arrangements for the diplomatic protection of the city's citizens while abroad. However, as the Plan was not implemented, Jordan annexed the eastern part of Jerusalem which fell under its control in 1948 and granted its citizenship to East Jerusalem's inhabitants on the same basis as the rest of the West Bankers. The western side of the city became part of the State of Israel since Israel controlled that part and granted its Jewish inhabitants Israeli citizenship. The Arab inhabitants of West Jerusalem were expelled.

After its occupation of the West Bank in 1967, Israel annexed East Jerusalem in 1980. The international community did not recognize the annexation of East Jerusalem, adopting a number of Security Council and General Assembly resolutions to that effect. Moreover, most States did not recognize Jerusalem as the capital of Israel. However, Israel proceeded with its unilateral actions, considering the city as part of its territory. It closed off Jerusalem from the rest of the West Bank. West Bankers now required entry permits to enter Jerusalem, just like other parts of Israel. In contrast to the West Bank, Israel extended its law and the jurisdiction of its courts to East Jerusalem.

Israel did not annex the Arab inhabitants of East Jerusalem and did not confer its citizenship on them. Nor did it treat them as West Bankers or Gazans in terms of residency. The inhabitants, who were counted in the Israeli census conducted on 19 June 1967, were deemed to be foreigners permanently residing in Israel. Israel provided them with blue identity cards as a permit for permanent residency. Inhabitants could acquire an Israeli travel document (*laissez passer*), which was valid for three years, to travel abroad. Jerusalem Arab inhabitants could participate in the Jerusalem local (municipality) elections, live anywhere in Israel, and acquire social security benefits such as pension and health insurance. They hired taxis in the same way as Israeli citizens. But they could not participate in the Israeli legislative elections or perform national service.

If East Jerusalemites move outside Jerusalem or Israel for three years or more, their residency in Jerusalem is revoked. Thereafter, they cannot return to the city. Such persons may then become stateless. Inhabitants may also lose their Jerusalem status if they acquire the citizenship of other States.

If East Jerusalemites move to the West Bank, irrespective of the length of their stay, their residency in East Jerusalem is also withdrawn. Residency and housing in the West Bank is effectively open to East Jerusalemites; many of whom live there without informing the authorities (see below). East Jerusalem women who marry West Bank men face the threat of withdrawal of their identity cards. If Jerusalemites' residence in the West Bank is discovered by Israel, their residency in Jerusalem may be revoked. Israel expels people to the West Bank and revokes their residency in East Jerusalem for political reasons, as it did in the case of four Palestinian parliamentarians who were removed to Ramallah in 2011. Moreover, a large number of East Jerusalemites have found themselves physically outside the city in recent years after the completion of the separation wall between East Jerusalem and the West Bank. These residents are threatened with withdrawal of their Jerusalem identity cards and many cards have indeed been withdrawn. In all these cases, the persons concerned become stateless, having on the one hand lost their Jerusalem status and, on the other, failed to acquire West Bank identity cards. Their number is estimated in the thousands. The Palestinian Authority is not in favour of granting Palestinian identity cards to such persons in order to discourage Israel from undertaking further expulsions. As stateless persons, they are unable to travel abroad or to acquire identity papers, a state of affairs which has adverse implications in areas such as marriage, property ownership, registration of children, practising of professions, or the conduct of business. The situation of this *de facto* stateless group is comparable to that of unrecognized Palestinian refugees in Lebanon, whose case will be addressed under separate heading below.

The Israeli government's practice in dealing with the Arab inhabitants of East Jerusalem originates from the *Awad v. Yitzhak Shamir et al.* case decided by the Israeli High Court of Justice on 5 June 1988. In this case, the Court held that permanent residency status is not citizenship and may be revoked due to residency abroad. This decision was used against the inhabitants, restricting their departure from the city and their acceptance of foreign nationalities or residency abroad. In 2008, for example, the residency of about 4,600 Jerusalemites was revoked, according to HaMoked, through the policy that became known as 'quiet deportation.' Family reunification for East Jerusalemites whose spouses are from outside the city, notably from the OPT, is granted in rare cases. In short, the status of 'permanent residence' for Arabs in Jerusalem is not guaranteed.

There are thousands of East Jerusalem identity card holders who are currently *de facto* residents of the West Bank. Many of them have never lived in Jerusalem but were registered in the city as part of the census undertaken by Israel on 19 June 1967. Members of such groups live their daily lives as West Bankers in terms of their homes, property, businesses, education, families, and so on. It is not uncommon to find West Bank families with a father holding a West Bank identity card and a mother holding an East Jerusalem card, and vice versa. According to Israeli law, members of this group are deemed to be residents of East Jerusalem for residence purposes. Yet, as noted above, if Israel were to discover their presence in the West Bank, their residence in East Jerusalem would be revoked. For the Palestinian Authority, the treatment of these persons may sometimes differ from that of West Bank identity card holders in terms of court and police jurisdiction—Palestinian police cannot issue traffic fines against East Jerusalemites, for example. Yet the Authority treats such persons as ordinary West Bankers in terms of, for instance, the practising of professions, ownership of property, and public employment. The status of East Jerusalemites is anomalous. This anomaly is a result of the Israeli policy of reducing the Arab population of Jerusalem to the absolute minimum. East Jerusalem status places the inhabitants in a peculiar situation. They can still get temporary Jordanian passports without being considered as Jordanians, as in the case of West Bankers. As mentioned above, they have the right to apply for Israeli citizenship. For the Palestinian Authority, Jerusalem inhabitants are considered to be Palestinians, notwithstanding minor exceptions such as those mentioned in the previous paragraph.

Under normal conditions, i.e. if East Jerusalem were to become part of the State of Palestine, the inhabitants of East Jerusalem would automatically acquire Palestinian citizenship, as in the case of West Bankers and Gazans. However, given the complex statuses that have been wilfully engineered by Israel in order to minimize the number of Palestinians in the city, the future citizenship of East Jerusalemites needs to be examined in detail. The granting of citizenship to the Arab Jerusalemites should be carefully worded and the implications carefully considered because Israel would use the acquisition of such citizenship as a pretext to revoke the inhabitants' residency in Jerusalem. This scenario would apply if East Jerusalem were to remain under Israeli control.

Palestinians displaced in 1967

This group of Palestinians was displaced from the West Bank and the Gaza Strip during and after the 1967 Arab-Israeli war. Over 400,000 persons belonging to this category left the Occupied Palestinian Territory in 1967, according to the Palestinian Central Bureau of Statistics (2007). It is difficult to estimate the exact number of those currently displaced, as there is no central institution capable of collecting data regarding individuals belonging to this group in various parts of the world. Yet if one considers that the population of the OPT has increased over fourfold since 1967 and if this figure is used as an analogy for the group under consideration, it may be concluded that the group numbers at least 1.2 million. Another category belonging to this group consists of inhabitants of the West Bank or the Gaza Strip who were deported by Israel or who have been denied the right of return since 1967. The status of the latter category, commonly known as 'identity card losers,' was supposed to be settled within the five-year transitional period following the Oslo Accords. Oslo II provided (Annex II, Article 28, paragraph 3) the basis for such a settlement through the formation of a committee for the purpose. However, the transitional period has ended and the status of this category has yet to be resolved.

Under international law, and according to the United Nations Relief and Works Agency for Palestine Refugees and the Office of the United Nations High Commissioner for Refugees, these peoples are ordinary refugees. Their actual status today is similar to that of other ordinary refugees. This status in relation to Palestinian citizenship will be discussed under separate heading below. The difference is that refugees in this category do not have the right of return to Israel but to the West Bank or the Gaza Strip.

Once they settle in the State of Palestine and acquire Palestinian citizenship, members of this group should lose their refugee status. However, if Israel denies them entry to the State of Palestine in the event of ongoing Israeli control of the Palestinian border, the members of the group would continue to be refugees while residing abroad. Yet if they obtain Palestinian passports even before exercising their right of return to the West Bank or the Gaza Strip, these people should be granted Palestinian citizenship, be provided with diplomatic protection by Palestinian embassies, participate in referenda and elections, etc.

The State of Palestine is under an international legal obligation to allow the members of this group to return to their native homes. This obligation stems from the right of return under international law and from the law of State succession applicable to the current inhabitants of the West Bank or the Gaza Strip, as set out above. The acquisition of citizenship of other States should not derogate from their right to return to the West Bank or the Gaza Strip and to recover their residence there.

Palestinian Refugees

This category, which consists of those displaced from the parts of Palestine in which Israel was established in 1948, is the largest category of Palestinians. The number of such refugees registered by UNRWA totalled 4,820,229 in 2010, according to UNRWA. Thousands of other refugees (the exact number is unknown) are not registered with UNRWA. According to international law, as will be explained shortly, these refugees have the right to return to Israel and to become Israeli citizens. Israel will most likely continue to oppose the right of return to its territory, as it has done for the past six decades. The obligation of permitting the return of these refugees lies with Israel, not with the State of Palestine. Yet the latter State would have a historical/political/moral duty to defend their rights.

And some of the refugees might not be interested in returning and becoming Israeli citizens.

In the State of Palestine, such refugees would have the right to opt for Palestinian citizenship, as a general rule. The status of subcategories belonging to this group will be detailed below. One category that should be excluded from the outset from the scope of Palestinian citizenship is that of 'Palestine Refugees' registered by UNRWA who were non-Palestinian/foreign citizens under British rule in Palestine but were residing in the territory of Palestine between June 1946 and May 1948. These persons left Mandate Palestine as a result of the 1948 war and lost their source of income. This category has been attributed to Palestine by UNRWA only for the purpose of receiving assistance from the Agency that has no relevance to citizenship. UNRWA provides its assistance on a humanitarian and not necessarily a legal basis.

The right of return of Palestinian refugees would continue to exist even after conferment of Palestinian citizenship on such refugees by the State of Palestine. Indeed, substantial numbers of Palestinian refugees have already acquired the nationalities of other States but are still deemed to be refugees for a number of purposes, including obtaining UNRWA assistance. No serious legal position would deny the right of return of these naturalized refugees. The right of return should not be confused with the refugee status granted by UNRWA or UNHCR. This status is determined only for the purpose of receiving protection or assistance from such United Nations agencies as well as the recognition of refugee rights in the countries in which Palestinian refugees reside based on international law (chiefly the 1951 Convention relating to the Status of Refugees and its 1967 Protocol) and the applicable local law. As an individual right, the right of return cannot be compromised, even if the Palestine Liberation Organization surrenders it. The right has a number of bases in international law and can only be surrendered voluntarily by the refugee himself/herself. Such legal bases can be found in eight branches of public international law: (1) inter-State citizenship law, (2) the law of State succession, (3) human rights law, (4) humanitarian law, (5) the law of State responsibility, (6) refugee law, (7) United Nations law, and (8) natural/customary law. These bases are briefly highlighted here.

Inter-State, or comparative, citizenship law is the starting point for refugees' right of return. In international law, the key basis for the right of return is derived from the individual's citizenship, and the case of Palestinian refugees is no exception. Hence, the individual's possession of Palestinian citizenship prior to 14 May 1948, i.e. before the establishment of the State of Israel, constitutes the first basis for the right of return. The other bases for this right presented in the annex are derived from the bond of citizenship between the refugee and the territory in which he or she habitually resided before displacement. Thus, Palestinian citizens who left the area of Palestine that became Israel have the right to return, that is to recover their citizenship. It follows that each citizen who became a refugee has an individual right to acquire Israeli citizenship once he or she is allowed to return to the place of habitual residence from which he/she departed. Descendants of these refugees have an identical right. Negotiations between Israel and the Palestinian leadership might yield a political solution to the refugee problem by, for example, allowing these refugees to return to a State of Palestine established in the 1967-occupied territory. Such a solution would not alter the right of refugees to return to Israel. In other words, the right of return that is based on citizenship as it existed before 1948 can be exercised exclusively by each individual who once held Palestinian citizenship. The acquisition of Israeli citizenship is a right based on prior citizenship status that cannot, legally speaking, be suspended by a unilateral Israeli action or by political accords.

The law of State succession reflects the practice of States in regard to citizenship. In almost all peace treaties reached in modern history, individuals belonging to a former State have *ipso facto* acquired the citizenship of the succeeding State. The Treaty of Lausanne of 1923, under which Turkey relinquished its title to Palestine, provided the basis for the Palestine inhabitants' citizenship. It stipulated that Turkish subjects habitually residing in territories detached from Turkey would acquire the citizenship of the new State, namely Palestine. Effectively, the inhabitants were granted Palestinian citizenship when such detachment took place. Although Israel may grant its citizenship to whomever it wishes, it cannot, according to international law, deny the citizenship of Palestinians who were residing in the parts of Palestine that became Israel. In 1950, the Israel Law of Return granted Israeli citizenship to any Jew who was present in or immigrated to Israel. This was applicable regardless of whether the Jew was a Palestinian citizen or not. The Arab inhabitants of Israel, who had previously held Palestinian citizenship, were gradually granted Israeli citizenship based on the 1952 Israel Nationality Law. Israel could, however, decide that Palestinian citizenship had ceased to exist in the area under Israel's jurisdiction, but not beyond that area. Yet this freedom of decision is not unlimited. In accordance with international law, Israel could not withdraw the citizenship from Palestinian citizens who were displaced from their places of habitual residence in the territory of Palestine in which Israel was established—i.e. the 1947-1949 refugees. The right to obtain Israeli citizenship by the citizens of Mandate Palestine entails the right of return. This conclusion was clearly arrived at by the International Law Commission in its Draft Articles on Nationality of Natural Persons in relation to the Succession of States. Thus, Article 14, paragraph 2, of the Draft Articles states: 'A State concerned shall take all necessary measures to allow persons concerned who, because of events connected with the succession of States, were forced to leave their habitual residence on its territory to return thereto.'

The third basis for the right of return is the international law of human rights. This law has different manifestations relating to the right of citizenship, residency, the prohibition of citizen's deportation and the right to move freely within and outside one's country. Two international human rights instruments are relevant here. One is the Universal Declaration of Human Rights of 1948. Article 13, paragraph 2, of the Declaration States that: 'Everyone has the right to leave any country, including his own, and to return to his country.' This provision, just as the rest of the instrument's content, represents a declaration of binding international law recognized by almost all States in the world. It entails the freedom of Palestinians to leave their country, regardless of whether they have left that country (i.e. Mandate Palestine) as refugees or in other capacities, and to return thereto; hence it constitutes a response to those who deny the human right of return on the ground that Palestinian refugees left Palestine voluntarily, since the Declaration lays down a general principle with regard to that right. Israel or any other State established in Mandate Palestine would definitively be the country of Palestinian refugees to which they would be entitled to return. The second instrument is the International Covenant on Civil and Political Rights of 1966. Article 12, paragraph 4, of this Covenant provides that 'No one shall be arbitrary deprived of the right to enter his own country.' Obviously, Palestine or any of its successor States, including Israel, is considered for each refugee as his own country. These are explicit human right rules governing return for Palestinian citizens, including refugees.

International humanitarian law is the fourth basis for the right of return. It is a well-established rule of humanitarian law that protected persons, i.e. civilian citizens of occupied territory, should not be removed from that territory. If they leave the territory wilfully or as a result of an armed conflict, civilians should be readmitted. This is an obligation incurred by the authority exercising power in the territory. Thus, Article 49, paragraph 1, of the 1949 Geneva Convention IV relative to the Protection of Civilian Persons in Time of War provides that: 'Individual or mass forcible transfers, as well as deportations of protected persons from occupied territory to . . . any other country, occupied or not, are prohibited, regardless of their motive.' Similarly, the right of return, as a matter of principle, has been incorporated in Article 26 (family reunification), Article 35 (right to leave the territory), and Article 45 (transfer to other countries) of the same Convention. 'The prohibition [of deportation] is absolute and allows of no exceptions,' as pointed out by the commentator on the article cited above. Even when the occupier undertakes total or partial evacuation of a given area, as paragraph 2 of the same article puts it: 'Persons thus evacuated shall be transferred back to their homes as soon as hostilities in the area in question have ceased.' 'This clause naturally applies both to evacuation inside the territory and to cases where circumstances have made it necessary to evacuate the protected persons to a place outside the occupied territory,' the aforementioned commentator adds. The denial of return to one's home constitutes, in effect, deportation. Deportation is considered, by Article 147 of the same Convention, as one of the grave breaches of the Convention.

When the State denies refugees the right to return, it means that other States are forced to accept them. In international law, no State has an absolute obligation to accept citizens of other States. The admission of a foreigner is rather a privilege that the State may grant or withhold. Any State may, with certain restrictions, expel foreigners (migrants, travellers, refugees) from its territory, in coordination with the Office of the United Nations High Commissioner for Refugees, the International Organization for Migration or other humanitarian institutions, and transfer them back to their country. If the State refuses to admit its citizens, or those who ought to be recognized by that State as its citizens under international law (e.g. law of State succession, citizenship law), such a State commits an internationally wrongful act against the State that received the refugee. These general principles apply to Palestinian refugees, as rights holders, and to the State of Israel, as a duty bearer with respect to the right of return to its territory. Hence, Israel would be internationally responsible vis-à-vis the States in which Palestinian refugees are residing, such as Jordan, Lebanon, Syria, and even the future State of Palestine. This responsibility entitles such States to adopt countermeasures under international law to remedy damages sustained as a result of the Israeli refusal to readmit Palestinian refugees, including restitution (by demanding actual return) and compensation. This right exists for the States involved; it also implies that refugees enjoy the right to return to their homeland.

A key role for international refugee organizations, particularly the Office of the United Nations High Commissioner for Refugees (UNHCR), just like its predecessor the International Refugee Organization, is the repatriation, or return, of refugees to their countries of citizenship. This is obvious from provisions 1, 8, and 9 of the UNHCR Statute of 14 December 1950. In practice, one of UNHCR's major functions has been to assist governments and other organizations in repatriating refugees. Although the 1951 Convention relating to the Status of Refugees provides alternative solutions to repatriation for refugees, such alternatives are mainly humanitarian in character and were stipulated for the purpose of providing options for the protection of refugees by any State willing to assume such protection in lieu of the State of original citizenship. Such solutions by no means eliminate the right of return.

United Nations law, namely the myriad resolutions on Palestine, including on the issue of refugees, renders the right of return unquestionable. It should first be noted that the question of Palestine is the responsibility of the General Assembly as the successor to the Council of the League of Nations, which issued and supervised the Palestine Mandate. The General Assembly recognized the existence of two States in Palestine, an Arab State and a Jewish State, in Resolution 181(III) of 29 November 1947. In the same resolution, the Assembly imposed an obligation on both States to extend their citizenship to their habitual residents, regardless of their religion or race. Thus, Israel, the Jewish State, and the new State of Palestine, the Arab State, were required to grant their citizenship to all their inhabitants, Jews and Arabs. This right of citizenship, as prescribed by the General Assembly, imposed an obligation on the new States to readmit citizens who had left their territory for any reason. The right of return has been consistently confirmed by many General Assembly resolutions relating specifically to this right, the first of which is Resolution 194 of 11 December 1948. Paragraph 11 of this resolution states that 'the refugees wishing to return to their homes and live at peace with their neighbours should be permitted to do so at the earliest practicable date, and that compensation should be paid for the property of those choosing not to return and for loss of or damage to property which, under principles of international law or in equity, should be made good by the Governments or authorities responsible.' This resolution, which incorporates the customary international rule rendering return an individual choice by using the phrase 'wishing to return,' has been reaffirmed by the General Assembly on an annual basis. The most recent of these resolutions, just to give an indication, is Resolution 65/101 of 10 December 2010. The Security Council has also advocated the right of return, including in its Resolution 237 of 1967.

All the above-mentioned international legal bases prove that the right of return for Palestinian refugees is a customary rule. Such a right has long been deemed to constitute a natural entitlement for any citizen. For this reason, perhaps, the right of return has not during the course of history been subjected to questioning by States. It can thus be claimed that, due to the recognition of this right as part of inter-State citizenship law, the law of State succession, human rights law, humanitarian law, refugee law and domestic migration law, the right of return has become a peremptory international norm, or *jus cogens*. Given that the denial of return is a grave breach of humanitarian law, all States are entitled to prosecute those who violate this right. Besides, unlawful deportation or transfer has recently been considered as a 'crime against humanity' if committed in peacetime, or as a 'war crime' if committed during an armed conflict, according to Articles 7 and 8 of the 1998 Rome Statute of the International Criminal Court. As the question of Palestine as a whole is the responsibility of the international community, represented by the General Assembly as the body that inherited the issue from the Council of the League of Nations, and in view of the great number of General Assembly resolutions on the right of return, it may be safely concluded that the right of return of Palestinian refugees is an *erga omnes* rule. This rule renders the right of return a concern of all States. In view of the importance of the rights derived from the right of return, all States can be held to have a legal interest in its realization. States are consequently required to meet a set of obligations regarding the right of return. These obligations include, *inter alia*, the ongoing recognition of the right of return, assisting Palestinian refugees legally at the domestic level (e.g. by providing identity documents, travel and work facilities, refugee status, and refraining from their deportation) and financially (e.g. through UNRWA) until such time as the refugees can exercise their right of return to Israel. All States must express support for the right of return in diplomatic settings, such as the United Nations and regional organizations, and sanction the possibility of referring the question of such refugees to the International Court of Justice for a judgment or an advisory opinion.

General Assembly Resolution 3236 (XXIX) of 22 November 1974 defines the Palestinian refugee problem as being of a different legal character from the situation of other refugees. For this reason, a number of scholars have advocated the application of the mechanism of 'temporary protection' to Palestinian refugees. Temporary protection covers refugees fleeing major crises in their States. It is granted as an interim solution. Thereafter refugees will return home or, if return is undesirable, they will be offered permanent status either by the host or by a third State. Temporary protection may afford fewer rights than those guaranteed to refugees under the 1951 Convention. The norm has special significance for Palestinian refugees, since Palestinians have effectively been denied many of the rights available to other refugees under the Convention. Although the status of Palestinian refugees is deemed to be regulated by Article 1D of the Convention, the granting of 'temporary protection' would be consistent with that article. A number of States hosting Palestinians do grant them the rights spelled out in the 1951 Convention, including the right to choose voluntary repatriation, local integration, or resettlement (Article 30 of the Convention). As Palestinians were excluded by Article 1D in order to facilitate the international administration of the refugee issue, this reason should not supplant the legal obligation to grant such refugees the benefits set out in the Convention as a minimum requirement, as discussed above.

The social conditions of Palestinian refugees in host countries vary depending on the rights accorded and the restrictions applied to them locally. Palestinians have at no point been meaningfully integrated into Arab host countries because of practices prohibiting their naturalization on political grounds. Palestinian refugees have never been recognized as refugees in Iraq and have only been granted residence permits. Palestinian refugees have limited scope for integration into Lebanese society and poor prospects for the future. Half a million Palestinians reside in Syria, of whom about a quarter live in refugee camps, and they are not permitted to acquire Syrian citizenship. They have access to public services but no right to vote or to stand for election and their ownership rights are restricted. Even Palestinian refugees who live in Jordan with Jordanian citizenship, many of whom are still living in refugee camps, are practically and politically unequal with nationals of non-Palestinian origin.

The purpose of the above discussion is to show that responsibility for the refugee problem lies with the State of Israel and with the international community. The Palestinian leadership cannot be legally held accountable if it reaches an agreement with Israel that does not include the right of return. The utmost that the Palestinian leadership can do is to grant Palestinian refugees its citizenship once the State of Palestine is established, to protect them abroad, and to defend their right of return.

Palestinian Refugees in the West Bank and the Gaza Strip

This group originally came from the territory of Mandate Palestine that became Israel in 1947-1949 and afterwards and now reside in the West Bank, including East Jerusalem, or the Gaza Strip. Members of this category totalled some 1,910,677 persons in 2010, according to the United Nations Relief and Works Agency for Palestine Refugees in the Near East (UNRWA), i.e. almost half of the population of the occupied Palestinian territory. In effect, this group has similar local status to West Bankers, Jerusalemites and Gazans, as the case may be. The reason for covering this group in a separate section of this chapter is that its members have the right of return to Israel, as in the case of other Palestinian refugees.

Technically, had Mandate Palestine remained one entity as it had been under British rule, Palestinian citizens who moved eastwards (to the West Bank) or southwards (to the Gaza Strip) would have been considered as internally displaced persons. Part of this group still lives in refugee camps, while the other part lives in towns. However, in practice, as both the West Bank and the Gaza Strip were separated from the parts of Palestine in which Israel was established (particularly as the West Bank and the Gaza Strip are generally recognized to be the territory that would form a separate State from Israel, i.e. the State of Palestine), these Palestinians obtained refugee status under international law. Although they have been treated *de facto* by the authorities exercising power in the West Bank and the Gaza Strip as equal to the inhabitants (in terms of, e.g., residency, identity cards, passports, election, public employment), members of the group are registered by UNRWA as refugees. Consequently, such persons are simultaneously citizens of the West Bank or the Gaza Strip and refugees. As citizens of the latter areas, they have a status akin to the original inhabitants of the West Bank and the Gaza Strip, as shown above. As refugees, they are entitled to the rights enjoyed by other refugees: UNRWA's protection, return to Israel, and compensation.

Despite their integration into the local population of the West Bank and Gaza Strip, the members of this group should continue to be considered under international law as refugees for certain purposes, such as the right of return and being eligible for UNRWA's protection/ assistance, and as dual citizens. These refugees are at the same time *de facto*, i.e. according to the local law of the OPT, citizens of the West Bank or the Gaza Strip, and citizens of the State of Israel in the sense that they have a right to become citizens of that State based on the law of State succession and other branches of international law detailed in the annex. Yet Israel refuses to grant them Israeli citizenship or to let them return to their homes in its territory.

In other words, this group has simultaneously three separate statuses:

(1) Refugee status in accordance with international law and the practice of UNRWA;
(2) OPT citizenship in accordance with the applicable local law in the West Bank, East Jerusalem and the Gaza Strip, and the practice of local authorities there;

(3) Israeli citizenship, although non-effective at present, based on international law.

Under the citizenship law of the State of Palestine, this group should be granted citizenship on the same basis as the West Bankers and Gazans. (Members of the group who now reside in East Jerusalem should be treated as West Bankers, notwithstanding their right of return to their original places of residence inside Israel.) However, the question of their refugee status should continue to be raised. The State of Palestine would, in one sense, serve as a host country for these refugees on the analogy of other host countries. One might fear that the refugee status of the group, should they acquire Palestinian citizenship, would be effectively ended. That is not true. Under international law, their refugee status would persist. They would therefore continue to receive UNRWA aid and be entitled to claim the right of return. The Palestine Liberation Organization ought to continue defending the rights of these refugees in United Nations forums. The granting of citizenship to the group should in no way, from a legal perspective, undermine their status. Israel would continue to oppose their return, regardless of whether the group acquired other nationalities or not. Thus, the acquisition of the citizenship of the State of Palestine would not *per se* be a reason for ending the group's refugee status. Indeed, most Palestinian refugees have acquired nationalities of other States (with the exception of the refugees in Lebanon and Syria) and these naturalized persons, in the eyes of international law, are still refugees. Hence, their right of return is still on the international agenda and UNRWA's assistance is still in place—for example, in Jordan Palestinian refugees are assisted by UNRWA despite holding Jordanian citizenship.

Palestinian Refugees Acquired a Third State Citizenship

Technically, people in this group are not refugees according to the 1951 Convention relating to the Status of Refugees as they are citizens of other States and ought to be protected by the State that has recognized them as its citizens. Thus, Article 1C of the Convention provides that: 'This Convention shall cease to apply to any person . . . if . . . (3) He has acquired a new nationality, and enjoys the protection of the country of his new nationality.' However, as Palestinian refugees in general were excluded from the scope of the 1951 Convention based on its Article 1D, as will be shown below, and as the countries that are hosting the majority of Palestinian refugees (Jordan, Lebanon, Syria, and the future State of Palestine in the West Bank and the Gaza Strip) are not even parties to the said Convention, these people should continue to be regarded as refugees for various purposes, particularly for the right of return to Israel and the right of compensation for property loss. The majority of these refugees are in Jordan, but there are also substantial numbers in Arab, European, American and other countries. True, in the States in which the 1951 Convention is applicable these refugees would not be considered under local law and for the purpose of UNHCR protection as refugees. However, they would be considered as refugees pursuant to international law provisions (see the annex) relating to citizenship in the law of State succession, human rights law, humanitarian law, and United Nations resolutions on the question of Palestine in general, and the right of refugees in particular, as well as in the light of international refugee law relating to Article 1D of the 1951 Convention.

The State of Palestine has no legal obligation to grant its citizenship to this group of refugees, since the responsibility to permit them to exercise their right to citizenship lies with Israel. Nevertheless, as Israel refuses to grant members of the group its citizenship or to readmit them into its territory, and as the State of Palestine will be the guardian of the Palestinian people at large, these refugees might be offered the choice of acquiring the citizenship of Palestine. Members of the group might lose other nationalities, since the internal law of some States prohibits citizens from acquiring other nationalities.

For these reasons, the right to Palestinian citizenship should be accorded on a case-by-case basis and upon the request of the person concerned. Thus, if a person did not wish to apply for Palestinian citizenship, the State of Palestine should not, and in fact it could not, impose its citizenship on him/her. If persons did not wish to apply for Palestinian citizenship due to the fear of losing their other citizenship, the State of Palestine might decide to offer them special treatment based on their original link with Mandate Palestine. The refugees might therefore be treated as Palestinian citizens (particularly in relation to residency, election, and employment) despite the fact that they lacked Palestinian citizenship. If they acquired the citizenship of the State of Palestine, such people would effectively become dual/multiple citizens. The new State, with a view to preserving the rights acquired by Palestinians in various countries, may not oppose the principle of dual citizenship.

Stateless Refugees within UNRWA Areas of Operation

These refugees do not possess the citizenship of any State and are therefore 'stateless persons' within the meaning of Article 1, paragraph 1, of the 1954 Convention relating to the Status of Stateless Persons. The discussion in this section is confined to stateless Palestinians who reside in three areas in which UNRWA operates—Lebanon, Syria and Jordan. It excludes refugees in the West Bank and the Gaza Strip (although these are also UNRWA areas of operation) whose status was addressed above. Stateless Palestinians reside mainly in Lebanon and Syria. A smaller number can be found in Jordan, but the vast majority of Palestinian refugees in Jordan have acquired Jordanian citizenship as discussed above. The acquisition of Palestinian citizenship by stateless refugees is more urgent than for all other groups. On acquiring such citizenship, members of the group may be protected by the State of Palestine, participate in referenda, vote and be elected to representative bodies such as the parliament and the Palestinian National Council. The group would most likely continue to receive UNRWA assistance as the Agency does not provide its services based on citizenship. There are millions of 'Palestine Refugees' who are still receiving UNRWA's assistance despite holding Jordanian, Lebanese, Syrian and other nationalities. There is no legal reason why UNRWA would cease to offer its assistance if such refugees were to acquire Palestinian citizenship. Palestinian Stateless refugees are registered by UNRWA as 'Palestine Refugees' and, as such, protected by UNRWA in cooperation with the Syrian, Lebanese and Jordanian governments. These governments treat Palestinian refugees as legal residents and provide them with identity cards indicating their status as Palestinian refugees residing in the country. The refugees hold travel documents/passports issued by the said governments in order to depart from, and return to, their State of refuge.

In addition to the general group of stateless Palestinians, there is a group of Palestinian refugees whose residency is considered illegal by host governments and is not registered by UNRWA. The members of this sub-group are commonly known as 'non-recognized' Palestinian refugees. The phenomenon exists mainly in Lebanon but it can also be found in other countries such as Syria and Jordan. Let us take the group in Lebanon as a case in point. Non-recognized refugees in Lebanon number about 35,000 persons. Their situation may be attributed to two factors: ambiguity of local law and UNRWA regulations.

In Lebanon, Palestinian refugees were first regularized under a decree enacted in 1959, which did not precisely define those eligible for residency. In 1962, the Lebanese Minister of the Interior enacted another decree that allowed Palestinian refugees to regularize their status until September of that year. Palestinians who arrived in Lebanon after that date, in other words the majority of non-recognized refugees, were not covered. They were then registered by the Palestine Liberation Organization (PLO) in accordance with the 1969 Cairo agreement signed between the Organization and Lebanon, pursuant to which the PLO issued identity documents to Palestinian refugees. Upon the PLO's withdrawal from Lebanon in 1982, the Lebanese government abolished the Cairo agreement and annulled the PLO's identity documents based on it. However, there is no specific provision in Lebanese law preventing the regularization of those who arrived after 1962. The matter was left to the discretion of the Lebanese security personnel, who generally refrain from registering additional refugees. Having nowhere else to go, these refugees were left without Lebanon-recognized identity cards and were deemed to be illegal immigrants.

There are four reasons for the non-registration of Palestinian refugees by UNRWA. One is that UNRWA's 'Palestine Refugee' criterion incorporates those persons, irrespective of their citizenship, 'whose normal place of residence was Palestine during 1 June 1946 to 15 May 1948, and who lost both home and means of livelihood as a result of the 1948 conflict.' This definition excludes: (a) persons who left Palestine before June 1946; (b) persons who fled the territory of Palestine that became Israel after 15 May 1948; and (c) refugees who left the occupied territory after 1967. The criterion stems from an internal UNRWA definition. A number of General Assembly resolutions gave the Agency a wider mandate that can be interpreted to include all Palestinian refugees. These resolutions include: 2252(ES-V) (1967), 37/120(I) (1982), 56/54 (2001), and 59/118 (2004). The latter resolution, for example, requested UNRWA to provide assistance 'to persons . . . who are currently displaced . . . as a result of the June 1967 and subsequent hostilities.' Secondly, UNRWA fears that the registration of non-recognized refugees might be perceived by the Lebanese government as a means of increasing the number of Palestinians in the country, an undesired phenomenon given the sectarian balance issue in that State. Thirdly, UNRWA is concerned that further registration of Palestinians would require an increase in its budget. Thus, if non-recognized refugees are added to the roughly 400,000 Palestinians who are already registered, a budget increase of approximately 10% would be required. Donor countries might not be prepared to allocate this amount. Lastly, many Palestinian refugees in Lebanon (their numbers are uncertain) became non-recognized as a result of procedural complications. UNRWA has revealed that perhaps as many as half of the non-recognized were refugees registered by other UNRWA areas of operation. The difficulty of transferring their files from these areas to Lebanon is due to the fact that registration requires the approval of the host government and

Lebanon is not ready to accept fresh UNRWA registrations, as just explained.

Non-recognized refugees face a variety of human rights abuses. To travel abroad, non-recognized refugees obtain a one-year travel document, which requires its holder to apply for a return visa, while ordinary refugees hold a five-year travel document without any need for a return visa. Even worse, refugees without identity cards, who number in the thousands, are deemed to be illegal immigrants: they cannot legally marry or acquire birth or death certificates; are unable to move within or outside Lebanon; and if caught by the police are liable to arrest. According to an UNRWA fact-sheet of March 2007, these refugees do not receive food and cash subsidies, shelter rehabilitation, primary health care or hospitalization. UNRWA provides schooling only after approval by its country director on a case-by-case basis. United Nations treaty bodies have confirmed that Lebanon is bound by the human rights conventions to which it is a party to regularize the status of non-recognized refugees. In 2004, the United Nations Committee on the Elimination of Racial Discrimination requested Lebanon to 'remove all legislative provisions and change polices that have a discriminatory effect on the Palestinian population in comparison with other non-citizens.' In 2006, the Committee on the Rights of the Child requested Lebanon to ensure that 'all . . . children of Palestinian refugees without identity documents, are registered immediately after birth. Meanwhile, children whose births have not been registered and who are without official documentation should be allowed to access basic services, such as health and education, while waiting to be properly registered.'

UNRWA has the primary responsibility for Palestinian refugees. However, the aforementioned UNRWA definition of who constitutes a 'Palestine refugee' has excluded thousands of Palestinians from its scope, so that they become, as a result, non-recognized. UNRWA, like all United Nations agencies, is bound by universal human rights principles, including non-discrimination. UNRWA's own definition that requires it to provide unequal services to the same refugee population may be seen as discriminatory. UNHCR currently does not assist Palestinian refugees in Lebanon, since its mandate excludes those who receive protection or assistance from other United Nations agencies, in accordance with Article 1D of the 1951 Convention relating to the Status of Refugees. However, UNHCR may consider that its mandate covers non-recognized refugees based on the second sentence of Article 1D, since non-recognized refugees do not receive protection or assistance. UNHCR confirmed this in its 2009 revised Note on the Applicability of Article 1D, indicating that when UNRWA's 'protection or assistance has ceased for any reason . . . these persons shall *ipso facto* be entitled to the benefits of this [1951] Convention.'

Non-recognized refugees need to acquire some form of legal status as a prerequisite for the enjoyment of basic rights. They must enjoy full access to UNRWA services. In the short term, Lebanon should consider registering non-recognized refugees as ordinary refugees and issue them with identity cards and travel documents. As a longer-term solution, UNRWA should consider changing its criteria concerning 'Palestine refugees.' The term may be redefined as follows: 'A Palestinian refugee is any person who held Palestinian nationality before 15 May 1948, including his or her descendants, and who is unable or, owing to fears of persecution based on his or her racial or religious or political affiliation, unwilling to return to his or her original place of residence in the territory of Palestine that was under the mandate of Great Britain.' This definition is consistent with the concept of a 'refugee' in international law—a key element of a refugee's definition is the fact that the person is residing outside the country of his or her citizenship and is unable or unwilling to return. If UNRWA is unable to register a Palestinian refugee, UNHCR may consider providing protection instead by reaching an agreement on the matter with Lebanon, aside from its Memorandum of Understanding that was signed in September 2003. UNHCR may develop a Standard Operating Procedure on the processing of Palestinian individual cases as it did in Egypt in May 2002, notwithstanding the fact that Egypt is a party to the 1951 Convention and Lebanon is not.

The most sustainable solution for these refugees is the acquisition of a citizenship. The State that is obliged to grant all 1948 Palestinian refugees its citizenship is Israel, as shown above. Israel also continues to be responsible for the return of these persons to its territory. Alternatively, however, the State of Palestine might grant its citizenship to these refugees based on humanitarian, not legal, grounds. The State of Palestine is only obliged to return refugees who left the West Bank and the Gaza Strip, i.e. the refugees of 1967 and its aftermath, as discussed above.

The host countries of stateless refugees should understand that the mere fact of acquiring the citizenship of the State of Palestine does not necessarily entail automatic return to that State, especially if Israel retains its control over the Palestinian border. The Palestinian leadership probably needs to reach bilateral agreements with Lebanon and Syria as well as with Jordan to this effect. Under such agreements, these three countries should agree to continue hosting Palestinian refugees until such time as they can return to their original places of habitual residence in Israel, not only to the State of Palestine. In fact, legally speaking, return to the State in the West

Bank and the Gaza Strip does not constitute an exercise of the right of return. In this sense, the new State might be regarded as a refugee host country.

Conferring Palestinian citizenship on this group of refugees would enable them to return to the State of Palestine or to be protected by Palestinian embassies as citizens, to hold a Palestinian passport, and to enjoy meaningful national affiliation.

Stateless Refugees Outside UNRWA Areas of Operation

Thousands of Palestinian refugees who do not hold the citizenship of any State (and are hence 'stateless persons' within the meaning of Article 1, paragraph 1, of the 1954 Convention relating to the Status of Stateless Persons) reside outside the areas in which UNRWA operates. These persons include Palestinian refugees in Iraq, Egypt, Libya, the Gulf States and other Arab countries as well as in Europe, Australia, the Americas and elsewhere. The majority of these persons are second- or third-time refugees from Palestinian communities in the five UNRWA areas of operation — the Gaza Strip, Lebanon, Jordan, Syria, and the West Bank. These refugees are protected by the Office of the United Nations High Commissioner for Refugees (UNHCR), according to Article 1D of the 1951 Convention relating to the Status of Refugees (hereinafter 'the 1951 Convention'), as non-Palestinian refugees. The aim here is to assess the extent to which the granting of Palestinian citizenship to these refugees would affect their international legal status.

Article 1, paragraph D, of the 1951 Convention stipulates: 'This Convention shall not apply to persons who are at present receiving from organs or agencies of the United Nations other than the United Nations High Commissioner for Refugees protection or assistance. When such protection or assistance has ceased for any reason, without the position of such persons being definitively settled in accordance with the relevant resolutions adopted by the General Assembly of the United Nations, these persons shall *ipso facto* be entitled to the benefits of this Convention.' This paragraph is intended to prevent the overlapping of competencies among United Nations agencies and to ensure continuity of protection for particular refugees. The first sentence excludes a specific category of persons from the Convention. The second brings such persons back under the Convention's coverage if the circumstances that justified their exclusion cease to exist. The drafting history of the Convention, as well as its application, reveal that Article 1D concerns only Palestinian refugees.

The content of the provision that subsequently became Article 1D was considered in connection with the question of whether to include or exclude Palestinian refugees from the Convention. On 26 January 1950, the United States was the first to propose the exclusion of Palestinian refugees from the Convention in order to exclude refugees whose case was taken care of by United Nations bodies other than UNHCR. Egypt, Lebanon, and Saudi Arabia seconded the American suggestion, but with a different purpose. These States wanted to maintain a special regime for Palestinian refugees based, in essence, on such refugees' right of return to their homes inside Israel. The three States proposed that the 'present Convention shall not apply to persons who are at present receiving from other organs or agencies of the United Nations protection or assistance' (General Assembly Resolution 429 (V), 14 December 1950). At the time, Palestinian refugees were receiving political assistance from the United Nations Conciliation Commission for Palestine (UNCCP) and humanitarian assistance from the United Nations Relief and Works Agency for Palestine Refugees in the Near East (UNRWA). States that were concerned that these refugees would be left without assistance if their special United Nations regime ceased to exist wished to ensure ongoing protection. This led to the adoption of the second sentence of Article 1D.

In the 1947-1949 period, approximately one million persons were displaced from the part of Palestine that became Israel and were dispersed all over the world. Since then, the United Nations has continued to assist Palestinian refugees and has called upon States to contribute to their relief. States were urged to coordinate their assistance collectively into a unified programme and a body named the United Nations Relief for Palestine Refugees (UNRPR) was established for that purpose on 19 November 1948. The General Assembly replaced UNRPR by UNRWA on 8 December 1949. The United Nations concurrently set up another body to provide durable solutions—namely UNCCP, which was established by General Assembly Resolution 194 (III) of 11 December 1948. Paragraph 11 of this resolution instructed UNCCP, inter alia, 'to facilitate the repatriation, resettlement and economic and social rehabilitation of the refugees and the payment of compensation.' UNCCP established an office in Jerusalem for repatriation, resettlement, rehabilitation, and compensation, and to work on 'the protection of the rights, property and interest of refugees' (General Assembly Resolution 394 (V) of 14 December 1950).

Today, the principal United Nations agency that assists Palestinian refugees is UNRWA, whose operations cover education, health, food and housing, guaranteeing a considerable number of refugees' basic rights. Despite the absence of the word 'protection' in its mandate, UNRWA has exercised over the years a mandate that can be characterized as protection. And the word 'protection' appeared explicitly in connection with UNRWA in General Assembly Resolution 37/120 (1982). Security Council Resolution 681 (1990) vested UNRWA with a mandate to monitor and observe the situation of Palestinians under Israeli occupation. UNRWA's mandate has proved flexible in order to allow its operations to evolve as the situation demands.

Article 1D excludes certain individuals from the Convention's scope. But such persons are not prevented from being considered as refugees under other legal provisions or instruments at the local level or under international law. As a British court noted in 2008, the 'treatment of Palestinian refugees must be considered against the human rights norms that are applied to other recognised refugees' (*Lebanon v. Secretary of State for the Home Department*). These provisions or instruments include the prohibition of *non-refoulement* as a customary international rule and pursuant to Article 3 of the Convention against Torture, and the right of return as enshrined in the 1948 Universal Declaration of Human Rights and the 1966 International Covenant on Civil and Political Rights; domestic legislation, such as alien regulations and asylum laws; standards of regional human rights and refugee bodies; or resolutions of the United Nations, particularly those relating to self-determination, the right of return and compensation. Thus, persons who have the characteristics of refugees can only be excluded from the 1951 Convention because their case is being handled by other United Nations bodies. These persons will continue to be refugees and should therefore be treated as such.

UNHCR has been increasingly approached by Palestinian refugees. UNHCR's policy is that Palestinians outside UNRWA areas of operation meet the inclusion provision of Article 1D and are therefore of concern to UNHCR. The refugee agency intervenes where such Palestinians encounter difficulties in renewing identity/travel documents, facing deportation or detention. In 1984, UNHCR made an appeal to States to prevent the forcible return of Palestinian refugees holding Lebanese travel documents. The essential point remains that, whichever organization provides protection to Palestinian refugees, the protection of the United Nations as a whole should be equivalent to that of UNHCR protection provided to other refugees. UNHCR's 2009 Note confirms that Palestinian refugees should enjoy the rights and entitlements attributed to refugees under the 1951 Convention and provided for in Articles 2 to 34 of that Convention. A 1992 New Zealand Refugee Status Appeals Authority decision held that the benefits of the 1951 Convention refer to 'each and every one of the articles of the Convention.' Likewise, the Federal Court

of Australia in 2002 held that the 'benefits of the Convention are those
benefits, such as the non-expulsion provisions of Article 32 and the *non-
refoulement* provisions of Article 33.'

States have approached the interpretation of Article 1D in five distinct
ways: (1) Article 1D excludes only Palestinians in UNRWA areas of
operation and Palestinians elsewhere enjoy normal refugee status (New
Zealand); (2) Palestinians everywhere, within or outside UNRWA areas,
are excluded from refugee status under the 1951 Convention (Australia);
(3) Palestinians enjoy recognition as refugees when they are outside
UNRWA areas of operation and cannot return thereto (Germany, 1990);
(4) Palestinian refugee recognition can be accorded only if UNRWA
ceases to exist (Germany, 1988); (5) Article 1D does not play a role in the
refugee determination process at all and Palestinians are to be treated as
ordinary refugees (Denmark, Sweden, and France). Case law also varies
from one State to the next. The New Zealand Refugee Status Appeals
Authority interpreted the *ipso facto* provision as applying only in 'the
situation where UNRWA assistance ceases to operate at all' (1997).
Hence, Article 1D would not deny refugee status to a Palestinian who
voluntarily leaves an UNRWA area of operation. A United States court
held in *Faddoul v. Immigration and Naturalization Service* (1994) that the
statelessness of a Palestinian alone does not warrant asylum and that such
persons must demonstrate the same well-founded fear as refugees with
nationalities. In *Kelzani v. Secretary of State for the Home Department*, a
British court decided in 1978 that the Palestinian was to be seen as a
'stateless person' and not as a 'refugee' as he had obtained a travel
document from Egypt. This shows that there is no fixed pattern in the way
States, courts or governments treat Palestinian refugees. Each State deals
with Palestinians according to its laws and politics, with or without
consistency with international law.

A key requirement for the application of the 1951 Convention to
Palestinian refugees is that the problem has not been definitively settled.
As long as the question of Palestinian refugees has not been solved, it
should continue to be a matter of United Nations responsibility. The full
settlement of the refugee problem cannot be achieved save with the
refugees' return to Israel. The 'relevant United Nations resolutions,'
including General Assembly Resolution 194 (III), envisage a
comprehensive settlement for the Palestinians as a people, whereby they
are entitled to repatriation and compensation for property loss. General
Assembly Resolution 2452 (XXIII) of 1968 urged the 'Government of
Israel to take effective and immediate steps for the return without delay of
those inhabitants who have fled the areas since the outbreak of hostilities.'

The General Assembly has mandated UNRWA to assist Palestinian refugees, as per its Resolutions 302 (IV) of 1949 and 2252 (ES-V) of 1967 and subsequent resolutions endorsing or extending UNRWA's mandate and activities. Even Palestinians who are granted citizenship rights remain vulnerable and can hardly be called 'definitively settled.' There are numerous instances of expulsion of Palestinians from host States. Jordan stripped thousands of Palestinians of its citizenship in 1988. Kuwait expelled close to 350,000 Palestinians after the events of 1990. In 1995, Libya expelled thousands of Palestinians. After the 2003 occupation of Iraq, hundreds of Palestinian refugees were forced to leave.

The foregoing shows that the case of Palestinian refugees, as a collective issue, is different from that of other refugees. The international community represented by the United Nations is obliged to bear responsibility until a final settlement is reached in accordance with international law: return, acquisition of Israeli citizenship, compensation. At the individual level, States treat Palestinians in different ways depending on local law and on their political attitudes towards the Israeli-Palestinian conflict at large. What the Palestinian leadership can do, through bilateral agreements and diplomacy, is to advocate for the adoption of certain policies towards Palestinian refugees, to call for the granting of more rights to the refugees, and to advocate for recognition of the right of return to Israel. The acquisition of other nationalities would affect the recognition of such persons as refugees in the domestic jurisdiction of some States or halt their recognition as refugees for certain international law purposes, such as the termination of UNHCR protection. But the acquisition of a citizenship would not prevent such persons from being recognized as refugees for other international legal purposes, particularly the right of return and compensation. Conferring the citizenship of the State of Palestine on refugees originating from Israel would be equivalent to acquisition of the nationalities of other States; a State in the West Bank and the Gaza Strip is not the State to which the 1948 refugees have the right to return.

Although it would not be legally bound to do so, the State of Palestine should grant stateless Palestinians with citizenship as a matter of priority for humanitarian considerations (i.e. to reduce the suffering they encounter) and because the State would be the guardian of the population of Mandate Palestine. By acquiring citizenship, the persons concerned would be protected abroad. They might no longer be refugees, for the purpose of the 1951 Convention, if they returned to the State of Palestine. But they might continue to receive UNHCR protection, especially if they were unable to enter that State in the event that Israel maintained its occupation. At all events, the mere fact of acquiring Palestinian citizenship would not end the right of return. This right is based on a number of international legal provisions and instruments (see annex) that cannot be altered by naturalization.

Palestinians Stripped of their Citizenship after 1925

The citizenship of this group, which incorporates persons born in Palestine who were residing abroad when the 1925 Palestinian Citizenship Order was enacted, is not widely known. Unlike Ottoman subjects residing in Palestine in 1925 who automatically became Palestinian citizens, the citizenship of this group raised legal concerns. The debate concerning the group continued until the end of the Mandate period. The formidable developments which occurred after the end of that period, particularly the problem of Palestinian refugees during and after the 1948 war, overshadowed the significance of this group despite its ongoing legal relevance.

Palestine's inhabitants travelled abroad as part of overall Ottoman emigration outside the Empire. People travelled as traders, students and for pleasure. In the nineteenth and early twentieth century, the difficult economic conditions in the Empire, coupled with the frequent wars, motivated citizens to seek job opportunities abroad. It is not possible to determine accurately the total number of Palestinian natives who were residing abroad on 6 August 1924, as precise statistics are lacking. But available data suggest that the total number of emigrants from what was then Greater Syria, including Lebanon and Palestine, to both North and South America in the period from 1860 to 1914 amounted to about 600,000 persons. See, for instance, Karpat's *The Ottoman Emigration to America* (1985: 185). Historically, and down to the present day, the inhabitants of Palestine account for about one-fourth of the inhabitants of the Levant (*Al-Sham*—Syria, Lebanon, Jordan, Palestine). It may therefore be roughly presumed that 150,000 Ottoman emigrants from the region were originally from the territory that became known as Palestine after the British occupation. These emigrants, in turn, constituted about 20% of Palestine's natives at the time. A French consular report published in 1907 mentioned that emigrants from Palestine to the United States totalled 4,000 persons in ten years. Half of these emigrants from Palestine brought their families over afterwards. Orfalea (*The Arab Americans*, 2006: 109) suggests that between 1920 and 1930 a total of 2,933 Palestinians arrived in the United States, while 7,047 Palestinians arrived in the following decade. Yet most of Palestine's immigrants headed for Latin America, notably Argentina, Brazil, Chile, Honduras, Mexico and El Salvador. In 1927, it was estimated by the Committee of the Defenders of the Rights of Palestine Arab Emigrants in Palestinian Naturalization, in a memorandum submitted to the High Commissioner for Palestine, that the number of Palestine's natives in Europe and the Americas totalled 25,000. By 1936 this figure had reached 40,000, according to the British-led Palestine Royal Commission. That is to say, there was an increase of 15,000 in ten years. One may estimate from all these statistics that the number of Palestine's natives residing abroad stood at somewhere between 10% and 25% of the total population at the end of British rule. Given that the number of Arab Palestinians in 2011 is about 11 million, according to the Palestinian Central Bureau of Statistics, the number of Palestine's pre-1948 emigrants might at present amount to as many as one million. This accounts for the number of Palestinians in Chile, for instance, who are mostly nineteenth and early twentieth century emigrants. They have been estimated at 350,000, according to Holston's *Proud Palestinians of Chile* published in 2005. It is estimated that about 250,000 Palestinians reside in the United States (Orfalea: 152).

The problem of this group arose from Article 2 of the 1925 Palestinian Citizenship Order: 'Persons of over eighteen years of age who were born within Palestine and acquired on birth or subsequently and still possess Turkish nationality and on the 1st day of August 1925, are habitually resident abroad, may acquire Palestinian citizenship by opting in such manner . . . subject to the consent of the Government of Palestine which may be granted or withheld in its absolute discretion. . . . This right of option must be exercised within two years of the coming into force of this Order.' Thus, the right of individuals belonging to this group to opt for citizenship had to be exercised between 1 August 1925 and 31 July 1927. On 12 November 1925, however, the British High Commissioner for Palestine decided by a Proclamation gazetted on 16 November 1925 that the right of option should begin retroactively from 6 August 1924. The time limit to opt for citizenship was thus terminated on 5 August 1926, one year after the enactment of the Citizenship Order. In effect, it was only possible to exercise the right of option when the amendment of the Order was gazetted on 16 November 1925. The persons concerned had effectively less than nine months, i.e. from the latter date until 5 August 1926, to opt for Palestinian citizenship.

In formulating Article 2 of the Order, the drafters narrowly interpreted Article 34 of the 1923 Treaty of Lausanne, the peace treaty whereby Palestine was separated from Turkey. This article gave 'natives of territory detached from Turkey,' including Palestine, the right to 'opt for the citizenship of the territory of which they are natives.' Article 2 replaced the phrase *'native* of Palestine' as it appeared in the Treaty with *'born* within Palestine.' This limitation deprived the descendants of those born in Palestine, whose birth had occurred in a foreign country, of the right to opt for Palestinian citizenship, even if their parents had been born as Turkish citizens and the descendants themselves possessed Turkish citizenship.

Article 4 of the Citizenship Order added more conditions which served to make the acquisition of Palestinian citizenship by persons of this group even more difficult. It provided, *inter alia*, that the person concerned should have resided in Palestine for not less than six months immediately prior to the date of making the application for Palestinian citizenship. It is hard to see why a person belonging to this group should be unable to acquire Palestinian citizenship if he or she had not resided in Palestine for at least six months. This residence condition has been described as an 'obvious paradox' and an unnecessary stipulation to the Treaty of Lausanne; see Stoyanovsky's *The Mandate for Palestine: A Contribution to the Theory and Practice of International Mandates* (1928: 274).

From a juridical standpoint, the problem of those residing abroad lay in the interpretation of the expression 'habitually resident abroad.' The expression was interpreted by the Supreme Court of Palestine on 16 December 1927 in *Kattaneh v. Chief Immigration Officer.* The petitioner, who had been born in Palestine as an Ottoman subject, was then residing in Lebanon. He applied for a Palestinian passport on the assumption that he was a Palestinian citizen. His application was rejected by the Government. This decision was upheld on 1 July 1927 by the Supreme Court, which denied Mr. Kattaneh's application to become a Palestinian. The Court concluded that if a person was physically present in a place, for any reason, he would be considered to have been 'habitually resident' for the purpose of the acquisition of Palestinian citizenship.

It is relevant to refer to the situation of Ottoman citizens who were natives of other territories detached from Turkey and were residing abroad. Such persons were given more guarantees of retention of the citizenship of their native country than Article 2 of the Palestinian Citizenship Order. Article 7 of the Iraq Nationality Law of 9 October 1924 gave any 'native' who was residing abroad, even if s/he had not been born in the country, the right to opt for Iraqi citizenship. Such persons were allowed almost two years from 6 August 1924 to declare their intention to acquire Iraqi citizenship, not just nine months as had been the case with Palestine. The most flexible legislation among Palestine's neighbouring countries was the Trans-Jordan Nationality Law of 1928, which gave any Ottoman born in Trans-Jordan before 6 August 1924, regardless of his place of residence and without a deadline, the right to become a citizen (Article 5). Similarly, Article 5 of the nationality legislation of both Syria and Lebanon gave 'natives' who held Ottoman citizenship and had been residing abroad the right, within a two-year period, to opt for the citizenship of their native territory. These natives were further given the choice of declaring their desire to opt for Syrian or Lebanese citizenship to the diplomatic agents of France in the State where such persons were resident. No residence condition was applicable to the exercise of the right of option in Iraq, Syria, Lebanon or Trans-Jordan. The strict rules of Article 2 of the Order did not exist in any legislation in force in Palestine's neighbouring countries, in spite of the fact that all such legislation, including the question of option, was derived from the same source— Article 34 of the Treaty of Lausanne.

It should be noted, with regard to State practice relating to territorial succession at the time, that most of the multilateral peace treaties concluded in the early twentieth century recognized the right of option for citizens residing abroad. In particular, almost all of the peace treaties that ended World War I contained a provision whereby all persons born in the territory affected by succession, who had not acquired the citizenship of another State, automatically became citizens of the State of their birth, wherever their residence might be. Article 65 of the Treaty with Austria, for instance, stated: 'All persons born in Austrian territory who are not born nationals of another State shall *ipso facto* become Austrian nationals.' An identical article can be found in the treaties with Bulgaria, Czechoslovakia, Hungary, Poland, Romania, and the Serb-Croat-Slovene State.

For most affected persons, the nine-month period afforded to apply for Palestinian citizenship was inadequate. For example, representatives of natives residing in Mexico complained, in a letter sent to the British Secretary of Foreign Affairs dated 9 September 1929, that the 1925 Citizenship Order 'did not become known to Palestinians resident abroad because the Palestinian Government would not authorize advertisements in foreign countries to bring the instructions to their notice.' Even when conditions for acquiring citizenship were fulfilled, the Government 'in its absolute discretion,' as Article 2 of the Citizenship Order put it, could choose ultimately whether to grant or withhold Palestinian citizenship. In effect, the Government had refused most of the applications: of 9,000 applications submitted between 1925 and 1936, 'not more than 100 were accepted,' according to the Palestine Royal Commission. British consulates outside Palestine had rejected applications for Palestinian citizenship. Thus, it was reported in 1927 by a letter of the Committee of

the Defenders of the Rights of Palestine Arab Emigrants in Palestinian
Naturalization that

> 'British Consuls in Europe and America have asked . . . Palestinian
> emigrants to make application for the maintenance of their Palestinian
> nationality. Applications were duly submitted, and the Palestinian residents
> abroad in the belief of having complied with the law, awaited the issue of
> the proper nationality certificates. They were greatly surprised to learn from
> their Consuls that the Palestine Government had refused its approval, on the
> plea that the applicants did not reside in Palestine the required [six-month]
> period.'

These people, like any stateless persons, had endured difficult conditions
in their countries of residence. They were unable to travel without
Palestinian passports. No diplomatic protection, which was particularly
essential in the revolutionary countries of Latin America at the time, was
afforded to them. Many were subjected to deportation from countries
which refused to admit stateless persons, such as Chile and Mexico. In
certain countries, such as Panama, previous Turkish citizens were
explicitly precluded from seeking naturalization: 'Chinese, Turks, Syrians
[including Palestine's natives at the time] . . . and any other aliens whose
immigration is prohibited are not included [in the naturalization provisions]'
(Article 1 of the Panama Law of 9 November 1926). In July 1927, the
authorities in El Salvador requested foreigners to present documents to
prove their citizenship as a condition for conducting business, a
requirement that jeopardized the livelihoods of Palestine's natives residing
in that revolutionarily country (Musallam, *Folded Pages from Local
Palestinian History in the 20th Century*, 2002: 49). Palestine's natives
were also precluded from obtaining visas even to visit their relatives or to
look after their property in Palestine. As indicated in a letter from the
Centro Social Palestino in Mexico to the British Minister of Foreign
Affairs on 9 September 1929, those who applied for visas 'received advice
of rejection of their application . . . thus making it physically impossible
for them . . . [to] travel to Palestine.' In justifying its refusal to grant
Palestinian citizenship, the British Government asserted that the intention
of such natives was solely to receive diplomatic protection from the
British authorities, not to return home, as reported in a letter sent by
Palestine's natives residing in Honduras to the Permanent Mandates
Commission of the League of Nations on 28 October 1928.

On several occasions, persons who were not permitted to return
protested to the British Government. When their efforts failed, they
petitioned the Permanent Mandates Commission of the League of Nations.

In 1927, for instance, eleven Arab natives of Palestine then residing in Honduras, El Salvador and Mexico complained that they had applied for Palestinian citizenship and that their applications had been refused. The applicants stated that they

> 'were all born in Palestine and that they had not during their absence changed their nationality. Those residents in Honduras added that they still owned land in Palestine, and that, although their engagement in commerce had hitherto prevented their return to Palestine, they expected to return home at some future date. The residents of El Salvador complained that they have been refused passports to visit or return to Palestine. The petitioners of Mexico, represented by the Palestinian Association in Mexico which had membership of more than 3,000 Palestinians, asked to be informed of what it meant that native born Palestinians could acquire citizenship in their native land. All the petitioners protested against the decision of the Government of Palestine that rejected their applications for Palestinian citizenship . . . .'

The British Government maintained that it would entertain options for Palestinian citizenship only for those who maintained a substantial connection with Palestine. This principle was embodied in a rule according to which Turkish nationals, natives of Palestine but resident abroad, could acquire Palestinian citizenship only if they had emigrated from Palestine during or after the year 1920, or if, having emigrated before 1920, they had since returned to Palestine and resided there for not less than six months. This latter's condition is explained by the undesirability of creating a class of persons permanently resident abroad who are entitled to British protection' (Permanent Mandates Commission, *Minutes of the Twelfth Session*, 1927: 128). The Mandates Commission expressed the hope that the British Government would show a 'liberal spirit' in dealing with these persons. No further action was taken.

A small number of persons born in Palestine and residing abroad had acquired Palestinian citizenship by other means, such as naturalization. For example, only 78 out of 4,713 persons naturalized in 1928 were persons who had been born in Palestine and then resided abroad; the rest were foreign Jews, according to a British report on the administration of Palestine. In 1937, the same source reported that 64 persons belonging to the former category had been able to acquire Palestinian citizenship, while, just as an example of the self-evident purpose of this practice, 21,542 non-Palestine-born Jews from Poland, Germany and Russia had been naturalized and obtained Palestinian citizenship. In the following year, just 92 persons acquired citizenship by the former method, whereas 17,988 immigrant Jews became Palestinian citizens during the same year.

A recommendation designed to resolve the citizenship problem of
these persons was presented to the British Government in 1936 by the
Royal Commission, which had visited Palestine to investigate the causes
of the disturbances of that year and to propose a solution. The Commission
suggested that at least 'those who are able to establish an unbroken
personal connection with Palestine and who are prepared to give a definite
formal assurance of their intention to return, should be admitted to
Palestinian citizenship.' On 31 August 1939, an amendment to the 1925
Palestinian Citizenship Order was introduced to allow these persons to
return to Palestine and to obtain Palestinian citizenship within two years.
On 2 November 1939, special regulations were enacted to that effect. The
Government of Palestine then advised the inhabitants, by a public notice
gazetted on 21 November 1939, to inform their relatives and friends
abroad that they should apply for Palestinian citizenship through this
newly opened channel. On 11 June 1942, another amendment to the
Citizenship Order (gazetted on 16 July) was passed, extending the time
limit for applications for citizenship to six years. This Order gave natives
residing abroad the right to apply for Palestinian citizenship, provided that
they could establish an unbroken personal connection with the country.

In practice, only a limited number were able to obtain citizenship. In
1946, it was reported that only 465 persons born in Palestine and residing
abroad had succeeded in acquiring Palestinian citizenship since 1925,
while the cases of 87 others remained under consideration (Survey I: 206).
This situation can be explained by two factors. One is the wording of
Article 1 of the 1939 amendment, which gave the Government of Palestine
absolute discretion to accept or refuse applications from these persons, and
the fact that the Government insisted that applicants should prove an
unbroken connection with Palestine, which was apparently a difficult task
to be performed from abroad. Secondly, the period during and immediately
after World War II (1939-1948) led to the imposition of severe restrictions
on entry and immigration into Palestine. The citizenship of this group and
their descendants has therefore remained unresolved until now. It follows
that this group of Palestine's natives constituted the first generation of
Palestinian refugees.

British practice with respect to the citizenship of this group of
Palestinians was contrary to the international law of State succession.
While Article 8, paragraph 1, of the International Law Commission's Draft
Articles on Nationality of Natural Persons in Relation to the Succession of
States imposes no obligation on a successor State to attribute its
citizenship to citizens of the predecessor State 'if they have their habitual
residence in another State,' the same paragraph restricts that provision by

inserting as a condition that such citizens should have the citizenship of another State. In other words, such persons should not be rendered stateless as a result of State succession. They are entitled to exercise the right of option for citizenship and the successor State 'should provide a reasonable time limit for the exercise of the right of option' (Article 11, paragraph 5, of the Draft Articles). As noted by the International Law Commission, a 'reasonable time limit' is a period 'necessary to ensure the effective exercise of the right of option.' As proved by the facts following the adoption of the 1925 Citizenship Order, the nine-month time-limit was unreasonable and the majority of the persons concerned had become stateless at the time. These persons should have enjoyed the right to opt for the citizenship of any State that would be created in Mandate Palestine at any time in the future by the citizenship legislation of the State of Israel or the State of Palestine, or through an agreement between the two States, depending on their former habitual residence.

The citizenship of this group and their descendants has therefore remained unresolved until now. These persons should enjoy all refugee rights pending the final settlement of their status by legislation or by treaty between the future State of Palestine and the State of Israel. However, as most of them have presumably acquired other nationalities with the passage of time, their main right would consist in the right of return on the same footing as other Palestinian refugees. Ultimately, this group, who are mostly descendants of Palestine natives, should be able to recover Palestinian citizenship. Members of the group belong to various areas of pre-1948 Palestine. If they were habitual residents of those parts of Palestine in which Israel was established, they should be allowed to return thereto and to acquire Israeli citizenship. Alternatively, they should be granted the citizenship of the State of Palestine like other refugees. If members of the group were habitual residents before 1948 in the areas of Mandate Palestine that are now the West Bank or the Gaza Strip, they should be granted the citizenship of the State of Palestine on a similar basis to persons originating from the 1967-occupied territory.

It may be relevant to note that the 1954 Jordanian Nationality Law included a provision concerning the granting of Jordanian citizenship to members of this group. Article 5 of the Law stipulated: 'His Majesty, upon the nomination of the Council of Ministers, may confer Jordanian citizenship on any emigrant who submits a written declaration by which he opts for Jordanian citizenship, providing that such emigrant renounces any former citizenship that he might have been holding prior to the submission of the aforementioned declaration.' Article 1 of the same law defined the term 'emigrant' as: 'Any Arab who has been born in the Hashemite

Kingdom of Jordan [including the West Bank at the time] or in those occupied parts of Palestine [in which Israel was established] and emigrated from the countries [Jordan or the parts of Palestine in which Israel had been established] or was forced to leave. This definition includes descendants of such emigrant regardless of their place of birth.' As this article set no time-limit for the granting of Jordanian citizenship to such persons, many of the persons concerned have effectively applied and acquired that citizenship since the 1950s. The names of these persons, who are mostly Palestinian natives or their descendants, have been published in the Jordanian Official Gazette. The citizenship law of the State of Palestine ought to take this provision as a precedent.

Inhabitants of Israel

As of May 2011, the number of Israeli citizens totalled 7,746,000, according to the Israeli Central Bureau of Statistics. Of these, 5,837,000 were Jews (nearly 75.3%) and 1,587,000 were Arabs (about 20.5%); the rest were classified as 'others.' These citizens (Jews and Arabs) belong to a single group as far as citizenship, in the legal sense, is concerned. In another sense, i.e. based on racial/ethnic affiliation, Israeli citizens may be divided into two sub-groups: Jews and Arabs. However, Israeli citizens are divided in this section into five sub-groups in the light of their relevance to Palestinian citizenship as it has evolved, legally and in practice, over past decades in order to define their status in relation to citizenship in the State of Palestine.

Israeli Arabs in their Places of Origin

Members of this group are part of the Arabic-speaking people who held Palestinian citizenship before the establishment of Israel. They remained in their original places of habitual residence inside the parts of Palestine that became Israel such as the Negev, Jaffa, Haifa, Nazareth, and the Galilee. On its establishment in 1948, Israel made it difficult for the Arab inhabitants to acquire Israeli citizenship. It used the technique of obliging any Arab applicant for Israeli citizenship to prove his or her Palestinian citizenship through Palestinian identity cards or passports that were not possessed by the majority because, first, the possession of such documents was optional under the mandate and, secondly, the Israeli military reportedly destroyed most such documents found with Arabs at the beginning of its seizure of Arab towns in 1948. These inhabitants, who were under military rule until 1966, were treated as foreigners in their native land. Their status at the time is comparable to that of Jerusalemites since the Israeli occupation in 1967. In 1980, however, Israel amended its citizenship law and enabled these inhabitants to acquire Israeli citizenship. Although they are now considered to be *de jure* Israeli citizens, they are discriminated against in Jewish-dominated institutions/society.

As a general rule, this group should be excluded from the citizenship of the State of Palestine. There is no legal reason for its members to become citizens of that State because, according to the law of State succession, they could only be Israeli citizens, yet 'Arab' in terms of ethnic affiliation. There is no need for the group to acquire Palestinian citizenship, since its right to citizenship, as well as the rights derived therefrom, are guaranteed by Israeli law—despite the aforementioned discrimination against them, which is a separate issue from citizenship as a legal concept.

Yet the group in question may be given the option of acquiring Palestinian citizenship. This option would be based on two grounds. One is family reunification, i.e. naturalization by marriage to a Palestinian citizen, man or woman. The second ground would involve a provision for special naturalization, upon application, which should be facilitated for those wishing to become Palestinian citizens. A provision to this effect might be inserted in the citizenship law without a residency requirement, or with a shorter requirement than the general residency period required for naturalization by citizens of other States. Any previous residency in the West Bank and Gaza should be taken into consideration in this regard, as there are considerable numbers of Arab Israelis who have been living in the Palestinian territory for many years without being currently considered as Palestinian citizens under the applicable local law in the territory. When an Arab Israeli acquires Palestinian citizenship, he or she might become a dual citizen of the State of Israel and the State of Palestine.

In all cases, i.e. even when members of this group continue to hold Israeli citizenship, they should be treated as Palestinians within the State of Palestine in terms of most citizens' rights, not least as regards admission, residency, ownership of immovable property, work, profession and business. One exception could be participation in legislative elections. Thus, the status of this group, which stems from the historical ties connecting all the 'Palestinian Arab People' as opposed to the 'Jewish People,' in the ethnic sense of the terms, would be similar to the favourable nation treatment that exists in international relations between States — like the status of a German citizen in France, for example, or a Qatari citizen in Oman. Such treatment can be afforded with or without reciprocity between Palestine and Israel.

Israeli Arabs Internally Displaced within Israel

The status of this group is quite similar to the previous one. The difference is that members of the group moved from one given place inside the territory of Palestine that became Israel to another during or after the 1948 Israeli-Arab conflict. As internally displaced persons within Israel, they are citizens of Israel according to Israeli law, and Israeli law has jurisdiction to determine their status. According to international law, however, the group should be accorded the right to return to their places of former residence from which they were displaced before the establishment of the State of Israel. They would ultimately be excluded from the scope of Palestinian citizenship in the State of Palestine. However, their question should remain part of the negotiations between Israel and the Palestine Liberation Organization, because their status has been created in the context of the overall Israeli-Palestinian conflict. This group, like the preceding one, should be given the option of acquiring the citizenship of the State of Palestine based on family reunification and naturalization. Its members should be treated as Palestinians in terms of most citizens' rights. This is, again, not a legal obligation but a political position.

Israeli Jews who were Native Palestinians

In 1925, there were 7,143 Jews residing in Palestine as Ottoman subjects. They then acquired Palestinian citizenship *ipso facto* based on the Palestinian Citizenship Order. After the establishment of Israel, this group acquired Israeli citizenship. There are no existing data on members of the group because Israel does not provide such statistics. Yet one may arrive at an approximate total by comparing data at the end of the Mandate with that relating to the current population of the West Bank and the Gaza Strip. In 1947, the number of Jews who expected to be habitual residents of the Arab State that was proposed by the United Nations Partition Plan was some 10,000, or about 1.4%. This figure included native Jewish Palestinians and naturalized Jewish Palestinians, foreigners as well as refugees. As the West Bank and the Gaza Strip constitute almost half of the area allocated to the Arab State, half of the above-mentioned percentage of Jews, or 0.07% of the total population of the OPT today, would remain there. As almost half of the Jews residing in Palestine at the end of the Mandate were foreigners (see below), the total number of Palestinian Jews residing in the West Bank and the Gaza Strip would be about 0.035%, or 2,500 persons. Comparing the figures proportionally with the current population of the West Bank and the Gaza Strip, which totals about 4.17 million, and assuming that the number of Jews has increased at the same rate, the total number of Jews assumed to be Palestinian citizens would not now exceed 15,000 at best. One third of these would probably be native Jewish Palestinians and two thirds naturalized Jews. In other words, the total number of native Jewish Palestinians and their descendants in the West Bank and the Gaza Strip who would be eligible to acquire Palestinian citizenship in the State of Palestine would be about 5,000.

This group, by and large, would not be given Palestinian citizenship, since most of its members were habitually resident in the territory of Palestine that became Israel — just like Arab Israelis in their original places of residence. However, Jewish Palestinians who were resident in the area that became known as the West Bank, mainly in the old cities of Jerusalem and Hebron, as well as the Gaza Strip, should be given the right to opt for the citizenship of the State of Palestine, as in the case of any refugee. These persons could be considered as 'Palestinian-Jewish refugees in Israel' who can return to their original places of habitual residence in the State of Palestine. They would in that case become dual Israeli-Palestinian citizens. Yet the granting of Palestinian citizenship to members of this group would be somewhat symbolic since, effectively, only a small number of them would be interested in acquiring such citizenship. There are two reasons for this assumption. One is that this group has been fully integrated into the Jewish community of Israel, so that one might be unable to distinguish them from other Israelis for the purpose of developing criteria for granting citizenship. The second reason relates to evidentiary difficulties, since most of this group's members are of the second, third or even fourth generation for which proof of original pre-Israel citizenship would be difficult to find.

Israeli Jews Naturalized in Palestinian Citizenship

Naturalization, as regulated by the Citizenship Order, was designed to grant Palestinian citizenship to foreign Jews who immigrated into Palestine. Article 7 of the Order, *inter alia*, provided that: 'The High Commissioner may grant a certificate of naturalisation as a Palestinian citizen to any person who makes application therefor and who satisfies him: (*a*) That he has resided in Palestine for a period not less than two years out of the three years immediately preceding the date of his application: (*b*) That he is of good character and has an adequate knowledge of either the English, the Arabic or the Hebrew language: (*c*) That he intends, if his application is granted, to reside in Palestine.' Based on this provision, a massive number of foreign Jews acquired Palestinian citizenship. At the end of the Mandate, the total number of persons who had acquired Palestinian citizenship by naturalization was estimated at 132,616; about 99% of them were Jews (Survey I: 208).

To give effect to Article 7 of the Palestine Mandate, the naturalization provisions of the 1925 Palestinian Citizenship Order were 'framed so as to facilitate the acquisition of Palestinian citizenship by Jews who take up their permanent residence in Palestine.' Naturalization was the key aspect of the said Citizenship Order. This fact was summarized by the Supreme Court of Palestine on 28 February 1929 in *Palevitch v. Chief Immigration Officer*. The case related to an immigrant Jew from Italy who had applied for naturalization in Palestine. It was held that Article 7 of the Mandate 'is concerned with the enactment of a citizenship law in which, so says this Article of the Mandate, there are to be included provisions framed so as to facilitate the acquisition of Palestinian citizenship by Jews who take up their permanent residence in Palestine. This has been done by the passing of the Palestine Citizenship Order, 1925, in which there are embodied, in Article 7(1), a number of qualifications which are required before the High Commissioner [for Palestine] may grant a certificate of naturalisation.' Shortly after the enactment of the Order, the British Government reported in 1925 that the 'qualifications for naturalization are simple: two years' residence in Palestine out of the three years preceding application . . .; knowledge of Hebrew is accepted under the literacy qualification. In special cases the High Commissioner is empowered to grant naturalisation even if the period of residence has not been within the three years preceding application. Special naturalisation offices have already been opened . . . and an officer is visiting the Jewish agricultural settlements . . . to receive applications on the spot.'

Officially, the Jewish Agency and the Zionist Organization were in favour of the naturalization of Jews in Palestine. For instance, according to a British report to the League of Nations, the increase in the number of Jews applying for naturalization in 1935 was a result of, *inter alia*, 'the campaign of the several Jewish representative institutions to encourage naturalization among members of the Jewish community.' More specifically, in 1936, Britain reported that 'the [Jewish] General Council (*Vaad Leumi*) conducted an energetic campaign for the naturalisation as Palestinian citizens of Jewish immigrants, who are qualified therefore by residence, and gave much assistance to the Department of Migration in the acceptance of applications for certificates of citizenship under the Palestinian Citizenship Order, 1925.' Yet not all Jews applied individually for naturalization. At the end of 1936, the Palestine Royal Commission reported that out of 292,000 Jews qualifying for Palestinian citizenship 'about 166,000 had acquired Palestinian citizenship and the remaining 126,000, or about 43 per cent of the qualified population, were not Palestinian citizens.' The reason, continued that Commission, was that many 'Jews have not availed themselves readily of the opportunity afforded them of becoming Palestinian citizens and this is accounted for by the fact that their chief interest is in the Jewish community itself and allegiance to Palestine [is a] minor consideration[s] to many of them.'

Britain enacted and applied immigration laws in order to bring Jews into Palestine, supporting their settlement in the country and ultimately naturalizing them there. The systematic collaboration between the Zionist Organization and Britain was recognized in Article 4 of the Mandate which stated that: 'An appropriate Jewish agency shall be recognised as a public body for the purpose of advising and co-operating with the Administration of Palestine in such economic, social and other matters as may affect the establishment of the Jewish national home and the interests of the Jewish population in Palestine. . . . The Zionist organization . . . shall be recognised as such agency.' Thus, as the British Government stated in its report to the League of Nations in 1925, while 'the regulations under the Immigration Ordinance, 1925, set up a statutory procedure for the introduction of Jewish immigrant labour into Palestine . . . the Palestinian Citizenship Order in Council, 1925, facilitates the acquisition of Palestinian nationality by persons settling in the country.'

Another naturalization provision was added to the Citizenship Order to serve a specific group of Jews who were already residing in Palestine and who temporarily naturalized in order to participate in the legislative elections of 1922. Thus, Article 5(1) of the Citizenship Order read: 'Persons who have made a declaration of their intention to opt for Palestinian citizenship in accordance with Article 2 of the Palestine Legislative Council Election Order, 1922, and have received provisional certificates of Palestinian citizenship . . . shall . . . be deemed to be entitled to acquire Palestinian citizenship.' Although this provision did not mention 'Jews,' the British Government confirmed in a 1925 report that 'Article 5 of the Order facilitates the acquisition of citizenship by Jews who opted therefor under Article 2 of the Palestine Legislative Council Election Order in Council, 1922.' Moreover, the Government added in 1932 that 'special facilities have been granted to Jewish students resident abroad to obtain citizenship, if qualified, without being required to present themselves in person at Jerusalem [to apply for naturalization].' Article 13 of the 1925 Palestinian Citizenship Regulations laid the material basis for this practice by authorizing British consuls to grant Palestinian citizenship to Jewish students abroad.

An intensified process of naturalization of Jewish soldiers serving in the British forces in Palestine had been conducted during and after World War II. This process started on 19 November 1940, when Britain amended the Palestinian Citizenship Order. This amendment was followed by a series of regulations to the same effect. Such naturalization continued through the later stages of the war and thereafter during the period leading to the end of the Mandate. Persons who were present in Palestine and participated in military service were overwhelmingly Jews. It was estimated that the number of Jews who participated in the British forces during World War II in Palestine amounted to some 27,000 men: 7,000 regular soldiers and 20,000 volunteers (Bentwich, *The Mandated Territories under the Second World War*, 1944: 165). In addition, there were '35,000 Civil Defence Workers. There were also about 1,500 Jews from Palestine and the Middle East in the R.A.F. [Royal Air Force] . . . [and] 15,000 were serving as special policemen in Palestine,' according to the ESCO Foundation for Palestine's *Study of Jewish, Arab, and British Politics* (1947: 1028). These naturalized soldiers presumably later joined the Israeli army.

Consequently, the vast majority of naturalized foreigners in Palestine were Jews, with minor exceptions. In 1931, for example, the British Government told the League of Nations that out of 'the 17,477 individuals and families, representing about 27,000 souls, who have acquired the Palestinian citizenship . . . nearly 95 per cent are Jews.' Another 1946 statistic estimated the naturalization of non-Jews throughout the Mandate period at 'approximately 1% of the total' (Survey I: 208). Immigrants arrived in Palestine from about 61 countries. The vast majority came from Europe.

Naturalization constituted the chosen formula for increasing the number of Jews in Palestine and legalizing their presence there. As indicated above, in mid-1925 the number of Jews who were Ottoman subjects and who then became *naturalized* Palestinians did not exceed 1% of the total population. Upon the establishment of Israel, Jewish Palestinians were converted into Israeli citizens and ceased to be Palestinians. Foreign Jews who were resident in Palestine also became Israeli citizens. These naturalized Jews formed the bulk of Israeli citizens. Article 4 of the Israeli Law of Return of 6 July 1950 gave every Jew who came to Palestine/Israel as a permanent immigrant the right to obtain an immigration certificate. Article 2(*a*) of the Israeli Nationality Law of 1 April 1952 considered every immigrant under the Law of Return to be an

Israel citizen. Article 2(*b*)(1) of the latter law regarded any immigrant Jew who entered Palestine before the establishment of Israel as an Israeli citizen.

Pursuant to the law of State succession, naturalized persons of the predecessor State should acquire the citizenship of the successor State(s). Israel, as seen in the preceding paragraph, granted such persons its citizenship. This point has therefore has been settled. Yet if the habitual residence of some of these naturalized Jewish Palestinians was in the West Bank or the Gaza Strip before 1948, then such persons may be able to acquire Palestinian citizenship. Article 1 of the International Law Commission's Draft Articles on Nationality of Natural Persons in relation to the Succession of States provides that the predecessor State's citizens acquire the citizenship of one of the successor States, 'irrespective of the mode of acquisition of the nationality.' Commenting on this provision, the Commission said that an 'element which is stated expressly in article 1 is that the mode of acquisition of the predecessor State's citizenship has no effect on the scope of the right of the persons referred to in this provision to a nationality. It is irrelevant in this regard whether they have acquired the nationality of the predecessor State at birth . . . or by naturalization.' The same conclusion was reached by the 1929 Draft Convention on Nationality of Harvard Law School, namely 'there is no reason whatsoever for drawing a distinction between persons who have acquired nationality at birth and those who have acquired nationality through some process of naturalization.'

Today, as discussed above, some 10,000 persons in this category would be eligible to acquire the citizenship of the State of Palestine based on their habitual residence in the West Bank and the Gaza Strip before 15 May 1948. The purpose of including this group in this chapter is to offer guidance to Palestinian policy-makers regarding this group's status in order to include or exclude it from the citizenship law of the State of Palestine based on clear policy reasoning. Effectively, as pointed out with respect to the group of original Jewish Palestinians, it is expected that the number of such persons interested in the acquisition of Palestinian citizenship would be small. Members of this group have been fully integrated into the Jewish community of Israel and most of them are descendants of naturalized Palestinians for whom the task of proving their original Palestinian citizenship would not be easy.

Newcomer Israelis

This category incorporates two types of people. The first are Jews who arrived in Palestine before 1948 (as legal or illegal immigrants or as Jewish refugees) and did not acquire Palestinian citizenship because they were not interested in obtaining it or due to their failure to satisfy the citizenship requirements of the 1925 Palestinian Citizenship Order. This group acquired Israeli citizenship after 1948. The second component of the category consists of Jews who have been immigrating into Israel since 1948. Neither component, irrespective of their habitual residence in Mandate Palestine or in Israel or the West Bank or the Gaza Strip, should be granted Palestinian citizenship. They have no legal ground for such citizenship unless, of course, they apply for naturalization like other foreigners. They have never been Palestinian citizens, even those who were resident in the West Bank or the Gaza Strip before 1948 or those who settled in the West Bank after 1967, i.e. in the settlements (as their residence there is contrary to international law). However, if the outcome of the negotiations results in an agreement to keep certain settlements in the West Bank under Palestinian sovereignty, then the citizenship law of the State of Palestine may consider naturalizing individuals belonging to this group, since citizenship depends on the status of the territory.

Conclusion

It will be a challenge for the State of Palestine to settle such a complicated question as Palestinian citizenship. However, if international legal criteria are applied, the status of persons who have the right to acquire Palestinian citizenship can be relatively straightforward. Without the application of international law, the regularization of Palestinian citizenship would be confusing and ambiguous. This chapter sets out a framework concerning who has the right to become a citizen of Palestine. Some persons should have the right to acquire Palestinian citizenship *ipso facto*, by operation of law; these are mainly the inhabitants of the West Bank and the Gaza Strip. Others may acquire Palestinian citizenship as a matter of choice, with a view to preserving their acquired rights in the States in which they have obtained a status; these include East Jerusalemites, if Jerusalem remains under Israeli occupation, Palestinian refugees who have acquired the citizenship of States that prohibit citizenship change, and refugees who fear that the acquisition of Palestinian citizenship might undermine their refugee status.

To develop criteria for Palestinian citizenship in the State of Palestine, one should begin from the point at which the territory of Mandate Palestine was separated from the Ottoman Empire. From that point on, a 'Palestinian' can be defined as any person who was a Turkish citizen and was habitually resident in the territory of Palestine upon its separation from the Ottoman Empire on 6 August 1924 based on the Treaty of Lausanne concluded between Turkey and Britain. The descendants of those who have the right to acquire Palestinian citizenship are included as well. All the groups discussed in this chapter can be assessed in accordance with such criteria and hence be included in or excluded from the scope of Palestinian citizenship. However, certain realities that have subsequently emerged during the various periods through which Palestine has passed should also be considered as bases for the granting of Palestinian citizenship. These realties include: naturalization through the acquisition of Palestinian citizenship under British rule; the acquisition of Jordanian citizenship under the Jordanian Citizenship Law in the West Bank; and family reunification cases approved under the Israeli occupation of the West Bank, including East Jerusalem, and the Gaza Strip.

Palestinian citizenship had become a full citizenship by the end of British rule. The fact that Palestine did not constitute an independent State does not derogate from that status. Modern history has witnessed instances of non-independent States conferring nationalities. For instance, nationalities were recognized in protected States such as Egypt and Morocco. Countries controlled by Great Britain had a distinct citizenship based on local legislation, including Canada, India, New Zealand, and South Africa. No doubts have been raised regarding the existence of the Iraqi or Afghan nationalities under the recent occupation. As far as citizenship is concerned, Palestine constituted a State under the Mandate. If Palestine had gained its independence at that time, Palestinian citizenship would not have differed from the citizenship of independent States. It follows that succeeding States in parts of Mandate Palestine would be under an international obligation to accept the status of Palestinian citizenship as it existed under the Mandate as a basis for the future determination of the inhabitants' status.

Due to the *de facto* sovereignties that Palestine has experienced, various statuses have affected its inhabitants. Certain statuses emerged as a result of the policies and legislative acts undertaken unilaterally by individual States. Almost every country in which Palestinians ended up accorded them domestic status. Hence Palestinians became 'citizens,' 'dual nationals,' 'permanent residents,' 'refugees,' 'immigrants,' 'returnees,' 'emigrants,' 'stateless,' 'internally displaced persons,' 'non-identified,'

'Gazans,' 'West Bankers,' 'Jerusalemites,' 'Arab Israelis,' or 'Jewish Israelis.' International law has a standpoint on all these statuses, regardless of the stand of various local citizenship laws in this respect.

Broadly speaking, people who relate to Palestine may be divided into three categories: (1) the inhabitants of the occupied Palestinian territory of the West Bank and the Gaza Strip; (2) refugees who left the area of Mandate Palestine in which Israel was established; and (3) the inhabitants of Israel. These categories can, in turn, be sub-categorized. The inhabitants of the occupied territory comprise three groups: West Bankers and Gazans; East Jerusalemites; and the 1967 refugees. Palestinian refugees may be divided into five groups: 1948 refugees residing in the occupied territory; those who acquired other nationalities; stateless refugees residing in UNRWA areas of operation; stateless refugees outside those areas; and persons stripped of their citizenship in 1925. Those holding Israeli citizenship include: Arabs in their original locations; Arabs who were internally displaced; native Palestinian Jews; naturalized Palestinian Jews; and newcomer Israelis.

The over four-million West Bankers and Gazans hold *de facto* Palestinian citizenship today; they can exercise most citizens' rights, such as residency, travel abroad, election, public employment, and ownership of immovable property. The State of Palestine is under an obligation pursuant to international law to grant its citizenship to these inhabitants, irrespective of the mode of acquisition of their present status. If the establishment of the Palestinian State is practically delayed, or if Israel continues its occupation, the Palestine Liberation Organization can in effect develop a Palestinian citizenship law, issue passports and exercise diplomatic protection by concluding bilateral agreements with States.

Although the some three-hundred-thousand East Jerusalemites are part of the West Bank, they constitute a separate group from the rest of the population due to the status that Israel has unilaterally created for them. In the State of Palestine, East Jerusalemites should be given the choice of opting for Palestinian citizenship. Special account should be taken of residents whose identity cards were withdrawn and who currently live in the West Bank without identity documentation. Such persons should be given Palestinian citizenship as a matter of priority. East Jerusalemites whose residency was revoked by Israel and who now live abroad should be given Palestinian citizenship and allowed to return to the State of Palestine if Israel opposes their return to Jerusalem—in case of Israel's on-going control of Jerusalem. As to those Jerusalemites living in the West Bank who still hold Jerusalem identity cards, care should be taken to preserve their acquired rights in the West Bank, on the one hand, and to protect their residence in Jerusalem, on the other. Jerusalemites who have acquired Israeli citizenship should be given the choice of obtaining Palestinian citizenship on request with a view to preserving their acquired rights in Israel. If Israel continues to exert control over Jerusalem, the State of Palestine should maintain the *status quo* regarding the city's inhabitants; Jerusalemites should retain Israeli identity cards and travel documentation, continue residing in Jerusalem and, at the same time, be treated as Palestinian citizens for the purpose of entry, residency, elections, referenda, ownership, etc., without having formal Palestinian citizenship. This may prevent Israel from using the acquisition of Palestinian citizenship as a pretext to revoke residency in the city.

Persons displaced in 1967 from the West Bank and the Gaza Strip now number at least 1.2 million. Those deported by Israel or denied the right of return since 1967 have a similar status. The State of Palestine is under an international legal obligation to allow the members of this group to return to their native homes. Once they have settled in the State and acquired Palestinian citizenship, these persons will cease to be refugees. If Israel denies them entry into Palestine in the event of ongoing occupation, the group will continue to be refugees. Even before their return, such persons may be granted Palestinian citizenship, offered diplomatic protection abroad, allowed to participate in referenda and elections, etc. Acquisition of the citizenship of other States should not derogate from the right of members of this group to return to the West Bank or the Gaza Strip and to recover their residence there.

Palestinian refugees displaced from the parts of Palestine in which the State of Israel was established on 15 May 1948 are the largest category of Palestinians. Those refugees registered by UNRWA now number about five millions. Thousands of other refugees are not registered with the Agency. According to international law, these refugees have the right to return to Israel and become Israeli citizens. Israel will most likely continue to oppose the right of return to its territory. The State of Palestine has no obligation to admit these refugees, but it has a political duty to defend their rights.

In the State of Palestine, Palestinian refugees may have the right to opt for Palestinian citizenship if they wish. The right of return of these refugees will not end after they acquire that citizenship. Substantial numbers of Palestinian refugees have already acquired the citizenship of other States and their refugee status is not denied. The right of return should not be confused with the refugee status granted by UNRWA or UNHCR, which is determined for the purpose of affording these agencies' assistance. As an individual right, the right of return cannot be politically compromised. It may solely be surrendered by the will of the refugee concerned. Responsibility for the refugee issue lies with Israel and the international community. The Palestinian leadership can reach an agreement that does not include the right of return. The utmost that the State of Palestine can do is to grant refugees its citizenship once the State is established, to protect them abroad, and to advocate their right of return to Israel.

The 1948 Palestinian refugees now residing in the West Bank and the Gaza Strip number two millions. In practice, this group has similar local status to West Bankers, Jerusalemites or Gazans, as the case may be. Under the citizenship law of the State of Palestine, this group should be granted Palestinian citizenship. The State would become, in a sense, like a host country for these refugees. The conferment of citizenship on such a category would in no way, from a legal perspective, undermine their status. Israel would in any case continue to oppose their return, regardless of whether they acquired other nationalities. Thus, the acquisition of Palestinian citizenship would not *per se* be a reason for ending this category's refugee status. Indeed, most Palestinian refugees have already acquired the nationalities of other States, but they remain refugees in the eyes of international law. For example, Palestinian refugees in Jordan are assisted by UNRWA despite holding Jordanian citizenship.

Palestinian refugees who have acquired the citizenship of other States are, technically speaking, no longer refugees according to the 1951 Convention relating to the Status of Refugees, since such persons can be protected by the State that recognizes them as its citizens. Yet they should continue to be regarded as refugees for various purposes, particularly for the right of return to Israel and the right of compensation for property loss. The majority of these persons are in Jordan, but substantial numbers live in other countries. True, in the States in which the 1951 Convention is applicable these refugees would not be considered as refugees in the eyes of local law and for the purpose of UNHCR protection; but they are still refugees pursuant to the international law of State succession, human rights law, humanitarian law, United Nations resolutions, and refugee law surrounding Article 1D of the Convention.

The State of Palestine has no legal obligation to confer its citizenship on this group of refugees, since responsibility for granting them a citizenship when they exercise the right of return lies with Israel. Nevertheless, given the Israeli refusal to grant its citizenship to members of the group or to readmit them to its territory and given that the State of Palestine will be the guardian of the Palestinian people at large, these refugees may be given the choice of acquiring the citizenship of the State of Palestine. Members of the group, after acquiring Palestinian citizenship, may lose other nationalities where internal laws prohibit dual citizenship. For this reason, the right to Palestinian citizenship should be accorded on a case-by-case basis and at the request of the person concerned. Thus, if a person did not wish to apply for Palestinian citizenship, the State of Palestine should not, and in fact could not, impose its citizenship on him/her. In such cases, Palestine might, as an alternative, accord special treatment to these refugees based on their original link to Mandate Palestine. They might therefore be treated as Palestinian citizens in relation to entry, residency, elections, and employment, despite the fact that they lack Palestinian citizenship. If they acquired the citizenship of the State of Palestine, they would effectively become dual/multiple citizens. The new State, with a view to preserving the rights acquired by Palestinians in various countries, may not oppose the principle of dual citizenship.

Most stateless Palestinian refugees who reside in the UNRWA areas of operation and do not possess the citizenship of any State are to be found in Lebanon and Syria; a smaller number can be found in Jordan. Acquisition of the citizenship of the State of Palestine by these refugees is more urgent than for other categories of Palestinians. They can thus be protected by the State of Palestine, participate in referenda and vote, and be elected to representative bodies. This group would most likely continue to receive UNRWA's assistance, as the Agency does not make its services conditional on citizenship status. There are millions of 'Palestine Refugees' who are still receiving such assistance despite being holders of Jordanian, Lebanese, Syrian and other nationalities. There is no legal reason why the Agency would cease to offer its assistance if such refugees become Palestinian citizens.

In addition to the general category of stateless Palestinians in UNRWA areas of operation, there is a group of Palestinian refugees whose residency is deemed to be illegal by the host governments and who are not registered by the Agency. The members of this sub-category of stateless Palestinians are commonly known as 'non-recognized' refugees. The sub-category exists mainly in Lebanon but some of its members are also to be found in other States such as Syria and Jordan. In Lebanon alone, such refugees number about 35,000. The most sustainable solution for them is to acquire a citizenship. The State that is obliged to grant its citizenship to all the 1948 refugees, including this sub-category, is Israel. Alternatively, the State of Palestine might confer its citizenship on them based on humanitarian grounds. The State would be bound to return only those persons who left the West Bank or the Gaza Strip, namely the 1967 refugees.

The mere fact of acquiring the citizenship of the State of Palestine does not necessarily entail a person's automatic return to that State, especially if Israel retains control over the Palestinian border. The Palestine Liberation Organization may reach bilateral agreements with Lebanon, Syria and Jordan to continue hosting refugees until such time as they are able to return to their original places of habitual residence in Israel, not only to the State of Palestine. Legally speaking, return to the State in the West Bank and the Gaza Strip does not constitute an exercise of the right of return. Hence, the State of Palestine would have virtually the same standing as one of the refugee host countries regarding the 1948 refugees.

Palestinian refugees who do not hold the citizenship of any State and who reside outside UNRWA areas of operation are treated by States in various ways depending on the States' local laws, international law commitments and their political stance *vis-à-vis* the Israeli-Palestinian conflict at large. The acquisition of a citizenship affects refugee status in the jurisdiction of some States or leads to the termination of UNHCR protection. But acquiring a citizenship does not affect the right of return, as just mentioned. Thus, the granting of Palestinian citizenship would be equivalent to the acquisition of the nationalities of other States. Again, a State in the West Bank and the Gaza Strip is not the territory to which the 1948 refugees have the right of return.

The citizenship of Palestine's natives who were residing abroad upon the enforcement of the 1925 Palestinian Citizenship Order and were denied the right to acquire Palestinian citizenship at that time should be resolved. Theoretically, this category may opt for the citizenship of any State created in Mandate Palestine: the State of Israel or the State of Palestine, depending on the applicant's former place of residence. If persons belonging to this category habitually resided in the parts of Palestine in which Israel was established, they should be allowed to return to Israel and to acquire its citizenship. Alternatively, they might acquire the citizenship of the State of Palestine like other Palestinian refugees. If members of this category habitually resided before 1948 in the areas of Mandate Palestine that now constitute the West Bank or the Gaza Strip, they should be granted, as a matter of right, the citizenship of the State of Palestine. The citizenship law of that State might take the provision of the 1954 Jordanian Nationality Law relating to such emigrants as a precedent.

Israeli Arabs residing in their places of origin would be excluded from the citizenship of the State of Palestine. There is no legal reason for this group to acquire the citizenship of the new State, nor is there a humanitarian need for such acquisition. Their citizenship is guaranteed by Israeli law. Yet this category may be accorded the option of acquiring Palestinian citizenship based on family reunification and naturalization. Naturalization should be facilitated for members of this category who wish to become Palestinian citizens without residency or with residency for a shorter period than is generally required for standard naturalization. Even when they continue to hold Israeli citizenship, members belonging to this category may be treated as Palestinians in the State of Palestine in terms of most citizens' rights, except those relating to legislative elections. Such treatment can be applied without reciprocity from Israel.

The status of Israeli Arabs internally displaced within Israel is quite similar to the previous one. The difference is that members of this category moved from a given place inside the territory of Palestine that became Israel to another during or after the 1948 Israeli-Arab conflict. Hence, these persons, in accordance with Israeli law, are citizens of Israel and Israeli law has the jurisdiction to determine their status. According to international law, however, the members of this category should be accorded the right to return to their places of former residence. They would ultimately be excluded from the scope of Palestinian citizenship in the State of Palestine. But their question may remain part of Israeli-Palestinian negotiations. This category should be given the option of acquiring the citizenship of the State of Palestine based on family reunification and naturalization. They should be treated as Palestinians in terms of most citizens' rights. This is, again, not a legal obligation but a political stance.

Jewish native Palestinians whose place of residence before 1948 was in the West Bank or the Gaza Strip should be eligible to acquire the citizenship of the State of Palestine. The number of persons belonging to this category at the present time may be estimated at about 5,000. These persons could be considered as 'Palestinian-Jewish refugees in Israel' and could return to their original places of habitual residence in the State of Palestine. They might become dual Israeli-Palestinian citizens. Yet the conferment of Palestinian citizenship on members of this category would be rather symbolic as, effectively, there would only be a small number of them interested in acquiring Palestinian citizenship, since the group has been fully integrated into Israel.

Some 10,000 Palestinian Jews who acquired Palestinian citizenship by naturalization under the Mandate would be eligible to acquire the citizenship of the State of Palestine based on their habitual residence in the West Bank or the Gaza Strip before 15 May 1948. As in the case of the previous category, it is expected that there would only be a small number of such persons interested in the acquisition of Palestinian citizenship.

Newcomer Israelis comprise two types of people. The first are Jews who arrived in Palestine before 1948 and did not acquire Palestinian citizenship because they were not interested in obtaining it or due to their failure to satisfy the citizenship requirements of the 1925 Palestinian Citizenship Order. This category acquired Israeli citizenship after 1948. The second category consists of Jews who have been immigrating into Israel since 1948. Neither category, irrespective of its members' place of residence (in Mandate Palestine, Israel, the West Bank or the Gaza Strip), should be granted Palestinian citizenship. But if the Israeli-Palestinian negotiations yield an agreement to keep certain settlements in the West Bank under Palestinian sovereignty, then the citizenship law of the State of Palestine may consider naturalizing such settlers (see Chapter Seventeen of this book).

The various categories of persons addressed in this chapter may overlap, and one individual may have a number of statuses simultaneously. Take, for example, a Palestinian born in the United States whose mother is a permanent resident of Ramallah with a West Bank identity card. The mother also possesses French citizenship. The father is originally a refugee from Haifa and currently a permanent resident of East Jerusalem with an Israeli identity card. Both parents then move to live and work in Syria. This person might have the following statuses: (1) a 'Palestinian refugee' from an area in which Israel was established, given the father's refugee status (Haifa); (2) a 'West Banker,' based on the mother's status (Ramallah); (3) a 'Jerusalemite,' based on the father's current status (East Jerusalem); (4) a 'French citizen,' based on the mother's citizenship; (4) an 'American citizen,' based on the citizenship attaching to the person's place of birth; (6) a 'resident' of Syria, where his parents are working; moreover, (7) the person might later marry a Jewish-Israeli woman and acquire Israeli citizenship. Another conceivable case is that of a Palestinian refugee in Gaza who was originally from Jaffa and became a second-time refugee when he moved to Lebanon in 1967 and is now living in China after marrying a Chinese-Canadian lady whom he met when studying in Canada.

The citizenship of the State of Palestine may be conferred on any person who meets the qualifications (even if just one) of the various Palestinian statuses addressed under any category discussed in this chapter. A person might claim the status that appeals to him/her under the national law of the States to which he/she is connected. The Palestinian in the first example given in the previous paragraph might acquire Palestinian citizenship based on his mother's permanent residency in Ramallah or his father's origin from Haifa or status in Jerusalem. He could claim and enjoy citizenship rights as a French citizen in France and as an American citizen in the United States. He would still be considered as a Palestinian refugee for the purpose of the right of return to Haifa. In Syria, he could reside in Damascus as an American citizen or a French national or as a Palestinian holding a passport issued by the Palestinian Authority. He would retain his UNRWA registration card as a Palestinian refugee. While in another country, such as Japan, he might be protected by the French or American embassies or by both. After the establishment of the State of Palestine, this person might also be protected by the Palestinian embassy in Tokyo.

Juridical and policy actions suggested in this chapter should be reflected in a citizenship law to be passed by the Palestinian Legislative Council. In the continued absence of the Council, as at the present time, the law can be enacted by the Palestinian President in the form of a Decree-Law under Article 43 of the 2003 Amended Palestinian Basic Law. The citizenship law can be broadly divided into two parts. Part I would incorporate the recommended policy actions presented in the various sections of this chapter. Part II would include the technical citizenship provisions normally found in the citizenship laws of any State. In this connection, the Palestinian citizenship law should reflect new developments in comparative and international law, particularly human rights law relating to the citizenship of children and equality between the sexes/spouses. The law should be accompanied by institutional structures for its implementation. Such structures would include a set of by-laws, a series of bilateral agreements with States, appointing immigration and passport personnel in Palestine, highly qualified diplomatic staff abroad, and budget allocations.

The first technical issue that the Palestinian citizenship law should address is the adoption of *jus soli* or/and *jus sanguinis* as bases for citizenship. *Jus soli*, which is predominant in the Anglo-Saxon States, confers citizenship on any person born in the country. *Jus sanguinis*, or the blood connection that is predominant in civil-law States and in all Arab countries, establishes citizenship on the fact of birth to a citizen of the State, regardless of the State of birth. All States in the world, including *jus soli* countries, rely on the latter principle and provide citizenship to children born to nationals anywhere. The question to be raised with the Palestinian legislator is whether or not to adopt the *jus soli* principle and to grant Palestinian citizenship to any child born on Palestinian soil. This is a matter of policy that should be decided by policy-makers. Palestinian legislators may adopt *jus soli* if they wish to increase the number of

Palestinians in the State. Otherwise, the law can be based on *jus sanguinis*, which is closer to Middle Eastern legal culture in this regard.

Dual/multiple citizenship should be permissible in the State of Palestine in order to protect citizens' rights acquired by Palestinians who have been living in the diaspora and to encourage them to return to Palestine in order to contribute to its social and economic life. Such citizens should be treated in the State as Palestinians only; i.e. they should not be allowed to claim protection by States to which they belong in order to avoid a return to the 'capitulation' era or avoid opening the door to foreign intervention in the internal affairs of the State. This approach is in line with international customary law as codified in Article 4 of the 1930 Hague Convention on Certain Questions Relating to the Conflict of Nationality Laws which stipulates: 'A State may not afford diplomatic protection to one of its nationals against a State whose citizenship such person also possesses.' Similarly, Palestine would not be able under international law to extend its diplomatic protection to Palestinian citizens in other States when they hold the citizenship of the States concerned — such as protecting Palestinian-Jordanians in Jordan or Palestinian-Chileans in Chile. On the other hand, when Palestinians reside in a State whose citizenship they do not possess, Palestinian diplomatic missions may intervene on behalf of fellow citizens and protect them abroad even if the citizens concerned hold other nationalities.

Naturalization should be fixed in such a way as to allow those who reside for a reasonable period of time in the State of Palestine and prove their social integration to acquire Palestinian citizenship. The residency period required for naturalization varies from one State to the next and may range from two to fifteen years. A reasonable period could be between three and five years, provided that the applicant is a legal resident, of good conduct, has ongoing residency and knows the official language of the State of Palestine. The citizenship law may allow for the granting of Palestinian citizenship by naturalization to certain persons although they do not satisfy the residency requirements, if they have provided significant service to the State. Naturalization by marriage should be framed in such a way as to facilitate family reunification and thus to confer citizenship on spouses of Palestinian citizens. With this objective in mind, residency in Palestine might not be required for the granting of Palestinian citizenship to such spouses. Yet the passage of a certain period following marriage, such as one or two years, might be required before citizenship is granted in order to ensure that the marriage is sustainable. A foreign spouse might also be granted Palestinian citizenship in the event that he or she begets a child with a Palestinian citizen. In no case should

Palestinian citizenship be imposed. Any interested person should file an application requesting the State of Palestine to grant its citizenship to him or her.

Equality between men and women should underlie the citizenship law of the State. Such equality should be envisaged in particular between husbands and wives. A Palestinian woman should be empowered to pass on her citizenship to her non-Palestinian husband and *vice versa*. Children born to at least one Palestinian citizen, mother or father, should be entitled to acquire Palestinian citizenship. By adopting gender equality, the Palestinian law will be consistent with modern international human rights law and the citizenship laws of developed States.

Citizens who wish to renounce their Palestinian citizenship for any reason should be allowed to do so by the citizenship law. Laws in some States require persons who apply for their citizenship to renounce former nationalities. The State of Palestine can facilitate this task by approving applications for renunciation of citizenship. In particular, a specific provision should be included in the law to allow children, once they have attained the age of majority, to renounce the Palestinian citizenship that they have acquired pursuant to the naturalization of their parents.

A special provision should be adopted in the citizenship law regarding babies born in the territory of Palestine to unknown parents or found therein. This would be an application of the *jus soli* principle. Children born to stateless parents in Palestine should also be granted Palestinian citizenship. Such provisions would render the Palestinian law consistent with the international approach to reduction of statelessness and with human rights law, which makes possession of citizenship a human right.

The withdrawal of citizenship or its revocation should not be exercised by Palestine as a general rule. However, in exceptional circumstances, citizenship might be revoked under a number of strict conditions: (1) that the person in question would not become stateless; (2) that he or she had committed serious acts against the State that should be exclusively and concretely specified in the law; and (3) that the revocation decision is taken by a final judgement of a court in which a right of appeal is guaranteed.

Annex

The Foundations of Palestinian Citizenship
in International Law

The international law foundations of Palestinian citizenship must be understood in the context of the legal developments that have affected the territory of Palestine. These developments stem, *inter alia*, from inter-State citizenship law, the law of State succession, United Nations law (mainly the United Nations Partition Plan), and the right of self-determination. The relevant foundations are tackled here in relation to citizenship.

Citizenship law pertaining to the succession of States is the first and by far the most decisive factor in determining inhabitants' citizenship. Let us now review the changes of sovereignty over Palestine in order to assess how they affected Palestinian citizenship.

The land of Palestine formed part of the Ottoman Empire from 1516. By the end of the sixteenth century, Turkish rule extended westwards into Europe as far as the border of Austria and along the southern rim of the Mediterranean Sea into Algeria. During this period, there was no political entity called 'Palestine.' Rather, parts of this land fell under various Turkish administrative divisions. In 1874, towards the end of the Empire, Jerusalem and its surrounding towns became a separate district governed directly from Istanbul. This division did not change the status of Palestine. In the midst of World War I, during which Britain and Turkey were enemies, the territory that become known as Palestine fell in 1917-1918 under British occupation. Under the Ottomans, the inhabitants of Palestine were Turkish citizens. Those known later as 'Palestinians' had no particular legal status. Hence, a distinct 'Palestinian people' did not exist at the time. The 'Palestinians' constituted a component of the 'Ottoman people.'

To acquire Palestinian citizenship at the outset, one was required to hold the status of an Ottoman subject or citizen. Upon the entry into force of the Treaty of Lausanne, the international instrument whereby Palestine was legally separated from Turkey on 6 August 1924, Ottoman citizens who resided in the territory of Palestine became *ipso facto* 'Palestinian citizens.' This was domestically confirmed by the Palestinian Citizenship Order, which was enacted by Britain in 1925. Hence, it is imperative to study the transition from Ottoman to Palestinian citizenship.

Turkish citizenship was first codified by the Ottoman Nationality Law of 19 January 1869. This law constituted the only legislation governing citizenship under the Empire. It was the legislative instrument that governed the citizenship of Palestine's inhabitants on the eve of the British occupation. Ottoman citizens who wished to travel abroad were required to hold Ottoman passports. With the enactment of the 'Regulations Relative to the Passports Offices in the Empire' on 17 July 1869, Ottoman passports began to be issued on a systematic basis. The passport legislation that was operative in the final days of the Empire was the Ottoman Passport Law of 9 June 1911. This law continued to be valid in Palestine after the British occupation. Palestine's inhabitants held Ottoman passports. Ottoman citizenship was well established in Palestine, since the Empire was independent and effectively controlled its territory. Other States recognized the Empire's independence, concluded treaties, exchanged diplomatic envoys with it, and treated its subjects as Ottomans. No State denied the Empire's supremacy over its territory and subjects. No other State claimed sovereign rights over Palestine. The Empire's sovereignty over, and Ottoman citizenship in, Palestine cannot be legally contested.

Under international law, when a State is dissolved and new States are being established, 'the population follows the change of sovereignty in matters of citizenship,' as concluded by Brownlie in 1963 in *The Relations of Nationality in Public International Law*. As a rule, citizens of the former State should automatically acquire the citizenship of the successor State(s) in which such former citizens habitually resided. Upon its detachment from the Ottomans, the territory of Palestine simultaneously became distinct from its neighbouring countries. This separation started as a matter of fact between Palestine and the newly created Arab States: Trans-Jordan, Egypt, Syria and Lebanon. Soon thereafter, Palestine's frontiers acquired permanent recognition through bilateral agreements with its neighbours. On the basis of the international legal framework established by the 1923 Treaty of Lausanne that ended Ottoman sovereignty over the eastern Mediterranean, each of the four countries developed a separate citizenship for its population through domestic legislation. Nationalities in the countries concerned had since become well established. It is therefore imperative to examine the boundaries of Palestine in order to define the territory in which Palestinian citizenship was established. This determination will clarify, by exclusion, who was entitled to hold Palestinian citizenship.

The eastern border of Palestine with Trans-Jordan was of particular significance. The Palestine Mandate originally incorporated the territory of Trans-Jordan within the scope of 'Palestine.' Article 25 of the Mandate accorded Britain the power 'to postpone or withhold application of such provisions of this mandate as . . . it may consider inapplicable to the existing local conditions.' On 16 September 1922, by a resolution adopted at the League of Nations, Trans-Jordan was excluded from the scope of Palestine and the border between Palestine and Trans-Jordan was fixed. Trans-Jordan had earlier been excluded from Palestine by Article 86 of the 1922 Palestine Order in Council, the Constitution that Britain applied: 'This Order in Council shall not apply to such parts of the territory comprised in Palestine to the east of the Jordan [River] and the Dead Sea.' Britain reached an agreement with Trans-Jordan in 1928, whereby the former recognized the existing autonomous government of Trans-Jordan. After concluding a treaty of alliance with Britain in 1946, Trans-Jordan declared its independence, settling the course of the lengthiest section of Palestine's border.

Trans-Jordan developed a citizenship for its own population which was distinct from that of Palestine. To begin with, the aforementioned resolution of the Council of the League of Nations of 16 September 1922 resolved, *inter alia*, that Article 7 of the Palestine Mandate relating to Palestinian citizenship would not be applicable to Trans-Jordan. That territory's inhabitants were then expressly excluded from the scope of Palestinian citizenship by Article 21 of the 1925 Palestinian Citizenship Order. Trans-Jordan eventually enacted its own citizenship law on 1 May 1928. Article 1 of this law conferred Trans-Jordanian citizenship on Ottoman subjects residing in Trans-Jordan retroactively as of 6 August 1924— the date on which the Treaty of Lausanne came into force. Trans-Jordanian citizenship constituted a separate citizenship from that of Palestine in law and in practice throughout the mandate. Trans-Jordanians, for example, were required to obtain permission or a visa to enter Palestine.

The relationship between the Palestinian and Trans-Jordanian nationalities arose in a case before the Supreme Court of Palestine on 14 December 1945. In *Jawdat Badawi Sha'ban v. Commissioner for Migration and Statistics*, Mr. Sha'ban, who was a Palestinian citizen and had acquired Trans-Jordanian citizenship by naturalization, argued that 'Trans-Jordan is a territory and not a State . . . in any case it is not a foreign State [in relation to Palestine].' The Court, in a decision that summarized the status of Palestine *vis-à-vis* Trans-Jordan and addressed the question of citizenship, held: 'Now, Trans-Jordan has a government entirely independent of Palestine . . . Trans-Jordan can, as in this case, grant a person naturalisation, *i.e.* grant an alien or foreigner Trans-Jordan nationality which is a separate nationality and distinct from that of Palestine citizenship . . . *Palestinians and Trans-Jordanians are foreigners* . . . Trans-Jordan must be regarded as a foreign State in relation to Palestine' (emphasis added).

With regard to the northern border of Palestine, Britain signed an agreement in 1920 with France, the then Occupying Power of Syria and Lebanon, settling initial issues relating to the Palestinian-Syrian-Lebanese border. In 1926, the previous agreements were replaced by the '*Bon Voisinage* Agreement to Regulate Certain Administrative Matters in Connection with the Frontier between Palestine and Syria [and Lebanon].' Both Syria and Lebanon regulated their nationalities on 30 August 1924. The two nationalities were formulated by separate Ordinances: 'Ordinance Concerning Turkish Subjects Established in Syria' and 'Ordinance Concerning Turkish Subjects Established in Greater Lebanon.' The Syrian and Lebanese nationalities were finally confirmed by two detailed orders issued on 19 January 1925. Syrian and Lebanese citizens were treated as foreigners in Palestine, as shown, for example, by the decision of the Supreme Court of Palestine of 31 October 1938 in *Nahas v. Kotia*.

The south-western border of Palestine with Egypt dates from the late nineteenth century. This border was originally drawn when the Ottomans recognized Egypt's autonomy. Two border agreements between Turkey and Egypt were concluded in 1906. The first is the 'Exchange of Notes between Britain [which had been controlling Egypt since 1882] and Turkey relative to the Maintenance of the *Status Quo* in the Sinai Peninsula.' The second is the 'Agreement between Egypt and Turkey for the fixing of an Administrative Line between the Vilayet of Hejaz and the Governorate of Jerusalem and the Sinai Peninsula.' The separation of Egypt from Turkey (Palestine, in this instance) as of 5 November 1914 was ultimately recognized by the 1923 Treaty of Lausanne. Egypt regulated its own citizenship by a Decree-Law on 26 May 1926. On 19 February 1929, a detailed Decree-Law concerning Egyptian Nationality was enacted which confirmed, in its first article, that Ottoman subjects who on 5 November 1914 had their habitual residence in Egypt had become Egyptian citizens.

From 9 December 1917 until the adoption of the Palestine Mandate on 24 July 1922, the international legal status of Palestine remained undetermined. The citizenship of the inhabitants of Palestine was similarly undefined. Britain's occupation did not alter, in law, the status of Palestine as an occupied Turkish territory. Britain declared a unilateral mandate over Palestine in July 1920 and established a civil administration that replaced military rule. Palestine remained nominally an Ottoman territory. Britain itself accepted this legal proposition. In May 1922, the Legal Secretary of the British-run Government of Palestine, Norman Bentwich, wrote in his article *Mandated Territories: Palestine and Mesopotamia (Iraq)* (1922: 53) that: 'The principles enunciated in the Mandate await the beginning of realisation when the Council of the League of Nations shall at last have given its decision. And it is only when that step has been taken that the sovereign powers of the Mandatory can be effective, and the '*damnosa hereditas*' from the Ottoman Empire . . . can be finally discarded. . . . The Mandatory . . . will be entrusted with the control of the foreign relations of the Mandated State, and will have the right to afford diplomatic and consular protection to citizens of Palestine outside its territorial limits. Palestine will have a separate Government and form a separate national unity with its particular citizenship.'

Palestine's inhabitants continued to be Ottomans but, in practice, Ottoman citizenship had become ineffective. The validity of Ottoman citizenship at the time can be explained by the international rule that occupation does not provide title to the occupant over the occupied territory. This is in line with international humanitarian law. Article 43 of both the 1899 Hague Regulations respecting the Laws and Customs of War on Land, and the 1907 Hague Regulations concerning the Laws and Customs of Land Warfare, requires the occupant to respect 'the laws in force in the country.' The inhabitants began to be gradually regarded as Palestinians. Britain became responsible for Palestine's international relations and for protecting its inhabitants abroad. While routinely employing the terms 'Palestinian' and 'Palestinian citizen,' for example in its 1922-published report on the administration of Palestine, Britain undertook measures that indicated the existence of the new citizenship. It issued provisional certificates of citizenship, which served as an indication of Palestinian citizenship. The certificates allowed their holders to receive protection from British consular officers abroad. To qualify for a citizenship certificate, the applicant had to: (1) be born in Palestine; (2) have expressed the intention to opt for Palestinian citizenship once a new law was passed; and (3) be willing to reside permanently in Palestine.

Inhabitants were able, from the outset, to leave Palestine using a travel document (*laissez-passer*) issued by the occupied authorities. An early proclamation issued by the British military in Palestine on 30 March 1918 prescribed, in its Article 10, that: 'No person shall attempt to enter or leave Occupied Enemy Territory [i.e. Palestine] without complying with the passport regulations for the time being in force.' The passport regulations in question were the Ottoman Passport Law of 9 June 1911. At the end of 1918, 'no one was allowed to cross to the east side of the Jordan, unless provided with a military pass,' wrote McCrackan in *New Palestine* (1922: 220). A preliminary system of Palestinian passports and travel documents was set up in August 1920 by the Palestine Passport Regulations. While passports were granted to Ottoman citizens residing in Palestine, a form of emergency *laissez-passer* was issued to foreigners and refugees whose countries were unrepresented in Palestine. Palestinians and foreigners had to request, in addition to either a passport or a travel document, a permit to leave the country. In a case before the Anglo-Turkish Mixed Tribunal in December 1927, *N. N. Berouti v. Turkish Government*, 'the claimant produced a *laissez passer*, dated 16 March 1920, and issued by the British military authorities . . . which described him as '*sujet palestinien, protégé britannique.*' The inhabitants were thus treated by other States as both 'Palestinian citizens and British protected persons,' as the French terms in this case indicate.

This practice was in line with British policy towards Palestine as reflected in a Statement made to the British Parliament by the Secretary of State for the Colonies on 23 June 1922, according to which 'it is contemplated that the status of all citizens of Palestine in the eyes of the law shall be Palestinian, and it has never been intended that they, or any section of them, should possess any other juridical status.'

Between the adoption of the Palestine Mandate on 24 July 1922 by the League of Nations and the enforcement of the Treaty of Lausanne on 6 August 1924, a new era on citizenship emerged. In its Article 7, the Mandate established the framework for Palestinian citizenship: 'The Administration of Palestine shall be responsible for enacting a citizenship law. There shall be included in this law provisions framed so as to facilitate the acquisition of Palestinian citizenship by Jews who take up their permanent residence in Palestine.' Obviously, the objective of regulating citizenship was to turn immigrant Jews into Palestinian citizens. However, the citizenship framework presumed the existence of a legal relationship between individuals and Palestine as a State. Palestinian citizenship was not based upon racial or religious considerations. Indeed, as pointed out by Ghali in *Les nationalités détachées de l'Empire ottoman à la suite de la guerre* (1934: 19), 'Palestinian citizenship is not a Jewish nationality' nor 'an Arab nationality.' Moreover, the Permanent Mandates Commission noted at its 1937 extraordinary session on Palestine that: 'Nationality law . . . showed that the Palestinians formed a nation, and that Palestine was a State, though provisionally under guardianship.'

The British-run Government of Palestine had naturalized certain groups of foreign residents in the country to enable them to participate in the legislative elections of 1922. These residents, as Norman Bentwich reported in 1926, were 'mostly immigrants Jews.' Most of them had immigrated into Palestine during the period 1920-1922. A proclamation was made on 1 September 1922 'providing that any person of other than Ottoman nationality, habitually resident in Palestine on that date, might within two months apply for Palestinian Citizenship.' As a result, according to the Report on the Administration of Palestine published by Britain, '19,293 Provisional Certificates of Citizenship were granted in respect of 37,997 persons, wives and minor children being included on certificates issued to heads of families' (1922: 5).

The Treaty of Peace between the Allied Powers and Turkey that officially ended the First World War was signed in Lausanne, Switzerland, on 24 July 1923. The Treaty acquired the force of law in Palestine on 6 August 1924. The status of Palestine and the citizenship of its inhabitants were finally settled by the Treaty from an international law perspective. In this regard, the British Government pointed out in its report submitted to the League of Nations that the 'ratification of the Treaty of Lausanne in Aug., 1924, finally regularised the international status of Palestine.' Thereafter 'Palestine could, at last, obtain a separate nationality' (1924: 6).

Most of the post-First World War peace treaties embodied citizenship provisions, and the Treaty of Lausanne was no exception. The Treaty addressed the citizenship of the inhabitants in the territories detached from Turkey in Articles 30-36. Elaborating the framework for citizenship, Article 30 of the Treaty of Lausanne stated that 'Turkish subjects habitually resident in territory which in accordance with the provisions of the present Treaty is detached from Turkey will become *ipso facto*, in the conditions laid down by the local law, nationals of the State to which such territory is transferred.' To qualify for Palestinian citizenship pursuant to this article, a person was required to meet two conditions. He or she should, first, be a Turkish subject or citizen. Secondly, the person concerned had to be habitually resident in Palestine as of 6 August 1924, the day on which the Treaty came into being. Article 30 is of great significance. It constitutes a declaration of existing international law. Weis concluded in his *Nationality and Statelessness in International Law* (1956: 149) that, as a rule, 'States have conferred their nationality on the former nationals of the predecessor State.' The inhabitants of Palestine, as the successors in that territory, henceforth acquired Palestinian citizenship even if there was, presumably, no treaty with Turkey.

Palestinian citizenship was regulated by the Treaty in a similar way to the nationalities of other mandate territories in the Middle East. The Iraq Nationality Law defined Iraqi citizens as Ottoman subjects who were habitually resident in Iraq on 6 August 1924. Likewise, the Trans-Jordan Nationality Law considered all Ottoman subjects habitually resident in Trans-Jordan on the aforementioned date to be citizens. In Syria and Lebanon under the French, inhabitants residing there on 30 August 1924 (the day on which the Treaty of Lausanne was ratified by France) were deemed to be Syrian or Lebanese. In Egypt, as noted earlier, the Treaty entered into force retroactively on 5 November 1914 and Ottoman inhabitants were considered to be Egyptians from that date.

Palestinian citizenship first came into being, according to international law, on 6 August 1924. Hence, 'treaty nationality in Palestine runs from that date,' as stated by the British-run Government of Palestine (*A Survey of Palestine*, 1946 — hereinafter 'Survey,' I: 206). The Treaty transformed the *de facto* status of Palestinian citizenship into a *de jure* status from the standpoint of international law. Meanwhile, the Ottoman Empire had ceased to exist. On 6 August 1924, for the first time ever, international law certified the birth of the 'Palestinian people' as distinct from all other peoples.

Article 30 of the Treaty of Lausanne stipulated that the new citizenship should be acquired in accordance with 'the conditions laid down by the local law.' This meant that the future citizenship legislation, i.e. the 1925 Citizenship Order, should comply with the Treaty. The Order's twenty-seven articles contained three key provisions that shaped the inhabitants' status. One related to the automatic conversion of Ottoman citizenship into Palestinian citizenship. The second dealt with Palestine's natives residing abroad at the time. The third was framed to grant Palestinian citizenship to immigrant Jews by naturalization.

The automatic, or *ipso facto*, change from Ottoman to Palestinian citizenship was dealt with in Article 1, paragraph 1, of the Citizenship Order. This provision declared that 'Turkish subjects habitually resident in the territory of Palestine upon the 1st day of August, 1925, shall become Palestinian citizens.' To qualify for Palestinian citizenship by virtue of this provision, the person had to be: (1) a Turkish subject or citizen; and (2) habitually resident in Palestine. While Palestinian citizenship in accordance with international law (i.e. the Treaty of Lausanne) was created on 6 August 1924, as just discussed, Palestinian citizenship based on domestic law was effectively created on 1 August 1925 (i.e. the Palestinian Citizenship Order). The Government of Palestine's Immigration and Travel Section developed procedures for obtaining evidence to prove Ottoman citizenship. They were set forth in the 'Instructions to Immigration Officers' (1930) which were sent to immigration officials stationed at Palestine's crossing points and to British consulates abroad. Under the heading 'Evidence of Ottoman Nationality,' the Instructions provided that evidence of Ottoman citizenship included, *inter alia*, the possession of an Ottoman passport or birth certificate which indicated clearly that the person was born as an Ottoman subject, or the possession of a naturalization certificate demonstrating that the individual had acquired Ottoman citizenship.

One month before the enforcement of the Citizenship Order in August 1925, the British-run Government of Palestine estimated through censuses the total population of Palestine at 847,238. This figure included both Turkish subjects and foreigners who were registered as permanent residents in the country. There is no available data on the population's citizenship. One may, however, obtain quite accurate figures for Turkish subjects by deducting the number of foreigners from the overall population of Palestine. The total number of registered foreign immigrants in Palestine between 1920 and 1925 was 79,368. Another figure for foreigners should also be subtracted from the total population, namely the 37,997 persons who were granted provisional naturalization in September 1922 in order to vote in the legislative elections. The remaining inhabitants were Turks. This calculation reveals that the total number of Turkish subjects in Palestine was as follows: 847,238 − (79,368 + 37,997) = 729,873. These persons accounted for the bulk of those who acquired Palestinian citizenship based on Article 1, paragraph 1.

A further calculation is required to establish the number of Arab and Jewish Turks residing in Palestine. According to British official data, the number of Arabs in the total population in mid-1925 stood at 717,006: 641,494 Muslims and 75,512 Christians. There were also 8,507 persons classified as 'others,' mainly Druze, Bahais and Samiries — all in fact were Arabs. Immigrant Arabs who entered Palestine and were registered as residents in the 1920-1925 period numbered 2,783. Thus, the net number of Arabs who were Ottomans, and automatically acquired Palestinian citizenship, was as follows: (717,006 + 8,507) − 2,783 = 722,730, i.e. more than 99%. On the other hand, the number of Jews in the total population, at the same time, stood at 121,725. Of these, the majority were foreigners: 37,997 who had acquired provisional Palestinian citizenship in 1922, as just mentioned, plus 76,585 registered immigrants who had entered Palestine between 1920 and 1925. Thus, the net number of Jews who were Turkish and then became Palestinian citizens was: 121,725 − (37,997 + 76,585) = 7,143, or just under 1% of the Ottomans in Palestine.

The 1925 Palestinian Citizenship Order incorporated the common rules of comparative citizenship law. Besides dealing with the natural transition from Ottoman to Palestinian citizenship and naturalization, the Order addressed citizenship by birth, declaration and marriage, and in respect of minor children. It adopted the *jus sanguinis* principle whereby children born to a Palestinian father would become Palestinian citizens, regardless of where they were born. The Order partially recognized the *jus soli* principle, unlike the 1914 British Nationality Law from which the Order derived a significant proportion of its provisions. Thus, the Order deemed children born to a stateless father, an unknown father or unknown parents, i.e. foundling children, to be Palestinians. Married women acquired the citizenship of their husbands. Women had no right to extend their Palestinian citizenship to their husbands. Revocation of citizenship was made possible through: (1) acquisition of another citizenship abroad upon the request of the Palestinian citizen; (2) submission of an application by a person who no longer wished to be a Palestinian citizen; (3) governmental withdrawal of citizenship as a result of the absence of the naturalized person; and (4) withdrawal due to disloyal acts such as collaborating with the enemy. By making the acquisition of foreign citizenship a ground for loss of Palestinian citizenship, the Order rendered dual citizenship impossible. Yet dual citizenship was still possible in the following cases: (1) those who had acquired Palestinian citizenship by naturalization, since it was not up to the Government of Palestine, in practice, to withdraw former nationalities; (2) those who had acquired citizenship as a result of different citizenship laws elsewhere in the world, for example a child born to a Palestinian father in the United States would become a Palestinian citizen based on the *jus sanguinis* principle adopted in the Palestinian law and at the same time an American citizen pursuant to United States law which is based on *jus soli*; (3) those Palestinians who had acquired the citizenship of other States without submitting an application, for instance where the citizenship of a foreign State was granted *en masse* to all residents.

Under the Mandate, States recognized Palestinian citizenship on the same basis as the nationalities of independent States. This recognition shows the extent to which citizenship was effective. States in which Palestinians resided treated them as citizens of a foreign country. Domestic courts recognized the existence of ordinary Palestinian citizenship. As early as 15 December 1925, a Palestinian citizen was recognized as a foreigner in Egypt in *Saikaly v. Saikaly*. The Egyptian court, in a judgment that summarized international practice with respect to citizenship in mandated territories, concluded that: 'Ottoman territories placed under a Mandate have the character of regular States, and their inhabitants possess the citizenship of these States in accordance with Article 30 of the Treaty of Lausanne. The plaintiff, therefore, has Palestinian nationality, and is a foreign subject in Egypt.' In the United States, Palestinians were considered to be ordinary foreigners on 10 March 1949. In *Klausner v. Levy*, the court stated that during 'the mandate Palestine could and did extend citizenship to its inhabitants, grant naturalization to immigrants and issue them passports for travel. Both native and naturalized nationals, at home and abroad, received the protection of the British Government.' In *Petition of Ajlouny*, also in the United States, the court held on 23 April 1948 that 'the petitioner, a native and citizen of Palestine, sought naturalization as a citizen of the United States.' In Uruguay (1928), a court decided that the inhabitants of Palestine were not British citizens for the purpose of extradition.

Palestinian citizens were treated as foreigners in Britain. The appellant in *The King v. Ketter* (1939) was born as an Ottoman subject and became Palestinian. He travelled in 1937 to Britain and overstayed, claiming that he was a British citizen and, as such, did not need to extend his residence permit. After being convicted of an immigration offence, he appealed. He submitted that, under Article 30 of the Treaty of Lausanne, 'Palestine was transferred to Great Britain and every Turkish subject resident in Palestine became *ipso facto* a subject of Great Britain.' In rejecting his plea, the English High Court held that the provisions of the said Treaty made the inhabitants of the territories detached from Turkey citizens of the detached territories. It concluded that 'nothing has been done in law to make him a subject of Great Britain.' From the outset, Britain treated the Palestinians as foreigners in its territory. In 1929, the League of Nations Mandates Commission asked whether residence in Palestine qualified as residence for naturalization in Britain. The British Government replied that: 'Residence in Palestine was a qualification only for Palestinian naturalisation.' Palestinians were considered to be foreigners and required permission to enter Britain. In British territory, a Palestinian citizen had no political rights, no voting power and was not subject to national service. During World War II, Palestinian citizens in Britain were issued with certificates of alien registration. For its part, the Supreme Court of Palestine repeatedly decided that Palestinians were foreigners in Britain. As early as February 1925, in *Attorney General v. Goralschwili and Another*, it was held that 'subjects of the Mandated territory did not become British subjects.' The same court, in *Sheinfeld v. Officer Commanding No. 3 Court Martial* of 16 February 1945, reaffirmed that 'Palestinians are not British subjects.'

Further evidence of a distinct Palestinian citizenship was the existence of Palestinian passports. As noted above, a system of passports was initially introduced in Palestine in 1920. Recognizing the fact that a passport is inherently linked to citizenship, the Government of Palestine enacted the Passport Ordinance on 16 December 1925. Regular Palestinian passports were then printed in 1926. Palestinians were entitled to request passports from British embassies or consulates abroad. The British Government reported to the League of Nations that 11,900 Palestinian passports had been granted in 1927, including 767 issued by British consuls. From the time of its inception, the rate of issuance of Palestinian passports was relatively high. In the last three months of 1926, when passports began to be printed on a regular basis, the Government of Palestine issued 1,314 Palestinian passports. During the period from 1926 to 1935, some 70,000 Palestinian passports were issued, according to a British report to the League of Nations. A form of temporary passport, or travel document, was granted to foreign residents in Palestine as of 1925. This document was known as an 'Emergency Certificate.' It was defined in Article 2 of the Passport Ordinance of 1925 as 'a document of identity issued under the authority of the High Commissioner for the purpose of travel outside Palestine.' Palestinian passports were recognized abroad, including in Britain, as being akin to other ordinary passports. Thus, once abroad Palestinians who presented their passports were treated as British protected persons.

The protection of individuals abroad is inherently related to citizenship. It is well established in international law, as decided for instance by the Permanent Court of International Justice in its 1939 judgement concerning the *Panevezys-Saldutiskis Railway*, that it is 'the bond of citizenship between the State and the individual which alone confers upon the State the right of diplomatic protection.' Similarly, however, the delegation of protection of citizens to another State is an accepted practice in international relations, as the International Court of Justice decided in 1955 in the *Nottebohm* case. Palestine's inhabitants had been considered to be British protected persons since December 1917 and remained so until the end of the Mandate. As early as June 1919, it was envisaged that the native inhabitants of the territories of mandates would be 'entitled to the diplomatic protection of the Governments exercising authority over those territories' under Article 127 of the Treaty of Versailles with Germany. In 1922, Britain informed the League of Nations that such natives 'are entitled to diplomatic protection by the Mandatory Power and that under the Foreign Office Consular Instructions natives of territories under British Mandates are already being treated as British-protected persons.' To this end, Article 12 of the Palestine Mandate stated that Britain is 'to afford diplomatic and consular protection to citizens of Palestine when outside its territorial limits.' Although this status was similar to that of British citizens and inhabitants of British–controlled territories, Britain was providing this service on behalf of Palestine in the same way as States provide such protection to citizens of other States.

Another direct result of any citizenship is the admission of foreigners into the country. Foreigners entered Palestine as travellers or immigrants. Travellers were obliged to acquire an entry visa to land in Palestine. Many travellers, however, had extended their stay there and acquired the status of permanent residents. Immigrants constituted the bulk of foreigners who entered and remained; most of them were Jews. Between 1920 and 1945, the total number of persons registered as immigrants was estimated at 401,149. Of these, 367,845 (about 91%) were Jews. In addition, almost half of all Jews entered or remained illegally, i.e. without permission from the Government of Palestine. Thus, about one-fourth of Palestine's inhabitants, citizens and foreigners, were immigrants at the end of the Mandate. Immigration constituted the first step towards the acquisition of Palestinian citizenship by naturalization. Britain had systematically used immigration laws and collaborated with the Zionist Organization to bring Jews, especially from Europe, into Palestine to settle there.

The foregoing legal foundations offer incontrovertible evidence that Palestinian citizenship had become a complete citizenship, i.e. like the citizenship of any other State, by the end of British rule. The fact that Palestine had not constituted an independent State does not derogate from that status. Modern history has witnessed many instances in which non-independent States have conferred citizenship on their inhabitants. Nationalities were recognized in protected States such as Egypt and Morocco before their independence from Britain and France, respectively. Countries controlled by the British Empire had distinct nationalities based on locally enacted legislation, including in the British dominions (e.g. Canada, New Zealand, and South Africa) and the British colonies, notably India. Distinct nationalities were recognized for the inhabitants of mandated territories. No doubts were expressed regarding the existence of Iraqi or Afghan nationalities under the recent occupation. History has witnessed other cases of nationalities granted by non-State entities, as shown by Grossman in *Nationality and the Unrecognized State* (2001). As far as citizenship is concerned, Palestine constituted a State. If Palestine had gained its independence after the end of the Mandate, Palestinian citizenship would not have differed from the citizenship of independent States. It follows that any succeeding State(s) in parts of Mandate Palestine would have been under an international obligation to admit the status of Palestinian citizenship as it existed under the Mandate as a basis for the future determination of the inhabitants' status.

Although citizenship is essentially a matter of local law, the competence of States in this regard should be exercised within the limits of the international law of State succession. In the 1923 Advisory Opinion of the

Permanent Court of International Justice on the *Nationality Decrees Issued in Tunis and Morocco*, the Court held that the right of the State to use its discretion regarding citizenship may be restricted by obligations that it may have incurred towards other States, so that its jurisdiction is then limited by rules of international law. In the 1930 Convention on Certain Questions relating to the Conflict of Nationality Laws (Flournoy, *Nationality Convention, Protocols and Recommendations Adopted by the First Conference on the Codification of International Law*, 1930: 467), Article 1, as a rule codifying existing State practice, left it 'for each State to determine under its own law who are its nationals.' Yet such determination should be limited, added the same article, to the extent that the internal law 'is consistent with international conventions, international custom, and the principles of law generally recognized with regard to nationality.' As noted by the United States of America at the 1929 Conference for the Codification of International Law: 'The scope of municipal laws governing nationality must be regarded as limited by consideration of the rights and obligations of individuals and of other States.' The International Law Commission stated in its commentaries to the Draft Articles on Nationality of Natural Persons in relation to the Succession of States, adopted by General Assembly Resolution 55/153 of 12 December 2000, that 'in the specific context of a succession of States, international law has an even larger role to play, as such situation may involve a change of nationality on a large scale.' In other words, domestic citizenship legislation should be consistent with international law in order to generate legitimacy. In the present case, therefore, States succeeding to the territory of Mandate Palestine should determine their citizenship based on international law.

The relevance of the international law of State succession to Palestinian citizenship may be inferred from the aforementioned International Law Commission Draft. Article 1 contains the key provision, from which other provisions are derived, concerning the acquisition of citizenship as a result of State succession. It provides that: 'Every individual who, on the date of the succession of States, had the nationality of the predecessor State, irrespective of the mode of acquisition of that nationality, has the right to the nationality of at least one of the States concerned.' The obligation of the successor State is based on the individual's former citizenship. As noted in the commentaries to the same article, citizenship should be conferred by 'either the successor State, or one of the successor States when there are more than one, or, as the case may be, the predecessor State.' Article 5 of the Draft establishes the criterion whereby the citizenship of the successor State should be conferred. It states that 'persons concerned having their habitual residence in the territory affected by the succession of States are presumed to acquire the nationality of the successor State on the date of such succession.' The commentary to Article 5 adds that 'habitual residence is the test that has most often been used in practice for defining the basic body of nationals of the successor State.' Although recent (1999), these provisions codify a long-standing practice of States that can amount to customary law. It may be gathered from the commentaries to the Draft Articles that many of the cases invoked and the references cited in connection with the drafting of the Articles relate to various parts of the world and occurred for the most part in the first half of the twentieth century.

As a result of the British and League of Nations policies in Palestine, Palestinian citizens and other inhabitants of the country had been converted at the end of the Mandate into two *de facto* 'nationalities' or peoples: Arabs and Jews. This situation was recognized when the future of Palestine was examined by the United Nations General Assembly in its Resolution 181(III) of 29 November 1947, known as the 'Partition Plan.' According to the Plan, Palestine was to be divided, *inter alia*, into an Arab State and a Jewish State. Racial and religious criteria had been formally adopted in determining the inhabitants' citizenship. According to statistics relied upon prior to the drafting of the Plan, the inhabitants of Palestine were estimated as of 31 December 1946 at 1,972,560, comprising 1,212,840 Arabs and 608,230 Jews and others (A/AC.14/32 and Add. 1, 11 November 1947). 'Palestinian Arabs' were persons who belonged chiefly to the Muslim and Christian religions. These Arabs, as already noted above, were originally Ottoman subjects who had become Palestinian citizens through the natural change of citizenship on 1 August 1925. 'Palestinian Jews' comprised two categories: (1) native Palestinian Jews who were, like the Arabs, Ottoman subjects and afterwards became natural Palestinian citizens; and (2) Jews who became Palestinian citizens by naturalization. Another group of Jews consisted of foreigners residing in Palestine as either legal residents or illegal immigrants, according to the immigration laws applicable in Palestine at the time.

Defining the citizenship of the inhabitants of both the Arab State and the Jewish State, the Plan stated that: 'Palestinian citizens residing in Palestine . . . as well as Arabs and Jews who, not holding Palestinian citizenship, reside in Palestine . . . shall, upon the recognition of independence, become citizens of the State in which they are resident and enjoy full civil and political rights. Persons over the age of eighteen years may opt, within one year from the date of recognition of independence of the State in which they reside, for citizenship of the other State, providing that no Arab residing in the area of the proposed Arab State shall have the right to opt for citizenship in the proposed Jewish State and no Jew residing in the proposed Jewish State shall have the right to opt for citizenship in the proposed Arab State.' The Plan's principle with respect to citizenship in post-Palestine States was thus straightforward. Palestinian citizens, irrespective of their religion, residing in the Arab State would become citizens of that State. Likewise, Palestinian citizens, also regardless of their religion, residing in the Jewish State would become citizens of that State. The principle was consistent with international law relating to citizenship at the time of territorial succession. Before reaching its recommended solution, the United Nations Special Commission on Palestine, which drafted the Plan, had examined previous proposals to solve Palestine's problem, including the proposal made by the Palestine Partition Commission of 1938 (the 'Woodhead Commission'), which also suggested the creation of Arab and Jewish States. With regard to the inhabitants' citizenship, the 1938 proposal stated: 'A Palestinian habitually resident in the Jewish State would automatically cease to be a Palestinian citizen . . . and would *ipso facto* become a citizen of the Jewish State. Similarly, a Palestinian habitually resident in the Arab State would *ipso facto* become a citizen of that State.' This proposed solution was the origin of the automatic change from Palestinian citizenship to the nationalities of the Arab and Jewish States. However, it should be noted that this proposal, unlike the Partition Plan, was based on two legal criteria: Palestinian citizenship and habitual residence in one of the two projected States; foreigners residing in the Arab State or the Jewish State, whether Arabs or Jews, could not become citizens of either State.

Reaffirming an existing rule of international law, the Plan incorporated the principle of automatic change from the citizenship of the predecessor State into one of the nationalities of the successor States. As already illustrated above, this rule has been adopted in various peace treaties leading to territorial change and 'is believed to express a rule of international law which is generally recognized' (*Harvard Research on Nationality*, 1929: 61). In the absence of an agreement between the Arabs and Jews of Palestine, the General Assembly decided that the inhabitants of the predecessor territory (Palestine) should acquire the citizenship of the successor territories. In other words, Palestinians should acquire either: (1) the citizenship of the Arab State (but not an 'Arab nationality' — in the sense that the Arab State citizenship should not be given solely to persons belonging to the Arab race); or (2) the citizenship of the Jewish State (but not a 'Jewish nationality' — which means that the citizenship of the Jewish State could be granted to non-Jews). Thus, the Plan merely applied an established rule of international law, whatever the legal validity of the Plan itself. It was not the only case in which General Assembly resolutions had embodied international legal rules. Indeed, the Assembly had often 'adopted resolutions declaring what it finds to be an existing rule of international law' (Sloan, *The Binding Force of a 'Recommendation' of the General Assembly of the United Nations*, 1948: 24). The Plan had merely declared the legal rules governing the future nationalities in the Jewish State and the State of Palestine, which later became the State of Israel and the State of Palestine respectively. It did not create these nationalities.

By granting citizenship to foreigners who were residing in post-Palestine States, the Plan created an exception to established international rules. To understand the reason for this, one should examine who the foreigners in Palestine were. A considerable number of foreign Jews (about 261,975) were present in Palestine at the end of the Mandate. This figure included three categories: (1) legal residents, namely immigrants who were permitted to reside in Palestine but did not constitute Palestinian citizens; they were estimated at 192,445, a figure reflecting the total number of registered Jewish immigrants during the period 1925-1945, which was 325,061 (Survey I: 185), minus the total number of Jews who acquired Palestinian citizenship by naturalization, which was 132,616; (2) illegal immigrants, according to the applicable immigration law at the time, who were estimated at between 50,000 and 60,000 (Survey I: 210); (3) refugees: some 14,530 European refugees, mostly Jews, entered and remained in Palestine during World War II (Survey I: 223). The total number of foreign Arabs in Palestine stood at 16,148 (6%). The proportion of foreign Jews was 94%. Hence, the reason for conferring citizenship on foreigners was actually to regularize the status of foreign Jews. Granting citizenship to foreigners is an unusual practice in cases of State succession.

The right of option corresponded to the fact that Arabs and Jews were dispersed in the cities, towns and villages of Palestine in such a way as to make the complete division of land between the two sides impractical. The United Nations Special Commission on Palestine, basing itself on the population data provided by Britain, characterized this situation as follows: 'There is no clear territorial separation of Jews and Arabs by large contiguous areas. Jews constitute more than 40 per cent of the total population in the districts of Jaffa (which includes Tel Aviv), Haifa and Jerusalem. In the northern inland areas . . . they represent between 25 and 34 per cent of the total population. In the inland northern districts . . . Jews form between 10 and 25 per cent of the total population, while in the central districts and the districts south of Jerusalem they constitute not more than 5 per cent of the total.' The population of the area allocated to the Arab State was presumed to include some 725,000 Arabs and 10,000 Jews. It had been assumed that the population of the area assigned to the Jewish State would comprise about 498,000 Jews and 407,000 Arabs. 'In addition, there will be in the Jewish State about 90,000 [Arab] Bedouins.' Thus, while a small minority of Jews was expected to reside in the Arab State, the Jewish State would incorporate a large minority of Arabs — almost half of the population. By giving the inhabitants belonging to the minority group in one State the right to opt for the citizenship of the other State, the Plan recognized a well-established rule of international law. The Plan, in one sense, had substituted itself for the absence of a treaty between the Arabs and Jews of Palestine. Moreover, by recognizing the right of option on an individual basis, the Plan differed from the approach adopted by the 1938 Partition Commission, which suggested an exchange of population between the projected Arab and Jewish States in lieu of the citizenship option. The Partition Commission took as a precedent the peace 'Convention concerning the Exchange of Greek and Turkish Populations' of 1923 that involved the transfer of persons of Orthodox religion residing in Turkey to Greece and the transfer of Muslims living in Greece to Turkey. Although the implementation of the right of option would require more complicated procedures than a population exchange, the option took the personal interest of individuals into account rather than the sole interest of States.

If the Palestine Mandate was valid, the Plan should likewise be deemed to be valid. There were two parties involved in the Mandate: the League of Nations and Britain. The League, as the supervisor of the Mandatory, had entrusted Britain with the administration of Palestine. As a natural successor to the Council of the League of Nations with respect to the mandated territories (according to an International Court of Justice finding of 11 July 1950), 'the General Assembly of the United Nations is legally qualified to exercise the supervisory functions previously exercised by the League of Nations with regard to the administration of the [mandated] Territory' (*International Status of South-West Africa:* 137). As Britain declared its intention to abandon its mandate on 2 April 1947, a lawful act under Article 28 of the Palestine Mandate, the United Nations assumed its responsibility. Hence, the General Assembly had the legal capacity to divide Palestine into two States. The Plan continues to be relevant, as reflected in many General Assembly resolutions, such as: 186 (S-2) (1948); 35/169(A-E) (1980); 43/177 (1988); 55/55 (2000); 57/107, (2003); 60/36 (2006); and 64/19 (2010).

Broadly ignoring the domestic citizenship law applicable in Palestine, the Plan attached greater importance to the Arab race and the Jewish religion (political criteria) than to the bond of citizenship (a juridical criterion) as bases for the future nationalities. However, the existence of a distinct Palestinian citizenship was not denied in principle in the Plan, and Palestinian citizens constituted the majority of the population anyway. It was envisaged, amongst other provisions of the Plan, that the citizenship stipulations should form part of the 'fundamental laws' of both the Arab and Jewish States. Hence, 'no law, regulation or official action shall conflict or interfere with these stipulations, nor shall any law, regulation or official action prevail over them' (the Plan, Part 1(c)). The Plan was to be the supreme reference in determining the future of post-Palestine citizenship. This shows the importance that the international community attached to the future nationalities of post-mandate Palestine. As the Plan was not implemented, international rules relating to the succession of States as codified by the International Law Commission, particularly the provisions that reflect customary law, should persist. Alternatively, the State of Israel (the Jewish State) and the future State of Palestine (the Arab State) may refer to the terms of the Partition Plan as the basis for settling any citizenship questions that may arise. Otherwise, the two States may reach an agreement on how to settle the question of citizenship.

Self-determination as a collective right of the Palestinian people constitutes an additional basis for Palestinian citizenship. This right has been recognized for peoples since the 1920s. The right of self-determination has been recognized as a *jus cogens* and *erga omnes* principle of international law, as demonstrated, *inter alia*, by the United Nations Charter (Article 55) and common Article 1 of the International Covenant on Economic, Social and Cultural Rights and the International Covenant on Civil and Political Rights, and by the jurisprudence of the International Court of Justice in the cases of *Namibia* (1970), *Western Sahara* (1975), *East Timor* (1995), and *the Wall* (2004). This chapter is not concerned with the right of self-determination *per se*, as many studies as well as countless General Assembly resolutions have confirmed this right for the Palestinian people (see Chapter One and Chapter Two of this book). What is significant, however, is the relevance of the right to citizenship. Self-determination is a collective right accorded to a given people. The legal element that binds members of a given people together, as one of the three pillars of any State set out in Article 1 of the 1933 Montevideo Convention on the Rights and Duties of States, is the bond of citizenship. Recognition of the right of self-determination for the Palestinian people entails recognition of their citizenship as the legal link that attaches the members of that people to the territory of Palestine. Without citizenship, Palestinian self-determination would become superfluous.

CHAPTER FOUR

RECOGNITION OF PALESTINIAN STATEHOOD: AN INTEREST FOR ALL

WINSTON P. NAGAN AND AITZA M. HADDAD

Introduction

Notwithstanding the commitment of major international constituencies to the idea that a solution to the longstanding conflict between Israel and the Palestinian people requires a two-State solution, this approach has being vigorously contested in international fora. Israeli authorities had worked on an assumption that a two-State solution was an agreed upon objective and that the only obstacle was the negotiation of the details of the settlement. Indeed, on the negotiations of the Camp David Accords the Israeli government accepted the idea in principle of a two-State solution.[1] Conservatives, like former United States (US) President George W. Bush for example,[2] also indicated in forthright terms that the US policy favours a two-State solution.[3]

However, when Palestinian leaders became frustrated with the stalling tactics in negotiations with Israel,[4] they began floating the idea that the

---

[1] A Framework for Peace in the Middle East Agreed at Camp David, Israel-Egypt, 1136 *United Nations Treaty Series* (UNTS) 196 (1978). See also Framework for the Conclusion of a Peace Treaty between Egypt and Israel, Israel-Egypt, 1136 UNTS 200 (1979).

[2] Y. Benhorin, 'Bush: Two-State Solution Will be Realized,' *YnetNews.com* (6 December 2008); G.W. Bush, 'Rose Garden Speech on Israel-Palestine Two-State Solution,' *American Rhetoric: Online Speech Bank* (24 June 2002).

[3] J. Ben-Ami, 'Statement by Jeremy Ben-Ami on Newt Gingrich Remarks on the Israeli-Palestinian Conflict,' *JStreet.org* (12 December 2011); H. Ibish and S. Sarsar, 'The Long Overdue State of Palestine,' *The Huffington Post* (17 July 2011).

[4] H. Siegman, 'Netanyahu's Freeze Scam,' *Huffington Post* (1 October 2011); N. Mozgovaya, 'Netanyahu: Only when Palestinians Recognize Israel as a Jewish

claim to the international recognition of Palestinian statehood would be indefinitely delayed by the Netanyahu regime's disinterest in a settlement.[5] They therefore floated the idea of appealing to the international community to recognize their right to self-determination, independence, and statehood.[6] The significant volume of support for their international claim galvanized the Netanyahu regime to mobilize the pro-Israeli 'lobby' in the US to generate a full court press on the Congress.[7] In response to this pressure, the Congress passed a Resolution insisting that the US should not support the claim of the Palestinians to national sovereignty.[8] As these pressures continued, they emboldened the Netanyahu regime to frustrate US policy makers in moving the negotiation process forward and essentially made the Obama administration comply with the Congressional mandate generated through its powerful lobby support in Washington not to support the Palestinian claim.[9] Since the US is a permanent member of the Security Council (UNSC),[10] the expectation is that, should the matter come before the Council, the US will veto Palestinian statehood.

State Will They be Ready for Peace - PM Tells Jewish Leaders that Peace Requires Security and that Israel's Security Needs Are Growing More and More,' *Haaretz* (2 September 2011).

[5] CMEP Bulletin, 'The Status of Negotiations: Looking Forward and Looking Back,' *Churches for Middle East Peace* (28 October 2011).

[6] M. Fisher, 'UN to Hear Palestinian Bid for Statehood,' *National Post* (16 September 2011); N. Mozgovaya, 'Abbas: Palestinian Independence Bid Does Not Contradict Peace Process with Israel,' *Haaretz* (16 September 2011).

[7] Some of these groups are considered to be lobbying bodies: American Israel Public Affairs Committee, Conference of Presidents of Major American Jewish Organizations, National Association of Arab-Americans, and Arabian American Oil Company. See M. Bard, 'The Israeli and Arab Lobbies,' *The Jewish Virtual Library* (31 January 2012); R. Lieberman, 'The Israel Lobby and American Politics,' 2 *Perspectives on Politics Perspectives on Politics* 7 (2009); W. Mead, 'Jerusalem Syndrome - Decoding the Israel Lobby,' *Foreign Affairs* 86 (2007).

[8] 'Congressional Resolutions Oppose Unilateral Palestinian State,' *Jewish Reporter* (8 July 2011); Jennifer Rubin, 'Is J Street Still Relevant?' *Washington Post* (16 December 2010).

[9] U. Avnery, 'Israel Lobby Humiliates Obama Administration,' *Counter Currents* (16 March 2009); B. Miller, 'Israel Lobby Drives America's Palestine Veto,' *Policymic* (26 September 2011); J. Lobe, 'US Politics Throws Palestine Under the Bus,' *Inter Press Service* (24 September 2011); S. Clemons, 'Obama Tells Palestinians to Stay in the Back of the Bus,' *The Atlantic* (22 September 2011).

[10] B. Fassbender, *UN Security Council Reform and the Right of Veto: A Constitutional Perspective* (Linden: Martinus Nijhoff, 1998); M. Scharf, 'Musical Chairs: The Dissolution of States and Membership in the UN,' 28 *Cornell International Law Journal* 29 (1995); L. Sohn, 'Voting Procedures in UN

The idea of a 'Greater Israel' remains a centrepiece of the agenda of the Netanyahu administration, which seeks to justify the idea on the basis that the ancient boundaries of Israel are legitimate boundaries that may trump Palestinian claims.[11] While the parties are negotiating on this matter, Israel has continued to support settlement expansion in Palestinian territories.[12] The Israeli right-wing has tremendous assets in Europe and the US, and has sought to mobilize those assets to block a decision in favour of Palestinian statehood. The Palestinians have managed to develop sympathy, good will, and ties in Asia, Africa, and Latin America.[13] Those assets appear to favour a speedy recognition of Palestinian statehood. Between these two postures, there is the significant revived level of international legal concern about this problem.[14] It is important that the legal concerns relating to these issues are understood in terms of the objective interests of all the stakeholders.

This chapter seeks to provide contextual background and a clearer picture of the interests of key stakeholders with regard to this issue, with a necessary exploration of the complex internal political dynamics in both Israel and the occupied Palestinian territories. We first provide a brief summary of the background to the conflict followed by a summary of the role of the relevant stakeholders. We conclude with some recommendations on how to move ahead to get an outcome that could satisfy the claims of the parties involved and the international community as a whole.

The Israel-Palestine Conflict: Background

Prior to World War I (WWI), Palestine was part of the Ottoman Empire;[15] a multi-ethnic empire incorporating territories and populations

Conferences for the Codification of International Law,' 69 *American Journal of International Law* 2 (1975).

[11] U. Avnery, 'Bibi and the Yo-Yos,' *OpEdNews* (25 May 2011); E. Karsh, *From Rabin to Netanyahu: Israel's Troubled Agenda* (Routledge, 1997).

[12] J. Slater, 'What Went Wrong? The Collapse of the Israeli-Palestinian Peace Process,' 116 *Political Science Quarterly* 2 (2001).

[13] T. Deen, 'Will Asia, Africa Follow Latin America on Palestine?' *Inter Press Service News Agency* (13 January 2011); C. Onians, 'Palestinians admitted to UNESCO as Full Member,' *The Jakarta Globe* (31 October 2011).

[14] R. Blecher, 'Palestine's Rocky Path to the UN,' *Foreign Affairs* (19 September 2011).

[15] M. Oke, 'The Ottoman Empire, Zionism and the Question of Palestine (1880-1908),' 14 *International Journal of Middle East Studies* 3 (1982).

in the Middle East.[16] During WWI Palestine was subject to British conquest. Prior to the Versailles Peace Treaty, international law held that territorial conquest was a valid means of acquiring territory.[17] The Peace Agreement generated the League of Nations.[18] The League of Nations created a Mandate System regarding the territories conquered by the allied powers.[19] The Palestine's territory was made subject to the Mandates' regime.[20] The Versailles Treaty changed the expectation that the European powers invariably owned the territories they conquered.[21] Britain, the conquering power, was mandated to administer Palestine.[22] One of the obligations of the mandatory powers was to secure the wellbeing and interests of the people under its control. This obligation became more complex because of Britain's Balfour Declaration, articulated in 1917 during WWI favouring Zionist interests for Jewish immigration and settlement in Palestine.[23]

What is most salient during this period is the lack of support for self-determination for the Palestinian Arabs by the United Kingdom (UK).[24] Palestine, which was a class A mandate, was somewhat distinctive in the sense that its mandate contained a clause that was not expressed in Article 22 of the League Covenant.[25] This clause involved the encouragement of Jewish immigration for the establishment of a national home for Jewish

[16] N. Bethell, *The Palestine Triangle: The Struggle Between the British, the Jews and the Arabs, 1935–48* (London: Deutsch, 1979).

[17] M. Boemeke, G. Feldman and E. Gläser, *The Treaty of Versailles: A Reassessment After 75 Years* (Cambridge: Cambridge University Press, 1998).

[18] L. Goodrich, 'From League of Nations to United Nations,' 1 *International Organization* (1947); P. Corbett, 'What is the League of Nations,' 5 *Britain Yearbook of International Law* 119 (1924).

[19] P. Potter, 'Origin of the System of Mandates under the League of Nations,' 16 *American Political Science Review* 4 (1922).

[20] N. Matz, 'Civilization and the Mandate System under the League of Nations as Origin of Trusteeship,' 9 *Max Planck Yearbook of United Nations Law* 47 (2005); E. Haas, 'The Reconciliation of Conflicting Colonial Policy Aims: Acceptance of the League of Nations Mandate System,' 6 *International Organization* 4 (1952).

[21] League of Nations, *Articles of the Palestine Mandate* (1922).

[22] S. Brooks, 'British Mandate for Palestine,' in S. Tucker, ed., *The Encyclopedia of the Arab-Israeli Conflict* (Santa Barbara: ABC- CLIO 2008), Vol. 3.

[23] J. Schneer, *The Balfour Declaration: The Origins of the Arab-Israeli Conflict* (Random House, 2010); J. Reinharz, 'The Balfour Declaration and Its Maker: A Reassessment,' 64 *The Journal of Modern History* 3 (September 1992).

[24] E. Said, *The Politics of Dispossession: Struggle for Palestinian Self-determination, 1969-94* (New York: Pantheon Books, 1994).

[25] E. Hertz, 'Mandate for Palestine: The Legal Aspects of Jewish Rights,' *Myths and Facts* (2005).

people. Jews were then a minority in Palestine.[26] Hence, there was an ostensible incompatibility between the Balfour Declaration and Article 22.[27] In correspondence with Prime Minister Lloyd George, Balfour wrote in 1919 that 'the weak point of our position of course is that in the case of Palestine we deliberately and rightly declined to accept the principle of self-determination.'[28] Thus, the mandate was administered with equivocal objectives; the conflicts between these objectives would never be clearly put on the table to rationally reconcile the precise terms of the original mandate.[29]

Unlike the mandates in Syria and Iraq, there was no progress through indigenous self-determination to statehood.[30] However, Palestine was a proto-State and that its latent sovereignty was rooted in the Palestinian inhabitants of the territory.[31] The UK was in a dilemma; fulfilling the Mandate's obligations required a repudiation of Balfour—and the Balfour promise repudiated the Mandate. This dilemma was never resolved.

When Britain requested in 1947 that the UN to consider the future dispensation of the territory defined by the Mandate, the UNGA created a special committee to investigate the international legal status of the Palestinian territory, which determined that the Mandate should be terminated and that independence should be granted.[32] The Committee, of which a majority was committed to partition of Palestine into a Jewish State and an Arab State, stipulated that the relinquishment of the territory to its populations should nevertheless be linked to an economic association, and that the status of Jerusalem should be a separate entity

---

[26] M. Rosenblit, 'International Law and the Jewish People's Collective Rights of Settlement and Self-Determination in the Land of Israel,' (2006).

[27] J. Quigley, *The Statehood of Palestine: International Law in the Middle East Conflict* (Cambridge University Press, 2010), p. 75.

[28] I. Friedman, *The Question of Palestine: British-Jewish-Arab Relations, 1914-1918* (New Jersey: Transaction Publishers, 1992), p. 325.

[29] Y. Rabin and R. Peled, 'Transfer of Sovereignty over Populated Territories from Israel to a Palestinian State: The International Law Perspective,' 17 *Minnesota Journal of International Law* 59 (2008); J. Quigley, 'Palestine Statehood: A Rejoinder to Professor Robert Weston Ash,' *Is There a Court for Gaza?* (2012), pp. 461-468.

[30] T. Primeau and J. Corntassel, 'Indigenous 'Sovereignty' and International Law: Revised Strategies for Pursuing 'Self-Determination,' 17 *Human Rights Quarterly* 343 (1995).

[31] United Nations, 'The International Status of the Palestinian People, Prepared for, and under the Guidance the Committee on the Exercise of the Inalienable Rights of the Palestinian People' (New York, 1981).

[32] UN Doc. A/RES/106 (S-1), 15 May 1947.

under international supervision.[33] By 1948, Britain ceded to the UN the mandate and attendant responsibilities.

Within the UN, a resolution known as Resolution 181 was adopted, providing for a partition of Palestine in order to establish a Jewish State (fifty-seven percent of the land) and an Arab State (forty-three per cent of the land).[34] The expectation of the international community then was that the partition lines constituted a legally binding definition of respective territorial claims.[35] Israel unilaterally declared itself a sovereign State in 1948, but without having adopted a constitution consistent with Resolution 181.[36] Although there was a Declaration of the Establishment of the State of Israel,[37] this declaration was not passed by the Knesset.[38]

In short, only one State was created and one State failed to be born. Armed conflict broke out between the newly born Jewish State and surrounding Arab States. To the historians of Israel, the resulting conflict became the War of Independence.[39] To the Palestinian historians, these events were catastrophic, or 'Nakba.'[40] The Israelis repelled Arab attacks and occupied territories beyond the partition lines. There remains a concern about the extension of Israeli sovereignty beyond the declared partition borders,[41] which were stabilized by the Armistice Agreements.[42]

---

[33] UN Special Committee on Palestine, *Report to the General Assembly*, UN Doc. A/364, 3 September 1947.

[34] UN Doc. A/RES/181(II), 29 November 1947.

[35] V. Kattan, *The Palestine Question in International Law* (British Institution of Comparative and International Law, 2008); R. Khalidi, 'International Law and Legitimacy and the Palestine Question,' 30 *Hastings International and Comparative Law Review* 174 (2007).

[36] J. Dorner, 'Does Israel Have a Constitution?' 43 *Saint Louis Law Journal* 1325 (1999); D. Sharfman, *Living without a Constitution: Civil Rights in Israel* (ME Sharpe, 1993).

[37] 'The Declaration of the Establishment of the State of Israel,' 1948, 1 LSI (Laws of the State of Israel) 3 (14 May 1948).

[38] R. Gavison, 'Legislatures and the Quest for a Constitution: The Case of Israel,' 11 *Review of Constitutional Studies* 345 (2006).

[39] C. Herzog and S. Gazit, *The Arab-Israeli Wars: War and Peace in the Middle East from the 1948 War of Independence to the Present* (Random House Digital, 2005).

[40] R. Lentin, *The Contested Memory of Dispossession: Commemorizing the Palestinian Nakba in Israel* (London: Zed Books, 2008).

[41] J. Cleary, *Literature, Partition and the Nation-State: Culture and Conflict in Ireland, Israel and Palestine* (Cambridge: Cambridge University Press, 2002).

[42] A set of agreements signed during 1949 between Israel and neighboring Arab States (Egypt, Lebanon, Jordan, and Syria) to put an end to the official hostilities of the 1948 Arab-Israeli war and to establish armistice demarcation lines between

140 Chapter Four

The US delegation to the UN was instructed to support Israel's request to keep the Negev, and the US considered that the Israeli borders were now a non-issue.[43]

On 28 May 1964, the first Palestinian National Council (PNC) convened in Jerusalem with 422 representatives. At the conclusion of this meeting, on 2 June 1964, the Palestine Liberation Organization (PLO) was founded with a Statement of Proclamation of the Organization[44] and the adoption of a Palestinian National Covenant.[45] Although the original Covenant did not expressly mention 'statehood,' it called for a right of return and self-determination for Palestinians. In 1968, the Covenant was amended to stipulate more clearly the Palestinians' aspirations.[46] In 1974, the PLO adopted a programme that made clearer the intention to declare an independent State in the territory of Mandate Palestine.[47] In the search for other strategies to advance its interests, the PLO sought to secure for its people diplomatic recognition,[48] stressing that the foundations of Palestinian statehood claims are founded on the principle of self-determination. The PLO also secured recognition of its role as representative of the Palestinian

Israeli forces and the forces in the West Bank held by Jordan, known as the 'Green Line.' See H. Levie, 'The Nature and Scope of the Armistice Agreement,' 50 *American Journal of International Law* 880 (October 1956); L. Beres, 'After the Scud Attacks: Israel, Palestine, and Anticipatory Self-Defense,' 6 *Emory International Law Review* 71 (1992).

[43] S. Spiegel, *The Other Arab-Israeli Conflict: Making America's Middle East Policy, from Truman to Reagan* (Chicago: University of Chicago Press, 1986).

[44] *Statement of Proclamation of the Organization* (Jerusalem: PLO, 28 May 1964).

[45] *The Palestinian National Charter: Resolutions of the Palestine National Council*, Articles 2 and 23, Palestine Liberation Organization (signed on 28 May 1964 and amended on 1-17 July 1968). See also M. Shemesh, *Arab Politics, Palestinian Nationalism and the Six Day War: the Crystallization of Arab Strategy and Nasir's Descent to War, 1957-1967* (Sussex Academic Press, 2008); M. Shemesh, 'The Founding of the PLO 1964,' 20 *Middle Eastern Studies* 4 (1984); D. Schiller, 'A Battlegroup Divided: The Palestinian Fedayeen,' 10 *Journal of Strategic Studies* 4 (1987); Y. Harkabi, *The Palestinian Covenant and Its Meaning* (London: Vallentine, Mitchell, 1979).

[46] That (1) Israel should be removed from its role as occupier of the West Bank and Gaza; (2) a Palestinian State is to be established thereto; and (3) the State of Israel is to be dismantled.

[47] *The Palestine National Council Programme of 1974* (8 June 1974).

[48] A. Yodfat and A. Yuval, *PLO Strategy and Tactics* (Saint Martin's Press, 1981).

people,[49] by gaining recognition by the Arab League and the majority of UN Members.[50]

This process has resulted in more than 122 States recognizing the PLO and over sixty States providing it with full diplomatic status. Fifty more States recognized the PLO but have not establishment Palestinian embassies, although some permit PLO offices to function under the name of the Arab League.[51] These developments do not indicate the existence of a Palestinian State or government in exile but instead focus on the PLO as the sole representative of self-determination rights.[52] As early as 1969, the UNGA began adopting resolutions that recognized the Palestinian right to self-determination as well as the PLO as the representative of the Palestinian people. The PLO was invited to participate in UN deliberations organized under the authority of the UNGA and UNSC.[53] The PLO has had observer status at the UN.[54]

The two key decisions of the UNSC concerning the Palestinian-Israeli conflict are Resolution 242 of 1967,[55] and Resolution 338 of 1973.[56] These resolutions imply that the right to self-determination involves rights of sovereignty, territorial integrity, and independence. They call for an end to Israeli occupation. But Israel forces have discriminated against Palestinians through the imposition of a complex regime. The problem with a policy that accentuates statelessness is that the longer it continues, the more difficult it is to manage a workable settlement.

The Partition Plan established criteria for citizenship without regard to religion or ethnicity. Subsequent Israeli legislation and practice has ignored the original citizenship requirement outlined in the Partition Plan,

---

[49] M. Madfai, *Jordan, the US and the Middle East Peace Process, 1974-1991* (Cambridge: Cambridge University Press, 1993) p. 21.

[50] S. Silverburg, 'The Palestine Liberation Organization in the UN: Implications for International Law and Relations,' 12 *Israel Law Review* 365 (1977).

[51] Up to this moment 122 UN Member States have recognized Palestine. See K. Jayakumar, 'Palestine and the UN: The Recognition Debate,' *Available at SSRN 2121011* (2011). See also PLO Negotiations Office, *Recognizing the Palestinian State on the 1967 border & Admission of Palestine as a Full Member of the UN* (2011); S. Vallejo, 'Recognition of the State of Palestine and the Hypocrisy,' *Committee in Solidarity with the Arab Cause* (2011).

[52] A. Cassese, 'The Israel-PLO Agreement and Self-Determination,' 4 *European Journal of International Law* 564 (1993).

[53] UN Doc. A/RES/3375, 10 November 1975.

[54] UN Doc. A/RES/3237 (XXIX), 22 November 1974.

[55] Resolution 242, 22 November 1967.

[56] Resolution 338, 22 October 1973.

generating a huge Palestinian refugee crisis.[57] Most recently, Israeli Prime Minister Netanyahu has sought to affirm the validity of internal Israeli practices on citizenship and statelessness by demanding that the PA agree that Israel is a Jewish State. There are some among Israeli ultranationalist political factions who propagate the notion that there is no such thing as a 'Palestinian.'[58] The Israeli Law of Return of 1970[59] effectively defines who is Jewish and, by implication, who is not.[60] Greater specificity is given to this definition in the Absentee Property Law of 1950, the Entering into Israel Law of 1952, and in Israeli Nationality Law of 1952. The Absentee Property Law defined most Palestinian Arabs as 'refugees' from territories that Israel conquered in the 1948 war. The law denies them the citizenship rights envisioned in Resolution 181 and the rights to their properties. The status of 'absentee' is inherited as well, meaning that children of Palestinian Arabs will also be considered 'absentees.' In effect, the status of absentee is a status of statelessness. The number of Palestinians who were expelled from Israel was estimated at 711,000 in 1949.[61] The descendants of these refugees are registered with the UN as Palestinian refugees. In 2010, the total population of refugees was 4.7 million,[62] about a third of the refugees live in refugee camps in States adjacent to Israel, and the rest live on the peripheries of cities and towns of

---

[57] D. Jefferis, 'Institutionalizing Statelessness: The Revocation of Residency Rights of Palestinians of East Jerusalem,' 24 *International Journal of Refugee Law* 202 (2011); L. Waas, *Nationality Matters: Statelessness under International Law* (Intersentia, 2008); J. Blackman, 'State Successions and Statelessness: The Emerging Right to an Effective Nationality under International Law,' 19 *Michigan Journal of International Law* 1141 (1998); U. Davis, *Citizenship and the State: a Comparative Study of Citizenship Legislation in Israel, Jordan, Palestine, Syria and Lebanon* (Garnet and Ithaca Press, 1997); L. Malkki, 'Refugees and Exile: From 'Refugee Studies' to the National Order of Things,' 24 *Annual Review of Anthropology* 495 (1995); E. Zureik, 'Palestinian Refugees and Peace,' 24 *Journal of Palestine Studies* 5 (1994); K. Radley, 'The Palestinian Refugees: The Right to Return in International Law,' 72 *American Journal of International Law* 586 (1978).
[58] R. Khalidi, *Palestinian Identity: The Construction of Modern National Consciousness* (New York: Columbia University Press, 2009).
[59] 'Law of Return,' Amendment No. 2, 1970, amending the Law of Return of 1950, 1970, 586 *Sefer HaChukkim* 34 (19 March 1970).
[60] S. Yehuda, 'The Definition of a Jew under the Law of Return,' 17 *Southwestern Law Journal* (1963).
[61] D. and C. Palley, 'The Palestinians,' *Minority Rights Group Report* 24 (1987) p. 10.
[62] *UNHCR Annual Report Shows 42 Million People Uprooted Worldwide*, Press Release (16 June 2009).

host countries. Some Israeli scholars maintain that the exodus of refugees from Israel was largely a response to the threats posed by the Haganah,[63] Lehi[64] and Irgun.[65]

The absentee status of Palestinians in Israel has had a major impact on the civil and socio-economic rights. By denying Palestinians their identity, the political propaganda is laying the groundwork for rejecting the Palestinians' claim to be a 'people' for the purposes of self-determination.[66] Another area that is particularly affected is that of land rights. Four cornerstones make up the legal basis of Israeli land policy[67] and together these laws exclude non-Jews from 92.6% of the land.

Israel also discriminates against Palestinians through a formidable array of defense regulations under a dual military-civilian system that is applicable to Palestinians only.[68] The emergency regulations, which were inherited from Britain, include the power to detain, the power to deport, the power to take possession of land, the power to forfeit and demolish property, and the power to declare closed areas.[69] Additionally, the Foundation of Legislation Law of 1980 further strengthened the powers of the Israeli State and weakened the rights of Palestinians as people.[70] For instance, a wide variety of goods are deemed to be 'war goods,'[71] such as sewing machines, and perishable Palestinian exports are delayed so that they are destroyed.[72] Palestinians income is restricted; Israeli law requires

---

[63] 'The Haganah,' *The Jewish Library* (31 January 2012). The Haganah was founded in June 1920.

[64] J. Heller, *The Stern Gang: Ideology, Politics, and Terror, 1940-1949* (Psychology Press, 1995).

[65] D. Niv, 'A short history of the Irgun Zevai Leumi,' *World Zionist Organization; Department. of Education and Culture* (1980).

[66] B. Bell, *Terror Out of Zion: Irgun Zvai Leumi, LEHI, and the Palestine Underground, 1929-1949* (New York: St. Martin's Press, 1977).

[67] *Basic Law: Israel Lands*, 14 LSI 48 (Israel, 1960); *Israel Land Administration Law*, 1960, 14 LSI 50 (Israel, 1960).

[68] M. Lissak, 'The Unique Approach to Military-Societal Relations in Israel and Its Impact on Foreign and Security Policy,' in *Peacemaking in a Divided Society: Israel After Rabin* by Sasson Sofer (2001), pp. 235-257.

[69] D. Kirshbaum, 'Israeli Emergency Regulations and the Defense (Emergency) Regulations of 1945,' *Israel Law Resource Center* (2007).

[70] *The Foundation of Law Act*, 1980, 34 LSI 181 (Israel, 1980).

[71] See S. Res. 102, 78th Cong. (1944); H. Res. 408, 78th Cong. (1944) (creating special committees on post-war economic policy and planning.

[72] E. Schechter, 'Legal Scholars Weigh in on Gaza Blockade, Flotilla Deaths,' *Carnegie Council* (28 June 2010); Y. Katz, 'Navy Commandos: 'They Came for War',' *Jerusalem Post* (31 May 2010).

Palestinian income to be twenty times less than that of Israelis.[73] Illegal
Israeli settlements and occupying forces also utilize military law to limit
economic and entrepreneurial activity that may compete with Israel. For
example, laws of military occupation disrupt Palestinian schooling,[74] and
the system of strategic roads makes the communications system a
nightmare.[75] The Israeli policy of targeted assassinations eliminates
educated and moderate Palestinians, making it difficult to create a competent
government authority.[76] Israel's control over airspace and waters prevents
Palestinian fishing operations in the Mediterranean;[77] its policies have also
led to the demolition of tens of thousands of homes,[78] and the destruction
of hundreds of thousands of fruit and nut trees.[79]

Water resources are also a major sought-after asset and a major
political issue in the Middle East.[80] The West Bank aquifer is considered a
major water resource.[81] Israel receives most of its water from two aquifers

[73] N. Kawach, 'Real Per Capita Income of Palestine Plunges,' *International
Solidarity Movement* (17 January 2010).

[74] I. Abu-Saad, 'State-Controlled Education and Identity Formation among the
Palestinian Arab Minority in Israel,' 49 *American Behavioral Scientist* 1085
(2006).

[75] T. Selwin, 'Landscapes of Separation: Reflections on the Symbolism of By-pass
Roads in Palestine,' in *Contested Landscapes: Movement, Exile and Place* by
Barbara Bender and Margot Winer (2001); A. Cordesman, 'Israel versus the
Palestinians: The 'Second Intifada' and Asymmetric Warfare,' *Center for Strategic
and International Studies* (July 2002), p. 66.

[76] G. Luft, 'The Logic of Israel's Targeted Killing,' *Middle East Quarterly* (2003),
pp. 3-13.

[77] 'Israel's Control of the Airspace and the Territorial Waters of the Gaza Strip,'
*B'Tselem; The Israeli Information Center for Human Rights in Occupied
Territories* (27 September 2010).

[78] B. Farrell, 'Israeli Demolition of Palestinian Houses as a Punitive Measure:
Application of International Law to Regulation 119,' 28 *Brooklyn Journal of
International Law* 871 (2003).

[79] A. Alwazir, *Uprooting Olive Trees in Palestine*, ICE Case No. 110 (November
2002); M. Kehat, 'Threat to Date Palms in Israel, Jordan and the Palestinian
Authority by the Red Palm Weevil, Rhynchophorus ferrugineus,' 27
Phytoparasitica 241 (1999).

[80] G. Abouali, 'Natural Resources under Occupation: The Status of Palestine Water
under International Law,' 10 *Pace International Law Review* 411 (1998); E.
Benvenisti and H. Gvirtzman, 'Harnessing International Law to Determine Israeli-
Palestinian Water Rights: The Mountain Aquifer,' 33 *Natural Resources Journal*
543 (1993).

[81] M. Lowi, 'Bridging the Divide: Transboundary Resource Disputes and the Case
of West Bank Water,' *International Security* (1993).

which are underground and which extend into Palestinian territory. This generates conflict about the Israeli exploitation of Palestinian water resources. While Israelis use approximately 800 litters of water per day, Palestinians are allowed to use only 200 litters.[82] Israel prohibits Palestinians from drilling into the West Bank aquifer without permits. It even bans constructing catchment basins to collect rainwater.[83]

International law does not validate the acquisition of territory by the use of force.[84] The occupation of such territory may, over time, generate new facts and new expectations if the legal status of the occupation is not clarified. The Palestinians have reasserted their claim to statehood covering the territories now occupied by Israel—namely, Gaza and the West Bank. It is possible that some interests in Israel wish to incrementally change the facts on the ground by increasing settlement activity and strategically placing access routes for exclusive Israeli use, while limiting Palestinian social, economic, and political development in the process. [85]

The marginalization of Palestinians is further exacerbated by racism.[86] Jews have been millennial victims of racism, and there is great sensitivity to the concern that some elements in Israel promote a racist agenda. Right-wing organizations often engage in what in other contexts would be classified as racist rhetoric based on the Hebrew Bible. The occupation is a major contributor to the disturbing emergence of right-wing-inspired racism in Israel.[87] The discriminatory practices may even suggest that the occupying power is deliberately making life an impossible struggle for Palestinians. The Palestinians' resistance is equated with terrorism; if they

---

[82] World Bank, *West Bank and Gaza - Assessment of Restrictions on Palestinian Water Sector Development*, Report No. 47657-GZ (2009), p. 11; National Research Council, *Water for the Future: The West Bank and Gaza Strip, Israel, and Jordan* (Washington: The National Academies Press, 1999); D. Izenberg and E. Waldoks, 'Mekorot: Water Supply to West Bank is High,' *JPost.com* (30 June 2012).

[83] Human Rights Watch, 'World Report 2012: Israel/Occupied Palestinian Territories' (January 2012).

[84] S. Korman, *The Right of Conquest: the Acquisition of Territory by Force in International Law and Practice* (Oxford: Oxford University Press, 1996).

[85] W. Harris, 'Taking Root: Israeli Settlement in the West Bank, the Golan, and Gaza-Sinai, 1967-1980,' 1 *Research Studies Press* 223 (1980).

[86] U. Avnery, 'The Darkness to Expel!' *Uri Avnery's Column* (25 December 2010).

[87] Albert Memmi, *The Colonizer and the Colonized* (Earthscan/James & James, 2003).

resist with non-violence they accused of being not serious negotiating party.[88]

The Parties and their Perspectives of Reality

Israelis and Palestinians have differing perspectives about the conflict and the scope of a possible resolution. To constructively develop a shared narrative, for the purpose of finding a possible resolution, it is imperative that the commentator acknowledge the reality of the perspectives of the parties involved. The vastly ambitious doctrine of the 'Clean Break' best reflects the influence of the ultranationalist political factions in Israel on American neo-conservative political interests.[89] This doctrine, which sought to reshape the entire State structure of the Middle East, in effect implies that the Palestinian problem in Israel is a sideshow. The Clean Break Doctrine promoted the idea of regime change in the case of dictators on the basis that one could not make peace with authoritarian despots.[90] While events in Tunisia,[91] Egypt,[92] Libya,[93] Yemen[94] and Syria[95] indicate strong popular demands for democracy, it appears that Netanyahu may wish that he had not been taken so seriously on the democracy question.[96]

---

[88] T. Kapitan, 'The Terrorism of 'Terrorism',' *Terrorism and International Justice* (2003), pp. 47-66; A. Merari, 'Terrorism as a Strategy of Insurgency,' 5 *Terrorism and Political Violence* 213 (1993).

[89] R. Perle, D. Feith, and D. Wurmser, 'A Clean Break: A New Strategy for Securing the Realm,' *Arab American Institute* (1996)

[90] P. Ish-Shalom, 'The Civilization of Clashes: Misapplying the Democratic Peace in the Middle East,' 122 *Political Science Quarterly* 533 (2008); R. Jervis, 'Why the Bush Doctrine Cannot Be Sustained,' 120 *Political Science Quarterly* 351 (2005).

[91] R. Abouzeid, 'Bouazizi: The Man Who Set Himself and Tunisia on Fire,' *Time Magazine* (21 January 2011); B. Whitaker, 'How a Man Setting Fire to Himself Sparked an Uprising in Tunisia,' *The Guardian* (28 December 2010).

[92] J. Stacher, 'Egypt's Democratic Mirage,' *Foreign Affairs* (7 February 2011); L. Sustar, 'The Roots of Egypt's Uprising,' *SocialistWorker.org* (3 February 2011).

[93] D. Cutler and M. Golovnina 'Timeline: Libya's uprising against Muammar Gaddafi,' *Reuters* (21 August 2011).

[94] K. Fahim, 'Yemeni Uprising Opens a Door to Besieged Rebels in the North,' *The New York Times* (16 December 2011); T. Finn, 'Yemen Uprising: Sana'a Rocked by Night of Fierce Fighting,' *The Guardian* (17 October 2011).

[95] M. Chulov, 'Syria Uprising is Now a Battle to the Death,' *The Guardian* (9 February 2012).

[96] J. Cook, 'Israel's Grand Hypocrisy: Netanyahu Slams 'Anti-liberal' Arab Spring,' *OpEdNews* (1 December 2011).

Commentators have speculated as to whether Netanyahu now misses the stability of an authoritarian friend like Mubarak.[97] On the other hand, deeply rooted in the Israeli ultranationalist agenda is the idea of a return to an exclusively Jewish State without Arabs.[98] The current state of negotiations has floundered on the rock of Israeli settlement activity. The US has now admitted that it is incapable of generating inducements to Netanyahu for a settlement freeze.[99] Bu the freeze is the essential precondition for Palestinians negotiators.[100] It is unclear what further steps the US can take short of putting the squeeze on 'the Lobby' – a squeeze that is beyond the capability of the Obama Administration. This has renewed Palestinian interest in looking at an alternative strategy to secure its claim to statehood.

The advantages of a recognized State begin with the idea that a duly recognized State would sharpen the legal question of Israel's continued occupation. The occupation in the face of recognized statehood would be tantamount to the occupation of territory by the use of force in violation of the UN Charter, Article 2(4).[101] Resolution 242 would add, in the light of legally recognized statehood, to the illegality of occupation on the assumption that the Israeli military occupation is now that of an aggressor. A fully recognized State would make it difficult for Israel to negotiate or discuss matters entailing State responsibility which constitute violations of international law. The recognition of a sovereign State would improve the negotiating stature of Palestinian negotiators. These negotiations involve the complex map of Israel and Palestine, including settlements, the 'wall' surrounding Jerusalem and the West Bank,[102] as well as other issues of

---

[97] B. Ravid, 'Israel Urges World to Curb Criticism of Egypt's Mubarak,' *Haaretz* (31 January 2011); B. Lynfield, 'Israel Worried as Mubarak Teeters,' *Global Post* (29 January 2011).

[98] G. Biger, 'The Boundaries of Israel—Palestine: Past, Present, and Future: A Critical Geographical View,' 13 *Israel Studies* 68 (22 March 2008).

[99] J. Dougherty and E. Labott, 'US Ends Bid for Renewed Israeli Settlement Freeze,' *CNN* (7 December 2010).

[100] A. Khalil, 'Palestinians Say Full Settlement Freeze is Precondition to New Peace Talks,' *Correspondent of The Christian Science Monitor* (27 August 2009).

[101] UN Charter, Article 2(4).

[102] Y. Shiryaev, 'Circumstances Surrounding the Separation Barrier and the Wall Case and their Relevance for the Israeli Right of Self-Defense,' 14 *Gonzaga Journal of International Law* 1 (2011); S. Murphy, 'Self-Defense and the Israeli Wall Advisory Opinion: An Ipse Dixit from the ICJ?' 99 *The American Journal of International Law* 62 (2005).

geographic complexity.[103] They would have to work through central issues for the purpose of a complete peaceful settlement with Israel. Those issues include Jerusalem, settlements, borders, water, refugees, political prisoners, missing persons, economic relations, monetary affairs and claims resolution.[104] While we hold that respect for the international rule of law is the best alternative for all the parties involved, we shall now address the particular interests of the parties individually.

United States Interests and Ultra-nationalist Politics in Israel

A useful starting point for an appraisal of US policy and interests in the Middle East is the Camp David Accords, which were negotiated by President Jimmy Carter. The Accords, which included secret negotiations between the parties, resulted in two framework agreements. The first dealt with the status of the Palestinians and their territorial rights under international law. The second, which was a separate agreement, was a framework for the conclusion of a peace treaty between Israel and Egypt. The first of these framework agreements at Camp David placed US foreign policy squarely in line with the international law stipulations and provisions of UNSC Resolutions 242 and 338, which are particularly relevant as a foundation for the consistency of US policy with international law regarding the international status of the Palestinians. In light of the above history, the US has a clear foreign relations interest in settling the Israeli-Palestinian conflict. This interest implicates sensitive and vital national security interests. The US is involved with other players whose interests are not necessarily the same.[105] The US must also try to formulate its foreign policy in a manner that ensures that its strategies and tactics are reconcilable with the position of the other three members of the Quartet (European Union, Russia, and UN).

The continuing Israeli-Palestinian conflict has become an immediate national security issue. When *Al Qaeda* attacked the US on 11 September 2001, one of its justifications for the attack was the unconditional US

---

[103] PLO Negotiations Affairs Department, 'Israeli Human Rights Violations within the Occupied Palestinian Territory (OPT): January–May 2011,' *Media Affairs* (2011); PLO Negotiations Affairs Department, 'Israeli Policies in Occupied East Jerusalem: Colonizing the Land and the People,' *Media Brief* (June 2011).

[104] UN Doc. E/RES/2010/31, 23 July 2010.

[105] D. Singer, 'Quartet Quartered, Road Map Thwarted, Palestine Aborted,' EU info (15 July 2007), K. Archick, 'European Views and Policies Toward the Middle East,' *Library of Congress Washington DC Congressional Research Service* (2005).

support for Israel and its policies *vis-à-vis* the Palestinians.[106] The US response to 9/11 involved the nation in a high-intensity conflict in Iraq and Afghanistan. It has been recognized that a central motivating tool for the alienation of activist Muslims is the belief that Israel and its policies of occupation simply represent an extension of US policy. Unquestioning support for Israeli military policies continues to fuel an ostensible justification for anti-Americanism and an assumption that, fundamentally, the US, too, is anti-Muslim.

The Israeli-Palestinian occupation is a catalyst within such a large population pool for the transition from alienation to terrorism.[107] It appears that the Obama Administration and the US security establishment are aware of these issues. When the Obama Administration came to office in 2009, it was confronted with concerns that the continuing Israeli-Palestinian conflict served as a recruiting tool for alienated terrorists.[108] In response, the Administration recruited a team of talented negotiators to press for the restart of negotiations toward a settlement. The President even went to Cairo to address the billions of Muslims who may have experienced some alienation due to the polarizing nature of the international Israel/Palestine debate. However, US foreign policy regarding Israel is significantly conditioned by the over twenty-five ultranationalist pro-Israeli lobby groups in Washington, DC. These groups are attentive to the needs of Israel's ultranationalist political interests. Domestic Israeli lobby groups pressured the US government and Congress to block the recognition of a Palestinian State and to ensure that the US would veto any resolution to that effect.

The influence of 'The Lobby' in the US can be seen in the recent House Resolution No. 1765. This Resolution emphasized the principle that a lasting peaceful solution will only come about through the negotiations of both parties, i.e. the State of Israel and the representatives of the Palestinian people. What the Resolution does not address is the inability of the Palestinian representatives to negotiate any solution with Israel in the face of such inequality in the status of the parties. Moreover, in condemning the efforts of the Palestinian people to seek statehood—even

---

[106] D. Kellner, 'Globalization, Terrorism, and Democracy: 9/11 and Its Aftermath,' *Frontiers of Globalization Research* 243 (2007).

[107] 'Palestine Population,' *Maps of the World* (January 2012); 'Muslim Americans: No Signs of Growth in Alienation or Support for Extremism,' *Pew Research Center for the People and the Press* (30 August 2011); D. Downing, *Conflicts of the Middle East* (Gareth Stevens, 2006).

[108] A. Soliman, 'President Obama: A new hope for Israel/Palestine?' *Strategic Foresight Group* (2008).

by purely peaceful and legal means—outside of negotiations with Israel, the US House undermines US treaty obligations to support the achievement of statehood for the Palestinians. This successful lobbying effort on behalf of Israel reveals two aspects of the US Israeli Lobby. First, it can powerfully refocus the attention of the US. Second, the US Israeli Lobby does not engage with the US government for US interests but rather in the interest of Israel.[109] Here the simplistic idea is that Israeli and US interests are the same. A more discriminating view would be that Israel has discreet interests.[110] It has been reported that well-placed neoconservative political appointees and elected officials pass on sensitive information to Israeli officials on the assumption that they are not really passing on secrets.[111]

The breakdown in talks between the Palestinians and Israelis and the effort to undermine US mediation efforts have prompted some of America's most distinguished public servants to issue a widely publicized document under the title *'A Letter to President Obama.'*[112] The authors of this letter, who are extremely disquieted by the failure of US Middle East diplomacy, urge a renewed American effort to revive its role in Middle East diplomacy. The letter provides a profoundly realistic summary of the central problems that confront the concerned parties and recommends a framework for a permanent status accord that provides a promising starting point for the Palestinians; however, it presents issues that may be anathema to the current right-wing extremist fringe led by Netanyahu and his acolytes.[113]

Uri Avnery holds pessimistic views with regard to the current leadership in Israel.[114] According to Avnery, the interjection into the negotiations of the recognition of Israel as a Jewish State has no coherent intellectual content, and is used by Netanyahu 'as a trick to obstruct the establishment of the Palestinian State.'[115] He would then declare that 'the

---

[109] L. Rennert, 'Crisis over Palestinian Statehood bid is all Israel's fault,' *American Thinker* (16 September 2011).

[110] R. Blackwill and W. Slocombe, 'Israel: A True Ally in the Middle East,' *Los Angeles Post* (31 October 2011).

[111] 'Obama Secretly Sold Israel Bunker-Busting Bombs (VIDEO),' *Jspace* (26 September 2011); Y. Ibrahim, 'Israeli Spying On US Unravels - Franklin Sings Like Canary,' *The Washington Times* (24 December 2004).

[112] L. Hamilton, D. Boren, Zbigniew Brzezinski, F. Carlucci, and W. Fallon, 'A Letter to President Obama; January 24, 2011,' 58 *The New York Review of Books* 11 (2011), p. 67.

[113] N. Mozgovaya, 'Netanyahu: Palestinians making 'Terrible Mistake' by not Resuming Peace Talks,' *Haaretz* (27 September 2011).

[114] U. Avnery, 'Interim Forever,' *OpEdNews* (3 January 2011).

[115] U. Avnery, 'Deny! Deny!' *OpEdNews* (18 June 2011).

conflict has no solution.' Avnery adds that in the right-wing voice box to deny 'the Jewish character' of the State is tantamount to the worst of all political felonies: to claim that Israel is a 'State of all its citizens.'[116] He explains how Netanyahu's Foreign Minister, Lieberman, amplifies his position to excess.[117] A continuation of conflict may suggest to the ultranationalist factions in Israel that conflict favours them in the long haul, because there are 400 lethal nuclear arsenals in Israel. These arsenals are a destabilizing force, which becomes even more dangerous when the levels of conflict sporadically spiral out of control. They create an incentive for the States surrounding Israel to acquire nuclear weapons capabilities. But the Israeli ultranationalist contingency is engaged, energized, and fanatical.[118]

Israel and the US have divergent interests regarding military intervention in the Middle East and sustaining the role of international law regarding such interventions. The Bush Administration allied itself with Israeli interests in the Middle East, and the US ended up fighting wars both of questionable benefit to US interests and of questionable legality under international law.[119] The US policy leaders at the time invested in extravagant security ideas originally generated by the Likud, such as the 'Clean Break' doctrine.[120] This doctrine found itself mutated after 9/11 into the 'Bush Doctrine.'[121] Nevertheless, the roots of the desire to attack Iraq came from the Likud's Clean Break Doctrine and the Likud's interest in regime change emerged from a view of Saddam Hussein as a serious security challenge to Israel. With Saddam gone, there has been a relentless campaign for regime change in Iran.[122] It is not in the national interest of

---

[116] U. Avnery, 'The Dwarfs,' *OpEdNews* (12 March 2011).

[117] J. Kay, 'Avigdor Lieberman: Palestinian Statehood Would Set a Dangerous Precedent,' *National Post* (20 September 2011).

[118] Sasson Sofer, *Peacemaking in a Divided Society: Israel After Rabin* (Psychology Press, 2001); N. Shelef, *Evolving Nationalism: Homeland, Identity, and Religion in Israel, 1925-2005* (Cornell University Press, 19 August 2010).

[119] M. Plitnick, Joel Beinin and Cecilie Surasky, 'Did Israel Lead the US into the War on Iraq?' *Jewish Voice for Peace* (20 December 2011).

[120] A. Shapiro, E. Williams, and Dawoud, *Neocon Middle East Policy: The 'Clean Break' Plan Damage Assessment* (Institute for Research, March 2005).

[121] H. Karoui, 'Conservative Revolution against America; The Bush Legacy: Debate about a doctrine and its Tributaries,' 1 *Social Sciences and Humanities* 3 (2010); W. Lang, 'Drinking the Kool-Aid,' 11 *Middle East Policy* 2 (2004).

[122] R. Howard, *Iran in Crisis? Nuclear Ambitions and the American Response* (Zed Books, 2004); P. Buchanan, 'Whose War? A Neoconservative Clique Seeks to Ensnare Our Country in a Series of Wars That Are Not in America's Interest,' 24

the US at this time to start a new war in the Middle East. Notwithstanding the unpopular attitude of the Iranian regime, it is unlikely that the majority of the American people would support a new neoconservative adventure.[123] It would be of value for the Obama Administration to repudiate those aspects of the Bush Doctrine that are controversial and challenge international law.

The US supplies Israel with the most advanced military technology, but in the future such support may not be in the best interests of the US. Despite the history of good relations in the past, Israel and the US have been on a rocky footing in recent times.[124] The US could not influence the Israeli government to halt settlements no matter how many of the highest-grade fighter planes it offered them.[125] Nor could the US induce Israel to behave with transparency in conformity with international standards regarding the proliferation of nuclear weapons. Israel has a significant market for its weapons sales and few friends.[126] In this sense, Israeli weapons technologies may well be deployed against US troops in the future.

The state of high-security crisis in Israel is funded largely by US assistance.[127] In addition to sources of funding from US private sector, there is enormous pressure on the US government to increase aid to Israel from 10-billion to at least 20-billion dollars a year.[128] It is estimated that Israel has received some 2 trillion dollars from American taxpayers since 1967. As vast billions of US dollars are being borrowed to fund the security needs of the State of Israel, this debt is passed on to the children of America's future, along with mounting unrest in a region under occupation. A dramatic move toward the recognition of Palestinian

---

American Conservative (2003); P. Buchanan, 'Whose War is this?,' 20 *Washington Report on Middle East Affairs* 6 (2001).

[123] J. Vaïsse, 'Why Neoconservatism Still Matters,' *Perspectives; Lowy Institute for International Policy* (2010); J. Krismer, *Our Puppet Government* (Ccb Publishing, 2008).

[124] C. Addis, 'Israel: Background and US Relations, *Library of Congress Washington DC Congressional Research Service* (2011).

[125] B. Ravid and N. Mozgovaya, 'US Offers Israel Warplanes in Return for New Settlement Freeze,' *Haaretz* (13 November 2011).

[126] M. Chossudovsky, 'Nuclear War against Iran,' 3 *Global Research* (2006); M. Chossudovsky, 'The Dangers of a US Sponsored Nuclear War,' *Global Research* (30 January 2006).

[127] M. Bard, 'US Aid to Israel,' *The Jewish Virtual Library* (January 2012); J. Sharp, *US Foreign Aid to Israel* (DIANE Publishing, 2010).

[128] 'Israel May Ask US for $20 Billion More in Security Aid, Barak Says,' *Haaretz* (8 March 2011).

statehood as a step toward an accelerated peaceful settlement would lessen Israel's security anxieties and the need for assistance from borrowed trillions now owed by US taxpayers.

US policy and the interest groups should be very discriminating about which groups they support in the Middle East and in Israel, to ensure that ultranationalist political interests do not hold US interests in peace and security hostage. In terms of contemporary international relations, Israeli ultra-nationalism is a danger to regional peace and security. It is quite possible that Israeli interests and US interests are the same, but the interests of the current Israeli leaders are different. The critical challenge for pro-Israel individuals, communities, and lobby groups in the US is to determine which of their activities support US interests in the region.

Israeli Interests in the Recognition of Palestine Statehood

Israeli interests are complex on the question of the recognition of a Palestinian State. We reject the idea that the majority of Israelis will opt for a state of continual insurrectionary, low-level conflict, which is precisely the danger involved in undermining the political development of appropriate institutions of good governance in the Palestinian territories. It is therefore in Israel's interest that the recognition of a Palestinian State, along the lines of good governance principles, will diminish the prospect of that governing authority being influenced by shadowy third-party forces. This type of government will provide the Israelis with the highest level of security, something that most Israelis, including Netanyahu, agree is as an important part of any settlement. In short, constitutional good governance for the Palestinians with the prospect of entrepreneurial freedoms could produce a stable and important political entity, which would significantly stabilize the prospects for peace and security in the region.[129] The alternative is simply to deny any right to self-determination, which will most certainly carry destructive consequences in the long term.[130]

There are two fundamental Israeli interests in the success of a negotiated settlement with the Palestinian leadership. The first is Israel's security interest, an interest that is still dependent on US support and could be in jeopardy if US efforts at mediation are sabotaged by the extreme

---

[129] J. Graham, B. Amos and T. Plumptre, 'Principles for Good Governance in the 21st Century,' *Policy Brief* 15 (2003).

[130] M. Walt and O. Seroo, 'The Implementation of the Right to Self-Determination as a Contribution to Conflict Prevention,' *Report of the International Conference of Experts held in Barcelona* (1998).

right-wing political forces in power within Israel. Failure in this regard
would compromise both US and Israeli security interests. The second
major interest of Israel is Israeli defence and promotion of the 'legitimacy'
of the State of Israel. This is an issue that is extremely sensitive to the
current Israeli leadership and their supporters in the diaspora community.
The issue of legitimacy emerged in part from the effort on the part of
Israeli detractors to suggest that Israeli policies regarding non-Jewish
inhabitants of the State were analogous to some aspects of the grand
design of Apartheid.[131] For example, efforts to create a boycott of Israeli
trade and cultural exchanges were vigorously opposed by Israeli State
interests.[132] However, the problems of legitimacy seem now to be tied to
the beliefs, the ideology, and the policies of the extreme right-wing
political factions in Israel. And these policies, which have racial overtones,
are committed to the *Eretz Israel* idea, an idea which itself seems wedded
to a repudiation of international-law-supported boundaries and to a
repudiation of the idea that sovereigns cannot acquire territory through
conquest; hence these policies only exacerbate the problems of legitimacy.

Any Israeli security interest could be advanced through the recognition
of Palestinian statehood. Israel has argued that rocket and terrorist attacks
from the Occupied Palestinian Territories give it a right of self-defence
and to respond to such attacks.[133] However, this claim has not met with an
approval that carries a global consensus. The technical argument against
Israel's assertion of the right of self-defence is based on the principle that
the occupied territories under Palestinian control are not recognized as a
nation State.[134] It is therefore maintained that Israel cannot assert its right
of self-defence against an entity that is not a sovereign State in
international law. The US Congress has enacted legislation to suggest that

---

[131] A. Bakan and Y. Abu-Laban, 'Israel/Palestine, South Africa and the 'One-State
Solution': The Case for an Apartheid Analysis,' 37 *Politikon* 331 (2010); J. Carter,
Palestine: Peace Not Apartheid (Simon and Schuster, 2006); D. Glaser, 'Zionism
and Apartheid: A Moral Comparison,' 26 *Ethnic and Racial Studies* 403 (2003);
M. Bisharah, *Palestine/Israel: Peace or Apartheid: Occupation, Terrorism and the
Future* (Zed Books, 2002); M. Marshall, 'Rethinking the Palestine Question: The
Apartheid Paradigm,' 25 *Journal of Palestine Studies* 15 (1995).
[132] A. Bakan, 'Israeli Apartheid: A Socialist View,' *Uruknet.info* (7 March 2011).
[133] S. Murphy, 'Self-Defense and the Israeli Wall Advisory Opinion: An Ipse Dixit
from the ICJ?' 99 *American Journal of International Law* 62 (2005).
[134] International Court of Justice, *Legal Consequences of the Construction of a
Wall in the Occupied Palestinian Territory: Summary of the Advisory Opinion*, 9
July 2004, para. 139.

Israel does have a right of self-defence under these circumstances.[135] The Congress may of course declare international law; but the currency of its declaration (which is essentially unilateral) would seem to require acceptance internationally for it to be seen as reflecting a statement of positive international law. If the Palestinians were granted sovereign nation status, there would be no ambiguity regarding the assertion of the right of self-defence. At the same time, the right to self-defence in international law clearly imposes corresponding obligations, of proportionality and others, on the Palestinian State, and spells out the consequences to follow if these obligations are unmet.[136] To the extent that the right of self-defence is clarified by Palestinian sovereignty, the mutual security interests of each body politic are significantly enhanced.[137]

A growing concern in Israel is the emergence of racism fuelled by the extremist right-wing political parties. The first point here is that Israeli intellectuals and human rights campaigners are embarrassed by this. Jews in the diaspora had been millennial victims of vicious racism/'anti-Semitism.' The practices against Jews fuelled by the banner of anti-Semitism culminated in the worst racist disaster the global community has ever experienced, the Holocaust. It is a great embarrassment to many Jews that some extremists in Israel feel free to exhibit the worst behaviour of pathological racism. The non-settlement with the Palestinians fuels this level of insecurity. It therefore seems to be a matter of some national urgency in Israel that a settlement be expedited. The two-State solution seems to be one of the most achievable objectives in a settlement and is a matter of national interest for Israel.

Israel has been recently wracked with internal social justice protests. Commentators suggested that Israeli protests were at least in part inspired

---

[135] 'Congress Affirms Israel's Right to Self-Defense,' *Near East Report* (12 July 2010).
[136] M. Franck, 'The Future of Judicial Internationalism: Charming Betsey, Medellin v. Dretke, and the Consular Right Dispute,' 86 *Boston University Law Review* 515 (2006); T. Franck, 'On Proportionality of Countermeasures in International Law,' 102 *American Journal of International* 715 (2008); M. Nabati, 'International Law at a Crossroads: Self-Defense, Global Terrorism, and Preemption (A Call to Rethink the Self-Defense Normative Framework),' 13 *Transnational Law & Contemporary Problems* 771 (2003); W. Fenrick, 'The Rule of Proportionality and Protocol in Conventional Warfare,' 98 *Military Law Review* 91 (1982).
[137] Y. Shiryaev, 'Circumstances Surrounding the Separation Barrier and the Wall Case and their Relevance for the Israeli Right to Self-Defense,' 14 *Gonzaga Journal International Law* 1 (2011).

by the lessons generated by the 'Arab Awakening.'[138] These internal
events have run parallel to events in the surrounding Arab States, which
have created apprehension in the government coalition in Israel. Israel's
alliance with the Mubarak regime in Egypt significantly buttressed its
strategic influence,[139] and the collapse of Mubarak removed a core pillar
that supported its strategic posture. The democratic movement in Egypt
sees the Mubarak legacy as decrepit and corrupt, and its government is
cautious about Israeli intentions. Israel's northern border is still recovering
from the recent Israeli attack on Lebanon.[140] And Israel's long-time ally in
the region, Turkey, has now largely rejected Israeli ties after the Israeli
attack on a Turkish humanitarian mission.

In an odd twist of fate, Netanyahu, the prime author of the Clean Break
Doctrine, which argues for regime replacement and the imposition of
democracy as a pathway to peace, has now seen his objective close to
realization, but without using the methods of regime replacement that he
had in mind. The emergence of a popular democratic movement will make
it difficult for Israel to resist the Palestinian push for self-determination.
There is a perspective emerging that the current elite will simply not have
the vision, the tools, or the will to provide for a realistic understanding
from an Israeli point of view of how to take the next steps forward.[141]

In sum, the greater the success of the democratic Arab Spring, the
more diminished are Israel's strategic options for avoiding a settlement
with the Palestinians. The essential reality is a radically new regional
environment in which the moral foundations of democratic expectation
stress the values of basic human rights and dignity. Israel must adjust its
position or be seen as a regime that is a leftover from the debris of the
dictators of Egypt, Tunisia and Libya.[142] It would be of great value if the

---

[138] K. Pollack, A. Al-Turk, M. Doran, D. Byman, and P. Baev, *The Arab Awakening: America and the Transformation of the Middle East* (Brookings Institution Press, 2011).
[139] R. Springborg, *Mubarak's Egypt: Fragmentation of the Political Order* (Westview Press: Boulder, Colorado, 1989); M. Azzam, 'Egypt: The Islamists and the State under Mubarak,' *Islamic Fundamentalism* (1996), pp. 109-122.
[140] E. Inbar, 'How Israel Bungled the Second Lebanon War,' *Middle East Quarterly* (Summer 2007), pp. 57-65; L. Beres, 'Israel, Lebanon, and Hizbullah: A Jurisprudential Assessment,' 14 *Arizona Journal of International & Comparative Law* 141 (1997).
[141] 'What Are You Willing to Die For?' *ShrinkWarapped* (18 February 2010).
[142] D. Levy, 'Israel and the Arab Uprisings: Challenges in a Changing Middle East: Remarks to the Council on Foreign Relations: The David Rockefeller Studies Program Roundtable Series,' *New America Foundation* (20 January 2012); D. Levy, 'Israeli Democracy in Peril: Why Daniel Levy Thinks Israel's Policy toward

US could step back and encourage a freer and less ideological discourse in Israel to emerge as a constructive response to the new challenges of a new environment.

Palestine and the Process for Securing Statehood Recognition

In the interest of achieving a just and stable peace in the contested lands under the control of Israel, we make a few suggestions on policy matters. Most of these suggestions require action by the Palestinian officials. Nevertheless, transparency is crucial because all members of the world community – including Israel, members of the UNSC, individual States, and members of State associations – have important parts to play in the process of achieving a viable State of Palestine. One of the two paths to Palestinian statehood requires the help and guidance of Israel to create the type of Palestinian State indicated in the UN Resolution on Partition and the Oslo Accords.[143] Israel has long enjoyed the support of the world community, especially the United States, in its role of preparing for the final agreement on partition. However, the longer Israel delays this process, while simultaneously denying the Palestinian people the possibility of real inclusion in a unified society and defying agreements to remain within established borders through its settlement activities, the more it risks isolating itself from the external powers that have thus far refused to support any 'unilateral' recognition of a State of Palestine.

The negotiation process overseen by the Obama Administration has completely broken down recently. This is due to extraordinary contingencies that Israeli representatives have placed upon negotiations. For one, Israel demanded Palestinian recognition of Israel as an ethnically exclusive State. It also required acceptance of the premise that Jerusalem belongs to Israel, so that there should be no restraints on the building of settlements in East Jerusalem.[144] Because the Israelis continued to engage in settlement activity, the Palestinians refused to participate. Both President Obama and his Secretary of State condemned these contingencies and the continuing settlements, explaining that they were unhelpful to the negotiation

---

the Palestinians is poisoning the Jewish State from Within,' *Slate.com* (6 January 2012).

[143] 'Declaration of Principles on Interim Self-Government Arrangements' (13 September 1993).

[144] C. Migdalovitz, *Israeli-Arab Negotiations: Background, Conflicts, and U.S. Policy* (DIANE Publishing, 2010); J. Beinin and L. Hajjar, 'Palestine, Israel and the Arab-Israeli Conflict A Primer,' *Middle East Report* (2010).

process.[145] A more skeptical view is that these activities are 'deal breakers' and that the Israeli government *intends* to disappoint by recklessly undermining legitimate expectations that good faith negotiations with the Palestinian people will bring about a resolution to the problem. If such an assessment is correct, then the current Israeli leaders are actively blocking Palestinians' effort to achieve statehood, and the body governing the Palestinian people in the West Bank and Gaza must consider moving forward 'unilaterally.'[146] As long as the PA acts in compliance with contemporary standards of human rights and rule of law norms, the international community has an ethical obligation to support the Palestinians' efforts. In this sense, the PA should create a model government to replace itself in order to address the fact that the PA lacks sufficient control over Palestine. The PA should organize elections to a newly constituted parliamentary authority and this parliament should act to create a constituent assembly for the purpose of drafting a constitution that meets contemporary normative standards for the State of Palestine. In other words, the form of governance should be democratic, transparent, accountable, responsible, and founded on the rule of law.[147] We would suggest that the PA examine the Badinter Arbitration Commission's deliberations concerning the recognition of the statehood of the Balkan States, including Bosnia and Herzegovina.[148] The Badinter Commission carefully reviewed the constitutions of these new States for the purpose of recognition by the European Union and, later, by the UN. Such recognition was obtained on the basis that the constitutions made the rights and duties of individuals depend on citizenship rather than ethnicity or religious identity.

Recognition by the UN, in any event, is dependent on a showing that the entity claiming sovereignty has the willingness and capability of upholding the principles of the UN Charter.[149] In short, the entity must be

---

[145] J. Weinstein, 'The DC Analysis: Three Takeaways from Obama Admin's Willingness to Support Israel Condemnation at the United Nations,' *The Daily Caller* (21 February 2011).

[146] J. Rubenfeld, 'Unilateralism and Constitutionalism,' 79 *New York University law Review* 1971 (2004).

[147] A. Lichta, C. Goldschmidta and S. Schwartz, 'Culture rules: The Foundations of the Rule of Law and Other Norms of Governance,' 35 *Journal of Comparative Economics* 659 (2007).

[148] P. Radan, 'The Badinter Arbitration Commission and the Partition of Yugoslavia,' 25 *Nationalities Papers* 3 (1997).

[149] A. Orakhelashvili, 'Statehood, Recognition and the UN System: A Unilateral Declaration of Independence in Kosovo,' 12 *Max Planck Yearbook of UN Law* 1 (2008).

peace-loving and committed to human rights and the rule of law. In this sense, the PA should reaffirm the 1988 Declaration of Independence in light of the creation of a new government and a new constitution. This would stress the consistent, continuing demand to recognize the right of the Palestinian people to self-determination and independence and strengthen the perception of coherence and continuity in the development of a Palestinian national identity. The PA may also encourage regional organizations to recognize the new government and State, such as the African Union, the European Union, the Association of Southeast Asian Nations.[150] If a sizable number of individual States recognize Palestinian statehood, this would ease recognition in regional associations and strengthen the momentum of the sovereignty process before the UN.

A veto means that the matter is concluded before the UN. However, there is a procedure, invented by the US, to get around the exercise of a UNSC veto, if that veto undermines the importance of protecting international peace and security. This procedure is known as the 'Uniting for Peace Resolution' and it has been used when the Security Council, because of a veto, was incapable of performing its primary functions concerning the protection and promotion of international peace and security. This Resolution assumes that, since the problem relating to peace and security remains, there is a residual competence in the UNGA to pass a Resolution by a supermajority, permitting UN action to be taken to protect international peace and security.[151] If it is clear that there already is a supermajority that would support the use of the 'Uniting for Peace Resolution' to overcome the exercise of a US veto, the US administration may be less enthusiastic about exercising the veto. However, the PA should still prepare a strategy to sidestep a US veto. In this sense, it may still be of some value to have the UNGA issue a recommendation to the UNSC based on its findings of fact and conclusions of law that the Palestinian claim to statehood is well founded. Technically, UNGA Resolutions are, in general, non-binding. However, the Israelis acted on Resolution 181 to declare their independent status and thereby assumed that it was a legally binding instrument.[152] When the Palestinians present their case for statehood, they are simply asking for a reaffirmation of a pre-existing UNGA Resolution 181, which stipulated that Partition

---

[150] These would include organizations such as the Arab League, the Arab League Educational, Cultural and Scientific Organization, and the Economic and Social Council of the Arab League's Council of Arab Economic Unity.

[151] UN Doc. A/RES/377, 3 November1950.

[152] J. Quigley, *The Case for Palestine: An International Law Perspective* (Duke University Press, 2005), p. 53.

envisioned the creation of an 'Arab State.' It is possible that the issue could be referred for confirmation to the UNSC and, should that happen, it would be important for the PA to seek advance support from the Council. President Abbas' initiative on the admission of Palestine to the UN as an independent State was initially scheduled for consideration in September 2011.[153] However, the US was spared the headache of a veto because the Palestinians failed to gain a nine-vote majority.[154] Some diplomats have stated that, at the present time, Palestinians would only get eight votes in favour of independence and other countries would vote either against independence or abstain.[155]

Conclusion

There are clearly developments in international and human rights law that would benefit the global community with the establishment of a Palestinian State.[156] There is a problem with the UN Security Council veto system, which occasionally works to undermine the efforts of widely held global opinion. It would strengthen the UN, and, consequently, international law, to reinstitute the UNSC bypass mechanism in order to give practical power to the UN General Assembly's voice.[157] It is the next stage in the development of the UN that the united 'nations' include those people who possess all or nearly all the characteristics of a traditional State, but have not yet been recognized; and if statehood is the requirement for a 'nation' to have a meaningful vote, then all nations deserve to be recognized as such.

The Israeli right wing and its conservative political allies have in fact been waging a relentless war against the UN as an institution.[158] This is

---

[153] Fisher, *op. cit.*

[154] In the absence of a veto, a Council resolution still needs nine votes to pass.

[155] P. Worsnip, 'New UN Council no More Favorable to Palestinians: US,' *American Jewish International Relations Institute* (23 January 2012).

[156] W. Nagan and A. Haddad, 'The Legal and Policy Implications of the Possibility of Palestinian Statehood,' 18 *University of California Davis Journal of International Law & Policy* 343 (2012).

[157] C. Joyner, 'UN General Assembly Resolutions and International Law: Rethinking the Contemporary Dynamics of Norm-Creation,' 11 *California Western International Law Journal* 445 (1981); R. Falk, 'On the Quasi-Legislative Competence of the General Assembly,' 60 *American Journal of International Law* 782 (1966).

[158] T. Gedalyahu, 'Muslim Student Attacks UN Rights Council for Anti-Israel Bias,' *Israel National News* (5 April 2011); M. Bard, 'The United Nations and Israel,' *The Jewish Virtual Library* (12 September 2012).

not good for Israel, for the US or for the UN as governing bodies. The recognition of the Palestinian State holds within it the promise of actually moving all parties past this period of international acrimony and impasse.[159]

As scholars, jurists, and human rights practitioners, our ultimate loyalty lies not with any State, organization, or even community—but instead with the values of peace, wellbeing, and freedom from fear for all individuals. The recognition of the State of Palestine is essential for achieving the wider realization of these values, for the people of Palestine, for the people of Israel, and for the people of the United States.

---

[159] I. Scobbie, A. Margalit and S. Hibbin, 'Recognizing Palestinian Statehood,' *Yale Journal of International Affairs* (25 August 2011).

CHAPTER FIVE

THE *DE JURE* STATE OF PALESTINE UNDER BELLIGERENT OCCUPATION: APPLICATION FOR ADMISSION TO THE UNITED NATIONS

BASHEER AL-ZOUGHBI

Admission of New Member States: Law and Politics

The five conditions for admission of new members to the United Nations are traced in Article 4 of the UN Charter. The first paragraph of Article 4 stipulates that 'Membership in the United Nations is open to all other peace-loving States which accept the obligations contained in the present Charter and, in the judgment of the Organization, are able and willing to carry out these obligations.'[1] Hence, any State that is peace-loving, accepts the UN Charter obligations, and is able and willing to carry out the Charter obligations qualifies for membership of the UN. In any event, the assessment of whether an applicant fulfils the criteria mentioned in Article 4 of the Charter is largely subjective rather than objective and has become a political rather than a legal procedure. Rule 134 of the General Assembly Rules of Procedure provides that: 'Any State which desires to become a Member of the United Nations shall submit an application to the Secretary-General. Such application shall contain a declaration, made in a formal instrument that the State in question accepts the obligations contained in the Charter.'[2] The second paragraph of Article 4 of the UN Charter provides that: 'The admission of any such State to

---

[1] UN Charter, 26 June 1945, Article 4.
[2] Rules of Procedure of the General Assembly (New York: United Nations, 1985), embodying amendments and additions adopted by the General Assembly up to 31 December 1984, p. 29.

membership in the United Nations will be effected by a decision of the General Assembly upon the recommendation of the Security Council.'[3]

If and when the Security Council recommends an applicant State for membership, the General Assembly is the organ that acts on the recommendation by a two-thirds majority of its members. If and when the Security Council recommends an applicant State for membership but the General Assembly fails to decide by a two-thirds majority upon the admission of the recommended applicant State, the State cannot be admitted to the UN. Rule 136 of the General Assembly Rules of Procedure provides that, '[i]f the Security Council recommends the applicant State for membership, the General Assembly shall consider whether the applicant is a peace-loving State and is able and willing to carry out the obligations contained in the Charter and shall decide, by a two-thirds majority of the members present and voting, upon its application for membership.'[4] Hence, admission of new member States to the UN is an area of competence shared between the Security Council and the General Assembly.

It is the General Assembly that implements the membership decision by a two-thirds majority based upon the recommendation of the Security Council. If and when the Security Council fails to recommend an applicant State for membership, the General Assembly is not empowered to admit the applicant State. The International Court of Justice (ICJ) ruled in the *Competence of the General Assembly for the Admission of a State to the United Nations* advisory opinion that '. . . the admission of a State to membership in the United Nations, pursuant to paragraph 2 of Article 4 of the Charter, cannot be effected by a decision of the General Assembly when the Security Council has made no recommendation for admission. . . .'[5] Rule 137 of the General Assembly Rules of Procedure stipulates:

'If the Security Council does not recommend the applicant State for membership or postpones the consideration of the application, the General Assembly may, after full consideration of the special report of the Security Council, send the application back to the Council, together with a full record of the discussion in the Assembly, for further consideration and recommendation or report.'[6]

[3] UN Charter, Article 4.
[4] General Assembly Rules of Procedure governing the admission of new Members.
[5] Competence of Assembly regarding Admission to the United Nations, Advisory Opinion: ICJ Reports, 1950, p. 4.
[6] General Assembly Rules of Procedure governing the admission of new Members.

Failure to recommend the admission of an applicant State may be due
to the opposition of at least one State that is a permanent member of the
Security Council, i.e. a negative vote by at least one permanent member
State, and/or non-approval by the requisite majority of 9 votes in favour in
the Security Council. Articles 23 and 27 of the UN Charter were amended
in 1963 and entered into force in 1965.[7] Amended Article 23 increased the
members of the Security Council from 11 to 15.[8] According to amended
Article 27, the decisions of the Security Council on procedural matters
'shall be made by an affirmative vote of nine members [formerly seven],
and on all other matters by an affirmative vote of nine members [formerly
seven], including the concurring votes of the five permanent members.'[9]

Throughout the history of the UN, many applicant States have been
unsuccessful in their first applications for admission to UN membership.
States have been denied the right to UN membership and/or their
applications have been delayed for many years either because of the non-
support of the requisite majority of States in the Security Council and/or a
negative vote by at least one permanent member of the Security Council
on a draft resolution recommending an applicant. For example, Portugal
applied for UN membership in 1946; on 18 August 1947 nine members of
the Security Council supported a draft resolution recommending its
admission to the UN, but the draft resolution was opposed by one
permanent member State and hence Portugal was not admitted at that
time.[10] In fact, it was not admitted to the United Nations until December
1955. Ireland, Italy and Finland are also perfect examples of European
States that secured the support of the requisite majority in the Security
Council for their admission to the UN but were opposed by a permanent
member State. However, they were admitted to UN membership at a later
stage, i.e. in 1955. With regard to Austria's membership of the UN, the
draft resolution recommending its membership on 21 August 1947 was
supported by eight member States but opposed by one permanent member
of the Security Council.[11] However, Austria was eventually admitted to the
UN in 1955 in what came to be known as 'The Package Deal.'

On 15 November 1976, a draft resolution on Vietnam's membership of
the UN was supported by 14 member States of the Security Council but
was opposed by one permanent member State (the United States of

---

[7] United Nations Publications *Basic Facts About the United Nations* (New York:
United Nations, 1980), p.3.
[8] *Ibid.*
[9] *Ibid.*
[10] See, for example, General Assembly Resolution 113(II) D, 17 November 1947.
[11] See, for example, General Assembly Resolution 113(II) H, 17 November 1947.

America) and hence the Security Council could not recommend Vietnam for UN membership. Prior to unification, the draft resolutions recommending the admission of the Democratic Republic of Viet Nam (the north) and the Republic of South Viet Nam were vetoed by the United States of America in 1975. Vietnam was eventually admitted to the United Nations in September 1977. The People's Democratic Republic of Korea (North Korea), supported by the then Union of Soviet Socialist Republics (USSR), was denied admission in 1949, while the application of the Republic of Korea (South Korea) for admission to the UN was vetoed by the USSR. The People's Democratic Republic of Korea and the Republic of Korea were not admitted to UN membership until 1991, i.e., after the end of the cold war.

The foregoing are just a few examples of how some permanent members of the Security Council have opposed the admission of certain States to UN membership for their own reasons. The criteria for admission of new members to the UN are codified in the UN Charter and political intentions should not play a role under any circumstances when deciding on the admission of new member States. As a result of the systematic policy of excluding certain States from membership of the UN, the General Assembly sought an advisory opinion from the ICJ in 1947. The General Assembly requested the ICJ in resolution 113 (II) of 17 November 1947 for an advisory opinion on the following question:

> 'Is a Member of the United Nations which is called upon, in virtue of Article 4 of the Charter, to pronounce itself by its vote, either in the Security Council or in the General Assembly, on the admission of a State to membership in the United Nations, juridically entitled to make its consent to the admission dependent on conditions not expressly provided by paragraph I of the said Article? In particular, can such a Member, while it recognizes the conditions set forth in that provision to be fulfilled by the State concerned, subject its affirmative vote to the additional condition that other States be admitted to membership in the United Nations together with that State?'[12]

In the advisory opinion on *Conditions of Admission of a State to Membership in the United Nations (Article 4 of the Charter)*, the ICJ drew attention to the five conditions for membership of the United Nations explicitly mentioned in Article 4 of the Charter, namely: 'an applicant must (1) be a State; (2) be peace-loving; (3) accept the obligations of the Charter; (4) be able to carry out these obligations; and (5) be willing to do

---

[12] UN Doc. A/RES/113(II) B.

so.'[13] The ICJ further States in the advisory opinion on the *Conditions of Admission of a State to Membership in the United Nations (Article 4 of the Charter)* that:

> 'The natural meaning of the words used leads to the conclusion that these conditions constitute an exhaustive enumeration and are not merely stated by way of guidance or example. The provision would lose its significance and weight, if other conditions, unconnected with those laid down, could be demanded. The conditions stated in paragraph I of Article 4 must therefore be regarded not merely as the necessary conditions, but also as the conditions which suffice.'[14]

The admission of States to UN membership is decided by political organs of the UN and, unfortunately, not by its principal judicial organ or by an impartial depository. However, the political organs have a legal obligation to ensure that the criteria of membership are observed. The ICJ pointed out in the *Conditions of Admission of a State to Membership in the United Nations (Article 4 of the Charter)* that the member States of the Security Council or the General Assembly are '. . . not juridically entitled to make its consent to the admission dependent on conditions not expressly provided by paragraph 1 of the said Article.'[15] It further stated that: 'The political character of an organ cannot release it from the observance of the treaty provisions established by the Charter when they constitute limitations on its powers or criteria for its judgment.'[16] Hence, States are legally required to examine solely whether the rules which are codified in Article 4 of the UN Charter are fulfilled when voting on whether or not to admit an applicant State. If, for example, some States decide to vote against the admission of an applicant State on the basis of political considerations rather than the rules set out in the UN Charter, it may be concluded that such States are violating the UN Charter and abusing their power. States that are members of the Security Council and/or the General Assembly must act in good faith in general and when deciding on this specific matter in particular.

With regard to the application by the *de jure* State of Palestine for UN membership that was submitted to the UN Secretary-General on 23 September 2011, it will come as no surprise if the Security Council decides not to recommend the *de jure* State of Palestine for UN

---

[13] Admission of a State to the United Nations (UN Charter, Article 4), Advisory Opinion: ICJ Reports 1948, p. 57.
[14] *Ibid.*
[15] *Ibid.*
[16] *Ibid.*

membership due to the opposition of at least one permanent member State (the United States of America) and/or to non-approval by the requisite majority in the Security Council. The *de jure* State of Palestine application might even be adjourned *sine die*. The third paragraph of Rule 60 of the Provisional Rules of Procedure of the Security Council provides that: 'If the Security Council does not recommend the applicant State for membership or postpones the consideration of the application, it shall submit a special report to the General Assembly with a complete record of the discussion.'[17] It should be noted that the opposition to the admission of the *de jure* State of Palestine to the UN will be based upon political factors and not on legal ones. At any rate, it is the right of the *de jure* State of Palestine to present proof (a legal memo) that it fulfils the criteria set out in the first paragraph of Article 4 of the UN Charter and, if necessary, have the General Assembly request an advisory opinion on the status of the State of Palestine under international law and on whether it fulfils the criteria of Article 4, paragraph 1, of the UN Charter. General Assembly resolution 506 (VI) of 1952 stipulates that '. . . according to the principles of international justice, it is not possible to deny to States Candidates for membership in the United Nations the right to present proofs on facts such as those recited in the first paragraph of the preamble.'[18] The 'proofs on facts' mentioned in General Assembly resolution 506 (VI) are '. . .the maintenance of friendly relations with other States, the fulfilment of international obligations and the record of a State's willingness and present disposition to submit international claims or controversies to pacific means of settlement established by international law.'[19]

In response to the multiple incidents of blockage of certain States from UN membership as a result of non-recommendation by the Security Council, the General Assembly could not and did not admit them to the UN but urged the Security Council to reconsider their applications. For example, General Assembly resolution 113 (II) G of 1947 'Requests the

---

[17] Provisional Rules of Procedure of the Security Council (adopted by the Security Council at its 1st meeting and amended at its 31st, 41st, 42nd, 44th and 48th meetings, on 9 April, 16 and 17 May, and 6 and 24 June 1946; its 138th and 222nd meetings, on 4 June and 9 December 1947; its 468th meeting, on 28 February 1950; its 1463rd meeting, on 24 January 1969; its 1761st meeting, on 17 January 1974; and its 2410th meeting, on 21 December 1982. Previous versions of the provisional rules of procedure were issued under the symbols S/96 and Rev. 1-6).
[18] UN Doc. A/RES/506(VI) A, Admission of new Members, including the right of candidate States to present proof of the conditions required under Article 4 of the Charter.
[19] *Ibid.*

Security Council to reconsider the application of Finland, in the light of this determination of the Assembly.'[20] The General Assembly further requested an advisory opinion from the ICJ on the *Conditions of Admission of a State to Membership in the United Nations (Article 4 of the Charter)*, as has already been observed, and called on the Security Council to comply with the criteria set forth in the first paragraph of Article 4 of the UN Charter. General Assembly resolution 197 (III) of 1948 'Recommends that each member of the Security Council and of the General Assembly, in exercising its vote on the admission of new Members, should act in accordance with the foregoing opinion of the International Court of Justice.'[21] The General Assembly further established a Special Committee in 1952 to make a detailed study of the question of the admission of States to membership of the United Nations.[22] In addition, the General Assembly established a Committee of Good Offices in 1953 so as 'to consult with members of the Security Council with the object of exploring the possibilities of reaching an understanding which would facilitate the admission of new Members in accordance with Article 4 of the Charter.'[23] The General Assembly also sought another advisory opinion on the *Competence of the General Assembly for the Admission of a State to the United Nations*, as has already been observed.

The Privileges of UN Membership

To put it simply, membership in the UN means that States belong to the intergovernmental organization. A UN member State is also a party to the Statute of the International Court of Justice on an *ipso facto* basis. The first paragraph of Article 93 of the UN Charter States that: 'All Members of the United Nations are *ipso facto* parties to the Statute of the International Court of Justice.'[24] Nevertheless, a non-member State of the UN may become a party to the ICJ Statute. The second paragraph of Article 93 of the UN Charter provides that: 'A State which is not a Member of the United Nations may become a party to the Statute of the International Court of Justice on conditions to be determined in each case by the General Assembly upon the recommendation of the Security Council.'[25] At any rate, any non-UN member State which is a party to a

---

[20] General Assembly Resolution 113(II) G, 17 November 1947.
[21] General Assembly Resolution 197 (III), 8 December 1948.
[22] General Assembly Resolution 620 (VII), 21 December 1952.
[23] General Assembly Resolution 718(VIII), 23 October 1953.
[24] UN Charter, Article 93(1).
[25] *Ibid.,* Article 93(2).

contentious case is required to contribute to the expenses of the ICJ: '3. When a State which is not a Member of the United Nations is a party to a case, the Court shall fix the amount which that party is to contribute towards the expenses of the Court. This provision shall not apply if such State is bearing a share of the expenses of the Court.'[26] Any non-UN member State which desires to accede to the Statute of the International Court of Justice can do so by fulfilling the conditions determined by the General Assembly based upon the recommendation of the Security Council. Switzerland, Liechtenstein, Japan and San Marino complied with the conditions determined by the General Assembly and as a corollary became parties to the Statute of the ICJ[27] prior to becoming UN member States. Similarly Nauru became a State party to the ICJ Statute when it fulfilled the conditions determined by the General Assembly based upon the recommendation of the Security Council.[28] Nauru did not join the United Nations until 1999.

Moreover, a State that is neither a member of the UN nor a party to the ICJ Statute can still access the ICJ. Article 35, paragraph 2, of the ICJ Statute provides that: 'The conditions under which the Court shall be open to other States shall, subject to the special provisions contained in treaties in force, be laid down by the Security Council, but in no case shall such conditions place the parties in a position of inequality before the Court.'[29] Security Council Resolution 9 of 15 October 1946 resolves that:

> '1. The International Court of Justice shall be open to a State which is not a party to the Statute of the International Court of Justice, upon the following condition, namely, that such State shall previously have deposited with the Registrar of the Court a declaration by which it accepts the jurisdiction of the Court, in accordance with the Charter of the United Nations and with the terms and subject to the conditions of the Statute and Rules of the Court, and undertakes to comply in good faith with the decision or decisions of the Court and to accept all the obligations of a Member of the United Nations under Article 94 of the Charter.'[30]

Hence, the *de jure* State of Palestine can lodge a general declaration stating that it accepts the jurisdiction of the ICJ with the Registrar of the Court. In any event, being a party to the ICJ Statute would be of little

---

[26] Statute of the International Court of Justice, 26 June 1945, Article 35(3).

[27] General Assembly resolutions 91 (l); 363 (iv); 805 (VIII); 806 (VIII).

[28] See Security Council Resolution 600, 19 October 1987 and General Assembly Resolution A/RES/42/21, 18 November 1987.

[29] Statute of the International Court of Justice, *op. cit.*, Article 35 (2).

[30] Security Council Resolution 9, 15 October 1946.

value in terms of the Palestinian–Israeli situation, although it would in no way harm it. Even if it became a State party to the ICJ Statute, the *de jure* State of Palestine could not, in contentious proceedings, file an application with the ICJ against the State of Israel simply because such proceedings require the consent of the other party (Israel). Israel will obviously not agree to recognize ICJ jurisdiction with respect to the Palestinian-Israeli situation. Furthermore, Israel has not made a declaration recognizing the jurisdiction of the ICJ as compulsory. Article 36, paragraph 2, of the ICJ Statute provides that: 'The States parties to the present Statute may at any time declare that they recognize as compulsory *ipso facto* and without special agreement, in relation to any other State accepting the same obligation, the jurisdiction of the Court in all legal disputes. . .'[31] With regard to advisory opinions, the ICJ can deliver such opinions on legal questions even if they concern non-UN member States, as in the case of the advisory opinion on the *Legal Consequences of the Construction of a Wall in the Occupied Palestinian Territory* delivered in 2004. Article 96, paragraph 1, of the UN Charter provides that: 'The General Assembly or the Security Council may request the International Court of Justice to give an advisory opinion on any legal question.'[32]

If and/or when the *de jure* State of Palestine is admitted to the UN, it will have a right to vote on General Assembly draft resolutions just like any other member State. Article 18, paragraph 1, of the UN Charter provides that: 'Each member of the General Assembly shall have one vote.'[33] In addition, Palestine may become a temporary member of other principal organs of the United Nations, including the Economic and Social Council and the Security Council if and/or when it is admitted to the UN. It is worth bearing in mind that UN membership also entails financial obligations. Article 17, paragraphs 1 and 2, of the UN Charter provide that: '1. The General Assembly shall consider and approve the budget of the Organization. 2. The expenses of the Organization shall be borne by the Members as apportioned by the General Assembly.'[34]

Blocking Palestine's admission to the United Nations will not alter its *de jure* statehood under international law. As noted above, Austria, Italy, Finland and Portugal are just some of the countries that were blocked from admission to the UN for many years, but this conduct did not undermine their statehood under international law. Moreover, Switzerland was admitted to the UN only in 2002 when it expressed the desire for

---

[31] Statute of the International Court of Justice, *op. cit.*
[32] UN Charter, Article 96.
[33] *Ibid.*, Article 18.
[34] *Ibid.*, Article 17.

membership. Very few countries have decided against membership of the United Nations. They include the Holy See and the Cook Islands, but this has in no way diminished their statehood under international law.

'The question of whether the Cook Islands was an 'independent' entity, i.e. a State, was also raised. For a period of time . . . it followed that the status of the Cook Islands was not one of sovereign independence in the juridical sense . . . However, in 1984, an application by the Cook Islands for membership in the World Health Organization[35/] was approved by the World Health Assembly. . . . In the circumstances, the Secretary-General felt that the question of the status, as a State, of the Cook Islands, had been duly decided in the affirmative by the World Health Assembly, whose membership was fully representative of the international community. The guidance the Secretary-General might have obtained from the General Assembly, had he requested it, would evidently have been substantially identical to the decision of the World Health Assembly.'[36]

The United Nations does not recognize States; the United Nations admits States to membership based upon recommendations of the Security Council that are carried into effect by the General Assembly, as has been observed. States as subjects of international law were established before the United Nations and even long before the League of Nations came into being. States created the United Nations by ratifying the UN Charter, but the United Nations did not and does not create States but merely admits them to membership. The United Nations is certainly the most prominent intergovernmental organization, but it is not the only one. Indeed, the statehood of the Cook Islands was established and affirmed without the necessity of being a member of the UN. The issue of recognition of States is subject to the jurisdiction of States. Article 7 of the Montevideo Convention on the Rights and Duties of States provides that: 'The recognition of a State may be express or tacit. The latter results from any act which implies the intention of recognizing the new State.'[37] In any event, a State does not necessarily and/or precisely need to be a member of the United Nations to accede to or to ratify the overwhelming majority of the international treaties under public international law, including international humanitarian law, international human rights law, international criminal law and international diplomatic law.

[35] 754 United Nations Treaty Series (UNTS) 73.
[36] UN Office of Legal Affairs, *Summary of Practice of the Secretary-General as Depositary of Multilateral Treaties* (New York: United Nations, 1999), p. 24.
[37] Montevideo Convention on the Rights and Duties of States, 26 December 1933.

Joining International Treaties

International Diplomatic Law

The *de jure* State of Palestine can and must accede to treaties under international diplomatic law and the law of treaties. Thus, the *de jure* State of Palestine can easily accede to the Vienna Convention on Diplomatic Relations of 1961, the Vienna Convention on Consular Relations of 1963 and the Vienna Convention on the Law of Treaties of 1969. The *de jure* State of Palestine's admission to UNESCO membership on 23 November 2011 has made it easier to accede to these conventions. Article 48 of the Vienna Convention on Diplomatic Relations of 1961 reads as follows:

'The present Convention shall be open for signature by all States Members of the United Nations or of any of the specialized agencies or Parties to the Statute of the International Court of Justice, and by any other State invited by the General Assembly of the United Nations to become a Party to the Convention, as follows: until 31 October 1961 at the Federal Ministry for Foreign Affairs of Austria and subsequently, until 31 March 1962, at the United Nations Headquarters in New York.'[38]

Article 50 of the Vienna Convention on Diplomatic Relations further provides that: 'The present Convention shall remain open for accession by any State belonging to any of the four categories mentioned in Article 48. The instruments of accession shall be deposited with the Secretary-General of the United Nations.'[39] Hence, the *de jure* State of Palestine must deposit an instrument of accession with the Secretary-General of the United Nations based on category number 2, i.e. its membership of a UN specialized agency. Similarly, the Vienna Convention on Consular Relations of 1963 stipulates that accession or signature is open to all States Members of the United Nations or of any of its specialized agencies, or States parties to the Statute of the International Court of Justice, or by any other State invited by the General Assembly to become a party.[40] The Vienna Convention on the Law of Treaties of 1969 stipulates that

---

[38] Vienna Convention on Diplomatic Relations, 18 April 1961, 500 UNTS 95, Article 48.
[39] *Ibid.*, Article 50.
[40] Vienna Convention on Consular Relations, 24 April 1963, 596 UNTS 261, Articles 74 and 76

accession is open to all States belonging to any of the above categories and further to any State member of the International Atomic Energy Agency.[41]

> 'Since that difficulty did not arise with regard to membership in the specialized agencies, where there is no 'veto' procedure, a number of those States became members of specialized agencies, and as such were in essence recognized as States by the international community. Accordingly, and in order to allow for as wide a participation as possible, a number of conventions then provided that they were also open for participation to States members of specialized agencies. This type of entry-into-force clause was called the 'Vienna formula.' Thus, whenever a treaty specified, under the Vienna formula or otherwise, which entities could become parties thereto, the Secretary-General had no difficulty in complying with the participation provision of the treaty concerned.'[42]

Even if Palestine was not a member of any of the UN specialized agencies, it could easily secure an invitation from the General Assembly to accede to any of the said conventions. 'The 'practice of the General Assembly' referred to in the above-mentioned understanding is to be found in unequivocal indications from the Assembly that it considers a particular entity to be a State even though it does not fall within the 'Vienna formula'.'[43] The accession of the *de jure* State of Palestine to the said conventions under international diplomatic law is crucial, as Palestine has been recognized by more than 130 States. The *de jure* State of Palestine must further invite those third States to establish diplomatic missions in its *de jure* capital, i.e. East Jerusalem although it is under occupation, and the head of the mission of the sending State must present his or her credentials to the receiving State, i.e. to the *de jure* State of Palestine. The immunities and inviolabilities of the members of the mission and their premises and other objects recognized under conventional and/or customary international diplomatic law must be respected, protected and implemented even in an occupied territory.

Security Council resolution 478 of 20 August 1980 called upon '[t]hose States that have established diplomatic missions at Jerusalem to withdraw such missions from the Holy City'[44] on account of the enactment by the Israeli Knesset of a basic law in 1980 entitled 'Jerusalem, Capital of

---

[41] Vienna Convention on the Law of Treaties, 23 May 1969, 27 January 1980, 1155 UNTS 331, Articles 81 and 83.
[42] UN Office of Legal Affairs, *Summary of Practice of the Secretary-General as Depositary of Multilateral Treaties* (New York: United Nations, 1999), p. 22.
[43] *Ibid.*, p. 23.
[44] UN Doc. S/RES/478 (1980), 20 August 1980.

Israel.' Jerusalem became a city without embassies by virtue of the principle that the diplomatic missions of the sending States in the receiving State (Israel) must not be located in the occupied section of Jerusalem. The opening of embassies in the occupied section of Jerusalem would be legal only if the sending States' diplomatic relations were to be established with the *de jure* receiving State, i.e. Palestine. In this case, the head of the mission would have to present his/her credentials to the *de jure* State of Palestine and not to Israel, the occupying power. Following any accession to the Vienna Convention on Diplomatic Relations, the *de jure* State of Palestine must accede to its 1963 Optional Protocol concerning the Compulsory Settlement of Disputes. Article I provides that: 'Disputes arising out of the interpretation or application of the Convention shall lie within the compulsory jurisdiction of the International Court of Justice . . . .'[45] Accession by the *de jure* State of Palestine to the 1963 Optional Protocol concerning the Compulsory Settlement of Disputes will show that the *de jure* State of Palestine is willing under all circumstances to submit to the available mechanisms for the peaceful settlement of disputes.

International Human Rights Law

The *de jure* State of Palestine can accede without UN membership to eight of the nine core international human rights treaties. The International Covenant on Economic, Social and Cultural Rights, the International Convention on the Elimination of All Forms of Racial Discrimination and the International Covenant on Civil and Political Rights are open for signature by 'any State Member of the United Nations or member of any of its specialized agencies, by any State Party to the Statute of the International Court of Justice, and by any other State which has been invited by the General Assembly of the United Nations to become a Party to the present Covenant.'[46] Hence, the *de jure* State of Palestine, though not a member of the UN, can accede to such treaties by virtue, *inter alia*, of its membership of any UN specialized agency.[47]

---

[45] Optional Protocol concerning the Compulsory Settlement of Disputes, 24 April 1963, 596 UNTS 487, Article 1

[46] International Convention on the Elimination of All Forms of Racial Discrimination, General Assembly Resolution 2106 (XX) of 21 December 1965, Article 17. See also of the International Covenant on Economic, Social and Cultural Rights, General Assembly Resolution 2200A (XXI) of 16 December 1966, Article 26.

[47] On 31 October 2011 the General Conference of UNESCO voted to admit Palestine as a Member State of UNESCO.

Meanwhile, the Convention on the Rights of the Child, the Convention against Torture and Other Cruel, Inhuman or Degrading Treatment or Punishment, the Convention on the Elimination of All Forms of Discrimination against Women, the Convention on the Rights of Persons with Disabilities and the International Convention on the Protection of the Rights of All Migrant Workers and Members of Their Families are open to accession by all States, regardless of whether they are members of the United Nations. Article 26 of the Convention against Torture and Other Cruel, Inhuman or Degrading Treatment or Punishment stipulates that: 'This Convention is open to accession by all States. Accession shall be effected by the deposit of an instrument of accession with the Secretary-General of the United Nations.'[48] Hence, the *de jure* State of Palestine must, without delay, deposit an instrument of accession to all these conventions with the Secretary-General of the UN. Article (18) of the Third Draft Constitution for a Palestinian State provides that: 'The State of Palestine shall abide by the Universal Declaration of Human Rights and shall seek to join other international covenants and charters that safeguard human rights.'[49] The *de jure* State of Palestine, under colonial occupation, is certainly eligible to accede to the aforementioned conventions:

'. . . a number of treaties adopted by the General Assembly were open to participation by 'all States' without further specifications . . . In reply to questions raised in connection with the interpretation to be given to the all States formula, the Secretary-General has, on a number of occasions,[50] stated that there are certain areas in the world whose status is not clear. If he were to receive an instrument of accession from any such area, he would be in a position of considerable difficulty unless the Assembly gave him explicit directives on the areas coming within the 'any State' or 'all States' formula. He would not wish to determine, on his own initiative, the highly political and controversial question of whether or not the areas whose status was unclear were States . . . . He therefore stated that when

---

[48] Convention against Torture and Other Cruel, Inhuman or Degrading Treatment or Punishment; General Assembly Resolution 39/46 of 10 December 1984, Article 27(1).

[49] Constitution of the State of Palestine, revised third draft of 4 May 2003. Quoted in Nathan J. Brown, *The Third Draft Constitution for a Palestinian State: Translation and Commentary*, Palestinian Centre for Policy and Survey Research, 2003, p. 14.

[50] See, *inter alia*, the Statement of the Secretary-General at the 258th plenary meeting of the General Assembly, at the eighteenth session, on 18 November 1963 (Official Records of the General Assembly, Eighteenth Session, 258th plenary meeting); and the Statement by the Secretary-General at the 918th meeting of the Sixth Committee, on 25 October 1966 (*ibid.*, Sixth Committee, 918th meeting).

the 'any State' or 'all States' formula was adopted, he would be able to
implement it only if the General Assembly provided him with the complete
list of the States coming within the formula, other than those falling within
the 'Vienna formula,' i.e. States that are Members of the United Nations or
members of the specialized agencies, or Parties to the Statute of the
International Court of Justice.'[51]

Hence, the *de jure* State of Palestine is *ipso facto* and *ipso jure* listed
under the 'all States formula' as a corollary of the 'Vienna formula.'
Based on its membership of the World Health Organization and other UN
specialized agencies, 'the Secretary-General considered that the Cook
Islands could henceforth be included in the 'all States' formula, were it to
wish to participate in treaties deposited with the Secretary-General.'[52] The
International Convention for the Protection of All Persons from Enforced
Disappearance is only open to accession by member States of the UN.
Article 38, paragraph 3, of the International Convention for the Protection
of All Persons from Enforced Disappearance reads as follows: 'This
Convention is open to accession by all Member States of the United
Nations. Accession shall be effected by the deposit of an instrument of
accession with the Secretary-General.'[53] Be that as it may, the *de jure*
State of Palestine will still be bound, like any other non-UN member State,
by the customary provisions of the Convention, notwithstanding its non-
accession. Moving from international human rights law to the law of the
sea, we find that the United Nations Convention on the Law of the Sea is
open for accession by all States. According to Article 305, paragraph 1, of
the United Nations Convention on the Law of the Sea: 'This Convention
shall be open for signature by: (a) all States.'[54] Article 307 of the
Convention provides that: 'This Convention shall remain open for
accession by States and the other entities referred to in article 305 . . . .
The instruments of accession shall be deposited with the Secretary-
General of the United Nations.'[55]

---

[51] United Nations, Prepared by the Treaty Section of the Office of Legal Affairs,
Summary of Practice of the Secretary-General as Depositary of Multilateral
Treaties (New York: United Nations, 1999), p. 23.
[52] *Ibid.*, p. 24.
[53] International Convention for the Protection of All Persons from Enforced
Disappearance, entered into force on 23 December 2010, Article 38.
[54] UN Convention on the Law of the Sea, 10 December 1982.
[55] *Ibid.*

International Humanitarian Law

With regard to international humanitarian law treaties, there is no condition which requires States to be members of the UN in order to ratify or accede to the treaties on the laws and customs of war. The first treaties under international humanitarian law were obviously codified long before the existence of the UN. Even after the establishment of the UN, ratification or accession of international humanitarian law treaties was not limited to UN member States. Article 156 of the Fourth Geneva Convention provides that: 'Accessions shall be notified in writing to the Swiss Federal Council, and shall take effect six months after the date on which they are received.'[56] Article 94 of the Protocol Additional to the Geneva Conventions of 12 August 1949, and relating to the Protection of Victims of International Armed Conflicts (Protocol I, 1977), provides that: 'This Protocol shall be open for accession by any Party to the Conventions which has not signed it. The instruments of accession shall be deposited with the depositary.'[57] The Swiss Federal Council is the depositary of Additional Protocol I and the four Geneva Conventions.

In its letter of 21 June 1989, the Permanent Observer of Palestine to the United Nations Office at Geneva informed the Swiss Federal Council that the Executive Council of the Palestine Liberation Organization (PLO) had decided on 4 May 1989 to accede to the four Geneva Conventions of 1949 and their two Protocols of 1977.[58] The Swiss Federal Council reply on 13 September 1989 was relatively neutral. It stated that the Council was not in a position to decide whether the letter sent by the Permanent Observer of Palestine to the United Nations Office at Geneva constituted an instrument of accession, 'due to the uncertainty within the international community as to the existence or non-existence of a State of Palestine.'[59] The PLO had also previously attempted to accede to the four Geneva Conventions and had expressed its formal position and decision to accede both to the Conventions and to Additional Protocol I. In 1969 the PLO informed the Swiss Federal Political Department of its decision to accede

---

[56] Geneva Convention IV relative to the Protection of Civilian Persons in Time of War, 12 August 1949.

[57] Protocol Additional to the Geneva Conventions of 12 August 1949, and relating to the Protection of Victims of International Armed Conflicts (Protocol I), 8 June 1977.

[58] States party to the Geneva Conventions and their Additional Protocols, available at: http://www.icrc.org/ihl.nsf/WebSign?ReadForm&id=375&ps=P.

[59] *Ibid.*

to the four Geneva Conventions.[60] In 1974 the PLO reiterated its
declaration that it wished to accede to the Geneva Conventions.[61] On 7
June 1982, the PLO made a unilateral declaration to the Swiss Federal
Council that it would accede to Additional Protocol I.[62] A remarkable
aspect of the 1989 PLO decision to accede to the four Geneva Conventions
of 1949 and their two Additional Protocols is that it was communicated to
the States parties to the Geneva Conventions by the Swiss Federal
Council. It should, moreover, be noted that the 1989 PLO decision
followed the proclamation of the State of Palestine on 15 November 1988.

Palestine's attempt to accede to the four Geneva Convections
notwithstanding its status as a *de jure* State under occupation is not
without precedent under international law. The Provisional Government
of the Algerian Republic acceded to the 1949 Geneva Conventions on 20
June 1960 even though Algeria only became an independent State in July
1962 after it was liberated from French occupation. The decision of
Palestine to accede to the four Geneva Conventions and their Additional
Protocols must be reiterated before the Swiss Federal Council. It must be
backed up by the legal argument that a *de jure* State of Palestine, albeit
under belligerent occupation, exists under international law and by a
reference to the emergence of a customary international law presumption
that the Occupied Palestinian Territory (OPT) of 1967 is a *de jure* State of
Palestine, a conclusion supported by the State practice of recognizing the
State of Palestine, and that Israel has the status of an occupying colonizing
power in the OPT. The Cook Islands and the Holy See are perfect
examples of States parties to international conventions, including the four
Geneva Conventions of 1949, although they are non-UN member States.

The Convention on the Prohibition of the Use, Stockpiling, Production
and Transfer of Anti-Personnel Mines and on their Destruction of 18
September 1997 does not require a State that wishes to accede to the
Convention to be a member of the UN. Article 16, paragraph 2, provides
that: 'It shall be open for accession by any State which has not signed the
Convention.'[63] Article 21 stipulates: 'The Secretary-General of the United

---

[60] G. McDougal, 'Palestinian Prisoners Captured in the Israeli Invasion of
Lebanon: Are They Prisoners of War?' *The Seventh United Nations Seminar on the
Question of Palestine*: 'The inalienable rights of the Palestinian people,' 9-13
August 1982, Dakar, Senegal.
[61] Rosas, *The Legal Status of Prisoners of War* (Helsinki, 1976), p. 208, quoted in
McDougal, *op. cit.*
[62] *Ibid.*
[63] Convention on the Prohibition of the Use, Stockpiling, Production and Transfer
of Anti-Personnel Mines and on Their Destruction, Oslo, 18 September 1997.

Nations is hereby designated as the Depositary of this Convention.'[64] The Chemical Weapons Convention is a further example of a treaty to which any State can accede without being a member of the UN. Article XX of the Chemical Weapons Convention provides that: 'Any State which does not sign this Convention before its entry into force may accede to it at any time thereafter.'[65] Article XXIII of the Convention stipulates: 'The Secretary General of the United Nations is hereby designated as the Depositary of this Convention . . . .'[66] Moreover, membership of the UN is not a prerequisite for a State to sign and/or ratify or accede to the Convention on Certain Conventional Weapons (CCW). Article 4 of the Convention provides that:

'1. This Convention is subject to ratification, acceptance or approval by the Signatories. Any State which has not signed this Convention may accede to it.
2. The instruments of ratification, acceptance, approval or accession shall be deposited with the Depositary.'[67]

Article 10 of the Convention stipulates:

'1. The Secretary-General of the United Nations shall be the Depositary of this Convention and of its annexed Protocols.'[68]

The *de jure* State of Palestine should also accede to the Convention for the Protection of Cultural Property in the Event of Armed Conflict, the Protocol to the Convention for the Protection of Cultural Property in the Event of Armed Conflict of 1954, and the Second Protocol of March 1999 to the Hague Convention of 1954 for the Protection of Cultural Property in the Event of Armed Conflict. Article 32 of the Convention for the Protection of Cultural Property in the Event of Armed Conflict provides that:

'From the date of its entry into force, the present Convention shall be open for accession by all States mentioned in Article 30 which have not signed

---

[64] *Ibid.*
[65] Convention on the Prohibition of the Development, Production, Stockpiling and Use of Chemical Weapons and on their Destruction (Chemical Weapons Convention), Paris, 13 January 1993.
[66] *Ibid.*
[67] The Convention on Prohibitions or Restrictions on the Use of Certain Conventional Weapons Which May Be Deemed to Be Excessively Injurious or to Have Indiscriminate Effects, 21 December 2001.
[68] *Ibid.*

it, as well as any other State invited to accede by the Executive Board of
the United Nations Educational, Scientific and Cultural Organization.
Accession shall be effected by the deposit of an instrument of accession
with the Director-General of the United Nations Educational, Scientific
and Cultural Organization.'[69]

International Criminal Law

Turning now to international criminal law, it should be noted that the
Rome Statute of the International Criminal Court (ICC) is open for
accession by any State, regardless of whether it is a UN member. Article
125, paragraph 3, of the Rome Statute of the ICC provides that: 'This
Statute shall be open to accession by all States. Instruments of accession
shall be deposited with the Secretary-General of the United Nations.'[70] On
21 January 2009 the Government of Palestine made a declaration
recognizing the jurisdiction of the International Criminal Court in
conformity with Article 12, paragraph 3, of the Rome Statute.

The Office of the Prosecutor issued a Statement in 2012 to the effect
that it was not in a position to determine whether Palestine is a State for
the purpose of accepting the declaration that had been made in line with
Article 12 of the Rome Statute. It subsequently claimed that: 'In
interpreting and applying Article 12 of the Rome Statute, the Office has
assessed that it is for the relevant bodies at the United Nations or the
Assembly of States Parties to make the legal determination whether
Palestine qualifies as a State . . . .'[71] It further stated that: 'The Rome
Statute provides no authority for the Office of the Prosecutor to adopt a
method to define the term 'State' under article 12(3) which would be at
variance with that established for the purpose of article 12(1).'[72] It seems
that the Office of the Prosecutor ignored the fact that the *de jure* State of
Palestine belongs to the 'Vienna formula' and *ipso facto* and *ipso jure* to
the 'all States formula,' as has been shown above. Be that as it may, the
situation of Palestine is clearly that of a *de jure* State under *de facto*
colonial occupation. The *de jure* State of Palestine must accede to the
Rome Statute of the ICC under Article 125 by depositing its instrument of
accession with the Secretary-General of the UN. The instrument of

---

[69] Convention for the Protection of Cultural Property in the Event of Armed
Conflict, 14 May 1954.
[70] Rome Statute of the International Criminal Court, 1 July 1998.
[71] The Office of the Prosecutor, International Criminal Court, *Situation in
Palestine* (3 April 2012).
[72] *Ibid.*

accession to the Rome Statute should preferably be submitted after it has acceded to international human rights law and international diplomatic law treaties under the 'Vienna formula,' taking into consideration the particularity of the *de jure* State of Palestine.

Many Israeli individuals, both members and non-members of the armed forces, have been involved in war crimes. Grave breaches of the Geneva Conventions of 1949 and other serious violations of international humanitarian law have been committed by Israeli nationals. Thus, wilful killing, torture, inhuman treatment, extensive destruction or appropriation of property without military necessity, unlawful deportation or transfer, and unlawful confinement constitute, *inter alia*, grave breaches of the Fourth Geneva Convention and entail individual criminal responsibility. Other serious violations of international humanitarian law also constitute war crimes under international criminal law. For example, transferring the occupant's civilian population into an occupied territory entails individual criminal responsibility as a serious violation of international humanitarian law and is further codified as one of the grave breaches of Additional Protocol I.

Israeli war crime suspects have not hitherto faced trial in criminal courts, either nationally or internationally, even though every State party to the Fourth Geneva Convention is under a legal obligation to 'search for persons alleged to have committed, or to have ordered to be committed, such grave breaches, and shall bring such persons, regardless of their nationality, before its own courts.'[73] Resolution XXIII adopted by the International Conference on Human Rights in 1968 notes the failure of States to ensure respect for international humanitarian law. Resolution XXIII of 1968 notes in its preamble that 'States parties to the Red Cross Geneva Conventions sometimes fail to appreciate their responsibility to take steps to ensure the respect of these humanitarian rules in all circumstances by other States, even if they are not themselves directly involved in an armed conflict.'[74] In light of the foregoing, Israel fears any prosecution of its nationals, including State officials, as suspects in the national courts of third States or in competent international criminal courts or tribunals such as the ICC.

The *de jure* State of Palestine must also accede to the International Convention on the Suppression and Punishment of the Crime of Apartheid. Article XIII of the International Convention provides that: 'The present Convention is open for signature by all States. Any State which

---

[73] Article 146, Geneva Convention IV, *op. cit.*
[74] Human Rights in Armed Conflicts, Resolution XXIII adopted by the International Conference on Human Rights, Tehran, 12 May 1968.

does not sign the Convention before its entry into force may accede to it.'[75] Article XIV, paragraph 2, stipulates: 'Accession shall be effected by the deposit of an instrument of accession with the Secretary-General of the United Nations.'[76] Palestine can also accede to the Convention on the Non-Applicability of Statutory Limitations to War Crimes and Crimes Against Humanity notwithstanding its non-UN membership.[77] The same applies to the Supplementary Convention on the Abolition of Slavery, the Slave Trade, and Institutions and Practices Similar to Slavery of 7 September 1956. Based on its UNESCO membership, the *de jure* State of Palestine is *ipso jure* entitled to accede to the Supplementary Convention.[78]

UN Specialized Agencies

The *de jure* State of Palestine can also approach UN specialized agencies to apply for membership without being a member State of the UN. Palestine applied for membership of the World Health Organisation (WHO) in 1989 but its application was postponed in a compromise decision of the World Health Assembly, which was adopted by 83 votes to 47, with 20 abstentions. This compromise vote was as a result of the exercise by the United States of America of political and economic pressure on WHO member States and the WHO *per se*. Article 3 of the WHO Constitution stipulates: 'Membership in the Organization shall be open to all States.'[79] Moreover, Article 6 of the WHO Constitution reads:

'Subject to the conditions of any agreement between the United Nations and the Organization, approved pursuant to Chapter XVI, States which do not become Members in accordance with Articles 4 and 5 may apply to become Members and shall be admitted as Members when their application has been approved by a simple majority vote of the Health Assembly.'[80]

---

[75] International Convention on the Suppression and Punishment of the Crime of Apartheid 1974, 1015 UNTS 243.

[76] *Ibid.*

[77] Convention on the Non-Applicability of Statutory Limitations to War Crimes and Crimes Against Humanity, UN General Assembly Resolution 2391 (XXIII), annex, 23 UN GAOR Supp. (No. 18) at 40, UN Doc. A/7218 (1968), Articles 5 and 7

[78] Supplementary Convention on the Abolition of Slavery, the Slave Trade, and Institutions and Practices Similar to Slavery, 7 September 1956, Article 11(2)

[79] Constitution of the World Health Organization, 22 July 1946.

[80] *Ibid.*

On 5 October 2011, the Executive Board of the United Nations Educational, Scientific and Cultural Organization (UNESCO) voted on a recommendation to admit Palestine to the Organization. Article II, paragraph II, of the UNESCO Constitution provides that 'States not members of the United Nations Organization may be admitted to membership of the Organization, upon recommendation of the Executive Board, by a two-thirds majority vote of the General Conference.'[81] UNESCO's General Conference voted on 31 October 2011 to admit Palestine as a member State of UNESCO.[82] The *de jure* State of Palestine, under colonial occupation, became a member State of UNESCO on 23 November 2011.

Palestine's attempts to join UN specialized agencies must be amplified. The *de jure* State of Palestine must also attempt to join the International Telecommunication Union. This is possible without being a member of the UN: 'If the State is not a Member of the United Nations: the application for membership needs to have secured approval by two-thirds of the Member States of the Union.'[83] Palestine must also join the Universal Postal Union (UPU): 'Any non-member country of the United Nations may become a UPU member provided that its request is approved by at least two-thirds of the member countries of the UPU. The UPU has now 192 member countries.'[84] Article 5, paragraph 1, of the Statutes of the World Tourism Organization provides that: 'Full membership of the Organization shall be open to all sovereign States.'[85] Moreover, Article 5, paragraph 3, of the Statutes stipulates that: 'Other States may become Full Members of the Organization if their candidatures are approved by the General Assembly by a majority of two-thirds of the Full Members present and voting provided that said majority is a majority of the Full Members of the Organization.'[86] The International Labour Organization is another UN specialized agency that the *de jure* State of Palestine must seek to join. Article 1, paragraph 4, of the ILO Constitution reads as follows:

---

[81] Constitution of the United Nations Educational, Scientific and Cultural Organization, 16 November 1945.

[82] The vote was carried by 107 votes in favour of admission and 14 votes against, with 52 abstentions.

[83] State Membership - How to become a Member State; available at: http://www.itu.int/members/mbStates2/index.html.

[84] UPU member countries; available at: http://www.upu.int/en/the-upu/member-countries.html

[85] Statutes of the World Tourism Organization, 27 September 1970.

[86] *Ibid.*

'The General Conference of the International Labour Organization may also admit Members to the Organization by a vote concurred in by two-thirds of the delegates attending the session, including two-thirds of the Government delegates present and voting. Such admission shall take effect on the communication to the Director-General of the International Labour Office by the government of the new Member of its formal acceptance of the obligations of the Constitution of the Organization.'[87]

Israel lives in fear of the peaceful submission of applications by the *de jure* State of Palestine to join significant international organizations such as the UN specialized agencies. Successful applications by the *de jure* State of Palestine to join international organizations will place it on an equal footing with other States. If and when it is admitted, the status of Israel, the occupying power, as a member State will be equivalent to that of another member State, i.e. the *de jure* State of Palestine under colonial occupation. Israel also fears that the *de jure* State of Palestine will accede to public international law treaties. As demonstrated above, the *de jure* State of Palestine is eligible to accede to many international treaties under international humanitarian law, international criminal law, international human rights law and international diplomatic law. Accession by the *de jure* State of Palestine to the Rome Statute of the International Criminal Court is one of Israel's greatest concerns and fears in this regard.

Israel also fears the growing number of State communiqués recognizing the existence of a *de jure* State of Palestine within pre-1967 Six-Day-War borders. The Icelandic Parliament, known as the Althingi, voted on 29 November 2011 to entrust the Government of Iceland with the recognition of the State of Palestine within pre-1967 Six-Day-War borders: 'Althingi resolves to entrust the government to recognize Palestine as an independent and sovereign State within the pre-1967 Six Day War borders.'[88] The Icelandic Foreign Ministry issued a diplomatic note on 15 December 2011 attaching an instrument of recognition of Palestine as an independent and sovereign State within the pre-1967 Six-Day-War borders.[89]

With regard to Palestinian refugees, their rights under international law are by no means prejudiced by the question as to whether the *de jure* State

[87] Constitution of the International Labour Organization, 1919, with amendments 1922-1972.
[88] Parliamentary Resolution on the recognition of the independence and sovereignty of Palestine, available at: http://www.mfa.is/media/MFA_pdf/Alyktun-Althingis-um-Palestinu_enska.pdf.
[89] Iceland Recognizes Palestine; available at: http://www.mfa.is/speeches-and-articles/nr/6847.

of Palestine is admitted to the UN. The rights of Palestinian refugees can never be undermined by the membership or non-membership of the *de jure* State of Palestine in any UN specialized agency, by its accession to international treaties or by its recognition or non-recognition by third States. Palestinian refugees are entitled to full reparations in accordance with customary international law, i.e. restitution, compensation and satisfaction. In its advisory opinion on *Questions relating to Settlers of German Origin in Poland,* the Permanent Court of International Justice (PCIJ) proclaimed that: 'Private rights acquired under existing law do not cease on a change of sovereignty . . . . It can hardly be maintained that, although the law survives, private rights acquired under it have perished.'[90]

In sum, the *de jure* State of Palestine must, without delay or any hesitation and notwithstanding its non-UN membership, deposit instruments of accession to treaties and other instruments under public international law, including international human rights law, international humanitarian law, international criminal law and international diplomatic law. As demonstrated above, the overwhelming majority of public international law treaties do not require the acceding State to be a member of the United Nations. The depositaries of the aforesaid international treaties must act in good faith and in accordance with the applicable law of accession and hence they must not preclude the accession of the *de jure* State of Palestine. The guidelines for the Secretary-General and any other depositary include compliance with: 'The provisions of the treaty; (b) Customary treaty law, including as it may be deemed codified by various conventions on the matter.'[91]

Accession by the *de jure* State of Palestine to the aforementioned treaties will show the international community that the *de jure* State of Palestine is not affected by non-UN membership; it will further provide assurances that Palestine, as a *de jure* State, is willing to assume its obligations under public international law and to work for its advancement under these international instruments. The *de jure* State of Palestine looks forward with confidence to the early ending of the Israeli colonial occupation of its State, i.e. the State existing on the 1967 borders. The successful attempt to join UNESCO constitutes one step forward in the process of becoming a member of other UN specialized agencies. Being a non-UN member State does not prejudice the status of the *de jure* State of Palestine under international law.

---

[90] Questions relating to Settlers of German Origin in Poland, PCIJ, Series B., No. 6, 1925.
[91] UN Office of Legal Affairs, *Summary of Practice of the Secretary-General as Depositary of Multilateral Treaties* (New York: United Nations, 1999), p. 4.

PART II

SPECIFIC IMPLICATIONS OF PALESTINE'S
UN MEMBERSHIP

This part examines a number of selected implications of the membership of Palestine in the United Nations. Each chapter tackles a different aspect of Palestine's admission to the UN, starting with the State's obligations towards the international community and to its inhabitants in terms of human rights. The ongoing applicability of international humanitarian law and the changes that might occur are also considered, with particular reference to conventions concerning prisoners of war and civilians. The legal status of Jerusalem following Palestine's admission is analysed and the question of water resources and potential disputes arising from their distribution is explored. The membership of Palestine in other international organizations is touched upon, with membership of the World Trade Organization being taken as a case in point. As indicated elsewhere, Palestine's membership has many more implications, but the chapters focus on substantive aspects of what may be expected to occur with respect to key issues.

Chapter Six explores the legal obligations of the State of Palestine to the international community, focusing on the International Covenant on Economic, Social and Cultural Rights (ICESCR) as a typical case. It reminds us that Palestine, in parallel with its efforts to become a member of the UN, needs to take the implications of joining such an organization seriously. Admission to the UN encompasses many rights, as shown in other chapters of this book, but it simultaneously establishes responsibilities. One of these responsibilities is to respect, protect and fulfil the human rights of those living under the State's jurisdiction. The inability of the State to guarantee such rights might entail its admission to the club of failing States. A key indicator of the State's readiness to comply with its obligations is the establishment of a legal system that is consistent with international human rights law. The chapter seeks to assess the applicable legislation in Palestine in the light of ICESCR provisions and suggests ways of reforming domestic law to align it with the State's global undertakings in order to create a successful State scenario.

Chapter Seven argues that the prospect of Palestine becoming a member of the UN may have crucial legal implications for the definition of the conflict between Palestine and Israel, and for the law that is applicable to the situation. In the short past, the characterization of the conflict between Israel and the occupied territories was controversial, as certain doctrinal interpretations tend to classify it as a non-international armed conflict. The chapter demonstrates that the consolidation of a Palestinian State would result in a change in the legal assessment of the conflict, leading perforce to its classification as an international armed conflict. The new situation would confer on Palestine the status of an 'occupied State' with the subjective right to have direct recourse to the Security Council. The Council might eventually have to take a decision demanding that Israel withdraw from the territory of Palestine in order to restore peace in the Middle East.

Chapter Eight addresses Palestine's efforts to trigger the jurisdiction of the International Criminal Court for international crimes committed on Palestinian territory commenced in the wake of Israel's so called 'Operation Cast Lead' offensive on the Gaza Strip in 2008-2009. The recent UN bid initiative has sought to support these efforts with further legal and political clout. This chapter provides a brief overview of the current state of affairs of Palestine's engagements with international law in relation to the triggering of ICC jurisdiction, which is one of the only remaining international mechanisms that could potentially reframe a long-standing political and legal power dynamic that is reflected in Israel's legitimacy battles, which have often resulted in turning the most fundamental tenets of international law on their head. Palestine has much to gain from the UN bid initiatives for claiming respect for Palestinian rights and compelling third States and global organisations to ensure the proper application of international law.

Chapter Nine demonstrates that, once Palestine becomes a member of the UN and eventually acquires the right to become a party to Geneva Convention III, the status of Palestinian prisoners in Israeli jails will certainly change from that of ordinary prisoners to prisoners of war. The purpose of this chapter is to evaluate how the situation of Palestinian prisoners in Israeli jails could benefit from the establishment of a Palestinian State. It discusses Israel's position concerning the non-existence of POW status in relation to the conflict with Palestine and elaborates on the significance of the State for POW status. It presents the possible scenarios for the treatment of Palestinians as POWs and the mechanisms available for Palestine to protect its citizens imprisoned in Israel.

Chapter Ten reviews the historical roots, current status and future prospects for Palestine statehood in light of international law, with specific reference to the status of Jerusalem after the admission of Palestine to the UN. It shows that Palestine's statehood dates from the end of World War I, when Palestine was established as a State upon the demise of the Turkish Empire. That statehood subsisted after 1948, even as secession led to the bulk of Palestine's territory being claimed by a new State, Israel. The 1967 occupation did not affect Palestine's statehood, which has been confirmed in the contemporary world by widespread diplomatic recognition and the membership of Palestine in the UNESCO and its admission by the General Assembly as a UN observer State. Palestine's admission to the full UN membership would entail no change in the status of Jerusalem, which is deemed to be undetermined at the international level. As residual sovereignty in Palestine remains with the State of Palestine, the best analysis is that Jerusalem, in its entirety, falls under the sovereignty of Palestine. Change could come about through negotiations between the relevant parties.

Chapter Eleven analyses the water claims of the State of Palestine in practice. It considers how freshwater claims of an independent Palestine with respect to the Jordan River could be reconciled with the existing freshwater claims of Israel, Lebanon, Syria and Jordan under international law. Against the background of a brief hydrographic introduction and a review of contemporary problems resulting from the Palestinian water shortage, the chapter argues that a Palestinian State would be entitled under customary international law to receive a significant portion of Jordan River waters. The chapter then identifies three legal problems a Palestinian State could face when attempting to realize its water claims and suggests how these problems could be overcome.

Chapter Twelve evaluates the attempt of Palestine to become a member of the World Trade Organization. In 2009 Palestine filed for the status of observer at the WTO. The chapter addresses the different areas relating to the admission of Palestine to the WTO, including advantages, drawbacks, the application process, the Palestine readiness plan and the overall economic status of Palestine. It concludes that the advantages of joining the WTO outweigh the drawbacks. However, lots of hard work needs to be undertaken to ensure that the Palestinian economy meets the requirements of WTO membership. As the existence of the State is a prerequisite for admission to the WTO as a full member, Palestine's membership, or the status of an observer State, in the UN will definitely boost its chances of being admitted to the WTO.

CHAPTER SIX

THE HUMAN RIGHTS OBLIGATIONS
OF THE STATE OF PALESTINE:
THE CASE OF THE INTERNATIONAL COVENANT
ON ECONOMIC, SOCIAL
AND CULTURAL RIGHTS

MUTAZ M. QAFISHEH

Introduction

In the light of Palestine's initiative aimed at securing membership of the United Nations, it is the time to start considering the obligations of this State towards the people under its jurisdiction and *vis-à-vis* the international community. On joining the UN, Palestine would have a set of rights under various branches of international law. It could become a member of regional and international organizations and courts, a party to treaties, establish full-fledged diplomatic relations, enter into alliances, enact its citizenship law, issue passports and protect its citizens abroad. Palestinian officials and scholars tend to be excited about the prospect of such rights.[1] What has been absent so far, however, is a discussion of the State's obligations in its international relations. This chapter attempts to fill in one aspect of this gap by focusing on the obligations arising from the International Covenant on Economic, Social and Cultural Rights (ICESCR),[2] adopted by the UN General Assembly on 16 December 1966.[3]

Article 26(1) of ICESCR provides that the 'present Covenant is open for signature by any State Member of the United Nations or member of any of its specialized agencies . . . .' Palestine's admission as a State to

---

[1] M. Qafisheh, ed., *Palestine Membership in the United Nations: Legal and Practical Implications* (Newcastle: Cambridge Scholars, 2013)—this book.

[2] 933 *United Nations Treaty Series* (UNTS) 3 (1977).

[3] Hereinafter referred to as 'ICESCR' or 'the Covenant.'

membership in the United Nations Educational, Scientific and Cultural Organization (UNESCO), a UN specialized agency,[4] on 31 October 2011,[5] has opened up the possibility for Palestine to accede to the Covenant.

This chapter tackles the obligations of Palestine based on ICESCR as a key human rights instrument on the global stage. It explores Palestine's obligations with regard to the applicable legislation in the Gaza Strip and the West Bank, the territory of the projected State. It evaluates such legislation and suggests measures that would bring domestic legislation into conformity with the following rights under this instrument: work, social security, food, housing, health, education and cultural life. The role of institutions and policies and Palestine's administrative or procedural obligations under the Covenant are beyond the scope of this chapter.

The Right to Work

The right to work is addressed in two articles of ICESCR. While Article 6 requires States to recognize the right to work in principle, Article 7 introduces specific sub-rights arising from the right to work.

Palestinian legislation recognizes the right to work as a matter of principle in Article 25 of the Amended Palestinian Basic Law of 18 March 2003:[6] '1. Every citizen shall have the right to work, which is a duty and honour. The Palestinian National Authority shall strive to provide work for any individual capable of performing it. 2. Work relations shall be organized in a manner that guarantees justice to all and provides workers with welfare, security, and health and social benefits. 3. Organization of unions is a right that shall be regulated by the law. 4. The right to conduct a strike shall be exercised within the limits of the law.' Specific rules on

---

[4] Agreement between the United Nations and the United Nations Educational, Scientific and Cultural Organization, approved by the General Conference on 6 December 1946 and by the General Assembly of the United Nations on 14 December 1946; UNESCO, *Manual of the General Conference* (Paris: UNESCO, 2002), p. 147, article 1. This article States: 'The United Nations recognizes the United Nations Educational, Scientific and Cultural Organization (UNESCO) as a *specialized agency* responsible for taking such action as may be appropriate under its basic instrument for the accomplishment of the purposes set forth therein' (emphasis added).

[5] UNESCOPRESS, *General Conference admits Palestine as UNESCO Member State*, 31 October 2011.

[6] Palestine Gazette, Special Edition, 19 March 2003, p. 5; hereinafter referred to as the 'Basic Law.'

the right to work are laid down in Labour Law No. 7 of 30 April 2000.[7] Article 2 of this Law reaffirms the said article of the Basic Law by stipulating that 'work is a right for each citizen who is capable thereof. The National Authority shall provide work on the basis of equal opportunities and without any kind of discrimination whatsoever.'

While conforming to Article 6(1) of the Covenant, these two provisions confine the right to work to citizens. This might contradict a clause in the said paragraph that describes work as a human right that should be enjoyed by citizens and non-citizens alike. Yet the Palestinian government, pursuant to Article 14 of the Labour Law, regulates the work of aliens via the *Regulation on the Granting of Work Licenses to Non-Palestinians* of 22 March 2004.[8] Aliens should henceforth acquire work permits from the Ministry of Labour. The Ministry can grant or withhold permits upon its absolute discretion.[9] Permits may be granted if the alien's work does not compete with the Palestinian workforce and if there is a real need for the worker.[10] The Ministry may take its decision subject to the principle of reciprocity.[11] Work permits can be issued for a maximum term of one year and are renewable subject to fresh approval by both the Ministry and the employer.[12] Permits may be denied without assessment of the grounds.[13]

These rules may lead to the loss of work by non-citizens without legitimate grounds and thus to the abuse of workers' rights by employers, violating the *human* right enshrined in Article 6(1) of ICESCR. Should it wish to remove any doubts about the compliance of its Labour Law with the latter stipulation of the Covenant, the Palestinian legislator ought to adopt equitable rights for all persons working in Palestine without discrimination based on citizenship or reciprocity.

Article 3(2) of the Labour Law excludes 'domestic workers and those in similar situations' from the scope of the Law's application. The paragraph adds that the Minister of Labour shall regulate the status of such workers by issuing a regulation. Twelve years on, this regulation has not yet been issued, leaving domestic workers without legal protection. The gap in the regulations governing the status of domestic workers in Palestine is similar to the legislation of other Middle Eastern countries,

---

[7] Palestine Gazette No. 39, 25 November 2001, p. 7.
[8] Palestine Gazette No. 52, 18 January 2005, p. 118.
[9] Article 1.
[10] Article 2(1).
[11] Article 2(2).
[12] Article 5.
[13] Article 4(3).

such as Lebanon. This gap has been deemed to constitute a violation of the right to work by, for example, the UN Committee on the Elimination of Discrimination against Women:[14] 'The Committee expresses concern that Article 7 of the [Lebanese] Labour Law excludes domestic workers from its scope of application thereby depriving them of a range of critical labour protections and making them vulnerable to all forms of exploitation.'[15] The Committee recommended that Lebanon should 'speedily enact the draft law regulating the employment of domestic workers.'[16] The same recommendation, *mutatis mutandis*, applies to Palestinian labour law.

The 2000 Labour Law can be modified by the mere removal of its Article 3(2) in order to bring domestic workers within its scope. The goal might alternatively be achieved by enacting the regulation referred to in the preceding paragraph. This regulation should give domestic workers all the rights enjoyed by ordinary workers as set out in the Labour Law, probably in addition to particular protection measures for domestic workers. At that point, Palestine would approach the boundaries of the recent *Convention concerning Decent Work for Domestic Workers* of 16 June 2011.[17]

With regard to the protection mechanisms for workers indicated in Article 6(2) of the Covenant, the Labour Law contains a set of techniques. It considers its labour guarantees to be non-derogable minimum rights. In the event of derogation by contracts or internal regulations of any establishment, the law prevails in favour of the worker.[18] The Law created an 'Employment Policy Committee' composed of workers, employers and the government, and vested it with the mandate of supervising the Law's proper implementation.[19] The Law established governmental 'labour offices' in various districts to assist workers, free of charge, in finding jobs by acting as an intermediary between employers and job-seekers.[20] It

---

[14] *Concluding comments of the Committee on the Elimination of Discrimination against Women: Lebanon*: UN Doc. CEDAW/C/LBN/CO/3, 8 April 2008.

[15] *Ibid.*, para. 30.

[16] *Ibid.*, para. 31.

[17] ILO Convention No. 189.

[18] Article 6.

[19] Article 7 of the Labour Law. The Labour Policies Committee was established by Decision of the Council of Ministers No. 4 of 17 August 2003, Palestine Gazette No. 49, 17 June 2004, p. 77. This decision is a local implementation of the Convention concerning Labour Administration: Role, Functions and Organisation of 26 June 1978 (ILO Convention No. 150).

[20] Articles 8 and 10-12.

established a ministerial committee[21] to compile systematic statistics on workforces and unemployment.[22]

The Law assigns additional rights to workers. It exempts cases involving workers from court fees.[23] The Law requires every employer to provide the labour office on a monthly basis with detailed information concerning workers' status and any vacant positions.[24] Establishments are obliged to ensure that at least 5% of their staff are workers with disabilities.[25] Workers may substantiate labour contracts through any means of proof, with or without written documents.[26] The Law protects workers against arbitrary dismissal,[27] establishes conditions for collective bargaining,[28] and deems that workers' financial credits constitute a right of lien.[29] The right to strike is recognized with specific procedures and a

---

[21] Decision of the Council of Ministers No. 16 of 24 February 2004 concerning the Rules of Procedure of the Committee on Unemployment, Palestine Gazette No. 49, 17 June 2004, p. 220.

[22] Article 9. *Cf.* Convention concerning Labour Statistics of 25 June 1985 (ILO Convention No. 160).

[23] Article 4.

[24] Article 12. This can be considered as a form of local application of the Convention concerning Vocational Rehabilitation and Employment (Disabled Persons) of 20 June 1983 (ILO Convention No. 159).

[25] Article 13. This can be considered as a form of national application which requires inspectors to be 'duly qualified technical experts and specialists, including specialists in medicine, engineering, electricity and chemistry' (Article 9); requires that the 'number of labour inspectors shall be sufficient to secure the effective discharge of the duties of the inspectorate' (Article 10); that inspectors shall be furnished with 'local offices, suitably equipped in accordance with the requirements of the service, and accessible to all persons concerned,' and with 'the transport facilities necessary for the performance,' and requires labour inspectors to be reimbursed 'any travelling and incidental expenses which may be necessary for the performance of their duties' (Article 11).

[26] Articles 24 and 28.

[27] Articles 39-48. *Cf.* Convention concerning Termination of Employment at the Initiative of the Employer of 22 June 1982 (ILO Convention No. 158).

[28] Articles 49-53. It seems, given their similar language and substance, that these articles have been drafted on the basis of the Convention concerning the Application of the Principles of the Right to Organise and to Bargain Collectively of 1 July 1949 (ILO Convention No. 98) and the Convention concerning the Promotion of Collective Bargaining of 8 June 1981 (ILO Convention No. 154).

[29] Article 85. This article is an application of the Convention concerning the Protection of Workers' Claims in the event of the Insolvency of their Employer of 23 June 1992 (ILO Convention No. 173).

timeline.[30] Specific penalties are imposed to ensure effective implementation of the rules.[31]

Vocational and technical training is regulated by the Law 'to guide workers towards available work and training opportunities that suit their skills, preferences and capabilities' and 'to produce workers for the development needs, enabling them to acquire sustainable skills.'[32] The Law assigns the Ministry of Labour the role of formulating vocational training polices in coordination with other ministries in order to train youth for market-oriented careers.[33] Conditions governing vocational training centres, which are directly run by the Ministry or by private employers, are laid down.[34] A regulation has been issued whereby procedures to enrol candidates in vocational and technical programmes have been formulated, including conditions of enrolment, application procedures, and the rights of trainees.[35] A licensing system for private employers to conduct vocational training under the Ministry's supervision has been put in place.[36] The existence of such a vocational and technical system brings Palestine into line with Article 6(2) of the Covenant, which requires States to adopt 'technical and vocational guidance and training programmes, policies and techniques.'[37]

Working hours are limited to forty-five hours a week.[38] In 'hard or dangerous jobs'[39] or for night work,[40] working time is reduced by one hour

---

[30] Articles 66 and 67.

[31] Articles 131-138.

[32] Article 18.

[33] Articles 19 and 20.

[34] Article 22.

[35] Decision of the Council of Ministers No. 169 of 12 July 2004 concerning the Regulation of Vocational Instructions and Training, Palestine Gazette No. 53, 28 February 2005, p. 286.

[36] Decision of the Council of Ministers No. 168 of 12 July 2004 concerning the Regulation of the Conditions and Procedures of the Licensing of Private Vocational Training Institutions, Palestine Gazette No. 53, 28 February 2005, p. 283.

[37] *Cf.* Convention concerning Vocational Guidance and Vocational Training in the Development of Human Resources of 23 June 1973 (ILO Convention No. 142).

[38] Labour Law of 2000, Article 68. This provision is below the standard adopted by the Convention concerning the Reduction of Hours of Work to Forty a Week of 22 June 1935 (ILO Convention No. 47).

[39] The hard and dangerous jobs have been listed in Decision of the Minister of Labour No. 3 of 6 May 2004 on Works of Reduced Daily Working Hours, Palestine Gazette No. 54, 23 April 2005, p. 147.

per day.[41] Workers are given the right to one hour of rest each working
day and should not work for five consecutive hours without a break.[42]
Workers may agree with employers on overtime, which should not exceed
twelve hours a week,[43] with 50% payment as compensation for the added
time.[44] Workers have the right to rest for at least twenty-four consecutive
hours a week.[45]

Various types of leave have been regulated. Workers have the right to
two to three weeks of paid annual leave,[46] depending on the difficulty of
the work,[47] paid national and religious holidays,[48] one paid week of
'educational leave,'[49] two paid weeks of 'pilgrimage holiday,'[50] fully paid

---

[40] Night has been defined in Article 1 of the Labour Law: 'A period of consecutive
twelve hours which compulsorily include the period between eight post meridiem
until six ante meridiem.' It should be noted that this definition is more favourable
to workers than international standards which define 'night' as 'a period of at least
eleven consecutive hours, including the interval between ten o'clock in the evening
and five o'clock in the morning.' See, among other conventions, Article 3(3) of the
Convention concerning Employment of Women during the Night of 28 November
1919 (ILO Convention No. 6).
[41] Article 69. Cf. Convention Limiting the Hours of Work in Industrial
Undertakings to Eight in the Day and Forty-eight in the Week of 28 November
1919 (ILO Convention No. 1).
[42] Article 70.
[43] This is below the eight extra hours fixed in the Convention Limiting the Hours
of Work in Industrial Undertakings to Eight in the Day and Forty-eight in the
Week of 28 June 1930 (ILO Convention No. 30).
[44] Article 71.
[45] Articles 72 and 73. This provision is taken from Article 2(1) of the Convention
concerning the Application of the Weekly Rest in Industrial Undertakings of 17
November 1921 (ILO Convention No. 14), and Article 6(1) of the Convention
concerning Weekly Rest in Commerce and Offices of 26 June 1957 (ILO
Convention No. 106).
[46] Article 74.
[47] Two weeks' holidays is less than the minimum three-week holiday fixed by
Article 3(3) of the Convention concerning Annual Holidays with Pay (Revised) of
24 June 1970 (ILO Convention No. 132).
[48] Article 75. These holidays were fixed by Decision of the Council of Ministers
No. 16 of 22 December 2003 concerning the Regulation of the Determination of
the Paid Religious and Official Holidays, Palestine Gazette No. 49, 17 June 2004,
p. 161.
[49] Article 76. Cf. Convention concerning Paid Educational Leave of 24 June 1974
(ILO Convention No. 140); Convention concerning Occupational Health Services
of 22 June 1985 (ILO Convention No. 161); Convention concerning the
Promotional Framework for Occupational Safety and Health of 15 June 2006 (ILO
Convention No. 187).

sick leave for fourteen days and half-paid sick leave for a further fourteen days a year,[51] and incidental leave.[52] Women have the right to maternity leave for ten weeks,[53] to a breast-feeding break for an hour a day for one year following delivery,[54] and the right to special leave without pay for one year.[55]

Such stipulations are in line with Article 7(6) of the Covenant, which accords workers the rights to rest, 'leisure and reasonable limitation of working hours and periodic holidays with pay, as well as remuneration for public holidays.'

The Palestinian Labour Law dedicates four sections/chapters to safe and healthy working conditions. They are entitled: 'occupational safety and hygiene,' 'child labour,' 'working women,' and 'work injuries and occupational diseases.'

Pursuant to Article 90 of the Labour Law, a series of safety measures have been adopted by executive orders. These measures relate to the installation of medical first-aid kits in workplaces,[56] the conduct of regular medical checks for workers,[57] the taking of safety precautions for construction workers,[58] workers dealing with chemical materials,[59] and workers employed in places where there are radioactive materials,[60]

---

[50] Article 77.

[51] Article 79.

[52] Article 78.

[53] Article 103. This period is below the international standard of a minimum of fourteen weeks pursuant to Article 4(1) of the Convention concerning the Revision of the Maternity Protection Convention (Revised), 1952, of 15 June 2000 (ILO Convention No. 183).

[54] Article 104.

[55] Article 105.

[56] Regulations concerning First Aid Medication in Work Installations No. 17 of 22 December 2003, Palestine Gazette No. 49, 17 June 2004, p. 163.

[57] Decision of the Council of Ministers No. 24 of 22 December 2004 concerning the Regular Medical Examination, Palestine Gazette No. 49, 17 June 2004, p. 191.

[58] Instructions of the Minister of Labour No. 1 of 20 February 2005 on the Precautions to Protect Workers in Construction and Engineering Structures, Palestine Gazette No. 55, 27 June 2005, p. 214. These instructions correspond to the standards laid down in the Convention concerning Safety and Health in Construction of 20 June 1988 (ILO Convention No. 167).

[59] Instructions of the Minister of Labour No. 2 of 20 February 2005 on the Safety Standards and Levels of Harmful Chemicals and Dusts Permitted at Workplaces, Palestine Gazette No. 55, 27 June 2005, p. 231. *Cf.* Convention concerning Safety in the use of Chemicals at Work of 25 June 1990 (ILO Convention No. 1990).

[60] Instructions of the Minister of Labour No. 3 of 20 February 2005 on the Annual Permitted Doze for Workers in Ionic X-Ray, Palestine Gazette No. 55, 27 June

massive noise,[61] light,[62] or heat,[63] and workers in gas or petroleum stations.[64]

In line with Palestinian Child Law No. 7 of 15 August 2004[65] and the ILO Convention concerning Minimum Age for Admission to Employment of 26 June 1973,[66] Article 93 of the Labour Law prohibits the recruitment of children under fifteen years of age. It outlaws the hiring of children for harmful jobs and for work at night[67] or in remote areas.[68] The Law imposes reduced working hours and more holidays for children[69] and instructs employers to conduct compulsory medical examinations for juveniles before they start work.[70] Employers should post the rules on child labour in workplaces.[71] These rules conform to a number of relevant ILO child standards.[72]

2005, p. 244. *Cf.* Convention concerning the Protection of Workers against Ionizing Radiations of 22 June 1960 (ILO Convention No. 115).

[61] Instructions by the Minister of Labour No. 4 of 20 February 2005 on the Safe Levels the Extremity of Noise at Workplaces, Palestine Gazette No. 55, 27 June 2005, p. 247.

[62] Instructions of the Minister of Labour No. 5 of 20 February 2005 on the Safe Levels of the Brightness of Light at Workplaces, Palestine Gazette No. 55, 27 June 2005, p. 249.

[63] Instructions of the Minister of Labour No. 6 of 20 February 2005 on the Safe Levels of Temperatures at Workplaces, Palestine Gazette No. 55, 27 June 2005, p. 251.

[64] Instructions of the Minister of Labour No. 7 of 20 February 2005 on the Protection of Workers in Gas and Petroleum Materials, Palestine Gazette No. 55, 27 June 2005, p. 254. *Cf.* Convention concerning the Protection of Workers against Occupational Hazards in the Working Environment Due to Air Pollution, Noise and Vibration 20 June 1977 (ILO Convention No. 148); Convention concerning Safety in the Use of Asbestos of 24 June 1986 (ILO Convention No. 162).

[65] Palestine Gazette No. 52, 18 January 2005, p. 13, Article 4.

[66] ILO Convention No. 138, Article 2(3).

[67] *Cf.* ILO Convention No. 6, *supra* note.

[68] Article 95.

[69] Article 96.

[70] Article 98.

[71] Article 94.

[72] Convention concerning the Prohibition and Immediate Action for the Elimination of the Worst Forms of Child Labour of 17 June 1999 (ILO Convention No. 182); Convention concerning Medical Examination for Fitness for Employment in Industry of Children and Young Persons of 9 October 1946 (ILO Convention No. 77); Convention concerning Medical Examination of Children and Young Persons for Fitness for Employment in Non-Industrial Occupations of 9 October 1946 (ILO Convention No. 78); Convention concerning the Restriction of Night Work of

In addition to maternity leave and breastfeeding, as indicated above, the Labour Law incorporates a considerable number of rules for the protection of working women: prohibition of discrimination between men and women with regard to work;[73] a ban on the recruitment of females in harmful jobs; a prohibition on employers requiring pregnant women to perform extra working hours; and prevention of women from working at night except when necessary,[74] for instance in hospitals, airports or the media.[75]

Lastly, the Law provides detailed guarantees, including health insurance and compensation, for workers against work-related injuries and occupational diseases.[76]

The penalties imposed in respect of the foregoing measures in the event of non-compliance underscores the importance that the Law attaches to the enforcement of labour standards.[77]

It may be concluded from this review of the Labour Law and its executive measures that the Palestinian labour system conforms to Article 7(b) of the Covenant relating to 'safe and healthy working conditions.' It further confirms Palestine's effective compliance with the Convention concerning Occupational Safety and Health Convention and the Working Environment of 22 June 1981[78] and the Convention concerning the Prevention of Major Industrial Accidents of 22 June 1993.[79]

A minimum wage for workers has yet to be fixed despite the provision of Article 89 of the Labour Law which States that the 'salary of the worker may not be less than the minimum limit which is legally fixed.' Non-compliance with this article stems from the fact that responsibility for fixing the minimum wage has been assigned to the 'Committee of Wages,' which is composed of representatives of the government, workers and employers.[80] The Committee was supposed to propose a minimum wage

---

Children and Young Persons in Non-Industrial Occupations of 9 October 1946 (ILO Convention No. 79); Convention concerning the Night Work of Young Persons Employed in Industry of 10 July 1948 (ILO Convention No. 90).

[73] Article 100.

[74] Article 101. *Cf.* Convention concerning Employment of Women during the Night of 28 November 1919 (ILO Convention No. 4).

[75] Decision of the Council of Ministers No. 14 of 22 December 2003 concerning the Work of Women Overnight, Palestine Gazette No. 49, 17 June 2004, p. 152.

[76] Articles 116-128.

[77] Articles 134 and 136.

[78] ILO Convention No. 155.

[79] ILO Convention No. 174.

[80] Labour Law of 2000, Article 86.

for workers to be adopted by the Council of Ministers.[81] While the Committee itself has been formed,[82] the decision fixing the minimum wage has yet to be taken.[83] The lack of such a wage opens the door to exploitation and different treatment of workers for the same job. This, in turn, leads to a breach of the part of Article 6 of the Covenant that gives everyone the right to enjoy '[f]air wages and equal remuneration for work of equal value without distinction of any kind.'[84] Thus, the Palestinian legislator should expedite the adoption of a minimum wage, thereby possibly paving the way for Palestine to become a party to the Convention concerning Minimum Wage Fixing, with Special Reference to Developing Countries of 22 June 1970.[85]

As discrimination against women in workplaces, particularly in terms of lower salaries compared with men, does exist in Palestine; the legislator should adopt measures to ensure equality between the sexes.[86] Such measures may include: (1) introducing a specific provision concerning equal wages between men and women instead of leaving the rule subject to the general wording of Article 100 of the law on general equality; (2) punishing gender discrimination regarding wages with appropriate penalties, such as high fines or even imprisonment, with retroactive compensation for a woman who suffers from such discrimination for the entire period in which she serves the employer; and (3) expediting the fixing of the minimum wage for women and men. By adopting such legislative measures, Palestine would comply with Article 7(a)(i) of the Covenant, which requires, *inter alia*, that 'women [are] guaranteed conditions of work not inferior to those enjoyed by men, with equal pay for equal work.' That would facilitate compliance with the ILO Convention concerning Discrimination in Respect of Employment and Occupation of 25 June 1958[87] and, more specifically, the Equal Remuneration Convention of 29 June 1951.[88]

---

[81] Article 87(2).

[82] Decision of the Council of Ministers No. 46 of 22 March 2004 concerning the Formation of the Committee of Wages, Palestine Gazette No. 52, 18 January 2005, p. 120.

[83] It should be noted that Article 57 of the Labour Law envisaged the possibility of fixing minimum wages through an agreement reached between workers and employers via collective bargaining.

[84] Article 6(a)(i).

[85] ILO Convention No. 131.

[86] 'Report on the Elimination of Discrimination against Working Women [in Palestine],' *Al-Ayyam*, No. 5476, 12 April 2011, p. 20.

[87] ILO Convention No. 111.

[88] ILO Convention No. 100.

The Labour Law established an inspection mechanism affiliated to the Ministry of Labour, called the 'Labour Inspection Commission' in order to ensure compliance with labour rules.[89] The Commission has been vested with policing authority and has jurisdiction to receive complaints and to conduct investigations.[90] It may enter workplaces, interview workers, request or open files and records, test materials used by workers to ensure compliance with health standards, and remove unhealthy objects from places of work.[91] Anyone who resists the labour inspectors is punishable by the removal of the contravention as well as with a fine.[92]

The Law does not, however, guarantee the effective performance of the inspectors. It does not require, for example, that a specific number of inspectors be hired to meet the needs of the workforce in each district. Nor does it require specific qualifications for inspectors rather than 'proper academic and professional qualifications.'[93] One might expect that the number, qualifications and rules of procedure applicable to inspectors would be materialized by enacting bylaws, but the Ministry has not issued any such bylaws as the Law requires.[94] And, unlike a number of its other provisions, the Labour Law does not set any penalties to ensure compliance with the stipulations relating to the labour inspection mechanism.

One may thus doubt the efficiency of the labour inspectors. One may even cast doubt on respect in practice for a number of other standards enumerated in the Labour Law itself and in Articles 6 and 7 of the Covenant. It is recommended that the bylaws relating to the inspection mechanism be enacted and contain specific qualifications for inspectors; the number of inspectors should be proportionate to the labour force in each district; and measures and penalties should be applicable to the inspectors themselves in cases of non-compliance with the inspection processes. Palestine would then satisfy the rules set forth in the Convention concerning Labour Inspection in Industry and Commerce of 11 July 1947.[95]

---

[89] Article 107.

[90] Article 110.

[91] Article 111.

[92] Article 135.

[93] Article 107(1).

[94] In Article 111(4) and Article 115.

[95] ILO Convention No. 81. This Convention requires labour inspectors to be 'duly qualified technical experts and specialists, including specialists in medicine, engineering, electricity and chemistry' (art 9); that the 'number of labour inspectors shall be sufficient to secure the effective discharge of the duties of the

In order to be fully compliant with international labour standards, Palestine needs to adopt further rules, such as protection against unemployment,[96] provision for social security (e.g. old-age benefit, invalidity benefit, and survivors' benefit),[97] compulsory health insurance,[98] protection for specific groups of workers, including workers in the fishing sector,[99] seafarers,[100] agricultural workers,[101] dock workers,[102] nursing personnel,[103] hotel and restaurant workers,[104] migrant workers,[105] and home workers.[106] The lack of specific regulations regarding these workers might lead to the non-applicability of labour law in some sectors of employment and, as a result, to non-compliance of Palestinian law with the labour rights enshrined in Articles 6 and 7 of the Covenant.

---

inspectorate' (art 10); and that the labour inspectors should be furnished with 'local offices, suitably equipped in accordance with the requirements of the service, and accessible to all persons concerned,' and 'the transport facilities necessary for the performance;' a further requirement is 'to reimburse to labour inspectors any travelling and incidental expenses which may be necessary for the performance of their duties' (art 11).

[96] Convention concerning Employment Promotion and Protection against Unemployment of 21 June 1988 (ILO Convention No. 168).

[97] Convention concerning Minimum Standards of Social Security of 28 June 1952 (ILO Convention No. 102).

[98] Convention concerning Medical Care and Sickness Benefits 25 June 1969 (ILO Convention No. 130).

[99] Convention concerning Work in the Fishing Sector of 14 June 2007 (ILO Convention No. 188).

[100] Convention concerning Minimum Standards in Merchant Ships of 19 October 1976 (ILO Convention No. 147).

[101] There are a number of conventions relating to agriculture, including: Convention concerning Workmen's Compensation in Agriculture of 12 November 1921 (ILO Convention No. 12); Convention concerning Labour Inspection in Agriculture of 25 June 1969 (ILO Convention No. 129); Convention concerning Safety and Health in Agriculture of 21 June 2001 (ILO Convention No. 184).

[102] Convention concerning the Social Repercussions of New Methods of Cargo Handling in Docks of 25 June 1973 (ILO Convention No. 137).

[103] Convention concerning Employment and Conditions of Work and Life of Nursing Personnel of 21 June 1977 (ILO Convention No. 149).

[104] Convention concerning Working Conditions in Hotels, Restaurants and similar Establishments of 25 June 1991 (ILO No. 172).

[105] Convention concerning Migration for Employment of 10 July 1949 (ILO Convention No. 97).

[106] Convention concerning Home Work of 20 June 1996 (ILO Convention No. 177).

The foregoing Palestinian standards would suffice, however, for the purpose of guaranteeing the right to work under the Covenant. After Palestine's accession to the Covenant, the Committee on Economic, Social and Cultural Rights (CESCR) would be in a position to assess the scope of its legal development in the field of labour rights and to recommend, in its concluding observations, relevant actions to be taken by Palestine and international organizations, particularly the ILO, to provide technical support in this field.

Article 8, paragraph 3, of the Covenant relates to labour unions. If we assume that Palestine would be interested in becoming a party to the Convention concerning Freedom of Association and Protection of the Right to Organize of 9 July 1948,[107] which is mentioned in paragraph 3, it follows that Palestine would be obliged to grant specific rights to associations of labour unions in accordance with the Convention. Palestine should grant workers and employers 'the right to establish and, subject only to the rules of the organisation concerned, to join organisations of their own choosing without previous authorisation.'[108] 'Workers' and employers' organisations shall not be liable to be dissolved or suspended by administrative authority.'[109] Nothing in the Labour Law prevents workers' or employers' associations from forming unions. Article 53(3) of the Law on collective bargaining between unions of employers' associations and unions of workers' associations implies that workers or employers may establish unions.

The Labour Law defines the term 'association' as 'any professional organization in accordance with the law of unions.'[110] This law of unions has not yet been enacted. Article 8(3) of the Covenant is closely linked to the envisaged 'law of unions.' If the Palestinian legislator is interested in complying with global human rights and labour standards, unions may not be subjected to the general restrictions of the Law of Associations.[111] Unions should be ruled in accordance with the said 1948 Convention, which does not allow any authority to intervene in the affairs of labour unions. Moreover, there is no need to obtain governmental permission for union operations and the authorities are precluded from restricting or dissolving such unions.

---

[107] ILO Convention No. 87.

[108] Convention concerning Freedom of Association and Protection of the Right to Organize, *supra* note. Article 2.

[109] *Ibid.*, Article 4.

[110] Article 1.

[111] Law No. 1 concerning Charitable Associations and Civil Society Organizations of 16 January 2000, Palestine Gazette No. 32, 29 February 2000, p. 71.

It should finally be noted that the Palestinian Labour Law of 2000 repealed Jordanian Labour Law No. 21 of 14 May 1960[112] that was applicable in the West Bank. The latter Law included detailed provisions concerning workers' and employers' unions.[113] As just noted, the 2000 Law is silent regarding such unions. It merely refers to a law that has not yet been adopted. This has left labour unions without any clear regulations, a step backward from the forty years older Jordanian law. In the Gaza Strip, however, labour unions are regulated by Labour Unions Order No. 331 of 24 October 1954,[114] which was enacted under Egyptian rule. This law is still applicable in Gaza, as its provisions were not included in Gazan Labour Law No. 16 of 14 November 1964,[115] which was applicable under the Egyptian administration. The 1954 law escaped being repealed by the 2000 Law, which revoked the said Gazan Labour Law. This situation has led to the application of different rules to labour unions in Gaza and the West Bank. This odd situation should be changed by adopting a modern law on labour unions based on the aforesaid 1948 ILO Convention.

Social Security

Article 9 of ICESCR relates to social security. Its reads: 'The States Parties to the present Covenant recognize the right of everyone to social security, including social insurance.' In this connection, Article 22 of the 2003 Palestinian Basic Law provides that: '1. Social, health, disability and retirement insurance shall be regulated by law. Maintaining the welfare of families of martyrs, prisoners of war, the injured and the disabled is a duty that shall be regulated by law. The National Authority shall guarantee these persons education, health and social insurance.'

The legislation of greatest relevance to social security in Palestine concerns retirement. This legislation includes: General Retirement Law No. 7 of 26 April 2005[116] and the Law of Insurance and Pensions of the Palestinian Security Forces No. 16 of 28 December 2004.[117] These two laws provide for compulsory retirement benefits for public servants. The Palestinian Parliament attempted to pass a new law that introduces social security benefits for private-sector workers by adopting Social Insurances

[112] Jordan Official Gazette No. 1491, 21 May 1960, p. 511.
[113] Articles 68-89.
[114] Palestine Gazette No. 41, 15 November 1954, p. 1039.
[115] Palestine Gazette, 15 December 1964, p. 1859.
[116] Palestine Gazette No. 55, 27 June 2005, p. 16.
[117] Palestine Gazette No. 53, 28 February 2005, p. 94.

Law No. 3 of 19 October 2003.[118] This instrument incorporates special insurance equivalent to that of public employees for workers in the non-governmental sector, including benefits for disabilities resulting from work incidents, for old age, and for natural disabilities and death. However, the Law was subsequently repealed by Decree-Law No. 6 of the Palestinian President on 23 August 2007,[119] leaving private-sector workers without social security benefits. Yet the Council of Ministers, in the absence of Parliament, enacted Regulations No. 16 of 9 August 2010 whereby it extended the benefits of the General Retirement Law to workers in the non-governmental and private sectors.[120]

The applicable law in Palestine grants retirement rights as a general rule to the widow of a deceased male worker. Women cannot pass retirement rights to their widower. This rule is drawn from a number of laws relating to retirement. Article 36 of the aforementioned Law of Insurance and Pensions of the Palestinian Security Forces of 2004 provides that 'persons entitled to pension . . . shall be 1. The widow [in Arabic 'armalah'] or widows of the beneficiary . . . .' Similar provisions are to be found in Article 32 of the 2005 General Retirement Law and the Regulation relating to the Retirement of Lawyers No. 1 of 1 January 1998.[121] Such rules imply that women are dependent on men and that it is the man who works, not the woman. This is inconsistent with the actual situation, since women account for 20% of the workforce in Palestine.[122] It denies women retirement rights despite the fact that they are obliged to pay retirement dues at the same rate as men. Such provisions should be changed to guarantee equality between men and women in terms of retirement rights and obligations so that Palestinian law is consistent with the human rights and labour standards set out above.

There are other pieces of legislation in force relating to social security in Palestine. They include, *inter alia*, support by the State for the following marginalized categories: orphans,[123] people with disabilities,[124]

---

[118] Palestine Gazette No. 48, 29 January 2004, p. 7.

[119] Palestine Gazette No. 73, 13 September 2007, p. 21.

[120] Decision of the Council of Ministers concerning the Benefit of the Employees of Local Councils, Civil Society Institutions, Private Sector, Employees and Members of Professional Institutions from the General Retirement Law, Palestine Gazette No. 89, 1 January 2011, p. 63.

[121] Palestine Gazette No. 25, 24 September 1998, p. 58.

[122] Palestinian Central Bureau of Statistics, *Survey of Workforces in Palestine* (Ramallah, 2012), p. 24.

[123] Law on the Administration and Development of Orphans' Properties Institution No. 14 of 28 September 2005, Palestine Gazette No. 60, 9 November 2005, p. 22.

the poor,[125] alimony for dependants whose head of family is unable to provide,[126] prisoners,[127] prisoners liberated from Israeli jails,[128] unemployed persons,[129] families of those killed, injured or imprisoned by the Israeli occupying forces and persons whose homes are demolished by Israel.[130]

It may be concluded from the above survey of the applicable legislation that Palestine complies with Article 9 of the Covenant. Local legislation not only tries to meet global standards, for instance regarding pensions and social assistance to disabled persons; it also addresses the

---

[124] Rights of People with Disabilities Law No. 4 of 9 August 1999, Palestine Gazette No. 30, 10 October 1999, p. 36. This law includes the following social rights for the benefit of people with disabilities: rehabilitation programmes at low or no cost (Article 5), exemption from taxes, customs and fees (Article 6), free health care (Article 10), and requiring buildings and policies to meet the needs of persons with special needs (Articles 12-17). See also Decision of the Council of Ministers No. 50 of 23 May 2006 on the Establishment of the Disabled Fund for Lending and Employment at the Ministry of Social Affairs, Palestine Gazette No. 68, 7 March 2007, p. 97.

[125] Law concerning the Ministry of Social Affairs No. 14 of 23 February 1956, Jordan Official Gazette No. 1265, 17 March 1956, p. 1367, Article 4; Decision of the Council of Ministers No. 96 of 10 September 2007 concerning the Exemption of Children of Poor Families and Children of Unemployed Persons from School Fees, Palestine Gazette No. 77, 9 October 2008, p. 156; Decision of the Council of Ministers No. 206 of 4 December 2004 concerning the Establishment of the Committee of the Administration of Aids to Citizens in Need, Palestine Gazette No. 54, 23 April 2005, p. 138.

[126] Law of Alimony Fund No. 6 of 26 April 2005, Palestine Gazette No. 55, 27 June 2005, p. 10.

[127] Decision of the Council of Ministers No. 21 of 28 June 2010 on Securing the Needs of Prisoners in Israeli Custody, Palestine Gazette No. 90, 30 March 2011, p. 98; Regulations No. 23 of 28 June 2010 concerning the Prisoners Salary, Palestine Gazette No. 90, 30 March 2011, p. 103.

[128] Decision of the Council of Ministers No. 19 of 4 January 2010 concerning the Exemption of Liberated Prisoners from School and University Tuition, Fees of Health Insurance and Rehabilitation Programs, Palestine Gazette No. 90, 30 March 2011, p. 93.

[129] Decision of the Council of Ministers No. 157 of 6 September 2005 concerning Remunerations for the Aid of Unemployment and Temporary Employment, Palestine Gazette No. 64, 31 May 2006, p. 306; Presidential Decree concerning the Establishment of the Fund for Employment and Social Protection for Workers No. 9 of 20 May 2003, Palestine Gazette No. 46, 16 August 2003, p. 17.

[130] Decision of the Council of Ministers No. 127 of 18 September 2006 concerning Compensation for Demolished Houses, Palestine Gazette No. 69, 27 April 2007, p. 192.

particular social challenges resulting from the Israeli occupation of Palestinian territory, as the legislation lays the basis for assisting families of persons killed by Israel and those whose homes are demolished.

Yet many of the legislative instruments dealing with the issues mentioned above are of an executive nature and are applied on an *ad hoc* basis. Unlike parliamentary law which is thoroughly discussed as part of the legislative process, executive orders can cease to exist or be withdrawn at the individual behest of the issuing official. Such legislation ought to be systematically regularized to ensure ongoing benefits for the lives of those impacted. Palestinian legislation could include more effective measures, as in the case of developed countries, to ensure social benefits such as benefits for old people, the unemployed, sick or homeless, refugees, mothers, widows and orphans. The Palestinian legislator is hereby called upon to reactivate the 2003 Social Insurances Law. Each State develops its social security according to its policies and economic abilities. Although more can be done, it can generally be said that Palestinian legislation guarantees at least minimum standards relating to social security which meet the already minimal requirements of the Covenant concerning social security.

The Right to Food

The right to food is the core provision of Article 11 of ICESCR. The article requires States to recognize this right and to adopt measures towards its realization. As CESCR noted in its General Comment No. 12 of 12 May 1999, entitled the 'Right to Adequate Food,'[131] the 'human right to adequate food is of crucial importance for the enjoyment of all rights.'[132] According to CESCR, the right to adequate food, like a number of other rights, encompasses three levels of obligation on States: 'to respect,' 'to protect' and 'to fulfil.'[133] While respecting the right to food is merely a passive obligation, i.e. to refrain from taking measures that prevent access to food sources,[134] the obligations to protect that right and to fulfil it on behalf of needy people require positive actions including the adoption of relevant legislation. Let us therefore assess how the right to

---

[131] UN Doc. HRI/GEN/1/Rev.7 ('Compilation of General Comments and General Recommendations Adopted by Human Rights Treaty Bodies'), 12 May 2004, p. 63.
[132] Para. 1.
[133] CESCR's General Comment No. 12, *op. cit.*, para. 15.
[134] *Ibid.*

adequate food is being protected and fulfilled/provided, as shown by the applicable legislation in the Palestinian territory.

A series of legislative instruments aiming to protect the quality of food are in force in Palestine. Food Control Ordinance No. 4 of 19 March 1942,[135] enacted during British rule in Palestine, is applicable in both Gaza and the West Bank. It vests the government with the power to monitor the price of basic food items, to fix maximum prices for certain products, and to prevent the monopoly of any party over basic goods. The government reserves the jurisdiction to issue permits for importing or exporting food, to inspect places producing or selling food, to review or confiscate documentation thereof, and to sanction those who violate the food control instructions. The Merchandise Marks Ordinance of 29 February 1929,[136] applicable in the Gaza Strip, and the Merchandise Marks Law No. 19 of 29 December 1953, applicable in the West Bank, punish any person who changes the names of products, trademarks, business names, ingredients or the date of expiry of any product, including food items, with the aim of preventing forgery or fraud. Public Health Law No. 20 of 27 December 2004[137] assigns to the Ministry of Health, *inter alia*, the mandate to issue permits for food-related professions and industries, to monitor places used for locally produced food, to check imported items at the borders, and to issue regulations relating to food safety.[138] Food producers are under an obligation to provide the Ministry with information on food ingredients, means of preservation, distribution, and samples of products.[139] The Law further prohibits the distribution of harmful food, such as expired or polluted goods,[140] and gives the Ministry the right to destroy such products.[141] Palestinian Standards Law No. 6 of 7 September 2000[142] established the Palestinian Standards Institution, which is a correspondent (observer) member of the International Organization for Standardization, to accredit and ensure the quality of industrial products, including food, based on scientific health and environmental standards with the aim of protecting customers. Consumer Protection Law No. 21 of 1 November

---

[135] Palestine Gazette, Supplement 1, No. 1178, 19 March 1942, p. 5.
[136] R. Drayton, ed., *The Laws of Palestine in Force on the 31st Day of December 1933* (London: Waterlow and Sons, 1934), p. 1,039.
[137] Palestine Gazette No. 54, 23 April 2004, p. 14.
[138] Article 2.
[139] Article 16.
[140] Articles 19 and 20.
[141] Article 27.
[142] Palestine Gazette No. 36, 19 March 2001, p. 63.

2005[143] offers detailed measures to protect consumers' health or to protect them from falling victim to fraud or exploitation. It ensures transparency in economic transactions that affect customers. Lastly, Agriculture Law No. 2 of 5 August 2003,[144] which relates to a key source of food, including plants and livestock as well as fishing, protects local agricultural products and supports those working in the agricultural sector.[145]

This survey of applicable laws and a series of executive orders that monitor food products[146] shows that the local legislation in the country has endeavoured to protect the right to food. This may in turn be regarded as a step towards compliance with international standards relating to the obligation of States to protect the right to adequate food for everybody who lives under the State's jurisdiction.

For CESCR, the obligation to fulfil the right to food means that the State must proactively engage in activities that facilitate and strengthen people's access to and utilization of food resources. And 'whenever an individual or group is unable, for reasons beyond their control, to enjoy the right to adequate food by the means at their disposal, States have the obligation to *fulfil (provide)* that right directly. This obligation also applies for persons who are victims of natural or other disasters.'[147]

---

[143] Palestine Gazette No. 63, 27 April 2006, p. 29.

[144] Palestine Gazette No. 47, 30 October 2003, p. 23.

[145] See further Decree-Law on the Repression of Fraud and Adulteration No. 11 of 10 June 1966, Palestine Gazette, Special Edition, 10 August 1966, p. 3; Marketing Agricultural and Animal Products Law No. 88 of 21 September 1966, Jordan Official Gazette No. 1956, 16 October 1966, p. 2,079; Natural Resources Law No. 1 of 24 January 1999, Palestine Gazette No. 28, 13 March 1999, p. 10; Environment Law of 1999, *op. cit.*

[146] Regulations of Food Inspection and Limitation of Prices No. 33 of 10 August 1959, Jordan Official Gazette No. 1439, 1 September 1959, p. 769; Decision of the Minister of Supply on Frozen Meat No. 3 of 3 July 1999, Palestine Gazette No. 31, 13 December 1999, p. 41; Ministerial Decree on the Analysis Samples of Food Materials and Chemical Products No. 1 of 25 September 2002, Palestine Gazette No. 44, 31 March 2002, p. 82; Ministerial Decree on Food Materials and Commodities No. 1 of 23 March 2003, Palestine Gazette No. 45, 24 May 2003, p. 83; Decision of the Minister of Agriculture No. 1 of 28 August 2004 on the Registration and Types of Permitted Agricultural Blights Herbicides, Palestine Gazette No. 52, 18 January 2005, p. 302; Decision of the Minister of Economy No. 6 of 5 May 2010 on the Price of Bread, Palestine Gazette No. 88, 15 December 2010, p. 144.

[147] CESCR's General Comment No. 12, *op. cit.*, para. 15 (emphasis in the original).

As discussed under Article 9 of ICESCR above, Palestine has enacted a number of laws designed to relieve those who are unable to secure adequate sources of living, including food, such as the poor, orphans, people with disabilities, widows, the unemployed, and the families of those killed, imprisoned or injured by the Israeli military. These enactments do not exclusively relate to the right to food; they are associated with various economic difficulties affecting marginalized groups in society. As has been noted earlier, most of these enactments are applied on an *ad hoc* basis, i.e. not systematically or in a sustainable manner. They are mostly administered by the Ministry of Social Affairs on the basis of humanitarian considerations, i.e. as a matter of charity and not as a matter of right, often relying on funds derived from external donors.

In order to conform to Article 11 of the Covenant, Palestine should 'consider the adoption of a *framework law* as a major instrument in the implementation of the national strategy concerning the right to food. The framework law should include provisions on its purpose; the targets or goals to be achieved and the time frame to be set for the achievement of those targets; the means whereby the purpose could be achieved described in broad terms, in particular the intended collaboration with civil society and the private sector and with international organizations; institutional responsibility for the process; and the national mechanisms for its monitoring.'[148]

The Right to Housing

The right to adequate housing encompasses not merely a roof over one's head, but also a number of requirements that together constitute adequate standards of living, as indicated by CESCR in its interpretation of Article 11 of the Covenant. In its General Comment No. 4 of 13 December 1991, entitled 'The right to adequate housing,'[149] the Committee enumerates seven requirements to be met by States in order to realize the right to adequate housing: (1) legal security of tenure; (2) availability of services, materials, facilities and infrastructure; (3) affordability; (4) habitability; (5) accessibility; (6) location; and (7) cultural adequacy.[150]

In Palestine, Article 23 of the 2003 Basic Law endorses the right to housing in principle by stating that 'every citizen shall have the right to

---

[148] *Ibid.*, para. 29 (emphasis in the original).
[149] UN Doc. HRI/GEN/1/Rev.7, *op. cit.*, p. 19.
[150] *Ibid.*, para. 8.

proper housing and the Palestinian National Authority shall secure housing for those who are without shelter.'

In concrete terms, while the applicable legislation in Palestine satisfies some of the above requirements indicated by CESCR, others require further legislative action. For example, the question of 'legal security of tenure,' which 'takes a variety of forms, including rental (public and private) accommodation, cooperative housing, lease, owner-occupation, emergency housing and informal settlements, including occupation of land or property;'[151] is met by a number of laws. These include the Land Code,[152] the Landlords and Tenants Law,[153] and the Ownership of Floors, Apartments and Shops Law.[154] The law does not allow eviction from, or confiscation of, property, except for public projects, pursuant to the law and after taking a series of administrative and judicial measures and with equitable compensation.[155] The task of ensuring the availability of services and infrastructure is assigned to various ministries, e.g. education, health, economy, finance, public works and housing, and internal affairs. Municipalities are vested with the mandate to provide various components of services and infrastructure, such as water, electricity, sanitation, hygiene, roads, and construction licensing, pursuant to Local Government Law No. 1 of 12 October 1997.[156] Certain administrative decisions facilitate the purchase and construction of houses at decreased prices for

---

[151] *Ibid.*

[152] Ottoman Land Code of 12 July 1858; Aref Ramadan, ed., *Completion of Laws: Ottoman Laws Valid in Arab States Detached from the Ottoman Government* (Beirut: Science Press, 1928), Vol. 3, p. 7; Land Transfer Ordinance No. 39 of September 1920, Drayton, *op. cit.*, p. 1001.

[153] Law No. 62 of 6 April 1953, Jordan Official Gazette No. 1140, 16 April 1953, p. 661. This law strictly limits the eviction of tenants to cases such as non-payment of rent or inflicting damage on the property. In the absence of one of these grounds, the tenant may remain in the rented property indefinitely. This approach in the Law might affect the right of owners to obtain equitable reimbursement of the actual value of the rent and might discourage investments in this sector. For this reason, the Law ought to be replaced with a view to striking a balance between the rights of landholders and tenants.

[154] Law No. 1 of 6 January 1996, Palestine Gazette No. 11, 11 February 1996, p. 22.

[155] Land Acquisition for Public Purposes Ordinance No. 24 of 10 December 1943, Palestine Gazette No. 1305, 1 December 1943, p. 50; and Land Acquisition for Public Schemes Law No. 2 of 18 December 1952, Jordan Official Gazette No. 1130, 1 January 1953, p. 433.

[156] Palestine Gazette No. 20, 29 November 1997, p. 5.

certain needy segments of the community.[157] Other executive orders provide for emergency shelters for victims of war and natural disasters.[158] Yet full compliance with Article 11 of the Covenant requires, according to CESCR, further efforts which might be beyond the capacity of even the most economically advanced States,[159] let alone developing countries and a 'State' that is still at the stage of emergence like Palestine.

The reference in Article 11(1) of ICESCR to 'the essential importance of international co-operation' is of particular relevance to the effective exercise of the right to housing. Such cooperation might be achieved with regard to Palestine, for instance, through housing projects that the international community, represented by international organizations and individual States, ought to offer, particularly as the issue of Palestine is a global issue that the international community has an obligation to resolve. Issues such as refugee displacement outside their original places of residence, confiscation of land by Israel, the construction of Jewish settlements in the West Bank, the ongoing displacement of inhabitants from their places of residence and eviction from their houses, particularly near settlements and the separation wall, and the demolition of houses entail violations of various aspects of the right to adequate housing as defined by ICESCR.[160] Palestine would nevertheless continue to be responsible for formulating policies directed towards the realization of the

---

[157] Housing Cooperative Societies Regulation No. 42 of 27 September 1959, Jordan Official Gazette No. 1447, 17 October 1959, p. 881; Decision on the Allocation of State Lands for Housing Cooperative Societies No. 45 of 2 April 1997, Palestine Gazette No. 17, 30 April 1997, p. 47; Decision of the Minister of Public Works and Housing No. 1 of 19 February 2004 on the Regulation of Selling and Leasing of Real Estates Owned by the Ministry, Palestine Gazette No. 49, 17 June 2004, p. 223; Decision of the Minister of Public Works and Housing No. 1 of 9 April 2012 on the Regulation of Selling of Houses in the Ministry's Housing Projects, Palestine Gazette No. 96, 10 June 2012, p. 67.

[158] Decision of the Council of Ministers No. 127 of 18 September 2006 concerning the Compensation for Demolished Houses, *op. cit.*

[159] CESCR's General Comment No. 4, *op. cit.*, para. 4.

[160] Report of the Special Rapporteur on Adequate Housing, visit to occupied Palestinian territories, UN Doc. E/CN.4/2003/5, 10 June 2002, paras. 79 and 80. After concluding that Israel has failed to fulfil its obligations under ICESCR (para. 82), the UN expert said that 'the international community of States remains duty bound to intervene to protect the Palestinian community, their homes and lands from further destruction and to ensure that the occupying Power is held to account for breaches of humanitarian law and other treaty obligations so as to ensure restitution of the Palestinian's human right to housing, including their public and private lands and other natural resources' (para. 83)..

right to adequate housing, adopting a national housing strategy,[161] approaching international donors, placing the question of housing on its list of priorities, reforming existing legislation and enacting new statutes that contribute to the full crystallization of that right for needy people.[162] As the said General Comment puts it, 'the role of formal legislative and administrative measures should not be underestimated in this context.'[163]

The Right to Health

In its General Comment No. 14 of 12 May 2000, entitled 'The right to the highest attainable standard of health,'[164] CESCR notes that 'the right to health embraces a wide range of socio-economic factors that promote conditions in which people can lead a healthy life, and extends to the underlying determinants of health, such as food and nutrition, housing, access to safe and potable water and adequate sanitation, safe and healthy working conditions, and a healthy environment.'[165] To assess compliance with the right to health standards set out in Article 12 of ICESCR, one should review pieces of legislation relating to these areas of service and others, since the obligations under Article 12(2) are just some examples of State obligations.

The following is a brief survey of the applicable legislation in this area.

Right to Child and Maternal Health

'The provision for the reduction of the stillbirth-rate and of infant mortality and for the healthy development of the child' (Article 12(2(a)) of the Covenant) is dealt with in a number of applicable laws. The Palestinian Child Law of 2004[166] prescribes a range of provisions aiming to protect and improve the health of children. The Law obliges the Ministry of Health to issue a 'Health Card' to every child for the purpose of regular

---

[161] CESCR's General Comment No. 4, *op. cit.*, para. 12.

[162] *Ibid.*, paras. 13,14 and 19.

[163] *Ibid.*, para. 15. See also paragraph 17 for more concrete legislative actions that States are obliged to undertake in order to meet the requirements of Article 11(1) of ICESCR.

[164] UN Doc. HRI/GEN/1/Rev.7, *op. cit.*, p. 86.

[165] CESCR's General Comment No. 14, *op. cit.*, para. 4.

[166] *Op. cit.*

health checks.[167] The vaccination of children is made free of charge.[168] The Law requires spouses to conduct medical checks before marriage to ensure the non-transmission of diseases to children.[169] The Law incorporates declaratory rules[170] on the protection of children from pollution, use of the media for public awareness relating to the prevention of transmittable diseases, the promotion of school health,[171] and action against the use of tobacco, alcohol and drugs by children.[172] The Regulation on Governmental Health Insurance No. 113 of 9 August 2004[173] makes medical treatment of children under the age of three free of charge, regardless of whether the child is insured or not.[174]

Other legislation adds specific measures concerning maternal and infant health. The Public Health Law of 2004[175] offers free vaccination to pregnant women, provides for child prophylactic vaccination, compels parents or legal guardians to comply with vaccination programmes established by the Ministry of Health, provides for penalties in the event of non-compliance, and includes instructions on child health awareness.[176] Anti-Smoking Law No. 25 of 28 March 2005[177] prohibits smoking, subject to sanctions, in schools and kindergarten or nursery terraces or playgrounds, and the importing or selling of cigarette-like toys.[178] The regulations pertaining to the transportation law comprise rules on the safety of children while travelling in motor cars, such as the compulsory use of security belts and safety seats.[179] The Regulation of the Licensing of the Radio, Television, Satellite and Wireless Stations of 2004[180] prohibits

---

[167] Article 23. Paragraph 2 of this article directs the Minister of Health to issue a regulation that specifies the form and content of this card. The regulation has not been enacted so far.
[168] Article 22(2).
[169] Article 24.
[170] The Law does not provide for sanctions for non-compliance with these provisions.
[171] Article 26.
[172] Article 27.
[173] Palestine Gazette No. 52, 18 January 2005, p. 263.
[174] Article 6(A).
[175] *Op. cit.*
[176] Articles 4-8 (child health rights) and Articles 80 and 81 (penalties for those who break the law).
[177] Palestine Gazette No. 68, 7 March 2007, p. 10.
[178] Articles 5, 9, 12 and 13.
[179] Regulation No. 393 of 13 September 2005 concerning Transportation Law No. 5 of 2000, Palestine Gazette No. 66, 22 July 2006, p. 45, Articles 226 and 246.
[180] Palestine Gazette No. 54, 23 April 2005, p. 90.

media outlets from publishing or broadcasting any material that contains photos, stories or news harmful to children's physical or mental health.[181] As noted above, the Midwifery, Motherhood and Childhood Care Occupation Law of 1959[182] protects women during child delivery. The Labour Law of 2000 grants paid maternity leave and breast-feeding breaks, and prohibits requiring pregnant women to work extra hours; moreover, mothers are provided with free primary medical care by the Childhood and Motherhood Care Centres of the Ministry of Health.

Rules on various aspects of children's health can also be adduced from criminal law, which severely punishes crimes against children such as rape, sexual harassment, abandonment, and failure to provide food, housing, shelter or clothing.[183] The juvenile justice law (which, e.g., offers probation and psychological treatment and prohibits torture);[184] the prisons law (e.g. the separation of children from adults and rehabilitation programmes);[185] the personal status laws (e.g. provisions governing the minimum age of marriage, alimony, and shelter and clothing for children);[186] and the regulations applicable to alternative families;[187] are all instances of legislation that contains rules relating to child protection.

---

[181] Article 12(iv)(5). See also Instructions of the Quality of the Environment Authority on the Protection of Food from Radiation Contamination of 7 April 2003, Palestine Gazette No. 45, 24 May 2003, p. 113.

[182] Jordan Official Gazette No. 1413, 14 February 1959, p. 173.

[183] Penal Code Ordinance No. 74 of 14 December 1936, Palestine Gazette, Supplement 1, No. 652, 14 December 1936, p. 399, e.g. Articles 165, 167, 184-188, 226-229, 253 and 260 (Gaza Strip); Penal Code No. 16 of 10 April 1960, Jordan Official Gazette No. 1487, 1 May 1960, p. 374, e.g. Articles 279, 287-291, 298, 305, 314 and 331 (West Bank).

[184] Juvenile Rehabilitation Law No. 16 of 29 April 1954, applicable in the West Bank, Jordan Official Gazette No. 1182, 16 May 1954, p. 396; Juvenile Offenders Ordinance No. 2 of 18 February 1937, applicable in the Gaza Strip, Palestine Gazette No. 667, Supplement 1, 18 February 1937, p. 187.

[185] Rehabilitation and Correction Centers ('Prisons') Law No. 6 of 28 May 1998, Palestine Gazette No. 24, 1 July 1998, p. 87, Articles 28, 29 and 60.

[186] Family Law (Order No. 303) of 10 February 1954, Palestine Gazette (Gaza Strip), No. 35, 15 June 1954, p. 869; Personal Status Law No. 61 of 1 December 1976, Jordan Official Gazette No. 2668, 1 December 1976, p. 2,756; Personal Status and Endowments of the Arab Anglican Community Law of 1954 (a scanned copy of this law is available at the *Palestinian Legal and Judicial System* 'Al-Muqtafi,' Institute of Law, Birzeit University, Palestine; it does not provide the name of the publisher or the publication date); Code of Cannon Law of 25 January 1983 (London: Collins Liturgical Publishers, September 1983).

[187] Alternative Families Regulations No. 70 of 20 July 1963, Jordan Official Gazette No. 1704, 15 August 1963, p. 1,053.

The above discussion clearly shows that the applicable legislation in Palestine endeavours to meet international standards relating to children's right to health.

The Right to Healthy Natural and Workplace Environments

'The improvement of all aspects of environmental and industrial hygiene' (Article 12(2-b) of ICESCR) requires in the view of CESCR: (1) preventive measures against occupational accidents and diseases; (2) an adequate supply of potable water, public hygiene and sanitation; (3) a reduction of the population's exposure to harmful substances such as radiation, harmful chemicals or other detrimental environmental conditions; and (4) action to discourage the abuse of alcohol, tobacco and drugs.[188]

The applicable system has addressed these issues by a series of laws. The Labour Law of 2000 and its bylaws comprise preventive measures in respect of accidents and diseases, under the titles 'occupational safety and hygiene,' 'child labour,' 'work of women,' and 'work injuries and occupational diseases,' as discussed above. The provision of potable water, public hygiene and basic sanitation are the responsibility of municipalities under the Local Government Law of 1997.[189] Towns and Villages Planning and Buildings Law No. 79 of 10 September 1966[190] lays down rules on planning for a suitable water supply and sanitation for any building as a prerequisite for obtaining a construction licence.[191] Environment Law No. 7 of 28 December 1999,[192] which provides for specific penalties in cases of non-compliance, deals with protection against dangerous garbage,[193] specifies standards for potable water,[194] lays the basis for the sanitation system,[195] and provides for precautions against the pollution of seawater.[196] Water Law No. 3 of 17 July 2002[197] elaborates in its 44 Articles on the mandate of the Water Authority, which includes inspecting water resources to prevent pollution and regulating the use of potable water and the use of water for commercial, industrial and

---

[188] CESCR's General Comment No. 14, *op. cit.*, para. 15.

[189] *Op. cit.*, Article 15(A), items 3, 5, 8, 9, 19, 23 and 24.

[190] Jordan Official Gazette No. 1952, 25 September 1966, p. 1921.

[191] Articles 14, 15, 19, 43, 48, 52, 60 and 67.

[192] Palestine Gazette No. 32, 29 February 2000, p. 38.

[193] Article 13.

[194] Article 28.

[195] Articles 29 and 30.

[196] Articles 37 and 38.

[197] Palestine Gazette No. 43, 5 September 2002, p. 5.

agricultural purposes. The Agriculture Law of 2003[198] sets out instructions for the use of non-potable water for agriculture,[199] prohibits the use of sewerage for irrigation,[200] and criminalizes those who pollute water resources.[201] It provides for concrete measures to ensure healthy animal and fish products.[202] The Public Health Law of 2004 requires the Ministry of Health to protect inhabitants from garbage, sewerage, and chemical and industrial toxics.[203] It introduces rules that protect wells, springs, rivers and beaches against pollution.[204] These legislative enactments, among others that have been discussed above,[205] contribute to the prevention or reduction of the population's exposure to harmful substances.

Action to discourage the abuse of alcohol, tobacco and drugs is dealt with in the Child Law of 2004 (see above), the Public Health Law of 2004,[206] the Anti-Smoking Law of 2005,[207] the Intoxicating Liquors Law of 1952,[208] anti-drugs rules,[209] and the penal codes.[210]

---

[198] *Op. cit.*

[199] Article 54

[200] Article 55.

[201] Article 65.

[202] Articles 67-76.

[203] Article 42.

[204] Article 45.

[205] Under Articles 6 and 7 on the right to work and Article 11 on the right to adequate standards of living.

[206] Article 44.

[207] *Op. cit.*

[208] No. 15 of 23 December 1952, Jordan Official Gazette No. 1131, 17 January 1953, p. 460. See also Food Control (Alcoholic Liquors) (Restriction of Manufacture) Order of 18 September 1943, Palestine Gazette, Supplement 2, No. 1290, 23 September 1943, p. 1087.

[209] Dangerous Drugs Rules of 12 September 1936, Palestine Gazette, Supplement 2, No. 635, 1 October 1936, p. 1,392; Order on Dangerous Drugs (West Bank) No. 558 of 16 February 1975, *Proclamations, Orders and Appointments* (Israeli Occupation, West Bank), No. 34, 24 December 1975, p. 1,355; Presidential Decree No. 3 of 24 June 1999 on the Establishment of the High Committee for the Prevention of Illegal Drugs and Mental Inebriations, Palestine Gazette No. 62, 25 March 2006, p. 119.

[210] Penal Code of 1936, *op. cit.*, Articles 15, 101 and 234; Penal Code of 1960, *op. cit.*, Articles 390-392.

The Right to Prevention, Treatment and Control of Diseases[211]

This requirement of Article 12(2(c)) of ICESCR can be tracked through a number of laws applicable since the period of Ottoman rule in the country, starting with the Regulations on Prohibition of the Spreading of Contagious Diseases in All Schools of 23 February 1913,[212] which is still applicable in Palestine since it has never been replaced.[213] Legislative developments continued under the British mandate,[214] the Egyptian administration in the Gaza Strip,[215] Jordanian rule in the West Bank,[216] even under Israeli occupation,[217] and under Palestinian self-rule.

A number of laws from past periods relating to the control of diseases are still enforceable in Palestine. Others were subsequently replaced. The Public Health Law of 2004 contains provisions on the prevention of contagious diseases, including the obligation of inhabitants to notify the authorities about spreading diseases, the collection of data and statistics, the placing of people with contagious illness under quarantine, the monitoring of transport, the conduct of medical checks for travellers, animal farms, workplaces and food products, the conduct of public awareness programmes on best health practices, and action against sources of disease, such as garbage, sewage, industrial toxics, chemicals or radiation.[218] The Child Law of 2004, as mentioned above, incorporates measures to protect children from disease by means of compulsory vaccination and free medical care.[219] The Agriculture Law of 2003[220] incorporates various rules aimed at protecting the inhabitants against

---

[211] CESCR's General Comment No. 14, *op. cit.*, para. 16.

[212] Ramadan, *op. cit.*, Vol. 6, p. 380.

[213] Regulation of Contagious and Infectious Diseases of 13 April 1914, Ramadan, *op. cit.*, Vol. 6, p. 397.

[214] E.g. Accidents and Occupational Diseases Notification Ordinance of 12 May 1945, Palestine Gazette, Supplement 1, No. 1409, 13 May 1945, p. 93.

[215] E.g. Order Relating to Notification of Deaths and Births as well as Vaccination and Diseases No. 33 of 25 July 1948, Palestine Gazette No. 2, 31 March 1950, p. 54.

[216] E.g. Decision of the Council of Ministers on the Plan of Action for the Control of Prevalent Ocular Diseases of 15 October 1961, Jordan Official Gazette No. 1581, 16 November 1961, p. 1,513.

[217] Proclamation on the Public Health (Contagious Diseases) of 4 November 1984, *Proclamations, Orders and Appointments* (Israeli Occupation, Gaza Strip) No. 74, 15 October 1986, p. 7,933.

[218] Articles 9-45.

[219] Articles 24-28 and 45-47.

[220] *Op. cit.*

diseases that might be spread through animals, plants or food products. It vests the Ministry of Agriculture with the power to fight such diseases.[221] The Labour Law of 2000 provides for protective measures against contagious diseases in workplaces and regarding occupational accidents (see above).

Administrative orders have complemented some of these laws and introduced extra stipulations to protect workers' and inhabitants' health. Such orders include Decision of the Council of Ministers No. 47 of 22 March 2004 on the List of Risks of Work Injuries, Career Diseases, Grave Accidents . . .;[222] Decision of the Council of Ministers No. 49 of 22 March 2004 on the Preventive List of Work Hazards and Career Diseases;[223] Instructions by the Minister of Labour of 2005 on the Protection of Workers in Gas and Petroleum Materials;[224] Regulation of the Poultry Incubators of 26 December 2005;[225] Instructions by the Quality of Environment Authority on the Protection of Food Materials from Radiation Contamination of 2003;[226] Regulation No. 17 of 22 December 2003 on the First Aid Medical Kits in Institutions;[227] and Regulation concerning Agriculture Quarantine No. 18 of 29 September 2008.[228]

These examples show that Palestine embraces an established system of disease prevention comparable to that of neighbouring countries through legislation stemming from the various powers that ruled Palestine: Turkey, Britain, Jordan, Egypt and Israel. The Palestinian legislator has built on these historical laws, and has updated and modernized them in such a way as to meet the international standards enshrined in ICESCR, Article 12(2(c)).

---

[221] Article 2(3) and Articles 45-47. See also the Regulation of Licensing the Construction of Animal Yards of 10 July 2003, Palestine Gazette No. 44, 31 March 2003, p. 225; Council of Ministers Decision No. 243 of 20 October 2005 on Fish Protection, Palestine Gazette No. 64, 31 May 2006, p. 425.

[222] Palestine Gazette No. 52, 18 January 2005, p. 123.

[223] *Ibid.*, p. 144.

[224] *Op. cit.*

[225] Council of Ministers Decision No. 380, Palestine Gazette No. 65, 14 June 2006, p. 428, Article 13.

[226] *Op. cit.*

[227] Palestine Gazette No. 49, 17 June 2004, p. 163.

[228] Palestine Gazette No. 81, 9 May 2009, p. 67.

The Right to Health Facilities, Goods and Services[229]

These sub-rights have been dealt with in Palestine through the regulation of health institutions, hospitals, clinics, medical professions, medicine, and health insurance. The Public Health Law of 2004 is the most comprehensive legislation in this regard. With regard to medical institutions, the Law directs the Ministry of Health to ensure equitable geographical distribution of governmental hospitals, clinics and pharmacies throughout the country in order to guarantee 'the health needs of citizens.'[230] The Law prescribes a system for private hospitals, medical centres and clinics, including licensing, required qualifications of personnel, and control of service prices, and sets up inspection mechanisms for such institutions.[231] It requires those working in 'medical professions' (human medicine, dentistry, pharmacy) or 'auxiliary medical professions' (e.g. nursing, diagnostic radiology, medical laboratories, vision screening, processing of eyeglasses, hearing screening, midwifery, anaesthesia, physical therapy, dental laboratories)[232] to acquire a licence from the Ministry of Health as well as from the relevant professional associations.[233] The Law prohibits the distribution or sale of any medicine that has not been registered at, and endorsed by, the Ministry based on a unified 'medical constitution.'[234]

The Public Health Law is supplemented by other laws and executive acts relating to the health sector in both Gaza and the West Bank. Examples of such laws include the Pharmacists Ordinance of 14 November 1921,[235] the Pharmacists Dealing in Drugs and Poisons Law of 22 June 1927,[236] Medical Practitioners Ordinance No. 58 of 29 December 1947,[237] Dentists Ordinance No. 1 of 7 March 1945,[238] Medical Doctors Association Law No. 14 of 1954,[239] Dental Association Law No. 11 of 27 December 1956,[240] Pharmaceutical Association Law No. 10 of 18

---

[229] CESCR's General Comment No. 14, *op. cit.*, para. 17.

[230] Article 46.

[231] Articles 46-57.

[232] Article 1.

[233] Articles 62-64.

[234] Articles 65-72.

[235] Drayton, *op. cit.*, p. 1,286 (Gaza Strip).

[236] Jordan Official Gazette No. 168, 15 October 1927, p. 49 (West Bank).

[237] Palestine Gazette, Supplement 1, No. 1637, 30 December 1947, p. 404.

[238] Palestine Gazette, Supplement 1, No. 1395, 8 March 1945, p. 1.

[239] Jordan Official Gazette No. 1179, 17 April 1954, p. 322.

[240] Jordan Official Gazette No. 1265, 17 March 1956, p. 1,359.

February 1957,[241] and Veterinary Surgeons Law No. 7 of 27 January 1960.[242] Examples of executive acts include the Regulation on the Governmental Health Insurance of 2004,[243] the Decision on Cases of Illness Uncovered by the Governmental Health Insurance of 2007,[244] and the Decision on Reducing the Fees of Licensing Health Care Institutions of 2007.[245]

As may be seen from the legislation surveyed above; most laws applicable in Palestine date back to the British, Jordanian or even Turkish eras. With the exception of the Public Health Law of 2004, the Palestinian Authority has mostly enacted executive acts relating to the right to health based on older laws. Nothing prevents the Authority from modernizing the legal system relating to the health sector. Executive decisions are often enacted on an *ad hoc* basis and relate to particular cases, or they sometimes effectively lapse shortly after their issuance. Such enactments, even when they embody substantive rules, can easily be revoked by the issuing party, unlike parliamentary law, which is subject to adequate deliberation and cannot be rapidly changed, as indicated above.

This discussion reveals that the applicable legislation in Palestine generally meets the standards required to respect and protect the right to health. What remains to be fully achieved, however, is fulfilment of this right by providing health services to the most needy, particularly the poor who are not in a position to afford expensive medical treatment for serious illnesses or certain chronic diseases.[246] Palestine should update a number of its laws not only to meet international human rights standards but also to reflect new scientific developments. It needs modern laws on the medical profession and medicine, protection of those infected with HIV/AIDS, a health insurance system that supports those unable to afford medical treatment, a greater focus on mental health,[247] and public awareness of the right to health and best health practices.

---

[241] Jordan Official Gazette No. 1323, 17 March 1957, p. 283.

[242] Jordan Official Gazette No. 1476, 16 March 1960, p. 154.

[243] *Op. cit.*

[244] Council of Ministers No. 89 of 10 September 2007; Palestine Gazette No. 77 of 9 September 2008, p. 148.

[245] Council of Ministers No. 46 of 23 July 2007; Palestine Gazette No. 73, 13 September 2007, p. 139.

[246] CESCR's General Comment No. 14, *op. cit.*, paras. 33 and 50-52.

[247] For example, hospitals dealing with mentally ill people are still ruled by the Ottoman Law of Mentally Ill Hospitals of 26 March 1876, Ramadan, *op. cit.*, Vol. 5, p. 289.

These issues could be covered by framework legislation, preferably by a law adopted by parliament or by a presidential decree pursuant to Article 43 of the 2003 Basic Law when the parliament is absent, which can be formulated along the lines proposed by CESCR.[248] This legislation should be based on a national strategy 'to ensure to all the enjoyment of the right to health, based on human rights principles which define the objectives of that strategy, and the formulation of policies and corresponding right to health indicators and benchmarks. The national health strategy should identify the resources available to attain defined objectives, as well as the most cost-effective way of using those resources.'[249] The Plan of Action of the National Steering Committee for the Reform and Development of the Health Sector and System of Health Care, endorsed by Palestinian Council of Ministers Decision No. 6 of 3 January 2006,[250] already constitutes a good step towards the realization of the framework legislation. However, such a plan requires follow-up aimed at formulating a concrete legislative framework that translates these policies into a binding instrument.

The Right to Education

Article 13 of ICESCR deals with the right to education, which should be realized by States through institutional measures adopted, *inter alia*, by legislation. The framework of the right to education is set out in paragraph 1,[251] and the subsequent paragraphs of the Article specify concrete measures that should be taken at the levels of primary education, secondary education and higher education, measures to eradicate illiteracy, and measures pertaining to systems of fellowships, continuous education and private schools.

Article 24 of the 2003 Basic Law embraces most of these measures by stipulating: '1. Every citizen shall have the right to education. Education shall be compulsory until at least the end of the basic level. Education shall be free in public schools and institutions. 2. The National Authority shall supervise all levels of education and its institutions, and shall strive to upgrade the educational system. 3. The law shall guarantee the independence of universities, institutes of higher education, and scientific research centers in a manner that guarantees the freedom of scientific research as well as literary, artistic and cultural creativity. The National

---

[248] CESCR's General Comment No. 14, *op. cit.*, paras. 53 and 54.

[249] *Ibid.*, para. 53.

[250] Palestine Gazette No. 65, 14 June 2006, p. 522.

[251] This resembles Article 26(2) of the Universal Declaration of Human Rights of 10 December 1948; UN Doc. A/811, 16 December 1948.

Authority shall encourage and support such creativity. 4. Private schools and educational institutions shall comply with the curriculum approved by the National Authority and shall be subject to its supervision.'

Like the right to health, most of the applicable legislation concerning education in Palestine is inherited from past periods. The older laws comprise chiefly the Education Ordinance of 2 January 1933,[252] applicable in the Gaza Strip, and Education Law No. 16 of 11 May 1964,[253] applicable in the West Bank. These two instruments offer the framework for the education system in Palestine. A number of additional enactments complement these laws with respect to specific areas of education, such as Curricula and Textbooks Law No. 19 of 16 May 1963.[254]

It should be noted that these pieces of legislation were enacted before the evolution of international human rights law, particularly prior to the adoption of ICESCR. By this fact alone, it can *prima facie* be concluded that the applicable law in Palestine does not take into consideration international standards relating to education as set forth in the Covenant. It emerges, however, on a closer reading of such instruments, that a number of the rules they contain are compatible with international standards, such as the adoption of an educational philosophy comparable to that reflected in Article 13(1) of ICESCR, namely: 'development of human personality and the sense of its dignity;' 'protecting fundamental freedoms;' 'participating effectively in a free society;' 'promoting understanding, tolerance and friendship among all nations;'[255] laying the basis for private, non-governmental and religious schools;[256] adopting a basic system for continuous education;[257] having an 'adequate fellowship system;'[258] and encouraging fundamental education 'for those persons who have not received or completed the whole period of their primary education' by educational programmes for persons who are illiterate.[259]

With a few exceptions, chiefly in the field of higher education as we shall see shortly, the Palestinian Authority has tried to upgrade the education system using the vehicle of executive orders and practical actions rather than parliamentary enactments. Administrative decisions

---

[252] Drayton, *op. cit.*, p. 693.

[253] Jordan Official Gazette No. 1763, 26 May 1964, p. 720.

[254] Jordan Official Gazette No. 1688, 30 March 1964, p. 614.

[255] Education Law of 1964, *op. cit.*, Articles 3 and 4.

[256] Education Ordinance of 1933, *op. cit.*, Articles 4 and 5; Education Law of 1964, *op. cit.*, Articles 59-77.

[257] Education Law of 1964, *op. cit.*, Article 24.

[258] *Ibid.*, Articles 100-109.

[259] *Ibid.*, Articles 110 and 111.

cover various areas of education, such as the reform of the Ministry of Education[260] and decisions on constructing school buildings,[261] fellowships,[262] scientific research,[263] and vocational and technical education.[264]

Higher education has been comprehensively regulated by the adoption of Higher Education Law No. 11 of 2 November 1998.[265] The Law recognizes the right to higher education for all;[266] accords universities and research institutions independence from the government with separate juridical personality;[267] grants the Ministry of Higher Education the power to supervise higher education institutions in order to ensure a uniform system in Palestinian universities;[268] divides educational institutions into governmental,[269] non-governmental (or not-for-profit)[270] and private institutions;[271] defines the various academic decrees/diplomas (e.g. bachelor's, master's, doctorate) and the duration of teaching in each case;[272] and provides for the licensing of new educational institutions by the Ministry,[273] the accreditation of new academic programmes[274] and the administration of educational institutions.[275] The Law, by and large, served

---

[260] Decision No. 67 of 27 June 2006 on the Reformation of the Ministry of Education, Palestine Gazette No. 68, 7 March 2007, p. 114.

[261] Decision of the Council of Minister No. 1 of 4 January 2005 the Provision of Needs for Public Education including School Buildings, Palestine Gazette, No. 55, 27 June 2005, p. 190.

[262] Presidential Decree No. 162 of 10 August 2010, Palestine Gazette No. 88, 10 December 2010, p. 58; Presidential Decision No. 4 of 20 February 2005, Palestine Gazette No. 54, 23 April 2005, p. 61.

[263] Council of Ministers Decision No. 125 of 6 September 2005 on the Allocation of Annual Budget for the Council of Scientific Research, Palestine Gazette No. 63, 27 April 2006, p. 635.

[264] Council of Ministers Decision No. 145 of 24 May 2004 on the Implementation of the Regulation Relative to Vocational and Technical Training, Palestine Gazette No. 53, 28 February 2005, p. 235.

[265] Palestine Gazette No. 27, 8 December 1998, p. 28.

[266] Article 2.

[267] Articles 3 and 7.

[268] Articles 5, 6 and 19.

[269] Article 14. A separate regulation for governmental universities has also been adopted. Palestine Gazette No. 83, 1 November 2009, p. 75.

[270] Article 15.

[271] Article 16.

[272] Article 20.

[273] Article 17.

[274] Article 18.

[275] Articles 11-16.

to formalize the pre-existing situation of higher education in the country. While it generally conforms to Article 13(2(c)) of ICESCR, it fails to lay the foundations for, or even to mention, 'the progressive introduction of free education.'[276]

The education system in Palestine has advanced in practice well beyond existing legal texts. With the exception of higher education, the system lacks a developed legal framework.[277] For example, the law prescribes that primary education shall be compulsory for nine years[278] and secondary education for three years;[279] in practice, primary education lasts for ten years and secondary education for two years. The law requires the Ministry of Education to hold a formal examination and to grant an official diploma at the end of compulsory education;[280] such an examination and diploma no longer exist. In addition, there are certain contradictions between the law and the situation on the ground; while the Basic Law requires primary education to be free,[281] schools charge fees in practice.[282]

Palestine needs at least to codify and update its education system in the form of a law, covering philosophy, institutions, schools, curricula, personnel, etc. Such codification can be derived from the executive orders or internal instructions that are currently being used by education officials.[283] The country needs to unify its education system in the Gaza Strip and the West Bank; the 1964 law in the West Bank is more than

[276] However, the system of fellowships discussed above might bridge this gap.

[277] Rules relating to schools might be found in various laws, including Child Law of 2004, *op. cit.*, Articles 37-41; Public Health Law of 2004, *op. cit.*, Article 38; Rights of People with Disabilities Law of 1999, *op. cit.*, Articles 6 and 14; Environment Law of 1999, *op. cit.*, Article 4.

[278] Education Law of 1964, *op. cit.*, Articles 8 and 10.

[279] *Ibid.*, Article 16.

[280] *Ibid.*, Article 55.

[281] Also Education Law of 1964, *op. cit.*, Article 11.

[282] This may be gathered from Council of Ministers Decision No. 80 of 25 July 2006 on the Reduction of Fees at Governmental Schools, Palestine Gazette No. 68, 17 March 2007, p. 127; Council of Ministers Decision No. 96 of 10 September 2007 on the Exemption of the Students of Poor Families and whose Fathers Unemployed from School Fees, Palestine Gazette No. 77, 9 October 2008, p. 156. These decisions imply that students who do not belong to these categories should pay fees.

[283] If one looks at the various instructions, such as the system of diploma accreditation, posted on the website of the Ministry of Education (http://www.mohe.gov.ps), one finds no legal basis for the Ministry's work other than the internal instructions.

twenty years more developed than the 1933 law that is still enforced in Gaza.

The new education system ought to fill in the gaps that are still missing in light of Article 13 of ICESCR, including the establishment of an effective mechanism to ensure that education at the elementary/basic education level is free for all, prevention of non-recognition of the compulsory nature of elementary education, and punishment of those who ignore it, for instance those who cause school drop-out, including parents and employers.

These objectives could be realized, *inter alia*, by adopting the plan of action on primary education based on Article 14 of ICESCR as elaborated by CESCR's General Comment No. 11 of 10 May 1999;[284] taking new global developments in the right to education, such as the Convention on the Rights of the Child of 20 November 1989,[285][286] into account; integrating human rights education into curricula;[287] and adopting 'specific references to gender equality and respect for the environment.'[288]

Cultural Life

To assess the compatibility of the applicable legislation in Palestine with Article 15 of ICESCR, we shall first review legislation on various aspects of cultural issues that set out the framework for the country's cultural legal system. We shall then look in some detail at the legislation relating to scientific research and intellectual property.

There is no single law on culture or on the protection of cultural life in Palestine. However, there are also no legal provisions that restrict cultural activities. At the secondary legislation level, one can find a number of executive orders that protect culture. For instance, the establishment of the Ministry of Culture and its assignment, by Council of Ministers Decision No. 227 of 7 September 2004 on the Ministry of Culture Structure,[289] with a range of functions reflect the degree of importance attached to culture. The Decision gives the Ministry a mandate to preserve popular arts, and to promote the establishment of cultural centres, artistic initiatives, events

---

[284] CESCR, General Comment No. 11: 'Plans of action for primary education' of 10 May 1999, UN Doc. HRI/GEN/1/Rev.7, *op. cit.*, p. 60, paras. 6 and 7.
[285] 1577 UNTS 3 (1990).
[286] Article 29(1).
[287] CESCR, General Comment No. 13: 'The right to education' of 8 December 1999, UN Doc. HRI/GEN/1/Rev.7, *op. cit.*, p. 71, para. 5.
[288] *Ibid.*
[289] Palestine Gazette No. 58, 8 September 2005, p. 103.

involving women and youth, and openness towards other cultures by participating in global festivals and exhibitions and signing cultural agreements with other States.[290] It includes provisions on theatre, folklore, poetry, singing, handmade industries, historical manuscripts, translation, music, fine arts and cultural heritage. It lays down substantive rules that are equivalent to parliamentary law.

Other legislation confirms this official interest in promoting culture. Such legislation relates to the theatre,[291] the merging of a number of institutions (Palestinian Poetry House, National Libraries House, Higher Council for Educational, Culture and Science) with the Ministry of Culture,[292] and the establishment of independent artistic institutions.[293] There is also legislation inherited from past periods that protects the cultural heritage, such as the Antiquities Ordinance of 31 December 1929,[294] the Palestine Archaeological Museum Rules of 29 November 1937[295] and Antiquities Law No. 51 of 1966.[296]

Although its applicable legislation does not conflict with Article 15 of ICESCR, Palestine still needs to upgrade its legal system and to adopt a comprehensive law on culture. Following its recent access to membership of UNESCO, Palestine needs to undergo systematic legislative reform in order to meet its international obligations as set out in a number of treaties relating to culture, particularly the Convention concerning the Protection of the World Cultural and Natural Heritage of 16 November 1972.[297]

Although the legal system in Palestine does not contradict Article 15(1)(a) of ICESCR and satisfies the obligation of 'abstention' or 'non-interference with the exercise of cultural practices and with access to cultural goods and services,' as required by the CESCR's Comment No. 21, entitled '[r]ight of everyone to take part in cultural life' of 20

---

[290] Article 2.

[291] Decision of the Council of Ministers No. 95 of 12 July 2005 on the Affiliation of the Palestinian Children's Theatre to the Ministry of Culture, Palestine Gazette No. 63, 27 April 2006, p. 580.

[292] Decision of the Council of Ministers No. 124 of 11 September 2006 on the Merger of Artistic Institutions to the Ministry of Culture, Palestine Gazette No. 69, 27 April 2007, p. 189.

[293] Presidential Decree No. 5 of 3 April 2011 concerning the Establishment of *Alashekeen* Group for Arts and Culture [National Songs], Palestine Gazette No. 91, 10 October 2011, p. 19.

[294] Drayton, *op. cit.*, p. 30.

[295] Palestine Gazette, Supplement 2, No. 742, 9 December 1937, p. 1,509.

[296] Jordan Official Gazette No. 1936, 16 July 1966, p. 1,327.

[297] 1037 UNTS 151 (1977).

November 2009,[298] Palestine still needs to take proactive measures to upgrade its legislation relating to culture. It needs to adopt legislation on culture that not only respects cultural rights, but also protects such rights and obliges the government to establish museums, libraries, theatres, cinemas, monuments, heritage sites, and parks and to organize cultural events as well as to facilitate learning from and interaction with other cultures within the country and abroad, and to teach and open access to 'cultural goods,' such as history, music, poetry, traditions, folklore, traditional cooking, dancing, literature, language, and science. The legislation should particularly guarantee access to these cultural installations and goods by the poor, children, women, people with special needs, minorities, and communities in rural and deprived urban areas.[299]

Following its recent membership in UNESCO, Palestine needs to undertake systematic reform in order to discharge its international obligations as set out in a number of treaties relating to culture. As a historical turning point, on 8 December 2011 Palestine ratified the Convention concerning the Protection of the World Cultural and Natural Heritage of 16 November 1972,[300] leading to its entry into force on 8 March 2012.[301] It simultaneously became a party to other three treaties on cultural diversity,[302] intangible cultural heritage,[303] and underwater cultural heritage.[304] This is the first time that Palestine, as a State, has acceded to multilateral treaties. On 22 March 2012, Palestine ratified two additional treaties: the Convention for the Protection of Cultural Property in the Event of Armed Conflict of 14 May 1954,[305] and the Convention on the Means of Prohibiting and Preventing the Illicit Import, Export and Transfer of Ownership of Cultural Property of 14 November 1970.[306] Other UNESCO instruments that are now open for Palestine include

---

[298] UN Doc. E/C.12/GC/21, 21 December 2009, para. 6.
[299] Paras. 52-54 and 66-70.
[300] 1037 UNTS 151 (1977).
[301] Office of International Standards and Legal Affairs, 'Ratification by Palestine of the Convention concerning the Protection of the World Cultural and Natural Heritage' (Paris: UNESCO, 16 January 2012).
[302] Convention on the Protection and Promotion of the Diversity of Cultural Expressions of 20 October 2005; UNESCO Doc. CLT-2005/CONVENTION DIVERSITE-CULT REV.2.
[303] Convention for the Safeguarding of the Intangible Cultural Heritage of 17 October 2003; 2368 UNTS 3 (2007).
[304] Convention on the Protection of the Underwater Cultural Heritage of 2 November 2001; 41 *International Legal Materials* 40 (2002).
[305] 249 UNTS 240 (1956).
[306] 1037 UNTS 151 (1977).

treaties on diverse fields such as copyright,[307] protection of phonograms,[308] discrimination in education,[309] and the international exchange and circulation of publications of educational, scientific and cultural materials.[310] The application of these treaties requires enactments to execute them at the national level, including legislation that establishes institutions, allocates resources, and prescribes penalties for those who violate the instruments.

Freedom of 'scientific research and creative activity,' as required by Article 15(3) of ICESCR, has been recognized in principle by Article 24(3) of the 2003 Palestinian Basic Law, which states that the 'law shall guarantee the independence of . . . scientific research centers in a manner that ensures the freedom of scientific research as well as literary, artistic and cultural creativity.'

Concretely, the 1998 Higher Education Law recognized scientific research as an objective of higher education,[311] set up the Council of Scientific Research,[312] and laid the basis for the independence and licensing of research institutions.[313] Other legislation attaches importance to scientific research by allocating budgets for such research,[314] exempting certain scientific institutions from tax,[315] excluding such institutions from censorship measures that apply to imported publications,[316] prohibiting judges from expressing their views on judgments issued by other courts

---

[307] Universal Copyright Convention of 24 July 1971; 943 UNTS 178 (1974).

[308] International Convention for the Protection of Performers, Producers of Phonograms and Broadcasting Organizations of 26 October 1961; 496 UNST 43 (1964).

[309] Convention against Discrimination in Education of 14 December 1960; 429 UNTS 93 (1962).

[310] Agreement for Facilitating the International Circulation of Visual and Auditory Materials of an Educational, Scientific and Cultural character of 10 December 1948; 197 UNTS 3 (1954).

[311] Article 4.

[312] Article 22.

[313] Articles 3 and 23-25.

[314] Banks Law No. 2 of 31 May 2002, Palestine Gazette No. 41, 6 June 2002, p. 5, Article 31(4) (the possibility of allocating up to 2% of the banks' profit to scientific research); Decision of the Council of Ministers No. 125 of 6 September 2005 on the Allocation of an Annual Financial Sum for the Council of Scientific Research, Palestine Gazette No. 63, 27 April 2006, p. 635.

[315] Agriculture Law of 2003, *op. cit.*, Article 40.

[316] Press and Publication Law No. 9 of 25 June 1995, Palestine Gazette No. 6, 26 August 1995, p. 11, Article 38.

except for the purpose of scientific research,[317] and adopting a legal basis for specialized research on sectors such as agriculture,[318] health,[319] water,[320] statistics[321] and sports.[322]

Despite guaranteeing freedom of expression in principle,[323] Publication Law No. 9 of 25 June 1995[324] restricts freedom of publishing. Rules under this Law that impose restrictions include a series of governmental approvals to be obtained, such as approval for any 'foreign finance' without specifying the meaning of this term,[325] the obligation of any seller to notify the Ministry of Information of the import of periodicals two weeks in advance,[326] the duty to acquire permits for the sale of any publications,[327] and the need for governmental bodies, universities and research institutions to acquire personal approval from the Minister for importing 'forbidden materials.'[328] It prescribes strict penalties for the so called 'publishing crimes.'[329]

The protection of authors' moral and material rights, in accordance with Article 15(1(c)) of ICESCR, has long been recognized in Palestine. The extension of the British Copyright Act of 16 December 1911 by Royal Order on 21 March 1924 marked the beginning of legal protection for

---

[317] Decision of the High Judicial Council No. 3 of 10 May 2006 concerning the Judicial Code of Conduct, Palestine Gazette No. 67, 19 October 2006, p. 75, Article 35.

[318] Decision of the Council of Ministers No. 111 of 3 August 2004 on the Regulation of the Palestinian National Centre for Agricultural Research, Palestine Gazette No. 52, 18 January 2005, p. 254.

[319] Higher Health Advisory Council Regulation No. 21 of 23 February 1966, Jordan Official Gazette No. 1908, 17 March 1966, p. 420, Article 4.

[320] Bylaws of the Palestinian Water Authority No. 66 of 5 June 1997, Palestine Gazette No. 18, 4 August 1997, p. 34, Article 9(B)(3).

[321] Decision of the Council of Ministers No. 198 of 1 November 2004 on the Formation of the Advisory Council of Official Statistics, Palestine Gazette No. 54, 23 April 2005, p. 116.

[322] Sports Decree-Law No. 11 of 1 December 2008, Palestine Gazette No. 79, 9 February 2009, p. 10, Article 4(10).

[323] E.g. Article 2 (right to express 'opinions freely by speaking, writing, filming and painting'), Article 4 (freedom of political parties, non-governmental organizations, newspapers), and Article 5 (right to own publishing institutions).

[324] Palestine Gazette No. 6, 29 August 1995, p. 11.

[325] Article 9.

[326] Articles 34 and 35.

[327] Article 36.

[328] Article 38.

[329] Articles 44-48.

authors' rights in the country.[330] The Act, which is still applicable in both the Gaza Strip and the West Bank, protects various authors' rights pertaining to literature, music, drama and 'artistic works,'[331] including books, novels, maps, charts, engineering drawings, oil paintings, cartoons, animations, movie direction, statues, photos, carvings, songs, inscriptions, dance tunes and plays.[332] Such protection includes publishing or re-publishing, lecturing, performing, translating, recording, broadcasting, playing in the cinema or the theatre,[333] selling, renting, distributing, granting as a gift or in the form of a will, and passing rights to heirs.[334]

A number of instruments provide specific protection for trademarks, commercial names, brands, symbols and industrial designs. These include the Patents and Designs Ordinance of 1 January 1925,[335] the Trademarks Ordinance of 21 November 1938,[336] and the Registration of Business Names Ordinance of 24 May 1935[337] in Gaza; as well as Patents and Designs Law No. 22 of 1953,[338] Trademarks Law No. 33 of 25 May 1952,[339] and Business Names Law No. 30 of 5 January 1953[340] in the West Bank.

These instruments, particularly the 1911 Copyright Act, meet the basic requirements of Article 15 (1(c)) of ICESCR, as defined by the CESCR's General Comment No. 17 of 25 November 2005, entitled the 'right of everyone to benefit from the protection of the moral and material interests resulting from any scientific, literary or artistic production of which he or she is the author.'[341] This Comment, *inter alia*, obliges States to adopt 'Adequate legislation and regulations, as well as effective administrative, judicial or other appropriate remedies, for the protection of the moral and material interests of authors.'[342] However, the over 100-year-old enactment needs to be updated and modernized to take into account subsequent

---

[330] Drayton, *op. cit.*, p. 3,204. The text of the Copyright Act of 1911 itself can be found in *ibid.*, p. 3,169.

[331] Article 1(1).

[332] Article 35.

[333] Article 1(2).

[334] Articles 2 and 5.

[335] Drayton, *op. cit.*, p. 1,233.

[336] Palestine Gazette, Supplement 1, No. 843, 24 November 1938, p. 156.

[337] Palestine Gazette, Supplement 1, No. 514, 27 May 1935, p. 175.

[338] Enacted on 30 December 1952, Jordan Official Gazette No. 1131, 17 January 1953, p. 491.

[339] Jordan Official Gazette No. 1110, 1 June 1952, p. 243.

[340] Jordan Official Gazette No. 1131, 17 January 1953, p. 522.

[341] UN Doc. E/C.12/GC/17, 12 January 2006.

[342] Para 18.

developments at the Palestinian and global levels, not only human rights developments, but also the need for consistency between the applicable law of the Gaza Strip with that enforced in the West Bank, and the need to ensure equal treatment, or 'non-discrimination,' of copyright holders in these two parts of the country.[343] The law likewise needs to be updated to reflect electronic and digital developments,[344] to protect cross-border copyright, and to lay the basis for bilateral and multilateral intellectual property treaties, such as those adopted under the auspices of UNESCO (see above) as well as the World Intellectual Property Organization (WIPO) in the fields of industrial property and design, artistic works, copyright, patents, trademarks, phonograms and new varieties of plants.[345] These enactments may fall under the obligation of the State to 'fulfil' its author's rights obligation which requires States 'to adopt appropriate legislative, administrative, budgetary, judicial, promotional and other measures towards the full realization of Article 15, paragraph 1 (c).'[346] Obviously, the launching of legislative reform in light of Article 15 (1(c)) of ICESCR could pave the way for Palestine to become a member of WIPO, another UN agency, to become a party to its series of treaties, and to learn from its technical expertise in the field of intellectual property.[347]

---

[343] *Cf. ibid.*, paras. 19-21: 'Non-discrimination and equal treatment.'

[344] *Ibid.*, para 31: 'States parties must prevent the unauthorized use of scientific,literary and artistic productions that are easily accessible or reproducible through modern communication and reproduction technologies, e.g. by establishing systems of collective administration of authors' rights or by adopting legislation requiring users to inform authors of any use made of their productions and to remunerate them adequately.'

[345] *WIPO Intellectual Property Handbook* (Geneva: WIPO, 2008), pp. 241-363. In this connection, CESCR's General Comment No. 17, *op. cit.*, para 49, stated that 'States parties may obtain guidance on . . . the right to the protection of the moral and material interests of the author, from the World Intellectual Property Organization (WIPO), the United Nations Educational, Scientific and Cultural Organization (UNESCO).' See also *ibid.*, paras. 56 and 57.

[346] CESCR's General Comment No. 17, *op. cit.*, para 28. See also paras 34, 39, 44-45 and 47-48.

[347] L. Shaver and C. Sganga, 'The Right to Take Part in Cultural Life: On Copyright and Human Rights,' 27 *Wisconsin International Law Journal* 637 (2010).

Conclusion

The path leading to Palestine's accession to international treaties is quite long, but at least the door has been opened. It is a historical juncture for Palestine to consider acceding to the two human rights covenants. The time has come to declare, by relevant actions, that Palestine and those under its jurisdiction deserve to live in a place in which global standards are implemented.

In short, Palestine is broadly qualified, in terms of its basic legislative structure, to become a party to the International Covenant on Economic, Social and Cultural Rights. With a view to bringing the country into full compliance with the Covenant and other international human rights instruments, a systematic legislative reform process should be launched.

CHAPTER SEVEN

LEGAL IMPLICATIONS OF THE MEMBERSHIP OF A PALESTINIAN STATE IN THE UN ON CIVILIANS IN THE LIGHT OF INTERNATIONAL HUMANITARIAN LAW

FLORIANA FABBRI AND JACOPO TERROSI

Introduction

The full recognition of Palestine as a State and the prospect of Palestine becoming a member of the United Nations may have crucial legal implications for the definition of the conflict between Palestine and Israel, and for the law that is applicable to the situation. At present the qualification of the conflict between Israel and the occupied territories is highly controversial, but some doctrinal interpretation tends to classify it as a non-international armed conflict. The present chapter demonstrates that the consolidation of a Palestinian State will result in a change in the legal assessment of the conflict, rendering it an international armed conflict. In particular, the new situation will confer on Palestine the status of an 'Occupied State' with the subjective right to have direct recourse to the Security Council. The Security Council will eventually have to take a decision to demand Israel to leave the territory of Palestine immediately in order to restore peace in the area. Basing itself on the changes in the status of Palestine and in the definition of the conflict, this chapter will discuss the change in the legal status of the population of the territory in the light of the Geneva Conventions.

According to Article 1 of the Montevideo Convention on the Rights and Duties of States (1933),[1] four criteria should be fulfilled for an entity to qualify as a State. The requirements are: a permanent population, a

---

[1] League of Nations Treaty Series (LNTS), Vol. CLXV, p. 25, 23 December 1933.

defined territory, a government and the capacity to enter into relations with other States.

The concept of a permanent population is not precisely defined in international law; it must therefore be interpreted in the light of the right to self-determination of peoples.[2] From this perspective, a population may be defined as a mass of individuals who are united by a common bond of solidarity, which is expressed in the fact that they permanently inhabit the same territory and have a formal link of nationality. The existence of a Palestinian population is undisputed, since Palestinians satisfy both the subjective and the objective concept of a nation. The first condition relies on the people's willingness to live together, while the *condition sine qua non* for the objective interpretation is the existence of real factors such as a common history or a shared culture.[3] The Palestinians clearly share all these factors. Furthermore, the existence of a genuinely permanent population in Palestine is supported by the International Court of Justice in its *Advisory Opinion on the Legal Consequences of the Construction of a Wall in the Occupied Palestinian Territory.*[4]

With regard to the government, the State must have a stable and independent political organization capable of taking political decisions and implementing them on its territory, thereby ensuring its autonomy and its independence from third States.[5] There is no doubt that Palestine has a stable and effective government. Public authorities have long been strong enough to assert themselves throughout the territory. The first stage in the process of reform implemented by the Palestinian Authority dates back to 2003. Later, in 2007, the government launched a new reform plan that was broader and more ambitious than the previous one and mainly affected the public administration sector and the security apparatus.[6] The peculiarity of Palestinian State-building stems from the fact that the process was launched before the official end of the conflict and formal independence. Nevertheless, the inverted chronological order of the peace agreement and

---

[2] The UN Human Rights Council affirms 'the inalienable, permanent and unqualified right of the Palestinian people to self-determination, including their right to live in freedom, justice and dignity and to establish their sovereign, independent, democratic and viable contiguous State.' UN Doc. A/HRC/13/L.27, 2010.

[3] *Cf.* the dissenting opinion of Judge Kreca: ICJ, *Case Application of the Convention on the Prevention and Punishment of the Crime of Genocide*, 11 July 1996.

[4] ICJ, *Advisory Opinion on the Legal Consequences of the Construction of a Wall in the Occupied Palestinian Territory*, 9 July 2004, para. 118.

[5] Kreca, *op. cit.*, para.13.

[6] See: http://www.mop-gov.ps/web_files/issues_file/PRDP-en.pdf.

institution-building reforms does not undermine the legitimacy of the Palestinian leadership or the effectiveness of their authority.

The third argument that must be taken into account to confirm the existence of Palestine as a State concerns its capacity to enter into relations with other States. It may be noted in this regard that Palestine has diplomatic relations with many Arab countries as well as with Western States and that it has acquired the status of an observer at the United Nations.

The most controversial element of the statehood definition is territory. The demarcation of Palestinian boundaries has long been questioned by Israel.[7] However, the uncertainty in defining the frontiers of Israel, a cause of disagreement with its Arab neighbours,[8] has not prevented many States and UN members from considering such an entity as a valid State. The same line of reasoning is applicable to the case of Palestine today. In light of this controversy, the issue of recognition by the international community plays a decisive role.

As is well known, the concept of recognition is ambivalent (declarative or constitutive); nevertheless, the relevant practice today requires that the act of recognition should be applicable to a factual situation that already exists. Although recognition by one State has only declarative legal effects, recognition by numerous States provides evidentiary support for the effective existence of statehood. The possibility of becoming a member of the UN is undoubtedly a proof of effectiveness for new States.

The Classification of the Conflict

The qualification of the conflict between Israel and Palestine has long been controversial because the Israeli presence in Palestinian territories is a special case. As a matter of fact, there is as yet no univocal interpretation in national and international jurisprudence or among legal scholars of the presence of an occupation in Gaza since the formal withdrawal of Israel in 2005. Moreover, the characterization of the insurgencies in Palestinian territories is also controversial.

Our first goal consists in understanding which law is applicable in this case; we shall therefore first analyse the plethora of positions advanced so far.

---

[7] The UN demanded on many occasions that Israel respect the borders fixed in the resolutions of 1947 (A/RES/181(II)) and of 1967 (S/RES/242).

[8] PCIJ, *Mosul Boundary Case*, Series B, No. 12, p. 21; ICJ, *Libya/Chad Case*, Reports, 1994, pp. 22-26.

Those who advocate considering the conflict as a non-international one emphasize that the confrontation between Israel and Palestine does not properly meet the definition of an international armed conflict contained in Article 2 of the Geneva Conventions. Indeed, a narrow interpretation of the term 'High Contracting Parties' requires that the conflict should involve only two or more States.[9] According to this interpretation, Palestine cannot be considered as a State entity yet, but the existence of an armed confrontation is not excluded. According to the decision of the International Criminal Tribunal for the Former Yugoslavia (ICTY) in the *Tadić* case, an armed conflict exists whenever there is recourse to armed force between States or there is protracted armed violence between governmental authorities and organized armed groups, or between groups within a State.[10] As international armed conflicts and non-international armed conflicts are mutually exclusive under international humanitarian law (IHL), a conflict which cannot be classified as an international armed conflict is a non-international armed conflict. The occurrence of a non-international armed conflict is determined by the existence of a high threshold of violence,[11] protracted violence over a period of time, and the presence of well-organized parties.[12] Applying these three criteria to the Palestinian context, we may certainly affirm that the level of intensity of the conflict is sufficiently high to consider this confrontation to be a non-international armed conflict. Indeed Palestine exercises command and control over territory and is highly organized and well equipped.[13]

Conversely, Palestine and the Supreme Court of Israel,[14] as well as some legal scholars, affirm that there is clear evidence of an international armed conflict, based on the definition of an international armed conflict.

---

[9] Moreover, in the light of the ordinary meaning of the terms used in common Article 3 of the Geneva Conventions, a non-international armed conflict necessarily takes place within the territory of a single State. Such an interpretation is supported by the ICRC commentary drawn up by J. Pictet, *The Geneva Conventions of 12 August 1949: Commentary to Convention III* (1952), p. 37.

[10] ICTY, *Prosecutor v. Tadić*, IT-94-1-AR72, Appeals Chamber, Decision of 2 October 1995, para. 70. Thus, the Appeals Chamber remedies the lack of a definition of a non-international armed conflict in Article 3 common of the Geneva Conventions. The concept was clarified more effectively by the same Tribunal in 2008 in the *Haradinaj* case, Merits, paras. 38 and 60.

[11] Additional Protocol II to the Geneva Conventions, Article 2.

[12] ICTY, *Prosecutor v. Haradinaj*, IT-04-84-T, Trial Chamber, Decision of 3 April 2008, para. 38.

[13] ICTY, *Prosecutor v. Haradinaj*, Merits, 2008, *supra*, para. 60.

[14] Israel High Court of Justice (HCJ), *Public Committee against Torture v. The Government of Israel*, HCJ 769/02, 14 December 2006, para. 18.

Article 2 of the Geneva Conventions of 31 August 1949 describes an international armed conflict as 'all cases of declared war or of any other armed conflict which may arise between two or more of the High Contracting Parties.' Paradoxically, Palestine and the Supreme Court of Israel reach the same conclusion from opposing preliminary remarks. Palestine considers itself to be a State occupied by Israel. If this view is applied, the confrontation between the parties assumes the characteristics of a fight for national liberation against an alien occupation, in exercise of the right of self-determination. Such wars are generally recognized as international armed conflicts, pursuant to Article 1(4) of Additional Protocol I of 8 June 1977 to the Geneva Conventions. On the other hand, in the 2006 *Targeted Killings* decision, the Israeli Court asserts that the law of international armed conflict 'applies in any case of an armed conflict of international character, in other words, one that crosses the borders of the State.'[15] Consequently, every transnational armed conflict should be considered to be international, regardless of whether it involves a non-State actor or not.[16]

In our opinion, the concurring result of the reasoning of Palestine and the Israeli Supreme Court concerning the conflict classification arises from two factors. First of all, Gaza is a *sui generis* area, inasmuch as Palestine is a State *in statu nascendi*. The jurisprudence has extended the application of international armed conflict rules beyond the cases strictly listed in Article 1(4) of Additional Protocol I. Indeed, the ICTY recently classified the conflict between the North Atlantic Treaty Organization (NATO) and the Federal Republic of Yugoslavia as an international armed conflict, confirming that such a conflict can occur between a State and an entity that is not a High Contracting Party to the Geneva Conventions.[17]

The third hypothesis with respect to the issue of classification involves considering the situation as one of occupation, in which Israel exercises control over the Palestinian territories. According to The Hague Regulations and Geneva Convention IV, a military occupation exists only if the occupying power has established and exercises effective control over the territory in which it has instituted its presence.[18]

---

[15] *Ibid.*

[16] HCJ, *Public Committee against Torture v. Government of Israel, op. cit.*, para. 21. See A. Cassese, *International Law* (Oxford: Oxford University Press, 2005), p. 420.

[17] ICTY, *Prosecutor v. Đorđević*, Trial Chamber, 23 February 2011, para. 1580.

[18] Article 42 of The Hague Regulations stated: 'Territory is considered occupied when it is actually placed under the authority of the hostile army. The occupation

To be precise, Article 42 of the Hague Regulations states that the occupying State is considered to be an occupying power if it exercises effective control over the territory. Correlating this article with the rules of Geneva Convention IV regarding occupation, we find that all the duties and obligations of the occupying power are derived from such specific control. In other words, the State is bound by the rules of occupation only if it has control over the territory; the stronger the State's power over the region, the stricter are the obligations. When the occupation is clearly declared and effective control is exercised, no problem arises from a legal point of view. On the other hand, when the State does not exercise effective control over all the territory, a critical situation arises on account of the lack of international provisions guaranteeing the protection of the territory and of local communities.

In the case of the Palestinian territories, several problems arise with respect to the recognition of an occupation. First of all, Israel has rejected the status of occupation. In particular, Israel is unwilling to be considered as an occupying power, thereby rejecting all obligations stemming from Geneva Convention IV. In Israel's view, if Geneva Convention IV were to be applied, the occupied territories should belong to one of the High Contracting Parties to the Convention. The Supreme Court of Israel partially confirms this view, maintaining that the occupation of Gaza definitely ended with the withdrawal in 2005. According to the Supreme Court, only the West Bank would be affected by the occupation.[19] However, the international community does not agree with this position. Indeed, several UN resolutions and the ICJ affirm that a State must apply Geneva Convention IV every time it occupies a territory that is not its own, regardless of whether any other subject has a 'title' over it.[20]

Finally, some authors, such as Dinstein,[21] cast doubt on the effectiveness of the Israeli withdrawal from Gaza, asserting that Israel maintains control over the airspace and borders, so that Gaza can also be classified as an occupied territory.

We shall examine in the next section how the admission of Palestine to

---

extends only to the territory where such authority has been established and can be exercised.'

[19] HCJ, *Mara'abe v. Prime Minister*, HCJ 7957/04, Judgment, 15 September 2005, para.14. and HCJ, *Jaber Al-Bassiouni v. Prime Minister*, HCJ 9132/07, Judgment, 30 January 2008, para. 12.

[20] Wall case, *op. cit.*

[21] Y. Dinstein, *The International Law of Belligerent Occupation* (Cambridge: Cambridge University Press, 2009), pp. 276–279.

the UN can definitively clarify the characterization of these territories.

Admission to Membership in the UN

Pursuant to Article 4 of the Charter of the United Nations, membership in the Organization is open to only a peace-loving State, which accepts and is able and willing to carry out all obligations flowing from the UN Charter, can acquire the status of a member of the organization, based on the exclusive judgment of the UN itself. The procedure for a State's admission as a member is subject to a decision of the UN General Assembly upon the recommendation of the Security Council. The ICJ addressed this procedural matter in 1948.[22] It reaffirmed the dualist role and powers of the two UN organs. According to the ICJ, the second paragraph of Article 4 makes a distinction between Security Council recommendations and General Assembly decisions. The particular choice of words is useful: the paragraph is designed 'to determine the respective functions of these two organs which consist in pronouncing upon the question whether or not the applicant State shall be admitted to membership after having established whether or not the prescribed conditions are fulfilled.'[23] Moreover, the Court highlighted that the political character of the UN organs cannot release them from observance of the provisions of the UN Charter when they impose limitations on their powers.[24] In the Palestinian case, the fact that the Security Council vetoes the admission request by Palestine does not prevent the General Assembly from taking a positive decision on the matter. The General Assembly has exclusive decision-making power regarding the admission. The ICJ clearly stated: 'To ascertain whether an organ has freedom of choice for its decisions, reference must be made to the terms of its constitution. In this case, the limits of this freedom are fixed by Article 4 and allow for a wide liberty of appreciation. There is therefore no conflict between the functions of the political organs, on the one hand, and the exhaustive character of the prescribed conditions, on the other.'[25]

Besides, the General Assembly decides by a two-thirds majority of its members about the admission of a new member. In reality, even if the Security Council imposes a veto, thereby attempting to influence the

[22] ICJ Reports, *Conditions of Admission of a State to Membership in the United Nations (Article 4 of the Charter)*, Advisory Opinion, 28 May 1948.
[23] *Ibid.*, pp. 64-66.
[24] *Ibid.*, p. 64.
[25] *Conditions of Admission of a State to Membership in the United Nations, op. cit.*, p. 64.

General Assembly decision, this does not prevent the General Assembly from recovering its freedom of choice by resorting to the mechanism established in the Uniting for Peace resolution.[26] The establishment of the United for Peace procedure in 1950 reflected the need to bypass a blockade imposed by a veto in the Security Council where there was a threat to the peace, a breach of the peace, or an act of aggression. In the Palestinian case, it may be presumed that any blockage of the admission of Palestine by the Security Council would imply a threat to the peace in the region.

Once Palestine acquires full membership in the UN, a change will occur in the legal assessment of the conflict, which will unequivocally become an international armed conflict. Under this circumstance, the State of Palestine would be considered to have peer status with Israel, and the relationship between them should be based on reciprocal respect in accordance with international law.[27] Thus, Israel would be forced to negotiate on a basis of parity with another State.

The new situation would render the occupied territories a part of the Palestinian State unlawfully occupied by Israel. According to international humanitarian law, the contemporary notion of occupation is based on its temporary dimension and on the need to defend the interests of the occupied population. An occupation is characterized by the presence of an armed conflict and effective control over the territory by the occupying power. Such conditions are cumulative requirements for the application of humanitarian law, specifically Geneva Convention IV and The Hague Regulations of 1899 and 1907.

The end of the occupation is determined by two situations. The first depends on the end of effective control over the territory by the occupying power, while the second is established by a peace treaty that defines the new situation in the area based on an agreement between the parties. This means that when the occupied State and the occupying power sign a peace treaty, they decide on the territory's future: the occupied State can decide to transfer the territory to the other party or, alternatively, the occupied territory can be given back to the original State, which never lost its sovereignty over it.

When Palestine becomes a member of the UN, it will acquire, as an occupied State, the subjective right to directly address the Security Council. It will be entitled to demand that the Security Council intervene and order Israel to leave its territory immediately. As a matter of fact, two

---

[26] General Assembly Resolution 377(V) (1950).
[27] General Assembly Resolution 2625 (XXV): 'The principle of sovereign equality of States.'

jus cogens norms are threatened by the unlawful occupation, i.e. the requirement to refrain from the use of force, pursuant to Article 2(4) of the UN Charter and General Assembly resolutions 2625 (1970) and 42/22 (1987) and the right to self-determination of peoples, pursuant to Article 1(2) of the UN Charter and General Assembly Resolution 2625 (1970).

In this specific case, the Security Council should take a serious decision aimed at ensuring peace and stability in the area pursuant to Chapter VII of the UN Charter and call for the immediate withdrawal of Israeli armed forces from the occupied territories. Israel should therefore act on Security Council resolutions requesting it to comply with its international obligations as a UN member: 'Every State has the duty to fulfil in good faith the obligations assumed by it in accordance with the Charter of the United Nations. Every State has the duty to fulfil in good faith its obligations under the generally recognized principles and rules of international law.'[28]

Legal Consequences of Recognition of the Occupation

Combatants versus Civilians

The classification of the armed conflict between Palestine and Israel is not solely of theoretical concern; it also influences the law that is applicable to the situation. Indeed, two different juridical regimes exist for an international armed conflict and a non-international armed conflict with respect to the protection of combatants and civilians. In the case of an international armed conflict, the rules of international humanitarian law are better developed. Many norms regulate the situation of lawful combatants and of civilians. Article 4(A) of Geneva Convention III recognizes two categories of status of prisoner of war (POW): that of lawful combatants who fall into 'the power of the enemy'[29] and comply with the cumulative provisions of the article, and civilians who participate in a '*levée en masse*' in order to resist the invading forces. In this case, recognition as a POW is strictly linked to the spontaneity of the popular reaction, the assumption being that people had insufficient time to organize themselves into regular armed units. Thus, persons who fall into the categories defined by Article 4(A) of Geneva Convention III should be recognized as POWs and enjoy all of the rights and guarantees pertaining

---

[28] General Assembly Resolution 2625 (XXV), 1970.
[29] Article 4 of Geneva Convention III: 'Prisoners of War, in the sense of the present Convention, are persons belonging to one of the following categories, who have fallen into the power of the enemy . . . .'

to such status.

With regard to the Palestinian territories, it is of fundamental importance to distinguish between two different actors who participate in the hostilities: armed forces of the Palestinian Authority, on the one hand, and insurgent groups in the occupied territories, on the other. This distinction will be essential for an understanding of which categories of Article 4 they fall into. Once Palestine acquires full statehood, and the conflict will be officially declared to be an international one, Geneva Convention III will become applicable as well as all related guarantees pertaining to the status of POW. It follows that the armed forces of the Palestinian Authority should be recognized as 'members of the armed forces of a Party to the conflict,' in accordance with Article 4(A)(1), while insurgent groups should be characterized as 'members of other militias and members of other volunteer corps,' such as 'organized resistance movements, belonging to a Party to the conflict,' in accordance with Article 4(A)(2). The latter norm is extremely relevant for the future situation because it applies regardless of the presence of an occupation of the territory affected by the resistance phenomenon. Moreover, the rule applies to both cases when the resistance movements are operating 'in' or 'outside their own territory,' so that it may be applicable to the resistance in Gaza as well as in the West Bank or any other Palestinian territory.

When Palestine is accepted as a member of the United Nations and its statehood is recognized, Palestinian combatants that fulfil the conditions of Article 4 of Geneva Convention III should be regarded as POWs when they fall into the power of the enemy. Israel will be under an obligation to guarantee them the full protection reserved for POWs by international humanitarian law.

Third-party Nationals and Diplomatic Protection

Third-party nationals are another category of civilians who can be considered protected persons in an international armed conflict if the cumulative conditions of Article 4 of Geneva Convention IV are fulfilled. In general, any third-party national in an occupied territory or in the territory of one of the parties to a conflict can be considered a protected person. Civilians who are third-party nationals should also be considered protected persons if their own State has no normal diplomatic relations with the belligerent State in which they find themselves. Moreover, if the third-party nationals are located in the occupied territory of a party to the conflict, they are immediately protected under all circumstances, regardless of the existence of normal diplomatic representation. The same kind of protection is guaranteed to the nationals of a co-belligerent State in both the territory affected by hostilities and in an occupied territory, provided that there are no diplomatic relations between the aforementioned State and the common enemy.

It is evident that Article 4 is construed essentially on the basis of nationality criteria. Once the statehood of Palestine is undisputed, Palestinians will fall into the category of 'nationals of a neutral State' or of a 'co-belligerent State,' depending on the circumstances. We can rule out the possibility that they would be considered as 'nationals of a State which is not bound by the Convention' since, in the light of the declaration sent by the Palestine Liberation Organization to Switzerland asking to accede to the Geneva Conventions, [30] we may suppose that the State of Palestine will ratify those instruments. Israel currently refuses to consider Palestinian accession as valid, but once Palestine becomes a State there will be no obstacle to accession.

Given the hypothetical possibility of a renewal of active hostilities between Israel and Lebanon, it may be interesting to analyse the kind of protection that Palestinian refugees in Lebanese camps would enjoy. In such circumstances, Palestinians would enjoy protected persons status based on Article 4 of Geneva Convention IV as third-party nationals if the State of Palestine declares its neutrality or becomes a co-belligerent with Lebanon, having previously interrupted its diplomatic relations with Israel. As beneficiaries of such protection, Palestinian refugees should be entitled to move away from hostility zones, as required by Article 35 of Geneva Convention IV and reaffirmed by the UN Security Council in resolutions 660, 661, 662 and 664 of 1990.[31] However, if Palestine and Israel both

---

[30] On 21 June 1989, the Swiss Federal Department of Foreign Affairs received a letter from the Permanent Observer of Palestine to the United Nations Office at Geneva informing the Swiss Federal Council 'that the Executive Committee of the Palestine Liberation Organization, entrusted with the functions of the Government of the State of Palestine by decision of the Palestine National Council, decided, on 4 May 1989, to adhere to the four Geneva Conventions of 12 August 1949 and the two Protocols additional thereto.' Nonetheless, the Swiss Federal Council informed the relevant States that it was not in a position to decide whether the letter constituted an instrument of accession, 'due to the uncertainty within the international community as to the existence or non-existence of a State of Palestine' (13 September 1989).

[31] The Security Council demanded that the immediate departure of nationals of third countries located in the territory of the hostilities should be permitted and facilitated and that such nationals should be granted immediate and continuing access to consular officials. It prohibited any action that might jeopardize the

maintain their normal diplomatic relations, protection under Geneva Convention IV for civilians within territories affected by hostilities would not be available.

The full statehood of Palestine will clarify the protection status of Palestinians. Today only the criteria of diplomatic representation could be invoked, due to the absence of a clear nationality. Where diplomatic protection is the only guideline available to identify a protected person, the results obviously differ unduly in terms of the identity of the States involved in the conflict and the presence of diplomatic relations between them. This might ultimately jeopardize the level of protection assured to civilians. Indeed, the legitimacy of the attribution of protection to Palestinians is still hotly debated, and different positions have been assumed by the ICJ and the Israeli High Court of Justice. If the broad interpretation of the International Committee of the Red Cross is applied,[32] Palestinians are protected since they do not possess any citizenship.[33]

Prisoners Accused of Criminal Offences

Clarification of the conflict between Israel and Palestine is of fundamental importance for the definition of the status of civilians in the occupied territories who are detained by Israel and charged with political crimes. Israel currently affirms its competence to detain, bring to trial and punish Palestinian individuals for political crimes under national law because it perceives them as national enemies. This point of view is made possible by Israel's refusal to recognize the existence of an international armed conflict, thereby also denying all recognized guarantees for protected persons in occupied territories. By defining the conflict as a non-international armed conflict, it considers itself free to detain, try and punish the civilian inhabitants of the occupied territories under national law and to limit their guarantees to those foreseen by common Article 3 of the Geneva Conventions.

On the other hand, when Palestine is recognized as a State and as a member of the UN, the conflict will be recognized as international, and the guarantees for civilians enjoyed by protected persons under a regime of occupation will have to be assured. In other words, if the conflict is recognized as international, civilians in the occupied territories will have to be considered as protected persons pursuant to Article 4 of Geneva

---

safety, security or health of third-party nationals. UN Doc. S/RES/664, 18 August 1990.
[32] See the ICRC commentary on Article 4.
[33] *Cf.* Chapter Three of this volume.

Convention IV, which establishes several rules aimed at guaranteeing the protection of the inhabitants of occupied territories, including protection before tribunals or courts martial of the occupying power. The purpose of Geneva Convention IV is to protect civilians from the abuse of authority by the occupying power. Indeed, the occupying power must guarantee order and security in the territories, enforcing the law applicable in the territories and introducing new laws only if the existing ones cannot be invoked to achieve its particular aim. This means that occupying powers cannot create new laws or, still worse, apply their national law in a territory over which they do not exercise sovereignty.[34]

Hence, Israel cannot, in the context of an international armed conflict, invoke its legislation to detain, prosecute or punish the protected persons for political crimes. Israel could only promote new laws in the occupied territories and detain or prosecute in accordance with those laws if there was no original law in the territory or if the existing law was incapable of maintaining or restoring safety and order in the region. Furthermore, according to Article 68(1) of Geneva Convention IV,[35] civilians can be detained only if this is absolutely necessary for the security of the detaining power or to guarantee the safety of civilians (Article 78). In point of fact, a protected person can be imprisoned exclusively when he/she has committed an offence intended to harm the occupying power, and the duration of such imprisonment must be proportionate to the offence committed.[36] Civilians cannot be indiscriminately interned for a political reason except where their actions, in the event of linkage to a political reason, may endanger the security of the occupying power.

When analysing provisions regarding detention, it is essential to make a clear distinction between detention and internment. Geneva Convention IV makes a clear distinction between the two forms of restriction of liberty. In the former case, the restriction of an individual's freedom of movement stems from criminal actions and is designed to protect the security of the occupying power.[37] Conversely, assigned residence or internment can be used only on grounds pertaining to the safety of the protected persons or the security of the occupying power.[38] The two

---

[34] The objective of this rule is to guarantee the sovereignty of the original State, which has not yet lost its sovereignty over the territory despite its temporary lack of control.
[35] 'Protected persons who commit an offence which is solely intended to harm the Occupying Power.'
[36] Geneva Convention IV, Article 68.
[37] *Ibid.*, Articles 5, 76 and 77.
[38] *Ibid.*, Articles 41, 42, 43, 46 and 78.

measures entail different sets of rights for the individual concerned. In particular, if Israel affirms the necessity of internment of a protected person, it has to base its statement on 'imperative reasons' of security entitling the occupying power to adopt assigned residence or internment measures. The decision of the occupying power, namely Israel in the present case, should respect regular procedures as established by international humanitarian law. In particular, the safety risk cannot be merely enounced; it has to be proven in terms of a real and imminent risk to the integrity of the protected persons. In addition, once the validity of the internment's reasons has been demonstrated and the protected persons are detained, such internment cannot be unlimited and has to be reviewed as soon as possible, and at least twice a year, by a court or administrative board (Article 78 of Geneva Convention IV).

Confiscation and Destruction of Property

When Palestine is recognized as a State and its conflict with Israel is recognized as an international armed conflict, the situation of civilians suffering the consequences of the construction of Wall will completely change. Civilians will be considered as protected persons pursuant to Article 4 of Geneva Convention IV, and any expropriation of land as a consequence of the building of the Wall will be subject to the law of occupation. The law of occupation is clear: it defends civilians who are considered as protected persons from abuse by the occupying power, especially from the expropriation of land and other assets without specific and necessary motivation.

Article 46 of The Hague Regulations insists that 'private property' must be respected and that it cannot be confiscated. The occupying power can administer the territories and land but it cannot confiscate assets and private property from its owners, especially for its own advantage and to the detriment of the local inhabitants (Article 52 of the Regulations). Expropriation is possible only in extreme situations or in rare exceptions, when the occupying power confiscates private property for reasons of public interest or military necessity,[39] and with adequate compensation.[40]

---

[39] B'Tselem, The Israeli Information Center for Human Rights in the Occupied Territories, *Information for the Consideration of Israel*, submitted to the UN Committee on Economic, Social and Cultural Rights, 47th session (14 November–2 December 2011), September 2011.

[40] Article 53 of Geneva Convention IV states that the destruction of real or personal property is prohibited 'except where such destruction is rendered absolutely necessary by military operations.'

All the rules established to protect the right of civilians in occupied territories are easily applicable in an international armed conflict, in which the legal institution of occupation exists, while is formally missing in the regime of non-international armed conflict. In our opinion, the construction of the Wall cannot be invoked as one of the rare exceptions for which Israel could confiscate private property because it is not motivated by public interest or military necessity.[41] It constitutes a violation of international humanitarian law rules regarding the protection of private property.

Another problem associated with the confiscation of private property of civilians concerns the fate of the assets expropriated after the end of hostilities, which is covered by Article 53(2) of the 1907 Hague Regulations. It is clear that confiscated land or property must be restored to the original owner, who must also receive economic compensation for the expropriation. In other words, when an international armed conflict between the parties is finally recognized and the end of hostilities brings a final peace treaty between the two States, Israel must restore expropriated property to the civilians concerned.

The other issue that must be analysed is Israel's policy of demolishing houses in the occupied territories as a sanction against families and those who support the actions of individuals who resist the Israeli occupation. Collective penalties and reprisals against the population are prohibited.[42] The Israeli house demolition policy clearly constitutes a punitive measure against civilians without being motivated by reasons of imperative military necessity.[43] Article 33 of Geneva Convention IV is also violated inasmuch as it expressly prohibits the punishment of protected persons for offences that they have not personally committed. According to Article 33, acts promoted by other persons, in particular by persons who are considered to be saboteurs, do not imply joint participation in acts against Israel by the population of the occupied territories.

Protected persons who are not actively engaged in activities hostile to Israel cannot be considered responsible for an act committed by a saboteur because, as stipulated in Article 33, vicarious individual responsibility of

---

[41] In *Tabib et al. v. Minister of Defense et al.* (HCJ 202/81, 1981) the Israel Supreme Court affirmed that the occupying power can use expropriation to construct roads that facilitate the movement of troops.

[42] Article 50 of the 1907 Hague Regulations: 'No general penalty, pecuniary or otherwise, can be inflicted on the population on account of the acts of individuals for which it cannot be regarded as collectively responsible.' See also Article 5 of Geneva Convention IV.

[43] As required by Article 53 of Geneva Convention IV.

one person for the act of another is inadmissible.[44] As stated in the ICRC commentary on Article 33 of Geneva Convention IV, the responsibility is exclusively personal and responsibility for an act committed by one person cannot be attributed to the community. It may be concluded that under these circumstances the policy of house demolition involves covert punitive purposes and fails to meet the conditions for the lawful destruction or confiscation of private property, which are mainly military, in accordance with the principle of proportionality under international humanitarian law.

Forcible Transfer of Civilians

In recent years Israel has been implementing a new policy in the West Bank aimed at expelling Bedouin communities, especially those located in Area C.[45] This type of policy can be clearly defined as a forcible transfer and as such is prohibited by both international humanitarian law and human rights law. According to international humanitarian law, if protected persons in occupied territories wish to leave the territories, the occupying power must let them go.[46] Article 49 of Geneva Convention IV prohibits forced expulsion from the occupied territory or mass deportations from one area to another against the will of the individuals concerned. Under international humanitarian law norms, the occupying power is not only banned from deporting or transferring protected persons during an occupation but commits a grave breach when it engages in such practices (see Article 147 of Geneva Convention IV).

When Palestine is recognized as a State, the situation will thus change completely and the applicability of international humanitarian law regarding occupation can no longer be denied. While Israel can still invoke the non-applicability of Geneva Convention IV because it does not recognize Palestine as a State and therefore refuses to apply Article 2 of Geneva Convention IV, it will no longer be able to so after full recognition of Palestinian statehood. Israel will have to accept the decisions and demands of the UN concerning the withdrawal of Israeli troops from occupied territories and will have to fulfil all obligations applicable to an occupying power until such time as the areas in which it exercises its power are liberated.

---

[44] Dinstein, *op. cit.*, p. 154.
[45] B'Tselem, *Israel Plans to Expel Bedouin Communities from Area C, West Bank*, 10 October 2011.
[46] Geneva Convention IV, Article 48.

An occupying power is bound by the provisions prohibiting any alteration in the demographic composition of territory by transferring its own population to the occupied territory. Article 49 of Geneva Convention IV and customary law[47] prohibit forcible displacement within the borders of a country and across international borders. The only exception to such a prohibition occurs when the displacement of civilians has a temporary nature and is justified by imperative military necessity or reasons related to the civilian security. Article 147 of Geneva Convention IV stipulates that unlawful deportation or transfer constitutes a grave breach. The criminal character of deportation acts by the occupying power has been reinforced by the Statute of the International Criminal Tribunal for the Former Yugoslavia,[48] and by jurisprudence,[49] as well as by the Rome Statute of the International Criminal Court.[50] The Israeli Supreme Court has justified the expulsion of individual Palestinians from the occupied territories by citing security reasons, and has justified Israeli settlements by arguing that they are private initiatives,[51] but Geneva Convention IV renders such reasoning inconsistent.

Conclusion

Since the end of the Second World War, assessments of the situation with respect to the State of Israel and Palestine have been highly controversial, and tensions between Israelis and Arabs have increased from year to year. Several wars have been fought in the course of the past sixty years and many UN resolutions have been adopted demanding an end to the hostilities and the creations of two States, one Israeli and one Arab. However, while full recognition of the State of Israel was easily accomplished in a few years, the same cannot be said regarding Palestine. Nevertheless, a new situation seems to be materializing today for Palestine, and the international community now appears to be ready to officially recognize Palestine as a State among its peers. Our analysis has

---

[47] ICRC, Rules 129 and 130 of customary international humanitarian law (2005).

[48] ICTY Statute, Article 2 (g) and Article 5 (d).

[49] ICTY, *Prosecutor v. Blagojević and Jokić*, Trial Judgment, IT-02-60-T, January 2005, para. 596.

[50] Deportation as part of a widespread or systematic attack on any civilian population may constitute a war crime or a crime against humanity, pursuant to Article 7(d), and Article 8, para. 2(a)(viii) and (b) (viii), of the Rome Statute. Even though this Statute is not binding on Israel, it can be taken into account as proof of customary law.

[51] Israeli Supreme Court, *Afu*, HC 785/87, HC 27/88 (1998).

shown that this official recognition will bring sweeping changes in international relations and in the legal implications for relations between Israel and Palestine, Palestine and other States, and Palestine and the United Nations.

The most radical change will concern the status of Palestinian civilians and the definition of the conflict. The first innovation will be a clarification of the conflict between Israel and Palestine, which may henceforth be defined exclusively as international, erasing any doubts about the matter. Thus, the applicability of all rules of international humanitarian law governing an international armed conflict, especially those governing occupation, will become clear. The application of such rules guarantees greater protection for civilians in the occupied territories, notably those who will be considered protected persons, pursuant to Article 4 of Geneva Convention IV. These people may not be detained, tried and punished pursuant to Israeli national law. They cannot be subjected to the Israeli policy of construction of the Wall and demolition of houses.

Israel has hitherto denied the applicability of Geneva Convention IV on the basis of a literal interpretation of the terms of Article 2, according to which Palestine cannot be considered a Contracting Party. Following the full recognition of Palestine as a State by the international community and its admission to membership of the UN, it will be extremely difficult to reject the applicability of Geneva Convention IV by invoking Article 2. Thus, greater protection for civilians will be ensured and violations of the rules of international humanitarian law concerning occupation will no longer be justified. In the end, Israel will be obliged to grant lawful combatants who fall into its power the status of prisoners of war and civilians in occupied territories the status of protected persons with all the guarantees provided by Geneva Convention IV.

CHAPTER EIGHT

TELL IT TO THE JUDGE:
PALESTINE'S UN BID
AND THE INTERNATIONAL CRIMINAL COURT

VALENTINA AZAROV

Introduction

On 29 November 2012, Palestine obtained 'non-member State observer' status in the General Assembly, which 'accord[s] to Palestine non-member observer State status in the United Nations.'[1] The resolution is a parallel move to Palestine's pending application for full UN membership submitted in September 2011, which was shelved by the Security Council later that year for lack of agreement amongst the Council members. The efforts to trigger International Criminal Court (ICC) jurisdiction for international crimes committed on Palestinian territory are multifaceted – they started with Palestine's Article 12(3) declaration to the Court in January 2009, and continued with the recommendations of the report of the Fact-Finding Mission on the Gaza Conflict, which urged the UN to consider referral to the Court.

Some of these initiatives have not had the support of the Palestinian representatives, who have been subjected to the very political pressures these initiatives have sought to defy. The absence of access to local mechanisms for justice and accountability for Palestinian victims of international law and human rights violations has resulted in the creation of a culture of impunity and contempt towards the right to human dignity of the Palestinian people. While the Israeli government and its institutional practice were, at least for some time, beyond reproach, Palestine's recent engagements through international law have held considerable sway over this long-standing dynamic.

---

[1] UN Doc. A/RES/67/19, 29 November 2012, para. 2.

This chapter considers the efforts to bring international crimes from the Palestinian-Israeli context before the ICC with the purpose of bringing the Court into the conflict, and thereby the conflict into the Court, in the hope that this would, at the very least, have a deterrent effect on Israel's predatory institutional practices and stimulate action by governments and international organisations to ensure protection for the rights of the Palestinian people; especially those who have become victims of international law violations. Beyond evoking the role of international institutions, these tactics could provide further clout for holding third States, who have or are considering engagements with Israel, accountable for undermining their obligations under international law, and in some cases also their ability to maintain the integrity of their domestic legal orders. This somewhat ambitious 'tour de France' of the current state of affairs commences by describing the legal narratives and battles engaged in by both sides as the backdrop to the UN bid, which in turn seeks to internationalise the conflict in order to shift the power dynamic that has for so long characterized the Palestine-Israel context.

Shifting Legal Narratives

The November 2012 Israeli offensive in Gaza, which media channels reported as a 'war,' was in fact another episode in Israel's enforcement of its 'effective control' over the Gaza Strip, as a long-standing Occupying Power of the territory – a position firmly maintained by the international community. During belligerent occupation, such instances of the use of force should have the purpose of enforcing the control of the occupier over the territory and restoring public life and safety.[2] Even when directed against organised acts of resistance mounted by the occupied population, the occupier must account for its inherent control over the territory by using the least harmful means to achieve a military advantage. If Israel's position *vis-à-vis* the Gaza Strip is assumed – namely, that it is no longer an Occupying Power in the Gaza Strip since the 'disengagement' of its settlements and military bases from inside the Gaza Strip in 2005 – each and every instance of an Israeli land incursion and any single attack on the territory of the Gaza Strip (such as the killing of a 13-year-old boy on 8

---

[2] As per Article 43 of the Convention IV respecting the Laws and Customs of War on Land, 18 October 1907 (Hague Regulations): 'The authority of the legitimate power having in fact passed into the hands of the occupant, the latter shall take all the measures in his power to restore, and ensure, as far as possible, public order and safety, while respecting, unless absolutely prevented, the laws in force in the country.'

November 2012 that triggered the recent escalation)[3] should be examined through the lens of relevant international law and practice on aggression.[4] This would be an undesirable outcome for Israel, who would most probably be found responsible for committing acts of aggression on numerous occasions.

Israel's official justification for the use of disproportionate force under the 'right to self-defence' during its recent operation is nonviable, as States cannot invoke self-defence for acts that defend an unlawful situation, which they are responsible for creating in the first place. Israel cannot invoke this right, an international norm usually applicable in time of peace, due to the on-going international armed conflict with the Gaza district of Palestine, continuing its belligerent occupation while systematically violating international humanitarian law and imposing an unlawful siege on Palestine's Gaza district, which constitutes collective punishment.[5] Having created a situation that only instigates violence through its own defaults as an occupier, resulting in the emergence of resistance, Israel is arguably limited in its ability to invoke a right to violently repress the occupied population's resistance, and is, moreover, under an obligation to examine all other means to quell resistance that are less harmful to the civilian population, including the possibility of reasserting control over the territory.

Aside from condemning the Security Council or General Assembly for their defaults in maintaining a deadlock on all collective measures *vis-à-vis* the Palestine-Israel context, individual States have done little to fulfil their obligations not to recognize or assist in violations of international law, often due to the fact that these questions are ceded to the political ranks. Third States that recognise or lend support to Israel's unlawful conduct through engagements and cooperation with Israeli institutions, however, are often unaware of how they render themselves unable to respect their own laws and foreign policy objectives by relying on Israel to apply international law in accordance with reasonable legal interpretations. Israel, in turn, has consistently refused the *en bloc* application of the law of occupation, conceding only to some of its 'humanitarian provisions,'

---

[3] Human Rights Watch, 'Israel/Gaza: Avoid Harm to Civilians,' 15 November 2012.

[4] The definition of aggression was elaborated in General Assembly Resolution 3314 (XXIV), adopted on 14 December 1974.

[5] International Committee of the Red Cross, 'Gaza: No End in Sight to Hardship and Despair,' 20 May 2011.

which Israel's Supreme Court, the High Court of Justice, has subjected to 'dynamic' interpretations to serve the State authorities' needs.[6]

While the European Union (EU) and its member States have long asserted a foreign policy interest and a legal obligation to ensure compliance with international humanitarian law and respect human rights,[7] enshrined in EU law through the Treaty of Lisbon, the EU and its member States have only just acknowledged the need to examine and remedy all areas of EU-Israel engagement in order to ensure that the EU could rely on Israel to make the internationally-accepted territorial distinctions and ensure that other Israeli institutional practices are in line with international law.[8] Thus, in a resolution adopted on 10 December 2012, the EU Council held that EU-Israel engagements should clearly stipulate that their application does not extend to Israel's unlawful activities in the Palestinian territory.[9] Third State responsibility was also evoked judicially by Public Interest Lawyers and Al-Haq, a leading Palestinian human rights non-governmental organization, in a suit for judicial review of the UK's arms sales to Israel after 'Operation Cast Lead,' that was later denied due to judicial deference to UK foreign policy.[10] Importantly, the basis for these obligations goes beyond the positivist legal arena to include law-like obligations based on rights that are established through accumulated

---

[6] D. Kretzmer, *The Occupation of Justice: The Supreme Court of Israel and the Occupied Territories* (New York: SUNY Press, 2002). See for a recent example of such 'dynamic' interpretations, V. Azarov, 'Exploiting A 'Dynamic' Interpretation? The Israeli High Court of Justice Accepts the Legality of Israel's Quarrying Activities in the Occupied Palestinian Territory,' *European Journal of International Law: Talk!,* 7 February 2012. See also J. Reynolds, 'Legitimising the Illegitimate: The Israeli High Court of Justice and the Occupied Palestinian Territory,' *Al-Haq* (2010).

[7] 'European Union Guidelines on Promoting Compliance with International Humanitarian Law,' *Official Journal* C 327, 23 December 2005.

[8] European Parliament resolution on the proposal for a Council decision on the conclusion of the regional Convention on pan-Euro-Mediterranean preferential rules of origin (2012/2519(RSP)).

[9] 'The European Union expresses its commitment to ensure that – in line with international law – all agreements between the State of Israel and the European Union must unequivocally and explicitly indicate their inapplicability to the territories occupied by Israel in 1967;' Council conclusions on the Middle East Peace Process, 3209th Foreign Affairs Council meeting, Brussels, 10 December 2012, para. 4.

[10] Al-Haq, 'Al Haq *v.* UK Secretary of State for Foreign & Commonwealth Affairs *et al.*: Denial of Claim,' 8 March 2010.

practice, and are subject primarily to political and not judicial enforcement.

Israel's Legitimacy Battles

These legal nuances were missing from the barrage of statements issued by Israel's official political and military outlets during its recent operation in the Gaza Strip – labelled, in Hebrew, with the biblical phrase 'Pillar of Cloud.' Footage taken by drones and fighter planes, and constant updates on socialmedia sites were all geared towards enhancing Israel's international legitimacy and crafting a narrative of self-defence against 'terrorism.' Israel's legal strategy, particularly since its operation 'Cast Lead' in 2008-2009 has hinged on exploiting the 'grey areas' of the law, including the proportionality debate on targeting military objectives and the soldier's right to life,[11] in order to justify the use of greater force against potential threats to protect human life of greater value than that of the enemy, based on the State's inherent obligation to its citizens. A strategy of warnings was implemented throughout the November 2012 military campaign against the Gaza Strip through phone calls, leaflets and 'roof knocks' by small missiles usually launched by drones a warning of an ensuing attack. However, neither the issuance of such warnings, nor the fact that Hamas's armed forces or other groups might have been conducting combat activity from the vicinity of civilian areas, thereby putting civilians at risk of counterattacks, justifies Israel's overwhelmingly indiscriminate attacks.[12]

Local and international human rights groups are currently examining physical evidence and collecting testimonies to ascertain the legality of the recent attacks under international humanitarian law, the law on the conduct of hostilities. Once the evidence is documented and placed in the public domain, it will be arrayed against Israel's version of events,

---

[11] See on the Kasher/Yadlin military doctrine prepared for the Israeli army before its 'Operation Cast Lead' in the Gaza Strip, which classifies the whole of the population there as culpable for supporting the Hamas regime, J. Kot, 'Israeli Civilians versus Palestinian Combatants? Reading the Goldstone Report in Light of the Israeli Conception of the Principle of Distinction,' 24 *Leiden Journal of International Law* 4 (2012).

[12] Strong indications have already been released by human rights groups, including Human Rights Watch, about Israel's use of large weapons and its unnecessary targeting of civilian locales for no apparent reason and at a time and in a manner that render such attacks unlawfully disproportionate. Human Rights Watch, 'Israel/Gaza: Israeli Airstrike on Home Unlawful,' 7 December 2012.

occasionally supported by foreign former military officers,[13] claiming the targeting of militants and the inevitability of civilian deaths due to the use of 'human shields' and the reality of 'asymmetric warfare.' Indeed, Israel is not the first to claim that an accidental civilian death is not a violation,[14] based on necro-economic calculations of the 'least of all possible evils.'[15] Its position has extensively relied on the necessity of self-defence, under *jus ad bellum*, evoking the 'means-end test' to justify violations of the laws of the conduct of hostilities (*jus in bello*).[16] Such claims, however, fail to provide substantive facts about the necessity of the use of military force against certain targets, which in some cases could have been captured and placed under Israel's control through less harmful means, resulting in core tenets of international humanitarian law being turned on their head. These debates play out within a particular contextual normative framework, which does not meddle with critical issues that pertain to the overall legality of Israel's continued occupation or presence in the Palestinian territory.

The relative success of Israel's efforts to deflect accusations and reproaches by international actors for its internationally unlawful conduct has waned as a result of increased Palestinian engagement through international law. A notable achievement was the growing fear about the potential vulnerability of Israel's immunity and its susceptibility to domestic universal jurisdiction laws in foreign jurisdictions, beyond the domain of political discretion, to which the Israeli government reacted with a fierce political response resulting in legislative changes in Belgium, Spain and the United Kingdom. Since Palestine submitted a declaration in January 2009 to the International Criminal Court under Article 12(3) of the Court's Statute, asking it to exercise jurisdiction over international

---

[13] Israel Defence Forces weblog, 'Col. Richard Kemp: IDF protects civilian rights,' 18 November 2012.

[14] The US has made such claims in calculating its attacks on Iraq and Afghanistan; M. Benjamin, 'When is an Accidental Civilian Death not an Accident?' *Salon*, 20 June 2007.

[15] E. Weizman, *The Least of All Possible Evils* (Verso, 2012). See also M. Benjamin, 'When is an Accidental Civilian Death not an Accident?' *Salon*, 30 July 2007.

[16] D. Kretzmer, 'The Inherent Right to Self-Defence and Proportionality in Ius Ad Bellum,' *European Journal of International Law* (2012). See also J. Moussa, 'Can *jus ad bellum* Override *jus in bello*? Reaffirming the Separation of the Two Bodies of Law,' 90 *International Review of the Red Cross* 872 (2008).

crimes committed in Palestine since 1 July 2002, Israel has been fully aware of the looming threat presented by the ICC.[17]

Israel's wariness has increased so much so, over the last few years, that in September 2012 the Israeli Turkel Commission, tasked with the appraisal of the 'Maritime Incident of 30 March 2011,' the Israeli navy's attacks on the *Mavi Marmara* flotilla and its aftermath, published a legal opinion it had commissioned from a German international law professor, Dr. Claus Kress, examining the emergence and practice of the ICC principle of complementarity.[18] The complementarity principle serves to ensure that priority is given to national systems in enforcing international criminal law; if they are deficient, by being either unwilling or unable to conduct proper investigations in accordance with the standards of international law, the national justice mechanisms should be 'complemented' by the ICC. While the opinion does not discuss the specific application of the principle to the case of Israel, it presents a detailed account of existing practice, while seemingly assuming that Israeli officials would not be susceptible to the Court's jurisdiction.

Several local and international human rights groups have released reports examining Israel's institutional practice and policies of investigating and prosecuting violations of international law, including war crimes.[19] Reflecting on their conclusions in a recent article, Sharon Weill and I assess Israel's legal practice in light of the measures it undertook in follow-up to the report of the Fact-Finding Mission on the

---

[17] T. Keenan and E. Weizman, 'Israel: The Third Strategic Threat,' *Open Democracy*, 7 June 2010.

[18] C. Kress, 'The Principle of Complementarity under the Rome Statute of the International Criminal Court,' A Legal Opinion Submitted to the Israeli Independent Public Commission to Examine the Maritime Incident of 31 May 2010, headed by Supreme Court Justice J. Turkel ('Turkel Commission').

[19] Israel's systematic unwillingness to investigate and prosecute international crimes may be seen in the biased role and practice of the Israel High Court of Justice, lack of access to civil remedies, and the absence of investigations and prosecutions by the authorities. See, e.g., S. Weill and V. Azarov, *Shielded from Accountability: Israel's Unwillingness to Investigate and Prosecute International Crimes*, International Federation for Human Rights, September 2011. See also Palestinian Centre for Human Rights, *Genuinely Unwilling* (2010; and 2011 update); Human Rights Watch, *Turning a Blind Eye: Impunity for Laws-of-War Violations during the Gaza War* (2010); and Human Rights Watch, *Promoting Impunity: The Israeli Military's Failure to Investigate Wrongdoing* (2005).

Gaza Conflict (the 'Goldstone report').[20] Israel has failed to initiate independent and impartial investigations. Instead, its army conducted an internal operational debriefing, governed by the Military Advocate General. Many investigations have been delayed or closed in an opaque manner, other complaints have been processed deficiently, through failure to promptly collect evidence and witness statements and the dismissal of complaints due to the context in which they occurred, in time of combat or other 'exceptional circumstances.'[21] The analysis concludes that neither States nor the ICC can rely on comity – an underlying presumption of mutual recognition between States in international cooperation – to recognise Israel's application of international criminal law norms either formally or substantively, since its practice has resulted in shielding the high echelons and initiating a small number of low-level prosecutions for mostly minor offences, *inter alia*. A similar conclusion was reached by the UN Human Rights Council on 25 March 2011, when it called upon the General Assembly to transfer the Gaza Conflict fact-finding mission's report to the ICC, considering the deadlock at the UN Security Council.[22]

The ICC's Role in the Palestine-Israel Context

Thus far, the deficient reaction of international law's mechanisms to Israel's offensive on the Gaza Strip during December 2008 and January 2009, with its 100:1 Palestinian-to-Israeli casualty ratio,[23] and countless claims by international groups and governments about the overwhelming need to investigate the possible commission of war crimes and crimes against humanity, has left thousands of victims with no access to justice and alleged perpetrators unaccountable. As such, great hopes lie in the role of the ICC with respect to the Palestine-Israel conflict: ever more so given that political pressures have undermined universal jurisdiction. Prosecutorial politics have become the standard in most States, effectively preventing victims from having direct recourse to justice.

---

[20] V. Azarov and S. Weill, 'Israel's Unwillingness? The Follow-Up Investigations to the UN Gaza Conflict Report and International Criminal Justice,' 12 *International Criminal Law Review* 5 (2012).
[21] *Ibid.*
[22] UN Doc A/HRC/16/L.31.
[23] R. Falk, 'The Goldstone Report and the Goldstone Retreat: Truths Told by Law and Reviled by Geopolitics,' in C. Meloni and G. Tognoni, *Is There A Court For Gaza? A Test Bench for International Justice* (The Hague: T.M.C. Asser Press, 2012), p. 88.

In light of these restrictions, the ICC is one of the only avenues for Palestinian recourse to justice that has yet to be fully explored. In the foreword to a volume released last year by Meloni and Tognoni, entitled 'Is There a Court for Gaza?,' Professor Schabas writes: 'Indeed, there are at least two courts capable of addressing the armed conflict in Gaza that took place in December 2008 and January 2009: the International Court of Justice and the International Criminal Court. The challenge, then, is to resolve the difficulties in establishing jurisdiction.'[24] He adds that the consequence of a claim that insulates Palestine from the ICC 'leads to an absurdity, or at least to a proposition that defies the very object and purpose of the Rome Statute' – 'to put an end to impunity.'

The ICC has a critical role to play in enforcing rights and forcing compliance with international law.[25] Notwithstanding its limitations, the ICC is guaranteed to change the dynamics of the conflict. At the very least, the ICC's jurisdiction could reduce the intensity and number of violations. Already, the possibility that Israeli officials, political and military leaders, could be exposed to prosecution, and the plausible threat of punishment by the ICC, has triggered significant diplomatic initiatives by Israel and other States, including the US. The ICC also plays an important role in promoting the peaceful resolution of conflicts and strengthening or restoring international peace and security. Peace and justice are not mutually exclusive, and their false dichotomization in the Israel-Palestine conflict has kept justice hostage to politics, particularly those of Israel and its allies, undermining the function of the Court.[26] There is a strong case to be made for the importance of the ICC's role in the conflict, by filling an accountability gap that would put an end to the current climate of impunity, including Israel's systematic unwillingness to investigate and prosecute international crimes committed by its nationals.

On 21 January 2009, the Palestinian Ministry of Justice submitted a declaration to the ICC under Article 12(3) of the ICC's Rome Statute. The Court asked questions concerning the declaration and Palestine's status, starting a rigorous and thorough substantive examination of the issues it framed as critical to the decision on whether to accept the declaration. A

---

[24] *Ibid.*

[25] The Prosecutor has also held that its office role, under the principle of indirect complementarity, is to indirectly trigger cooperation by inducing States to investigate and prosecute violations within their domestic system in order to avoid having their nationals being brought before the ICC.

[26] This view is supported by the classic statement of the Nuremberg International Military Tribunal: 'only by punishing individuals who commit such crimes can the provisions of international law be enforced.'

fervent academic debate ensued providing insights not only into the incoherent applications of international law to Palestine, but equally into the politics of the Court. Examining the validity of Palestine's declaration, Professor Alain Pellet's expert brief, signed by a list of acclaimed international law experts, which was presented to the Office of the Prosecutor, adopted a functional, teleological approach to the interpretation of the Rome Statute, the object and purpose of which is to ensure universal access to justice. The brief asserted that if the Court were to decisively refuse Palestine's access to the Court, international crimes committed in Palestine would be placed in an international criminal law vacuum, having been reprimanded by Israel's legal system. Professor Pellet held that Palestine's declaration fulfils the Statute's conditions for jurisdiction, and that in accepting the declaration, the Court does not need to pronounce itself on the question of Palestine's statehood status.[27]

A number of prominent publicists have argued that the Court was under an obligation to adopt the functional approach that brings about the function of the Statute and safeguards its underlying object and purpose (under a teleological interpretation), as entrusted by the international community – namely, to fight impunity. Only such an approach could do justice to the importance of the role of the ICC in filling the accountability gap in the region. All the same, a pragmatic approach to conceptualizing the Court's role should be adopted. The ICC can provide primarily symbolic, retributive justice to a limited number of victims through the prosecution of the high political and military echelons, often referred to as the 'big fish' in the jargon of international criminal law. Its practice of providing other forms of reparation to victims remains under-developed, having recently been subject to fervent debate following the Court's first reparations decision in the *Lubanga* case.[28]

Palestine's Road to the ICC

Several steps have been undertaken over the recent years to attempt to trigger the Court's jurisdiction in the case of Palestine. In parallel to the submission of the Article 12(3) declaration, the report of the UN Fact-Finding Mission on the Gaza Conflict recommended that the Court examines its *prima facie* findings. A decision by Palestine to accede to the

---

[27] A. Pellet, 'The Effects of Palestine's Recognition of the International Criminal Court's Jurisdiction,' in C. Meloni and G. Tognoni, *op. cit.*, pp. 424-425.
[28] Redress, 'Lubanga Case - Q & A on ICC Landmark Decision on Reparations for Victims,' *Victim's Rights Working Group*, 14 August 2012.

Rome Statute as a full State Party is not mutually exclusive to the acceptance of its Article 12(3) declaration, and could serve to extend the temporal scope of the Court's jurisdiction back to 1 July 2002. Another option, previously contemplated by Palestine's legal services, is that of referral of the Palestinian case to the Court by a third State party to the Statute. Moreover, cases of nationals of State parties to the Statute, who were involved in the commission of international crimes in the context of the conflict, such as the case of South African nationals who were enlisted in Israel's armed forces and participated in its 'Operation Cast Lead' offensive on the Gaza Strip, should be subject to further examination.[29] It is therefore an important moment to ensure that the ICC's Office of the Prosecutor reopens its examination of Palestine's cases.

The right question was not whether Palestine is a 'State' but rather whether it has the capacity to enter into relations and to assume jurisdiction over the crimes set forth in the Rome Statute, so as to validly transfer that jurisdiction to the Court.[30] There was never any place for the Prosecutor to examine whether Palestine is a State in general terms, as no objective definition of a State exists in international law. Statehood is a relativist, bilateral matter of pure fact and politics, and States and international organisations are left to decide individually whether they treat an entity as a State for their specific purposes. Although Palestine has been treated as a State by at least 132 States and a range of international organisations, since the relevant question is whether Palestine should be considered a 'State' for the purposes of the Rome Statute, it is for the Court and its various organs to make this decision.

Instead, on 3 April 2012, the Prosecutor decided 'not to proceed' with the examination of the case of Palestine and deferred the determination of Palestine's statehood status to the UN and the Court's Assembly of State Parties.[31] This decision was particularly surprising since, after all, it was the Prosecutor who, over the course of three years, presented the Palestinian legal services with elaborate, substantive questions; called for the submission of expert opinions to the Court by various practitioners and institutions; and initiated an extensive academic debate surrounding legal issues concerning Palestine's capacity to trigger the Court's jurisdiction. The Prosecutor's framing of the issues, however, contained a number of flaws that have since been highlighted by prominent publicists.

---

[29] I. Garda, 'South Africa's legal war over Gaza,' *Al-Jazeera*, 1 November 2009.

[30] M. Kearney, 'Palestine and the International Criminal Court: Asking the Right Question,' *UCLA Human Rights and International Criminal Law Online Forum* (2010).

[31] Office of the Prosecutor, 'Situation in Palestine,' 3 April 2012.

Professor Schabas has noted that the Prosecutor was wrong to think that the Assembly of State Parties is charged with this decision,[32] particularly considering that the main facets of the Assembly's mandate pertain to budgetary issues. Chantal Meloni adds that the Prosecutor should have referred this question to the judges, as per Article 19(3) of the Rome Statute, which states: '[t]he Prosecutor may seek a ruling from the Court regarding a question of jurisdiction or admissibility.'[33] Moreover, as Amnesty International pointed out, 'delegating this decision to a political body undermines the vital independence of the Court and exposes the ICC to political influence over justice issues.'[34] Amnesty's position, which called 'for an independent judicial determination of the issue by the ICC judges rather than a political determination by external bodies,' is that 'the ICC Pre-Trial Chamber is currently the only judicial body that can conduct such a legal process.'

Although the Prosecutor cannot set the Assembly's agenda, as Schabas noted, it can be reasonably expected that upon a request by the Prosecutor the issue would be brought up for discussion. It was not, however. In response to a request letter sent by several academics, including Professor Schabas and Professor Dugard, the former UN Special Rapporteur on Palestine, asking the Assembly to include the issue on its agenda, the Assembly's President explained that 'for any items to be included on the agenda of the Assembly they would have to be proposed by a State Party, the Court or by the United Nations.'[35] The bottom line is that the issue of whether or not an entity is a 'State' for the purpose of the Statute is, as Schabas holds, 'a jurisdictional fact to be assessed and debated within the Court, at various stages of the procedure . . . [which] may be raised by the Prosecutor, by the judges and even by a defendant.'[36]

The uncertain practice concerning the procedure for the Prosecutor to make a determination on the statehood status of an entity clearly does not

[32] W. Schabas, 'Palestinian Statehood and the International Criminal Court: A Curious Condition from Whitehall,' *PhD Studies in Human Rights*, 27 November 2012.

[33] C. Meloni, 'Palestine and the ICC: Some Notes on Why It Is Not a Closed Chapter,' *Opinio Juris*, 25 September 2012.

[34] Amnesty International, 'Questions and Answers: Amnesty International's Response to the ICC Office of the Prosecutor's Statement that it cannot investigate crimes committed during the Gaza conflict,' 4 April 2012.

[35] W. Schabas, 'Palestinian Statehood and the International Criminal Court: A Curious Condition from Whitehall,' *PhD Studies in Human Rights*, 27 November 2012.

[36] *Ibid.*

mean that the Prosecutor has nowhere to turn for guidance. In practice, the indeterminacy of the question of statehood status in international law has been managed in practice through procedural avenues, such as the example of the UN Secretary-General's practice in his role as a depositary of international treaties who, in deciding whether to consider an entity a 'State,' either seeks guidance from the General Assembly or looks at whether the entity was admitted to a UN agency, *inter alia*.[37] The Secretary-General's interpretation of the so-called 'All States' clause, found in the majority of treaties for which he acts as depositary, is a telling example of the ways in which certain procedural gateways within the international legal order have emerged to re-formalize the de-formalized definition of a 'State' in international law, re-injecting this hollow shell with context-specific, operational content.

While the Prosecutor may be expected to 'look around' at the determinations of other international actors in relation to a specific entity, it arguably cannot delegate the decision to another body altogether. What exactly made the Prosecutor retract its commitment to examine Palestine's case so abruptly, arguably in abuse of the procedural standards that the Prosecutor's Office is bound to uphold, and in defiance of the legitimate expectations it had created over the course of three years of deliberations, remains unknown. As Kearney has noted, 'such a strange statement inevitably raises more questions than it can answer.'[38] Be that as it may, the content of the decision is indicative of an intention to avoid a serious examination of Palestine's case and to effectively remove it from the Court's docket.[39]

Palestine's UN Bid and the ICC

Despite Palestine's overwhelming treatment as a State, the recent General Assembly resolution is an important 'rubber stamp' that affords further clout to the legal position that Palestine is a State in international law. The resolution was voted for by 138 States (with 9 against and 41 abstentions), including some EU States that have yet to grant Palestine explicit bilateral recognition. In reaction to the resolution, major international human rights groups called on Palestine to ratify the ICC

---

[37] UN Office of Legal Affairs, *Summary of the Practice of the Secretary-General as Depositary of Multilateral Treaties* (1994).
[38] M. Kearney, 'The Situation of Palestine,' *Opinio Juris*, 5 April 2012.
[39] V. Azarov, 'ICC Jurisdiction in Palestine: Blurring Law and Politics,' *The Jurist*, 9 April 2012; W. Schabas, 'The Prosecutor and Palestine: Deference to the Security Council,' *PhD Studies in Human Rights*, 9 April 2012; Meloni, *op. cit.*

Statute along with other international instruments, so as to affirm its commitment to respect for international law. However, curiously, little mention was made of Palestine's Article 12(3) declaration, which grants the Court retroactive jurisdiction since July 2002. The examination of Palestine's Article 12(3) declaration was suspended by the Prosecutor until further guidance was obtained from the UN or the Assembly of State Parties. As such, the 29 November General Assembly resolution arguably provides the Prosecutor with 'fresh evidence' to reopen Palestine's file. It is hard to believe that, with the matter settled by the UN General Assembly, the Prosecutor would be able to continue to press against a decision in favour of the Court's exercise of jurisdiction over Palestinian territory.

However that may be, a ratification of the Statute by Palestine should be considered in parallel, not only because it could grant the Court retroactive jurisdiction over international crimes committed on Palestinian territory since 1 July 2002, otherwise only applicable from the moment of ratification, but also because the power to accept ratification by Palestine lies in the hands of the UN Secretary-General, and not the Court's organs, including the Office of the Prosecutor. Indeed, Palestine has been eligible to ratify the Statute – under the *Summary of the Practice of the Secretary-General as Depositary of Multilateral Treaties*, which considers 'All States' to be entities who are members of a UN specialised agency – as of November 2011 following its acceptance as a member of UNESCO.[40]

At the end of the day, whether the international judiciary, the International Court of Justice and the International Criminal Court, plays a role in litigating the case of Palestine depends primarily on whether Palestine is treated as a State by either of these bodies.[41] However, once triggered by Palestine, the ICC is expected to consider a number of further questions of varying relevance: the specific date from which Palestine will be considered a State, for the purpose of exercising retroactive jurisdiction; the result of the applicability of the complementarity principle to Israel's investigative practice and the availability of national remedies through the Israeli and Palestinian legal and judicial systems and practice; as well as, potentially, the need to seek investigative cooperation from local authorities, including both Israel and Hamas. As for the Hamas government, the Court might also see the need to determine whether

---

[40] *Summary of the Practice of the Secretary-General as Depositary of Multilateral Treaties, op. cit.*
[41] V. Kattan, 'Litigating 'Palestine' Before International Courts and Tribunals: The Prospects of Success and Perils of Failure,' 35 *Hastings International and Comparative Law Review* 1 (2011).

jurisdiction over the whole of Palestinian territory, the West Bank and the Gaza Strip, is transferred by virtue of new or existing Article 12(3) declarations.

Conclusion

The UN bid and its prospects for the exercise of ICC jurisdiction over Palestinian territory have become the focal point for Israel's efforts to contend with the proper application of international law. These efforts have recently manifested, amongst other things, in Israel's twists and turns before the US administration to amend the recent General Assembly resolution – however, to no avail.[42] Amid discussions on the EU's position – and having been of the view only a year ago that Palestine should abandon its ICC aspirations in favour of the 'peace process' – the British government distinguished itself by conditioning its support for Palestine's bid on Palestinian assurances that it would not turn to the ICC; on the pretext that doing so would jeopardise the so-called 'peace process.'[43] This proposition and its intended result are however misleading.

Strictly legally speaking, a State's right to join international treaties and organisations cannot be neutered, either through political agreements or General Assembly resolutions, at least not in accordance with international law. One can safely assume, in the light of recent historical developments that Israel's efforts to deflect ICC jurisdiction have not ceased – the 'low profile' it kept during the vote at the General Assembly is most probably part of a broader strategy to contest the involvement of international justice mechanisms. In this regard, Kearney has stated: 'Premising recognition of statehood on a condition that you absent your new State from rights or responsibility under international law is to make a mockery not just of the process of statehood, but of the very notion of human rights.'[44] Those who maintain the stance that Israel should be immunised from the ICC's jurisdiction seem to disregard the fact that the ICC is the only remaining international justice mechanism to redress the accountability gap in the Palestinian-Israeli context – particularly since universal jurisdiction laws have ceded their authority to prosecutorial

---

[42] B. Ravid, 'Palestinians refuse clause in UN draft barring criminal charges against Israel,' *Haaretz*, 27 November 2012.

[43] 'Foreign secretary says UK will abstain unless Palestinians commit to unconditional return to talks with Israel,' *The Guardian*, 26 November 2012.

[44] Comments to: Kevin Jon Heller, 'Britain to Support Palestine's UNGA Resolution?' *Opinio Juris*, 26 November 2012.

politics, partly due to the very Palestinian efforts that have sought to gain access to international justice.

The support granted by EU States to the General Assembly resolution of 29 November 2012 is a strong indication of the fact that Israel's legal and political narrative is becoming increasingly unconvincing. This change in the state of affairs makes it high time for States to ensure the proper application of international law to the question of Palestine, which has long remained on the periphery of international law. Despite political currents, maintained by civil society and international actors who continue to cede to politics key 'overarching questions' of international law, including Palestine's statehood, prolonged occupation and building settlement by Israel,[45] Palestine's present-day status 'need[s] to be considered in the context of the undeniable increase in the 'legalisation' of the diplomatic, cultural, political and military aspects of the conflict.'[46]

While some publicists have warned of the political dangers of the ICC wading into the Palestinian-Israeli context, and the likelihood of Palestinian violations being first in line,[47] most probably together with Israel's war crime of transferring, directly or indirectly, its civilians into the occupied territory, which was recently condemned by a Human Rights Council established inquiry committee,[48] this very logic, which ostensibly seeks to protect the political legitimacy of the Court, is most likely to result in a decline in its international legal authority. If it proceeds correctly and carefully, Palestine has much to gain from the recent developments brought about by its UN bid, particularly in terms of claiming respect for Palestinian rights. Most prominently, the normative facts that have been produced by Palestine's engagements through international law have made the obstacles intended to bar Palestine from accessing the ICC increasingly untenable, since maintaining these barriers is exacting a heavy toll on the integrity of both the international legal order and the legal orders of individual States.

---

[45] M. Kearney, 'Why Statehood Now: A Reflection on the ICC's Impact on Palestine's Engagement with International Law,' in C. Meloni and G. Tognoni, *op. cit.*, p. 394.

[46] *Ibid*, 393.

[47] K. Heller, 'Britain to Support Palestine's UNGA Resolution?' *Opinio Juris*, 26 November 2012.

[48] UN Doc A/HRC/19/2, 16 August 2012. UN News, 'Independent UN Inquiry Urges Halt to Settlement in Occupied Territory,' 31 January 2013. Israel decided to end its cooperation with the Council following the decision to establish the inquiry committee; 'Israel ends contact with UN Human Rights Council,' *BBC News*, 26 March 2012.

CHAPTER NINE

PALESTINIAN PRISONERS IN ISRAELI JAILS IN LIGHT OF THE THIRD GENEVA CONVENTION: FROM JAILS TO PRISONER OF WAR CAMPS

MAGDALENA A. PULIDO

Introduction

International humanitarian law (IHL) stipulates, with reference to international armed conflicts, that every person who finds himself in the hands of the opposing party is entitled to a certain status, either prisoner of war (POW) status, which is governed by the Third Geneva Convention [1] or protected civilian status, which is governed by the Fourth Geneva Convention.[2] The fact that there is no possibility of a gap between the two Conventions precludes the creation of an 'intermediate status.'[3] In the case of Palestinians detained by Israel, POW status and protective treatment have been refused, as their detention is deemed to be governed by a different set of rules that permits prolonged imprisonment and minimum respect for their human dignity. This regime is based on considerations of national security and is regulated with that end in view at the domestic

---

[1] Convention III relative to the Treatment of Prisoners of War (Geneva Convention III), Geneva 12 August 1949.
[2] Convention IV relative to the Protection of Civilian Persons in Time of War (Geneva Convention IV), Geneva 12 August 1949.
[3] ICTY, *Prosecutor v. Delalić, 'Celebici Case,'* (Judgement), Case No. IT-96-21-T, 16 November 1998, para. 271, quoting the Commentary to the Fourth Geneva Convention.

level. This policy, added to the effects of long-term occupation of Palestine, affects the application of IHL.[4]

The purpose of the present chapter is to discuss how the situation of Palestinian prisoners in Israeli jails could benefit from the establishment of a Palestinian State. The first part of the chapter will discuss Israel's position regarding the non-existence of POW status in relation to the conflict with Palestine. The second part will elaborate on the importance of the existence of the State of Palestine for POW status, while addressing possible scenarios in which its existence would provide either for the status and treatment of Palestinian prisoners as POWs, or for other mechanisms whereby Palestine could protect its nationals imprisoned in Israel.

Palestinians Imprisoned in Israel

The Geneva Convention relative to the Treatment of Prisoners of War (GC III), most of which is deemed to constitute customary law,[5] governs the status granted to combatants who have taken part in hostilities and have fallen into the hands of the enemy.[6] Combatants are considered to have a 'license to kill or wound enemy combatants and destroy enemy military objectives;'[7] and they are not liable to punishment for their mere participation in hostilities or for acts that do not violate IHL.[8] The purpose of their detention is not to reprimand them, but rather to prevent their continuing participation in the conflict.[9] A series of protection guidelines are applicable to POW status in order to prevent abuse by the detaining power.

---

[4] Geneva Convention IV, *op. cit.*, Article 6, which stipulates that only a specific set of articles continue to apply one year after the general close of military operations.

[5] L. Green, *The Contemporary Law of Armed Conflict* (Manchester: Manchester University Press, 1993), p. 188; H. Fischer, 'Protection of Prisoners of War,' in D. Fleck, *The Handbook of Humanitarian Law in Armed Conflicts* (Oxford: Oxford University Press, 1995), p. 325.

[6] *Op. cit.* Geneva Convention III, Article 4.

[7] Inter American Commission on Human Rights, *Report on Terrorism and Human Rights*, OEA/Ser.L/V/II.116 Doc. 5, 22 October 2002, para. 68.

[8] International Committee of the Red Cross (ICRC), *Study on Customary International Humanitarian Law*, Rule 106. Conditions for Prisoner of War Status, Customary Study IHL.

[9] M. Sassòli, *et al., How Does Law Protect in War?* (Geneva: ICRC, 2011), Vol. I, Chapter 6, p. 10.

In the context of the armed conflict between Israel and Palestine liberation groups, Palestinians who participate in the ongoing armed activities are considered to be either 'terrorists' or 'unlawful combatants,'[10] meaning that they are denied the status and treatment awarded to combatants by the rules of IHL. Even though IHL does not recognize the categories of 'terrorist' or 'unlawful combatant,' domestic regulations have ruled on the matter so that Israel may 'lawfully' permit prolonged detention and reduce guarantees.

Application of the Law Governing the Determination of Combatant and POW Status

IHL contemplates a legal procedure for determining combatant-POW status and Israel is obliged to abide by this procedure as a party to the Geneva Conventions. The determination and status of combatants should be settled in accordance with the following three-pronged test that will be further expanded upon below:

- The nature of the conflict, which must be of an international character;
- The detaining power must evaluate the character of the opposing force through individual and group considerations;
- If any doubt arises, detainees must be presumed to have POW status, and a competent tribunal must determine each detainee's claim.

Nature of the Conflict

An international armed conflict traditionally involves States and is regulated by the Geneva Conventions of 1949 and possibly Additional Protocol 1 as a whole or the provisions reflecting customary law.[11] Moreover, international humanitarian law, which was originally limited to States, has evolved to include groups fighting for national liberation against a dominant power.[12] Thus, according to Professor Cassese, 'an

---

[10] The origin of the term 'unlawful combatant,' advanced by the United States, has been developed outside IHL.

[11] J. Pejic, *Status of Armed Conflicts*, in E. Wilmshurst, ed., *Perspectives on the ICRC Study on Customary International Humanitarian Law*, 2001, p. 77.

[12] Protocol Additional to the Geneva Conventions of 12 August 1949 and relating to the Protection of Victims of International Armed Conflicts (Protocol I), 8 June 1977, Article 1(4). S. Vite, 'Typology of Armed Conflicts in International

armed conflict which takes place between an Occupying Power and rebel or insurgent groups - whether or not they are terrorist in character - in an occupied territory amounts to an international armed conflict.'[13] In the present case, there is an ongoing occupation[14] by Israel of the Palestinian territories, which has co-existed with different theatres of hostilities aimed at putting an end to the occupation.

Notwithstanding the foregoing, the fact that certain armed groups are not identified with a specific State has been a key argument used by Israel in support of the alleged non-applicability of the law of international armed conflict, thereby excluding them from POW determination.[15] This was stressed in the *Targeted Killings* case, in which it was determined that 'terrorists and their organizations, with which the State of Israel has an armed conflict of international character, do not fall into the category of combatants. They do not belong to the armed forces, and they do not belong to units to which international law grants status similar to that of combatants. Indeed, the terrorists and the organizations which send them to carry out attacks are unlawful combatants. They do not enjoy the status of prisoners of war.'[16]

The concept of 'unlawful combatant' has accordingly been defined as 'a person who took part in hostilities against the State of Israel, whether directly or indirectly, or who is a member of a force carrying out hostilities against the State of Israel, who does not satisfy the conditions granting a prisoner of war status under international humanitarian law.'[17] The purpose of highlighting terrorist activities and unlawful combatants is to prevent the application of IHL. As stated by the International Committee of the Red Cross (ICRC), 'when a situation of violence amounts to an

---

Humanitarian Law: Legal Concept and Actual Situations,' *International Review of the Red Cross*, 2009, p. 73.

[13] A. Cassese, *International Law* (2005), p. 420.

[14] A territory is occupied 'when it is placed under the authority of the hostile army. The occupation extends only to the territory where such authority has been established and can be exercised,' as defined in Convention IV respecting the Laws and Customs of War on Land and its annex, The Hague, 18 October 1907, Articles 42 and 43; and Geneva Convention IV, Article 47.

[15] Israeli Ministry of Foreign Affairs, *The Operation in Gaza, 27 December 2008-18 January 2009: Factual and Legal Aspects*, July 2009, para. 29, p. 10.

[16] High Court of Justice (Israel), HCJ 769/02 '*1. The Public Committee against Torture in Israel, 2. Palestinian Society for the Protection of Human Rights and the Environment v. The Government of Israel et al.: The Targeted Killings* case,' 13 December 2006, para. 25.

[17] Supreme Court sitting as Court of Criminal Appeals, *1. A and 2. B v. State of Israel*, 11 June 2008, para. 6, quoting 'Internment of Unlawful Combatant Law,' 2.

armed conflict, there is little added value in calling such acts 'terrorism'.'[18] These actions create uncertainty as to whether such 'terrorist acts' fall outside IHL regulations; equating a struggle with terrorism 'is unnecessary and has been recognized as a stumbling block.'[19]

Israel tries in this way to remove activities that are permitted and regulated during an armed conflict from the scope of application of IHL in order to justify a restrictive approach. Overall, it is important to stress that it is on account of the existence of an armed conflict that both parties are entitled to carry out certain activities which are prohibited in peacetime and that armed forces are punishable for the commission of war crimes despite POW status.

Israel has therefore developed a generalized method of classification to determine the non-existence of combatants who are entitled to POW status. The classification is based on the origin of the groups of which the detainees may claim membership and focuses on the absence of a State.

Evaluation of Individual and Group Considerations

The law applicable to the determination of POW status is contained in Article 4A(2) of the Third Geneva Convention and is elaborated by Articles 43 and 44 of the First Additional Protocol (API), which modify the requirements for POW status. Article 4 requires those to whom it is applicable to comply with the following conditions: to have an effective chain of command, to bear distinctive signs, to carry arms openly and to conduct operations in accordance with the laws and customs of war.[20] Special attention is thus given to (i) compliance with IHL and (ii) the element of distinction. In practice, violations of IHL have not been treated as a key ground for refusing POW status;[21] priority is given instead in conferring such status to the need to guarantee proper treatment of combatants. With a view to covering national liberation movements, API highlighted the obligation of 'carrying arms openly' rather than imposing a

---

[18] ICRC, *Challenges for IHL-Terrorism: Overview*, 29 October 2010.
[19] J. Paust, *Terrorism's Proscription and Core Elements of an Objective Definition*, University of Houston, p. 60.
[20] Geneva Convention (III), Article 4A (2).
[21] Protocol I, Article 44 (2). M. Sassoli, 'La Guerre contre le terrorisme, le droit international humanitaire et le statut de prisonnnier de guerre,' 39 *Canadian Yearbook of International Law* (2001), p. 14.

strict distinction based on clothing. It thus gave irregular armed forces greater space for compliance.[22]

Unfortunately, there is no clarity regarding which criteria are to be evaluated on an individual or collective basis[23] and this leaves too much leeway for a State to deny combatant status to all members of a group.[24] This is evident in the case of Israel, as indicated by the Israeli Supreme Court, which has stated that Palestinian armed groups are not homogenous and that '[t]hey include groups, which are not necessarily identical to each other in terms of the willingness to abide by fundamental legal and human norms.'[25] While it is conceded that certain groups may comply with the requirements, the Court ensures overall failure by interfering with the possible identification of groups that may be able to comply, opting instead for a generalized approach. Furthermore, it actually acknowledges the existence of groups who 'fight the army' as opposed to those who act against civilians, but it fails in practice to allow benefits to those fighting solely against the army.

Presumption of POW Status

POW status is to be conferred upon capture. If the combatant is denied such status, he may be tried for the commission of belligerent acts; it is therefore important for a competent tribunal to determine his status.[26] Given the asymmetrical nature of the present conflict, regular conditions that would permit an impartial evaluation of a person's qualification for POW status by a military tribunal of the State do not apply in practice. This measure should therefore be neutralized. It has been argued with reference to the presumption of doubt of POW status that 'States should not be able to unilaterally decide that no doubt has arisen for an entire

---

[22] D. Hacker, 'The Application of Prisoner of War Status to Guerillas under the First Protocol Additional to the Geneva Conventions of 1949,' *2 B.C. International and Comparative Law Review* 131 (1978).

[23] K. Watkin, 'Combatants, Unprivileged Belligerents and Conflicts in the 21st Century,' in *International Humanitarian Law Research Initiative*, January 2003, p. 9.

[24] W. Mallison, 'The Juridical Status of Irregular Combatants under IHL,' 9 *Case Western Reserve Journal of International Law* 39 (1977), pp. 58-63, where there is acknowledgment of the 'relative ability of regular versus irregular armed forces to fulfill all the requirements of IHL.'

[25] Targeted Killings Case, *op. cit.*, Vice-President E. Rivlin, p. 45.

[26] ICRC, *Commentaries to the Geneva Conventions of 12 August 1949 and Protocols Additional to the Geneva Conventions*, Commentary to Article 5 of Geneva Convention III.

group of captured persons who have taken part in hostilities,'[27] since the purpose of the relevant article is to maintain and emphasize as much as possible the protection afforded by IHL. Moreover, where a judiciary that is connected to the military, as in the present case, is called upon to determine the status, the Inter-American Court has recognized that 'the impartiality of the judge is affected by the fact that the armed forces have the dual function of combating insurgent groups with military force, and of judging and imposing sentence upon members of such groups.'[28]

Where States have been involved in intra-State armed conflicts, no doubt has been cast on the applicability of the law relating to POWs, notwithstanding differences of opinion regarding compliance with requirements such as distinction by uniform and implementation of IHL. Nevertheless, certain States, when involved in armed conflicts with non-State actors, have agreed to grant treatment resembling POW status, as in the cases of the Spanish civil war,[29] the Algerian war of independence, the war between Nigeria and Biafra, and some of the conflicts in the former Yugoslavia.[30] This means that it is actually possible to concede POW status to combatants at some point during the conflict and to allow them to benefit from some sort of immunity, although the question of temporality must be stressed in respect of the lengthy duration of the armed conflict at hand.[31] This approach finds stronger support in the context of national liberation wars and where people are fighting for self-determination,[32] as evidenced by the position endorsed by the United Nations General Assembly in resolutions concerning the treatment of POWs.[33] It is evident from this recognition that, while political motives may initially underlie

---

[27] Y. Naqvi, 'Doubtful Prisoner-of-War Status,' 84 *International Review of the Red Cross* (2002), pp. 574-575.

[28] *Case of Cantoral Benavides v. Peru, Inter-American Court of Human Rights*, Judgment (Merits), 18 August 2000, para. 108.

[29] N. Padelford, 'International Law and the Spanish Civil War,' 31 *American Journal of International Law* 226 (1937).

[30] Yugoslavia/Croatia, Memorandum of Understanding of 27 November 1991, para. 3; Bosnia and Herzegovina, Agreement No. 1 of 22 May 1992, para. 2(4).

[31] S. Sivakumaran, 'Lessons for the Law of Armed Conflict from Commitments of Armed Groups: Identification of Legitimate Targets and Prisoners of War,' 93 *International Review of the Red Cross* (2011), pp. 18-19.

[32] UN Doc. E/CN.4/Sub.2/2004/40, Specific Human Rights Issues: New priorities, in particular Terrorism and Counter-terrorism, Terrorism and Human Rights, Final report of the Special Rapporteur, Kalliopi Koufa, 25 June 2004, p. 13. E. Kwakwa, *International Law of Armed Conflict: Personal and Material Fields of Application* (Kluwer, 1992) p. 81.

[33] General Assembly resolutions 2396, 2395 (1968), 3103 (1973).

the refusal to grant POW status, its conferral remains primordial, since it encourages combatants to abide by the law and to offer the same treatment to captured soldiers.[34] It is certainly preferable to the maintenance of a convenient air of confusion regarding which law to apply.

Even where the above-mentioned examples cannot be deemed to fall under customary international law, they illustrate Israel's persistent unwillingness to act and the limited scope for action by Palestine as a non-State.

Results of the Non-application of POW Status

Administrative Detention

Where an occupation is established in the context of an international armed conflict, detention is used by the occupying power as a tool to secure civilians who pose a security threat. Detention may be considered to some extent as a tool that assists the occupying power in complying with its obligation to provide for control and security,[35] but it is also well established that occupation constitutes the most severe measure that may be imposed[36] or, as clarified in the *Delalić* Case, as a method of 'last resort.'[37]

Article 78 of Geneva Convention IV deals with the detention of civilians and establishes as a prerequisite that 'the individual himself must pose a threat to security,'[38] which means that the ground for detention must be based on his personal situation, i.e. there should be no attempt to invoke other people's responsibility or to use him as a bargaining tool.[39] Moreover, detention should not constitute a punishment or constitute an alternative to criminal proceedings.[40]

Finally, detention must cease once the individual no longer poses a threat. As Jelena Pejic comments, 'the longer internment lasts, the greater

---

[34] Kwakwa, *op. cit.*, p. 82.

[35] Geneva Convention IV, *op. cit.*, Article 27.

[36] Geneva Convention IV, *op. cit.*, Article 41 and Article 78.

[37] *Prosecutor v. Delalić* Case, Judgement, IT-96-21-T P.10427, 16 November 1998, para. 572.

[38] R. Goodman, 'Editorial comment: The detention of civilians in armed conflict,' 103 *American Journal of International Law* (2009), p. 56.

[39] A. Deeks, 'Administrative Detention in Armed Conflict,' 40 *Case Western Reserve Journal of International Law* (1978), p. 407.

[40] J. Pejic, 'Detention: POWs and Security Detainees,' in *The Law of Armed Conflict: Problems and Prospects*, Chatham House (18-19 April 2005), p. 44.

the onus on a detaining authority to prove that the reasons for it remain valid.'[41] Recent case law has helped to confirm the above-mentioned provisions and has also established that the detention of civilians is unlawful in the following two circumstances:

'(i) When a civilian or civilians have been detained in contravention of Article 42 of Geneva Convention IV, i.e. they are detained without reasonable grounds to believe that the security of the Detaining Power makes it absolutely necessary;[42]

(ii) Where the procedural safeguards required by Article 43 of Geneva Convention IV are not complied with in respect of detained civilians, even when their initial detention may have been justified.'[43]

In the case under discussion, Israel has made use of administrative detention in order to detain Palestinians from the occupied Palestinian territories for prolonged periods under harsh conditions. Detainees are considered to be a security risk on grounds linked to the existence of the State itself rather than to the maintenance of the occupation, which constitutes the purpose of the IHL regulation. Detention is therefore undertaken in contravention of IHL, as evidenced by the practice of holding detainees outside the occupied territories.[44]

The Internment of Unlawful Combatants Law

Israel's failure to implement the laws governing international armed conflict, thereby preventing the recognition of combatant-POW status, seems to have brought a different model into operation. It has decided to develop other possibilities for detaining and otherwise dealing with Palestinians accused of engaging in hostilities. For instance, it has enacted an 'Internment of Unlawful Combatants Law,' the purpose of which is to detain Palestinians without trial. It envisages the application of the Law 'to foreign parties who belong to a terror organization that operates against

---

[41] J. Pejic, 'Procedural Principles and Safeguards for Internment/Administrative Detention in Armed Conflict and Other Situations of Violence' (2005), Vol. 87, No. 858, p. 382.

[42] *Prosecutor v. Delalić, 'Celebici Case* (Appeals Judgment, 2001), para. 322.

[43] *Delalić, op. cit.,* para. 583. *Prosecutor v. Kordić and Čerkez,* IT-95-14/2-T (2001), para. 291. Article 43 refers to the right to have the action reconsidered by a court or administrative board and reviewed at least twice a year.

[44] Geneva Convention (IV) Article 76, Amnesty International, Submission to the Human Rights Committee, 99th session, July 2010, p. 15.

the security of the State.'[45] This has made it possible to hold alleged 'unlawful combatants' until they are able to prove that they will not harm State security, which is a very difficult task for people who are detained and who, in many cases, are not fully informed of the allegations against them. Moreover, the conditions of detention are linked to an assessment by senior military officers of the state of hostilities, the aim being to ensure that their release would not endanger the State.

The Relevance of Being a State to the Condition of POW

International law is the reflection of a struggle between States to build support for each other while preserving their sovereignty. States have therefore laid down rules that permit them to exercise rights and that impose obligations. However, the system has been compelled to recognize other entities that also play a role and are 'entitled to benefits of international law,'[46] such as international organizations, insurgents and belligerents, national liberation movements and other entities.[47]

Despite the broadening of the scope of international law to reflect the importance of non-State entities in certain contexts, the State-centred model persists. The evolution has not permitted a fully synchronized response to matters that fall outside the elements created by States, and while there is recognition of the importance of non-State entities for the system of international law, they do not enjoy equality of arms in the international arena. In some areas, the correct implementation of the law can only be demanded through a State, and there is unfortunately still a heavy reliance on States for its application.[48]

The International Court of Justice (ICJ), while quoting the Vienna Convention on the Law of Treaties, recognized that, in the relations between States, an obligation of an international humanitarian character incurred by one party may not be terminated or subjected to conditions in response to the behaviour (breach) of its counterparty[49]. But the ICJ

---

[45] *A B v. State of Israel* case, *op. cit.,* p. 11.

[46] M. Shaw, *International Law* (Cambridge: Cambridge University Press, 2008), p. 46.

[47] *Ibid.*, pp. 197, 245-246.

[48] A. Carswell, *Classifying the Conflict: A Soldier's Dilemma*, 91 *International Review of the Red Cross* (2009), p. 153.

[49] Vienna Convention on the Law of Treaties, 23 May 1969, 1155 UNTS 331, Article 60(5). International Court of Justice, *Legal Consequences for States of the Continued Presence of South Africa in Namibia (South West Africa)*

Advisory Opinion on the *Legal Consequences of the Construction of a Wall* is an interesting example of a case in which the Court, referring to the situation in the occupied territories, drew attention to the continued armed conflict, and the indiscriminate violence and repressive measures, and called on both Israel and Palestine, as a non-State actor, to observe the rules of IHL.[50] The problem continued to be that Palestine, as a non-State, remained a step behind in the struggle to counteract the rules set by Israel in its capacity as a State. A further example is how commitments by the Palestinian side to apply IHL have been rejected, and have been described as 'missed opportunities . . . to push forward the agenda of compliance.'[51]

Moreover, in an area of law such as that governing prisoners of war, problems arise when it comes to determining the applicable laws when unequal sides are pitted against one another. As the traditional POW regime tries to protect the honour of those serving their countries and to prevent unnecessary harm once they are out of the battlefield, the lack of any connection to States in the case of armed groups contributes to the establishment of a limbo. The acceptance among States of a right to self-defence and the importance attached to regular armed forces critically affect the access of non-State entities to protection. This is accentuated by States' application of a misinterpreted version of the law. Any attempt to apply these legal interpretations to relations with non-State entities merely exacerbates the situation to the detriment of the imprisoned. It would appear at times that legal constructs created for the purpose of protection are stressed with a view to obtaining political gain. Furthermore, rules of international law seem to present an ongoing obstacle when it comes to ensuring respect for individual rights, especially in cases where the lack of statehood can be of direct relevance to the treatment meted out to those fighting to obtain a State.

The State of Palestine: Protection for Prisoners in Israel

Once there is a Palestinian State, it will be able to exercise its legal capacity 'to create . . . legal relations with other units as it sees fit' since it

---

notwithstanding Security Council Resolution 276, Advisory Opinion, 21 June 1971, para. 96.

[50] International Court of Justice, *Legal Consequences of the Construction of a Wall in the Occupied Palestinian Territory,* Advisory Opinion, 9 July 2004, para. 162.

[51] C. Bassiouni, 'The New Wars and the Crisis of Compliance with the Law of Armed Conflict by Non-State Actors,' 98 *Journal of Criminal Law and Criminology* (2008), p. 749.

will be 'unaffected . . . by dependence upon other States.'[52] Palestine will thus be able to assume international rights and duties,[53] to be heard by the international community and to demand the full exercise of the said rights. The State of Palestine will be able to protect its nationals.

It is important to stress that the establishment of the State of Palestine is not a mere case of State succession, i.e. 'replacement of one State by another in responsibility for the international relations of territory,'[54] but a complex matter of finally gaining access to the international legal arena and exercising the right to self-determination that has been suppressed in the case of Palestinians. Hence the applicable rules may reflect principles of customary law regulating State succession, but they must be placed in context.

The Montevideo Convention on Rights and Duties of States stipulates that the State should possess a permanent population,[55] which will have the nationality of the new State. Moreover, the link of nationality will lead to protection by the State and recognition of allegiance by nationals to their State. As each State is allowed to determine who is entitled to be its nationals,[56] provided that this is done in accordance with international law, the creation of the State of Palestine in the case under discussion entitles all individuals with a genuine connection to the State to be recognized.[57] It

---

[52] Permanent Court of International Justice, *Customs Regime between Germany and Austria (Protocol of 19 March 1931)*, Advisory Opinion, Individual Opinion of Judge Anzilotti, p. 57-8. Shaw, *op. cit.*, p. 202.

[53] UN General Assembly Resolution 2625, *Declaration on Principles of International Law concerning Friendly Relations and Co-operation among States in Accordance with the Charter of the United Nations*, 24 October 1970.

[54] Shaw, *op. cit.*, p. 959.

[55] The Montevideo Convention on Rights and Duties of States of 26 December 1933 provides in Article 1 that a State should possess a permanent population, defined territory, a government and capacity to enter into relations with other States.

[56] PCIJ, *Nationality Decrees issued in Tunis and Morocco (French Zone)*, Advisory Opinion, PCIJ Reports, Series B, No. 4, 1923, p. 24. The Hague Convention on Certain Questions Relating to the Conflict of Nationality Laws, 1930, Article 1.

[57] ICJ, *Nottebohm Case (Liechtenstein v Guatemala)*, 1955, pp. 22-23. In a modern take, the European Convention on Nationality (1997), in its Article 18, considers that in order to decide on the granting of nationality, a State shall take into account the genuine and effective link of the person concerned with the State, the habitual residence of the person, the will of the person and the territorial origin of the person concerned. International Law Commission, 'Draft Articles on Nationality of Natural Persons in relation to the Succession of States,' in 'Report of the International Law Commission on the Work of its 51st Session' (1999). Article 5

will therefore transform the situation for Palestinians, since they will
acquire access to a new set of protection guarantees which they have
hitherto lacked.[58]

Furthermore, in accordance with international law, the 'change in
ownership of a particular territory involves also a change in . . . the legal
authority governing the area . . . . The nationality of the inhabitants is
altered.'[59] Hence, the Palestinian authorities would be able to grant
nationality[60] to subjects on the basis of the following hypotheses: (i) those
born in the territory, (ii) those residing in the territory,[61] and (iii) those
born abroad to parents who are entitled to claim nationality, since in most
cases it would be the first time that the persons concerned obtained access
to a nationality and exercised the said right.[62]

The recognition of a State of Palestine may imply that the armed
conflict with Israel has been terminated and lead to an arrangement
whereby the well-established provisions relating to the release of POWs
will be implemented.[63] In the light of this chapter's main contention that
Israel has not permitted these provisions to be applied to combatants[64] and
since there is a possibility that the conflict will not be terminated, the
establishment of a Palestinian State will raise issues pertaining to the
release or ongoing detention of Palestinian prisoners in Israeli jails. Three
types of situation will therefore be analysed: first, the situation of
Palestinian combatants affected by the alleged inapplicability of IHL who,
once they have a State, should achieve POW status; second, the situation

---

refers to the presumption of nationality: 'persons having their habitual residence in
the territory concerned are presumed to acquire the nationality of the . . . State.'

[58] It is important to bear in mind that the constitution of a Palestinian State is
linked to the individuals in the Occupied Palestinian Territory and in Israel.

[59] Shaw, op. cit., p. 489.

[60] An objective of international law is to reduce the number of stateless
individuals; hence the creation of a State will immediately entail a nationality
effect.

[61] In the case of habitual residence, the Draft Articles on Nationality of Natural
Persons, op. cit., also establish that a new State is not obliged to grant its
nationality to persons with habitual residence in another State or against the will of
the persons concerned.

[62] The Universal Declaration of Human Rights, 10 December 1948, Article 15.

[63] Geneva Convention III, Article 118.

[64] R. Goldman and B. Tittemore, 'Unprivileged Combatants and the Hostilities in
Afghanistan: Their Status and Rights under International Humanitarian and Human
Rights Law,' American Society of International Law Task Force on Terrorism
(2002), p. 26; this analyses the position of the United States according to which
'unlawful combatants' were not to be released at the close of hostilities.

of Palestinian-Israeli nationals linked to the armed conflict, who could benefit from POW status; and third, if there is no acceptance of a new status for those detained, the possibility for Palestine to seek protection through other means, such as human rights mechanisms.

Consequences for Palestinians Deprived of IHL Guarantees

The existence of a State of Palestine can give rise to various arguments in support of modifications to the treatment of armed groups classified as unlawful combatants, such as the possibility to demand the review of compliance with the Geneva Conventions and human rights treaties. The existence of a State of Palestine cannot be ignored by Israel. Even if it does not desire to enter into relations or agreements, the international obligations that arise between Israel and the State of Palestine cannot be disregarded by either party, including the application of international humanitarian rules of a customary character, at least until Palestine accedes to the Geneva Conventions and their Additional Protocols. Israel's justificatory view that a balance is required between national security and human rights law,[65] which allows for a limitation of the conditions applicable to detainees and unilateral qualifications of POW rights by Israel on grounds of national security,[66] would no longer have any basis, since Palestine would be entitled to contest it and to demand compliance with IHL and adequate respect for the human rights of its nationals.

Furthermore, the existence of national armed forces would come into play, i.e. once Palestine takes steps to constitute its armed forces and their components, their existence can no longer be challenged. Therefore, 'the

---

[65] E. Gross, 'Human Rights, Terrorism and the Problem of Administrative Detention in Israel: Does a Democracy have the Right to Hold Terrorists as Bargaining Chips?' 18 *Arizona Journal of International and Comparative Law* (2001), pp. 726-727, citing *Administrative Detention Appeal Anon v. Minister of Defense*, where the Court stated that human rights cannot become a pretext for denying public and State security. A balance is needed— a sensitive and difficult balance-between the freedom and dignity of the individual and State and public security.

[66] J. Kastenberg, 'The Customary International Law of War and Combatant Status: Does the Current Executive Branch Policy Determination on Unlawful Combatant Status for Terrorists Run Foul of International Laws, or Is It Just Poor Public Relations?' 39 *Gonzaga Law Review* (2004), p. 533.

agreement between States primarily for the protection of the members of the national forces of each against the other'[67] enters into existence.

This issue has been addressed by L.C. Green who, referring to changes resulting from the proclamation of a State of Palestine, writes that 'if the Palestine National Council or the government of the State of Palestine declares that the various military groups associated with the PLO and resembling those considered in these two judgments constitute the 'army' of the State, it may become difficult for Israel . . . to continue to deny combatant status to such forces, or to refuse to treat captured members thereof as prisoners of war.'[68] In this new scenario, if the armed conflict continues, those detained will be awarded POW status, since the regular armed forces of the new State of Palestine will fall within the framework established for combatant-POW determination. It will therefore be important to review whether those classified as 'unlawful combatants' prior to the constitution of the State can benefit from assimilation to the new regular armed forces of Palestine.

Bearing this in mind, it is relevant to point out that, in State practice, members of insurgent groups become part of the national army if they succeed in their struggle. The question therefore arises whether the status of those still imprisoned without access to any effective protection can be modified so that their situation is equivalent to that of subsequent POWs from their own State.

Articles 10 and 11 of the rules governing the attachment of conduct by insurrectional or other movements to a new State developed by the International Law Commission[69] establish the norms whereby the conduct of insurrectional or other movements are attributable to a new State, in accordance with the principle of continuity between the national liberation movement and the new State and acknowledgment of the movement by the State.

The National Liberation Movement and the New State

It has been recognized that 'continuity [exists] between the organization of the movement and the organization of the State to which it

---

[67] T. Ho, 'The Relevancy of Nationality to the Right to Prisoner of War Status,' 8 *Chinese Journal of International Law* 397 (2009).

[68] L. Green, 'Terrorism and Armed Conflict: The Plea and the Verdict,' 19 *Israel Yearbook on Human Rights* (1989), p. 135.

[69] International Law Commission, 'Draft Articles on the Responsibility of States for Internationally Wrongful Acts with commentaries,' in *Report of the International Law Commission on the work of its 53rd Session*, 2001.

has given rise.'[70] Real and substantial continuity therefore needs to exist for this situation to arise.

In the light of the foregoing, it would be possible to claim that the forces struggling for the constitution of a State of Palestine would be recognized as members of its regular armed forces and could therefore be asked to join other captured combatants. The requirement of real and substantial continuity would demand a specific determination, which would probably result in very few groups bearing a resemblance to the official forces.

Acknowledgment by the State of the Armed Groups as its Own

While the focus of the article is the acknowledgement of acts as those of the State, the underlying principle is the possibility of attribution to the State of 'conduct that was not or may not have been attributable to it at the time of commission, but which is subsequently acknowledged and adopted by the State as its own.'[71] Hence, while it was previously impossible for Palestine to execute a fair petition in support of the acts of armed groups acting on its behalf, the acknowledgment of said groups as part of its own armed forces could permit some reconsideration of the manner in which they are held.

This specific point may be linked to a previous position adopted by the Government of Israel, when it stressed, in the *Military Prosecutor v Omar Mahmud Kassem and Others* case,[72] that lack of recognition of the acts of an armed group by a State with which it is at war precludes the application of international law. Hence, a petition on behalf of groups that are intimately related to the regular armed forces of the new State may secure certain level of recognition in the aftermath of the acts carried out, from which they can benefit during their ongoing detention.

The above examples stem from the legal implications of the constitution of the State of Palestine, which will undoubtedly have consequences in the sphere of individual rights; it follows that the difference in the time of apprehension should not change the underlying protection granted for such acts.

---

[70] Commentary to Article 10: *Conduct of an Insurrectional or other Movement, op. cit.*, para. 6.

[71] *Ibid.*, Commentary to Article 11: Conduct acknowledged and adopted by a State as its own.

[72] *Military Prosecutor v Omar Mahmud Kassem and Others*, 1969, I Is. Yb. On HR, 456, (1971).

Arab-Israelis Detained for Acts Against Israel

The determination of nationality as result of the establishment of a Palestinian State is of relevance to detainees of Israeli nationality and Palestinian origin who have been detained in connection with the armed conflict. Contrasting views exist on whether it is possible for the detaining power to grant POW status to a person who owes a duty of allegiance to it, or whether the person's acts can solely be judged as treason. The *Tadić* case emphasized the importance of substantial relations rather than formal bonds in determining nationality.[73] Thus, where nationality was granted by Israel to the inhabitants of the territory because of their presence in what eventually constituted the State,[74] lack of acknowledgment of a remaining allegiance to Palestine should not be invoked to limit the guarantees applicable to the treatment of these individuals. Palestinian combatants have stronger links and allegiance to Palestine than to an imposed nationality. Hence, IHL would become applicable to their relationship with Israel and demands for the application of Geneva Convention III to their treatment would be legitimate.

A claim of local allegiance based on a link due to the former residence of the imprisoned could be invoked as an argument, but it is precisely in this connection that preeminence should be given to the underlying values of IHL. As there is no IHL rule that deprives nationals of the detaining power of POW status on account of their nationality,[75] POW status should be granted. The imprisoned would benefit from the implementation of IHL in preference to measures stemming from political interests. Hence, where doubts exist, international protection, i.e. POW status, should prevail over domestic punishment for treason, and this is a clear example of a case in which pressure should be applied by third States to secure compliance.

Protection of Nationals on Grounds Other than IHL

In view of Palestine's inability as a non-State actor to secure proper implementation of the rules created by States to regulate the conduct of States, it is important to take into account the difference that would ensue once the State of Palestine is established. Palestine will be able, under these different circumstances, to demand better conditions of detention for

---

[73] ICTY, *Prosecutor v. Tadić* case, Judgment 15 July 1999, Case No. IT-94-1-A, 73, para 166.
[74] I. Brownlie, 'The Relations of Nationality in Public International Law,' 39 *British Yearbook of International Law* (1963), p. 318.
[75] T. Ho, *op. cit.*, p. 421.

its nationals in Israel. The following section will address the possibility of seeking ways to ensure compliance with international obligations through (i) the exercise of diplomatic protection by Palestine and (ii) accession to human rights treaties and international courts to demand compliance by Israel.

Failure to Provide a Fair Trial and Detention by Israel

If Palestinian prisoners remain in detention without securing compliance with international law and human rights, and if the detention can, moreover, be deemed to constitute cruel, inhuman or degrading treatment or punishment, Palestine will be entitled to exercise measures of protection on behalf of its nationals and to demand reparation from Israel.

Various arguments may be advanced and they need to be analysed in the light of the specific facts, but the general contention that the detention of individuals without a fair trial constitutes a breach of the relevant obligations which 'extends from the time the initial act has occurred until those obligations have been fulfilled'[76] could be invoked by Palestine without raising temporality issues.

Diplomatic Protection on Behalf of Palestinian Prisoners

Pursuant to the principle of diplomatic protection, which was recognized as customary international law by the Permanent Court of International Justice in the *Mavrommatis Palestine Concessions* case, States have the right to espouse claims on behalf of their nationals whenever they have been injured by acts of other States that are contrary to international law.[77] It may be exercised in judicial or arbitration proceedings. In order to exercise diplomatic protection, two conditions must be met: (i) the claimant must have the nationality of the State taking up his claim; and (ii) local remedies must be exhausted.[78] In the present case, Palestine would be able to exercise diplomatic protection and demand reparation for injuries on behalf of its nationals who were classified as unlawful combatants while in detention in Israel, since the requirement of nationality would be complied with and the requirement of exhaustion of

---

[76] P. Ornachea, 'Moiwana Village: The Inter-American Court and the 'Continuing Violation' Doctrine,' 19 *Harvard Human Rights Journal* 288 (2006).

[77] PCIJ, *The Mavrommatis Palestine Concessions Case (Greece v Great Britain) (Jurisdiction)* (1924), Series A No 2 12.

[78] ICJ, *Case Concerning Avena and other Mexican Nationals (Mexico v United States of America)* (2004), p. 26.

local remedies would be lifted, inasmuch as a remedy for the circumstances of detention is not available through ordinary channels.

Diplomatic protection remained inaccessible for a lengthy period for stateless persons, as evidenced in the *Dickson Car Wheel Company* case, which established that 'a State . . . does not commit an international delinquency in inflicting an injury upon an individual lacking nationality, and consequently, no State is empowered to intervene or complain on his behalf either before or after the injury.' However, once Palestine is a State, it will be entitled to offer diplomatic protection.

The development of international law should therefore permit the establishment of diplomatic protection by the new State on behalf of its nationals in order to protect human rights. Diplomatic protection conducted at inter-State level 'remains an important remedy for the protection of persons whose human rights have been violated abroad.'[79] If there is a persistent violation of nationals being held abroad (for example, detention that fails to meet human right requirements), diplomatic protection may serve as a mechanism to halt such violations. Palestinians imprisoned before the establishment of the State who have not benefited from a reassessment of their status could request the exercise of diplomatic protection on their behalf. This would mean that, notwithstanding the lack of POW status, the State could claim protection for individuals involved in the armed conflict. Moreover, requests for protection of persons linked to an armed conflict have already been made on behalf of detainees in Guantanamo.[80] While previous cases that have dealt with the matter involved requests by individuals for the exercise of diplomatic protection, it is possible in the present situation to envisage circumstances in which the State of Palestine can implement diplomatic protection.

While diplomatic protection cannot take the place of human right mechanisms, it would allow Palestine to demand respect for international

---

[79] International Law Commission, 'Draft Articles on Diplomatic Protection with commentaries' in 'Report of the International Law Commission on the Work of its 58th Session,' UN Doc A/61/10, 2006, p. 26.

[80] For example, *Khadr v. Prime Minister of Canada* case (2009) in which the Canadian Court of Appeal ordered the Canadian Government to request repatriation of a Canadian citizen imprisoned in Guantanamo. This has also been discussed in *Kaunda v. President of the Republic of South Africa* (2005) dealing with the possibility of requesting diplomatic protection for mercenaries captured and imprisoned in Zimbabwe.

obligations on behalf of its nationals and, in particular, to demand protection of their human rights.[81]

Accession to Human Rights Treaties and International Courts

In the light of continuing violations, the accession of Palestine to human rights treaties would permit it to demand compliance by Israel with its international obligations vis-à-vis Palestinian nationals detained in Israel. The accession of Palestine to human rights treaties such as the International Covenant on Civil and Political Rights, the International Covenant on Economic, Social and Cultural Rights, and the International Convention on the Elimination of All Forms of Racial Discrimination would enable it to demand compliance with the treaties by other States parties, such as Israel.

Accession of Palestine as a State party to the International Criminal Court and the International Court of Justice could lead to the application of review mechanisms to the status and conditions of detainees. While the International Criminal Court is already studying the acceptance by Palestine of the jurisdiction of the Court,[82] once the State is recognized by the United Nations its accession would no longer be delayed and would entitle the ICC to conduct investigations of possible violations committed in its territory and to determine individual responsibility for any crimes committed. Furthermore, the ICC would be able to characterize the conflict in its considerations and to determine whether war crimes have been committed such as the 'wilful deprivation of fair trial to POW or other protected persons.'[83] As an indirect effect, it would force the parties to reconsider the proper application of the law of armed conflicts in future hostilities.

The International Court of Justice, on the other hand, would require the agreement of both States in order to address the responsibility of the parties. While it is therefore a measure that seems less likely, the ICJ

---

[81] J. Dugard, 'Diplomatic Protection and Human Rights: The Draft Articles of the International Law Commission,' 24 *Australian Yearbook of International Law* 75 (2005).

[82] Ad hoc declaration recognizing the Jurisdiction of the International Criminal Court (under Article 12(3) of the Rome Statute), 21 January 2009.

[83] Rome Statute of the International Criminal Court, 17 July 1998, Article 8 2(a)(vi); Customary Study of International Humanitarian Law, *op. cit.*, Rule 100 Fair Trial Guarantees: No one may be convicted or sentenced, except pursuant to a fair trial affording all essential judicial guarantees.

would be able to conduct a review of the status and conditions of detainees and to provide further legal clarifications of the conflict.

Conclusion

The misinterpretation of IHL can entail dreadful consequences for prisoners. For example, the occupying power's right to detain based on security considerations is limited as follows: (i) detention is only for civilians; (ii) the measure is exceptional in character.[84] Moreover, the characterization of certain groups as 'terrorists' and 'unlawful combatants' is a tool expressly designed to exclude groups from the scope of international law. Any attempt to separate the impact of the occupation from the inability to exercise the right of self-determination, on the one hand, and from armed hostilities, on the other, has little chance of success. The difficult position that Israel has assumed in this regard has contributed to a critique by several authors of dynamic interpretations of the law by the court(s), which tailor it exclusively to meet the needs of the State; this is a clear reference to Israel's 'adaptations' of the applicable law.[85] The legal handling of the case of Palestinians imprisoned in Israel is no different: a partial or misguided application of IHL is not conducive to correct status and treatment.

The elevation of Palestine into a State will permit rectification of existing non-compliance with IHL in the context of the armed conflict with Israel. Palestine's new status will permit a review of the status and conditions of individuals imprisoned in Israel. While it is possible that other measures will be implemented between Palestine and Israel in order to terminate decades of conflict, such as bilateral agreements regulating either the exchange of prisoners or the ongoing detention of individuals, it is important to acknowledge the possibilities analysed above for a proper review of the conditions of detention applied to persons involved in the armed conflict.

As Israel has failed to determine the law applicable to the rights of individual detainees, a variety of issues will need to be considered once there is a Palestinian State, such as the continuity of armed forces,

---

[84] Commentary to Geneva Convention IV, *op. cit.*, Article 78.

[85] V. Azarov, 'Exploiting a 'Dynamic' Interpretation? The Israeli High Court of Justice Accepts the Legality of Israel's Quarrying Activities in the Occupied Palestinian Territory,' European Journal of International Law: Talk!, 7 February 2012; S. Darcy, 'An Enduring Occupation: The Status of the Gaza Strip from the Perspective of International Humanitarian Law,' *Journal of Conflict and Security Law* (2010), p. 14.

acknowledgment of armed groups by Palestine, and the need for a change in the strict conditions of detention imposed by Israel on the ground of national security considerations. Palestine will be able to discuss these matters as a party enjoying equal status with Israel, and if problems are encountered in this regard, Palestine will be able to have recourse to impartial bodies that will assist it in determining the applicable law and the status and treatment of Palestinian individuals in Israel.

It will be possible to assess the status and treatment of individuals not only in the light of international humanitarian law but also in the light of human rights law. Thus, new elements such as nationality and the exercise of diplomatic protection can be invoked to demand protection of human rights, while Palestine will be able to assert its right as a State to claim reparations.

Israel will be bound to revise the status of individual detainees in order to avoid further violations of continuing obligations and can use the new situation to adopt different perspectives on continued imprisonment. A key aspect of the change of Palestine's status is that it will permit equality in an area of law that still relies in large measure on the figure of the State to make rights and obligations executable.

CHAPTER TEN

THE STATUS OF JERUSALEM AFTER THE ADMISSION OF PALESTINE TO THE UNITED NATIONS

JOHN QUIGLEY

Palestine's admission to membership in the United Nations may have ramifications for Jerusalem in a variety of ways. Just how membership will alter Palestine's posture in the international community is hard to predict. Palestine will be able more effectively to assert its positions on major issues, including the issue of the status of Jerusalem.

As a technical matter, the admission of Palestine to membership in the United Nations in and of itself brings no change in the legal status of Jerusalem. Admission to membership in the United Nations is handled without regard to the boundaries of an applicant State. The General Assembly need determine only that the entity is a State, that it is peace-loving, and that it is willing and able to fulfil the obligations of UN membership. These are the requirements specified in the UN Charter.[1] To be a State, the entity must have territory, but precisely which territory is not determined when a vote is taken on admission. If the applicant State's borders are uncertain, if it has a dispute with a neighbouring State over a border, none of that is regarded as relevant in a decision about admission. A prime example is the admission of Israel to UN membership in 1949. That decision was taken despite the fact that Israel's claim to territory was uncertain. States that were members of the United Nations did not know just what Israel was claiming, or whether what it was claiming was properly Israel's. That was in particular true with regard to Jerusalem, as the member States were uncertain whether Israel was making a claim to Jerusalem. The Security Council, in recommending Israel's admission,

---

[1] UN Charter, Article 4.

made no finding regarding the extent of its territory.[2] Nonetheless the UN admitted Israel to membership.[3]

Whatever Jerusalem's legal status the day before admission, its status will be the same the day after admission. Change in Jerusalem's legal status may come about as a result of negotiations or as result of acknowledgment by the international community of a particular status. Until such occurs, Jerusalem's legal status will not change.

Legal Status of Jerusalem after World War I

The possibilities for change will be considered below. But first, one must inquire into the legal status of Jerusalem at present. The legal status of Jerusalem has not changed since Palestine became a State after World War I. Jerusalem being a part of Palestine, the question of Jerusalem's status must be examined in the context of the status of Palestine.

The officials responsible for devising a status for Palestine and for administering it regarded Palestine as a State. Jan Smuts, a member of Britain's Imperial War Cabinet during World War I, wrote the outline for the Covenant of the League of Nations, including provisions on mandates. Smuts referred to the mandate territories in his draft as 'not completely independent States.' Sir Herbert Samuel, who became Britain's High Commissioner in Palestine, referred to the mandates coming out of the Turkish Empire, including Palestine, as States.[4] So too did Norman Bentwich, Palestine's British-appointed Attorney General, who called Palestine an 'infant State.'[5] Smuts' characterization ('not completely independent States') made clear that in his view an entity may be a State even if not in full control of its affairs.

Territory in Palestine, including Jerusalem, came under the sovereignty of the State of Palestine from 1924 with the entry into force of the Treaty of Lausanne.[6] The Treaty referred to Palestine as a State detached from the territory of the Turkish Empire. Article 30 of the Treaty of Lausanne

---

[2] Letter from the President of the Security Council to the President of the General Assembly, 7 March 1949, UN Document A/818.

[3] UN General Assembly Resolution 273, 11 May 1949.

[4] Letter from Mr. Samuel to Earl Curzon, 2 April 1920, Enclosure: Syria, Palestine, Mesopotamia and the Arabian States, *Documents on British Foreign Policy 1919-1939*, First Series, Vol. 13 (London: Her Majesty's Stationery Office, 1963), p. 251.

[5] N. Bentwich, *The Mandates System* (London: Longman, 1930), p. 66.

[6] Treaty of Peace, Lausanne, 24 July 1923, League of Nations Treaty Series, Vol. 28, p. 11.

required Palestine to treat Ottoman nationals inhabiting Palestine as nationals of Palestine. Article 30 referred to the Ottoman Arab territories as 'States' being detached from the Ottoman Empire.

Palestine was accepted as a State from 1924 by the international community. It was regarded as a State by Great Britain and by outside States that had dealings with Palestine. It was regarded as a State by the Permanent Court of International Justice, which found it to be a successor in sovereignty to the Turkish Empire.[7] Pierre Orts was Chair of the Permanent Mandates Commission, which oversaw Britain's administration of Palestine. Orts, himself a highly regarded lawyer, called Palestine a State, 'though provisionally under guardianship.'[8] Like Smuts' statement, Orts' statement reflected the view, well accepted with respect to the mandates, that statehood did not require complete control over the State's affairs.

In 1932, when Great Britain tried to exempt Palestine goods entering its territory from British tariffs, it encountered objection from States with which Britain had most-favoured-nation treaties. Those States – including the United States, Italy, and Spain – said that Palestine was a State, therefore if Palestine goods entered Britain duty-free, so too should goods from their territories. The United States, in a diplomatic note to the British Government, referred to Palestine as a 'foreign country' in relation to Britain.[9] As a result of this reaction, Britain decided not to exempt Palestine goods from British tariffs.[10]

Malcolm Shaw cites my analysis of why Palestine was a State under mandate in my book *The Statehood of Palestine: International Law in the Middle East Conflict*, and says that my analysis 'does not hold water. In no situation was a mandated territory regarded as a sovereign State prior to the termination of the mandate over the territory in question.'

Shaw cites none of the State practice during the interwar period that shows that the former Ottoman territories were in fact regarded as sovereign

[7] *Mavrommatis Jerusalem Concessions*, Permanent Court of International Justice, Series A, No. 2, 30 August 1924.

[8] League of Nations, Permanent Mandates Commission, *Minutes of the Thirty-Second (Extraordinary) Session devoted to Palestine*, Geneva, 30 July-18 August 1937, including the Report of the Commission to the Council, Tenth Meeting, 5 August 1937, No. C.330.M.222.

[9] The Secretary of State to the British Chargé (Osborne), Washington, 27 August 1932, Document 641.67n3/11, in *Foreign Relations of the United States 1932* (Washington: US Government Printing Office, 1940), Vol. 1, p. 115.

[10] Committee on Imperial Preferences for Palestine, Report, C.P. 367(32), 28 October 1932, UK National Archives Reference No. CAB/24/234.

States under mandate. He does not cite the Treaty of Lausanne, which specifically identifies these territories as States. Shaw's only further statement in support of his position is as follows:

'None of the States that emerged from such territories . . . traces the commencement of its legal independence as a State from the date of the establishment of the mandate.'[11]

That Statement reveals Shaw's fundamental error. Of course, the independence of these States does not trace to the establishment of the mandate, at least in the sense of complete control over the territory. But that is not the issue. The issue is whether their statehood dates from the establishment of the mandate. And it does. The Palestine Declaration of Independence of 1988 references the Treaty of Lausanne and its phrase about the former Ottoman territories as being 'detached' from the Turkish Empire.[12]

Shaw makes no attempt to substantiate his requirement of independence, making only a reference to a work by James Crawford. In that work, Crawford makes the same point, but cites no adequate authority.[13] The practice of States during the mandate period in regarding the mandates as States shows that independence in the sense of factual control is not required. All that is required is that no other State has sovereignty, and with the mandates over the former Ottoman territories the mandatory did not hold sovereignty. Moreover, international practice, and specifically international practice during the era of the mandates over the former Ottoman territories, recognized protectorates as States even though they lacked factual control over their affairs. Scholars of the era analogized the situation of the mandate territories to territories under a protectorate to say that statehood did not require independence and that the former Ottoman territories were States.[14]

---

[11] M. Shaw, 'The Article 12(3) Declaration of the Palestinian Authority, the International Criminal Court and International Law,' 9 *Journal of International Criminal Justice* 301 (2011), pp. 306-307.

[12] Palestine National Council, *Declaration of Independence*, 15 November 1988, UN Doc. A/43/827, S/20278, Annex III.

[13] Shaw, *op. cit.*, p. 307, citing J. Crawford, *The Creation of States in International Law* (New York: Oxford University Press, 2006), pp. 575-577.

[14] J. Quigley, *The Statehood of Palestine: International Law in the Middle East Conflict* (Cambridge: Cambridge University Press, 2010), pp. 70-74.

Legal Status of Jerusalem after 1948

A faulty analysis about the legal status of Palestine as it emerged after World War I leads to a faulty analysis about the legal status of Jerusalem. As part of Palestine, Jerusalem fell under the sovereignty of Palestine. Upon Britain's withdrawal on 14 May 1948, Palestine was a State whose territory included Jerusalem. In that year, a new State was proclaimed in the territory of Palestine and eventually gained acceptance by the international community. That State, calling itself Israel, seceded from Palestine. Hence, whatever territory pertained to Israel became deleted from the territory of Palestine. But the acceptance of Israel as a State involved no determination of how much of Palestine's territory was so deleted. The United Nations first proposed that Jerusalem be an internationalized entity, hence not part of a Jewish State.[15] UN General Assembly Resolution 181, which embodied the proposal, was abandoned, but the proposal for an internationalized Jerusalem did not die. When Israel was being considered for UN membership in 1949, the issue of Jerusalem carried great prominence. The international consensus was that Jerusalem was not part of the territory that Israel could claim. A number of UN member States were concerned that Israel might claim Jerusalem, and that that claim might hinder resolution of the Question of Palestine, which remained high on the UN agenda. So when Israel was being scrutinized for UN membership, member States were anxious to secure an assurance from Israel that it was not claiming Jerusalem, even though by then Israel exerted factual control over the western sector of the city.

The United Kingdom announced in the UN Security Council that it opposed UN admission for Israel for its refusal to clarify its position in regard to Jerusalem. The United Kingdom found Israel's position on Jerusalem (along with its position on repatriation of Palestine Arabs displaced in 1948) to be inconsistent with UN policy. The concern was that Israel's position on these issues was inconsistent with the requirement for membership that an applicant State be peace-loving. If Israel were to claim Jerusalem, this would show that it was not peace-loving.

On the basis that Israel had not specifically indicated it would not claim Jerusalem, the United Kingdom opposed UN admission for Israel. The United Kingdom announced, however, that despite its negative view on Israel's qualifications for membership, it would not vote in the negative in the Security Council vote on Israel's admission. That stance on the part of the United Kingdom related to the fact that the United Kingdom did not

---

[15] UN General Assembly Resolution 181, 29 November 1947.

regard it as appropriate for a permanent member to vote in the negative (considered a veto) on an applicant State that enjoyed majority support in the Security Council. Aware that Israel would command a majority, the United Kingdom announced that it would abstain on the vote, rather than vote in the negative.[16]

The UK stance reflected the fact that Jerusalem was not regarded as territory of Israel. This view with regard to Jerusalem became even clearer when Israel's membership application moved from the Security Council to the General Assembly. Hearings were held in the General Assembly on Israel's application in the spring of 1949. Abba Eban, as Israel's foreign minister, was quizzed pointedly on the same two issues that troubled the United Kingdom, namely, the displaced Palestine Arabs and Jerusalem. The representative of Belgium in particular sought from Eban an assurance that Israel was making no claim of sovereignty over Jerusalem.

At a meeting of the Ad Hoc Committee of the UN General Assembly held at Lake Success, New York, on 6 May 1949, Foreign Minister Abba Eban was questioned on the displacement and on Jerusalem, to determine if Israel qualified as 'peace-loving.' The Belgian representative, Mr. Nisot, posed to Eban the following question:

'Could the representative of Israel tell us whether, if Israel were admitted to membership in the United Nations, it would agree to co-operate subsequently with the General Assembly in settling the question of Jerusalem and the refugee problem or whether, on the contrary, it would invoke Article 2, paragraph 7, of the Charter which deals with the domestic jurisdiction of States?'

Article 2, paragraph 7 reserves to States those issues that are matters of domestic jurisdiction. Thus, Nisot was asking Eban if the status of Jerusalem was a matter that Israel regarded as falling under its domestic jurisdiction. Eban answered as follows:

'The government of Israel will co-operate with the Assembly in seeking a solution to those problems. Once again, I do not wish rashly to commit myself to legal theories, being perhaps the least juridically versed of any present, but I do not think that Article 2, paragraph 7, of the Charter, which relates to domestic jurisdiction, could possibly affect the Jerusalem problem, since the legal status of Jerusalem is different from that of the territory in which Israel is sovereign.'[17]

---

[16] UN Security Council, Official Records, 4th year, No. 17, 414th meeting, 4 March 1949, UN Doc. S/PV.414, pp. 2-3.

[17] UN General Assembly, Ad Hoc Committee, 47th meeting, 6 May 1949, UN Doc. A/AC.24/SR.47.

Eban was saying that Israel did not claim Jerusalem as part of its territory, even though it did claim the rest of the territory it took militarily in 1948. Eban said further that 'the territory of Jerusalem . . . has not the same juridical status as the territory of Israel.' Jerusalem, Eban was affirming, was not in the same status as the other territory that the Israel Defence Force had by then occupied, and over which it did claim sovereignty. Despite the fact that west Jerusalem was then under IDF control, Israel was making no claim to any part of Jerusalem.

Israel's declaration of statehood of 14 May 1948, referred, as a principal legal basis, to Resolution 181. Under that resolution Jerusalem was not to fall to Israel. Many UN member States accepted Eban's assurance and voted Israel to membership. Mr. Nisot, the Belgian representative, remained unsatisfied. Belgium abstained on the vote to admit Israel to UN membership.

Israel's Claim and its Rejection

Once Israel was safely admitted to UN membership, as it was in May 1949, it reneged on Eban's assurance that Israel did not regard the status of Jerusalem as a domestic matter. Eight months after Eban gave Israel's assurance to the United Nations, Israel's parliament declared west Jerusalem to be Israel's capital, impliedly claiming sovereignty.[18] This claim was directly contrary to the assurance Eban gave the United Nations that Israel had no claim to Jerusalem and that Israel would cooperate with the UN in resolving Jerusalem's status.

The international community regarded Israel's claim as a hindrance to UN efforts to resolve the Question of Palestine. The Knesset's action was not regarded as lawful. States that recognized Israel did not recognize sovereignty for Israel over west Jerusalem. When some governmental offices of the new State of Israel were relocated there, and Jerusalem began to function as a centre of administration, most States declined to locate their embassies there, despite Israel's urging. Only a few States located embassies in Jerusalem but subsequently moved them to Tel Aviv. Despite Israel's *de facto* control of west Jerusalem since 1948, the international community has not recognized its claim.

---

[18] Emergency Regulations (Land Requisition-Accommodation of State Institutions in Jerusalem) (Continuance in Force of Orders) Law, *Laws of the State of Israel*, Vol. 4, p. 106 (1950); *Jerusalem Named Capital of Israel*, New York Times, 24 January 1950, p. A1.

Consulates in a foreign State are normally subordinated to the sending State's embassy in the State's capital city. States declined to subordinate their consular missions in Jerusalem to their embassies in Tel Aviv – to avoid giving the appearance that Jerusalem was lawfully part of Israel. The United Kingdom, for example, maintains a consulate-general in Jerusalem that does not report to the U.K. embassy in Tel Aviv. Normally as well, a sending State presents credentials for a new consul to the government of the receiving State. The United Kingdom pointedly presents no credentials to the Government of Israel for the appointment of its consuls-general in Jerusalem.

The United States maintains a consulate-general in Jerusalem, located in the eastern sector of the city, but with jurisdiction over the entirety of the city, including west Jerusalem, where it maintains a consular office. The consulate-general reports directly to the Department of State in Washington, rather than to the US embassy in Tel Aviv. The consulate in west Jerusalem reports to the consulate-general in east Jerusalem. The United States, like the United Kingdom, regards Jerusalem, in its entirety, as territory not under the sovereignty of Israel.[19]

Court Cases on West Jerusalem: Canada and USA

The issue of the status of Jerusalem, specifically west Jerusalem, came before a court in Canada a few years ago when a man born in west Jerusalem who acquired Canadian nationality demanded that the Government of Canada write 'Jerusalem, Israel' in the box on his Canadian passport that calls for place of birth. Normally the name of the State of birth is inserted. The Canadian government, however, as a matter of policy, did not insert the name of any country if the person was born in west Jerusalem. Instead, it inserted the name of the city: 'Jerusalem.' This was in keeping with the Canadian government's position, similar to that of the United Kingdom and the United States, that Israel's claim to Jerusalem is not recognized.

The man sued in the Federal Court of Canada to demand that the word 'Israel' be inserted. The Government of Canada responded, consistent with its policy, that Canada did not regard west Jerusalem as falling under Israel's sovereignty, and that were it to insert 'Israel' it might be taken to recognize Israel's claim. The Federal Court took evidence and then issued

---

[19] L. Lee and J. Quigley, *Consular Law and Practice* (2008), p. 100.

a decision against the man. The court refused to order the Government to insert 'Israel.' The decision was affirmed on appeal.[20]

The same issue has arisen in the United States. The policy of the US Department of State in issuing passports to persons born in Jerusalem after 1948 is the same as Canada's. The word 'Jerusalem,' rather than the name of a State, is entered in the box for place of birth. In 2002, the US Congress adopted a legislative bill requiring that 'Israel' be used if it is requested by the applicant.[21] President George Bush signed the bill into law, not because he agreed with this provision, but because it was written by the Congress into a much larger bill that appropriated funds for the operations of the United States elsewhere in the world. As he signed the bill, President Bush wrote a Statement to the effect that the question fell within the authority of the executive branch of government, not of the Congress.

Taking its cue from President Bush, the State Department did not implement the statute, arguing that the issue is one that falls to the executive branch rather than to the Congress. The State Department continued to write 'Jerusalem' and nothing else in the box for place of birth for applicants born after 1948 in west Jerusalem. In one instance, the parents of a boy born in west Jerusalem in 2002 applied for a passport for him and asked that 'Jerusalem, Israel' be written in the box for place of birth. The State Department refused. The parents filed suit against the State Department. The lower courts said that the matter was one within the authority of the executive branch of government and ruled that the matter was not subject to judicial consideration because it involved a political issue. The US Supreme Court ruled in 2012 that the matter could be considered judicially and returned the case to the lower courts to decide whether the matter properly falls to the executive branch or to the Congress. The Supreme Court expressed no view on that issue.[22]

The case stands to be resolved in the lower courts, less on the question of the proper status of Jerusalem than on the question of which branch of government in the United States has the authority. But throughout the litigation, the State Department has taken the position that west Jerusalem is not deemed by the United States to fall under the sovereignty of Israel.

---

[20] *Veffer v. Canada*, Federal Court No. T-149-05, *Federal Court Reports* (2006), Vol. 4, p. D 26, 1 May 2006. *Veffer v. Canada*, Federal Court of Appeal No. A-252-06, *Federal Court Reports* (2008), Vol. 1, p. 641, 25 June 2007.
[21] Foreign Relations Authorization Act, Fiscal Year 2003, Public Law No. 107-228, US Congress, *Statutes at Large*, Vol. 116, p. 1350 (2002).
[22] *Zivotofsky v. Clinton*, Supreme Court Reporter, Vol. 132, p. 1421 (2012).

Status of West Jerusalem Unchanged

The status of Palestine as a State from mandate times has not changed; hence Jerusalem's status must still be analyzed in that light. Shaw argues that Palestine is not presently a State. Shaw assumes that a requirement for statehood is independence in the sense of not being under the factual control of another State. By that requirement, any State whose territory is occupied militarily would cease to be a State. Shaw incorrectly finds Palestine as not being a State for lack of having a government, ignoring the fact that Palestine's territory is occupied.[23]

Shaw further cites the fallacious argument made by the Foreign Ministry of Israel that the PLO agreed in the Interim Agreement that it would not 'take any step that will change the status of the West Bank and the Gaza Strip' pending the outcome of negotiations. Shaw ignores the provision in the same article of the Interim Agreement that the Interim Agreement was concluded without regard to the claims of either party. Palestine statehood was a claim on the Palestinian side, and in any event was not a change in status.[24] Shaw wrote prior to the UNESCO vote, in which 107 States indicated their view that Palestine is a State, because they voted it to membership, statehood being a requirement for membership. Whatever validity Shaw's arguments may have had when he wrote, they no longer 'hold any water,' to use his term.

Israel's claim of sovereignty in Jerusalem not having been accepted by the international community, the logical conclusion is that the prior sovereignty subsists. Therefore, until some change is made, Jerusalem (in its entirety) falls under the sovereignty of Palestine. It is territory of Palestine that is not included in whatever territory attaches to the State, Israel, that seceded from Palestine in 1948.

Just as the UN act in admitting Israel was taken without a determination of its territory, so too a UN act in admitting Palestine will be without a determination of its territory. All that the UN need determine is that Palestine is a State, that it seeks membership, that it is peace-loving, and that it is willing and able to fulfill the obligations of UN membership. The determination that Palestine is a State requires a finding of sovereignty over territory, and on this score Palestine has qualified since 1924.

Jerusalem's status could change if the international community changed its view and were to accept Jerusalem as having a new status. That could hypothetically occur were Jerusalem, or a part of it, to be

[23] Shaw, *op. cit.*, p. 307.
[24] *Ibid.*, p. 308.

accepted as Israel's territory. The more likely change would come through Palestine-Israel negotiations that could lead, in principle, to the formation of a single State in the territory of (mandate) Palestine, hence that Jerusalem would fall under the territory of such a State. Or there could be agreement that Israel and Palestine accept each other. In that case the territory of Jerusalem could be divided, or some other accommodation might be made, for example a status that would regard Jerusalem as territory both of the State of Israel and of the State of Palestine.

None of these changes, it needs to be repeated, would be involved in the admission of Palestine to membership in the United Nations. The act of admission would have no effect on the status of Jerusalem.

Legal Status of East Jerusalem

When in 1967 Israel occupied east Jerusalem, along with the entirety of the West Bank, the UN General Assembly met to cope with the crisis. The Security Council had taken no action beyond a call for a ceasefire, so the General Assembly held an emergency special session. While the session was in progress, the Knesset adopted legislation saying that 'the law, jurisdiction and administration of the State' of Israel 'shall extend to any area of Eretz Israel designated by the Government by order.'[25] The Knesset authorized the minister of the interior to extend the boundaries of any municipality to include any area designated by government order,[26] and the minister expanded the borders of east Jerusalem to include a substantial sector of West Bank territory to the north and east.[27] The government then merged east Jerusalem with west Jerusalem to form a single administrative entity.[28]

The adoption of this legislation and regulations caused outrage among UN member States attending the General Assembly's emergency special

---

[25] Law and Administration Ordinance (Amendment No. 11) Law, *Laws of the State of Israel*, Vol. 21, p. 75 (1967). Implementing this law, the government ordered that Israeli law should apply. *Kovetz HaTakanot* (Official Gazette), No. 2064, 28 June 1967, p. 2690, in S. Jiryis, 'Israeli Laws as Regards Jerusalem,' in H. Köchler ed., *The Legal Aspects of the Palestine Problem with Special Regard to the Question of Jerusalem* (1981), pp. 181-182.

[26] Municipalities Ordinance (Amendment No. 6) Law, *Laws of the State of Israel*, Vol. 21, p. 75 (1967).

[27] Official Gazette, No. 2063, 28 June 1967, p. 2670.

[28] Municipalities Ordinance (Declaration on the Enlargement of Jerusalem's City Limits), Official Gazette, No. 2065, 28 June 1967, p. 2694, in 'Order Unites Holy City,' *Jerusalem Post*, 28 June 1967, p. 1.

session. Aware of the international reaction, the Government of Israel was careful to specify that these enactments did not amount to a claim of sovereignty over east Jerusalem. It told the United Nations:

'The [legislative] measures adopted relate to the integration of Jerusalem in the administrative and municipal spheres, and furnish a legal basis for the protection of the Holy Places of Jerusalem.'[29]

The United Nations, however, viewed the legislative measures as a disguised annexation, despite Israel's protestations to the contrary. On that basis, the UN condemned Israel for a *de facto* annexation.[30]

In 1980, the Knesset dispensed with any *caveat* and declared by statute that 'Jerusalem, complete and united' was 'the capital of Israel.'[31] This enactment did not claim sovereignty in so many words, but it would make little sense to have a capital in territory not under the State's sovereignty. An Israeli court has held that the 1980 legislation was intended to and did put east Jerusalem under Israel's sovereignty, as a matter of Israel's domestic law.[32] The United Nations found the 1980 law to be unlawful, on the same basis as it had earlier found the 1967 enactments unlawful.[33]

In 1990, the Government of Israel made its claim to east Jerusalem even more explicit. After a shooting incident in east Jerusalem in which Israeli police killed seventeen Palestinians, the Security Council asked the UN Secretary-General to propose appropriate measures in response.[34] The Secretary-General proposed sending investigators. Israel objected, however, saying that:

'Jerusalem is not, in any part, 'occupied territory;' it is the sovereign capital of the State of Israel. Therefore, there is no room for any

---

[29] Report of the Secretary-General, p. 3, UN Doc. A/6753 (1967) (quoting Abba Eban, Foreign Minister of Israel, letter to UN Secretary-General).

[30] UN Security Council Resolution 252, 21 May 1968. UN Security Council Resolution 267, 3 July 1969. UN General Assembly Resolution 2253, 4 July 1967. See also Report of the Secretary-General, 10 July 1967, p. 3, UN Doc. A/6753 (1967) (Abba Eban stating in letter to Secretary-General that the term 'annexation' was 'out of place').

[31] Basic Law: Jerusalem, Capital of Israel, *Laws of the State of Israel*, Vol. 34, p. 209 (1980).

[32] *Temple Mount Faithful Association v. Attorney General*, High Court No. 4185/90, Piskei Din, Vol. 47(5), p. 221 (1993), in A. Landau, 'Israel's Rights on Temple Mount Undisputed,' *Jerusalem Post*, 15 November 1993, p. 7 (finding that Israel's town planning and antiquities laws are applicable to Muslim *Waqf's* activities in old city of Jerusalem on the basis of the 1980 Basic Law).

[33] UN Security Council Resolution 478, 20 August 1980. UN General Assembly Resolution 35/169(E), 15 December 1980.

[34] UN Security Council Resolution 672, 12 October 1990.

involvement on the part of the United Nations in any matter relating to Jerusalem.'[35]

In a follow-up resolution, the Security Council expressed 'alarm' at Israel's view that east Jerusalem was not occupied territory.[36]

This position represented an explicit claim, made to the United Nations, that east Jerusalem fell under Israel's sovereignty. This position represented complete repudiation of the commitment Abba Eban gave to the United Nations in 1949 that Jerusalem was not a domestic issue for Israel. Having reneged with regard to west Jerusalem in 1950, Israel now reneged with regard to east Jerusalem.

Palestine within 1967 Borders

Palestine has, to be sure, put forward a position that would see its territorial extent limited to the territory that Israel seized in 1967. While Palestine's UN membership application is silent on the issue of territory, President Abbas included with the application an additional letter, which the Secretary-General apparently forwarded to the Security Council, in which President Abbas briefly stated the case for Palestine statehood. The letter refers to the Palestine National Council's declaration of 15 November 1988, to UN General Assembly Resolution 181 of 1947, to UN Security Council Resolution 242 of 1967, to the International Court of Justice Advisory Opinion of 9 July 2004, and to the large number of bilateral recognitions of Palestine. These bilateral recognitions, the letter recited, were made 'on the basis of the 4 June 1967 borders with East Jerusalem as its capital.'[37]

The '4 June 1967 borders' would not include west Jerusalem. The UN General Assembly Resolution 67/19 of 29 November 2012 gives a similar formulation of Palestine's territory, referring to the 'State of Palestine on the Palestinian territory occupied since 1967.' To date, the claim by Palestine to territory taken in 1967 remains an offer, conditional on acceptance by Israel of terms that Israel has yet to accept.

---

[35] Report Submitted to the Security Council by the Secretary-General in Accordance with Resolution 672, para. 3, UN Doc. S/21919 (1990).

[36] UN Security Council Resolution 673, 24 October 1990. See also J. Brinkley, 'Labor Party Rejects Likud Terms for Palestinian Talks,' *New York Times*, 6 March 1990, p. A3 (in objecting to Israel's plans to build housing in east Jerusalem for newly arriving immigrants from the Soviet Union, the US Department of State reaffirmed that east Jerusalem was part of the West Bank, not of Israel).

[37] UN Doc. S/2011/952, Annex II.

The claim to the 1967 territory is strong, of course, not only because the two sectors – Gaza Strip and West Bank – remain Palestine territory from 1924, but because they were taken in a situation of belligerency, and beyond that, through an act of aggression. That proposal is part of an overall proposal that involves other issues, prominently the refugee issue. So while that proposal has been made, no cession of territory can be inferred. If Palestine and Israel do agree on a two-State solution with a border in Jerusalem that divides the city east and west, that agreement will be legally binding. Palestine will have ceded west Jerusalem.

A potential cession of west Jerusalem in Palestine-Israel negotiations should be regarded as precisely that – an issue on which Palestine is giving up its own legal claim, which is considerably more solid than that of Israel. Palestine need not simply acknowledge Israel's long-time control of west Jerusalem as a control to which Israel is presently entitled. Indeed, as seen above, the international community does not regard Israel's control of west Jerusalem as giving it sovereignty.

Enhanced Capacity to Gain an Acceptable Status for Jerusalem

Apart from any issue of legal status, UN membership for Palestine would put Palestine in a stronger position to advocate for a fair and appropriate status for the city. To be sure, Palestine already has capacity to do so in its status as an observer, but membership will bring Palestine into closer contact with other UN member States. The range of interaction presently is limited to issues directly affecting Palestine. As a member State, Palestine will interact with UN member States across the entire range of issues that arise at the United Nations. Other States will seek its support on issues of interest to them. Palestine will be in a position to seek support in return for issues of interest to it. That will include issues relating to Jerusalem. More active involvement of the General Assembly on the issue of Israeli settlements in Jerusalem is one potential issue of this sort. There is much more the General Assembly could do. It could organize, at least by recommendation, the imposition of economic and diplomatic sanctions. The condemnations issued against Israel for exertion of sovereignty over east Jerusalem could be enhanced and reinforced with sanctions.

With the Security Council as well, Palestine as a member will be in a stronger position to lobby for action to protect Jerusalem. With both the Security Council and the General Assembly, Palestine may be able to revive the issue of Jerusalem to the level of attention it received in 1947.

The Security Council has been remiss in its approach to Jerusalem. It has never made the simple but obvious statement that Jerusalem was captured by Israel through an act of aggression, when Jordan came to the defense of Egypt, then under aggression by Israel. It is the role of the Security Council to deal with breaches of the peace and acts of aggression. Yet the Security Council has never addressed the question of how east Jerusalem came under Israel's control. The failure of the Security Council, either in the aftermath of the hostilities or in Resolution 242, to condemn Israel for aggression is widely taken by legal analysts in Israel and in the West as condonation of Israel's action in taking east Jerusalem. The same is true of the failure of the General Assembly to condemn Israel for aggression in its emergency special session of July 1967.

The view of such analysts typically rests on the votes taken on Soviet-proposed resolutions to condemn Israel for aggression. The defeat of these draft resolutions is taken as condonation. Yet if one reads the record of proceedings of the Security Council and of the General Assembly, one sees that not a single State, other than Israel, spoke up to justify Israel's attack on Egypt and its subsequent attacks on Jordan and Syria. Not even the United States, which well knew the details of how Israel came to the decision to invade Egypt, said a word to support Abba Eban when he said that Egypt had attacked first on the morning of June 5, 1967, or when he said that Israel was entitled to invade because of Egypt's restrictions on shipping in and out of the port of Eilat, or when he said that Israel faced an imminent invasion from Egypt.

Nonetheless, the failure of either the Security Council or the General Assembly to condemn Israel for aggression has left the path open to such disingenuous assertions of the legality of Israel's action in invading Egypt and then Jordan and Syria. East Jerusalem came under Israel's control in an act of aggression, yet the world body that was established to preserve the peace has yet to make a statement to that effect. Palestine membership at the United Nations will make it more difficult for the world body to evade its responsibilities on war and peace issues in relation to Palestine.

Enhanced Capacity to Protect Jerusalem via Treaties

Palestine as a member of UNESCO is already developing a strategy to protect cultural sites.

If Palestine accedes to human rights treaties, it will be able to invoke procedures to bring attention to violations of rights for which Israel is responsible.

If Palestine accedes to the Statute of the International Criminal Court, it will be in a stronger position to seek prosecution for war crimes, crimes against humanity, or genocide that may be committed in relation to Jerusalem. In particular, prosecution can be sought for the establishment and maintenance of civilian settlements in Jerusalem, an act specifically designated as a war crime.[38]

Even without UN membership, Palestine has the legal capacity to confer jurisdiction on the International Criminal Court. In January 2009, Palestine conferred jurisdiction on the ICC over any internationally defined crimes committed in the territory of Palestine since 1 July 2002. To date, however, the Office of the Prosecutor has declined to commence an investigation of any such crimes. As a State party to the Rome Statute of the ICC, Palestine would be in a stronger position to require action in the ICC. The Office of the Prosecutor has taken the position that it will await UN General Assembly action on Palestine statehood before initiating any investigation. This action in fact was taken by the General Assembly in Resolution 67/19 of 29 November 2012, stating that the status of Palestine as an observer is that of a non-member State.

Jurisdiction attaches in the ICC for acts committed in the territory of a State from the date the State becomes a party. However, in the case of a State like Palestine, which has previously filed a declaration accepting ICC jurisdiction for acts committed in its territory, such declaration remains in force. The Palestine declaration filed in January 2009 grants jurisdiction from the ICC opening date, which was 1 July 2002.

Enhanced Capacity to Advocate for Repatriation of Jerusalemites

One issue of importance for Jerusalem is the situation of Jerusalemites who were forced to leave in 1948. Along with other Palestine Arabs forced from territory that Israel seized, they have not been repatriated by Israel. As a State, Palestine may be in a stronger position to advocate for their repatriation. The repatriation of any of the Palestine Arabs displaced in 1948 has proved an intractable issue. Despite yearly resolutions of the UN General Assembly calling for implementation of the Assembly's Resolution 194 of 1948, the matter remains unresolved. As a UN member State, Palestine can raise the issue in the Human Rights Council, on the basis that the International Covenant on Civil and Political Rights

---

[38] Rome Statute of the International Criminal Court, 2187 *UN Treaty Series* 90, Article 8(2)(b)(viii).

acknowledges a right to return to one's country.[39] Return has been regarded largely as a political matter, and in particular as a matter that can be handled only by negotiation. But human rights are implicated, and the matter falls within the purview of human rights institutions. Israel, as a party to the International Covenant on Civil and Political Rights, must report to a Human Rights Committee on its compliance with human rights standards. To date, the issue of repatriation has not been a subject of attention. The forced flight of Arabs from west Jerusalem began with the bombing of the Semiramis Hotel by the Haganah in January 1948 and continued in the ensuing months. Repatriation remains to be accomplished.

Conclusion

Israel's qualification to join the United Nations was challenged in 1949 on the basis of two issues on which a number of States found Israel deficient. One was the displaced Palestine Arabs. The other was Jerusalem. On neither has Israel given a satisfactory response. On each it has in fact violated international norms even more egregiously than it had as of 1949. It has failed to repatriate the Palestine Arabs, even though its original excuse was that peace should first be achieved with the Arab States. Now Israel has peace treaties with two neighbouring States, and in the context of negotiating with Palestine continues to refuse to repatriate even if a peace treaty is achieved. On Jerusalem, Israel first laid claim to the portion of the city it held from 1949. Then in 1967 it extended its administrative regulation to the rest of the city and in 1980 asserted a claim to it. Israel has acted with impunity in taking action that was considered in 1949 to call into question its character as a peace-loving State.

The status of Jerusalem should not be determined by negotiations between two entities, one of which enjoys military, political, and financial predominance over the other. For the status of Jerusalem, like other issues in controversy, to be resolved in a manner consistent with international norms, a process like that contemplated in the 1980s by the UN General Assembly – a multilateral process – is required. Given that that process was derailed by Israel with the backing of the United States, and given that the United States beginning from 1991 was able to orient matters into an inequitable bilateral process, the likelihood of a renewed multilateral process is remote. That unfortunate circumstance does not, however,

---

[39] International Covenant on Civil and Political Rights, 999 *UN Treaty Series* 171, Article 12.

derogate from the reality of what Jerusalem's status actually is. Despite Israel's claims first to the western sector, then to the eastern sector, the international community has stood firm in refusing to accept these claims, even as Israel exercises factual control over the entirety of the city.

But the United Nations should be doing much more to reverse Israel's illegal actions. Palestine as a member State will have a stronger voice to urge the United Nations to fulfil its obligations.

CHAPTER ELEVEN

WATER CLAIMS OF AN INDEPENDENT PALESTINE IN PRACTICE: RECONCILING CONFLICTING WATER CLAIMS IN THE REGION

VALENTIN JEUTNER

Introduction

In the arid regions of the Middle East fresh water is one of the most valuable resources. It is a source of both life and conflict. In light of Palestine's[1] recent bid to join the United Nations, this chapter seeks to show that water can also be a source of cooperation and peace. The interests of riparians of shared water resources are, compared with other natural resources, inextricably linked. No State can manage and benefit from a shared water resource successfully without taking the concerns of its neighbours into account.

International law provides a framework within which the competing interests of water-sharing States can be reconciled. There are limits to the utility of international law, especially in a region beset by conflict such as the Middle East. However, tried and tested legal rules can demarcate the parameters that guide negotiations concerning water claims.

This chapter aims to outline the international law applicable to the shared water resources of an independent Palestine, with a special focus on the River Jordan. The chapter further highlights potential legal problems

---

[1] For the purposes of this chapter and notwithstanding the current legal character of the Palestinian entity, the Palestinian entity is treated as a State in order to evaluate the potential water claims of a future Palestinian *State*. The final section considers briefly the position of a Palestinian non-State entity. [This chapter has been written before the UN General Assembly statehood vote of 29 November 2012—the editor.]

related to the realization of Palestinian water claims in practice. The focus is in many respects a broad one and the analysis set out below thus cannot claim to be complete. While many details will have to be worked out by the parties concerned, it is nonetheless hoped that the following pages can serve as a starting-point for inevitable future negotiations.

The analysis comprises four parts. The first part introduces the hydrological features of the territory that an independent Palestine would probably occupy. Against this hydrological background, the second part outlines the current availability of water to the Palestinians. It will become apparent that water supplies are very limited at present and entail three main problems related to vital human needs, environmental pollution and economic development. The third part considers a strategy to remedy the current problems based on the equitable allocation of water, the identification of additional water sources, and the establishment of joint management structures. This strategy can only be successful if the interests of all regional actors are taken into account. The analysis will therefore involve consideration of the concerns of Syria, Lebanon, Jordan, Israel and Palestine, especially with respect to the River Jordan. The final part evaluates three potential legal obstacles pertaining to the law of treaties that need to be overcome in order to implement the new strategy.

Hydrological Background

This section places the analysis set out below in its hydrological geographic context and provides a brief introduction to the freshwater sources of the territory that an independent Palestine would likely occupy. The political and legal realities as well as the current allocations of water will be considered in the following sections.

The territory of an independent Palestine would probably be situated in today's Gaza Strip and the West Bank (a combined area of ca. 6,000 km^2).[2] Such a Palestinian State would be located in one of the world's most arid regions. The area's climate is mostly of Eastern Mediterranean character, with rainy and cold winters, but it would also include deserts in the east and south. Rainfall varies greatly within and between the West Bank and Gaza. Precipitation in the West Bank ranges from 90 to 375 mm/year in the Jordan Valley and 150 to 300 mm/year in the Eastern

---

[2] United Nations Food and Agriculture Organization (FAO), AQUASTAT (Occupied Palestinian Territories), 2008.

Slopes region to 300-600 mm/year in the Central Highlands in the north.[3] Rainfall in Gaza ranges from 200 to 400 mm/year.[4] Apart from precipitation, the area's freshwater sources are groundwater aquifers and surface water streams to which we shall now turn.

Groundwater

There are four main groundwater resources that would be situated, at least in part, within the territory of an independent Palestine: the Coastal Aquifer[5] in the Gaza Strip and the Mountain Aquifer, which consists of a western,[6] northern,[7] and eastern[8] basin, in the West Bank. Taken together, all four aquifers have renewable freshwater supplies in excess of 1,000 MCM/year.[9] Most of the Mountain Aquifer's recharge area is located in Palestine, while the storage areas (from which water can be withdrawn) are predominantly located in Israel.[10] The quality of water sourced from the Mountain Aquifer basins is generally good.[11] However, only 5 to 10% of the Coastal Aquifer meets drinking water standards.[12] These groundwater

---

[3] Strategic Foresight Group, *Blue Peace: Rethinking Middle East Water*, 2011, p. 77. See also FAO, *op. cit.*, which uses slightly higher figures ranging from 100 to 700 mm/year.

[4] By comparison: German annual average precipitation in 2011 was 718 mm/year.

[5] Size: 2,000 km^2; renewable water supply: 330 MCM/year.

[6] Size: 6,000km^2; renewable water supply: 375 MCM/year.

[7] Size: 1,044km^2; renewable water supply: 147 MCM/year.

[8] Size: 3,080 km^2; Renewable water supply: 196 MCM/year.

[9] For a comprehensive review of the shared groundwater resources of the Palestinian entity, see V. Jeutner, 'Water Claims of an Independent Palestine,' 24 *Georgetown International Environmental Law Review* (2012).

[10] E. Benvenisti and H. Gvirtzman, 'Harnessing International Law to Determine Israeli-Palestinian Water Rights: The Mountain Aquifer,' 33 *Natural Resources Journal* 555 (1993); World Bank, *West Bank and Gaza: Assessment of Restrictions on Palestinian Water Sector Development* (World Bank, *World Bank Report*, No. 47657-GZ, 2009), p. 9.

[11] Jordan Ministry of Water and Irrigation, Palestinian Water Authority, Israeli Hydrological Service, *Overview of Middle East Water Resources: Water Resources of Palestinian, Jordanian, and Israeli Interest* (1998), p. 16; Coastal Aquifer: 'generally good;' *ibid.*, p. 18; Eastern Mountain Aquifer: 'excellent quality with some salt and gypsum intrusion;' *ibid.*, p. 20; North Eastern Mountain Aquifer: 'water quality deteriorated, surface contamination, agriculture, wastewater, salt water intrusion due to over pumping;' *ibid.*, p. 22; Western Mountain Aquifer: 'generally good quality;' *ibid.*

[12] World Bank, *op. cit.*, p. 27. The situation is exacerbated by the fact that the Coastal Aquifer is subject to severe over-pumping due to general water scarcity.

aquifers are currently the only major freshwater resource available to the inhabitants of the West Bank and the Gaza Strip.[13] This is so despite the existence of certain surface water resources on the borders of the Palestinian territory. These will be considered next.

Surface Water

Apart from a few surface water streams such as the Faria in the West Bank or Wadi Gaza near Gaza,[14] the River Jordan (250 km) is the area's most significant surface water resource. Its basin covers an estimated area[15] of 18,000 km^2 and transcends the boundaries of Lebanon, Jordan, Israel, Syria and Palestine.[16] The Upper Jordan derives its flow from groundwater springs in Mount Hermon (Lebanon) and three surface water tributaries,[17] which merge and form the Upper Jordan before flowing into Lake Tiberias (Lake Kinneret, Sea of Galilee). South of Lake Tiberias, the Lower Jordan receives significant recharge from Syria's Yarmouk River[18] (ca. 130 MCM/year)[19] before emptying into the Dead Sea.[20] While the river's total estimated flow is ca. 1,578 MCM/year,[21] its water quality

---

[13] With the exception of minor surface water streams such as the Faria or the Qidron.

[14] For more information on the Faria river see, e.g., S. Shaddeed *et al.*, *Management Options of Wadi Faria Baseflow* (Eleventh International Water Technology Conference, 2007), pp. 129-143.

[15] Forty per cent of which are located in Jordan, 37% in Israel, 10% in Syria, 9% in the West Bank and 4% in Lebanon.

[16] B. Lehner *et al.*, *New Global Hydrography Derived from Spaceborne Elevation Data* (Transactions American Geophysical Union, 2008), pp. 93–94.

[17] The Hasbani (Lebanon) contributes 138 MCM/year, the Dan (Israel) contributes 245 MCM/year, the Banias (Syria) contributes 121 MCM/year. The Upper Jordan Basin (Israel/Syria) contributes 150 MCM/year. See further S. McCaffrey, *The Law of International Watercourses* (2007), p. 308.

[18] J. Dellapenna, 'The Waters of the Jordan Valley: The Potential and Limits of the Law,' 5 *Palestine Yearbook of International Law* 20 (1989).

[19] M. Haddadin, 'Diplomacy on the Jordan: International Conflict and Negotiated Resolution,' *Natural Resource Management and Policy* 219 (2002).

[20] Green Cross Italy, *Water for Peace: The Jordan River Basin* (2006).

[21] A modest volume compared, e.g., to the Nile's ca. 74,000 MCM/year. Cf. K. Frenken and AQUASTAT, *Irrigation in the Middle East Region in Figures* (UN FAO Water Report, 2008), p. 34; McCaffrey, *op. cit.*, p. 308; Deutsche Gesellschaft für Internationale Zusammenarbeit, *The MENA Water Portal (Factsheet Palestine)*, 2012; Dellapenna, *op. cit.*, p. 10.

varies greatly[22] and is virtually unusable by the time it reaches the banks located in Palestine.[23] The next section will show that in any event Palestinians do not access the waters of the river Jordan at present.[24]

Present Distribution and Present Problems

Against the background of the brief hydrological introduction, the first sub-section reviews the contemporary allocation of fresh water to Palestine. The second sub-section introduces three main problems related to the current water shortage in Palestine, namely the difficulty of satisfying vital human needs, a deteriorating environment and an underdeveloped economy.

Present Allocation

The data on the respective allocations of water is not uniform. Indeed the values given by different actors are so inconsistent that one might question the usefulness of displaying any figures at all.[25] The table below, compiled by synchronizing a number of statistics,[26] is thus merely designed to give the reader a rough idea of the dimensions of the water

---

[22] Jordan Ministry of Water and Irrigation, Palestinian Water Authority, Israeli Hydrological Service, *op. cit.*, p. 19: 'varies greatly, brackish in south, north fresher.'

[23] AQUASTAT (Jordan River), *op. cit.*, p. 16.

[24] D. Phillips *et al.*, *The Jordan River Basin: 2. Potential Future Allocations to the Co-Riparians*, 23 *Water International* 39 (2007), p. 44.

[25] At least for the purposes of a legal analysis of the fresh water question.

[26] The table displays the averaged data provided by the following studies: H. Shuval, 'Is the Conflict over shared Water Resources between Israelis and Palestinians an Obstacle to Peace?' in E. Matthews, ed., *The Israel-Palestine Conflict: Parallel Discourses* (UCLA Center for Middle East Development, 2011), p. 102; A. Aliewi *et al.*, *Palestine Water: Between Challenges and Realities*, in *ibid.*, p. 121; A. Rouyer, *Turning Water Into Politics: The Water Issue in the Palestinian-Israeli Conflict* (2000); J. Lautze and P. Kirshen, 'Water Allocation, Climate Change, and Sustainable Water Use in Israel/Palestine: The Palestinian Position,' 34 *Water International* 189 (2009), p. 203; U. Shamir, 'Water Agreements Between Israel and Its Neighbors,' in J. Albert *et al.*, ed., *Transformations of Middle Eastern Natural Environments: Legacies and Lessons* (1998), p. 274; Israel Water Authority, *The Issue of Water Between Israel and the Palestinians* (2009), p. 8; Israel Ministry of Environmental Protection, *Israel's Second National Communication on Climate Change* (2010), p. 39.

currently available to Palestinians (2011). The table also shows the Israeli figures in order to place the numbers in context.

Water withdrawal in Israel and Palestine (in millions of cubic metres (MCM)/year)

Total renewable	Total withdrawn	Israel	Palestine	Water Source
570	700	700	0	Jordan
375	385	340	45	*Western* Aquifer
147	133	105	28	*Northern* Aquifer
196	81	40[27]	41	*Eastern* Aquifer
330	555	430	125	Coastal Aquifer
300	301	300	31	Other[28]
220	220	220	0	Reused water
2138	2375	2135	270	Total
		754-767[31]	177-178[30]	Litre/person/day [29]

---

[27] In settlements.

[28] Includes: minor runoff, cisterns, desalination.

[29] Israel: 7.62 million (World Bank, 2012) - 7.75 million (Israeli CBS, 2009); Palestine: 4.15 million (World Bank, 2012) - 4.17 (Palestinian CBS, 2011). Note that the Palestinian values include both the West Bank and Gaza.

[30] The actual output of water may be lower, as the figures provided include water below drinking water quality (e.g. brackish water) and water lost due to poorly maintained infrastructure.

[31] In its 2009 Report the Israeli Water Authority (Israel Water Authority, *op. cit.*, p. 1) reaches results that are significantly lower (for Israel: ca. 3,20l/pc/day) and higher (for Palestine: ca. 2,73l/pc/day) than those presented in this table. This is partly due to the fact that the report excludes the Palestinian inhabitants of the Gaza Strip (pp. 17 and 20 of the report) from the equation when calculating the availability of water per capita/year. The reason for the lower Israeli figure is, in the absence of a water consumption breakdown by source (which the report does not contain), difficult to identify. The report does point out, however, that it refers only to the 'consumption of fresh, natural water' (p. 17), presumably excluding reused water and water from desalination plants, which would bring the overall available water down. Finally, it should be noted that other official Israeli sources (e.g. the Israel Ministry of Environmental Protection, *op. cit.*, p. 26) present somewhat different and higher figures regarding Israeli per capita consumption. According to this report, water consumption in 2007 totalled ca. 2,200 MCM and per capita consumption reached more than 1,000 MCM/year (all figures *ibid.*, p. 39 of that report).

Again, it must be reiterated that this table does not contain objective truths, but merely aims to give the observer a basic understanding of the current situation. Leaving aside the debates surrounding specific figures, the table indicates at least three things. First, Palestinians currently receive no water from the River Jordan. Second, the Palestinians currently engage in virtually no reuse of water.[32] And, third, Palestinians have access to significantly less water than their Israeli neighbours.[33]

Resulting Problems

The current allocation of fresh water to Palestine results in three major problems. First, vital human needs cannot be satisfied. Second, the limited amount of available water impacts negatively on the environment as effective wastewater treatment is difficult and aquifers are over-pumped. Third, the absence of water hinders economic development.

Vital Human Needs

The current amounts of water allocated to the West Bank and Gaza make it extremely difficult to satisfy the population's drinking-water needs. The commonly accepted absolute water scarcity threshold is set at 500 m³/year.[34] The average availability of water *per capita* in Palestine is ca. 70 m³/year.[35] Approximately ten per cent of the West Bank's population does not receive a regular water supply at all.[36] The situation is likely to worsen as the population grows,[37] and as the available amount of fresh water decreases.[38] The water crisis entails two related challenges.

---

[32] Only one out of five wastewater treatment plants in the West Bank is fully functional, Strategic Foresight Group, *op. cit.*, p. 79.

[33] This latter conclusion does not mean that the allocation of water between the two parties is *per se* inequitable.

[34] M. Matlock, *A Review of Water Scarcity Indices and Methodologies* (Sustainability Consortium, 2011), p. 1.

[35] *Ibid.*

[36] Strategic Foresight Group, *op. cit.*, p. 76.

[37] The Israel National Climate Change Report forecasts an estimated 40% decrease in water supply levels by 2100, and in the last 15 years the Palestinian population doubled. See, e.g., World Bank, *op. cit.*, p. v; and Lautze and Kirshen, *op. cit.*, p. 195.

[38] Rapid urbanization decreases, e.g., the aquifers' recharge zones. See Strategic Foresight Group, *op. cit.*, p. 76; Over-pumping of the Coastal Aquifer leads to seawater intrusion and increasing salination, making the aquifer's water undrinkable. See AQUASTAT (OPT) 2008, *op. cit.*

First, there is increasing food insecurity due in part to the difficulty of sustaining large-scale domestic agriculture in light of scarce water resources. Second, the absence of functional wastewater treatment plants leads to an increased risk of water-borne diseases in the area.[39] Furthermore, the absence of efficient wastewater treatment severely affects the environment.

Environmental Concerns

The 1995 Oslo Accord II (Annex 3, Article 12)[40] already acknowledged the interrelationship between the fresh water question and environmental concerns. However, the situation has not improved significantly since then. The World Bank estimates that 25 MCM of 'untreated sewage are discharged to the environment' annually in the West Bank alone.[41] Moreover, the Coastal Aquifer in Gaza is subject to increasing pollution.[42] One study suggests that 70 to 80% of untreated domestic wastewater is discharged into the environment in Gaza.[43] The consequences of the release of untreated wastewater are felt by all users of the shared water resources. This problem therefore underscores the need for cooperation in solving the water crisis.

Economic Development

Finally, the availability of water is also an essential condition for economic development in the Palestinian territories.[44] This is especially

---

[39] A. Abunaser et al., 'Relation of Nitrate Contamination of Groundwater with Methaemoglobin Level Among Infants in Gaza,' 13 Eastern Mediterranean Health Journal (2007). 26% of disease in Gaza is water-related. See further World Bank, op. cit., p. 23; Wash MP 2004: 64 and Statement by the UN Humanitarian Coordinator for the Occupied Palestinian Territory of 3 September 2009.

[40] Israel-Palestine Liberation Organization: Interim Agreement on the West Bank and the Gaza Strip, 1995, 36 ILM 551 (1997).

[41] World Bank, op. cit., p. 20. See also Strategic Foresight Group, op. cit., p. 81.

[42] World Bank, op. cit., p. 23.

[43] A. Alfarra and S. Lubad, Health Effect Due to Poor Wastewater Treatments in Gaza Strip (Israel/Palestine Centre for Research & Information, Water Conference, 2004). See also E. Burleson, 'Middle Eastern and North African Hydropolitics: From Eddies of Indecision to Emerging International Law,' 18 Georgetown International Environmental Law Review 385 (2006), p. 401.

[44] A. Abedrabbo and A. Tal, Water Wisdom: Preparing the Groundwork for Cooperative and Sustainable Water Management in the Middle East (2010), p. 113; O. Al-Jayyousi and G. Bergkamp, 'Water Management in the Jordan River

true in light of the fact that agriculture in Palestine still constitutes ca. 25% of Palestine's GDP.[45] The World Bank estimates that the limited availability of water accounts for an annual loss of up to 10% of GDP.[46] Furthermore, high water costs for businesses and families present an obstacle to economic development in addition to the limits placed on Palestine's agriculture.[47] Palestine is in the same situation as its neighbour Jordan,[48] where water scarcity is the 'single most important constraint' on the country's economic development.[49] Sustainable water resource management is an absolute prerequisite for future economic development.

The Future – Equitable and Reasonable Utilization

This section argues that the most sustainable strategy for resolving the water dispute in the region requires the taking of two steps. First, the existing water resources need to be allocated in an equitable and reasonable manner. This includes the identification and utilization of alternative water resources. Second, the water resources need to be managed in a spirit of cooperation by joint institutions, and specific dispute settlement procedures need to be put in place. We shall now address each of these steps in more detail.

Equitable and Reasonable Utilization of Water Resources

We suggest that the best methodology for allocating the waters of the River Jordan among the riparians is to apply the equitable and reasonable standard described in Article 6 of the 1997 UN Convention on the Non-Navigational Uses of International Watercourses ('the Convention').[50]

Basin: Towards an Ecosystem Approach,' in Olli Varis *et al.,* eds., *Management of Transboundary Rivers and Lakes* (2008), p. 120.

[45] World Bank, *Brief Overview of the Olive and the Olive Oil Sector in the Palestinian Territories* (2006); A. Biswas *et al., Water as a Human Right for the Middle East and North Africa* (2008), p. 98; Water Wisdom, *op. cit.,* p. 11.

[46] Potentially a loss of 10% of GDP; World Bank, *op. cit.,* p. 26.

[47] Burleson, *op. cit.,* pp. 390–391.

[48] Aix Group (Joint Palestinian-Israeli-International Economic Working Group), Economic Development of the Jordan Valley (2009), pp. 28–29.

[49] The Hashemite Kingdom of Jordan (Ministry of Environment), *Jordan's Second National Communication to the United Nations Framework Convention on Climate Change* (2009), p. 17.

[50] UN Doc. A/RES/51/229, 21 May 1997.

In the context of the regional conflict in which hardly any claim or statement goes uncontested, a general allocation standard grounded in international law has the benefit of being beyond the reach of any one party. The language of the law facilitates a productive discourse between the parties and one that is free to the largest extent possible from unhelpful polemical statements. Some might question this rather idealistic depiction of the law.

However, all riparians of the River Jordan have indicated that they accept this allocation standard of the UN Convention. Although the Convention has not yet entered into force, Jordan, Lebanon and Syria are parties to it and are obliged to act in accordance with the Convention's object and purpose.[51] Israel abstained in the vote on General Assembly Resolution 51/229, but stated clearly in its explanation of vote that it supported 'the compromise reached with regard to Articles 5, 6 and 7.'[52] Israel's governmental Water Authority recently reiterated this position.[53] Moreover, the Palestinian Authority has stated that it will sign the Convention upon gaining independence.[54] It could further be argued that the factors listed in Articles 5 and 6 represent customary international law and would as such be of legal significance irrespective of the Convention.[55]

Even though the seven Convention indicators may appear vague,[56] and even though it is not yet entirely clear to what extent each of the specific factors also represents custom,[57] the merits of having the guidance of an independent framework that strives to ensure a holistic approach to water

---

[51] Vienna Convention on the Law of Treaties, 27 January 1980, 1155 UNTS 331, Article 18.

[52] Oral Statement by Ms. Kidron, 'Israel supported the compromise reached with regard to Articles 5, 6 and 7. Nevertheless Israel would have preferred a more explicit balance between the principle of no harm and the principle of reasonable and equitable utilization.'

[53] Israel Water Authority, *op. cit.*, p. 27.

[54] Statement by Shaddad Attili (Head of the Palestinian Water Authority) at the closing session of the 2011 Stockholm Water Week on 27 August 2011.

[55] McCaffrey, *op. cit.*, p. 1; S. Schwebel, *Second Report on the Law of the Non-Navigational Uses of International Watercourses* (1980), UN Doc. A/CN.4/332 and Corr.1 and Add. 1, p. 189.

[56] Dellapenna, *op. cit.*, p. 43.

[57] Note, however, that none of the governments commenting on the International Law Commission (ILC)'s Draft Articles objected to any of the factors listed in Article 6, with many emphasizing the list's non-exhaustive nature, and that some suggested adding further factors.

allocation outweighs the shortcomings of letting the parties negotiate entirely unaided.[58]

Against that background we may now proceed to apply the Convention's factors to the River Jordan and its riparians. It should be pointed out, however, that the following analysis can only attempt to indicate trends and a relative size of water shares. Ultimately, it is up to the parties to work out the details of the water allocation in light of the exact data and their individual priorities.

Before we turn to the seven factors in Article 6 of the Convention below, two final preliminary issues need to be addressed. First, we must establish that the Convention applies to the River Jordan. Second, the starting point for allocation of water needs to be determined.

The Jordan: An International Watercourse

According to Article 1 of the Convention, a water resource engages international law if it is an international watercourse. An international watercourse is a system 'of surface waters and groundwaters constituting by virtue of their physical relationship a unitary whole parts of which are situated in different States and normally flow into a common terminus.'[59] So there are three main elements to the definition of an international watercourse. First, the water resource must be a system of surface waters and groundwaters constituting a unitary whole; second, parts of the resource must be situated in different States; and third, normally there has to be a common terminus. The River Jordan satisfies this definition. Deriving its flow from groundwater springs in Mount Hermon and numerous surface water tributaries,[60] the river constitutes a system of groundwaters and surface waters. As the river's different components

---

[58] *Cf.* S. Hillel, who specifically rejects an open-ended, largely unguided approach in D. Brooks and J. Trottier, eds., *A Modern Agreement to Share Water Between Israelis and Palestinians: The Friends of the Earth Middle East Proposal* (2010), p. 51.

[59] Convention on the Law of the Non-Navigational Uses of International Watercourses, *op. cit.*, Articles 2(b), 2(a).

[60] The Hasbani (Lebanon) contributes 138 MCM/year, the Dan (Israel) contributes 245 MCM/year, the Banias (Syria) contributes 121 MCM/year and the Upper Jordan Basin (Israel/Syria) contributes 150 MCM/year. See further McCaffrey, *op. cit.*, p. 308.

(such as tributaries and lakes)[61] are interrelated,[62] they constitute a unitary whole. The Dead Sea is the system's common terminus. As the river flows through Lebanon, Syria, Israel, Jordan and Palestine, parts of the watercourse are situated in different States. Hence, the River Jordan is an international watercourse.

Guaranteed Minimum Amount of Water

It is unlikely that the riparians would engage in open-ended negotiations without assurances that they will be guaranteed at least a certain minimum amount of water. Such minimum guarantees would provide the starting-point for an equitable and reasonable allocation analysis. Numerous ways of determining the size of a country's guaranteed minimum share are conceivable. The size of the minimum share could be linked to (a) the amount of water contributed by each country; (b) the minimum *per capita* needs of each country based on an objective standard; or (c) the minimum *per capita* needs of the respective countries' populations living in the Jordan river basin.

It is the second approach (b) that has received the most support.[63] Indeed, it is likely that this approach, which ensures that, on average, all inhabitants of the region receive at least the same minimum amount of water, is most agreeable to all parties concerned. Compared to the third option, the second approach preserves the ability of riparians to determine independently how to distribute the water within their borders. Severe difficulties arise, however, in connection with the method of calculating the minimum amount of water required. Current proposals include annual minimum needs of 75 m^3, 125 m^3, and 150 m^3,[64] but it is not entirely clear which kinds of water demands are included in these calculations. It would

---

[61] Report of the ILC on the Work of its Forty-Sixth Session, *Yearbook of the International Law Commission*, Vol. 2 (1994), UN Doc. A/49/10; A/CN.4/Ser.A/1994/Add.1 (Part 2), p. 90.

[62] McCaffrey, *op. cit.*, p. 308.

[63] Phillips *et al.*, *op. cit.*, p. 46; D. Brooks and O. Mehmet, *Water Balances in the Eastern Mediterranean* (International Development Research Centre, Canada, 2000), p. 75; H. Shuval and H. Dweik, *Water Resources in the Middle East: The Israeli-Palestinian Water Issues: From Conflict to Cooperation* (2007), Chapter 1; J. Isaac, 'Core Issues of the Palestinian-Israeli Water Dispute, Environmental Crisis,' in K. Spillmann and G. Bachler, *Regional Conflicts and Ways of Cooperation* (1994).

[64] *Cf.* P. Gleick, *Basic Water Requirements for Human Activities: Meeting Basic Needs* (1996), pp. 21, 83 and 88; Shuval and Dweik, *op. cit.*, Chapter 1; Brooks and Mehmet, *op. cit.*, p. 75.

be especially important to include, at least in part, agricultural and industrial needs that are closely linked to the overall ability to sustain human life. However, guaranteeing a minimum amount of water is sensible in principle and the following analysis will thus deal with the allocation of water required beyond this minimum level.

The Factors

With that in mind, we shall now turn to the Convention's seven factors. While all factors should be given equal weight (Article 6(3)), Article 7 requires all parties to take all 'appropriate measures to prevent the causing of significant harm,' and Article 10 states that uses of an international watercourse to satisfy vital human needs should be given special regard. Israel emphasized the importance of these provisions in its explanation of vote.[65] It has been shown,[66] with reference to case law[67] and international instruments,[68] that the obligation not to cause significant harm is qualified to the extent that the harm caused must be significant and unreasonable and should in that sense be taken into account when reviewing the seven factors.[69]

---

[65] Oral statement by Ms. Kidron, *op. cit.*

[66] McCaffrey, *op. cit.*, p. 419.

[67] Trail Smelter Case, 16 April 1939 and 11 March 1941, see 3 *UN Reports of International Arbitration Awards* (1941), pp. 1911 and 1938. See also S. Schwebel, *Second Report on the Law of the Non-Navigational Uses of International Watercourses* 92 (1980), UN Doc. A/CN.4/332 and Corr.1 and Add. 1; ICJ, *Corfu Channel* (UK *v.* Albania), *ICJ Reports*, 1949, p. 4; Lake Lannox (Spain *v.* France), 16 November 1957, *Revue Générale de Droit International Public*, Vol. LXII, 1958, pp. 79 and 107, translation from *Yearbook of International Law Commission*, Vol. 2, 1974, Part 2, p. 197.

[68] UN Conference on the Human Environment 1972 (UN Doc. A/CONF.48/14), Principle 21; Rio Declaration 1992 (UN Doc. A/CONF.151/26), Principle 2; UN Framework Convention on Climate Change (UN Doc. FCCC/INFORMAL/84), Preamble, 1992; Convention on Biological Diversity, 1992 (UN Doc. UNEP/Bio. Div/N7INC.5/4), Article 3; UN Environment Programme (UNEP), *Governing Council Decision on Principle of Conduct in Field of the Environment for the Guidance of States in the Conservation and Harmonious Utilization of Natural Resources Shared by Two or More States* (Official Record of the General Assembly, Thirty-third Session, Supplement No. 25 (A/33/25), Annex 1), Principle 1, 1978.

[69] McCaffrey, *op. cit.*, p. 445.

Factors of a Natural Character

The geographic and hydrographic factors, as defined by the International Law Commission which drafted the UN Convention,[70] have already been discussed above. They are relevant here to the extent that they identify the River Jordan as an international watercourse and Israel, Jordan, Lebanon, Palestine and Syria as the river's riparians.

Hydrological factors require the consideration of: first, the properties of the water resource such as quality; second, the contributions each State makes to the waters; and third, the relative importance of the resource to the respective riparian States.[71]

The River Jordan's water quality varies greatly.[72] Indeed, towards the south the river contains hardly any water and virtually none of drinkable quality.[73] Rather than favouring one riparian, this factor alerts the parties to the fact that an equitable allocation needs to take these realities into account and that it would not, for example, suffice to allocate the river's run-off to the Palestinians or to Jordan.

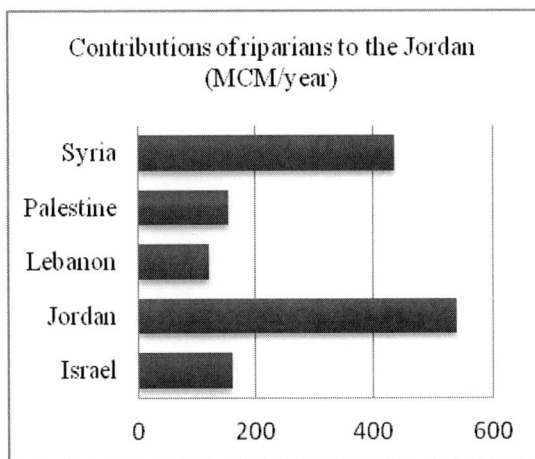

---

[70] *Ibid.*

[71] Report of the ILC on the Work of Its Forty-Sixth Session, *Yearbook of the International Law Commission*, Vol. 2 (1994), UN Doc. A/49/10; A/CN.4/Ser.A/1994/Add.1 (Part 2), p. 97.

[72] Jordan Ministry of Water and Irrigation, Palestinian Water Authority, Israeli Hydrological Service, *op. cit.*, p. 19.

[73] Amnesty International, *Troubled Waters - Palestinians Denied Fair Access to Water* (2009), p. 13.

All riparian States contribute to the Jordan's flow. Jordan contributes ca. 530 MCM/year (41.2% of the basin area), Syria contributes ca. 435 MCM/year (37.3% of the basin area), Israel contributes ca. 160 MCM/year (9.7% of the basin area), Palestine contributes ca. 155 MCM/year (8.2% of the basin area) and Lebanon contributes ca. 120 MCM/year (3.6% of the basin area).[74]

These contributions of States to the river via tributary streams and precipitation are an important consideration. Indeed, it has been suggested that disparities between riparian States' contributions and eventual water allocations may be one reason why the 1955 Johnson Plan for the redistribution of the waters of the Jordan was rejected.[75] However, there is no automatic entitlement to a specific share of water deriving from contribution alone. The 'Harmon Doctrine,' which favoured such an approach, has been universally rejected.[76]

The final hydrological factor addresses the relative importance of the River Jordan in the water household of the five riparians. This factor is significant, because it helps to discern the real value of the water resource for the respective riparians. The chart below shows, for example, that the Jordan is of least significance to Syria (2.5%) despite Syria's significant contributions to the river. Moreover, Palestine, which comes fourth in the context of contributions, comes second with respect to the importance of the river (19.7%). The significance of the river to Lebanon (2.6%), Israel (8.9%) and Jordan (56.5%) does, however, roughly correspond to the countries' contributions to the river. This factor strengthens the case of Palestine and Jordan in particular, whose hydrographic and hydrological properties make them especially dependent on the River Jordan. The claims of Syria and Lebanon, however, are weakened, as they hardly rely on the river at all.

---

[74] Phillips *et al.*, *op. cit.*, p. 42.
[75] *Ibid. Cf.* M. Haddadin, *The Jordan River Basin: Water Conflict and Negotiated Resolution* (UNESCO, 2003).
[76] McCaffrey, *op. cit.*, p. 308.

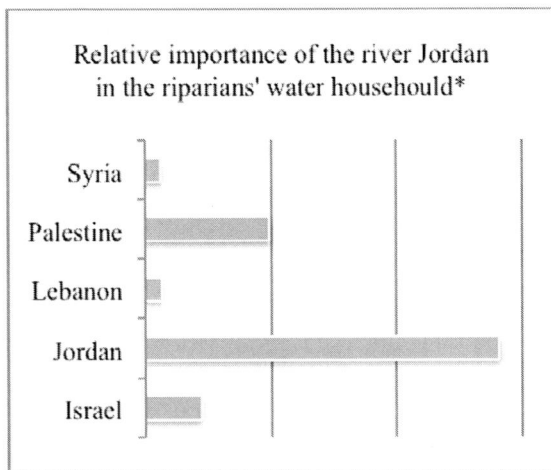

Relative importance of the river Jordan in the riparians' water househould*

*In per cent of total long-term renewable water resources. All data from AQUASTAT, 2009, http://www.fao.org.

The final factor to be considered within the context of Article 6(a) relates to the climatic conditions in the region under review. Rather than favouring a single party, this factor underlines the urgency with which a sustainable water management strategy needs to be developed in this water-scarce region of the world. The latest reports of the Intergovernmental Panel on Climate Change (IPPC) predict that the region will become even warmer and drier in the future and that both surface and groundwater availability is likely to decrease.[77] These observations are echoed in the Climate Change reports of Israel,[78] Jordan,[79] Lebanon[80] and

---

[77] IPCC, *Climate Change and Water* (IPCC Technical Paper VI, 2008), p. 87.

[78] Israel Ministry of Environmental Protection, *op. cit.*, p. 74.

[79] The report observes: 'Jordan's remarkable development achievements are under threat due to the crippling water scarcity, which is expected to be aggravated by climate change.' The Hashemite Kingdom of Jordan (Ministry of Environment), *op. cit.*, p. 29.

[80] The report observes: 'A reduction of 6 to 8% of the total volume of water resources is expected with an increase of 1°C and 12 to 16% for an increase of 2°C.' Republic of Lebanon (Ministry of Environment), *Lebanon's Second National Communication to the United Nations Framework Convention on Climate Change* (2011), p. XV.

Syria,[81] and the report prepared on the Palestinians' behalf by the UN Development Programme.[82]

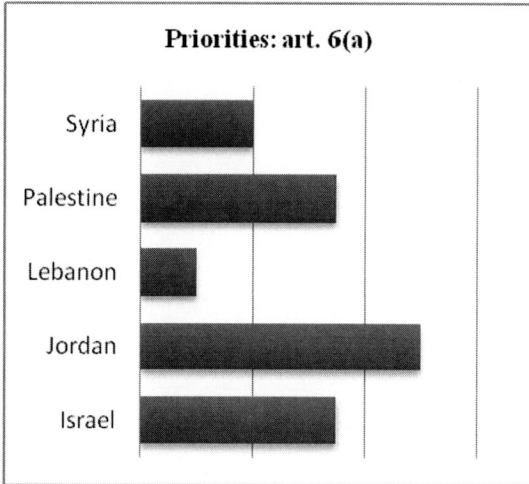

In light of the factors considered within the context of Article 6(a), priority should be given to the interests of the riparians in the following preliminary order. First, Jordan, as it both contributes the most water and relies on it to the greatest extent; Second, Israel and Palestine. Although they do not contribute as much as Syria, the river is of significant importance to them. Third, Syria, which does not rely on the Jordan as much as Palestine and Israel but contributes significant amounts of water; and, fourth, Lebanon which neither contributes much nor relies too heavily on the Jordan.

---

[81] The report observes: 'The per capita share of water is expected to worsen in the future: it might drop to 500 m3 in 2025.' Syrian Arab Republic (Ministry of State for Environment Affairs), *Initial National Communication under the United Nations Framework Convention on Climate Change* (Damascus, 2010), p. 72.

[82] The report observes: 'Freshwater resources in the oPt are predicted to become scarcer as climate change causes decreases in annual participation.' UNEP, *Climate Change Adaption Strategy and Programme of Action for the Palestinian Authority* (2010), p. XI.

The Social and Economic Needs of the Watercourse States

The riparians' social needs are to be measured narrowly by considering the availability of sufficient water to sustain human life.[83] The international water poverty threshold is set at 1,369 lpcd (or 500 m^3/pc/year).[84] Of the five riparians, Syria (2,250 lpcd)[85] and Lebanon (3,110 lpcd)[86] fare best regarding the availability of water. Both are more or less comfortably above the minimum level. Israel (639 lpcd),[87] Palestine (552 lpcd),[88] and Jordan (424 lpcd)[89] are, however, already dramatically below the threshold. It must be remembered that these figures represent average values and that local water availability might at times be even lower. A recent World Bank study found, for example, that in 2009 25% of the West Bank's population connected to the water network lived on less than 50 lpcd and 7% on less than 20 lpcd.[90] Water-related social needs further include health risks, which are more severe in regions with a limited supply of water.

---

[83] See UN Watercourse Convention's Working Group Statement of Understanding (36 ILM 1997), p. 719, defining vital human needs, in accordance with Article 10 of the Convention, as being determined by paying special attention to the provision of sufficient water to sustain human life, including both drinking water and water required for the production of food in order to prevent starvation.

[84] E. Barbier, *Natural Resources and Economic Development* (2007), p. 259; G. Schneier-Madanes and M. Courel, *Water and Sustainability in Arid Regions: Bridging the Gap between Physical and Social Sciences* (2009), p. 209.

[85] Total actual renewable water resources: ca. 16,797 MCM (AQUASTAT, *Country Profile: Syria*, 2009, p. 34); Population: ca. 20,446,609; World Bank, *Indicators: Population* (2010).

[86] Total actual renewable water resources: ca. 4,800 MCM (AQUASTAT, *Country Profile: Lebanon*, 2009, p. 34); Population: ca. 4,227,597 (World Bank).

[87] Total actual renewable water resources: ca. 1,780 MCM (AQUASTAT, *Country Profile: Israel*, 2009, p. 34); Population: ca. 7,624,600 (World Bank).

[88] Total actual renewable water resources: ca. 837 MCM (AQUASTAT, *Country Profile: West Bank and Gaza* (FAO, *Water Report*, 2009, p. 34); Population: ca. 4,152,102 (World Bank).

[89] Total actual renewable water resources: ca. 937 MCM (AQUASTAT, *Country Profile: Jordan*, 2009, p. 34); Population: 6,047,000 (World Bank).

[90] World Bank, *West Bank and Gaza: Assessment of Restrictions on Palestinian Water Sector Development*, *op. cit.*, p. 17. Note: ca. 1/3 of these quantities is lost along the way due to poor water infrastructure so that in reality water availability is even lower than the mentioned percentages. According to the World Bank, the average water supply in the West Bank is 97 lpcd.

With regard to the economic needs of the riparians, we shall again
adopt a narrow approach and consider the riparians' GDP. Based on their
GDP, the riparians would be ranked in the following order: Israel (2009:
USD 195.4 billion; 2012 estimate: ca. 249.0),[91] Syria (2009: USD 53.9
billion; 2012 estimate: USD 68.3 billion),[92] Lebanon (2009: USD 34.9
billion; 2012 estimate: 45.5 billion),[93] Jordan (2009: USD 25.1 billion;
2012 estimate: USD 32.9 billion)[94] and Palestine (2009: USD 5.9 billion;[95]
2012: ca. USD 7 billion[96]). Eventually, a holistic approach will also have
to take into account the importance of water for the respective economies.
It is particularly important to consider national reliance on agriculture,
which is especially high in Syria[97] and Palestine,[98] while accounting for
2% of Israel's GDP[99] and only slightly more in Jordan.[100]

We may therefore draw the following conclusion under paragraph (b):
there would be two groups of riparians with equal demands: first, Jordan
and Palestine, and second, Israel, Syria and Lebanon.

[91] International Monetary Fund, *World Economic Outlook Database* (2011).
[92] *Ibid.*
[93] *Ibid.*
[94] *Ibid.*
[95] UN Statistics Division, *Country Report: Occupied Palestinian Territory* (2009).
[96] Based on IMF estimates. See, e.g., International Monetary Fund,
Macroeconomic and Fiscal Framework for the West Bank and Gaza (Seventh
Review of Progress, 2011), p. 3.
[97] Syria's agriculture sector employs about a third of the work force and
contributes a third of the country's GDP. *Cf.* Syrian Arab Republic (Ministry of
State for Environment Affairs), p. 77; AQUASTAT, *General Country Profile:
Syria* (2008).
[98] AQUASTAT, *General Country Profile: Occupied Palestinian Territory* (2008).
[99] Phillips *et al.*, *op. cit.*, p. 43.
[100] Jordan's agricultural sector contributed 2.3 percent of GDP in 2004. *Cf.* The
Hashemite Kingdom of Jordan (Ministry of Environment), *op. cit.*, p. 32.

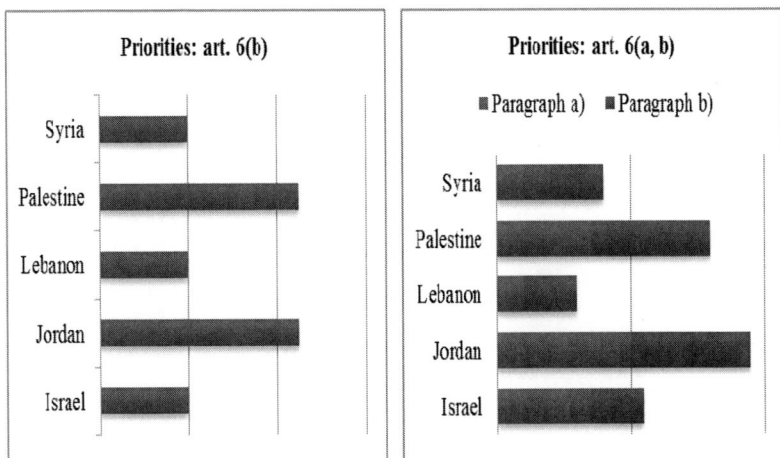

Population Dependent on the Watercourse in Each State

The wording of this factor suggests that what needs to be considered is the number of people who depend on the specific watercourse rather than the overall number of inhabitants of a country. This makes sense in practice. Otherwise, every Russian living at the eastern edge of the Asian continent would influence the balance in a dispute between, say, Estonia and Russia concerning a local river in the extreme west of the country. It seems appropriate, therefore, to consider and compare the populations who actually depend on the basin.[101] This approach leads to the following hierarchy of claims (assuming that no other significant water resources exist in the area): Jordan,[102] Syria,[103] Palestine,[104] Lebanon,[105] Israel.[106] Future negotiations must also account for the projected rapid population growth.

---

[101] Phillips *et al.*, *op. cit.*, p. 43.

[102] 54% of ca. 6.04 million (World Bank, *Indicators: Population, op. cit.*) living in basin equals: ca. 3,265,380 people.

[103] 11% of 20.04 million (*ibid.*) living in basin equals: ca. 2,249,127 people.

[104] 39% of 4.15 million (*ibid.*) living in basin equals: ca. 106,464 people.

[105] 8% of 4.22 million (*ibid.*) living in basin equals: ca. 338,207 people.

[106] 4% of 7.62 million (*ibid.*) living in basin equals: ca. 304,984 people.

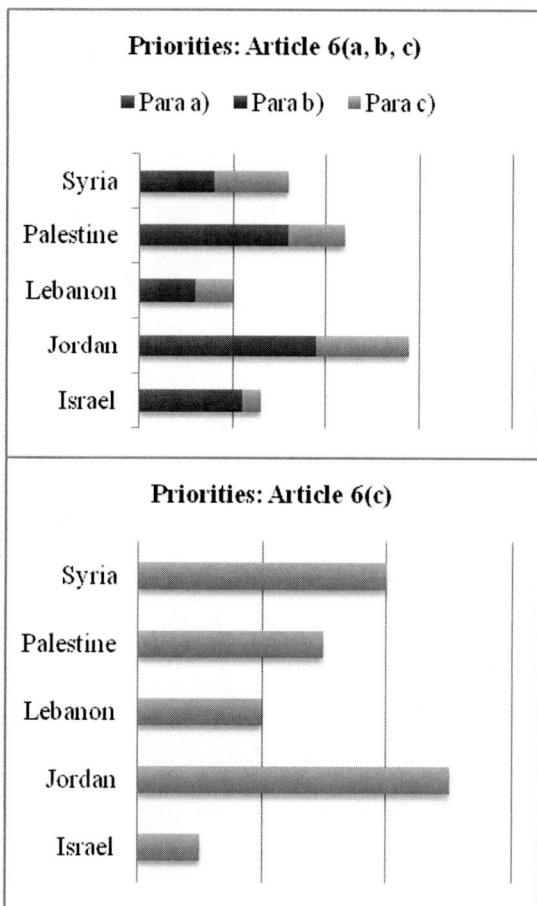

Priorities: Article 6(a, b, c)

■ Para a)   ■ Para b)   ■ Para c)

Syria

Palestine

Lebanon

Jordan

Israel

Priorities: Article 6(c)

Syria

Palestine

Lebanon

Jordan

Israel

Effects of the Use of the Watercourses in One State on Another

This factor, which the Convention and the 1994 International Law Commission's report leave largely undefined,[107] does not favour specific riparians. Rather, it urges the negotiating parties to consider the impact of water uses within their borders on the other riparians. This factor would be of particular relevance in the context of dam-building projects or the

---

[107] Report of the ILC on the Work of Its Forty-Sixth Session, 2 *Yearbook of the International Law Commission* (1994), UN Doc. A/49/10; A/CN.4/Ser.A/1994/Add.1 (Part 2).

construction of reservoirs, which could severely limit the river's flow temporarily or permanently.

Existing and Potential Uses of the Watercourse

This factor refers to both existing and potential uses. It should be emphasized that neither is to be given priority and it should also be recognized that 'one or both might be relevant in certain cases.'[108]

In light of the significant potential uses of the less developed riparians, including Palestine, which could not access the Jordan in the past at all, and those riparians who have substantial existing uses, both types of use are relevant here. In practice, however, giving equal weight to existing and potential uses cannot work without a reduction in the water shares currently allocated to riparians in the context of existing uses. Assuming that 100% of the Jordan waters are currently allocated and that Palestine is then granted access to and use of the Jordan, the water Palestine withdraws will inevitably have to be deducted from other riparians' existing uses. Depending on the size of the potential uses, and their calculation will certainly be very difficult, there could then be a *prima facie* conflict with the obligation not to cause significant harm (Article 7). However, the harm caused to the other riparians would arguably not meet the 'unreasonableness' threshold. Furthermore, international law derived from State practice, judicial decisions[109] and academic commentary[110] has rejected the argument that existing uses entail an entitlement to a fixed amount of water. This means in practice that the present riparians might have to accept a reduction in their shares (subject to at least the minimum guaranteed amount of water) in order to allow Palestine in particular to realize at least some of its potential uses. A transitional period could limit the detrimental effects of the limitation of current uses.[111]

---

[108] *Ibid.*

[109] Lake Lannox Arbitration (France *v.* Spain), 2 *Yearbook of International Law Commission* (1974), Part 2, p. 197. See also Colorado *v.* New Mexico, 467 US 176 and Kansas *v.* Colorado 206 U.S 46.

[110] L. Oppenheim and A. Watts, *Oppenheim's International Law* (1992), p. 584; H. Smith, *The Economic Uses of International Rivers* (1931), p. 174.

[111] D. Phillips *et al.*, *Factors Relating to the Equitable Distribution of Water in Israel and Palestine* (2nd Israeli-Palestinian International Conference on Water for Life in the Middle East, October 2004).

Resources of the Watercourse and the Costs of Measures Taken

As in the case of the last two factors, this factor is also unlikely to favour any one party. With regard to the conservation and protection of water resources, all riparians need to acknowledge that only a concerted effort will halt the ongoing pollution[112] and salination of the River Jordan,[113] which not only limits the availability of drinking water, but also has a negative impact on the entire region's ecosystem by threatening, for example, one of the world's most important flyways for migratory birds.[114]

Similarly, consideration of the development and economy of use of water resources does not favour one riparian in particular. Rather, the factor serves to urge all riparians to review and improve their water use efficiency. While Israel uses its scarce resources extremely efficiently,[115] with a recycling rate of more than 70% (ca. 500 MCM),[116] the remaining four riparians have considerable potential to improve.[117] In Jordan the public sewage system is steadily expanding and most of the water used by the agricultural sector is treated wastewater.[118] In Lebanon, however, about one third of all dwellings are not yet connected to public sewage networks.[119] Syrian average irrigation efficiency has been estimated at less than 40%.[120] Most problematic is the situation in Palestine, where more

---

[112] See, e.g., recent news reports in: H. Sherwood, 'Pollution Fears at River Jordan Pilgrimage Spot,' *The Guardian* (26 July 2010); S. Udasin, 'Sewage Clogs Jordan River South of Baptism Site,' *The Jerusalem Post* (23 December 2010).

[113] EcoPeace/Friends of the Earth Middle East, *Projects – Jordan River: Introduction* (2012).

[114] Friends of the Earth Middle East, *The Jordan River Valley: A Vital Migratory Flyway* (2012).

[115] Phillips *et al.*, *The Jordan River Basin: 2. Potential Future Allocations to the Co-Riparians*, *op. cit.*, pp. 43-44.

[116] Israel Ministry of Foreign Affairs, *The Water Issue between Israel and the Palestinians* (5 March 2012). See also *Israel Ministry of Environmental Protection*, *op. cit.*, pp. 39 and 70.

[117] Phillips *et al.*, *The Jordan River Basin: 2. Potential Future Allocations to the Co-Riparians*, *op. cit.*, p. 44.

[118] The Hashemite Kingdom of Jordan (Ministry of Environment), *op. cit.*, p. 32.

[119] Republic of Lebanon (Ministry of Environment), *op. cit.*, p. 24.

[120] Syrian Arab Republic (Ministry of Agriculture and Agrarian Reform) and A. MunlaHasan, *Water Use Efficiency in Syrian Agriculture* (National Agricultural Policy Centre, 2007), pp. 5-6. Note, however, that Syria has pledged to improve its water use efficiency significantly: Syrian Arab Republic (Ministry of State for Environment Affairs), *op. cit.*, pp. 2, 77, 93 and 133.

than one third of the water supply is lost to a rundown pipe system.[121] Furthermore, a low water supply does not permit the efficient operation of sewage systems, so that wastewater treatment is almost non-existent.[122] While large-scale infrastructural improvements are necessary to improve the current situation, Israel has shown that domestic 'soft measures' linking tax benefits to water consumption can also be very successful.[123]

This factor should not directly influence the amount of water allocated to the specific parties, but the final negotiations should consider ways to address the significant costs of the necessary improvements. One possibility could be to devise a regional incentive scheme that would offer lucrative loans for water efficiency improvement projects.

The Availability of Alternatives to a Particular Use

This paragraph asks riparians to consider not just existing alternative water sources but also whether needs currently satisfied by the use of water could be satisfied by other means.

With regard to existing alternatives, an equitable and reasonable allocation would have to take into account the fact that both Lebanon[124] and Syria[125] have extensive additional water resources apart from the River Jordan.[126] Moreover, Israel can access additional water resources stored mainly in the groundwater aquifers shared with Palestine[127] and Lake Kinneret. Jordan and Palestine have more limited access to alternative resources[128] due to the hydrographic properties of their territories, and both

---

[121] World Bank, *West Bank and Gaza: Assessment of Restrictions on Palestinian Water Sector Development, op. cit.*, p. 17.

[122] See above table 'Water withdrawal in Israel and Palestine.'

[123] A. Ben-David, 'July: Water Consumption Drops Sharply,' *Yedioth Ahronoth* (8 April 2009).

[124] The main freshwater sources include the rivers Awali and Litani as well as the Orontes (shared with Syria).

[125] Apart from the River of Jordan, Syria has access to the waters of the Tigris, the Euphrates and the Orontes (shared with Lebanon).

[126] Phillips *et al.*, *The Jordan River Basin: 2. Potential Future Allocations to the Co-Riparians, op. cit.*, p. 39.

[127] *Ibid.*, p. 44.

[128] Jordan's main alternative water sources are the confined (non-rechargeable) Disi aquifer, which is already being mined at an unsustainable rate, and the Jafer Basin. *Cf.* AQUASTAT, *General Country Profile: Jordan* (2008).

States rely heavily on the river.[129] The latter two should therefore receive shares of the water that acknowledge their limited alternatives.

Furthermore, a detailed analysis of alternative means of satisfying current needs must be a crucial part of the multilateral negotiations. It is not unlikely that the riparians would agree to an external (non-binding) review of how they could optimize their domestic water use by moving towards less water-intense production cycles and irrigation methods.

However, even if current uses are optimized and the efficiency of water uses is increased (see also the discussion relating to Article 6(f) above), climate change and population growth will necessitate the identification of additional resources.[130] Apart from the overall reduction of water consumption and the optimization of current uses, there are two main freshwater sources: first, desalination, and second, the importation of water by channels or other means.

For those riparians with access to the Mediterranean Sea (Palestine (Gaza), Israel, Lebanon, Syria) or the Red Sea (Jordan), desalination of seawater could provide long-term water security. Indeed, Mekorot – Israel's National Water Company – estimates that Israel will have a water surplus from 2014 onwards due to the construction of two additional desalination plants at Ashdod and Soreq.[131] The construction of Jordan's desalination plant at Aqaba is also under way,[132] and the Palestinian Energy Authority intends to expand desalination projects in Gaza.[133] In addition to seawater desalination, the cheaper[134] processing of brackish water sources in the riparians' hinterlands could provide at least some interim relief.[135]

Desalination is not, however, without problems. There are numerous unresolved concerns regarding the environmental impact of desalination

---

[129] Phillips *et al.*, The Jordan River Basin: 2. Potential Future Allocations to the Co-Riparians, *op. cit.*, p. 44.

[130] Dellapenna, *op. cit.*, p. 36.

[131] Mekorot's CEO Shimon Ben Hamo speaking to the Knesset's Economic Affairs Committee on 7 February 2012. See Y. Azulai, 'Mekorot CEO Promises Surplus Water in 2014,' *Globes* (7 February 2012); Z. Lavi, 'Israel to Have Water Surplus within Decade,' *Yedioth Ahronoth* (2 September 2012).

[132] M. Tyseer, 'Jordan Receives Two Bids for Red Sea Water Desalination Project,' *Bloomberg* (13 February 2012).

[133] UNEP, *op. cit.*, p. XII.

[134] IPCC, *op. cit.*, p. 46.

[135] Y. Dreizin, *Water Development and Management in Israel and the Region: The Overall Perspective* (2nd Israeli-Palestinian International Conference on Water for Life in the Middle East, October 2004); S. Arlosoroff, *Water Demand Management – A Strategy to Deal with Scarcity. Israel – A Case Study* (*ibid.*)

plants, their high use of energy,[136] and the comparative costliness of desalinated water.[137] However, the first solar-powered desalination plants are being constructed,[138] and there are hopes that the use of 'crystalline lagoons, which dissipate the heat [from desalination plants] through a closed cooling circuit'[139] will reduce the negative environmental effects of desalination.[140] The costliness of desalination[141] will certainly have to be considered, but desalination is getting cheaper and the costs of water scarcity are in any event greater than those related to desalination.

The importation of water is also frequently discussed. Proposals include the construction of a Red Sea-Dead Sea Canal (including a hydropower plant),[142] an Israel-Palestine Water Carrier, the transport of water, *inter alia* by ship, from Turkey to Israel,[143] a Gaza-Nile pipeline,[144] and Turkey's Peace Pipeline linking the Euphrates with northern Jordan.[145] The feasibility of these alternatives is uncertain. So far the Red Sea-Dead Sea Canal is the only project making any progress.

The consideration of alternatives concludes the review of the seven Article 6 factors. Far from being an exhaustive analysis, this part served to illustrate the operation of the factors in practice and to tentatively indicate the relative proportions of the different riparians. Taking the hydrographic availability of alternatives into account, the order of shares, from the

---

[136] IPCC, *op. cit.*, pp. 10 and 96.

[137] *Ibid.*, p. 46.

[138] B. Kader and S. Zaman, 'Solar Desalination Plants in Abu Dhabi to Curb Water Production Costs,' *Gulf News* (20 January 2012).

[139] J. Milnes, *Crystalline Lagoon Technology to Cool Power Plants, Regeneration and Air Conditioning Magazine* (2 February 2012).

[140] T. Laylin, 'New Cooling Lagoons Could Save the Gulf's Marine Enviornment,' *Green Prophet* (28 January 2012)

[141] T. Younos, 'The Economics of Desalination,' 132 *Journal of Contemporary Water Research & Education* 39 (2005).

[142] E. Benvenisti, *Addressing the Dead Sea Basin Issues* (2nd Israeli-Palestinian International Conference on Water for Life in the Middle East, October 2004).

[143] I. Gürer and M. Ülger, *Manavgat River Water as a Limited but Alternative Water Resource for Domestic Use in the Middle East* (2nd Israeli-Palestinian International Conference on Water for Life in the Middle East, October 2004); M. Rende, *Water Transfer from Turkey to Water-Stressed Countries in the Middle East* (*ibid.*)

[144] A. Lesch, *Transition to Palestinian Self-Government: Practical Steps Toward Israeli-Palestinian Peace* (American Academy of Arts and Sciences, 1992), pp. 132-133.

[145] G. Gruen, 'Turkish Waters: Source of Regional Conflict or Catalyst for Peace?' *Water, Air and Soil Pollution* (2000), pp. 556 and 575.

largest to the smallest, should be as follows: Jordan, Palestine, Israel, Syria, and Lebanon.

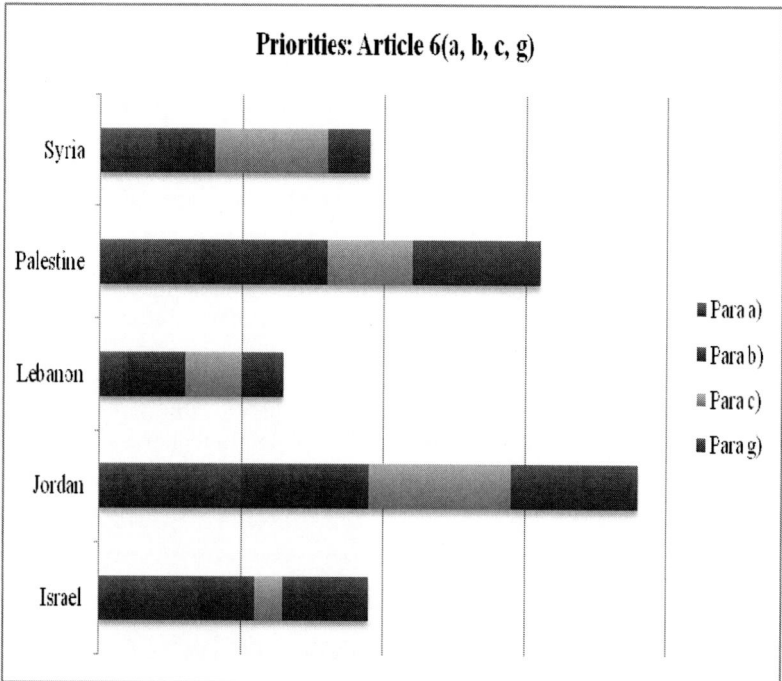

Again, it should be pointed out that the chart merely indicates rough estimates. In any event, the size of the water shares would have to be constantly re-evaluated, taking into account fluctuating water needs and surpluses. While the analysis has given all factors equal weight, it should be borne in mind that, according to Article 10 of the UN Convention, special regard should be given to vital human needs.

A Spirit of Cooperation[146]

Beyond the adoption of the principle of equitable and reasonable allocation of shared water resources, the riparians would be well advised to establish certain institutions tasked with the implementation and

---

[146] Dellapenna, *op. cit.*, p. 36.

facilitation of the outcomes of the eventual negotiations. The parties should also agree upon a dispute settlement mechanism.[147]

There are numerous proposals as to how the present institutional landscape, including, for example, the Joint Water Committees of Israel-Palestine and Israel-Jordan, could be reformed.[148] Ultimately, however, only the riparians themselves can determine the eventual shape of the institutional landscape. A basin-wide structure including all five riparians would certainly be the best solution. More important than the exact institutional design, however, is that all parties should be willing to enter the negotiations in a spirit of cooperation (Article 6(2)). Sustainable management of the Jordan basin will necessarily require the exchange of data and information and an acknowledgement that none of the parties can utilize the Jordan successfully if they disregard the other riparians' interests. This does not mean that the riparians must accept any limitation of their sovereign rights to their natural resources. On the contrary, it means that the riparians must realize that they can optimize the use of their sovereign resources only if they cooperate with each other.

An agreed dispute settlement procedure has the potential to facilitate the peaceful and expedient solution of conflicts. The exact design of such a procedure needs to be worked out by the parties, but it is conceivable that, depending on the frequency of disputes, a mechanism based on ad hoc arbitration staffed with arbitrators selected by the parties would be a workable solution. Arbitration would be an impartial and flexible procedure. Compared to unregulated open-ended negotiations, law-based arbitration proceedings offer predictability, certainty and the protection of certain minimum expectations.[149]

This concludes our observations regarding the ideal allocation of water in the future. The next and final part will consider the types of obstacles that the Palestinians could face in the process of implementing their water claims in practice.

---

[147] Phillips *et al.* (*The Jordan River Basin: 2. Potential Future Allocations to the Co-Riparians, op. cit.*, p. 5) suggested, for example, the establishment of Water Bank, which could facilitate regional freshwater resources development. Other institutions, such as the World Bank, which is already active in the area, could play a crucial role in the eventual implementation of a water agreement.

[148] Compare, e.g., Brooks and Trottier (*op. cit.*) with Geneva Initiative; H. Shuval, *A Regional Peace Plan: The Geneva Initiative Annexes* (Annex 10 - Water), 2009, pp. 231–249.

[149] See the recent case before the Permanent Court of Arbitration between India and Pakistan relating to India's Kishenganga Project (KHEP), available at: http://www.www.pca-cpa.org.

Obstacles

In the ideal scenario, a new regional treaty would implement Palestinian water claims in a manner that does justice to the water interests of all riparians. This section will evaluate three potential legal obstacles that could make such implementation difficult. First, some have suggested that if Palestine remains a non-State entity,[150] it could not enter into binding legal agreements and would therefore be unable to become a party to a new regional treaty or to enjoy any protection under international law. Second, even if Palestine acquires statehood, the riparian States may refuse to renegotiate and insist instead on the agreements currently in place. Third, whether or not Palestine becomes a State, Palestine's claims may be limited by agreements entered into by the Palestinian non-State entity prior to Palestine's independence.

Treaties between States and Non-states

According to the 'myth regarding non-State-actors,'[151] non-State entities are excluded from international law.[152] While it is true that treaties are traditionally concluded between States,[153] Article 3 of the 1969 Vienna Convention on the Law of Treaties does not preclude the legal force of treaties concluded by States with 'other subjects of international law.'[154] The Vienna Convention does not define such 'other subjects,' nor does it set out the principles governing the treaties concluded with those subjects.[155] However, despite the vagueness of the 1969 Vienna Convention, it is clear that agreements with 'other subjects of international law' can have legal force.[156]

---

[150] Either because the Palestinian's UN membership bid fails or because one holds the view that UN membership does not suffice to bestow statehood upon the Palestinians.

[151] J. Paust, 'Nonstate Actor Participation in International Law and the Pretense of Exclusion,' 51 *Virginia Journal of International Law* 977 (2011), p. 978. For an extensive list of examples of treaties concluded between States and non-State actors, see *ibid.*, p. 979, note 4; and p. 982 note, note 8.

[152] Brooks and Trottier, *op. cit.*, p. 2.

[153] Vienna Convention on the Law of Treaties, *op. cit.*, Article 1.

[154] *Ibid.*, Article 3.

[155] S. Rosenne, *Developments in the Law of Treaties, 1945-1986* (1989), p. 22; M. Fitzmaurice *et al.*, *Contemporary Issues in the Law of Treaties* (2005), p. 18.

[156] M. Villiger, *Commentary on the 1969 Vienna Convention on the Law of Treaties* (2009), pp. 103-104; E. Cannizzaro and M. Arsanjani, *The Law of Treaties Beyond the Vienna Convention* (2011), p. 307; J. Quigley, 'The Israel-

With respect to the Palestinian entity, it is already apparent that three of the potential treaty parties (Syria, Lebanon, Jordan) recognize a Palestinian State and therefore acknowledge the Palestinian entity as a subject of international law.[157] Israel does not currently go so far. However, Israel and the Palestinians have concluded numerous agreements in the past. As they accuse each other of breaching the agreements, it can be assumed that both parties intended the agreements to have binding force.[158] The United Nations Security Council shares this view and has urged the two parties to 'fulfil their obligations, including the agreements already reached.'[159] Similarly, the International Court of Justice (ICJ) recently referred to 'a number of agreements [that] have been signed since 1993 between Israel and the Palestine Liberation Organization imposing various obligations on each party.'[160]

So even if Israel has not treated the Palestinian entity as a State in past negotiations,[161] the Palestinian non-State entity has certainly been treated as a subject of international law by the riparians (including Israel) and the international community. Thus, the mere possibility that Palestine may not achieve statehood[162] should not prevent the regional actors from concluding an agreement with binding legal force.[163]

PLO Interim Agreements: Are They Treaties?' 30 *Cornell International Law Journal* 717 (1997), p. 730.

[157] The PNA is presumably perceived as the representative of the Palestinian State, although the issue of who would be the legitimate representatives of such a State gives rise to a host of questions. See Chapter Two of this volume (the editor).

[158] *Ibid.*, p. 740.

[159] UN Doc. S/RES/904 (1994), reprinted in 33 ILM 548 (1994).

[160] ICJ, *Legal Consequences of the Construction of a Wall in the Occupied Palestinian Territory* (Advisory Opinion), *ICJ Reports*, 2004, pp. 136 and 77; UN Secretary-General, *Agreement on International Roads in the Arab Mashreq*, UN Doc. E/ESCWA/TRANS/2001/3 (2001); UN Secretary-General, *Multilateral Treaties Deposited with the Secretary-General: Status as at 1 April 2009* (2009), p. 520.

[161] R. Falk, *Some International Law Implications of the Oslo/Cairo Framework for the PLO/Israeli Peace Process* (1994), pp. 8, 19 and 29. He questions whether the agreements reached by the PLO and Israel are treaties in the 'technical sense,'

[162] Irrespective of the meaning given to this term.

[163] However, if Palestine does not become a State, it may be unable to show that it is a watercourse State entitled to certain water shares based on customary international law.

Chapter Eleven

Customary International Law *v.* Treaties

More challenging from the Palestinian point of view would be a situation in which the Palestinians achieve statehood but are prevented from implementing their water claims by the other riparians' refusal to renegotiate the treaties that currently allocate the water amongst the existing riparian States.[164] One example is the 1994 Peace Treaty between Jordan and Israel, which limits the extent to which Palestine's water claims can be implemented in its provisions concerning water allocations. The forthcoming analysis assumes that Palestine's water claims would be based on customary international law predating the latest regional bilateral agreements and codified in 1997 in the UN Watercourses Convention.[165]

If the present riparians refused to renegotiate, there would be a *prima facie* conflict of norms between Palestine's entitlement to certain water shares based on the customary rule of equitable and reasonable allocation of water resources and the bilateral treaties of the present riparians. There is a conflict because of the lack of a *prima facie* hierarchy of sources in international law,[166] with the exception of *ius cogens* norms[167] and possibly Article 103 of the UN Charter,[168] none of which, however, apply to this scenario.

With respect to the three riparians that have ratified the UN Watercourses Convention (Lebanon, Jordan, Syria), it could be argued that a refusal to renegotiate would breach the States' obligation to act in accordance with the object and purpose of the Convention[169] and that they would be

---

[164] Treaty of Peace between the State of Israel and the Hashemite Kingdom of Jordan, 34 ILM 43 (1995); Al Wehdah Dam Agreement between Syria and Jordan (23 November 1987, Law No. 32 (Syria), Official Gazette of 9 December 1987). See AQUASTAT, *Chronology of Major Events in the Jordan River Basin Table* (FAO, 2009), p. 41; R. Stephan, 'Legal Framework of Groundwater Management in the Middle East (Israel, Jordan, Lebanon, Syria and the Palestinian Territories),' in H. Shuval and H. Dweik, eds., *Water Resources in the Middle East: Israel-Palestinian Water Issues - From Conflict to Cooperation* (2007), p. 30.

[165] A Palestinian claim based on the UN Watercourses Convention instead is unlikely to succeed, as Article 3 of the UN Watercourses Convention makes it clear that the Convention does not affect existing treaties. Israel has emphasized this point: *Oral Statement by Israel's Delegate Ms. Kidron, op. cit.*

[166] M. Villiger, *Customary International Law and Treaties: A Study of Their Interactions and Interrelations, with Special Consideration of the 1969 Vienna Convention on the Law of Treaties* (1985), p. 35.

[167] Vienna Convention on the Law of Treaties, *op. cit.*, Article 53.

[168] UN Charter, 24 October 1945, 1 UNTS XVI, Article 103.

[169] Vienna Convention on the Law of Treaties, *op. cit.*, Article 18.

obliged to modify their treaties to the extent that Palestine could utilize at least some water, for example of the Jordan. The three riparians could, however, point out in their defence that Article 3 of the Convention explicitly states that the Convention does not affect existing treaties. So it is questionable whether an argument based on the Convention alone could succeed and we shall therefore consider how the conflict of norms could be resolved under general international law.

The general rule is that treaties do not 'directly impair customary law on the same subject matter,'[170] and that such customary rules remain valid with respect to States that are not parties to the treaty under review.[171] States parties to treaties that conflict with customary international law would thus be 'obliged to apply the original customary rules *vis-à-vis* non-parties.'[172] The treaties would remain valid between the treaty parties as *leges speciales*, but they could not bar claims based on general customary international law as long as the customary norm continued to exist and as long as the treaty parties were not persistent objectors and hence arguably not bound by the general customary norm.[173]

The application of these rules to the case at hand shows that even though the validity of the bilateral agreements between the riparians would remain unimpaired, these treaties would not affect the riparians' obligations under customary international law *vis-à-vis* Palestine, which is not a party to the existing treaties. This would apply unless the riparians could show that they were persistent objectors to the customary international law norm on which Palestine relied. That is not the case here, as all four riparians have made known their support for the customary norms on which Palestine relies.[174]

This conclusion makes sense. It would be impossible to preserve the legal character of both the customary norms and the treaties if both remained valid in times of conflict. The result would be that neither norm could command authority *vis-à-vis* the other. Accepting, with respect to

---

[170] M. Villiger, *Customary International Law and Treaties: A Manual on the Theory and Practice of the Interrelation of Sources* (1997), p. 160; R. Wetzel and D. Rauschning, *The Vienna Convention on the Law of Treaties: Travaux Préparatoires* (1978), p. 8; R. Jennings, 'The Progressive Development of International Law and Its Codification,' 24 *British Yearbook of International Law* 301 (1947), p. 305.

[171] Villiger, *Customary International Law and Treaties, op. cit.*, pp. 161–162.

[172] *Ibid.*

[173] *Ibid.*, p. 209.

[174] This is underscored by the fact that all four riparians have declared their support for the customary rules codified by the UN Watercourses Convention.

third parties, the continued validity of the customary norm, based on State practice and *opinio juris*, when it conflicts with a bilateral treaty entered into by States that acknowledge the validity of the customary norm, is in full conformity with international law,[175] which allows for the modification or disappearance of customary norms only in light of sufficient State practice and *opinio juris* to that effect (and not through the mere conclusion of bilateral agreements). If, of course, a great number of States were to conclude treaties that were in conflict with a customary norm, the customary norm would ultimately be modified, be replaced by a new norm, or vanish.

In conclusion, it is unlikely that Palestine's water claims based on customary international law could be barred by a refusal of the present four riparians to renegotiate their bilateral treaties.

Treaties Prior to Palestine's Statehood

Finally, we shall briefly consider whether an independent Palestine could be bound by water agreements entered into by the Palestinian non-State entity prior to Palestinian acquisition of statehood and, more specifically, whether the water allocations of the 1995 Israeli-Palestinian Interim Agreement (Annex 3, Article 40),[176] entered into by Israel and the Palestine Liberation Organization, could limit the parties' water negotiations. The answer appears to be straightforward. Article 31(6) of the 1995 Accords makes it clear that: 'Neither Party shall be deemed, by virtue of having entered into this Agreement, to have renounced or waived any of its existing rights, claims or positions.'[177] Similarly, Article 40(1) of Annex 3 of the Accords indicates that the water allocations are not designed to be permanent, but are to be determined by later negotiations between the parties.[178] Hence, neither Israel nor Palestine would be limited in the course of renegotiations by the allocations of the 1995 Accords.

With regard to continuing treaty obligations of an independent Palestine aside from the Oslo Accords, one needs to consider the law relating to State succession in respect of treaties. Unfortunately, the law in

---

[175] Villiger, *Customary International Law and Treaties*, *op. cit.*, p. 206. *Cf.* N. Kontou, *Termination and Revision of Treaties in the Light of New Customary International Law* (1995), p. 30.

[176] Israel-Palestine Liberation Organization: Interim Agreement on the West Bank and the Gaza Strip, 1995, *op. cit.*

[177] *Ibid.*, Article 31(6).

[178] *Ibid.*, Annex 3, Article 40(1).

this area is less than clear.[179] Positions range from the assumption that, on the one hand, any independent State comes into existence with a 'clean slate' and as such is not bound by any previous treaty obligation,[180] and, on the other, that previous treaty obligations generally remain applicable,[181] to more complex approaches according to which the situation depends on the character of the independent State that comes into existence, e.g. whether the new State is a 'newly independent State.'[182]

There is, however, considerable support for the argument, based on Article 12 of the 1978 Vienna Convention on Succession of States in respect of Treaties,[183] that, in any event, treaties concerning boundaries

---

[179] P. Menon, 'The Newly Independent States and Succession in Respect of Treaties,' 18 *Korean Journal of Comparative Law* 139 (1990), p. 142; D. Vagts, 'State Succession: The Codifiers View,' 33 *Virginia Journal of International Law* 275 (1993), pp. 294–295; D. O'Connell, *State Succession in Municipal Law and International Law* (1967), pp. 9–14; D. Mekonnen, 'State Succession in Africa: Selected Problems,' *Recueil de Cours International*, Vol. V (1986), pp. 103–108; G. Hafner and E. Kornfeind, 'The Recent Austrian Practice of State Succession: Does the Clean Slate Rule Still Exist?' 1 *Austrian Review of International and European Law* 1 (1996), p. 2; I. Brownlie, *Principles of Public International Law* (1998), p. 650.

[180] Restatement (Third) of the Foreign Relations Law of the United States, para. 210; E. Williamson, 'State Succession and Relations with Federal States,' 86 *Proceedings of the Annual Meeting of the American Society of International Law* 1 (1992), p. 11; A. Keith, *The Theory of State Succession, with Special Reference to English and Colonial Law* (1907), p. 17; H. Tichy, 'Two Recent Cases of State Succession – An Austrian Perspective,' 4 *Austrian Journal of Public and International Law* 117 (1992), pp. 123–124; M. Kamminga, 'State Succession in Respect to Human Rights Treaties,' 7 *European Journal of International Law* 469 (1996), p. 472.

[181] See the statement by Sir Humphrey Waldock in the *Yearbook of the International Law Commission*, 1974, Vol. II, Part 1, p. 169; G. Marston, 'United Kingdom Materials on International Law,' 69 *British Yearbook of International Law* 433 (1998), p. 483; H. Wilkinson, 'The American Doctrine of State Succession' (1934), p. 14: 'Max Huber championed the theory of continuity. According to him, the new State assumes the rights and obligations of the predecessor State as if they were its own.'

[182] Vienna Convention in Succession of States in Respect of Treaties, UN Doc. A/CONF.80/31, 22 August 1978, reprinted in 17 ILM 1488 (1978), Article 16. See further Williamson, *op. cit.*, pp. 11-12; J. Crawford, 'State Succession and Relations with Federal States,' 86 *Proceedings of the Annual Meeting of the American Society of International Law* 1 (1992), p. 21.

[183] Vienna Convention on Succession of States in Respect of Treaties, *op. cit.*, Article 12(1).

and 'attaching to'[184] territories, including water rights,[185] are not affected
by State succession.[186] Although this view concerning water treaties is not
undisputed,[187] most States,[188] with few exceptions,[189] accept this approach
and the International Court of Justice has confirmed that Article 12 of the
1978 Convention[190] reflects customary international law.[191]

---

[184] *Ibid.*, Article 12.

[185] ICJ, *Case Concerning the Gabcikovo-Nagymaros Project* (Hungary *v.*
Slovakia), *ICJ Reports*, 1997, p. 72; M. Shaw, *International Law* (2008), p. 970; S.
Salman, *The Present State of Research Carried Out by the English-Speaking
Section of the Centre for Studies and Research, Water Resources and International
Law* (Centre for Studies and Research in International Law and International
Relations, 2002), p. 112; J. Klabbers, 'Cat on a Hot Tin Roof: The World Court,
State Succession and the Gybcikovo-Nagymaros Case, 11 *Leiden Journal of
International Law* 345 (1998); 'Report of the International Law Commission to the
General Assembly,' *Yearbook of the International Law Commission* (1974), Vol.
II, Part One, p. 206.

[186] A. Aust, *Modern Treaty Law and Practice* (2007), p. 370; A. McNair, *The Law
of Treaties* (1961), p. 39; I. Sinclair, *The Vienna Convention on the Law of Treaties*
(1984), pp. 105–106; O. Dörr and K. Schmalenbach, *Vienna Convention on the
Law of Treaties: A Commentary* (2012), p. 1245; A. Zimmermann, 'State
Succession in Treaties,' 13 *Max Planck Encyclopedia of Public International Law*
(2006). More cautiously (with respect to former colonies in particular), ILC,
'Succession of States and Governments,' *Yearbook of International Law
Commission* (1968), Vol. II., p. 113; Official Records of the UN Conference on the
Succession of States in respect of Treaties, Vol. III, doc. A/CONF.80/16/Add.2, p.
27, para. 2.

[187] I. Brownlie, *Principles of Public International Law* (2008), p. 663. See also S.
Rosenne, 'Automatic Treaty Succession,' in J. Klabbers and R. Lefeber, eds.,
Essays on The Law of Treaties (1998), p. 97; D. Mekonnen, 'The Nile Basin
Cooperative Framework Agreement Negotiations and the Adoption of a 'Water
Security' Paradigm: Flight into Obscurity or a Logical Cul-de-Sac?' 21 *European
Journal of International Law* 421 (1998), p. 433; D. O'Connell, 'Reflections on the
State Succession Convention,' 39 *Zeitschrift für ausländisches öffentliches Recht
und Völkerrecht* 725 (1979), p. 736.

[188] In addition to the 22 State Parties. See 'Succession of States in respect of
Treaties,' *Yearbook of the International Law Commission* (1974), Vol. II, Part
One, p. 73.

[189] Afghanistan, Nigeria, Romania, Somalia. *Ibid.*

[190] Vienna Convention in Succession of States in Respect of Treaties, *op. cit.*,
Article 12(1).

[191] ICJ, *Case Concerning the Gabcikovo-Nagymaros Project, op. cit.*, p. 72: 'The
Court considers that Article 12 reflects a rule of customary international law; it
notes that neither of the Parties disputed this.'

It follows that Palestine would in any case remain bound by agreements relating to water rights and by obligations entered into by the Palestinian non-State entity.

Ultimately, however, the significance of these legal answers to this complex dispute may be questioned and the present author agrees with the observation that it would be illusionary to hope that 'rules of State succession can be devised that will replace the processes of management and negotiation.'[192] However, legal rules help to structure the negotiation discourse and they can bring to light the underlying rationale for a certain position. In the case at hand, the applicable law can provide guidance and a framework for the eventual decisive negotiations between all parties concerned.

Conclusion

Regardless of the underlying political questions and whether or not Palestine becomes a State, the most important conclusion of this chapter must be that cooperation is the only way in which all regional actors can optimize the use of their scarce water resources. At present all riparians strive for water security, yet none can claim to have achieved it. The only sustainable solution in the long term is a regional agreement that considers the interests of all States concerned. Some might question the likelihood of such an agreement ever becoming a reality, citing the deep tensions between the different parties. Some may entirely reject the utility of international law in facilitating the resolution of the water conflict. But those who are sceptical of the regional actors' commitment to cooperation need to acknowledge that there is no alternative. If the parties do not cooperate, the problems mentioned above will simply continue to grow, leading to severe environmental, economic and political complications, since thirsting populations are certainly not a fruitful ground for peace in a region that is already shaken by international and also, more recently, by domestic tensions. Those who question the utility of international law due to its vagueness and the difficulty of ensuring its enforcement need to acknowledge that alternative political solutions will be even vaguer and entail neither an accepted enforcement mechanism nor reliable dispute settlement procedures.

The only way forward is to convince the regional players that every one of them stands to benefit from a regional agreement. While academic studies certainly do not change the world, human beings do. If the insights

---

[192] Crawford, *op. cit.*, p. 21.

contained in these pages can support the arguments of those who engage in dialogue with the respective regional players, the present chapter's mission will have been more than accomplished.

CHAPTER TWELVE

PALESTINIAN MEMBERSHIP OF THE WORLD TRADE ORGANIZATION: BREAKING INTERNATIONAL TRADE BARRIERS

NAEL SAYED-AHMAD

Introduction

The first step on the road to the World Trade Organization (WTO) consists in the filing of a request for observer status for the next five years; acceptance of this request is based on the fact that existing members possess enough background about the country and its general economic profile (WTO communications 2009). The next stage is to answer all questions from existing members about the economy in general and the trade policies implemented within the country. This would involve 157 existing members, who would decide on the ability of Palestine to enter their markets and to deal with their respective private sectors, as the Palestinians hope to be able to use the WTO and its system to resolve some existing economic disputes with the Israeli State (WTO communications 2010).

Palestine seeks to proceed towards full integration into the world trading system. Following its participation as an *ad hoc* observer in the session of the WTO Ministerial Conference held in Hong Kong in 2005, Palestine is now seeking to obtain 'full' WTO observer status, i.e. observer status in the General Council and its subsidiary bodies as an interim step on the way to achieving WTO membership.

Palestine is on the way to becoming a normal member of the international community. A logical aspect of this normalization is the country's integration into universal systems, including international economic systems. Palestine specifically seeks integration as a normal player into the rules-based world trading system under the umbrella of the WTO, with the resulting rights and obligations. Palestine is ready to play by the rules, and wishes to rely on the rules when trading with its partners. Integration into the world trading system also entails the establishment of a firm basis and reference for current and future bilateral and regional trading arrangements.

While continued and growing trade with Israel as a neighbour will remain a key element of Palestine's current and future economic policy, Palestine's producers, traders, service providers and intellectual property owners are adopting a global outlook in order to gain and retain competitiveness in the future. WTO rules will provide an essential underpinning for their activities by guaranteeing important rights such as market access under agreed terms, non-discrimination and respect for proper administrative procedures. These rights will apply in relations with all trading partners, except to the extent that the bilateral or regional agreements specifically determine otherwise (WTO communications 2010).

WTO: An Overview

The establishment of the World Trade Organization was not foreseen when talks began in the Uruguay Round in 1986, but as the talks progressed it was proposed as the necessary institutional framework to ensure the implementation of the final agreements. At the Marrakech Ministerial Meeting on 15 April 1994, the Final Act embodying the results of the Uruguay Round of Multilateral Trade Negotiations was signed by all Contracting Parties to the General Agreement on Tariffs and Trade (GATT). A total of 111 countries out of 125 formal participants in the Uruguay Round signed the Final Act. By mid-1996 the Organization had 116 members and 37 countries had observer status.[1] The WTO now has 157 members and over 30 observers awaiting full membership of the Organization. The WTO provides the common institutional framework for the conduct of trade relations among its members in matters related to the agreements contained in the Final Act of the Uruguay Round. The key features and functions of the Organization are highlighted below.

WTO is a single institutional framework encompassing GATT as modified by the Uruguay Round negotiations and all agreements and arrangements concluded under it. It is headed by a Ministerial Conference which meets once every two years. The General Council of the Organization oversees the Organization's operations and its ministerial decisions, and

---

[1] K. Bagwell and R. Staiger, *The WTO: Theory and Practice,* WTO Economic Research and Statistics Centre, Staff Working Paper ERSD-2009-1, November 2009, p. 12.

acts as a dispute settlement body and a trade review mechanism. The General Council establishes subsidiary bodies: a Goods Council, a Services Council, and a Council on Trade-Related Aspects of Intellectual Property Rights (TRIPS Council). The WTO framework ensures a single undertaking approach to results from the Uruguay Round; thus, membership in the WTO involves accepting all the results of the Round without exception.[2]

The WTO facilitates the implementation, administration and operation of the Uruguay Round agreements. It provides a forum for negotiations among members concerning their multilateral trade relations in matters under the annexed agreements, as well as a forum for further negotiations concerning multilateral trade relations. A related role involves providing the necessary implementation framework for agreements reached in these negotiations. The Organization administers the integrated dispute settlement mechanism linking rights and obligations in trade in goods with those in services and intellectual property rights. While undertake the administration of the Trade Policy Review Mechanism (TPRM), the WTO initiates cooperation with other multilateral institutions such as the IMF, the World Bank and its affiliated agencies.[3]

The WTO dispute settlement system solves complaints filed in one of the following two ways: (1) the parties find a mutually agreed solution, particularly during the phase of bilateral consultations; (2) through adjudication, including the subsequent implementation of the panel and Appellate Body reports, which are binding upon the parties once adopted by the Dispute Settlement Body.[4]

Benefits of Joining the WTO for Palestine

A great deal of research has been conducted on the benefits accruing to many countries from membership of the WTO. The literature suggests that many members would be likely to acquire more power in terms of

---

[2] R. Anderson, P. Pelletier, K. Osei-Lah, and A. Müller, *Assessing the Value of Future Accessions to the WTO Agreement on Government Procurement: Some New Data Sources, Provisional Estimates, and an Evaluative Framework for Individual WTO Members Considering Accessions,* WTO Economic Research and Statistics Centre, Staff Working Paper ERSD-2011-15, October 2011, p. 3.

[3] Bagwell and Staiger, *op. cit.,* p. 17.

[4] R. Torres, *Use of the WTO Trade Dispute Settlement Mechanism by the Latin American Countries: Dispelling Myths and Breaking down Barriers,* WTO Economic Research and Statistics Centre, Staff Working Paper ERSD-2012-03, February 2012, p. 7.

improvement of the domestic economy, expansion of trade and markets, and other similar benefits. The following is a brief discussion of some of these benefits and how they apply in the Palestinian context.[5]

Being a Member Means International Recognition

For the past ten years or so the Palestinian government has been trying to have the membership of Palestine approved, as a means of getting the international community to recognize that a Palestinian State truly exists. In other words, the Palestinians, by promoting peace and good governance, hope that their economic conditions will change, thus mobilizing funds for their markets and reinvigorating the economic development process.[6]

However, an argument may be advanced about the outlook for such a process and the number of years it will take before Palestine makes it into the WTO. In other words: what should the Palestinians do until their membership is approved? What about the consequences of international recognition?[7] As the WTO is not about enforcing equality between member countries, Palestinians are looking for an international body that would assume responsibility for making their State equal to that of Israel.

As this is not the WTO's job, it would seem unbeneficial for Palestine to seek such membership. This may indeed be true in light of the fact that the WTO is controlled to some extent by older and stronger members who are in turn favourites of the Israeli State.[8]

---

[5] F. Monge-Arino, *Costa Rica: Trade Opening, FDI Attraction and Global Production Sharing,* WTO Economic Research and Statistics Centre, Staff Working Paper ERSD-2011-09, May 2011; R. Ossa, *A 'New Trade' Theory of GATT/WTO Negotiations,* WTO Economic Research and Statistics Centre, Staff Working Paper ERSD-2009-08, November 2009; Yann Duval, *Cost and Benefits of Implementing Trade Facilitation Measures under Negotiations at the WTO: An Exploratory Survey,* Asia-Pacific Research and Training Network on Trade, Working Paper Series, No. 3, January 2006; and Simon J. Evenett and Jonathan Gage, *Evaluating WTO Accessions: The Effect of WTO Accession on National Trade Flows,* 2005.

[6] Ossa, *op. cit.,* p. 12.

[7] Monge-Arino, *op. cit.,* p. 23.

[8] A. Abdelrahman and A. Draghmah, *The WTO and Palestine,* Ministry of National Economy, Palestine, December 2003, p. 19.

Promoting a Better Economy

When it becomes a member of the WTO, Palestine is going to become economically bigger and stronger due to the opening of the borders for the international free flow of products, services and manpower. This will also promote Palestinian products internationally and make prices more competitive, thus increasing profit margins for local producers.[9] More importantly, becoming a member of the WTO will help Palestinians to cut their cost of living, as the prices they pay for everything they consume are affected by trade policies. The services industry could be one of the most important sectors affected by such policies: phone calls, for example, would be cheaper. The group of economists led by Robert Stern also considers that lowering services barriers by one third under the Doha Development Agenda would raise developing countries' income by around $60 billion.[10]

This is also true in terms of increasing income. As the barriers are lower among members of the WTO, it is expected that both national and personal incomes would increase. This would make it easier for many consumers to access products and services which were somewhat expensive for them in the past. It would make the product range wider, and the possibility of saving from buying and of buying by saving would have a stronger appeal for a larger portion of society.

Another economic advantage of WTO membership would consist in the fact that WTO members enjoy free movement of workers. Hence, a drop in unemployment could be expected as well as higher salaries and better opportunities for sharing experience among member States. The Palestinians possess a very high level of intelligence in terms of manpower. Unfortunately, however, a very high rate of unemployment is inherent in the economy, and moving employees into the international markets has always been a major challenge for the local community and policy-makers alike. So by joining the WTO, Palestinians could look forward with relative confidence to unemployment rates falling, incomes rising, foreign funds being channelled into local investments by business owners and international investors, economic growth being stimulated, and life becoming easier for the community in general.[11]

---

[9] Z. Drabek, and S. Laird, *Can Trade Policy Help Mobilize Financial Resources for Economic Development?* WTO Economic Research and Statistics Centre, Staff Working Paper ERAD-2001-02, August 2001, p. 15.

[10] Ossa, *op. cit.*, p. 14.

[11] Monge-Arino, *op. cit.*, p. 26.

As the Israelis are aware of all of the above, they are continuously working towards non-approval of Palestinian membership of the WTO. They fear that their markets would suffer from a lack of acceptance of their merchandise within the Palestinian territory even if prices were lowered and tariffs cut, as the Palestinians would find an alternative to Israeli markets and products within the WTO.

Drawing on Others' Experiences

Palestinians are keen to receive international aid, not just in the form of international financial support but also through the sharing of experience, which would support Palestinian community reforms and enable Palestinians to benefit from the more advanced countries' history of addressing and surmounting financial and social dilemmas.

The Palestinian Authority, through its different ministries, seeks to channel all the aid it can get into shaping a new country and bridging the gaps between different sectors. So WTO membership would ease the flow of aid into the country and make it easier for the competent authorities to overcome obstacles relating to the type of aid received and where it should be channelled.

Although Palestine's entry into the WTO is expected to boost its attractiveness to foreign investors because it promises not only market openings but also increased policy transparency, better governance and greater business predictability, some research suggests that the acquisition of Western experience would be highly unlikely to serve the interests of Palestine. Different cultures and norms exist in such an equation.

Others argue that Palestine (as a Muslim country) has its own way of dealing with socio-economic problems and that if any help is sought, it should come from other Muslim countries and not from those with different social and cultural systems. However; it is crystal clear that many Muslim countries have greatly benefited in managing crises from the help of Western countries and that the WTO is at all times neutral on such issues, as it tries to channel the help of members to other members who are in need.[12]

Better Access to Developing Country Coalitions

Many coalitions have been formed within the WTO to enhance the position of the developing countries in the Organization, starting with the Group of 77 (G77) in 1964 and including, more recently, Non-Agricultural

---

[12] Evenett and Gage, *op. cit.*, p. 26.

Market Access (NAMA-11). The Palestinian State would find it beneficial to join such sub-groups in order to enhance its economy and the social welfare of its citizens. It is argued that access to any of the sub-groups would itself constitute a huge advance for Palestine, as it currently seems to be singlehandedly combating financial and political problems. If we take a look at Palestinian foreign trade, we find that Palestinians clearly trade certain products with certain countries, and that they actually find it easier to stay with these countries instead of broadening their import-export prospective. By entering coalitions, Palestinians would manage their trade in goods and services in a much easier way, as they would be forced to trade them with other members and, in turn, gain privileges such as lower customs tariffs, wider market segments, and greater free publicity for Palestinian products among the countries concerned.[13]

Why Not Join the WTO?

By contrast, many scholars view any developing country's membership in such organizations as a destructive step for its society and a barrier to the likelihood of resolving internal problems. This position is briefly discussed below.

The WTO is not a Policy-maker

It might look as though the WTO is a body that makes and implements policy for the sake of member States and, given that the Palestinians might wish to have such a body formulate and implement policies for their benefit, it is important for them to realize that it is a member-driven organization and that trade policies are based solely on the negotiations conducted between member countries. So if policies are perceived not to favour any member State, the matter is referred to a Dispute Settlement Body which makes rulings by adopting the findings of a panel of experts or an appeal report.[14]

The WTO is Not about Free Trade at any Cost

The real question is which countries are willing to bargain with each other, and to engage in a process of give and take, and of offer and request. In other words, the WTO is concerned about development rather than free

---

[13] Ossa, *op. cit.*, p. 14.
[14] Monge-Arino, *op. cit.*, p. 9.

trade, and Palestinians need to reflect on which countries can benefit them in terms of free trade and mobilizing funds for their country. Any misunderstanding of this concept might deprive Palestinians of the privileges to be gained from joining the WTO.[15]

Misunderstanding the Concepts Inherent in the WTO

It is of great importance for the Palestinian State to understand such concepts as: small countries are powerless; the WTO destroys jobs and widens the gap between rich and poor; commercial interests take priority over environmental and development issues; the WTO is not a tool of powerful lobbies; and the WTO is not undemocratic. It should be clear that many of them would actually operate to the detriment of the Palestinians and that they are unlikely to achieve the advantages they seek along these lines. Palestinians cannot seek improvements from the Organization unless they are prepared to take positive action. They should present themselves to other members as a State from which the latter stand to benefit in order to join the different member State coalitions and be in a position to subscribe to any agreements to be signed in the future. It will be a long, hard process and it is essential for Palestinians to take a closer look at their capabilities and their willingness to proceed with such an important step towards economic globalization.[16]

The WTO is not a Political Body

Palestinians should not seek any political benefits from membership of the WTO. While it is true that politics and economics are interrelated, this does not mean that the two should be mixed in order to achieve personal objectives at the local or international level. Palestinians should realize that the Palestinian State is a political body and that it will not achieve international recognition through the WTO or any of its members or subgroups. Hence, before joining the WTO Palestinians should have their own State. The WTO is an economic organization that seeks to develop international trade for the benefit of members which are already established as free States, which have their own borders and roles in international trade, their own trade agreement, and which are freely willing to participate (both politically and economically) in international coalitions.[17]

---

[15] Abdelrahman and Draghmah, *op. cit.*, p. 5.

[16] *Ibid.*, p. 6.

[17] Monge-Arino, *op. cit.*, p. 11.

The WTO Unit of the Ministry of National Economy

Palestinian efforts to join the WTO had to be organized through a collective body composed of different sectors and people responsible for the progress of Palestine towards WTO membership. After almost 10 years of work within the Ministry, the WTO Unit was established in 2011 as the body responsible for coordinating all activities and documentation related to the process. It also performs counselling work, providing advice about international trade systems and carrying out research, training activities and workshops about the issue.[18]

The Unit works hand in hand with other national ministries and governmental bodies to achieve WTO membership. It engages in many activities to that end, including:

1. Coordination of the efforts of different advisory, technical and specialized teams to provide proposals and suggestions concerning the process of joining the WTO;
2. Training of Palestinian teams to engage in negotiations on the right of Palestine to join the WTO;
3. Advisory services on trade issues and the WTO;
4. Preparation of the memorandum on Palestinian trade policies and coordination of efforts in that regard;
5. Collection and analysis of all data required for the process;
6. Follow-up to different meetings at both the national and international levels and feedback about progress achieved in the process;
7. Serving as a point of contact between the Palestinian Authority and the different WTO committees;
8. Evaluation of laws and regulations pertaining to the WTO and the national economy in order to ensure consistency with WTO requirements;
9. Participation in the process of planning and execution of all activities likely to win the approval of WTO members for Palestine's membership.[19]

The Ministry also established the so-called 'national team for participation' and the 'technical advisory team;' the efforts of the teams are coordinated by the WTO Unit.

---

[18] Abdelrahman and Draghmah, *op. cit.*, p. 16.
[19] *Ibid.*, p. 18.

With regard to communications with the WTO, the Unit submitted its first communication in 2009, stating that Palestine was interested in WTO membership. Prior to that, Palestine had participated as an observer in meetings held in Hong Kong in 2005 and in Geneva in 2009 and 2011.

On the level of community support, Palestinians clearly support such an important step. The Unit works on the following four levels to achieve maximum support at both the national and international levels: communications with the ambassadors of member States; communications with representatives of member States within Palestine; communications with the WTO secretariat; and communications with WTO subgroups and coalitions (WTO communications, 2009 and 2010).

The WTO Unit in Palestine conducted several workshops to enhance the abilities of the teams working with and within the WTO Unit so as to acquaint them with WTO regulations and international trade concepts. The Unit revised many regulations in different sectors to ensure their consistency with WTO legal regulations.[20]

The Unit works side by side with other teams to achieve the overall objective of joining the WTO. It plans to take the following steps within the foreseeable future:

1. Revision of all regulations with the help of different responsible bodies;
2. Continuous communication with the WTO;
3. Continuous training of the Palestinian negotiating team;
4. Launching of campaigns at the community level to enhance public awareness of the benefits of joining the WTO;
5. Development of a database for researchers on the WTO and on work done in Palestine to date with the aim of joining this important international organization;
6. Preparation of readiness drafts for different sectors in Palestine and of the requisite schedules for completion of the application process for membership of the WTO (WTO overview 2012, p. 4).

---

[20] *Palestine Readiness Plan Formal Form*, Ministry of National Economy, Palestine, July 2007.

Palestine's Request for Observer Status[21]

Palestinians have been trying for the past ten years or so to have their observer status approved by the WTO. At the domestic level; the majority of Palestinians agree on the importance of joining the WTO since the benefits of membership of such an international body greatly exceed the drawbacks. The following is a brief overview of the request content and the areas of key importance for the success of the application process:

1. A brief introduction: The introduction specifies the country's name, governing body, responsible ministry (ministries), and the formal request for observer status in the WTO and its subsidiary bodies.
2. An overview of Palestinian economic policy and the foreign trade regime: The Palestinian economy is introduced in terms of territory, population and the different sectors (agriculture, industry, services, external trade and international aid).
3. Overall development plan: This is a presentation of different overall development strategies adopted by the Palestinian authorities, including the 2007 reform and development plan, and the 2009 development plan with its different focal areas.
4. Economic policies: Both fiscal and monetary policies are presented in the application, although significant shortcomings are evident and there is no central bank. This section also discusses the investment policies implemented in Palestine, focusing on investment incentives including, in particular, the 1998 law on the encouragement of investment. It also mentions the industrial estates and free zone law of 1997. Other focal areas are agricultural and industrial policies.
5. Foreign trade regime and policy: This section highlights the risks inherent in the Palestinian trading system, focusing on the governing body responsible for formulating and implementing trade policies, i.e. the Ministry of National Economy. The section also discusses tariffs and indirect taxes related to international trade and the countries that have already concluded trade agreements in support of the Palestinian economy and foreign trade. Other areas highlighted in the section are: customs and import licensing, the export regime, technical regulations and standards, and sanitary and phytosanitary measures.

---

[21] *Palestine Request for Observer Status Formal Form*, Ministry of National Economy, Palestine, October 2009; *Palestine Request for Observer Status Formal Form*, Ministry of National Economy, Palestine, April 2010.

6. Intellectual property and legal framework: Another focal area in the request is the legal framework whereby Palestinians govern their economic activities, which includes British Mandate law, Ottoman law, Israeli military orders still in effect, pre-1967 Jordanian laws and Palestinian laws issued after 1995. A legal reform process is under way, with enacted new laws replacing old laws and draft new laws pending approval by the Legislative Council.
7. Trade agreements: The final section of the application form includes a brief description of the trade agreements concluded to date by the Palestinian authorities, including the nature of the agreements, the countries involved, plans for expansion into other international markets and targets to be achieved in the near future.

Palestine Readiness Plan: Bridging the Gaps[22]

Palestine decided to apply for observer status in the WTO as part of the process of securing international recognition for its democratic State. This status would enable Palestinians to better understand WTO activities and the negotiating process leading to full membership. Full membership would assist the country in receiving both technical and financial aid conducive to more sustained development of its different sectors.

The Palestinian readiness plan is another step on the way to WTO membership. The key aim is to close the gaps created during the past 64 years or so by the Israeli occupation. It is also a huge step along the road leading to economic equality with other countries worldwide. The plan focuses on three areas, all of which are conducive to a better trade system and a more efficient development process. The three areas are:

1. Legislative reforms based on the system implemented in the WTO: With a view to joining the WTO, Palestine embarked on a reform process of all its laws, especially those focusing on trade, in order to identify the gaps relating to more than 60 agreements, decisions and mutual understandings. Three international agreements are regarded as pivotal for the WTO: the General Agreement on Tariffs and Trade (GATT), the General Agreement on Trade in Services (GATS) and the Agreement on Trade-Related Aspects of Intellectual Property Rights.
2. Institutional reforms based on the system implemented in the WTO: Palestinians need to bring about institutional reforms that

---

[22] Palestine Readiness Plan, *op. cit.*

will enable them to join the WTO. The focus here is mainly on performance capability and building a new institutional system that meets WTO requirements.

3. Training of human resources: It is crucial for the Palestinians to have a capable implementation team that can negotiate the terms for becoming a member of the WTO. They need all the help they can get in this area, including training, capacity-building, and planning and implementation strategies for different roles and legal reforms. Emphasis should be laid on Palestinians' negotiating abilities as the next step towards securing WTO membership, especially with respect to negotiations concerning trade policy and the trade system in general. Greater emphasis should also be laid on the flexibility of the WTO and the prospective benefits in terms of the greatest possible input from existing members into the national economy and the development process.

It should be possible, by focusing on the above three areas, to bridge existing gaps in the Palestinian system and to promote the process of reform of the national economy. It should be noted that Palestine, while taking steps to have its application for observer status approved, is also seeking admission to other groups that are active in the WTO. By dint of the work accomplished to date, Palestine hopes to achieve such approval and perhaps in the near future to become a full member of the WTO.

Conclusion

Palestine should think long and hard about the next step towards achieving membership of the WTO. It should focus on its readiness plan and ways of implementing it in the near future, as this would show other WTO members that the Palestinian State is serious about joining this international coalition.

It is crystal clear that the advantages of the WTO exceed its drawbacks, and that Palestine, like any other developing country, stands to benefit from becoming a member of the Organization and from joining the globalization movement in terms of trade and economics in general.

Emphasis should be laid on the need for more research on the status of the Palestinian national economy and for a formal State to govern the country and to lead the economic reform process at both the national and international levels

PART III

THE STATE OF PALESTINE: PAST AND FUTURE

This part examines issues that lie beyond the formal membership of Palestine in the UN. It reviews certain historical narratives, compares Palestine under Israeli occupation with the case of Namibia under the occupation of apartheid South Africa, projects the future of the modern legal, political and constitutional systems of the State and proposes radical alternatives to the two-State solution.

Chapter Thirteen reviews Palestinian 'citizenship' and Palestinian 'nationality' during the British Mandate and connects the concepts with the future status of the inhabitants of the State. It argues that the Palestinian 'national' has remained an enduring figure in the historical narrative of Palestine. In creating Palestinian citizenship, the British failed to take into account the Palestinians' own discourse concerning the nationality that belongs to a nation State. As a result, a conflict arose under the Mandate between the figures of the 'citizen' and the 'national' and this conflict persists to the present day. The early history of nationality and citizenship is a crucial component of the future statehood. The chapter claims that historians often focus on politics and negotiations and that the study of citizenship during the Mandate has been neglected despite its tremendous influence on modern concepts of citizenship, nationality and the nation State.

Chapter Fourteen compares the independence of Palestine with the independence of Namibia and analogizes the influence of American foreign policy in the two situations. The fact that both Namibia and Palestine were mandates under the League of Nations has had a dramatic effect on international law and relations. The chapter compares the character of South African apartheid with the character of the Israeli occupation. It concludes that the policies of the Israeli authorities show sufficient parallels to qualify as apartheid-like practices. These practices may amount to international crimes. The authors present summaries of the major strategies developed by the UN to bring non-violent pressure for change to bear on South Africa in order to bring about change. These strategies may be of value for the defence of Palestinian interests. The chapter highlights the Palestinian strategies in the context of US policy.

Chapter Fifteen suggests that Palestine's membership in the UN offers an opportunity for the young State to take advantage of opportunities to create a justice system that never was. It contends that UN membership presents critical opportunities for Palestine to enhance human dignity and expand economic opportunities. In addition to these obvious implications, UN recognition provides a unique opportunity to become a beacon among nations through the establishment of the 'rule of justice' in the new nation. Although many people talk about the 'rule of law,' what is really needed is the 'rule of justice' – a system that elevates fairness and equity above formalism. Such a 'justice' system consists of many parts. The chapter focuses on one aspect: the role of universities in educating tomorrow's lawyers, judges, and public officials.

Chapter Sixteen proposes key principles that the author believes should underlie the future constitution of the State of Palestine, which should be a federal and bi-national (Arab and Jewish) secular State. The chapter expresses regret that the Palestinians have been negotiating *vis-à-vis* their 'enemies, notably Israel and its prime backer, the US, promoting initiatives towards a settlement of the conflict for the past twenty odd years.' A party that initiates is also a party that inevitably makes mistakes. The Jewish-Palestinian author argues that Palestinians still have to hear from the PLO leadership that their most serious mistake since 1999 has been the assumption that their 'primary enemy, political Zionist Apartheid Israel, was ready for a historical compromise on the 1967 basis.'

Chapter Seventeen presents the 'divide-and-share' approach as a formula for the Palestinians and Israelis to coexist in the same already small land. The writer believes that the one-State solution is no longer a viable option as the majority of Israeli Jews oppose it. The two-State solution encounters difficulties due to the facts on the ground; it is almost impossible to establish a viable Palestinian State on the 1967 border, as the territory is small, lacks contiguity and the West Bank is full of Israeli settlements. The significantly revised two-State solution rests on two main ideas: first, sharing all the things that cannot be divided, above all Jerusalem; and, second, distinguishing between citizens and residents in order to creatively address the other two thorniest issues: Jewish settlers and Palestinian refugees. While the settlers may continue to reside in the State of Palestine as Israeli citizens, the refugees can return to reside in the State of Israel as Palestinian citizens.

CHAPTER THIRTEEN

THE PALESTINIAN CITIZEN
VS. THE PALESTINIAN NATIONAL:
PAST AND PRESENT*

LAUREN BANKO

'This legislative capacity [for nationality and citizenship] lies within the
sphere of the National Government as set up by the people.'
—*Palestinian delegation to the President of the League of Nations, 1921*

Introduction

In 1925, the British administration of Palestine announced the passage
of the Palestine Citizenship Order-in-Council, an order given by the power
of His Majesty the King of England to confer citizenship on both Ottoman
natives born and habitually resident in Palestine, and immigrant Jewish
settlers who had resided in Palestine for at least two years. For the first
time, the Palestinian Arabs were given a legal and internationally
recognized citizenship status. As is well known, this status lasted for over
two decades. Since the creation of the State of Israel in 1948, the
Palestinian citizen has ceased to exist. Rather, the Palestinian national,
both in the Diaspora and within the Occupied Territories, has taken the
place of the citizen as the internationally recognized identity status for all
Palestinians. The existence of only Palestinian nationality, and not
citizenship, has implications for the creation of Palestinian citizenship for

* A shortened version of this chapter was presented at Hebron University's
International Conference on 'Membership of Palestine in the United Nations:
Legal and Political Implications' in April 2012. The author is grateful for the
opportunity to present this work and for the comments and feedback which were
given.

a second time in history, at the time when a Palestinian State will be recognized by the United Nations.

The Palestinian national has remained an enduring figure in the historical narrative of Palestine. The British, in their creation of Palestinian citizenship, failed to take into account the Palestinians' own discourses of nationality and of belonging to a nation State. As a result, the figures of the citizen and the national conflicted not only during the Palestine Mandate, but in the sixty-four years since the creation of Israel. This chapter seeks to historicize the discourses of both identities from the time of the Palestine Mandate until today. In addition, it will analyse how the historical concepts of Palestinian citizenship and nationality affect on-going negotiations on Palestinian statehood, particularly in light of Palestinian emigrants and refugees.

Historians have often been left out of political negotiations on the situation of Palestine, and historians have themselves often neglected the study of Palestinian citizenship during the only time period when such a legal status existed—the colonial citizenship given to the Palestinians under the British Mandate administration. This chapter is mostly devoted to that very topic in order to historicise the Palestinian mandate leaders' discourses and practices of citizenship and nationality, and their conceptions of what both meant in a future independent Palestine. It seems that the leaders of today have been slow to build upon the notion of Palestinian citizenship and nationality which were in fact shaped in liberal, progressive terms beginning in the early 1920s. The following focuses more on the history of the discourses of citizenship in the mandate. It does not answer or argue large political questions on current nationality and citizenship issues. Instead, this chapter produces more questions than answers as to the current arrangements for citizenship and nationality which the Palestinian National Authority as well as the Hamas government in Gaza might have proposed before the September 2011 statehood bid—and indeed might propose in the future.[1]

Nationality and Citizenship under the Mandate

The British civil administration began in Palestine in 1920 under High Commissioner Herbert Samuel with a very clear policy plan for the facilitation of Jewish immigration and the creation of nationality status for Jewish immigrants into Palestine. No mention was made in the draft Palestine Mandate as to the nationality of the former Ottoman Arab

---

[1] *Cf.* Chapter Three of this volume (the editor).

majority. The entire process of inventing a legal Palestinian citizenship in the crucial early 1920s created an enormous amount of questions over the status, sovereignty and civic rights of subjects as opposed to nationals or citizens in a mandated territory. British notions of citizenship were imported into Palestine after approval by His Majesty's Government (HMG) in London and blended with existing Ottoman-era legislation, Palestinian municipal law and international laws of State succession and immigration.

The creation of citizenship in the Arab world during the post-World War I period of international mandates was a unique colonial process. In Palestine it was even more so, and the British needed to create as apolitical a citizenship as possible. Since the mandate included the Balfour Declaration, the establishment of a Jewish national home in Palestine was the driving force for early policy under the British administration. The mandate required the British to create a law for the acquisition of Palestinian nationality for the Jews. This nationality would give certain rights and obligations not only to the Jewish immigrants, but also to the majority Arab population since the mandate also stipulated that the Jewish national home policy could not prejudice the civil or religious rights of the existing majority population. Hence, the British had to walk a fine line in their legislation on nationality and citizenship and they needed to act as a colonial power rather than as a trustee and draft a colonial citizenship that gave only limited political rights.

In light of the mandate, the British feared giving explicit liberal citizenship rights and practices along with citizenship status. Since Palestine's population was ninety-three percent Arab when the mandate was ratified, these types of rights would give the Arabs control over Palestine and its government. Proposed democratic measures challenged the foundation of British policy in Palestine—the facilitation of a Jewish national home. Therefore, Palestinian citizenship had to be created in a way that would not allow for any civil, political or social rights or practices which threatened the Balfour Declaration as enshrined in the mandate.

The Palestinian national, populist leadership discussed Palestinian nationality and citizenship in ways that alluded to the concept of Palestinian nationality as a primordial status acquired by birth in the Arab lands or descent from Palestinian ancestors. In their discussions with British colonial leaders, the Palestinians, especially the first delegation to London in 1921, criticized the British notion that the Jewish immigrants were to be given a national status separate from the status of the Palestinian Arabs as 'former Ottoman nationals.' They asked that the

British create an equal citizenship for those residents of Palestine from before the First World War.

The difference between the Palestinians' concepts of nationality and citizenship was clear in their demand for national political and civil rights. They saw the British legislation of citizenship as colonial. It is useful to briefly explain the meanings of citizenship and nationality during the time before and during the mandate. In the study of the development of the nation, scholars have posited two types of nationhood whose roots lie in the eighteenth and nineteenth centuries. Nationhood and membership in the nation is either by descent, *jus sanguinis*, or by birth in the territory, *jus soli*. A nation was made up of people who shared the same ethnicity, or it was a State of its equal citizens within its territory, not always connected to ethnicity. On this point in the post-Ottoman Arab lands, Arab nationality is contrasted with territorial political citizenship such as Palestinian, Syrian and Iraqi citizenship.

The nation and, by extent, nationality and nationalism, depend on a political territory. The ultimate realisation of both is the nation State. Once the nation State comes into existence with sovereign borders and democratic political and legal structures, it then becomes responsible for legislating citizenship as a legal and regulating nationality. The State also becomes the grantor of rights and duties to its citizens and it decides who belongs.

National identities are more abstract concepts, and the existence of a State is not necessary since a nation can exist without a sovereign entity. The State, however, is essential to regulate citizenship and provide the proper identification to its citizens. The 'western' notion of citizenship refers to a legal relationship between an individual and the State. It is full membership in a community with civil, political and social rights and responsibilities.[2]

In the territory that became Palestine, the 1869 Ottoman Law of Nationality defined Ottoman citizenship: all subjects were to be Ottomans without religious distinction, and this nationality could be gained or lost according to conditions in the law.[3] After the British occupied Palestine in 1017/1918, the entire Arab region which had been part of the Ottoman Empire remained nominally part of that empire until the Ottomans signed a peace treaty. The Palestinian Arabs kept Ottoman nationality until the 1923 Treaty of Lausanne. During this time, the British administration in

---

[2] D. Miller, *Citizenship and National Identity* (Cambridge: Polity Press, 2000), p. 83.

[3] N. Salam, 'The Emergence of Citizenship in Islamdom,' *Arab Law Quarterly* 125 (1997).

Palestine and London debated the drafts of a nationality order. The Palestine Mandate, ratified in 1922, further defined the Palestinian nationals.

Mandate and citizenship draft legislation stated that all Ottoman subjects of Palestine would become Palestinian citizens at the date of ratification of the peace treaty and thereby lose their Ottoman nationality unless an individual notified the government within twelve months of his desire to keep Ottoman nationality and leave Palestine. The citizenship legislation drafts further specified that Ottoman subjects who usually reside in Palestine but were absent on the date of ratification of the peace treaty would become citizens if they returned to Palestine within twelve months and took up permanent residence. Meanwhile, Jewish immigrants who took up residence in Palestine within two years of the ratification of the mandate became Palestinian citizens. In what later became Article 7 of the Palestine Mandate, its draft stipulated that the government must enact a nationality law for the acquisition of Palestinian citizenship for Jews within two years after the ratification of the mandate. The mandate draft laid out very few points that could be used to construct a proper nationality law and indeed did not differentiate between nationality and citizenship.

Nationality or Citizenship?

The discussions of Palestine mandate nationality focused on the status of the Palestinians: were they meant to be treated as British-protected persons, Ottoman subjects, foreigners, or nationals of a mandate? Their status also needed to be valid outside Palestine. As for the Jewish immigrants, dependent on their country of origin, they were subjected to different consequences when they arrived in Palestine and applied for provisional certificates of nationality. They often lost their birth nationality. At the same time, the Arabs remained Ottoman nationals in lieu of a peace treaty.

As for Palestinians who travelled or lived abroad, British consulates treated them as former Ottoman nationals or even enemy aliens. Officially, the Palestinian Arabs were not entitled to British protection while abroad and so became stateless in the absence of the Ottoman Empire. Ottoman citizens who lived outside of Palestine but wanted Palestinian nationality could obtain proof of their nationality either with an Ottoman passport or with other identity documents that showed the individual's father was an Ottoman subject. If these individuals needed to apply for travel documents, they had to sign that they would opt for Palestinian nationality as soon as a law passed to enable them to do so, and this meant they would reside permanently in Palestine after arrival.[4]

In the early 1920s, the administration in Palestine and the government in London debated the framework and functions of an elected legislative council, but decided they could not pass any electoral law for it prior to ratification of the mandate; after that, they would still need an order-in-council to regulate Palestinian nationality. Without the latter, electoral registers for the territory could not be compiled and the British depended on such registers in order to properly divide the population and decide upon the system of secondary electors. A nationality law was necessary to define who was a Palestinian citizen in order to grant franchise.[5]

After the Mandate for Palestine came into effect in September 1922, Great Britain immediately finished its draft constitution and legislative council election orders. The Palestine Order-in-Council of 1922 served as the first constitution of the Palestine government but it did not repeal the 1869 Ottoman Nationality Order. However, the 1922 Palestine Electoral Order-in-Council defined a Palestinian citizen in order to identify the electorate only. Citizens were 'Turkish subjects' habitually resident in Palestine when the order started to be applied, and all other inhabitants not of 'Turkish nationality' who were habitually resident—the Jewish immigrants.

The 1922 Election Order-in-Council gave the first political and civil rights, those to vote and hold office, to Palestinians. But it defined political membership by religion. This division by religious communities did not reflect the socio-political reality in Palestine or any emerging trend towards equal citizenship.

From Nationality Law to Citizenship Order-in-Council

With the election order passed, the British concentrated on the draft nationality law. Its provisions had to be in accordance with the peace treaty signed between the Allies and the new Turkish Republic and had to meet the requirements for Palestine as a territory affected by the treaty. For example, the nationality draft order stated that Ottoman subjects in Palestine could not opt for the nationality of the Hijaz, Mesopotamia (Iraq) or Syria because the 'race' of the majority population in those countries

---

[4] Passports for Jews and Arabs of Palestinian or Syrian Origin, 5 July 1920, CO 323/831/81.
[5] Palestinian Nationality Memo, August 1921, CO 733/14/117.

was the same as in Palestine, defined as Arab.[6] Former Ottoman subjects could opt for the new Turkish nationality even if they automatically received Palestinian nationality. They had twelve months after the treaty ratification to do so. The British Home Office, which was responsible for naturalisation of foreigners, held the opinion that Palestinian nationality should be limited so that it did not pass indefinitely to future generations who were resident outside of Palestine. It recommended the limit of citizenship passed by blood to the second generation born outside of Palestine. This limit was in accordance with the British Nationality Act of 1914.[7]

The ordinance's drafts used the term 'Palestinian nationality' to indicate the international status of Palestinians, but Article 29 of the treaty used 'citizen' to mean the same thing. Later, the Foreign Office memo on the nationality draft noted that the phrase 'Palestinian citizen' should be used throughout as the author knew of no authorisation that stated that the term citizen was not used to denote a member of a State in international law.[8]

On the Arab side, some members of the High Commissioner's nominated Advisory Council had some knowledge of the draft nationality order. They objected to it. As early as November 1921, the Arab members refused to discuss the constitution or nationality. They argued that the nationality law quite obviously benefited the Zionist immigrants. For example, they opposed the short, two-year residency period required before an individual could be naturalised as a citizen.[9] In November 1921, during one of the Advisory Council meetings after an explanation of the constitution and nationality laws, one of the council's unofficial Arab members, Turkan Bey, declared to the British members that since the mandate and the peace treaty had not yet been approved, and because the Advisory Council was not an elected body, his Arab colleagues refused to discuss a basic law or constitution. He added that the nationality law seemed to only benefit the Zionist immigrants. He indicated the Arab opposition to the two-year residency period required before an individual could be naturalised as a citizen. He argued (not entirely correctly) that one reason for the opposition was that in every other country the residency requirement was at least five years. Turkan Bey argued for a rapid passage of the nationality law after consultation with the Arab leaders in order to

---

[6] Nationality Order-in-Council Draft Memo, 27 October 1921, CO 733/6/121.
[7] Palestinian Nationality Order-in-Council Memo, 8 May 1924, CO 733/80/48.
[8] CO 733/12/13-14 1921.
[9] CO 733/6/184-185.

benefit Palestinian Arabs who lived or travelled abroad.[10]

The Palestinian emigrants also had problems with their lack of nationality. In 1922, the Palestine Administration, HMG (His Majesty's Government) and the League of Nations started to receive petitions from Palestinians in South American countries, Mexico and Cuba. Since the British Foreign Office had not received definite instructions on Palestinian nationality, consuls sometimes refused to issue passports or visas to Palestinians in order to allow for their return to Palestine or to travel for business.[11]

In 1924, the Treaty of Lausanne ratification officially meant Palestinian nationality was recognised. The treaty ended the 'nominal' Ottoman citizenship. Former Ottomans came under the laws and regulations of the successor States. In order for Ottoman nationals in Palestine to be subject to the laws and regulations of the Palestine Mandate Administration as nationals of the territory, they had to prove their status as Ottoman subjects and be resident in Palestine on the date on which the Treaty of Lausanne came into force. For emigrants born in Palestine, the treaty stated that they could naturalise within two years of the treaty's ratification.

The Citizenship Order-in-Council and its Amendments

The King of England passed the Palestine Citizenship Order-in-Council on 1 August 1925. The Citizenship Order was enacted by the British Government, not by the government of Palestine. Until the middle of 1924, the order-in-council draft to regulate Palestinian citizenship was entitled Palestinian Nationality Order-in-Council. By July, the draft order had 'nationality' crossed out and replaced with 'citizenship.' The order draft had interchangeably used the terms 'national,' 'citizen,' and 'subject,' even though in previous discourses between officials these words had separate connotations.[12]

The Citizenship Order's first article declared Turkish subjects habitually resident in Palestine on 1 August 1924 to be automatically Palestinian citizens on 1 August 1925. This article did not account for inhabitants who had been given provisional nationality under the 1922 Legislative Election Order, who included non-Turkish subjects. It also did not account for Ottoman subjects resident abroad on 1 August 1924. However, Article 5 granted that non-Turkish residents were deemed citizens under Article 2 of

---

[10] Advisory Council meeting minutes, 4 November 1921, CO 733/6/184-185.
[11] CO 733/27 1922.
[12] CO 733/80/599 1924.

the Legislative Election Order subject to their intention to opt for citizenship. In total, the number of Ottoman citizens resident in Palestine on the date of the order who became Palestinian citizens was nearly 730,000.[13]

Palestinians with Ottoman nationality who lived abroad on 1 August 1925 could opt for citizenship in accordance with the regulation that they had been in Palestine for six months prior to opting in accordance with the Treaty of Lausanne and had not acquired a foreign nationality. This option was open to them for two years from the date of the order, until 31 July 1927. However, the difference in wording of Article 2 from its sister Article 34 in the Treaty of Lausanne was a cause for denial of citizenship to individuals who would have otherwise been considered Palestinian. In Article 34 of Lausanne, the phrase 'native of' Palestine had been used, whereas the Citizenship Order used 'born in Palestine.'[14] This slight change meant that these descendants of Palestinians with Ottoman nationality abroad were not given citizenship. This went against the 1869 Ottoman law which stated that children receive nationality by descent and it went against British naturalisation and nationality laws.

The High Commissioner used his power to make a drastic change in the Citizenship Order in November 1925: the date by which Ottomans residing outside of Palestine could opt for nationality changed. Rather than allowing them two years, beginning on 1 August 1925, the two-year option timeframe was put into effect retroactively, from 6 August 1924— the date of the Treaty of Lausanne. It meant that Palestinians who lived abroad in August 1924 had less than one year to opt for nationality.

Palestinian emigrants lost Ottoman citizenship with the Treaty of Lausanne and were unaccounted for in the Citizenship Order-in-Council. Similarly, those resident abroad on 1 August 1925 who could not return to opt for citizenship within the given time frame lost their Ottoman nationality and were not given a new nationality by the Palestinian Citizenship Order unless they returned to Palestine with six months to spare before the end of July 1926 to meet the residency requirement to apply for citizenship. Without a clear status, these Palestinians often could not get the proper travel documents to return to Palestine to reside. Emigrants in places such as Latin America, Cuba and Haiti were subjected to the greatest difficulty. These Palestinians could not simply reside

---

[13] M. Qafisheh, *The International Law Foundations of Palestinian Nationality: A Legal Examination of Nationality in Palestine under Britain's Rule* (Leiden: Martinus Nijhoff, 2008).
[14] *Ibid.*

anywhere since they had become stateless and without any diplomatic protection.[15]

The Palestinian Discourse of Nationality and Citizenship

The Palestinian Arab Executive leadership unanimously rejected the citizenship legislation on the basis that it denied citizenship to native-born Palestinians while it privileged Jewish immigrants and it neglected provisions for natural civil and political rights. This became especially clear in protests sent to Palestine from emigrants who were denied citizenship, yet still claimed Palestinian nationality, along with land and family in Palestine. Through his time as president of the Arab Executive, Musa Kazim Pasha al-Husayni defended his call for equal nationality and citizenship rights in Palestine and questioned British nationality legislation even before the ratification of the mandate.

In 1921, Musa Kazim wrote to Winston Churchill, British Secretary of State for the Colonies, that the native Jews of Palestine did have the duties, privileges and rights to citizenship. He wrote that the people of Palestine inherited their country as its native inhabitants. Musa Kazim and others debated the nationality status of Jews in Palestine and whether they were Jewish or English nationals, 'for it is obvious they cannot be both at the same time.' Musa Kazim then asked if 'Jew-ism' was in fact a nationality, and if so, what of the 'English-ism' of colonial officials who were also Jewish in Palestine? The threat that the Jews would have their own, separate nationality in Palestine was a rallying call against the mandate by the Palestinians. As to citizenship rights, Kazim argued for the political and civil rights that existed under Ottoman rule such as representative parliament, and the rights of free speech and assembly.[16]

At the time of the Citizenship Order in 1925, the Arabic press questioned the meaning of 'nationality' in light of the Balfour Declaration and the mandate. In the press, the order was referred to as the 'nationality law' (*qanoon al-jinsiyya* or *haq al-jinsiyya*) and Palestinians used the term *jinsiyya* in reference to the perhaps more legalistic 'citizenship' (*muwatina*). Citizenship was viewed as a legal status while nationality was deeper and primordial on the basis of ancestry in a certain territory.

---

[15] *Ibid.*

[16] *Watha'iq al-Haraka al-Wataniyya al-Filastiniyya min Awraq Akram Zu`aytir, 1918-1939* [Documents of the Palestinian National Movement from the Papers of Akram Zu'aytir] (Beirut: Institute of Palestine Studies, 1979), pp. 65-71.

Issa Bandak, a newspaper editor and populist national leader in Bethlehem, established the Committee for the Defence of Palestinian Arab Emigrant Citizenship Rights in 1926, and it lobbied into the 1930s against the citizenship order. The Palestinians argued that the order was unlawful because it was not enacted by a parliament elected by the people. Indeed, the Palestinians were never allowed to see any drafts of the order. They felt that the order remained illegal and benefited what was then still only the small minority of Jewish immigrants. Bandak concluded that the establishment of a Jewish national home, strengthened by the nationality order, would abrogate future Arab national control of the country. He pledged that the Palestinians would work to stop the law unless the British enacted a new law 'legitimately by constitutional means.'[17]

The Diaspora (numbering between 20,000 and 30,000 according to the Palestinians by the late 1920s) shaped the meaning of Palestinian citizenship. The emigrant communities in Latin America and Cuba constantly appealed beginning in 1927 to the British to give them their 'right of return'—over two decades before this term was used by refugees. The emigrants claimed their nationality as descendants of Ottoman nationals in Palestine, which meant they were entitled to have the right of citizenship and the right to return to Palestine to claim their citizenship regardless of whether they remained residents of Palestine.[18] They also claimed that the British denial of their citizenship was a form of 'ethnic cleansing' in order to decrease their numbers in Palestine. They felt their demonstration of Palestinian nationality was through retaining connections with Palestine, including paying taxes, owning land, and supporting the national movement, and that they should thus be entitled to legal citizenship in Palestine.[19] Indeed, their discussions framed the meaning of citizenship as a right that stemmed from Palestinian nationality.

The Palestinian Citizenship Order of 1925 was amended again in 1931: all Ottoman subjects habitually resident in Palestine on the date of the Lausanne Treaty 1924, and those who lived abroad on the date of the citizenship law in 1925, were given Palestinian citizenship. However, any Palestinians who lived abroad on the date of Lausanne, 6 August 1924, were *not* covered by the amendment.[20] The order was again amended in 1939 and 1941. The amendment gave the right to those Palestinians who had obtained another citizenship but kept connections with Palestine to apply for Palestinian citizenship.

---

[17] 'The law prejudices the rights of the Arabs,' *Mir'at al-Sharq*, 21 October 1925.

[18] Nationality of Emigrants, *Sawt al-Shaab*, 19 February 1927.

[19] 'Cry of Palestinians in the Diaspora,' *Sawt al-Shaab*, 9 March 1927.

[20] Qafisheh, *op. cit.*, p. 91.

Post-1948 Palestinian Citizenship and Nationality

On 29 November 1947, UN General Assembly Resolution 181 referred to Palestinian citizens in relation to elections for the proposed partitioned Arab and Jewish States. According to the UN, those given the right of the franchise, the most basic political right of citizenship, were to be those over the age of eighteen who were Palestinian citizens resident in Palestine, as well as Jews and Arabs resident in Palestine who were not yet Palestinian citizens but would sign a note of intention to become citizens. 'Citizens' continued to be mentioned in terms of rights and freedoms given to all residents of the future Arab and Jewish States. Chapter Three of the resolution then specifically focused on citizenship. Palestinian citizens, according to mandate legislation, in Palestine outside of Jerusalem and those Arabs and Jews without citizenship who lived in Palestine would become citizens of the State of their residence upon independence, and have all the civil and political rights of citizenship. The residents of Jerusalem were to become automatically citizens of the City of Jerusalem unless they stated their intention to opt for citizenship of the Arab State or Jewish State. Jerusalem citizens were to have the appropriate civil and political rights regardless of nationality.

After the creation of Israel, the Palestinians lost the only citizenship they had ever had as Palestinians under the mandate. From 1948 until the promulgation of the 1952 Nationality Law of Israel, Palestinian Arabs in Israeli territory were deprived of nationality and citizenship under international law—this was in clear contravention of the laws of State succession.[21] The Palestinians under Jordanian rule in the West Bank became Jordanian citizens. Under Egyptian rule, Palestinians in the Gaza Strip were given a separate citizenship identity from Egyptians. In the Arab States where Palestinians have sought refuge, they have not been given citizenship of their country of residence—this was initially based on the argument that not allowing naturalisation would protect the identity of the Palestinians. Under Israeli occupation, Palestinians have been issued with identity cards by Israel, but not with citizenship in any sense.[22] The Palestinian Authority (PA) after 1995 issued passports but, again, this is

---

[21] V. Kattan, 'The Nationality of Denationalized Palestinians,' *Nordic Journal of International Law* 74 (2005), p. 84.
[22] A. Khalil, 'Palestinian Nationality and Citizenship: Current Challenges and Future Perspectives,' CARIM Research Report (2007), p. 8.

not related to citizenship and passports are given only with Israeli approval.[23]

In 1968, the Palestinian National Charter included Article 4, which stated that Palestinian identity passed by blood, *jus sanguinis*, and that the aftermath of the expulsion in 1948 did not negate that identity or cause a loss of membership as Palestinians in the Palestinian community. Article 5 then defined the Palestinians, for the first time officially under a Palestinian quasi-government, as 'those Arab nationals who, until 1947, normally resided in Palestine regardless of whether they were evicted from it or have stayed there. *Anyone born after that date, of a Palestinian father—whether inside Palestine or outside it—is also a Palestinian*' (emphasis added). The following article stated that Jews who normally resided in Palestine before the opening of the country to Zionist settlement were also Palestinians. At the same time, the Charter declared the mandate over Palestine and everything based upon it as null and void, noting that Judaism was not an independent nationality and that Jews were citizens of the States to which they belonged originally. The Charter did not compensate pursuant to this declaration for the British-legislated citizenship order by providing their own, aside from the definition of a Palestinian.[24]

In 1995, the PA drafted a citizenship law, but it was not publicised or passed. Citizenship could not have been regulated by it anyway, since the PA operated under Israeli occupation.[25] The third Draft Palestine Constitution gave citizenship to any Palestinian resident of Palestine before 1948, on the basis of descent by father and mother and, importantly, it passed indefinitely. Further, all those with the right of return were to have Palestinian nationality. However, this was a draft constitution only.[26] The most recent official mention of Palestinians in the context of nationality is in the 2003 Basic Law of the PA but it does not define who is a Palestinian or state whether those outside of the West Bank and Gaza are to be given voting rights. Article 7 of the Basic Law states that 'Palestinian citizenship shall be regulated by law.' Citizenship-related political, civil and social rights are listed in Articles 21-33.[27]

---

[23] I. Jad, *Citizenship under a Prolonged Occupation: The Case of Palestine* (Berkley Electronic Press, 2004), p. 5.

[24] The Palestinian National Charter: Resolutions of the Palestine National Council, 1-17 July 1968.

[25] Khalil, *op. cit.*, 45.

[26] *Ibid.*, 46-47.

[27] Palestine Gazette, Special Edition, 19 March 2003, p. 5.

According to the Draft Constitution of 2003, Palestinian nationals who are not citizens will indeed have representation in a future Advisory Council.[28]

For decades, the status of the Arabs living inside Israel, including in East Jerusalem, has been one of either unequal citizenship due to their nationality, or of no proper rights as citizens at all in the case of the East Jerusalem residents. In the past decade, new government policies and discourses in Israel since the second intifada have created a consciousness that Arab citizens' citizenship is not real citizenship in the sense of civil and political rights. The Israelis see citizenship as a 'conditional privilege' for their Arab residents rather than a right.[29]

The legal opinion on Palestinian statehood, produced by Guy Goodwin-Gill of Oxford University, highlights the problem of citizenship for Palestinian nationals in the Diaspora. He notes that they will lose their representation with the coming of statehood as the Palestinian National Council, their official representative, will be dissolved. This means they will not have civil or political rights to participate in matters of government or the formation of the political identity of a Palestinian State.[30]

Conclusion

At the core of citizenship inclusion in the modern State is the status' regulation of power. Citizenship determines the criteria for membership in the decision-making processes of a State, and it determines who receives the State's assistance and benefits. In the case of an independent Palestinian State, the criteria for citizenship must be more than superficially stated in order to give Palestinian nationals—whether refugees or not—clear terms for membership in that State and hence access to its decisions and benefits. But what of the territorial fragmentation of Palestine and the fragmentation of those who claim to be nationals? Or of the legal argument of Victor Kattan that all Palestinians have been denationalized following the end of 1948, and remain without nationality due to the need for a Palestinian State to provide such nationality?[31]

As mentioned above, the British colonial officials in Palestine and London debated for two years over whether to pass a law to regulate Palestinian nationality before or after ratifying a constitutional order-in-

---

[28] Khalil, *op. cit.*, 17.
[29] N. Rouhana and N. Sultany, 'Redrawing the Boundaries of Citizenship: Israel's New Hegemony,' 33 *Journal of Palestine Studies* 10 (2003).
[30] See Chapter Two of this volume (the editor).
[31] Kattan, *op. cit.*, pp. 67-102.

council. They debated whether to first define the citizenry in order to give them the right to vote without a constitution, or whether to give citizenship first to allow for a constitution to be formed by elected representatives. The same issue applies to the current situation in the West Bank and Gaza Strip, and wherever Palestinian nationals have been scattered: should citizenship and the electorate in a Palestinian State be defined first without a constitution or basic law in order for the citizens to draft a constitution, or must citizenship be imposed first without representative decisions being made on its provisions?

As Asem Khalil notes, once a Palestinian State comes into existence, the relationship between Palestinian nationals and Palestinian citizens must be defined. He argues that those entitled to the power to draft a constitution and vote are the total of Palestinian nationals but those who actually have the power to actively do this are not the same—they are instead Palestinian citizens and the institutions which represent citizens. The regulation of citizenship is in the power of the legislature—in the case of democracy, representatives make up the legislature.[32] Therefore, the question again is what the criteria will be for citizenship in an independent Palestine. If nationality is the criterion, it is essential to recognize that the Palestinian national and the Palestinian citizen are two different statuses and nationality does not necessarily mean citizenship. If the right of return is the criterion for determining citizenship, due to international law all Palestinian nationals (as all have the right to return) will be deemed citizens.

In the 1920s and 1930s, the Palestinian Diaspora emigrants were denied citizenship, and demanded their 'right of return' to be given by Britain and the League of Nations. They believed that their Palestinian Arab nationality entitled them to have the right to return and be given Palestinian citizenship. In this way, the emigrants' discourse shaped the meaning of Palestinian citizenship under the mandate as a status that should be given on the basis of descent from Palestinian parents and ancestors, unconditionally. Palestinian national leaders such as Musa Kazim and Issa Bandak, and the press, agreed with this notion in their demands for the British to recognize Palestinian citizenship for all Palestinians.

Today, however, the situation has changed, despite the struggles of Palestinian emigrants under the mandate to achieve their right to citizenship on the basis of their nationality. The Palestinian refugees of post-1948 are not included in the plans for the future Palestinian State as

---

[32] Khalil, *op. cit.*, 6.

citizens. Their nationality is acknowledged but their civil and political rights are not. This is in line with modern, western practices of citizenship—but not in line with the history of Palestinian citizenship and nationality discourse. One must then ask, in an independent Palestinian State with UN membership, how much weight will be attached by the members of a Palestinian government to their ancestors' strong opinions that Palestinian nationality is a guarantee of the right of Palestinian citizenship in a nation State?

CHAPTER FOURTEEN

PALESTINIAN INDEPENDENCE VS. THE INDEPENDENCE OF NAMIBIA AND THE AMERICAN FOREIGN POLICY

WINSTON P. NAGAN AND AITZA M. HADDAD

Introduction

Namibia (earlier known as South West Africa), currently an independent democratic African State, has a history that has many important parallels and developments that may be of contemporary relevance to the struggle of the Palestinian people for self-determination and sovereign independence. The most important point of convergence between Namibia and Palestine is that both of these peoples and their territories were subjected to conquest by the allied powers during World War I.[1] The Namibian conquest was completed by the South African army.[2] The motivation for the South African effort to conquer German South West Africa was that it contemplated the annexation of South West Africa as a fifth province of the Union of South Africa.[3] In short, the campaign to conquer South West Africa assumed, in part, the continuance of the international law of rules that permitted the acquisition of territory by conquest.

Palestine, which during the early stages of World War I was under the 'imperium' of the Ottoman Empire, became, along with other parts of the Middle East, a strategic objective for British military conquest. The drive to conquer Palestine and defeat the Ottoman army was not an easy

---

[1] A. Anghie, 'Colonialism and the Birth of International Institutions: Sovereignty, Economy, and the Mandate System of the League of Nations,' 34 *New York University Journal of International Law and Politics* 513 (2002).

[2] R. Dale, 'The Armed Forces as an Instrument of South African Policy in Namibia,' 18 *Journal of Modern African Studies* 57 (1980).

[3] R. Green, K. Kiljunen, and M. Kiljunen, *Namibia, the Last Colony* (Longman, 1981).

conquest. In fact, Britain suffered serious defeats with huge losses of men and material before the conquest was finally concluded. Britain, too, like South Africa, considered that it would acquire title to the territories that it had conquered in the Middle East, with no small sacrifice, according to the international law principle of the acquisition of territory by conquest.[4]

The expectations of both Britain and South Africa were strongly resisted in the peace negotiations following the war and, in particular, by President Wilson's strong demand that colonial conquests should no longer be the currency of the world order after World War I.[5] Out of the peace proceedings that ended the war, there emerged the creation of an international organization, the League of Nations,[6] which invented a new institutional frame, namely Mandate System. This arrangement meant that the conquerors would retain administrative authority over their conquests, but their administration provided them with no 'imperium' or 'dominion' over these territories. The conquerors assumed the mandate as an international obligation, meaning that it was a gratuitous undertaking. This undertaking was to be performed in accordance with standard mandate agreements reached between the international community, represented by the League of Nations, and the mandatory States.

South West Africa was a class C mandate,[7] and Palestine was classified as a class A mandate.[8] The obligation of the administering power was to ensure that the mandate territory would be administered in the interest of the inhabitants who, it was assumed, had not achieved the level of collective maturity to stand independently in the world community.

---

[4] W. Werner, 'A Brief History of Land Dispossession in Namibia,' 19 *Journal of Southern African Studies* 1 (1993); L. Berat, 'Evolution of Self-Determination in International Law: South Africa, Namibia, and the Case of Walvis Bay,' 4 *Emory International Law Review* 251 (1990).

[5] S. Korman, *The Right of Conquest: The Acquisition of Territory by Force in International Law and Practice* (Oxford: Oxford University Press, 1996); G. Curry, 'Woodrow Wilson, Jan Smuts, and the Versailles Settlement,' 66 *American Historical Review* 968 (1961).

[6] F. Northedge, *The League of Nations: Its Life and Times, 1920–1946* (Leicester: Leicester University Press, 1986); C. Ellis, *The Origin, Structure & Working of the League of Nations* (Houghton Mifflin, 1928).

[7] S. Slonim, 'The Origins of the South West Africa Dispute: The Versailles Peace Conference and the Creation of the Mandates System,' 6 *Canadian Yearbook of International Law* 115 (1968); R. Bradford, *The Origin and Concession of the League of Nations' Class 'C' Mandate for South West Africa and Fulfilment of the Sacred Trust, 1919-1939* (Doctoral Dissertation, Yale University, 1965).

[8] S. Brooks, 'British Mandate for Palestine,' in S. Tucker, ed., *The Encyclopaedia of the Arab-Israeli Conflict*, Vol. 3, 2008, p. 770.

Additionally, the mandatory power had an obligation to promote the development of self-determination for the peoples of the mandated territories.

In the years before World War II, South Africa was a State in which racial discrimination was a part of the political culture.[9] These attitudes, policies, and practices influenced the way it carried out its mandate obligations in South West Africa.[10] Between 1922 and 1946, the budget of the territory was radically disproportionate in terms of its allocations to indigenous people.[11] The Germans had expropriated vast tracts of indigenous lands through expropriation.[12] Although thousands of Germans had left the territory, most of the land was given to white settlers with significant government subsidies. These settlers were ethnically Afrikaners. As the status of the territory was challenged, South Africa continued to apply as much of its new and ideologically invigorated ideas of white supremacy and black subjugation as it could to South West Africa. The political arrangements inside the territory vested local power in an all-white legislative assembly. This legislative assembly organized a petition to secure the transfer of the territory to South Africa. The pattern of mandate responsibility was largely racially discriminatory and was described by the American commentator, Allard Lowenstein, as a 'Brutal Mandate.'[13]

After World War II and the creation of the United Nations, the mandated territories under the authority of the League of Nations were transferred to the UN Trusteeship Council. South Africa contended that the UN was not a legitimate successor to the League, opposing the registration of South West Africa as a UN trusteeship territory. As these issues were developing, the extremist National Party came to power in 1948.[14] The new National Party declined to issue periodic reports concerning the status of the territory to the UN on the basis that the

---

[9] C. Feinstein, *An Economic History of South Africa: Conquest, Discrimination And Development* (Cambridge University Press, 2005).

[10] A. Rovine, 'The World Court Opinion on Namibia,' 11 *Columbia Journal of Transnational Law* 203 (1972).

[11] I. Evans, *Bureaucracy and Race: Native Administration in South Africa* (University of California Press, 1997).

[12] J. Noyes, *Colonial Space: Spatiality in the Discourse of German South West Africa 1884-1915* (Psychology Press, 1992).

[13] A. Lowenstein, *Brutal Mandate: A Journey to South West Africa* (1962)

[14] J. Dugard, *The South West Africa/Namibia Dispute: Documents and Scholarly Writings on the Controversy Between South Africa and The United Nations* (University of California Press, 1973); J. Dugard, 'The Revocation of the Mandate for South West Africa,' 62 *American Journal of International Law* 78 (1968).

mandate over the territory had lapsed, which carried the implication that South Africa owed no obligations to the international community regarding the status of Namibia. The matter was taken to the International Court of Justice (ICJ) in 1950. The ICJ ruled that, although there was no positive law that required South Africa to voluntarily transfer responsibility for South West Africa to the Trusteeship Council, nonetheless South Africa continued to have international obligations with regard to South West Africa.[15] The Court issued another ruling in which it maintained in an advisory opinion that South Africa's mandate would remain in force, and the UN was to receive the reports from South Africa.

Parallel to the efforts to clarify the legal status of South West Africa, the government of India put before the UN its concerns that the policies and practices of the discriminatory rule of South Africa were in fact targeting the minority population of Indian descent.[16] This was the wedge that India used to focus UN attention, because the victims of South African discrimination were South Africans of Indian origin. South Africa invoked a thick version of sovereignty and insisted that its policies were an internal matter and exclusively within its internal domestic jurisdiction.

UN Action and Apartheid

The General Assembly adopted resolutions from 1946 to 1950 concerning Namibia. The culmination of these resolutions was a recommendation that South Africa cease to enact discriminatory legislation and establish a commission to assist in negotiations with South Africa, India, and Pakistan on these matters. The General Assembly continued to take an interest in the problem and created a Commission to study the racial situation and report back to the General Assembly. The initial report of the Commission determined that the policy and practice of the governing party of South Africa contravened the UN Charter and the International Bill of Rights, and that apartheid was dangerous and could impair friendly relations among States, provoke conflict inside South

---

[15] E. Schwelb, 'The International Court of Justice and the Human Rights Clauses of the Charter,' 66 *American Journal International Law* 337 (1972).

[16] L. Lloyd, 'A Family Quarrel: The Development of the Dispute over Indians in South Africa,' 34 *The Historical Journal* 703 (1991); L. Lloyd, 'A Most Auspicious Beginning: The 1946 United Nations General Assembly and the Question of the Treatment of Indians in South Africa,' 16 *Review of International Studies* 131 (1990).

Africa, and impact on the stability of international relations.[17] While the Commission's second report confirmed this conclusion, its third report stated that apartheid was a serious and disturbing factor in international relations.[18]

South Africa ignored the UN. In 1960, a major massacre of blacks occurred in Sharpeville, South Africa.[19] This brought the Security Council into the picture because it considered that the conflict inside South Africa might endanger international peace and security.[20] During the ensuing period, both the Security Council and the General Assembly noted the serious international implications of apartheid. In this sense, the UN effort from 1946 to 1961 stressed the importance of South Africa coming into compliance with UN Charter obligations and human rights law. In 1962, the General Assembly began to consider not simply a clarification of obligations and recommendations for compliance, but other measures of coercion to pressure South Africa to comply.[21] The recommended pressures included: (1) breaking off diplomatic relations with the Government of the Republic of South Africa or refraining from establishing such relations; (2) closing ports to all vessels flying the South African flag; (3) enacting legislation prohibiting ships from entering South African ports; (4) boycotting all South African goods and refraining from exporting goods, including all arms and ammunition, to South Africa; (5) refusing landing and passage facilities to all aircraft belonging to the Government of South Africa and companies registered under the laws of South Africa.[22]

After 1962 and the creation of a UN Sub-Committee to monitor apartheid, apartheid became one of the most documented international delinquencies.[23] Meanwhile, conflict inside South Africa intensified. This led to more sanctions targeting South Africa generated by the General

---

[17] UN General Assembly, 'Report of the Committee on South West Africa,' UN Doc. A/RES/851, 23 November 1954.

[18] UN General Assembly, 'Procedure for the Examination of Reports and Petitions Relating to the Territory of South West Africa,' UN Doc. A/RES/844, 11 October 1954.

[19] W. Nagan and L. Albrecht, 'Judicial Executions and Individual Responsibility under International Law: The Case of the Sharpeville Six' (United Nations, 1988).

[20] *Ibid.*

[21] UN Doc. A/RES/1978, 16 December 1963.

[22] *Ibid.*

[23] I. Gassama, 'Reaffirming Faith in the Dignity of Each Human Being: The United Nations, NGOs, and Apartheid,' 19 *Fordham International Law Journal* 1464 (1996).

Assembly.[24] The General Assembly, taking advantage of its power to draw
the attention of the Security Council to situations that may endanger
international peace and security, referred the matter to the Council.[25] The
Security Council responded by supporting an internationally honoured
arms embargo against South Africa.[26] Perhaps the best expression of the
Security Council's posture is contained in Resolution 282 of 1970.[27]

The recommendations and decisions relating to both economic and
arms embargoes are among the most important actions to emerge from the
General Assembly and the Security Council. They are relevant to the
complex question of maintaining an economic presence in South Africa.
General Assembly Resolution 1881 (XVIII) of 1963 addressed the human
rights violations committed against South Africa's political prisoners.[28] In
1966, the General Assembly condemned apartheid as a crime against
humanity and criticized South Africa's main trading partners for their
collaboration with South Africa in the maintenance of the apartheid
system.[29] In 1967, the General Assembly expressed support for freedom
fighters against apartheid, demanding that they be treated as prisoners of
war under the Geneva Convention III.[30] In 1968, the UN supported a
cultural, educational, and athletic boycott of South Africa.[31]

In short, apart from condemning apartheid as a crime against humanity,
the General Assembly also targeted the treatment of freedom fighters,
political prisoners, repressive laws, bans on political organizations, and the
territorial initiatives to Balkanize South Africa and to denationalize the
blacks. There were renewed calls for a mandatory arms embargo and, most

---

[24] *Ibid.* See also M. Doxey, 'International Sanctions: A Framework for Analysis
with Special Reference to the UN and Southern Africa,' 26 *International
Organization* 527 (1972).
[25] N. Crawford and A. Klotz, *How Sanctions Work: Lessons from South Africa*
(Palgrave Macmillan, 1999); V. Gowlland-Debbas, 'Security Council Enforcement
Action and Issues of State Responsibility,' 43 *International and Comparative Law
Quarterly* 55 (1994).
[26] *Ibid.*
[27] UN Doc. S/RES/282, 23 July 1970.
[28] UN Doc. A/RES/1881, 11 October 1963.
[29] UN Doc. A/RES/2202, 16 December 1966.
[30] Commission on Human Rights, 'Establishment of the *Ad Hoc* Working Group of
Experts on Human Rights in South Africa,' UN Doc. E/CN.4/RES/2 (XXIII), 6
March 1967.
[31] D. Booth, 'Hitting Apartheid for Six? The Politics of the South African Sports
Boycott,' 38 *Journal of Contemporary History* 477 (2003); D. Booth, *The Race
Game: Sport and Politics in South Africa* (Psychology Press, 1998); M. Beaubien,
'The Cultural Boycott of South Africa,' 29 *Africa Today* 5 (1982).

importantly, the General Assembly declared that the South African government was 'an illegitimate minority racist regime.'[32] By 1985, the Security Council called for stronger measures targeting South Africa.[33]

In this context, the UN adopted an International Convention that criminalized apartheid in 1973.[34] The term the crime of *apartheid*, was defined as 'policies and practices of racial segregation and discrimination . . . for the purpose of establishing and maintaining domination by one racial group of persons over any other racial group of persons and systematically oppressing them . . . .' Now the Statute of the International Criminal Court includes within its jurisdiction the crime of apartheid.

Namibia and the Crime of Apartheid

In 1959, litigation involving Ethiopia and Liberia came before the ICJ.[35] In its preliminary ruling, the Court determined that it did have jurisdiction to proceed to determine the question of whether the application of apartheid violated an obligation rooted in the mandate or international law generally. The case then proceeded to arguments on the merits. In 1966, the Court ruled that, even though it had determined the jurisdictional question, there was still an issue that had to be determined after jurisdiction, but prior to the merits. This was the issue of whether Ethiopia and Liberia could establish a direct legal interest in the litigation, which the Court determined was an essential condition to have *locus standi in judicio*. The decision of the Court was divided 8 to 8. The President of the Court, Judge Spender, then voted twice to break the tie

---

[32] UN Doc. A/RES/38/39, 5 December 1983.

[33] UN General Assembly, 'International Convention against Apartheid in Sports,' UN Doc. A/RES/40/64 A., 10 December 1985.

[34] UN General Assembly, 'International Convention on the Suppression and Punishment of the Crime of Apartheid,' UN Doc. A/RES/3068(XXVIII), 30 November 1973.

[35] M. Pomerance, 'Case Analysis: The ICJ and South West Africa (Namibia): A Retrospective Legal/Political Assessment,' 12 *Leiden Journal of International Law* 425 (1999); E. Gross, 'Ethiopia and Liberia *vs.* South Africa: The South West Africa cases (1968); J. Stevenson, *South West Africa Cases* (Ethiopia *vs.* South Africa; Liberia *vs.* South Africa), Second Phase,' 61 *American Journal of International Law* 116 (1967); R. Falk, 'The South West Africa Cases: An Appraisal,' 21 *International Organization* 1 (1967); G. Wynne, 'Grounds for Revision of the Judgment of the International Court of Justice of 21st December, 1962, That It Had Jurisdiction to Adjudicate upon the South West Africa Case: Ad Hoc Judge Improperly Chosen as Liberia Had No Locus Standi,' 81 *South African Law Journal* 449 (1964).

and the case was dismissed. Implicit in the Court's reasoning was the idea that the issue on the merits was a political rather than a juridical issue.

The decision caused an international firestorm. The apartheid regime saw the case as a victory and at least some sort of validation of apartheid. The General Assembly was seized of the matter and it terminated the mandate by a resolution and declared South West Africa to be a direct responsibility of the UN. It should be noted that the UNGA had been studying the apartheid problem since the late 1940s and had early on determined that apartheid was incompatible with the UN Charter. In 1967, the General Assembly established a UN Council for South West Africa to administer the territory until independence.[36] In 1968, the Council was renamed the UN Council for Namibia in accordance with the wishes of the people in the territory.[37] In 1969, the Security Council recognized the termination of the mandate by the GA as legal, concluded that the presence of South Africa in the territory was unlawful and called for South Africa to withdraw. In 1970, the Council declared that all activity of South Africa after the termination of the mandate was 'illegal and invalid.'[38]

The matter was sent back to the ICJ to consider the consequences for the world community of the termination of the mandate by the UN. This effectually permitted the ICJ to adjudicate the merits of the case that it had avoided in 1966. The judgment of the Court was a path-breaking judgment in international law. It upheld the decision to terminate the mandate, determined that apartheid was incompatible with international law, including human rights law, and further determined that the Universal Declaration itself had gravitated from a moral obligation to a juridically enforceable customary international law standard. The Namibia litigation had far-reaching implications for the status of apartheid in international law, provided an impetus for the development of the idea that apartheid is an international crime.

The Namibian issue was sent again to the ICJ for a determination of the consequences for the rest of the world community of the termination of the mandate by the UN. The ICJ had to craft its decision by deciding that apartheid was a contravention of the most important legal expectations of modern international law. It was Namibia, a class C mandate, that

---

[36] 'United Nations: Report of UN Council for South West Africa,' 7 *International Legal Materials* (ILM) 104 (1968).

[37] United Nations Council for Namibia, *United Nations Council for Namibia: What It Is, What It Does, How It Works* (United Nations Office of Public Information, 1975).

[38] Y. Ronen, *Transition from Illegal Regimes under International Law* (Cambridge University Press, 2011), pp. 38-53.

highlighted the importance of a legal clarification of the application of policies of racial domination and subjugation of the apartheid State.

Palestine was a class A mandate and was considered to be a territory with a more advanced population on the pathway to self-determination. In the case of Namibia, it was assumed that the population would be less developed and more dependent on the mandatory power. Yet today, Namibia is a sovereign and independent State, and Palestine is not. Additionally, the policies and practices of apartheid reflecting domination and subjugation have many essential characteristics that resemble the policy and the practice of the occupying power over the occupied territories of Palestine today.[39] And such policies and practices were consistently and authoritatively declared to be violations of international law.

The Palestine Mandate and Subsequent Developments

Namibia is free. Palestine is under the occupation of Israel. Regardless of possible breaches of mandate responsibilities by the United Kingdom (UK), the mandate responsibilities were passed on to the United Nations by the UK and the UN proceeded to take a decision on how the Palestine territory would evolve. This was done in Resolution 181, which indicated that the territory would be divided between two States, one Jewish and one Arab.[40] It also specified the borders and conditions for the recognition and consolidation of statehood. These conditions reflected the importance of basic rights of persons who were not Arab or Jewish and who resided in those parts of the territory designated for Jewish or Palestinian statehood. The Israeli Declaration of Independence highlighted an intention to create a State that would secure the equality of all persons regardless of religion or gender.[41] Regrettably, the Declaration did not gravitate to the status of a constitutional mandate in Israel. In 1967, Israel occupied Gaza and the West Bank. It then instituted a regime of control, which minimized Palestinian interests and maximized those of Israel.

It has been claimed that the regime of occupation designed to control and regulate Palestine has many elements that are similar to the regime of

---

[39] W. Nagan and A. Haddad, 'The Legal and Policy Implications of the Possibility of Palestinian Statehood,' *University of California Davis Journal of International Law and Policy* 343 (2012).

[40] UN Doc. A/RES/181(II), 29 November 1947.

[41] 'The Declaration of the Establishment of the State of Israel,' 1948, 1 LSI 3 (14 May 1948).

white supremacy in South Africa.[42] There has been an assertion that Zionism is apartheid by another name.[43] We are not certain that the approach to understanding the elements that constitute the repression of the crime of apartheid are best understood in abstract ideological terms. From a legal point of view, it is important that we explore the main outlines of the policy and practice of apartheid that gave rise to the position it now holds as a violation of international law. In order to do this, we must have an adequate descriptive definition of apartheid as a policy and practice, and we must consider whether the regime of occupation by Israel has sufficient gravitas to fall for prescriptive purposes within the terms of the treaty that renders apartheid. We must provide an operating definition of apartheid and an illustration of its complex regulatory and repressive scheme and then consider those aspects of Israeli policy and practice that are similar and therefore fall within the prohibited conduct.

The Social Process of Apartheid

Apartheid was the policy and practice of the ruling party of South Africa prior to the establishment of a government of reconciliation. South Africa had historically been subject to both colonial and imperial dominance, and the ethnographic picture of South Africa that emerged after World War II represented the ascendancy of the dominant Afrikaner elite. When the National Party won the elections of 1948, it began a programme of systematic racial discrimination designed to cover every facet of human intercourse for which there might be trans-group contact or interaction.[44]

The justification for apartheid was founded upon the philosophy of so-called Christian nationalism and was further rationalized under a neo-Hegelian formula known euphemistically as 'separate development.'[45] The edifice of apartheid was constructed along the lines of two legislative and administrative pillars. The first pillar was the creation of legislative prescription covering every phase of social organization, such as power

[42] L. Hajjar, *Courting Conflict: The Israeli Military Court System in the West Bank and Gaza* (University of California Press, 2005).
[43] D. Glaser, 'Zionism and Apartheid: A Moral Comparison,' 26 *Ethnic and Racial Studies* 3 (2003); R. Stevens, 'Zionism, South Africa and Apartheid: The Paradoxical Triangle,' 32 *Phylon* 123 (1971).
[44] D. O'Meara, *Forty lost years: The Apartheid State and the Politics of the National Party, 1948-1994* (Randburg: Ravan Press, 1996).
[45] *Ibid.* See also H. Wolpe, 'Capitalism and Cheap Labour-Power in South Africa: From Segregation to Apartheid,' 1 *Economy and Society* 4 (1972).

and economic exclusion, lack of fundamental respect, employment and professional relations, exclusion from health and social services, family relations, educational rights, and freedom of conscience and belief. This comprehensive scheme of prescription covering every value process in the social order was unique for its breadth and the detail of human interaction it sought to control, regulate, and ultimately disparage. Such a system could not endure, except for a further framework of legislative and administrative prescription designed to repress resistance to the application of these prescriptions and to severely punish and proscribe alternative or internationally sensitive values for the prospect of an alternative to apartheid.

The administrative pillar of apartheid involved the creation of a vast bureaucratic structure to ensure that the legislative dictates would be given operational efficacy on the ground. Thus, the educational bureaucracy was completely reorganized and structured along hierarchical ethnic lines. For example, there was a Bantu education department, a coloured education department, an Indian education department, and a department that focused on white education. With regard to racial classifications, there was a board whose specialization was to classify, especially marginal classes, according to race. In the context of affective ties and family relations there was a bureaucracy within the framework of police practices which sought to vigorously enforce the so-called Immorality Act which prohibited sex across racial lines. Even the framework of national security was collapsed into an apartheid-conditioned security management system. Indeed, the political 'management' of black South Africans was reduced to the concept of Bantu administration. These examples illustrate the importance of the administrative components of the Apartheid State.

The international system kept apartheid on its agenda of concern for a very long time and proceeded to document in detail the extent to which apartheid was incompatible with the international rule of law and with the expectations of human dignity built into the Charter. In order to proscribe apartheid as a crime against humanity, the international system borrowed from the tradition of the Nuremberg Charter. Thus, the Nuremberg and international law principles of individual responsibility for crimes against humanity were codified in the Apartheid Convention. Article I(1) of the Convention declared that 'apartheid is a crime against humanity' and 'that inhuman acts resulting from the policies and practices of apartheid . . . are crimes violating the principles of international law, in particular the purposes and principles of the Charter of the United Nations, and constitute a serious threat to international peace and security.' Article I(2) declared 'criminal those organizations, institutions and individuals committing the crime of apartheid.' Article IV(b) requires the adoption of measures to 'prosecute, bring to trial and punish . . . persons responsible for or accused of' acts constituting crimes under the Apartheid Convention.

The inclusion of the Nuremberg principles in the Apartheid Convention extended those principles to human rights violations caused by the apartheid regime authorities. The principles would have likely remained relevant since the international community had increasingly recognized the South African struggle against the illegitimacy of the apartheid regime and its massive human rights violations, as well as the applicability of the principles of decolonization, self-determination, and independence. This legal-political characterization of the South African problem made the Nuremberg principles concerning crimes against humanity and personal responsibility under international law directly applicable to South Africa in appropriate circumstances.[46]

The essential condition in racial domination is a pattern of identification that distinguishes the target of domination from the dominant group.[47] In apartheid, the systematics of domination as official governmental policy, edict, and practice rather dramatically sharpened the distinction between the 'in-group,' or the dominator, and the 'out-group,' or the dominated.[48] The domination is so ubiquitous and all-encompassing that the preconditions of widespread atrocity targeted at the 'out' victim group are significantly enhanced. The prospect of conflict becoming genocidal in character by threat becomes more ominous. Of course, genocide can occur without the systematics of apartheid, but an apartheid State reinforces the conditions that make genocide a realistic expectation. The social tensions generated by the imposition of apartheid can lead to genocide if the predisposition to exterminate emerges as a critical part of the principle of group dominance. In the context of apartheid, what is implicit and unconscious is in fact explicit and brutally overt.

Contested Issues of Land and Demographics

Land and demographics were central policy concerns of apartheid. They are also central concerns of important Israeli policy makers. In South

---

[46] A. Sparks, *Beyond the Miracle: Inside the new South Africa* (University of Chicago Press, 2003), p. 160;   L. Graybill, *Truth and Reconciliation in South Africa: Miracle or Model?* (Lynne Rienner Pub, 2002).

[47] W. Nagan and A. Haddad, 'Genocide & The Shoah (The Holocaust): Intellectual Tools for Education & Public Policy Decision,' 12 *Global Jurist* 1 (2012).

[48] W. Nagan, 'South Africa in Transition: Human Rights, Ethnicity and Law in the 1990s,' 35 *Villanova Law Review* 11 (1990).

Africa, there were two vital aspects of apartheid related to the issue of land rights. First, when South Africa assumed its mandate responsibilities for South West Africa under the League, it tried to annex South West Africa to South Africa using indirect, creeping annexation practices, which were often buried under administrative regulations. They did not succeed.[49] Later, South Africa tried to annex Walvis Bay openly but this, too, failed.[50]

The second aspect of South Africa's land policy had its foundation in an earlier law, 'The Natives Land Act of 1913.'[51] This Act declared that 87% of the South African land mass would be for whites only; 13% was for blacks. The Act was a massive expropriation measure. The blacks lost their lands, a critical basis for material survival. The planned consequence was to force blacks into wage labour to service the urban commercial sector. The State managed the flow of labour by a policy of influx control. The black land was allocated to poor white farmers. When apartheid's doctrine became more developed, this dispensation became the cornerstone of the apartheid objective; most of the land would be exclusively for the benefit of whites and would secure their nationality and citizenship rights; and small portion of the land would evolve into black Statelets called Bantustans. The plan required the forced removal of blacks remaining in 'white South Africa' to one of the appropriate Statelets. The drift of policy meant that blacks in 'white South Africa' had no citizenship rights, and could only experience these in an assigned black Statelet. The ideological description given this experiment was called 'Grand Apartheid.'[52]

A less grand version targeted the black and non-white communities living in 'white South Africa,' whose homes and businesses were subject to an administrative regime set up by the 'Group Areas Act.'[53] These communities could have their districts declared 'white areas.' They were

---

[49] Dugard, 'The Revocation of the Mandate for South West Africa,' *op. cit.*
[50] G. Evans, 'Walvis Bay: South Africa, Namibia and the Question of Sovereignty,' *International Affairs* 599 (1990); A. Wing, G. McDougall, E. Landis, and W. Nagan, 'The Recurrence of Hostilities in Namibia on the Eve of Implementation of Security Council Resolution 435,' in *Proceedings of the Annual Meeting* (American Society of International Law, 1989), pp. 350-365.
[51] P. Wickins, 'The Natives Land Act of 1913: A Cautionary Essay on Simple Explanations of Complex Change,' 49 *South African Journal of Economics* 65 (1981); 'The Natives Land Act of 1913' (Subsequently Renamed Bantu Land Act, 1913 and Black Land Act, 1913), Act No. 27 (1913).
[52] P. Vale, ''New Ways to Remember . . .': Community in Southern Africa,' 18 *International Relations* 73 (2004).
[53] A. Mabin, 'Comprehensive Segregation: The Origins of the Group Areas Act and Its Planning Apparatuses,' 18 *Journal of Southern African Studies* 405 (1992).

given a limited period in which to remove or be forcibly removed and have their homes bulldozed. Compensation paid for removal was nominal. Such is the picture generated by Grand and Petty Apartheid.

Palestine did not have its land claims settled under the British mandate. The mandate permitted Jewish emigration and occupation of lands in the mandated territory.[54] After Britain relinquished its mandate responsibilities to the UN, the UN General Assembly by Resolution 181 drew the boundaries of a Jewish State and an Arab State. The boundary question remained unsettled. After the Israeli occupation of Gaza and the West Bank, the UN Security Council made it clear that Israel could not have acquired these territories by the use of force. It affirmed that the occupied territories were ultimately a matter of Palestine patrimony. However, right-wing interests in Israel saw the occupation as an important wedge into the furtherance of a long-held right-wing Israeli ideal: the creation of a Greater Israel. The Israeli right wing has not made this an obvious part of its foreign policy. It has sought, along the lines of South Africa's earlier policy in Namibia, to promote a form of creeping annexation.

Along with this form of creeping annexation, the Israeli government has insisted that Israel be an exclusively ethnic Jewish State. This means that Israelis of Arab race are not included in future civic status. Even more problematic is the idea that Palestinians in the occupied territories will, by definition, be non-Jewish and regarded as foreigners. To the extent that they remain present, they will have no civil and political rights. In this sense, the right-wing Israeli elite have the land ambitions that were identified with the Grand Apartheid scheme and the role of Statelets within that scheme. A programme of annexation will never be one of complete ethnic cleansing. There will be rather truncated, unviable pockets to house the Palestinian population in circumstances that secure the non-development of these unviable pockets of Palestinian existence. It was South Africa's contention that the Bantustans would be unviable pockets of black existence in the context of an 'Eretz South Africa.'

Discrimination, Repression, and Domination

The regime of Israeli occupation of Palestine has many similarities to the regime of white ethnic domination in South Africa and Namibia. Central to the system is the importance of the badges of cultural identity that distinguish the dominator from the dominated. How the policies and practices are set in motion is not exactly the same, but they have similar

---

[54] See *supra* note 74.

consequences. Parallels would have to be drawn with the law that assigns to certain classes of Palestinians the status of absentee. This status is a form of denationalization and it resembles the policy and practice of apartheid in the effort to Balkanize South Africa.

Prior to apartheid, the South African government enacted the 'Natives Land Act of 1913,' which was a massive act of uncompensated expropriation that reserved, as noted above, 13% of the land for blacks in which they could exercise ownership and 87% exclusively for whites. The apartheid regime sought to extend the implications of this Act by creating fictional States in which blacks could exercise national rights. At the same time, this meant that blacks living outside the 'homelands' had no rights. The parallels between the issue of land rights, absentee rights, and human rights abuses are not precise but they largely have the same civic and socio-economic consequences. Israeli pro-settler policy in the occupied territories also resembles an element of creeping annexation. As indicated earlier, South Africa tried to annex Walvis Bay in Namibia but the UN strongly denied it the right to do so.

Palestinians live under permanent national security emergency regulations imposed by Israeli army, which virtually mean the complete extinction of civil and political rights. South Africa under apartheid gravitated to such a position. Such situations leads to arrest without warrant, indefinite administrative detention, robust interrogation methods, often tantamount to torture, and other forms of cruel, unusual, and degrading treatment. The Israelis maintain thousands of prison populations of Palestinians and their treatment in these prisons is well below acceptable international standards. Control over the economy, in particular the labour market, implies that the conditions of labour for Palestinians are arduous, capricious, and sometimes coercive. Freedom of movement is so heavily monitored by Israeli security that to travel from one part of Palestine to another is both risky and often a nightmare. Access to healthcare is capriciously subject to the whims of roadblocks. Palestinians are often denied access to basic health care, frequently with lethal consequences. A more systematic approach to cataloguing the element of subjugation sufficient to constitute an international crime analogous to apartheid would be to look at the fundamental human rights issues in terms of value deprivations. Palestinians are denied the power of self-determination and correspondingly the power to declare statehood.[55]

---

[55] For more human rights violations by Israel in Palestine, see Chapter Four of this volume.

Resistance to Ethnic Cleansing

Just as South Africa generated a global antipathy to apartheid, there has been a growing antipathy to the policies and practices of Israeli hegemony, which are seen to have parallels to the policies and practices of apartheid. The policies and practices to further these objectives of an ethnically pure Israel and the importance of a programme to suppress the emergence of Palestinian identity and self-determination have the same general characteristics as apartheid at its height. Israeli policy makers have developed a systematic scheme for dominating and subjugating the Palestinian people which is reinforced by all the arsenals of a national security and garrison State. In this sense, the parallels to the apartheid regime are unmistaken. Like apartheid, the strategy of domination requires continual repression and fragmentation of the dominated. It includes the decapitation of leadership in order to destroy the will to survive and the will to struggle for the most important mandate and sacred trust of civilization, the right to self-determination and independence.

The right to self-determination is a peremptory principle of international law with *jus cogens* status. The policy currently pursued is one that carries many of the vestiges of colonialism and imperial conquest. These are matters that international law absolutely prohibits. It is therefore important that attention be drawn, not only to the activities of the Israeli security establishment, but also to those States and interest groups that aid and abet such activities in repudiation of some of key international law norms. Apart from the policy that undermines Palestinian identity and the right to self-determination, there are numerous other problems that also implicate fundamental international law standards: continuing occupation a breach of the right to peace; ongoing occupation an act of aggression against the Palestinian people; the rights of a protected people under humanitarian law violated; and routine human rights violations, including torture, extrajudicial execution, arbitrary detention, home demolition, restriction on freedom of movement, right to return and compensation for personal and property deprivations and land confiscation and expulsion of families.

These violations were characteristic of apartheid and were a vital inspiration for the development of the Convention that declares apartheid, and apartheid-like practices, to be crimes which violate international law. Since the concept and orientation of Grand Eretz Israel and Grand Eretz South Africa sought to create ethnically pure States via the strategies of ethnic cleansing and land appropriation, and then implemented these objectives by force, by ignoring humanitarian law, and by repudiating much of human rights law, the policies and practices of the Israeli right wing in the occupied territories have an apartheid-like character.

Conclusion

Netanyahu's position is amplified to excess by his Foreign Minister. 'The position of the Israeli Foreign Minister holds out even less hope for a settlement. Lieberman believes that the Palestinians cannot be a peace partner because they do not want peace. According to Lieberman, even 'if we offer the Palestinians Tel Aviv and they withdraw to the 1947 borders, they will find a reason not to sign the peace treaty.'' [56] Lieberman stresses that the Palestinians have no legitimate leaders. Lieberman states that in 'the present political circumstances, it is impossible for us to present a plan for a permanent settlement.' If Lieberman sees no final agreement, Netanyahu holds out for an interim agreement of multigenerational duration. The idea of an interim agreement simply means that settlement expansion will continue.

The most recent breaking development concerning settlement activity is that the Israeli government has apparently secured the assurance of a US veto.[57] The US has justified the veto on the ground that a resolution supporting a Palestinian State is an impediment to the process of direct negotiations between the Palestinians and Israel to secure a settlement. Israel rejected a US call for a temporary cessation of settlement-building in order to restart the negotiations. Israeli authorities have approved the construction of thousands of new Israeli housing units in East Jerusalem, on lands that ostensibly are within the dominion of the Palestinians.[58] Clearly, such a move undermines the representations made by the Israeli Prime Minister and the American President at the UN.

Only strong pressure, sufficiently significant to compel Israel to shift position, will make the difference. Without such pressure, Obama Administration is wasting its time. Critical to pressuring Israel will be a significant number of Congressional representatives, supporting the Administration and getting the major Jewish organizations in the US to be willing to support a realistic peace process. So long as the pro-Israel groups in the US provide support only to the Israeli ultranationalists, the greater will be the intransigence of the Israeli ultranationalists to commit

---

[56] U. Avnery, 'The Dwarfs,' *OpEdNews* (12 March 2011).
[57] A. Pfeffer, B. Ravid and S. Shamir, 'Palestinians Still Lack Security Council Majority for Statehood, UN Sources Say,' *Haaretz* (21 September 2011).
[58] H. Sherwood, 'Israel Approves New Settler Homes in East Jerusalem,' *The Guardian* (27 September 2011).

to a realistic peaceful settlement. This is not to say that Israeli ultra-nationalism is the exclusive stumbling block to a final resolution. But it certainly is a crucial threshold barrier.

Our discussion of the Apartheid Convention and its applicability to the regime of occupation by Israel of the Palestinian territories suggests that the Convention may influence opinion both inside and outside Israel to expedite the recognition of Palestinian statehood and independence. The price of ignoring the criminal implications of the regime's policy implies that the regime may be weakening its position in the international community, and skirting the line of international illegitimacy. There are other strategies that the UN General Assembly has promoted over the years to secure compliance with its mandate under international law.

The General Assembly produced a refined set of strategies: (1) desist from collaborating with the Government of South Africa, by taking steps to prohibit financial and economic interests under their jurisdiction from cooperating with the Government of South Africa and companies registered in South Africa; (2) prohibit airline and shipping lines registered in their countries from providing services to and from South Africa and deny all facilities to air flights and shipping services to and from South Africa; (3) refrain from extending loans, investments and technical assistance to the Government of South Africa and companies registered in South Africa; and (4) take appropriate measures to dissuade the main trading partners of South Africa and economic and financial interests from collaborating with the Government of South Africa and companies registered in South Africa.

Later the Security Council adopted a mandatory arms embargo against South Africa. It called for the total elimination of apartheid and urged UN members to adopt the following additional measures: (1) suspend all new investment in the Republic of South Africa; (2) prohibit the sale of Krugerrands and all other coins minted in South Africa; (3) restrict the field of sports and cultural relations; (4) stop guaranteed export loans; (5) prohibit all new contracts in the nuclear field; and (6) ban all sales of computer equipment that may be used by the South African army and police.

It remains for the Palestinian leadership and people to consider a very wide range of non-violent international strategies to secure statehood.

CHAPTER FIFTEEN

PALESTINE MEMBERSHIP
IN THE UNITED NATIONS:
OPPORTUNITIES TO CREATE A JUSTICE
SYSTEM THAT NEVER WAS

DAVID F. CHAVKIN

Introduction[*]

United Nations membership for Palestine presents critical opportunities to strengthen human dignity and expand economic opportunities in the West Bank and Gaza and throughout the region. In addition to these obvious implications, UN recognition also provides a unique opportunity for Palestine to become a beacon among nations through the establishment of a 'rule of justice' in the new nation.

In this chapter, I will discuss some of the characteristics of a true 'justice' system. Although many talk about the 'rule of law,' including representatives of the US Agency for International Development and the American Bar Association, what is really needed is a 'rule of justice' – a system that elevates fairness and equity above formalism. There are many parts to such a 'justice' system. While I will touch on a few of these parts, I will focus on the key role of universities in educating the lawyers, judges, and government officials of tomorrow.

Doing Justice

In the eulogy he delivered at the memorial service for his late brother and former United States Senator and Presidential candidate, Robert F.

---

[*] Allison Marie, my research fellow, provided valuable assistance in the development of this chapter.

Kennedy, Senator Edward M. Kennedy reminded the nation and the world
of the phrase perhaps most associated with his brother:

> 'As he said many times, in many parts of this nation, to those he touched
> and who sought to touch him: 'Some men see things as they are and say
> why. I dream things that never were and say why not'.'[1]

Imagine a justice system that does not yet exist in Palestine, in the
United States, or in any other country in the world – a justice system that
is modeled after the very struggle for freedom, independence, and human
dignity. Dr. Martin Luther King, Jr. remarked that, 'Human progress is
neither automatic nor inevitable . . . Every step toward the goal of justice
requires sacrifice, suffering, and struggle; the tireless exertions and
passionate concern of dedicated individuals.' Those who have sacrificed,
suffered, and struggled to get to this point in the life of a Palestinian State
know the truth of these remarks.

A Shared Vision of Justice

Whether one comes from an Islamic, Christian or, as in my case, from
a Jewish tradition, there is a shared vision of justice. The Qur'an contains
the following passage:

> 'Allah commands you to deliver trusts to those worthy of them; and when
> you judge between people, to judge with justice. Excellent is the
> admonition Allah gives you. Allah is All-Hearing, All-Seeing.'[2]

Similarly, in the Old Testament, the following passage appears:

---

[1] Address at the Public Memorial Service for Robert F. Kennedy, delivered 8 June
1968 at St. Patrick's Cathedral, New York. This phrase originates in a speech by
the 'Serpent' in *Back to Methusaleh*, a play written by George Bernard Shaw in
1921. The actual phrase that appears in the text of the play is as follows: 'THE
SERPENT. If I can do that, what can I not do? I tell you I am very subtle. *When
you and Adam talk, I hear you say 'Why?' Always 'Why?' You see things; and you
say 'Why?' But I dream things that never were; and I say 'Why not?'* I made the
word dead to describe my old skin that I cast when I am renewed. I call that
renewal being born.' *Back to Methuselah (A Metabiological Pentateuch)*, by
George Bernard Shaw, *available at* http://www.gutenberg.org/files/13084/13084-
8.txt (last visited 22 May 2012) (emphasis added). The original meaning is
therefore quite different from the more contemporary usage of the phrase as an
appeal to dream about a better future.
[2] *An-Nisa', 4:58.*

'What does HaShem require of you but to do justice, love mercy, and behave modestly?'[3]

And, in the New Testament, we are reminded of the parable of the unjust judge:

> 'And he spake a parable unto them to this end, that men ought always to pray, and not to faint; Saying, There was in a city a judge, which feared not God, neither regarded man: And there was a widow in that city; and she came unto him, saying, Avenge me of mine adversary. And he would not for a while: but afterward he said within himself, Though I fear not God, nor regard man; Yet because this widow troubleth me, I will avenge her, lest by her continual coming she weary me. And the Lord said, Hear what the unjust judge saith.'[4]

If we start from the goal that we want to produce - a justice system *that does justice* - how do we design it from the bottom up to produce that result? This approach is similar to the architectural concept of 'form follows function.'[5] We start with the end and then determine the means necessary to achieve those ends. These means necessarily begin with the

---

[3] *Micah* 6:8. The Talmud credits the prophet, Micah, with summarizing the Torah's 613 commandments in these three principles. Torah.org, *What Is Known About the Prophet Micah?*, available at
http://www.torah.org/qanda/seequanda.php?id=167# (last visited 22 May 2012). This passage is sometimes translated as 'What doth the Lord require of thee? Only to do justice and to love mercy, and to walk humbly with thy God.' *Micah* 6:8 (King James).

[4] *Luke* 18:1-6 (King James).

[5] The use of the phrase 'form follows function' is sometimes ascribed to the American sculptor Horatio Greenough. It is probably more accurate to credit the American architect Louis Sullivan. In his 1896 article, 'The Tall Office Building Artistically Considered,' Sullivan wrote 'form ever follows function.' The phrase appears in the article as: 'Whether it be the sweeping eagle in his flight or the open apple blossom the toiling work horse, the blithe swan, the branching oak, the winding stream at its base, the drifting clouds, over all the coursing sun, form ever follows function, and this is the law. . . . It is the pervading law of all things organic and inorganic, of all things physical and metaphysical, of all things human and all things superhuman, of all true manifestations of the head, of the heart, of the soul, that the life is recognizable in its expression, that form ever follows function. This is the law. Shall we, then, daily violate this law in our art?' The full text of the article appears at
http://academics.triton.edu/faculty/fheitzman/tallofficebuilding.html (last visited 15 March 2012).

essential process of selecting and educating future lawyers.[6] It is therefore especially appropriate that the conference that was the impetus for this article/chapter was sponsored by Hebron University, a university that is part of the effort in Palestine to educate more effective and responsible lawyers,[7] and included representatives of Al-Quds University, the first university to support a for-credit legal clinic in the Arab world.[8]

To return to the metaphor of 'dreaming,' it is important to recognize that models in other countries have proven to be woefully inadequate. Most legal educators have been incredibly timid in responding to the challenges presented in reports like the Carnegie Foundation Report.[9] Why

---

[6] By focusing on the role of legal education in improving the justice system in the new State I do not mean to suggest that other aspects of justice system reform are not also important. This chapter is necessarily limited in scope. However, the independence of Palestine presents opportunities to fundamentally alter the role of the Palestinian Bar from a self-protective guild to a public service-oriented entity that envisions law as a moral profession rather than an entity focused on the protection of the financial health of its members.

[7] The role of the Hebron University (HU) Legal Clinic as an organizer of this conference is especially relevant to my remarks on the importance of experiential education.

[8] D. Chavkin, 'Thinking/Practicing Clinical Legal Education from within the Palestinian-Israeli Conflict: Lessons from the Al-Quds Human Rights Clinic,' 18 *Human Rights Brief* 14 (2010).

[9] For a more detailed discussion of the Carnegie Foundation Report, see discussion below, The Carnegie and Best Practices Reports. The authors of the Carnegie Foundation Report concluded that, 'we think that practice-oriented courses can provide important motivation for engaging with the moral dimensions of professional life – a motivation that is rarely accorded status or emphasis in the present curriculum.' W. Sullivan, A. Colby, J. Wegner, L. Bond, and L. Shulman, *Educating Lawyers: Preparation for the Profession of Law* 88 (Carnegie Foundation for the Advancement of Teaching, 2007), hereinafter 'Educating Lawyers' or 'Carnegie Foundation Report.' They also concluded that, 'legal educators will have to do more than shuffle the existing pieces. The problem demands their careful rethinking of both the existing curriculum and the pedagogies that law schools employ to produce a more coherent and integrated initiation into a life in the law.' *Ibid.* at 147. In adopting the model proposed in this text, I am suggesting a very different model along the 'continuum of teaching and learning' than those identified by the Report authors. *Ibid.* Of course, the authors of the Carnegie Foundation Report were not the first to challenge legal educators to do better with regard to the teaching of skills and values. In 1984, the American Bar Association Board of Governors established a Commission on Professionalism, whose final report was released in 1986. American Bar Association, *Teaching and Learning Professionalism: Report of the Professionalism Committee* (ABA Section of Legal Education and Admission to the Bar, 1996).

should we tinker around the edges when a fundamental change in legal education is really necessary?[10] Would it not make more sense to build an 'andragogical' model for doctrinal, practice and formative goals that looks more like the clinical legal education model that I believe is the best model for inculcating skills and values?[11] And, should we not heed the warning sounded by Andrew Watson about the limitations of freestanding ethics

---

[10] See J. Frank, 'Why Not A Clinical-Lawyer School?' 81 *University of Pennsylvania Law Review* 907 (1933), p. 916 ('What would we think of a medical school in which students studied no more than what was to be found in such written or printed case-histories and were deprived of all clinical experience until after they received their M.D. degrees?').

[11] In using the term 'clinical legal education,' I mean the following: 'Clinical education is first and foremost a method of teaching. Among the principal aspects of that method are these features: students are confronted with problem situations of the sort that lawyers confront in practice; the students deal with the problem in role; the students are required to interact with others in attempts to identify and solve the problem; and, perhaps most critically, the student performance is subjected to intensive critical review.' *Report of the Committee on the Future of the In-House Clinic*, 42 *Journal of Legal Education* 508 (1992), p. 511. The essence of this model is learning by doing with critical reflection of both the learning and doing steps. This resonates with the ancient Chinese proverb that is often attributed to Confucius: 'I hear, and I forget. I see, and I remember. I do, and I understand.' In the western world, Aristotle's observations about learning by doing came approximately 100 years after Confucius and it was nearly another 400 years before Julius Caesar wrote in *De Bello Civili* (circa 52 B.C.) that 'Experience is the teacher of all things' and another 100 years after that before Pliny the Elder wrote in *Naturalis Historia* (circa 77 A.D.) that 'Experience is the most efficient teacher of all things.' Kenneth Kreiling has described the process of clinical education in the following way: 'Traditional classroom legal education primarily is concerned with the process of learning through information assimilation. Usually the information to be assimilated is applied within the narrowly circumscribed confines of the instructor-defined classroom. In contrast, clinical education is primarily concerned with the process of learning from actual experience, learning through taking action (or observing someone else taking action) and then analyzing the effects of the action. The data of learning are provided primarily by the students' actual performances and experiences with clients who have legal problems. Such problems arise in a world where some facts cannot be ascertained, where personal qualities and interpersonal relationships often are crucial, where the 'problem-solver' must take action and choose solutions while faced with unforeseeable contingencies. Clinical education provides a model of the multi-dimensional world of practice that traditional legal classroom education simply cannot provide.' K. Kreiling, 'Clinical Education and Lawyer Competency: The Process of Learning to Learn from Experience Through Properly Structured Clinical Supervision,' 40 *Maryland Law Review* 284 (1981), pp. 285-86.

courses and of attempting to alter the values of adults through classroom teaching:

> 'The present practice of giving a single course seems about as logical as keeping a medical student in laboratories during the four years of medical school and then turning him out upon an innocent population after a one-hour course in 'medical practice.' He would assuredly be lost, and so would his patients.'[12]

Commentators often focus on the differences between the 'American' model of legal education and the 'continental' model of legal education that Palestine has inherited through the collective influences of the Ottoman Empire, the British Empire, and numerous other imperialist regimes that have deprived Palestinians of self-government and national identity. However, the two systems are really far more similar than they are different. Whether targeted at undergraduate or graduate students, education in both models is largely passive and contrary to every principle of effective adult learning. Then, upon graduation, having largely abdicated their responsibilities to produce law graduates with the skills to be effective and the values to be responsible, law schools thrust on practicing lawyers and judges the responsibility for turning their graduates into lawyers. This process takes place with inadequate control of quality of experience, with varying levels of professional commitment to student development, and with inconsistent models of training in skills and values.

I am hardly the first person to indict university education generally or the model of legal education practiced in Palestine specifically. President Sari Nusseibeh of Al-Quds University has written:

'To quote Kant, it [the student body] was a crooked piece of timber that I now had to straighten out . . . . It was a daunting prospect to reform an institution dominated by a political-religious movement systematically throwing shackles on the mind . . . . I traced the source of the disease to a tradition of learning that embodied everything wrong with Palestinian education . . . . Rote learning was the norm at Al-Quds, a parrotlike repetition of facts closely aligned with social conformity. Students for the most part reproduced existing social norms, thus merely adding more conformists to a social system already resistant to change and criticism.'[13]

The product of this model of legal education is barely short of calamitous. Legal education by academics, who are generally unfamiliar

---

[12] A. Watson, 'Some Psychological Aspects of Teaching Professional Responsibility,' 16 *Journal of Legal Education* 1 (1964), p. 20.
[13] S. Nusseibeh and A. David, *Once upon a Country: A Palestinian Life* (Farrar, Straus & Giroux, 2007), p. 389.

with practice and often overtly hostile to it, focuses on the development of doctrinal knowledge that bears small relationship to the actual practice of law and that is often outdated before it is put into use. At the same time, the skills required for effective representation and the values required for responsible representation are largely ignored until after graduation. When they are addressed, whether through formal or informal apprenticeships, they are taught by practitioners whose primary responsibility is to clients and whose teaching and practice skills and values are often suspect.

Acknowledging my Assumptions about Legal Education

In challenging the current models of legal education and in suggesting a blueprint for change in an independent Palestine, it is important to acknowledge the assumptions about legal education that I bring to the table. Like views about religion, many of these assumptions are articles of faith that cannot be proven rationally and that are subject to challenge. At the same time, I do believe that they are correct and they therefore drive both my analysis and my daily work.

First, legal education has a responsibility to improve the profession. There are many law deans and faculty members, especially at law schools at which I have taught overseas, who disagree with this view. They believe that law schools, particularly those that are part of universities, have a responsibility that begins and ends with the development and dissemination of knowledge. I take a very different view of the responsibility of law schools. Without diminishing the importance of knowledge development and dissemination, I think that law schools can and must do more in making societies more just. That means that one of the values that law school teachers must inculcate in students is a public service ethic – a sense of responsibility to improve the justice system by improving the operation of that system and in making access to justice possible for more people. This responsibility belongs to all attorneys – those who practice public law and those who practice private law; those who practice in government and those who practice in the private sector; those who serve as judges, those who serve as prosecuting attorneys, and those who serve as defense attorneys.

Second, I believe that law schools need to develop law graduates who will be *effective* and *responsible* as attorneys. *Effective* lawyers have the skills necessary to practice effectively. These skills include interviewing, theory of the client development and implementation, fact investigation, counseling, negotiation, and trial skills.[14] *Responsible* lawyers have the values necessary to practice responsibly. These values include respect for client autonomy, respect for the rights of third persons, civility, and personal integrity. Law school curriculums would need to be reformed to develop these skills and values in law school.

Third, I believe that legal education needs to be made accessible to all qualified students. That means that financial costs leading to a law degree should not present an insurmountable barrier and that students should not graduate with such heavy debt loads that their career choices are necessarily circumscribed. It also means that non-financial barriers, like scheduling of classes solely in the day, need to be eliminated to increase access for students who work full-time in the day, for students who have child-care or adult-care responsibilities during daylight hours, or who have other daytime obligations.

Breaking the Current Pattern

The first step in breaking this pattern of irrelevant and mediocre legal education is to develop a consensus within our institutions (and, preferably, within academia more generally) about what we are trying to produce. Students come through our doors at the beginning of their legal education. They exit those doors at the end of three or four or five years in our institutions. How should they be different - inside and out?

I recently attended a conference sponsored by the Association of American Law Schools regarding curriculum reform. At various times throughout the conference presenters and discussants conflated topics of teaching goals, teaching techniques, teaching contexts, and teaching assessments. However, at no time was there a discussion of the basic outcomes we want to achieve in our students.[15] What values should they possess on graduation/commencement? What skills should they be able to bring to their first job? If, as is often stated by architects, form is to follow function, we must first develop a consensus regarding the function of legal

---

[14] These skills are described at greater length in D. Chavkin, *Clinical Legal Education* (Anderson Publishing, 2002).

[15] That is not to say that there was no discussion of values. For example, Professor Robert Gordon presented a paper entitled 'Core Values and Models of Legal Education.' Core values that we might share are important. However, they are simply not the same as educational outcomes for students that should drive curriculum reform and teaching models. This topic is discussed more in Conference on the Future of the Law School Curriculum, Association of American Law Schools (11-14 June 2011).

education. Today, too often, form follows financing in the design of curriculum, in the structure of classes, and in the excessive focus on doctrine.

Changing the Nature of the Legal Academy

Second, we need to develop a new cadre of what I will call 'academic practitioners.' These academic *practitioners* would come to academia with an extensive background in actual practice and they would renew these practice experiences periodically in settings relevant to their teaching and scholarship interests. However, as *academic* practitioners, they would spend full time working in academia with their primary commitment being the education of their students. Secondarily, they would be in a unique position, at the intersection of theory and practice, to develop scholarship that would guide the development of legal doctrine, practice skills, and values.

There are some academics who meet this description already. However, in general, academia does not value (and often aggressively devalues) practice experience, regarding it as something that sullies, rather than advances, academic effectiveness. And practitioners who enter academia in clinical teaching positions too often view their sinecure as an opportunity to be a social change agent, with little sense of responsibility to students. So, in many ways, we experience the worst of all possible worlds – academics without practical context and practitioners without theoretical perspective.

Building Legal Education on a Broad Base

I also believe that the primary legal degree should be a hybrid degree – between the graduate degree required in the United States and a few other countries and the undergraduate degree required in Palestine and many other countries. There are several reasons for this belief.

First, educating undergraduates in law ignores the fact that a large number (in many countries, a majority) of the students will never enter the practice of law. These students will enter business or some other field and make little use of the doctrinal lectures or Socratic dialogues that characterized their undergraduate years.

Second, educating undergraduates in law means that they are necessarily deprived of exposure to many subjects that are essential for a responsible and effective lawyer. These subjects include human psychology, macro- and micro-economics, philosophy, humanities, social sciences and natural sciences.[16] No lawyer can effectively and responsibly practice in any capacity without a basic grounding in these areas of knowledge.

I do not mean to suggest that undergraduate education in countries like the United States and Japan is entirely successful in providing a base on which to develop responsible and effective lawyers. Too many students in these systems either specialize too early or never learn basic knowledge about people and society that they will need in the practice of law. However, the chances are greater that this base of knowledge will be developed in an undergraduate education focused on breadth, not depth. A hybrid model will unite the best aspects of both the undergraduate and graduate models.

Shortening Undergraduate Education to Three Years

While I am a big believer in the benefits of a broad undergraduate education for lawyers and their clients, I do not believe that four years of undergraduate education are required to yield these dividends. In some ways, the standard of a four-year undergraduate education is both too much and too little. Students would certainly benefit from an even longer exposure to the humanities and social and physical sciences. However, at some point one must balance the incremental benefits of another year against the significant fiscal costs of another year. And, so much of the undergraduate period is spent in becoming an adult (and exploring extracurricular pursuits). For reasons of cost-effectiveness, I would therefore limit the broad grounding in law as part of the undergraduate degrees to three years.

Shortening the Legal Education Component to Two Years

Legal education is expensive. If lawyers, their clients, and society benefitted from the total time spent in law school, then one could justify these costs. However, it is hard to argue that anyone realizes sufficient benefits from a third year of legal education.

---

[16] The need for increased exposure to the humanities is an insight hardly unique to this author. See M. Nussbaum, *Not for Profit: Why Democracy Needs the Humanities* (Princeton University Press, 2010) (expressing her alarm at the degree to which the humanities are pushed aside in all educational systems around the world in favour of subjects more clearly linked to economic growth). The United States is certainly not a country to emulate in this area of education. See D. Vise, 'College Ratings Ignites Debate Over Core Requirements,' *Washington Post* (20 November 2010).

The American comment that 'First year they scare you; Second year they work you; Third year they bore you' is all too true. In too many law schools and for too many law students, legal education is a repetitive and relatively unproductive experience of drawing theory from the reading of appellate cases or the learning of doctrine that will change over the course of a career. Over and over again, the same skills are tested, even as the subject matter changes. With a clearer vision of the educational outcomes that we wish to produce and with a more effective educational model for achieving those outcomes, two years of full-time legal education should be sufficient.

Integrating Adult Learning Principles into Education

Legal education needs to incorporate adult learning theory through development of an andragogical model.[17] Unfortunately, learning is not always the goal of education. Too much education focuses on the transmission and temporary retention of information and not on the development of knowledge. I therefore adopt for these purposes the definition of learning articulated by L.D. and A. Crow:

'Learning involves change. It is concerned with the acquisition of habits, knowledge, and attitudes. It enables the individual to make both personal and social adjustments. Since the concept of change is inherent in the concept of learning, any change in behaviour implies that learning is

---

[17] The concept was popularized (perhaps a somewhat generous description) in the United States by Malcolm Knowles. M. Knowles, 'Andragogy, Not Pedagogy,' in 16 *Adult Leadership* (1968), pp. 350–86. Knowles enunciated six principles that are essential for adult learning: 1) The learners feel a need to learn; 2) The learning environment is characterized by physical comfort, mutual trust and respect, mutual helpfulness, freedom of expression, and acceptance of differences; 3) The learners perceive the goals of a learning experience to be their goals; 4) The learners accept a share of the responsibility for planning and operating a learning experience, and therefore have a feeling of commitment toward it. The learners participate actively in the learning process; 5) The learning process is related to and makes use of the experience of the learners; and, 6) The learners have a sense of progress toward their goals. M. Knowles, *The Modern Practice of Adult Education: From Pedagogy to Andragogy* (Cambridge Book Co. 1988), pp. 57-58. For a more comprehensive discussion of adult learning theory, see M. Knowles, E. Holton III, and R. Swanson, *The Adult Leader* (Butterworth-Heinemann, 2005). For a discussion of the application of these principles in the context of legal education, see F. Bloch, *The Andragogical Basis of Clinical Legal Education*, 35 *Vanderbilt Law Review* 321 (1982).

taking place or has taken place. Learning that occurs during the process of change can be referred to as the *learning process.*'[18]

In referring to 'habits, knowledge, and attitudes,' we might just as easily substitute the synonyms of 'practice, doctrine, and values.' In substituting these terms, I am incorporating the terminology used in the Carnegie Foundation Report in its critique of American legal education.

With this perspective on adult learning in mind, what should a legal education look like? As I answer that question, I am guided by the principle enunciated by John Dewey that 'All genuine education comes about through experience.'[19]

The Carnegie and Best Practices Reports

Fortunately, in reconceptualising the process of legal education,[20] we do not need to start with a blank slate. Two recent reports provide us with a blueprint for educational reform even as they criticize the current state of American legal education and, by implication, legal education around the world.

In 2007, the Carnegie Foundation for the Advancement of Teaching issued its report on American Legal Education – Educating Lawyers: Preparation for the Profession of Law.[21] Although I believe that the choice of language was unfortunate, the authors identified three 'apprenticeships'[22] for legal education:[23]

---

[18] L. Crow and A. Crow, 'Meaning and Scope of Learning,' in L. Crow and A. Crow, eds., *Readings in Human Learning* (1963), Vol. 1, p. 1.

[19] J. Dewey, *Experience and Education* 13 (Macmillan, 1938).

[20] I use the term 'process' purposefully because Knowles described the 'andragogical model' as 'a process model, in contrast to the content models employed by most traditional educators.' Knowles, Holton III, and Swanson, *op. cit.*, p. 115. As Knowles explained, 'The difference is not that one deals with content and the other does not; the difference is that the content model is concerned with transmitting information and skills, whereas the process model is concerned with providing procedures and resources for helping learners acquire information and skills.' *Ibid.*

[21] *Educating Lawyers, op. cit.* The Carnegie Foundation for the Advancement of Teaching has conducted numerous studies of professional education. *Educating Lawyers* is part of a series of reports on professional education issued by the Foundation through its Preparation for the Professions Program.

[22] As the authors explain, 'the metaphor of apprenticeship sheds useful light on the practices of professional education. . . . [W]e . . . extend it [the metaphor] to the whole range of imperatives confronting professional education. So we speak of three apprenticeships. The signature pedagogies of each professional field all have

'The first apprenticeship, . . . intellectual or cognitive, focuses the student on the knowledge and way of thinking of the profession . . . . The . . . second apprenticeship is to the forms of expert practice shared by competent practitioners. . . . The third apprenticeship, . . . identity and purpose, introduces students to the purposes and attitudes that are guided by the values for which the professional community is responsible.'[24]

Critical for my thinking was the recognition in the Carnegie Foundation Report that experiential learning is necessary to achieve the goals of the second and third apprenticeships.[25] And, while the Report did not mandate real-life client representation as the modality for the 'values' apprenticeship, it did acknowledge that 'Much of the humanizing and inspiring aspects of the law have always resided in actual contact with clients and their needs.'[26]

At the same time that the Carnegie Foundation Report was being prepared by adult learning theorists, a group of American legal educators and practitioners began working together to develop a statement of best practices in legal education.[27] Complementing the findings and recommendations of the Carnegie Foundation Report,[28] the Best Practices

---

to confront a common task: preparing students . . . to think, to perform, and to conduct themselves like professionals.' *Ibid.*, p. 27.

[23] My quarrel is with the choice of the word 'apprenticeship.' I worry that the term will conjure up the kind of post-graduate apprenticeship still used in many countries to compensate for the shortcomings of legal education. As discussed below, I am very critical of these apprenticeships – whether primarily informal as in the United States, or formal as in much of the rest of the world.

[24] *Educating Lawyers, op. cit.*, p. 28. In the Report, the authors later define the cognitive apprenticeship as '[t]he teaching of legal doctrine and analysis, which provides the basis for professional growth.' *Ibid.*, p. 194. The authors define the practice apprenticeship as '[a]n introduction to the several facets of practice included under the rubric of lawyering, leading to acting with responsibility for clients.' *Ibid.* The authors define the formative apprenticeship as '[a] theoretical and practical emphasis on inculcation of the identity, values, and dispositions consonant with the fundamental purposes of the legal profession.' *Ibid.*

[25] *Ibid.*, p. 28 ('In this second apprenticeship, students learn by taking part in simulated practice situations, as in case studies, or in actual clinical experience with real clients. . . . [The] lessons [of the third apprenticeship] are also ideally taught through dramatic pedagogies of simulation and participation.')

[26] *Ibid.*, 33.

[27] R. Stuckey, *Best Practices for Legal Education: A Vision and A Road Map* (Clinical Legal Education Association 2007). A description of the process used in preparing the report is available through the Clinical Legal Education Association website, http://www.cleaweb.org/best-practices (last visited on 4 June 2012).

[28] There was considerable cross-fertilization between the two reports. *Ibid.*, p. x.

Report concluded that: 'While law schools help students acquire some of the essential skills and knowledge required for law practice, most law schools are not committed to preparing students for practice.'[29] To counteract this shortcoming, the report authors recommended that: 'Law schools should help students acquire the attributes of effective, responsible lawyers including self-reflection and lifelong learning skills, intellectual and analytical skills, core knowledge and understanding of law, professional skills, and professionalism.'[30] In order to achieve this result, law professors need to incorporate learning theory into their teaching and recognize that: 'Optimal learning from experience involves a continuous, circular four stage sequence of experience, reflection, theory, and application.'[31]

This observation parallels the work of David Kolb, a Professor of Organizational Behaviour at Case Western Reserve University. In language similar to that used by Knowles, Kolb defined 'learning' as 'the process whereby knowledge is created through the transformation of experience.'[32] Building on the work of Kurt Lewin,[33] Kolb adapted and enhanced the 'Lewinian Experiential Learning Model' set forth below.[34]

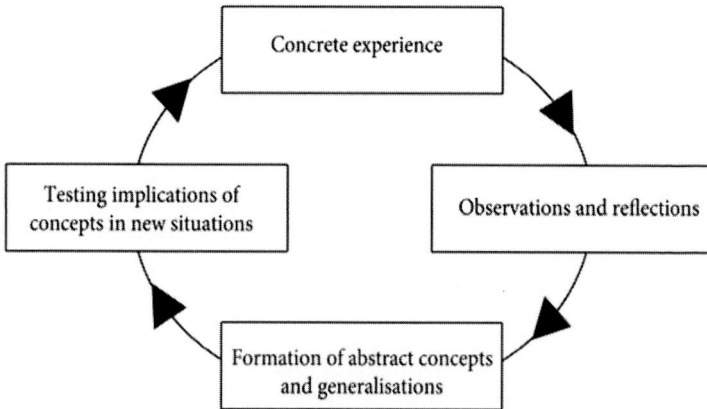

---

[29] *Ibid.*, p. 5.
[30] *Ibid.*, p. 6.
[31] *Ibid.*, p. 122.
[32] D. Kolb, *Experiential Learning: Experience as the Source of Learning and Development* (Prentice Hall, 1983), p. 38.
[33] Kolb described Lewin as the founder of American social psychology. *Ibid.*, p. 8.
[34] *Ibid.*, p. 21.

I will use this model as I describe the blueprint for a very different vision of legal education.

Reconceptualising the First Year

Let us start with the first year. Most law schools treat the subjects in the first year as if they were separate unrelated topics. However, a particular injury to a client might have elements of property law, of contract law, of tort law, of civil procedure, of constitutional law, and of ethics. Despite that fact, when students are tested in a contracts examination, they know that the answer will be a 'contracts' answer, not a 'con-torts' answer. This ignores the fact that clients seldom come into a lawyer's office with the word 'contracts' or 'torts' stamped on their forehead.

One way to better integrate the teaching of doctrine would be to design teaching modules that transcend these artificial categories and provide a context for understanding clients and their problems. By starting with a client problem and then building to its ultimate resolution, class discussions can teach doctrine, practice and values while cutting across arbitrary course titles.

One of my favourite examples is the situation that confronted the California Supreme Court in *Moore v. The Regents of the University of California*.[35] In this case, a doctor (Golde) practicing at the University of California in Los Angeles, a State university, treated a patient (Moore) for a blood disease. Early on in the course of treatment, the doctor discovered that Moore possessed certain traits and factors that had potential commercial value. Although the doctor removed the patient's spleen and withdrew numerous blood samples over time, all of which may have been medically necessary, he did not disclose the commercial value of these products and used them for his own financial gain.

Imagine, for a moment, that an actor playing the role of the patient (bolstered by the transcripts and exhibits in the case) came into class on the first day and described his discovery that the doctor had secured a patent named after the patient. The patient now wants to determine his rights and possible remedies. Without having read any cases, students would then be divided into four- to five-person work groups in class to collaborate on possible rights of the patient and possible remedies for redress of those rights. Students would be problem-solving together with a focus on what the law might be, not merely what they have been told it is

---

[35] 793 P.2d 479 (Cal. Sup. Ct. 1990).

through the reading of statutes (in a civil law jurisdiction) or cases (in a common law jurisdiction).

With little prompting from instructors, students will begin to identify a variety of possibilities. Perhaps the doctor should have been required to obtain informed consent from the patient before touching him (or, at least, once the commercial possibilities were identified). Without using the words 'contract law' or 'property law' or 'criminal law,' students can brainstorm together creatively about the possibilities of lawsuits against the doctor and against the medical centre. Without using the words 'intellectual property,' students can brainstorm together creatively about the nature of intellectual property. Without using the word 'ethics,' students can brainstorm together creatively about the potential obligations of doctors and, by extension, lawyers to share all material information with their patients/clients. The exercise could then be turned on its head with the simulated interview of the doctor in the case.

Integrated, context-based learning is necessary, but it is not sufficient to train responsible and effective lawyers. The traditional first-year courses also provide an opportunity to bring experiential learning into the curriculum. By creating well-designed simulations, every aspect of every course taught in the first year can be explored through experiential learning. Students learn by doing, not by listening. And, throughout the course students can learn research and writing skills not as mere academic exercises, but rather in the context of these simulated cases. Along the way, students integrate broad values discussions into their representation of their clients in the simulated case. Students could draft pleadings, conduct fact investigations and legal research, engage in oral advocacy, counsel simulated clients and negotiate on their behalf.

Because I teach clinic students who have gone through my Civil Procedure course (or Civil Procedure courses taught by others through experiential learning techniques) as well as students who have learned Civil Procedure in a more traditional lecture or Socratic model, I get an opportunity to see the impact of these different teaching models on the learning of the students involved. While admittedly not a 'double blind' or even 'single blind' experiment, it is impossible to avoid the conclusion that students learn better in an experiential, context-based teaching model. One need only compare the blank faces of students from the traditional model with the anxious but more confident students from the experiential context-based model when assigned their first clients. The difference is too dramatic to miss.

Reconceptualising the Upper-level Curriculum

By the second year in the American legal system, students have completed most of their required courses and are ready to begin their upper-level curriculum. Students in my mental health law course, which is often taught by others as a traditional doctrinal course, are given the opportunity to represent real-life clients in real commitment proceedings. These students are given the opportunity to combine theory and practice with real-life client experiences. Similar opportunities exist with other courses to integrate theory and practice by expanding experiential learning opportunities. While I believe that these experiential learning opportunities are critical to adult learning, they should not be confused with clinical legal education – the ultimate model of andragogical learning.

One required course that ordinarily carries over into the second year is the course in legal ethics. Too often, this subject is taught as a rule-based doctrinal course. The result is that students may learn the rules sufficiently to pass the Multistate Professional Responsibility Examination,[36] but have little or no ability to identify ethical issues or to apply the rules of professional conduct in practice.

By contrast, I teach legal ethics through a course entitled 'Professional Responsibility Theory and Practice.'[37] Although we cover all of the issues of a traditional course, I have built in an experiential component in which students confront such ethical issues as capacity, conflict of interest, and confidentiality in the context of real-life client representation. Students engage in real-life client interactions as they draft wills and advance directives for low-income elderly clients.[38] Students actually understand the rules of professional conduct through their need to use those rules as personal guides to their lawyer-client relationships. They develop knowledge, not merely the ability to recite the rules.

---

[36] This is a national examination developed by the National Committee of Bar Examiners. See National Conference of Bar Examiners, The MPRE: http://www.ncbex.org/multiState-tests/mpre (last visited 30 May 2012). It is usually a requirement for admission to practice in the various States.

[37] This course model is described more fully in D. Chavkin, *Experience is the Only Teacher: Bringing Practice to the Teaching of Ethics*, in M. Robertson, L. Corbin, F. Bartlett and K. Tranter, eds., *The Ethics Project in Legal Education* 63 (Routledge, 2011), p. 63.

[38] Advance directives include durable powers of attorney for financial and medical decision-making and living wills. Durable powers of attorney authorize specified individuals to act on their behalf in the event of disability; living wills represent the decisions of the elderly person in case the individual is in a coma or other terminal condition and cannot make decisions for himself.

Expanding Clinical Legal Education

By the second year, students are ready to take on the role of lawyer in adversarial contexts in a clinical setting.[39] In most clinics in the United States, students are certified under student practice rules to represent real-life clients with a wide range of civil and criminal legal problems.[40] The properly-designed clinic is the ultimate example of andragogical experiential learning in legal education.[41] Students learn to become responsible[42] and effective[43] lawyers by assuming the role of lawyer in a setting in which they have the opportunity and faculty resources to engage in guided self-reflection of the process of lawyering and their role in that process. Years ago, Donald Schön referred to this approach to the education of professionals as 'reflection on knowing in action.'[44] It has taken us far too many years to get this point and too many law students have been cheated of effective and responsible education in the interim. While I believe that all well-designed experiential learning has benefits for students, I also believe that the full benefits can only be achieved in models in which students assume personal responsibility for client work and fulfil those responsibilities in real-life settings with real-life consequences.[45]

---

[39] In beginning clinical education in the second year, I do not intend to criticize those law schools, like Yale Law School, that have successfully started clinical education in the first year. I do think, however, that there is so much going on for most students in the first year that expensive clinical resources are best spent beginning in the second year.

[40] For a discussion of student practice rules in the United States, see D. Chavkin, 'Am I My Client's Lawyer?: Role Definition and the Clinical Supervisor,' 51 *SMU Law Review* (1998), 1507

[41] I use the adjective 'properly-designed' because not every course described as 'clinic' meets this standard. I describe the elements of a 'properly-designed' clinical experience in D. Chavkin, *Spinning Straw Into Gold: Exploring The Legacy of Bellow and Moulton*, 10 *Clinical Law Review* 245 (2003).

[42] They become responsible by developing the values required of 'responsible' lawyers.

[43] They become effective by developing the skills required of 'effective' lawyers.

[44] D. Schön, *The Reflective Practitioner: How Professionals Think in Action* (Basic Books, 1984), pp. 276-278; D. Schön, *Educating the Reflective Practitioner* (Jossey-Bass, 1987), pp. 22-31

[45] Chavkin, *Experience is the Only Teacher, op. cit.*

Eliminating Articles or Apprenticeships

The final question for an international audience is why we cannot simply leave the development of responsible and effective lawyers to the profession in apprenticeships or articles. There are several answers to that question, all of which argue for the integration of andragogical experiential learning in the law school environment.

First, the law graduate experience in apprenticeships or articles is too uneven. Some students have excellent educational experiences in their post-graduate experience. However, far too many students describe hours spent photocopying or delivering documents or writing memoranda no different in content and with less effective feedback than the students experienced in law school.

Second, the post-graduate experience is supervised by lawyers or judges who may not be effective educators. Law school professors are selected for their ability to teach, in addition to their responsibilities to develop scholarship and provide service. By contrast, lawyers or judges supervising students in apprenticeships or articles may not be effective teachers in providing guidance and facilitating self-reflection.

Third, the priority within the law school experience is on the education of the student. In apprenticeships or articles, the focus is on the delivery of services, whether in the form of legal representation by lawyers or rendering decisions by judges. This inherent conflict means that maximizing education of the law graduate may and will often need to be sacrificed to the realization of other goals.

Fourth, as we know from the andragogical model, autonomy and personal responsibility are critical elements of adult learning. In most apprenticeship or articles settings, with the possible exception of law graduates placed in State prosecutor offices, autonomy and personal responsibility are necessarily sacrificed because of the setting. Clients have retained lawyers, not law graduates, and judges may not delegate their professional responsibility to their clerks. Education is therefore necessarily compromised.

One could go on with criticisms of the apprenticeship model. However, the point is probably made by these four areas of focus. These reasons explain, at least in part, why American legal education largely abandoned the apprenticeship model starting in the late 1800s and why American legal education brought the clinical experience into law schools starting widely in the late 1960s.

Conclusion

We can do a far better job of educating future lawyers than we are doing today. The key to this improvement is to combine the teaching of theory and practice through a staged model that integrates adult learning theory into legal education. Beginning with simulations in the first year, this model uses real-life contexts to bring clients and their problems into legal education. It culminates in a model in which students assume the role of lawyer under the supervision of skilled educators/practitioners (whom I describe as academic practitioners) to enable students to develop the reflective practice skills and values that will ultimately improve the profession. Only through this model can we develop graduates who will truly serve society in the years ahead.

But, improving the delivery of legal education is only one aspect of improving legal practice. Law schools need to do a better job of recruiting law students from under-represented populations and in supporting them (financially and emotionally) while they are in law school. Within the profession, we need to build bar associations that are more concerned about advancing social justice than about protecting the financial health of members. We need to mandate pro bono service by lawyers and to provide career paths to judicial appointment and government service that encourages community service and commitment to the best ideals of the profession.

Although the term 'rule of law' is bandied about by many, including many Americans involved in American Bar Association and US Agency for International Development projects, what we really should be working for is a 'rule of justice.' The 'rule of law' can be formalistic and it can often elevate the technical over the spiritual. To build a 'justice system,' we need to be far more ambitious in our dreams and far more revolutionary in our agenda. The improvement of legal education is a critical first step.

CHAPTER SIXTEEN

THIRTEEN THESES ON A CONSTITUTION FOR A FEDERAL REPUBLIC OF PALESTINE[*]

URI DAVIS

Introduction

In this chapter, I make a distinction between racism, discrimination or racial discrimination as defined in Article 1(1) of the UN Convention on the Elimination of All Forms of Racial Discrimination of 1966,[1] on the one hand, and apartheid as a political system that regulates racism through acts of Parliament and imposes racialist choices on the inhabitants under its rule through the law enforcement instruments of the State (police courts/jail and army), on the other hand.

In the initial version of this chapter was entitled 'Owning-Up to Our Mistakes.' I submit that we, the PLO, as representatives of the Palestinian people, still have to hear from our leadership that the most serious mistake we have made since 1999 was the assumption that our primary enemy, political-Zionist apartheid Israel, was ready for a historical compromise, let alone for a historical compromise on the basis of the pre-1967 borders.

The fact that governmental choices are informed by perceived so-called 'national interests' is an apparent truism. What is not always fully recognized, however, is that civil society mobilization often affects governmental choices and that, over time, governments respond to civil

---

[*] A previous version of this chapter was submitted at Al-Quds University, Faculty of Law Conference on 'Drawing-Up the Palestinian Constitutions: Aspects and Challenges,' 7-8 May 2011.
[1] 'Any distinction, exclusion, restriction or preference based on race, colour, descent, or national or ethnic origin which has the purpose or effect of nullifying or impairing the recognition, enjoyment or exercise, on an equal footing, of human rights and fundamental freedoms in the political, economic, social, cultural or any other field of public life.'

society interventions (e.g., the anti-Vietnam war resistance inside the US
and internationally; the international anti-apartheid mobilization against
apartheid South Africa; and, I am confident, the BDS mobilization against
apartheid Israel).

After 20 years of Oslo negotiations, we know that the so-called 'peace
process' has been skillfully manipulated by apartheid Israel to advance its
primary 'national interest,' that is, its primary political-Zionist apartheid
interests, namely, settler-colonial greed, and that the international
consensus on a 'two-State' solution based on the 1949 armistice lines has
led us nowhere.

We need to go back to the drawing board, reconsider the paradigm of
a 'two-State' solution in terms that are consistent with the values of the
Universal Declaration of Human Rights, standards of international law and
all UN resolutions relevant to the question of Palestine. This is what I
propose to do in this chapter by elaborating thirteen principles (theses) for
the constitutional system of the State of Palestine as I see it.

Thesis One

The two-State solution based on the demarcation of the 1949 armistice
agreements between the apartheid State of Israel and its neighbouring
countries (otherwise known as 'the Green Line' and/or the '1967 borders')
has long been a chimera.

Thesis Two

The Palestine National Council (PNC) has correctly defined the aim of
the Palestinian resistance as the achievement of a just and long-term
solution of the Israeli-Palestinian conflict on the basis of the implementation
of *all* UN resolutions relevant to the question of Palestine, namely, on the
basis of a two-State solution as stipulated by the said UN resolutions and
the conditions of the admission of the State of Israel as a member State to
the UN.

Thesis Three

The most serious mistake we have made since 1999 was the
assumption that our primary enemy Political-Zionist apartheid Israel was
already ready for a historical compromise, let alone for a historical
compromise on the basis of the '1967 borders.'

Thesis Four

A Constitution for a sovereign and democratic Republic of Palestine as a Member State of the United Nations is a Constitution informed by the values of the UN Universal Declaration of Human Rights, and is compatible with the standards of international law, the UN Charter and *all* UN resolutions relevant to the question of Palestine.

Thesis Five

A Constitution for a sovereign and democratic Republic of Palestine as a Member State of the United Nations that is a Constitution informed by the values of the UN Universal Declaration of Human Rights, and is compatible with the standards of international law, the UN Charter and *all* UN resolutions relevant to the question of Palestine must also be compatible with UN General Assembly Resolutions 181(ii) of 1947 and UN General Assembly Resolution 194(iii) of 1948.

Thesis Six

A possible Constitution for a sovereign and democratic Republic of Palestine as a Member State of the United Nations that is a Constitution informed by the values of the UN Universal Declaration of Human Rights; is compatible with the standards of international law, the UN Charter and *all* UN resolutions relevant to the question of Palestine; and is also be compatible with UN General Assembly Resolutions 181(ii) of 1947 and UN General Assembly Resolution 194(iii) of 1948 is, by definition, must also be a Constitution for a democratic Federal Republic of Palestine that comprise three constituent elements: the Arab State of Palestine, the Hebrew State of Palestine, and the *corpus separatum* of the City of Jerusalem.

Thesis Seven

The sovereignty of a democratic Federal Republic of Palestine is vested with the Federal Parliament. Citizenship of a Federal Republic of Palestine is Palestinian federal citizenship. All Palestinians, that is, all 1948 and 1967 Palestine refugees (*Lajiin* and *Nazihin* respectively) and their families, all Palestinian internally displaced persons (*Muhajjarin*) and their families, all residents in the 1967 Israeli occupied Palestinian territories and their families, and all Arab and non-Arab citizens of the apartheid State of Israel and their families are Palestinian federal citizens of a democratic Federal Republic of Palestine and equal before the Constitution.

Thesis Eight

Rather than start from scratch, a possible Constitution for a sovereign and democratic Federal Republic of Palestine as a Member State of the United Nations could take the 1996 Constitution of the Republic of South Africa and its Bill of Rights as a template, in which case State citizenship with any one of the two State components of a Federal Republic of Palestine, the Arab State of Palestine and the Hebrew State of Palestine, represents the locus of the federal citizen's ballot box as well as his or her provincial rights, provincial responsibilities and provincial duties.

Thesis Nine

A Preamble to a Constitution for a sovereign and democratic Federal Republic of Palestine could be based on the Preamble to the Constitution of the New South Africa and read:

Preamble
We, the peoples of Palestine,
Recognise the injustices of our past;
Honour those who suffered for justice and freedom in our land;
Respect those who have worked to build and develop our country; and
Believe that Palestine belongs to all who live in it, united in our diversity.
We therefore, through our freely elected representatives, adopt this Constitution as the supreme law of the Republic so as to:

- Heal the divisions of the past and establish a society based on democratic values, social justice and fundamental human rights;
- Lay the foundations for a democratic and open society in which government is based on the will of the people and every citizen is equally protected by law;
- Improve the quality of life of all citizens and free the potential of each person; and
- Build a united and democratic Federal Palestine able to take its rightful place as a sovereign State in the family of nations.

May this Constitution protect our peoples.

Thesis Ten

Founding Provisions of a Constitution for a sovereign and democratic Republic of Palestine could be based on the Founding Provisions of the Constitution of the New South Africa and read:

Founding Provisions

1. Federal Republic of Palestine

The Federal Republic of Palestine is one, sovereign, democratic member State of the United Nations founded on the following values:

A. Human dignity, the achievement of equality and the advancement of human rights and freedoms.
B. Non-racialism and non-sexism.
C. Supremacy of the constitution and the rule of law.
D. Universal adult suffrage, a federal common voters roll, regular elections and a multi-party system of democratic government, to ensure accountability, responsiveness and openness.

2. Supremacy of the Constitution

This Constitution is the supreme law of the Republic; law or conduct inconsistent with it is invalid, and the obligations imposed by it must be fulfilled.

3. Citizenship

(1) There is a common federal Palestine citizenship.
(2) All citizens are equally entitled to the rights, privileges and benefits of federal citizenship; and equally subject to the duties and responsibilities of citizenship.
(3) Federal legislation must provide for the acquisition, loss and restoration of citizenship.
(4) Federal anthem

The citizenship of the Republic is determined by the President by proclamation.

(5) Federal flag

The Federal flag of the Republic is green, white, black and red.

4. Languages

(1) The official languages of the Republic are Arabic, Hebrew, English, Russian and Amharic.

(2) Recognising the historically diminished use and status of the official languages of our peoples, the Republic must take practical and positive measures to elevate the status and advance the use of these languages.

(3) (a) The federal government and state governments including the *corpus separatum* of the City of Jerusalem may use any particular official languages for the purposes of government, taking into account usage, practicality, expense, regional circumstances and the balance of the needs and preferences of the population as a whole or in the province concerned; but the federal government and each state government (with the exception of the *corpus separatum* of the City of Jerusalem) must use at least two official languages. (b) The government of the *corpus separatum* of the City of Jerusalem may use the English language exclusively. (c) Municipalities must take into account the language usage and preferences of their residents.

(4) The federal government and state governments, by legislative and other measures, must regulate and monitor their use of official languages. All official languages must enjoy parity of esteem and must be treated equitably.

(5) A Pan Palestine Language Board established by federal legislation must (a) promote, and create conditions for, the development and use of all official languages; the Ladino, Yiddish and Jidi languages; sign language; and (b) promote and ensure respect for all languages commonly used by communities in Palestine, including all immigrant languages; and other languages used for religious purposes in Palestine.

Thesis Eleven

A Citizenship Law for a sovereign and democratic Republic of Palestine could be based on the Citizenship Provisions of the Constitution of the New South Africa and begin with the definition of a Palestinian federal citizen as follows: 'Palestine federal Citizenship is a right for anyone who:

1. Was born in Palestine, as defined by the territory covered by the British Mandate, or had the right to Palestinian citizenship according to the laws in force during that period;
2. Was born in Gaza or in the West Bank, including Jerusalem;
3. Irrespective of place of birth, has one or more direct ancestors that meet the requirements of paragraph (1) above;
4. Is the spouse of a Palestinian who meets the mentioned requirements;
5. Has Israeli citizenship.

Thesis Twelve

A Bill of Rights for a sovereign and democratic Federal Republic of Palestine as a Member State of the United Nations could be based on the Citizenship Provisions of the Constitution of the New South Africa and begin as follows:

1. Bill of Rights

(1) This Bill of Rights is a cornerstone of democracy in Palestine. It enshrines the rights of all people in our country and affirms the democratic values of human dignity, equality and freedom.
(2) The Republic must respect, protect, promote and fulfil the rights in the Bill of Rights.

2. Application

(1) The Bill of Rights applies to all law, and binds the legislature, the executive, the judiciary and all organs of the Republic.
(2) A provision of the Bill of Rights binds a natural or a juristic person if, and to the extent that, it is applicable, taking into account the nature of the right and the nature of any duty imposed by the right.

(3) When applying a provision of the Bill of Rights to a natural or juristic person in terms of subsection (2), a court

    a.   In order to give effect to a right in the Bill, must apply, or if necessary develop, the common law to the extent that legislation does not give effect to that right; and

    b.   May develop rules of the common law to limit the right, provided that the limitation is in accordance with other sections.

(4) A juristic person is entitled to the rights in the Bill of Rights to the extent required by the nature of the rights and the nature of that juristic person.

3. Equality

(1) Everyone is equal before the law and has the right to equal protection and benefit of the law.

(2) Equality includes the full and equal enjoyment of all rights and freedoms. To promote the achievement of equality, legislative and other measures designed to protect or advance persons, or categories of persons, disadvantaged by unfair discrimination may be taken.

(3) The Republic may not unfairly discriminate directly or indirectly against anyone on one or more grounds, including race, gender, sex, pregnancy, marital status, ethnic or social origin, colour, sexual orientation, age, disability, religion, conscience, belief, culture, language and birth.

(4) No person may unfairly discriminate directly or indirectly against anyone on one or more grounds in terms of subsection (3). Federal legislation must be enacted to prevent or prohibit unfair discrimination.

(5) Discrimination on one or more of the grounds listed in subsection (3) is unfair unless it is established that the discrimination is fair.

4. Human Dignity

Everyone has inherent dignity and the right to have their dignity respected and protected.

5. Life

Everyone has the right to life.

6. Freedom and Security of the Person

(1) Everyone has the right to freedom and security of the person, which includes the right

- Not to be deprived of freedom arbitrarily or without just cause;
- Not to be detained without trial;
- To be free from all forms of violence from either public or private sources;
- Not to be tortured in any way; and
- Not to be treated or punished in a cruel, inhuman or degrading way.

(2) Everyone has the right to bodily and psychological integrity, which includes the right

- To make decisions concerning reproduction;
- To security in and control over their body; and
- Not to be subjected to medical or scientific experiments without their informed consent.

7. Slavery, Servitude and Forced Labour

No one may be subjected to slavery, servitude or forced labour.

8. Privacy

Everyone has the right to privacy, which includes the right not to have

(1) Their person or home searched;
(2) Their property searched;
(3) Their possessions seized; or
(4) The privacy of their communications infringed.

9. Freedom of Religion, Belief and Opinion

(1) Everyone has the right to freedom of conscience, religion, thought, belief and opinion.

(2) Religious observances may be conducted at federal or State-aided institutions, provided that
- Those observances follow rules made by the appropriate public authorities;
- They are conducted on an equitable basis; and
- Attendance at them is free and voluntary.

(3) This section does not prevent legislation recognising marriages concluded under any tradition, or a system of religious, personal or family law; or systems of personal and family law under any tradition, or adhered to by persons professing a particular religion.

(4) Recognition in terms of paragraph (3) must be consistent with this section and the other provisions of the Constitution.

10. Freedom of Expression

(1) Everyone has the right to freedom of expression, which includes:

- Freedom of the press and other media;
- Freedom to receive or impart information or ideas;
- Freedom of artistic creativity; and
- Academic freedom and freedom of scientific research.

(2) The right in subsection (1) does not extend to:

- Propaganda for war;
- Incitement of imminent violence; or
- Advocacy of hatred that is based on race, ethnicity, gender, pregnancy, marital status, ethnic or social origin, colour, sexual orientation, age, disability, religion, conscience, belief, culture, language and birth, and that constitutes incitement to cause harm.

11. Assembly, Demonstration, Picket and Petition

Everyone has the right, peacefully and unarmed, to assemble, to demonstrate, to picket and to present petitions.

12. Freedom of Association

Everyone has the right to freedom of association.

13. Political Rights

(1) Every citizen is free to make political choices, which includes the right

- To form a political party;
- To participate in the activities of, or recruit members for, a political party; and
- To campaign for a political party or cause.

(2) Every citizen has the right to free, fair and regular elections for any legislative body established in terms of the Constitution.

(3) Every adult citizen has the right

- To vote in elections for any legislative body established in terms of the Constitution, and to do so in secret; and
- To stand for public office and, if elected, to hold office.

14. Citizenship

No federal citizen may be deprived of citizenship.

15. Freedom of Movement and Residence

(1) Everyone has the right to freedom of movement.

(2) Everyone has the right to leave the Republic.

(3) Every citizen has the right to enter, to remain in and to reside anywhere in, the Republic.

(4) Every citizen has the right to a passport.

16. Freedom of Trade, Occupation and Profession

Every citizen has the right to choose their trade, occupation or profession freely. The practice of a trade, occupation or profession may be regulated by law.

17. Labour Relations

(1) Everyone has the right to fair labour practices.

(2) Every worker has the right

- To form and join a trade union;
- To participate in the activities and programmes of a trade union; and
- To strike.

(3) Every employer has the right

- To form and join an employers' organisation; and
- To participate in the activities and programmes of an employers' organisation.

(4) Every trade union and every employers' organisation has the right

- To determine its own administration, programmes and activities;
- To organise; and
- To form and join a federation.

(5) Every trade union, employers' organisation and employer has the right to engage in collective bargaining. Federal legislation may be enacted to regulate collective bargaining.
(6) Federal legislation may recognise union security arrangements contained in collective agreements.

18. Environment

Everyone has the right to an environment that is not harmful to their health or well-being; and to have the environment protected, for the benefit of present and future generations, through reasonable legislative and other measures that prevent pollution and ecological degradation; promote conservation; and secure ecologically sustainable development and use of natural resources while promoting justifiable economic and social development.

19. Property

(1) No one may be deprived of property except in terms of law of general application, and no law may permit arbitrary deprivation of property.
(2) Property may be expropriated only in terms of law of general application for a public purpose or in the public interest; and subject to compensation, the amount of which and the time and

manner of payment of which have either been agreed to by those affected or decided or approved by a court.

(3) The amount of the compensation and the time and manner of payment must be just and equitable, reflecting an equitable balance between the public interest and the interests of those affected, having regard to all relevant circumstances, including the current use of the property; the history of the acquisition and use of the property; the market value of the property; the extent of direct federal or state investment and subsidy in the acquisition and beneficial capital improvement of the property; and the purpose of the expropriation.

(4) For the purposes of this section, the public interest includes the nation's commitment to land reform and to reforms to bring about equitable access to all of Palestine's natural resources; and property is not limited to land.

(5) The Republic must take reasonable legislative and other measures, within its available resources, to foster conditions which enable citizens to gain access to land on an equitable basis.

(6) A person or community whose tenure of land is legally insecure as a result of past political-Zionist discriminatory laws or practices is entitled, to the extent provided by an Act of Parliament, either to tenure which is legally secure or to comparable redress.

(7) A person or community dispossessed of immovable and movable property rights and/or inheritance rights including rights in lands, forests, rights of possession and other rights, easements and other property rights after 24 July 1922 as a result of past political-Zionist discriminatory laws or practices is entitled, to the extent provided by an Act of Parliament, either to restitution of that property or to equitable redress.

(8) No provision of this section may impede the Republic from taking legislative and other measures to achieve land, water and related reform, in order to redress the results of past political-Zionist discrimination.

(9) Parliament must enact the legislation referred to in subsection (6).

20. Housing

(1) Everyone has the right to have access to adequate housing.

(2) The Republic must take reasonable legislative and other measures, within its available resources, to achieve the progressive realisation of this right.

(3) No one may be evicted from their home, or have their home

demolished, without an order of court made after considering all
the relevant circumstances. No legislation may permit arbitrary
evictions.

21. Health Care, Food, Water and Social Security

(1) Everyone has the right to have access to health care services,
including reproductive health care; and sufficient food and water;
and social security, including, if they are unable to support
themselves and their dependants, appropriate social assistance.

(2) The Republic must take reasonable legislative and other measures,
within its available resources, to achieve the progressive realisation
of each of these rights.

(3) No one may be refused emergency medical treatment.

22. Children

(1) Every child has the right:

- To a name and citizenship from birth;
- To family care or parental care, or to appropriate alternative care
  when removed from the family environment;
- To basic nutrition, shelter, basic health care services and social
  services;
- To be protected from maltreatment, neglect, abuse or degradation;
- To be protected from exploitative labour practices;
- Not to be required or permitted to perform work or provide
  services that are inappropriate for a person of that child's age;
  or place at risk the child's well-being, education, physical or
  mental health or spiritual, moral or social development;
- Not to be detained except as a measure of last resort, in which
  case, in addition to the rights a child enjoys under sections 12
  and 35, the child may be detained only for the shortest
  appropriate period of time, and has the right to be kept
  separately from detained persons over the age of 18 years; and
  treated in a manner, and kept in conditions, that take account of
  the child's age;
- To have a legal practitioner assigned to the child by the Republic,
  and at Republic expense, in civil proceedings affecting the
  child, if substantial injustice would otherwise result; and

- Not to be used directly in armed conflict, and to be protected in times of armed conflict.

(2) A child's best interests are of paramount importance in every matter concerning the child.

(3) In this section 'child' means a person under the age of 18 years.

23. Education

(1) Everyone has the right to a basic education, including adult basic education; and to further education, which the Republic, through reasonable measures, must make progressively available and accessible.

(2) Everyone has the right to receive education in the official language or languages of their choice in public educational institutions where that education is reasonably practicable. In order to ensure the effective access to, and implementation of, this right, the Republic must consider all reasonable educational alternatives, including single medium institutions, taking into account equity; practicability; and the need to redress the results of past political-Zionist discriminatory laws and practices.

(3) Everyone has the right to establish and maintain, at their own expense, independent educational institutions that do not discriminate on the basis of race, ethnicity, gender, pregnancy, marital status, ethnic or social origin, colour, sexual orientation, age, disability, religion, conscience, belief, culture, language and birth; are registered with the Republic; and maintain standards that are not inferior to standards at comparable public educational institutions.

(4) Subsection (3) does not preclude Republic subsidies for independent educational institutions.

24. Language and Culture

Everyone has the right to use the language and to participate in the cultural life of their choice, but no one exercising these rights may do so in a manner inconsistent with any provision of the Bill of Rights.

25. Cultural, Religious and Linguistic Communities

(1) Persons belonging to a cultural, religious or linguistic community

may not be denied the right, with other members of that community, to enjoy their culture, practise their religion and use their language; and to form, join and maintain cultural, religious and linguistic associations and other organs of civil society.

(2) The rights in subsection (1) may not be exercised in a manner inconsistent with any provision of the Bill of Rights.

26. Access to Information

(1) Everyone has the right of access to any information held by the Republic; and any information that is held by another person and that is required for the exercise or protection of any rights.

(2) Federal legislation must be enacted to give effect to this right, and may provide for reasonable measures to alleviate the administrative and financial burden on the Republic.

27. Just Administrative Action

(1) Everyone has the right to administrative action that is lawful, reasonable and procedurally fair.

(2) Everyone whose rights have been adversely affected by administrative action has the right to be given written reasons.

(3) Federal legislation must be enacted to give effect to these rights, and must

- Provide for the review of administrative action by a court or, where appropriate, an independent and impartial tribunal;
- Impose a duty on the Republic to give effect to the rights in subsections (1) and (2); and
- Promote an efficient administration.

28. Access to Courts

Everyone has the right to have any dispute that can be resolved by the application of law decided in a fair public hearing before a court or, where appropriate, another independent and impartial tribunal or forum.

29. Arrested, Detained and Accused Persons

(1) Everyone who is arrested for allegedly committing an offence has the right:

- To remain silent;
- To be informed promptly of the right to remain silent; and of the consequences of not remaining silent;
- Not to be compelled to make any confession or admission that could be used in evidence against that person;
- To be brought before a court as soon as reasonably possible, but not later than 48 hours after the arrest; or the end of the first court day after the expiry of the 48 hours, if the 48 hours expire outside ordinary court hours or on a day which is not an ordinary court day; at the first court appearance after being arrested, to be charged or to be informed of the reason for the detention to continue, or to be released; and
- To be released from detention if the interests of justice permit, subject to reasonable conditions.

(2) Everyone who is detained, including every sentenced prisoner, has the right

- To be informed promptly of the reason for being detained;
- To choose, and to consult with, a legal practitioner, and to be informed of this right promptly;
- To have a legal practitioner assigned to the detained person by the Republic and at Republic expense, if substantial injustice would otherwise result, and to be informed of this right promptly;
- To challenge the lawfulness of the detention in person before a court and, if the detention is unlawful, to be released;
- To conditions of detention that are consistent with human dignity, including at least exercise and the provision, at Republic expense, of adequate accommodation, nutrition, reading material and medical treatment; and
- To communicate with, and be visited by, that person's spouse or partner; next of kin; chosen religious counsellor; and chosen medical practitioner.

(3) Every accused person has the right to a fair trial, which includes the right:

- To be informed of the charge with sufficient detail to answer it;
- To have adequate time and facilities to prepare a defence;

- To a public trial before an ordinary court;
- To have their trial begin and conclude without unreasonable delay;
- To be present when being tried;
- To choose, and be represented by, a legal practitioner, and to be informed of this right promptly;
- To have a legal practitioner assigned to the accused person by the Republic and at Republic expense, if substantial injustice would otherwise result, and to be informed of this right promptly;
- To be presumed innocent, to remain silent, and not to testify during the proceedings;
- To adduce and challenge evidence;
- Not to be compelled to give self-incriminating evidence;
- To be tried in a language that the accused person understands or, if that is not practicable, to have the proceedings interpreted into that language;
- Not to be convicted for an act or omission that was not an offence under either State, federal or international law at the time it was committed or omitted;
- Not to be tried for an offence in respect of an act or omission for which that person has previously been either acquitted or convicted;
- To the benefit of the least severe of the prescribed punishments if the prescribed punishment for the offence has been changed between the time that the offence was committed and the time of sentencing; and
- Of appeal to, or review by, a higher court.

(4) Whenever this section requires information to be given to a person, that information must be given in a language that the person understands.

(5) Evidence obtained in a manner that violates any right in the Bill of Rights must be excluded if the admission of that evidence would render the trial unfair or otherwise be detrimental to the administration of justice.

Thesis Thirteen

The implementation of all of the above propositions requires that our PLO leadership, both the Executive Committee and Palestine National Council (PNC), own up to our mistakes, notably, that we acknowledge what we all know to be the truth, namely:

- That at least since our 1988 PNC Declaration of Independence we recognize the State of Israel as a 'Jewish' State – but only in its 1947 borders and only in terms of *all* UN resolutions relevant to the question of Palestine, first and foremost UN General Assembly Resolution 194;
- That our enemy is not Judaism as a religion, not Jews as a religion, or as a Hebrew people, and not Israel as a 'Jewish State' but our enemy is 'Political Zionism,' namely the 'Jewish State' in its Political-Zionist apartheid interpretation and practice of settler-colonialism.

CHAPTER SEVENTEEN

A NON MODEST PROPOSAL FOR RESOLVING THE PALESTINE-ISRAEL CONFLICT: THE DIVIDE AND SHARE APPROACH

SAID ZEEDANI

Introduction

I have good reasons to believe that the desirable, fair, peaceful, final and agreed upon solution to the Palestine-Israel conflict should be predicated, *inter alia*, on respect for the following principles or pillars:

- Israel remaining a democratic and Jewish State; Jewish only in the sense that the majority of its actual citizens are Jews in the long run.
- The creation of an independent and viable Palestinian State alongside Israel, to the East of Israel, and in peace with Israel. Adjustments to the borders of 4 June 1967 should not in any way disfavour the Palestinian State.
- The free return of the Palestinian refugees, or those who wish to exercise their right of return, to their homeland, mainly, but not exclusively, to the Palestinian State. This is in addition to securing citizenship for the Palestinian refugees in their other places of residence.
- Respect for the attachments of both Palestinian Arabs and Israeli Jews to the whole country or to special places in it.
- Equal democratic citizenship for both Palestinian Arabs and Israeli Jews within the boundaries of either of the two States.
- Compensation for the loss of homes and private property and related suffering of the Palestinian refugees and the internally displaced Palestinian persons.

With these principles in mind, we are in a better position, I believe, to appraise the merits of the different, and competing, main options or proposals for peacefully resolving the century-old conflict between Palestinian Arabs and Israeli Jews, taking into account that the continuation of the occupation of Gaza and the West Bank, the status quo, any apartheid regime, or any agreed upon or unilaterally imposed transitional stage, is not tenable in the long run.

The One-State Solution

With or without federation or bi-nationalism, the one-State solution is not a live political option for the short and medium terms. Though the majority of Palestinians, inside and outside the Occupied Territories since 1967, might be in favour of such a solution, the overwhelming majority of Israeli Jews are strongly opposed to it, as it conflicts with their commitment to keep Israel as a democratic and Jewish State, with a majority of Jews as its actual citizens. For the majority of Israeli Jews, the one-State solution means no less than the end of Zionism. It is this ominous nightmare of the one-State solution that lurks behind, and accounts for, the declared commitment of the main political parties and movements of Jewish Israel to one version or another of the two-State solution.

I am aware, as I assume you are, of the variety of initiatives and arguments for the one-State solution, mainly advocated by Palestinian intellectuals, non-Zionist Israeli and non-Israeli Jews and others. It is not my intention here to enumerate these initiatives, old and new, or to evaluate the arguments for and against each of them. As a committed liberal democrat, my heart and mind are clearly in favour of some version of the one-State solution, primarily because it is the most accommodative to the needs and aspirations of the Palestinian refugees. This is, of course, in addition to its other manifest merits. But, as I said before, the one-State solution, as understood by the majority of Israeli Jews, their political representatives and supporters, heralds the end of Zionism. And this accounts for its rejection by them. Needless to say in this regard, the support of the majority of Palestinians derives less from their genuine commitment to the values and practices of liberal democracy than from their strong commitment, among other things, to a fair solution to the problem of the refugees of 1948 (whether inside or outside the boundaries of Historic Palestine). In any case, the one-State solution is not right around the corner. Nor will it be for the foreseeable future. The most we can do in this regard is not to block the road leading to it by creating insurmountable barriers.

The Two-State Solution

Call it what you wish. Call it the Nusseibeh/Ayalon Destination Map or the Geneva Initiative or the Clinton Parameters or the (Saudi) Arab Peace Plan or the Bush Vision or the peace plan endorsed by the UN Security Council Resolution. The two-State solution, as we all know, encounters formidable obstacles. Endless rounds of negotiations between the Israelis and Palestinians, direct and indirect, in the country and abroad, and for more than 20 years, have not yielded any significant tangible results so far. The majority of both Israeli Jews and Palestinian Arabs, as well as the international community at large, are supportive of some version or another of the two-State solution. But the facts on the ground created by the successive Israeli governments over the years, mainly in terms of settlement activity, the erection of the Separation Wall, and the creation of new Jewish neighbourhoods in Arab Jerusalem, make the establishment of a viable Palestinian State along the 4 June 1967 borders an almost impossible task. It is therefore no accident that with the passage of time the species of sceptics, Palestinians and others, about the viability of the two-State solution is growing in number. It does not follow, however, that the idea of the two-State solution should be discarded or abandoned. Rather, it is my settled view that this idea needs to be revisited and significantly revised.

The Divide and Share Approach

Since neither the one-State solution nor the two-State solution (according to the currently defended or endorsed versions) is right around the corner, intellectuals/academics/politicians have recently started the search for alternative solutions, final or otherwise. For example, the Centre for Middle East Studies at Lund University in Sweden came up last year with a proposal called 'The Parallel Two States Solution.' According to this new proposal, the two States would have jurisdiction over their respective populations: Israel would have jurisdiction over Israeli Jews (including those who live in settlements); Palestine would have jurisdiction over Palestinians (including the returning refugees and perhaps also the Palestinians in Israel). And the two States would create the needed legal/economic/security coordination and cooperation mechanisms. A less ambitious, though more daring, proposal is being advanced and advocated by Sari Nusseibeh in his most recent book '*What is a Palestinian State Worth?*' (2011). Fearing that occupation might continue for decades to come, and convinced that neither the one-State solution (his most desired option) nor the two-State solution (the second best option) is within reach, Nusseibeh comes up with a 'modest proposal' for a transitional phase, according to which Israeli Jews (the citizens) could run the whole country while the Palestinian Arabs (including the returning refugees) could at last enjoy living in it, the whole of it (as permanent residents in the main, but with equal civil and human rights). Under favourable conditions, one can imagine, such a transitional phase would most likely lead to the one-State solution, federated or otherwise.

However, I still believe that a significantly revised version of the two-State solution can accommodate the competing demands and claims of the two parties to the conflict, taking into account the big changes on the ground, especially in the West Bank (including Arab or East Jerusalem). The guiding idea in the following revised two-State proposal dawned on me toward the end of the first month of the Al-Aqsa intifada in the year 2000. The components or constituent elements of this revised version can be listed as follows:

- The creation of a democratic Palestinian State along the 4 June 1967 borders, with minor adjustments in favour of the State of Palestine.
- Recognizing Israel as a democratic and Jewish State; Jewish only in the sense that the majority of its actual citizens are Jews.
- Settlers who find themselves under Palestinian jurisdiction can become either equal Palestinian citizens or remain Israeli citizens with permanent resident status in Palestine (of course, without their current privileges).
- Palestinian refugees can freely return to the Palestinian State. Those refugees who opt to return to Israel can become permanent residents in Israel, but citizens of Palestine. Those Palestinians who opt to remain citizens of other States can still exercise their right of return to the Palestinian State when they so wish. Arrangements for dual citizenship should also be put in place. In any case, no Palestinian should be allowed to remain a stateless person thereafter.
- The two States commit themselves to the values and practices of liberal democracy, as well as to the principle of non-discrimination against ethno-cultural minority groups.
- Separation between the two States is to be mainly political rather than geographic/demographic. No monstrous walls or repulsive

fences are to separate the two States. Thus the unity of the one country could be preserved.

- The two States are to share fairly all things that cannot or should not be divided. Above all, they are to share fairly the city of Jerusalem, which shall remain united and open to all.
- Far-reaching cooperation and integration between the two democratic neighbouring States.
- An agreed-upon scheme of special minority rights for both Palestinians in Israel and Jews in Palestine. Such special minority rights are primarily intended to protect and sustain their respective ethno-cultural particularity.
- Respect for the attachments of both Palestinian Arabs and Israeli Jews to the whole country or to special parts of it or places in it. The attachments of non-Palestinian Arabs, Moslems and Christians, as well as those of non-Israeli Jews should also be taken into account.

The above revised two-State proposal rests on two important distinctions: one is between country and State; the other is between citizenship and (permanent) residency status. Accordingly, though I might end up as a citizen of either State, the whole country will be mine (as my attachment to it is being respected). In the other State, I am much more than a tourist or passer-by; I can work, move freely, reside, own property, and, above all, I can be a permanent resident enjoying equal civil rights. Thus, Israel can remain a Jewish and democratic State, while both Palestinian Arabs and Israeli Jews can enjoy the whole country. Needless to say, under more conducive conditions (especially when citizenship nationalism rather than ethno-cultural nationalism prevails), the two States can entertain the idea of a confederation or even a federation.

Conclusion

The one-State solution, attractive as it is from the perspective of committed liberal democrats, is not a viable political option for resolving the Palestine/Israel conflict in the foreseeable future. This is mainly because the overwhelming majority of Israeli Jews are still committed to Zionism, i.e., to the creation and sustenance of a democratic and Jewish State. In light of this, it does not help much to say, or threaten (as some Palestinian intellectuals tend to do), that the failure of the currently endorsed and defended two-State solution would or should give added impetus to the one-State solution. Far from it. The failure of the currently endorsed and defended two-State solution might entail the continuation of occupation or its replacement by some sort of an apartheid system of rule. Or, it might be replaced by unilaterally imposed Israeli interim arrangements (such as the unilateral withdrawal of Israeli forces from all Areas B and parts of Areas C). It is my considered judgment that what is most needed now is a revised vision of the two-State solution that takes seriously into consideration the Israeli-created facts on the ground, while turning them against their malicious creator(s). The revised two-State solution that I propose is intended to do just that. But, more importantly, it directly addresses almost all the moot core issues. It is with such an inclusive vision, I think, that we should approach both Israeli public opinion and the international community, including the UN system. It is with such a truly generous offer that we should apply for membership in the community of independent States.

Needless to say, I personally tend to believe that such a revised two-State proposal is not only academically or intellectually appealing, but also, and more importantly, politically practicable—in spite of initial impressions to the contrary.

INDEX

A